# A Latin American Music Reader

## Views from the South

Edited by Javier F. León
and Helena Simonett

Published in collaboration
with the Society for Ethnomusicology

UNIVERSITY OF ILLINOIS PRESS
Urbana, Chicago, and Springfield

Published in collaboration with the Society for Ethnomusicology (SEM) and produced under the guidance of its Board of Directors. For information about SEM, please see its website at www.ethnomusicology.org. Sponsored by the Research Institute for the Study of Man (RISM), a program of the Reed Foundation, through a grant to SEM.


Manufactured in the United States of America
1 2 3 4 5 C P 5 4 3 2 1
∞ This book is printed on acid-free paper.

Library of Congress Cataloging-in-Publication Data
Names: León, Javier F., editor. | Simonett, Helena, editor.
Title: A Latin American music reader : views from the south / edited by Javier F. León and Helena Simonett.
Description: Urbana : University of Illinois Press, published in collaboration with the Society for Ethnomusicology, [2016] | ?2016 | Includes bibliographical references and index.
Identifiers: LCCN 2016003066| ISBN 9780252040214 (hardcover : alk. paper) | ISBN 9780252081675 (pbk. : alk. paper)
Subjects: LCSH: Folk music—Latin America—History and criticism. | Folk music—Social aspects—Latin America. | Applied ethnomusicology—Latin America. | Ethnomusicology—Latin America.
Classification: LCC ML3549 .L38 2016 | DDC 780.98—dc23 LC record available at http://lccn.loc.gov/2016003066

Ebook ISBN 978-0-252-09843-7

To the memory of Michael Marcuzzi (1966–2012)

# Contents

# Preface

This volume is the result of two projects that fortuitously came together. The first grew out of an initiative proposed by our late colleague Michael Marcuzzi at the meeting of the Latin American and Caribbean Special Interest Group of the Society for Ethnomusicology in 2006. Michael was a passionate advocate of the better dissemination of the work of music scholars based in Latin America and the Caribbean, and to this end he proposed and took on the job of setting up a website where English-language translation of key texts could be made available to individuals unfamiliar with this body of scholarship. A few years later, members of the board of the Society for Ethnomusicology began to entertain the possibility of devoting a series of publications to English-language translations of ethnomusicological scholarship, which led to a joining of efforts to have that first publication devoted to Latin American and Caribbean literature.

Assembling a collection like this involved making choices regarding the scope and depth of the literature selected. The main aim has been to select pieces that would speak to contemporary research issues and concerns within the region, rather than adopting a more historical or geographically based approach. There are multiple reasons for this choice, ranging from the pragmatic to the political. Most important early studies in the region exist in the form of monographs, extended essays, and multivolume reference works that cannot be appropriately abridged or excerpted. Many of these are certainly of interest to scholars already working in Latin America and the Caribbean. Yet, they do not necessarily make the best entry points for individuals working outside of the region and who are more likely to be interested in current research trends and approaches that may be pertinent beyond Latin American and Caribbean contexts.

Furthermore, much of that earlier work, while not available in English, has been consistently available to Anglo-American and European scholars, many of whom are trained in Spanish and Portuguese, and who often engage with these languages in their own work. Although this practice has contributed to a general awareness about other research traditions among English-language scholars not working in the region, it has also had the unintended consequence of generating something akin to an epistemological version of an ethnographic present. The work of many of the founding figures of comparative musicology and ethnomusicology in the United States and Europe is regarded in retrospect as a product of and a response to scholarly concerns and research agendas of particular historical moments and places. The theories, methods, and perspectives associated with Latin American and Caribbean scholars, however, often lack that same type of historicization, instead being perceived as unchanging and inherent aspects of a more orthodox or old-fashioned counterpart scholarly tradition. Contemporary research by scholars based in Latin America and the Caribbean remains largely unknown among English-language scholars working outside of the region, even though there is a growing overlap of research interests and concerns. As such, the pieces in this volume constitute an initial survey of this literature, one that emphasizes some of the ways in which contemporary scholars engage with other music traditions outside the region as well as with the legacy of their own intellectual history.

This orientation is also in response to and in support of the changes that have been taking place within Latin American and Caribbean academia. Since the mid-1990s, there has been a growing interest in and institutional support for the study of local forms of music and dance in the region. New generations of students have a growing number of options from which to choose when considering the pursuit of advanced training in ethnomusicology and related fields that do not require them to emigrate to the United States, Canada, or Europe, including graduate programs in Brazil, Chile, Colombia, Mexico, and Venezuela. There has also been a proliferation of regional and international professional music societies, such as the Associação Brasileira de Etnomusicología (ABET, Brazilian Association for Ethnomusicology), the Latin American branch of the Society for the Study of Popular Music (IASPM-AL), and the Sociedad de Etnomusicología (SIBE, Ethnomusicology Society), that regularly sponsor conferences and other fora where Spanish and Portuguese scholars share their research. Research centers and archives, among them the Instituto Nacional de Música Carlos Vega (Argentina, Carlos Vega National Institute of Music), the Fundación Simón I. Patiño (Bolivia, Simón I. Patiño Foundation), the Casa de las Américas (Cuba, the House of the Américas), the Instituto de Etnomusicología (Peru, Ethnomusicology Institute), and the Centro Nacional de Documentación Musical Lauro Ayestarán (Uruguay, Lauro Ayestarán National Center for Musical Documentation), are responsible for a growing number of research publications, audio recordings, and video documentaries. These are complemented by a number of regional, peer-reviewed, and often multilingual journals, including the *Revista Musical Chilena* (Chilean musical review), the *Revista Transcultural de Música/Transcultural Music Review* (*TRANS*), *Música e Cultura* (Music and culture), and the *Latin American Music Review/Revista de Música Latino Americana* (*LAMR*).

Bringing this project to fruition has been the result of the hard work of a number of individuals and institutions whose contributions must be acknowledged. The membership of the Latin American and Caribbean Section of the Society for Ethnomusicology (LACSEM) was instrumental in suggesting potential pieces for inclusion in this book and for securing contact information for a number of potential contributors. Peter Manuel also provided much-needed advice and help vetting articles during the early stages. This book would also not have been possible were it not for the dedication of the colleagues who volunteered their own valuable time, specialized musical knowledge, and language skills to translate these articles. We are also indebted to the authors for agreeing to have their work translated and for their patience and flexibility through the lengthy revision and editing process. Stephen Stuempfle of the Society for Ethnomusicology as well as Laurie Matheson, Jennifer Comeau, and Amanda Wicks at the University of Illinois Press helped shepherd the manuscript through its various stages. Olivia Salzano provided expert assistance with the initial editing of the Portuguese language pieces. Deborah Oliver offered Helena and me precious advice and an expert guiding hand during the final stages of editing. Ned Sublette kindly granted permission to reproduce previously published material, and Lizette Alegre similarly allowed us to use her photographic work. The elegant dancer that graces the front book cover is an oeuvre of the Mexican painter "Kijano" Carlos Maciel, a dear friend of Helena's. We greatly appreciate his generosity for permitting us to utilize the image. The press's designers turned it into an outstanding cover art. The anonymous peer reviewers offered invaluable suggestions and insights that helped shape this book. Jim Cowdery and Jane Florine rendered crucial assistance following the untimely passing of our friend and colleague Michael Marcuzzi (1966–2012), whose passion and commitment to this project never faltered. We have dedicated this volume to his memory.

Finally, I would like to thank my wife, Molly Burke León, for her boundless patience and loving support during this project, especially during its last stages, which also saw the long-awaited birth of our daughter, Fiona. Helena wishes to thank her husband, Gieri Simonett, and her wonderful daughters, Oriana and Seraina, for their constant encouragement throughout.

Javier F. León
June 5, 2015

# A Latin American Music Reader

# One Hundred Years of Latin American Music Scholarship

## *An Overview*

HELENA SIMONETT
(WITH MICHAEL MARCUZZI)

"I'm not sure whether it makes sense to identify a Latin American school of ethnomusicology, given the size and diversity of the area," Bruno Nettl once remarked, mainly because "regional and national distinctions get in the way" and "the cultural configuration of [the area] contrasts with that of other continents."[1] Gerard Béhague, a musicologist-ethnomusicologist who had written prolifically about Latin American music scholarship, queried "the idea of 'Latin America' as a symbolic construction of general identity" and found "the concept of musical boundaries and borders within it [to be] equally perplexing."[2] He repeatedly warned that such a monolithic view of the continent as a whole would inevitably lead to simplistic, naive, and reductionist generalizations about music expressions.[3]

Why then try to outline the history of Latin American music scholarship, which by necessity must be general and concise, if some of the most eminent music scholars of the twentieth century seem to advise against it? With this introduction to the intellectual history of music research in Latin America, we want to help the reader situate the selected individual articles within their respective contexts and understand the complex dynamics of discussions across disciplinary and geographic boundaries. If Anglo-American and European ethnomusicologists seem notoriously concerned with defining and redefining their discipline and with searching for a legitimate place within academia, music scholars in Latin America are no better off. A variety of competing historical narratives have developed since the beginning of music research in Latin America, and many significant factors have contributed to the heterogeneity of music scholarship in the continent—not least of which, of course, are the heterogeneity of the area itself, as suggested by Nettl, and the immense riches of its musical practices that reject constraint into rigid academic categories.[4]

In establishing a baseline from which to outline the main trends in Latin American music scholarship, we must caution that any starting (or ending) point is fraught with some degree of arbitrariness. Nonetheless, we begin here with the turn of the twentieth century, a point at which the Brazilian Republic was roughly a decade old, the Spanish-American War had just ended Spain's rule over its last colonial territories in the Caribbean, and Mexico was about to embark on a major armed upheaval from which would emerge a modern nation. These historic shifts brought a sense of forward motion for many Latin Americans; yet at the same time, any profound political, social, or economic stability in Latin America seemed utterly elusive. Despite ongoing struggles the young nations were facing, this period was marked by a political and cultural fervor within the continent as a whole, effecting a surge of efforts to establish one's own estimable nationhood as one among equals in the international community, without recourse to a defining colonial patrimony. Cultural introspection and dialogue "inspired reform-minded activists to pursue cultural renovation to match the dynamics of a quickly evolving society."[5]

Although the upsurge of intellectual and artistic activity in Latin America was particular to each nation, it laid the foundation for a transnational cultural renaissance to come: the *entre guerre* years in Europe, abetted by a disdain for the social failures culminating in the Great War, brought about an international interest in the cultures beyond Europe. With their renewed sense of self-confidence, the Americas, particularly the metropolises—Mexico City, Havana, Buenos Aires, Rio de Janeiro, and New York—became sites of cultural, intellectual, and artistic inspiration. From this environment emerged the pioneers of Latin American music scholarship.

These pioneers came to effect the validation of all kinds of American musical forms, particularly those that by and large had previously remained unnoticed or considered unworthy of study. In fact, Béhague reminds that "the earliest history of ethnomusicology in Latin America dates back to the late nineteenth century when historians began to recognize the importance of local oral cultural phenomena, . . . a reaction against the domination of European and European-related music . . . that tended to obliterate the nationalizing qualities of local musical expression."[6] Admittedly, many of these scholars never departed fully from some of their earlier—and at times irreconcilable—theoretical orientations, not least of them being a reliance on exclusive, Eurocentric models of development and hierarchical readings of the social body so as to never escape entirely the trap of furthering the colonial legacy.[7] In spite of such shortcomings, however, these early scholars were transformative figures in the intellectual life of Latin America and crucial to the establishment of Latin American music scholarship.

## Pioneering Studies of Latin American Music

Any recognition of certain pioneering figures in Latin American music scholarship should not be understood here as an attempt to look past the many individuals along the way who have made qualitatively important contributions to the field. We hope to strike a balance with a brief look at the work of four towering figures in the early years of post-1900 Latin American musicology: Carlos Vega in Argentina, Mário de Andrade in Brazil, Fernando Ortiz in Cuba, and Carlos Chávez in Mexico.

Of these major pioneers, it was the Argentine musicologist Carlos Vega (1898–1966) whose intellectual influence was geographically most far-reaching. Trained as a violinist, guitarist, and composer, Vega's early research was on plainchant, and this focus would remain a continuing presence in his scholarly output even amidst the ever-expanding scope of his musicological interests as the years went on. His first major study was a musicological analysis of a colonial manuscript: *La música de un códice colonial del siglo XVII* (The music of a colonial codex of the seventeenth century), which was published in 1931 by the Instituto de Literatura Argentina at the Universidad de Buenos Aires (Institute of Argentine Literature, University of Buenos Aires). He was interested in the reconstruction of pre-Columbian musical systems and musical instruments, having been influenced by the ideas of British anthropologist Edward B. Tylor (1832–1917) on cultural survivals.[8] Vega was also influenced by the Berlin school of comparative musicology, having translated the Hornbostel-Sachs musical instrument classification system to Spanish as part of his own study on Argentinean musical instruments.[9] This translation would serve both as a primary source and as a template for a number of subsequent organological studies in Cuba, Venezuela, Peru, Mexico, and Bolivia.[10]

In the 1930s, Vega began to collect and study indigenous and folk (criollo and mestizo) repertories in Peru, Bolivia, and northern Argentina, and in the following decades expanding to Chile and Paraguay.[11] Also in the 1930s, he became interested in developing a theory of analysis of popular music based on melodic motives (which continues to be influential with some Argentinean scholars), establishing the classificatory schemes for Argentinean folk music genres and an accompanying theory of folkloristics, and conducting extensive work on the history and development of various dance genres in Argentina and neighboring countries.[12] Vega's growing reputation attracted numerous students of folklore and followers of his methods and theories. By the 1940s and 1950s, he had taken on as students the noted Argentinian folklorist and ethnomusicologist Isabel Aretz (1909–2005, who later married another of Vega's students, Luis Felipe Ramón y Rivera [1913–1993] of Venezuela), Uruguayan musicologist Lauro Ayestarán (1913–1966), and the Argentine Mario García Acevedo (1926–2013). Both Aretz and Ramón y Rivera later established themselves as the preeminent scholars in Venezuela, taking up Vega's mantle as mentors of a new generation of musicologists and ethnomusicologists during the latter twentieth century.

In 1931, Vega founded the Instituto Nacional de Musicología (National Institute of Musicology) in Buenos Aires, dedicated to the study of Argentine folk music and the music of Latin America. He also held positions on the Board of Musicology of the Museo Argentino de Ciencias Naturales (Argentine Museum of Sciences) and the Instituto de Musicología (Institute of Musicology) in the Ministry of Education. In addition to his work on medieval music, Vega continued to write extensively on the folk music of South America. Prominent among his works were two late studies: "Acculturation and Musical Traditions in South America," delivered at the Second Inter-American Conference on Ethnomusicology at Indiana University in 1965, and "Mesomusic: An Essay on the Music of the Masses," which promulgated an ethnomusicological role in the study of popular music.[13]

Although Vega never fully separated his theory and methods from the evolutionary and diffusionist concepts of the Berlin school of comparative musicology, Béhague considered him to be "one of the most eminent contributors to Latin American ethnomusicology in regard to practical study and knowledge of hemispheric traditional musics."[14] His work ultimately became a model around which most Latin American music scholarship coalesced in the first half of the twentieth century, with its shared focus on folk and vernacular music and dance genres.

Mário de Andrade (1893–1945) was a classically trained pianist, poet, novelist, and essayist whose eclectic influence in the artistic and intellectual history of his native Brazil was seminal. De Andrade held a professorship in music history, diction, and aesthetics at the Conservatório Dramático e Musical de São Paulo (Dramatic and Musical Conservatory of São Paulo), where he also studied in his youth, and undertook extensive fieldwork throughout Brazil, particularly during the 1920s. Prior to his appointment at the conservatory, de Andrade worked as a freelance writer for various newspapers and journals, and in 1935 he took on the directorship of the Departamento de Cultura da Municipalidade Paulistana (São Paulo Municipal Department of Culture), a post that was indicative of his longstanding concern for the city's artistic life.

De Andrade's studies of Brazil's folk music, with an emphasis on its Afro-Brazilian and Amerindian musics, were central to his vision of Brazil's national artistic direction. In musical terms, de Andrade was concerned with the relationship between concert music and the nation's folk music, advocating for a compositional approach from the synergy of the two. This new sense of *brasilidade* or Brazilianness, engaging folklore as both a creative source material and aesthetic inspiration, was collapsed onto his social persona of being "the most demanding presence for those pursuing artistic modernism."[15]

The point of convergence came in 1922 with the Semana de Arte Moderna (Week of Modern Art) in São Paulo. Although the exhibit was principally mounted by de Andrade and the painter Emiliano Di Cavalcanti, the week soon became associated with the famed Grupo dos Cinco (Group of Five), whose members opposed to the nation's cultural establishment, manifest in the Academia Brasileira de Letras (Brazilian Academy of Letters).[16] De Andrade's modernism was fiercely nationalistic insofar as it sought out a distinct identity for Brazilian culture on the world stage; yet his ideas were unquestionably tied to European trends in the literary and fine arts during the *entre guerre* years. The zeitgeist was best articulated in Oswald de Andrade's *Manifesto antropófago* (1928, *Cannibalist Manifesto*). This "call to arms" placed a defining stamp on this new course for Brazilian artistic expression with a rather overt, modernist aesthetic. The *Manifesto* proselytized for an engagement with intrinsically Brazilian cultural expressions—its traditional music—and a "cannibalizing" of the outside world for artistic elements and sensibilities, whereby the two could be appropriated and transfigured into forms and expressions uniquely Brazilian.[17]

Mário de Andrade's work exemplified the spirit of the *Manifesto*. His scholarly interest in Brazil's folklore led to the publication of his monumental *Ensaio sobre a música brasileira* (Essay on Brazilian music) and the equally influential novel *Macunaíma*.[18] Little could detract from his growing centralization in the artistic life of the nation, and though on the surface both of these 1928 works were wrought of different alloys, they emerged from Andrade's imagined crucible of cultural oppositions: Bahia and Scarlatti in musical tandem, the Amazon rain forest in São Paulo, and both of Brazil's official languages—Portuguese and "Brazilian."

In 1937, after Getúlio Vargas's declaration of Estado Novo (New State), de Andrade's position at the Departamento de Cultura (Department of Culture) was withdrawn. The following year, de Andrade left São Paulo to take up a post at the Universidade Federal do Rio de Janeiro (Federal University of Rio de Janeiro), where he oversaw the Congresso da Língua Nacional Cantada (Congress of National Musical Language), a major folklore and folk music initiative. He returned to São Paulo in 1941, where he remained until his passing three years later. His legacy remains astoundingly multifaceted: the indelible marks left on Brazil's national identity are unequalled by any cultural figure of the twentieth century.

The career of the Cuban scholar Fernando Ortiz Fernández (1881–1969) was many-sided to say the least, and his résumé at any stage of his career could have included one or more of the following titles: diplomat, lawyer, politician, criminologist, folklorist, ethnographer, activist, and, perhaps, organologist. His scholarly writing on Cuban culture remains unparalleled, and while musical subjects were foregrounded in his writings throughout his entire career, unlike de Andrade or Vega, this pioneer of Afro-Cuban studies had no formal musical training.[19] In addition to his numerous publications on Afro-Cuban culture, Ortiz was the founder of several academic societies and served in administrative roles and as the editor of numerous academic journals.[20] Ortiz was a member of the Cuban legislature from 1917 to 1927 and was nominated for the Nobel Peace Prize in 1955.

"Surrounded with a certain aura of inviolability," Ortiz's oeuvre has remained central to Afro-Cuban studies.[21] Robin Moore's assessment of the scholarly work of Ortiz is undoubtedly an ideal place to begin a reading of its legacy of which we would like to highlight two major oeuvres: the five-tome monograph of Cuban organology, published between 1950 and 1955, and, in terms of a larger contribution to the social sciences, *Contrapunteo cubano del tabaco y el azúcar* (*Cuban Counterpoint: Tobacco and Sugar*).[22] The former, one of the most comprehensive undertakings ever published on the musical life of a single nation, is formidable in its breadth as well as in its then-prescient approach to a more holistic inclusion of "sound-producing" instruments within the purview of organology. In the latter work, Ortiz introduced the notion of transculturation, which he described as the process of cultural change through contact whereby agency on the part of all players in the cultural sphere of contact effects a shift in state for all the parent-culture sources. That is, change appears in more than one direction, and not simply within the cultural milieu seeking social ascendancy. Ortiz's formulation emerged from his objections to the application of the concept of acculturation, which at the time was often applied indiscriminately and "based on its alleged Eurocentric implications, whereby 'the natives' are seen as having to acculturate themselves in order to receive the benefits of a superior Western culture, as if they have nothing to offer of their own."[23]

In 1995 the Cuban government established the Fundación Fernando Ortiz (Fernando Ortiz Foundation) for the preservation of his legacy and the continuation of the studies that he started, especially those of Afro-Cuban culture.

The central figure in the institutionalization of music scholarship in Mexico was Carlos Chávez, the seventh child of a mestizo family, who had formal instruction in harmony and piano playing but was self-taught in composition and orchestration.[24]

His career set off dramatically in 1921 with a concert of his own works, after which the secretary of public education commissioned him to write a ballet on an Aztec subject. This public recognition opened immediate access to influential circles for Chávez, who was already in tune with the prevailing official tide of cultural nationalism of the postrevolutionary years. In a 1928 lecture at the Universidad Nacional Autónoma de México (UNAM, National Autonomous University of Mexico), he praised the pre-Conquest virtues of Indian music as expressing "what is profoundest and deepest in the Mexican soul," and the musical life of pre-Columbian Indians as "the most important stage in the history of Mexican music."[25]

Mexico's postrevolutionary intellectual leaders had already formulated a strong nationalist political ideology that was to reshape Mexican identity through the arts, as seen in the work of the Mexican muralists like Diego Rivera, José Clemente Orozco, and David Alfaro Siqueiros. Chávez's brief visit to Europe and a prolonged stay in New York, where he befriended composer Aaron Copland, persuaded him to envision an American leadership of Western culture and to deconstruct the idea of universal music.[26] During his twenty-one years as music director and conductor of the Orquesta Sinfónica Nacional (National Symphony Orchestra), founded in 1928, Chávez promoted contemporary music and the works of Mexican composers. As a member of the International Composers' Guild and the Pan-American Association of Composers, he actively contributed to the development of Mexico City as an important musical center of the hemisphere.

Chávez profoundly influenced Mexican musical life from the 1920s to the 1950s not only as a composer, conductor, and teacher, but also as a writer on music and as a government official. Chávez published numerous essays on Mexican music and a monograph titled *Toward a New Music*.[27] The Charles Eliot Norton lectures he gave at Harvard University in 1958–59 were collected in *Musical Thought*.[28] As the director of the Conservatorio Nacional de Música (National Conservatory of Music, 1928–34) and of the Instituto Nacional de Bellas Artes (INBA, National Institute of Fine Arts, 1947–52), Chávez provided academic leadership in music education by initiating basic reforms of the curriculum, organizing concerts of all kinds, and by establishing research branches for the study of folk and popular music, of music history and bibliography, and of new musical possibilities. These research areas were the breeding ground for a group of young scholars who would come to shape the discipline in Mexico, among them Luis Sandi (1905–1996), Eduardo Hernández Moncada (1899–1995), Jesús C. Romero (1893–1958), Gerónimo Baqueiro Fóster (1898–1967), and Vicente T. Mendoza (1894–1964).

A number of other outstanding individuals established early music scholarship of their respective regions and nations and distinguished themselves through the quality of their research. The following pages are dedicated to some of those contributors, although this is by no means an inclusive list.

## Further Regional and National Developments

### MEXICO AND CENTRAL AMERICA

The early years of Mexican folk music research could not properly be contextualized without mention of the Departamento de Bellas Artes (Department of Fine Arts) of the Secretaría de Educación Pública (SEP, Secretariat of Public Education), founded in 1921 by the first postrevolutionary president, Álvaro Obregón. With Chávez appointed as the department's first director, the new initiative marked the beginning of focused documentation on the music of the nation's diverse regions. Within a decade, a series of highly influential tomes appeared—such as Rubén M. Campos's two books on Mexican musical folklore, Higinio Vázquez Santana's collection of Mexican song genres, and Gabriel Saldívar's history of Mexican music from pre-Columbian to colonial times—the result of intense fieldwork, transcription and archival initiatives.[29] By 1946 Luis Sandi had created the Sección de Investigaciones Musicales (Musical Research Section) of the Department of Music, which directed research in two categories: folklore and art music (*música culta*). By the end of that year, the research section had been subsumed into the newly decreed INBA.[30]

Of all these early scholars, special mention must be made of Vicente T. Mendoza. Mendoza was a student at the National Conservatory, but it was while working with the Comisión Nacional Forestal (National Forestry Service) throughout the 1920s that he began collecting and documenting the music and dance of Mexico's various regions.[31] By 1929 he had taken a professorship at the conservatory and soon began to establish himself within the international community of folklorists as an important figure in the Americas. Like his contemporary, composer and pianist Manuel Ponce (1882–1948), Mendoza was attuned to the aims of the earlier work of the Mexican ethnologist Nicolás León Calderón (1859–1929) in committing to the preservation and description of Mexican folklore.[32] While working as an inspector for elementary school music programs, Mendoza became dismayed at the paucity of resources on and attention to Mexico's own music.

Unlike other Mexican folklorists of the first half of the twentieth century, however, Mendoza's work aimed to move beyond a descriptive methodology, applying a more elaborate analytical apparatus. Mendoza sought to understand the historical bases for the emergence of Mexican musical genres, particularly coming from medieval Spain and pre-Columbian Mexico. Mendoza made convincing connections between the Mexican corrido and the antecedent epic poetry and ballads of Spain.[33] His penchant for historical study was a defining characteristic of his work, as was his focus on the connections between music and poetry. Mendoza's emblematic publications on the Mexican corrido are a detailed and nuanced typology of the folk ballads of the Mexican Revolution.[34] Mendoza became the founding president of the Sociedad Folclórica de México (Folklore Society of Mexico, 1938) and, with his second wife, Virginia Rodríguez Rivera, herself a prolific writer on Mexican folklore, established a more rigorous study of musical folklore in Mexico.[35] From the mid-1930s until his death, Mendoza principally worked from the Instituto de Investigaciones Estéticas (Institute of Aesthetic Research at UNAM), and his papers can be found in the archives of the Biblioteca Nacional de México (National Library of Mexico).[36]

Two other prominent contemporaries of Mendoza deserve mention here: musicologist, composer, and engineer Daniel Castañeda was chief of the Academia de Música Mexicana (Academy of Mexican Music) at the National Conservatory in the 1930s. His research was concerned with folklore, and together with Mendoza, Castañeda published a compendium of pre-Columbian instruments.[37] Spanish musicologist and critic Otto Mayer-Serra, who immigrated to Mexico in 1940, served as the artistic director of the Orquesta Sinfónica de Xalapa (Xalapa Symphony Orchestra). He was the first to publish an extensive study of twentieth-century Mexican music. His most influential work, however, is *Música y músicos de Latinoamérica* (Music and musicians of Latin America), which became a mainstay in Latin American musicology after its publication in 1947.[38]

Musicological activity in Central America in the first half of the twentieth century was utterly sparse. One of the few studies dealing with music was a two-volume monograph by María Baratta and Jeremías Mendoza: this study, which included music, dance, and an historical overview of Salvadorian traditional music, seems to have been a corrective to an earlier publication by the Salvadorian Ministry of Education that contained collections of folk repertories—games, songs, song texts, and poetry—without musical notation.[39]

Though proper Panamanian musicological work began with the 1930 publication of Narciso Garay's *Tradiciones y cantares de Panamá* (Traditions and songs of Panama), the foundations for more systematic work in Panamanian musical folklore were laid in the 1910s by the Panamanian novelist Octavio Méndez Pereira (1887–1954). The writer rose to prominence in Panamanian academic circles, eventually taking on the rectorship at the Universidad Interamericana de Panamá (Inter-American University at Panama City). It was during his tenure that Myron Schaeffer (1908–1965) became the director of the Instituto de Investigaciones Folklóricas (Institute of Folklore Research) at the university. In 1944, the institute devoted the first two issues of its *Boletín del Instituto de Investigaciones Folklóricas* to the music of Panama.[40] The first of these studies focused on the *tamborito*, the representative Panamanian dance form; the second was on the *mejorana*, an equally important song form. A note appeared in the second volume in which Méndez announced that the institute's work was being suspended pending a coordination of the financial contributions to be made by the participating government agencies. Schaeffer left the institute and continued on working elsewhere in Latin America.[41]

## THE ANDEAN REGION

Of the Ecuadorian composer and musicologist Segundo Luis Moreno Andrade (1882–1972), George List wrote in 1966: "No musicologist of comparable stature with a similar interest in traditional music has arisen to take his place in Ecuador."[42] Moreno, who had studied clarinet, bassoon, theory, and composition at the Conservatorio Nacional de Quito (National Conservatory in Quito) became in 1937 the founding director of the conservatory in Cuenca, a city in the south-central region of Ecuador, and served as director of the conservatory in Guayaquil from 1945 to 1952. Moreno was foremost an art music composer and wind band director, and though he investigated the music of Ecuador's three principal regions—the Pacific littoral, the mountainous Andean plateau, and the eastern Amazonian basin—most of his scholarly writing dealt with Amerindian traditions in the Andes, particularly those of the central Imbabura region where he was born. His 1930 published essay, "La música en el Ecuador" (Music in Ecuador), was the initial attempt at a comprehensive music history of the nation.[43]

Similar to Moreno's work is that of the Peruvian composer and folklorist Daniel Alomía Robles (1871–1942). Alomía Robles began his fieldwork after his appointment as subprefect of justice of the peace in Jauja, a city in central Peru, eventually collecting repertories among many different rural indigenous communities in Peru, and also neighboring Bolivia and Ecuador. He relocated to New York City in 1919 and returned to Peru fourteen years later to take up the directorship of the Sección Bellas Artes (Fine Arts Section) of the Ministry of Education in Lima.[44] Alomía Robles's field research inspired numerous compositions, perhaps the best known being the *kashua* section of his *zarzuela El cóndor pasa* (1913), which eventually became a stand-alone song covered by various folk, popular, and vernacular artists throughout the Americas.[45]

Moreno and Alomía Robles shared with other scholars at that time an interest in gaining glimpses into pre-Columbian Andean music systems by examining what were deemed to be their "remnants" as embodied in rural indigenous musics; perhaps the best known being the French husband-wife team Raoul d'Harcourt and Marguerite d'Harcourt, who were partly inspired to conduct this endeavor after meeting Robles in 1910.[46] The d'Harcourts conducted extensive research in the Andes; their influential 1925 *La musique des Incas et ses survivances* (The music of the Incas and its survivals), with its concern for and classification of pentatonic melodies, presented some of the most influential ideas concerning Latin American musicology in the region, as Raúl Romero notes in this volume.[47]

As mentioned above, these concerns with pre-Columbian and indigenous music systems also inspired the early work of Carlos Vega in Argentina, and even that of

Isabel Aretz, who initially studied with Vega because of her own interest in Inca music.[48] They also influenced the work of the violinist, composer, and musicologist Andrés Sas (1900–1967), another key figure of Peruvian musicology.[49] Born in Paris and raised in Belgium, Sas traveled to Peru in 1924 and in 1927 to teach violin at the Academia Nacional de Música Alcedo (Alcedo Music Academy; later the Conservatorio Nacional de Música). He remained in Peru after his return in 1929, the year he married the pianist Margarita María Lucila "Lily" Rosay. Together in that same year they founded the Academia de Música Sas-Rosay (Sas-Rosay Music Academy), which remained open until 1965, during which time hundreds of students passed through its ranks. In 1951, Sas assumed the directorship of the conservatory while continuing his studies of Peruvian folk music, which later became source materials for his compositions. Sas also provided the first study and transcription of the first known opera written in the Americas, Tomás de Torrejón y Velasco's *La púrpura de la rosa* (1701, The blood of the rose).

As a founding member of the Consejo Interamericano de Música (CIDEM, Inter-American Music Council), as well as a member of the Advisory Board of the Inter-American Institute for Musical Research at Tulane University, Sas was the most internationally known figure of Peruvian musicology at the time. In 1935, he founded the periodical *Antara*, which continued until 1956. His publications focused on the Amerindian music of Peru and the music of Peru's colonial period, though his essay on contemporary concert music is perhaps his most widely recognized work in North America.[50] Like Vega, Sas's work was informed by ideas about cultural diffusion and evolution that were popular with North American and European scholars of the time. In particular, he drew on the recent theory of Amerindian migration from Siberia to the Americas via the Bering Strait land bridge to posit the connection between Andean, East Asian, and South Asian pentatonic systems.[51]

A colleague of Sas, German composer Rodolfo (Rudolph) Holzmann (1910–1992), who settled in Peru in 1938, also came to study indigenous and mestizo music, an interest that grew out of his critiques of the overuse of pentatonic scales by Peruvian nationalist composers.[52] Upon his arrival in Lima, Holzmann began to teach at the Academia Nacional de Música Alcedo and became a member of the Orquesta Sinfónica Nacional (National Symphony Orchestra). His interest in the traditional music of Peru led to positions at the Casa de la Cultura (House of Culture) and the Escuela Nacional de Música y Danzas Folclóricas (National School of Folklore Music and Dance). Noteworthy of his publications are an overview of Peru's traditional musics and a study of Q'ero music, where he advocated a holistic approach by combining his formal analysis of musical structure with secondary archival recordings and ethnographic sources.[53]

Holzmann's career and research interest often crossed paths with those of Josafat Roel Pineda (1921–1987). An anthropologist by education, Roel Pineda was one of the founders of the Sociedad Peruana de Folclor (Peruvian Society of Folklore) in Cuzco and helped design the first Inti Raymi festival at the Inca site of Sacsayhuamán in Cuzco. While teaching folklore at the Escuela Nacional de Turismo (National School of Tourism) in that city, Roel Pineda participated in several ethnographic expeditions, including a research project with the Q'ero. After relocating to Lima, he served as head of ethnomusicology at the Conservatorio Nacional de Música, where he published a study about the *wayno* of Cuzco that was strongly influenced by Vega's theories of melodic analysis.[54] Later positions included a directorship of the Department of Folklore at the Casa de la Cultura and at the Centro de Estudio y Difusión del Folclor (Center of Study and Diffusion of Folklore; today Centro Universitario de Folklore) at the Universidad Nacional Mayor de San Marcos, Lima (National University of San Marcos).

Roel Pineda was also a frequent collaborator of the noted novelist, poet, anthropologist, and folklorist José María Arguedas (1911–1969). A prolific writer and passionate advocate for Andean folk traditions, Arguedas was instrumental in redefining what had previously been an interest in the study of an allegedly timeless "Inca" music into the study and promotion of extant regional forms of Andean musical dance.[55] His writings on a variety of folk practices, including songs in Quechua, the circulation of folk music, and profiles of vernacular musicians, stressed an ethnographic orientation.[56] Furthermore, as head of the Sección de Folclor y Artes Populares (Folklore and Popular Arts Section) of the Ministry of Education and the Instituto de Estudios Etnológicos del Museo de la Cultura Peruana (Institute of Ethnological Studies at the Museum of Peruvian Culture), and later director of the Casa de la Cultura, Arguedas was influential in documenting and establishing guidelines for the performance of regional music and dance traditions, helping foster the creation of a commercial recording industry devoted to regional Andean genres, and becoming a staunch ally and mentor to a number of the performers associated with that folkloric music circuit.

Arguedas's more ethnological and folkloristic orientation was paralleled by other scholars in the Andean region, who opted to focus more explicitly on descriptions and historical accounts of musical instruments, dances and ritual events centered on music, and dance in a given locality. In Bolivia, an early example of this type of scholarship is the work of Manuel Rigoberto Paredes (1870–1951), a lawyer and politician by profession with an avocation for ethnology, whose studies of Bolivian indigenous cultural practices provide a template for what would become the study and cultivation of various forms of Bolivian folklore.[57] There are also the organological studies of composer and poet Antonio González Bravo (1885–1962), a passionate student of the Aymara language and director of the Conservatorio Nacional de Música de La Paz (National Conservatory of Music of La Paz).[58] In neighboring Paraguay, musical scholarship was relatively sparse, although the historical work of Juan Max Boettner (1899–1958) on a broad range of indigenous, popular, and art musics, stands out as an important exception.[59]

Chile has also counted with a number of important scholars. Noted historian Eugenio Pereira Salas (1904–1979), who published on a variety of topics dealing with the arts, wrote the first general history of music in Chile.[60] The book is impressive in scope, covering from pre-Columbian musical survivals (as embodied in historical description of Araucanian, rather than Quechua or Aymara, dances and musical instruments), various types of colonial era musics, and a thorough account of the historical origins of several contemporary folk and popular genres.[61] Chile also counts with an impressive number of early studies devoted to Araucanian (Mapuche) music, with the work of composer-and-painter-turned-ethnographer Carlos Isamitt (1885–1974) particularly noteworthy.[62] Another prolific writer of the time is Carlos Lavín (1883–1962), who studied comparative musicology with Erich M. von Hornbostel (1877–1935) in Berlin, and who is well-known for his important organological study on the Chilean *guitarrón* and on a number of fiestas and ritual dances in the northern part of the country.[63]

The Instituto de Investigaciones Musicales de la Universidad de Chile (University of Chile's Institute of Musical Research), founded in 1943 as the Instituto de Investigaciones Folklóricas (Institute of Folkloric Research), played a key role in supporting this early scholarship through the publication of books and recordings, offering seminars, and organizing concerts, conferences and exchanges with foreign scholars.[64] In 1945, the university also sponsored the founding of the *Revista Musical Chilena* (Chilean musical review), which for seven decades has been one of the most important journals devoted to the publication of music scholarship in Latin America. The Universidad de Chile was also the academic home of Margot Loyola (1918–2015), a noted folklorist, performer, and dance educator.

Loyola began her studies at the Chilean Conservatorio Nacional de Música in the early 1950s, with her comparative-research interest eventually leading her to study also with José María Arguedas in Peru, Carlos Vega in Argentina, and Lauro Ayestarán in Uruguay. She is best known for her collection of songs and dances from a number of regions of Chile, including Rapanui (Easter Island), many of which then became a part of her performance repertoire or served as the basis for creating the choreographies for the folkloric dance troupes and performing ensembles that she was so instrumental in developing during the first decades of her career.[65] Loyola began to publish research based on her many years of collecting, focusing mainly on the documentation of regional genres like the cueca and the tonada.[66] Her field recordings, photographs, interviews, and other ethnographic materials have become a core part of the archives of the Fondo de Investigación y Documentación de Música Tradicional Chilena, Pontificia Universidad Católica de Valparaíso (Foundation for Chilean Music Research and Documentation at the Pontifical Catholic University of Valparaíso), which bears her name.

Arguably the most prominent contributor to the early literature on Colombian music was Emirto de Lima (1881–1970), a pianist and composer émigré from Curaçao living in Baranquilla on Colombia's northern coast. His publications were for the most part dedicated to discussions of folk and Amerindian music.[67] These initial studies by Lima, along with other antecedent Colombian studies, were instrumental in having "located Colombian music and songs in the international musicological literature."[68] Lima, who wrote on themes as diverse as the Colombian *bambuco* and the music of Debussy, was also a rather prolific composer.

The essays on Colombia's "national" music by Guillermo Uribe Holguín (1880–1971), composer and director of the Conservatorio Nacional de Música, were rather well-known at the time, mostly for their contentious reception.[69] In 1938, music educator and composer Daniel Zamudio (1885–1952) put forth an analytical study of song forms in Colombia that seems to have remained unpublished until 1949.[70] Finally, the sibling team of Delia Zapata Olivella (1926–2001) and Manuel Zapata Olivella (1920–2004) are believed to have been the first to produce tape recordings of Colombian folk music. Delia Zapata Olivella was a dance specialist who worked at the Departamento de Investigaciones Folklóricas del Instituto Popular de Cultura (Department of Folklore Research of the Popular Institute of Culture) in Cali, and her brother was a physician and novelist who published numerous articles on the folklore of Colombia. Together they organized a Colombian folkloric ensemble in the 1950s that toured throughout Europe, Asia, and Latin America.

### THE SPANISH-SPEAKING CARIBBEAN

The work of Fernando Ortiz has tended to eclipse much of the musical scholarship undertaken in Cuba in the first half of the twentieth century. Nevertheless, the work of Alejo Carpentier (1904–1980) and Lydia Cabrera (1899–1991) merit inclusion in this brief examination of some of the pioneering figures in Latin American musicology. Neither Carpentier nor Cabrera was best known as musicologists, but their contributions to our understanding of Cuban musical practices are indeed remarkable.

Carpentier was well traveled.[71] Born in Switzerland, he spoke fluent French, and even though he identified most with Cuban culture—his family moved to Havana soon after his birth—the years he later spent in Paris were particularly influential on his thinking. He had also traveled in Mexico and South America, spending many years in Venezuela, and was well integrated into the artistic and intellectual life of these regions. Best known as an essayist and novelist, Carpentier was also a pianist. His activities during the 1920s–'30s in Havana demonstrated many interesting parallels to de Andrade's career in Brazil. Carpentier was a founding member of *Revista de Avance* (1927–30), a journal concerned with Cuban nationalism, emerging trends in the arts, and rather radical departures from the social and political status quo. Akin to de Andrade's modernist agenda, Carpentier too was concerned with the integration of European and Latin American musical materials, particularly those of Afro-Cuban provenance.

Along with his musical confidante, the violinist and composer Amadeo Roldán (1900–1939), Carpentier organized concerts of new music in Havana with a focus on premieres of the music of European contemporaries such as Erik Satie, Darius Milhaud, Francis Poulenc, and Igor Stravinsky. Carpentier and Roldán also collaborated on a number of compositions. Both men were intimately concerned with the integration of Afro-Cuban musical materials in their works and instigating a rather modernist break from the reproduction of European musical forms in the Americas: their motto was "down with the lyre, up with the bongo!" (*¡abajo la lira, arriba el bongó!*).

Carpentier's writing integrated a variety of musical themes and literary devices (from French surrealism and magical realism to neo-Baroque), yet his recourse to Afro-Cuban sources as a cultural repository in the development of his personal writing style remained rather constant throughout his career, most notably in the application of colloquialisms, rhythmic play through alliteration, and the use of musical mimesis. Among his musicological works, his 1946 book, *La música en Cuba* (*Music in Cuba*), remains the most renowned. It is an examination of the musical life of Cuba from the sixteenth to the mid-twentieth century, with particular attention to the cultural contact of European, Amerindian, and African cultures in Cuba's musical history. Also noteworthy is Carpentier's 1977 essay, "América latina en la confluencia de coordenadas históricas y su repercusión en la música" (Latin America at the confluence of historical coordinates).[72] By any measure, it is a masterfully constructed analysis.

Lydia Cabrera was born into a prominent family in Havana: her father was a lawyer and writer; her mother was a socialite.[73] Her childhood was in part shaped by a close contact with the *criada negra* (black housemaid), and this formation would have a lasting effect on her scholarly work. Although Cabrera entered into a Cuban society in which few women achieved higher education, she eventually went to study in Paris. That experience allowed her to develop her very distinct gaze on Afro-Cuban culture, as well as remove herself from the object of her study.

Cabrera's publications on Afro-Cuban culture were filled with unique interpretive moves. The subject of her first two books was Afro-Cuban folktales, many of which she knew from an early age.[74] This was the beginning of her ethnographic technique of telling and retelling, which created a certain ambiguity between what could be loosely understood as fact and fiction, or between the ethnographic voice of her informants and her own autobiographical input. Her major work on Afro-Cuban religion was in many respects a settling of this ethnographic approach, and the catalog of Afro-Cuban medicinal plants contained within this tome came to be circulated and reintegrated into some of the most important religious treatises to be found in Afro-Cuban practices.[75]

Though musicology was neither the principal focus of her contributions nor a recurring theme in her written studies, Cabrera, along with the photographer Josefina Tarafa, collected and recorded a variety of Afro-Cuban music during the 1950s that was published in a fourteen-LP set of field recordings titled *Música de los cultos africanos en Cuba* (Music of African cults in Cuba). The recordings were accompanied by a nineteen-page liner note booklet that included song texts and photographs taken by Tarafa. Since 2000, Smithsonian Folkways reissued some of the Cabrera-Tarafa tracks, evidence of "the indelible character of the original project undertaken by Cabrera and Tarafa" in the mid-twentieth century.[76]

Cuba's most prominent music collector, lawyer and independent scholar Cristóbal Díaz Ayala (b. 1930), amassed throughout his lifetime numerous objects in relation to Latin American music, particularly of Cuba and Puerto Rico. His collection contains approximately a hundred thousand items in a variety of formats, including wax cylinders, 78rpm, 45rpm, and LP vinyl records, CDs, magnetic tapes, videos, photos, sheet music, and books. After Díaz Ayala donated his collection in 2001 to Florida International University, some of the materials have been digitized and are now available to the public.[77] He has written several books on Cuban music and a two-volume discography spanning the years 1898 to 2005.[78]

While the works of nineteenth-century Puerto Rican *costumbrista* writers would not normally be included as musicology, they remain some of the best sources for insight into early Puerto Rican musical life.[79] The works of writers such as Tapia y Rivera (1828–1882) and Manuel A. Alonso (1822–1889) provide some of the finest examples of this style of writing that also include descriptions of earlier musical activities in Puerto Rico.[80] Nonetheless, in the decades before and after 1900, assorted essays appeared on Puerto Rican music, particularly addressing the iconic danza. The renowned Puerto Rican writer and historian Salvador Brau (1842–1912) authored an early and influential study on the genre, as did the musician and composer Braulio Dueño Colón (1854–1934), a contemporary of the famed danza composer Juan Morel Campos (1857–1896).[81] In 1915 Fernando Callejo Ferrer (1862–1926) published the other notable study of this period, which dealt with the art and salon music milieu of the time.[82]

Most of the research undertaken on the traditional music of the Dominican Republic in the first half of the twentieth century coincided with the Trujillo Era

(1930–61). The 1927 publication by the Dominican composer Julio Arzeño is but one prominent exception antedating General Rafael Trujillo's rise to power.[83] Arzeño, like many of his contemporaries in Latin America, looked to the musical folklore of his native country for compositional inspiration. This nationalist sentiment among Dominican composers-cum-investigators was in part an attempt to emerge from the shadows of Puerto Rican danza composers such as Morel Campos, whose music had served as the model for Dominican musical composition for the salon since the late nineteenth century.[84]

Fieldwork undertaken by the U.S. musicologist Jacob M. Coopersmith (1903–1968) in 1944 led to a series of publications that provided some much-needed overviews of Dominican musical activities.[85] His more detailed monograph on Dominican music and musicians was written in two parts: the first considered the Spanish musical heritage in the Dominican Republic, with an emphasis on the history of Catholic church music; the second engaged with the nation's folkloric traditions, a direct result of Coopersmith's fieldwork endeavors. The text was written in a parallel Spanish-English format and published by the Pan American Union with an introduction by Charles Seeger. The second half of the tome provided an inventory of Dominican musical instruments, songs (with some transcriptions), and an invaluable bibliography with 123 entries as well as a discography of Dominican music.

The two other figures in the study of Dominican music who merit mention here are Flérida Lamarche de Nolasco (1891–1976), a musicologist whose publications first appeared in the late 1920s, and Edna Garrido de Boggs (1913–2010), whose work was crucial to the record of Dominican musical life and spanned a century of Dominican music making. De Nolasco's career was marked by an indefatigable commitment to the production of pedagogical materials, beginning with her early work *Cultura musical* (1927, Musical culture) and the influential *Grandes momentos de la historia de la música* (1957, Great moments in the history of music).[86] Garrido de Boggs, on the other hand, paid attention to the island's folk music; and although she spent most of her latter years in the United States, she frequently returned to the Dominican Republic where she served as the director of the folklore division at the Dirección General de Bellas Artes (General Office of Fine Arts). The 2007 collection of her texts, *Más allá del sur dominicano* (Beyond the Dominican south), is a fitting retrospective on her life's work.[87]

## BRAZIL

Despite de Andrade's initiatives in music research, Brazilian musicology has not yet produced leading figures after his passing. Mention nonetheless should be made of Luciano Gallet (1893–1931), a pianist and composer, who was one of the founders of the Associação Brasileira da Música (Brazilian Association of Music) in 1930. Heading the Instituto Nacional de Música (National Institute of Music), he planned the institute's integration in the Universidade Federal do Río de Janeiro (Federal University of Rio de Janeiro), which was realized in 1934. Gallet's 1934 published *Estudos de folclore* (Studies of folklore) provided an overview of Afro-Brazilian music, a noteworthy attempt of its time at a general set of observations on the subject, though its analysis was neither very nuanced, nor insightful in terms of any extensive field experience that was brought to bear on the study. Although de Andrade's main student, Oneyda Alvarenga (1911–1984), made the most overt attempts to follow in his pioneering footsteps, her own writings, such as the 1950 published survey *Música popular brasileira* (Popular Brazilian music), remained overwhelmingly descriptive. Perhaps her more important, and lasting, impact on Brazilian musicology was her organization and publication of de Andrade's manuscripts and the curation of the vast materials collected by the Missão de Pesquisas Folclóricas (Mission of Folklore Research) in 1938.[88]

The study of Luso-Brazilian music and dance fared somewhat better than other folk and popular music studies in the first half of the nineteenth century, particularly in the hands of the musicologists Rossini Tavares de Lima (1915–1987), founder of the periodical *Folclore* and co-organizer of the Centro de Pesquisas Folclóricas Mário de Andrade (Center for Folklore Research Mário de Andrade), and Luíz Heitor Corrêa de Azevedo (1905–1992)—in addition to the contributions by de Andrade himself on this subject. Corrêa de Azevedo assumed the chair of folklore at the Instituto Nacional de Música (National Institute of Music) as well as the executive directorship of the *Revista Brasileira de Música* (Brazilian music review), a flagship publication that circulated from 1935 to 1945. The journal was a site of collaboration for the major figures of Brazilian musicology of the period, including de Andrade, the composer Francisco Mignone, and Antônio Sá Pereira.[89] Corrêa de Azevedo's international prominence continued to grow: during the 1940s he was the Brazilian music advisor at the Pan American Union, Music Division, and music editor of the *Revista Cultura Política* (Political culture review). In 1951 he moved to Paris to become music commissioner for UNESCO, and while there he published his most influential monograph, *150 anos de música no Brasil: 1800–1950* (1956, 150 years of music in Brazil).

Since the repressive Vargas regime (1937–45) censored any critical intellectual engagement with Brazilian society, a strong nationalist orientation authenticating the country's folk traditions dominated musicological research. In the realm of folk music studies, scholars were foremost interested in collecting and rescuing folk music "to provide raw materials for the high arts."[90] The intersection of composition, musicology, and folklore was solidified during this period; it was reflected in the merging of art music and traditional music in the works of so many Brazilian composers.

## Latin American Music Research by Western Scholars

Latin American music scholars active in the first half of the twentieth century were generally concerned with safeguarding their respective national musical patrimonies, as well as working toward securing the social and political conditions that could benefit the musical lives of their countries. As they began to formulate the scope and direction of a homegrown discipline, the region had also become an object of interest for Western scholars.[91] As a result, much foreign research began to be carried out in Latin America. Although in many cases no links were forged between the works of local and foreign scholars, since the latter often worked from a privileged position and with a different research agenda, there were some instances of confluence. As Javier León points out with regard to Peru, "local and foreign scholars shared a number of research interests, for example, concerns over survivals of Inca musical practices, such as Pan-Andean pentatonicism. As such, both local and foreign researchers were seen as contributing towards 'our' understanding of Peruvian music."[92]

Foremost among European researchers in Latin America was the continuing efforts of German scholars to broaden the Berlin Phonogramm-Archiv, which had been founded in 1900, initiating an intellectual interest in the sound documents themselves, as well as numerous analytical studies from their transcription. One of the most significant studies was Erich M. von Hornbostel's analytic work of the recordings made by ethnologist Theodor Koch-Grünberg (1872–1924), who conducted research in northern Brazil and Venezuela between 1903 and 1905 under the sponsorship of the Baessler-Institut. Koch-Grünberg was appointed director of the Museum für Völkerkunde (Ethnographic Museum) in Stuttgart from 1914 until his death on an expedition in Brazil.[93] Particularly interesting for ethnomusicologists is the third volume of his meticulous ethnology, *Vom Roroima zum Orinoco* (From the Roraima to the Orinoco [River]), which describes the material and spiritual culture of a number of tribes, focusing mainly on the Taulipáng (Taurepan) but also covering the Shirianá, Waika, Yekuaná, and Guinaú.[94] It is illustrated by numerous photographs and sketches and includes an appendix written by Hornbostel on music, with descriptions of instruments, consideration of musical form and style, and transcriptions of thirty-seven melodies and songs taken from audio recordings. Koch-Grünberg's pioneering accomplishments also include the films he made of the *parishara* (hunting ritual) dance of the Taulipáng, using a cinematograph.[95] In 1934, the original cylinder recordings were transferred from the University of Berlin to the Museum für Völkerkunde in the same city. Federica de Ritter's Spanish translations of *Vom Roroima zum Orinoco*, including Hornbostel's appendix, were published in Venezuela.[96]

Colombia's earliest known field recordings were produced by the German ethnologist Konrad Theodor Preuss (1869–1938). These wax cylinder recordings from 1914 foregrounded the music of various Arhuaco groups from the Sierra Nevada de Santa Marta and the Amazonian Uitoto Amerindians, though only the latter constitute the core data for the monograph, *Die Musik der Uitoto* (Music of the Witoto), by German musicologist Fritz Bose (1865–1945).[97] Wax cylinder recordings of the Arhuaco and the Goajiro (Goajira Peninsula) Amerindian groups produced by the U.S. anthropologist J. Alden Mason (1885–1967) in 1923 are stored in the Indiana University Archives of Traditional Music.[98]

The 1935 organological study of South American indigenous sound instruments by Swedish anthropologist Karl G. Izikowitz (1903–1984) is a synthesis of numerous secondary-source materials.[99] It presents various museum holdings in Europe and the United States, with a special emphasis on the instrument collections available in Göteborg, Sweden; the second part of the study is a detailed overview of the ethnographic writings on Amerindian cultures and analyses of their musical instruments by historians, social scientists, travelers, and researchers. The parts of the study on Venezuelan Amerindian instruments are perhaps the most thorough of all the subjects addressed in this volume.[100]

Finally, as mentioned earlier, the French scholars Raoul d'Harcourt and Marguerite d'Harcourt figured prominently among foreign scholarly contributors to Latin American musicology, not only for their previously mentioned monograph published in 1925, but also for their later work with Aymara populations in Bolivia.[101]

## New Directions

As scholars grew more aware of the actual diversity of Latin American musics in the second half of the twentieth century, their studies began to depart from the rather simplistic view, and oft-repeated notion, that Latin America and its music was the result of a tripartite ethnic scheme: Amerindian, African, and European. Even though ethnomusicologists working in Latin America had been cognizant of the truly synergetic nature of popular and folk genres in Latin America before, the 1960s saw a departure from the search for origins or originary traits in the musical life of the regions in question, as well as a move away from the interest in parent sources of creole (mixture of African and European) or mestizo (mixture of Amerindian and European) musical cultures. This period was marked by an emerging interest in the movement of populations into and within the Americas, its minority populations, and reconfigurations or variations of the triethnic scheme in characterizing Latin American music—interests that could be observed in most Latin American music scholarship during the period among both Latin American and Anglo American specialists.

According to Béhague, after the mid-century, "researchers [also] became aware of the need for first-hand knowledge and experience in the musical traditions they sought to describe and interpret. Such an awareness made possible a better, more representative account of folk and traditional music."[102] This emergence of a more anthropological orientation in Latin American musical research coincided with a gradual opening of hemispheric lines of communication in the 1950s and 1960s. The resultant commitment to greater Pan-American activity also effected greater transnational institutional support. The shift toward more anthropological concerns and practices within Anglo-American ethnomusicology, particularly after the appearance of Alan P. Merriam's *Anthropology of Music* (1964), only intensified the parallel trend in Latin America.

Also characteristic of the post-1950 period was an unprecedented emergence of Latin American research institutions; many of these were soon clustered into webs or collectives of support for not only national projects, but also projects that were truly intra- and inter-American in their scope and financial backing. Although little funding or support was directly available to scholars with prospective research agendas, institutions contributed to the development of professional activities throughout the regions, formalized and realized national and inter-American programs, and the important archival work that they abetted.[103]

Many of these homegrown institutions were linked across national boundaries in Latin America. Their interconnectedness was often aided by the involvement of the Organization of American States (OAS; Organización de Estados Americanos, OEA) and UNESCO (United Nations Educational, Scientific and Cultural Organization).[104] Not only was the involvement of these international organizations important to many research institutions, but the number of monographs, series studies, and working papers produced by Latin American scholars also surged due to the conspicuous involvement of OAS and UNESCO, either directly or through institutional affiliates. The augmentation in publishing venues for scholars was likewise evident in the increase of institution-affiliated periodicals (as opposed to those of scholarly societies). Periodicals dealing with musical research or musical themes proliferated: *Actas del Folklore, Boletín Música, Anuario de la Fundación de Etnomusicología y Folklore, Inter-American Music Bulletin,*[105] *Páginas de Cultura, Revista Colombiana de Folclor,*[106] *Revista INIDEF, Revista Musical Chilena,* and *Revista Musical de Venezuela*, among others. Though a few of these journals first emerged in the late 1940s, their currency was very much a phenomenon of the period after the 1950s. Institutions and their publishing venues became indispensable for the growth of scholarly work throughout Latin America.

Before detailing some watershed moments in the inter-American institutionalization of musical research, we introduce some of the region's most important institutional initiatives and personalities of this time period. It is noteworthy that a growing number of Latin American scholars had been spending time abroad, either in Europe or the United States, or both, earning a degree at an institution of higher education, before returning home to put their experience in the service of instituting musical scholarship.

This was the case with María Ester Grebe (1928–2012), a musicology graduate of the Universidad de Chile who continued her studies at the University of California, Los Angeles, with Charles Seeger, Mantle Hood, and Klaus Wachsmann and later at Indiana University. She eventually wrote her doctoral dissertation under the direction of John Blacking at Queen's University Belfast.[107] Grebe's research interests were eclectic. Her early research on sixteenth-century vihuela music and its vestiges in Latin America distinguished her as a scholar of decided savvy.[108] Also known is her work on organology and the music and cosmology of the Mapuche and Aymara of Chile.[109] Her longstanding interest in the intersection of music, healing, and medicine singles her out as one of the earliest proponents of music therapy and medical musicology.[110] Grebe's husband, psychiatrist Juan Marconi Tassara, was a leading figure in establishing public mental health at the Universidad de Chile, and in the late 1960s, Grebe was invited to collaborate with the Facultad de Medicina (Faculty of Medicine) and was later named professor of medical anthropology. The cultural aspects of healing and music therapy were recurring themes in her scholarly output.[111] Grebe was active in the direction of the *Revista Musical Chilena* at various stages in her career and also served as the president of the Chilean branch of RILM (Répertoire International de Littérature Musicale; International Repertory of Music Literature).

Of a younger generation that refined its academic skills abroad, we mention a few representative individuals who have decisively shaped the field of music scholarship in their home countries and beyond. José Jorge de Carvalho, who studied composition at the Universidade de Brasília (University of Brasília), did his graduate work at the Queen's University Belfast and postdoctoral work at Rice University and the University of Florida. He was a researcher at the Universidad Central de Venezuela (Central University of Venezuela), and he later took a professorship in the Departamento de Antropologia of the Universidade de Brasília and a research fellowship at the Conselho Nacional de Desenvolvimento Científico e Tecnológico (CNPq, National Council of Scientific and Technological Development). He has also held a position at the University of Wisconsin–Madison. His work has principally been concerned with Afro-Brazilian communities, particularly for their sacro-musical practices.[112] Arturo Chamorro Escalante earned his doctorate at the University of Texas, Austin, under the direction of Gerard Béhague. The work of Chamorro Escalante, one of Mexico's most prolific scholars of his generation, encompasses Amerindian musical traditions, urban popular music, percussion instruments, and ethnographic theory and methods, and includes numerous genre-specific studies.[113] Peruvian scholar Raúl R. Romero received his doctoral degree from Harvard University and is currently director of the Instituto de Etnomusicología, Pontificia Universidad Católica de Peru (Institute of Ethnomusicology at the Pontifical Catholic University of Peru). His scholarly connections are as immersed in Peruvian ethnomusicology—from an intellectual and investigative tradition antedating the emergence of a U.S. ethnomusicology—as in the theoretical and methodological perspectives received from his American academic formation.[114] Romero's work demonstrates the continuing awareness among Latin American scholars of the vital contributions of homegrown scholarship on musical practices. Romero has also put forward more than a few challenges to U.S. scholars and scholarship that cut to the core of how Pan-American interconnectedness really might be shaping up.[115] Among the scholars of this younger generation is Chilean Juan Pablo González, who received his doctoral degree in ethnomusicology from the University of California, Los Angeles, before teaching at the Pontificia Universidad Católica de Chile. He served as the first president of the Sociedad Chilena de Musicología (Chilean Musicological Society) and decisively shaped the Latin American branch of the International Association of the Study of Popular Music (IASPM-AL). His own work reflects this interest in both musicology and the study of popular music.[116] Three seminal papers of this generation—by Carvalho, Romero, and González—have been translated for this volume.

## VENEZUELA AND BEYOND

A great number of Latin American scholars received their academic foundation in Venezuela under the tutelage of the husband-wife team of Luis Felipe Ramón y Rivera and Isabel Aretz, both of whom had studied with Vega in Buenos Aires. They relocated to Caracas at the invitation of the Venezuelan poet and folklorist Juan Liscano, who in 1946 had instituted the Servicio de Investigaciones Folklóricas Nacionales (SIFN, National Folkloric Research Service). The directorship of the music section was entrusted to Ramón y Rivera, and both he and Aretz began programs of fieldwork in Venezuela, which at the time focused greater attention on the nation's Amerindian musics. The following year, the couple returned to Buenos Aires, where Ramón y Rivera directed the Orquesta Americana (American Orchestra) and Aretz took a professorship in ethnomusicology at the Escuela Nacional de Danzas de Argentina (National School for Argentine Dance).[117] In 1953 they returned to Venezuela; Ramón y Rivera became director of the Instituto Nacional de Folklore (INAF, National Institute of Folklore, former SIFN) under the administration of the Ministry of Education.[118] The research team was expanded at the institute under his tenure: Aretz became a research fellow, as did many others. The institute housed a formidable archive, originally containing a considerable number of recordings of Venezuelan indigenous music made by Ramón y Rivera, Aretz, and Liscano, as well as Félix Cardona Puig and Abel Vallmitjana. The archive was quickly expanded after 1953 to include more recordings, as well as transcriptions, analyses, monographs, and other secondary sources both directly and indirectly related to Venezuelan folklore or to the study of folklore itself. By the mid-1960s, the archive housed over three thousand entries. Aretz had assumed the directorship of the Department of Folklore at the Instituto Nacional de Cultura y Bellas Artes (National Institute of Culture and Fine Arts) in 1965, remaining there until 1970.

Founded in 1971, Venezuela's Instituto Interamericano de Etnomusicología y Folklore (INIDEF, Inter-American Institute of Ethnomusicology and Folklore), the brainchild of Aretz and Ramón y Rivera, has arguably had the most lasting effect on Latin American musicology of any institution. Drawing on a wide array of international and institutional connections, the organization has reshaped the face of musicology throughout South and Central America since the 1970s owing to a commitment to the development of professional skills in folklore study and ethnomusicology for students from across these regions. An additional accomplishment of INIDEF was that it returned expertise back to the home countries of the scholars: the development of archives, the "publication of instructional materials and filed research results [provided] a base for future and even more meaningful scholarship."[119]

In 1986 Aretz became the president of the Fundación Internacional de Etnomusicología y Folklore (FINIDEF, International Foundation of Ethnomusicology and Folklore), and in 1989 she took the helm of the Centro para las Culturas Populares y Tradicionales (CCPYT, Center for Popular and Traditional Cultures), both based in Caracas. Ramón y Rivera was the founding director (1988–90) of the Fundación de Etnomusicología y Folklore (FUNDEF, Foundation for Ethnomusicology and Folklore), an institutional successor to the INIDEF; Aretz served as its director from 1990 to 1995, then returned to her native Argentina to serve as director of the Argentine FINIDEF in Buenos Aires.

One of the more prominent pupils trained at the INIDEF, the Peruvian Rosa Elena (Chalena) Vázquez departed from the description-driven publications of her Venezuelan musicological advisors, even though her contributions to Peruvian musicology do parallel those of many pioneers in Latin American musicology in the concern for social and political conditions that could benefit the musical life of Peru. For her 1982 published monograph on the musical practices of Peru's black population she received the Premio de Musicología Casa de las Américas (House of the Américas Musicology Award) in Havana.[120] She was particularly concerned with the development of a local tradition of ethnomusicological scholarship that deserved institutional support.

Guatemalan José Manuel Juárez Toledo (1931–1980), a music education specialist by training and the principal musicologist at the Centro de Estudios Folklóricos (CEF, Center for Folklore Studies) at the Universidad de San Carlos de Guatemala (USAC), went on to study folklore at the INIDEF in Caracas in 1976. His study on music and maize rituals in Guatemala remains his principal monograph.[121] In his home country, he served as the assistant director of the school for teachers' education and as the director of the Instituto Escuela Nacional de Bellas Artes. He was an active composer and published in a variety of genres, from symphonic poems to children's songs. Two other INIDEF graduates also helped shape music scholarship in Guatemala: Roberto Díaz Castillo, cofounder of the CEF and an active essayist and editor (serving *Editorial Nueva Nicaragua* for thirteen years), and Celso Lara Figueroa, a former director of the CEF and a recognized musician and historian. Their writings were concerned with a wider swath of folklore—beyond "traditional" music—while bringing in an additional focus on popular arts (in the case of Díaz Castillo) and oral history (in the case of Lara Figueroa).[122] The latter established ethnomusicology, musicology, and organology studies at USAC, and worked extensively as a researcher and advisor for various Latin American initiates through UNESCO and the OAS. Two journals have been associated with the CEF: *Tradiciones de Guatemala* (established in 1968; Guatemalan Traditions) and *La Tradición Popular* (Popular Tradition).[123]

Indeed, the graduate list of the INIDEF reads as a Who's Who of contemporary musicology in Latin America: in addition to the abovementioned individuals, it also includes Raúl Romero, Carlos Alberto Coba Andrade, José Jorge de Carvalho, among others. In our estimation, the work of these scholars have constituted some of the most important contributions to Latin American music scholarship, and this is so even beyond the merits of any locally situated research foci. In other words, the work of these individuals is commendable—if not for the diverse nature and efficacy of its applied musicological bent, then for the emergence of clear contributions to a truly American music scholarship in terms of theory, method, or locale-specific study. Irrespective of whether the research of the INIDEF alumni derives from the contingencies of locally situated musical practices or is generated from a bird's eye, collectively the work of this body of scholars has since come to represent irrefutable challenges to Béhague's longstanding criticisms of Latin American ethnomusicology and its paucity of contributions to the discipline at large.[124]

## MEXICO AND CENTRAL AMERICA

In fact, many scholars of the time worked diligently for institutional support of various kinds to strengthening the academic study of music in their respective countries and to establish research institutions that would serve as hubs of national ethnomusicological investigation. In Mexico, Carmen Sordo Sodi had taken the helm of the Musical Research Section of the Instituto Nacional de Bellas Artes (INBA, National Institute of Fine Arts). Her work led to the first exhibition of Mexican musical instruments (1966) and annual courses in ethnomusicology (1967–72). In 1974, the Musical Research Section of the INBA was subsumed under the Centro Nacional de Investigación, Documentación e Información Musical (CENIDIM, National Center of Investigation, Documentation, and Musical Information), the brainchild of Sordo Sodi. She was CENIDIM director until 1978, when Manuel Enríquez assumed the position. A composer and violinist, Enríquez's tenure was marked by the New Music Forum, the Composition Workshop, the Electroacoustic Music (E-A) Laboratory, the Indigenous Music and Dance Festival, and the conferences and concerts of colonial Latin American music (*Ciclo de Conferencias y Conciertos Panorama de la Música Virreinal en Latinoamérica*). During Enríquez's tenure, the center adopted the name "Carlos Chávez" and *Pauta*, a quarterly journal focusing on contemporary concert music, began its run (1981).

Under Leonora Saavedra's CENIDIM directorship, the Composition Workshop, the E-A Laboratory, and the Experimental Research Area transferred to the Conservatorio Nacional de Música, which also continued to publish *Heterofonía* (Heterophony), the principal Mexican musicology quarterly journal founded in 1968. The *Boletín Cenidim* began publication in 1986. The tenure of the center's fourth director, Luis Jaime Cortéz (1988–94), was marked by a surge in the historical studies of Mexican musics well as an increase in the overall print publications from the center. José Antonio Robles Cahero, CENIDIM's fifth director, organized the Encuentro Internacional de Músicas del Mundo (International Meeting of World Musics) and instituted the Jesús C. Romero Chair (Robert Stevenson won the first annual award for research). Lorena Díaz Núñez took over the directorship in 2002, instituting the Foro Nacional sobre Música Mexicana (National Forum on Mexican Music) and CENIDIM's Museo Virtual de la Colección de Instrumentos Musicales (Virtual Museum of the Collection of Musical Instruments).

The center holds numerous collections and archives. It continues its support of musicological research and publications, mostly through the coordination of numerous other institutional initiatives such as the Dirección General de Culturas Populares (DGCP, Office of Popular Cultures), Instituto Nacional de Antropología e Historia (INAH, National Institute of Anthropology and History), Instituto Nacional Indigenista (INI, National Indigenist Institute), replaced in 2003 by the Comisión Nacional para el Desarrollo de los Pueblos Indígenas (CDI, National Commission for the Development of Indigenous Peoples), and the Museo Nacional de Culturas Populares (MNCP, National Museum of Popular Cultures), among other affiliates of CENIDIM.[125]

In larger countries, such as Mexico, music scholars would often maintain affiliations with multiple research institutions, while also engaging in various musical activities beyond fieldwork, such as performing, composing, or pedagogy.[126] As one can imagine, these affiliations with the numerous research institutions not only represent the many hats worn by music scholars in Mexico, but they are also key to the developments of scholarly networks. It is impossible here to address in sufficient detail the veritable breadth of Mexican music scholars since the mid-twentieth century. We therefore refer to Steven Loza's study, the most comprehensive source for a survey of the field up to 1990.[127]

Without any intent to detract from the valuable work of so many Mexican scholars, any mention of Mexican music scholarship must include two important U.S. scholars: E. Thomas Stanford (b. 1929) and Robert Stevenson (1916–2012). Both have been at the forefront of archiving and cataloging the musicological record of Mexico in addition to the numerous publications in their respective areas of expertise in the music of Mexico: Stevenson's research has primarily focused on historical musicology and the art music of Mexico,[128] while Stanford has focused on vernacular music genres and ethnomusicological methods.[129] Their indefatigable work as researchers, editors (Stevenson for the *Inter-American Music Review* and Stanford for the *Anuário Interamericano de Investigación Musical*), and administrators cemented their position in the history of Mexican musicology and helped to foreground the music of Latin America in European and U.S. musicological and ethnomusicological circles.[130]

Comparatively, little music research had been undertaken in Central America during this period.[131] The organization of some early folk festivals held in Guararé, Panama, attributed to the pioneering efforts of the husband-wife team Manuel F. Zárate (1899–1968) and Dora Pérez de Zárate (1912–2001), has had a resonating effect since their inception in the 1950s. The first formal musicological initiatives in the second half of the twentieth century were, however, not really seen until the 1970s, first with the Primer Congreso Internacional de Folklorología (First International Congress of Folklore) in 1973 and then the Primer Seminario de Folkloristas (First Seminar of Folklorists) in Panama City in 1978. The former was sponsored by the Dirección Nacional del Patrimonio Histórico (National Directorate for Historical Heritage), affiliated with the Instituto Nacional de Cultura (INAC, National Institute of Culture), under the directorship of the anthropologist Reina Torres de Araúz; the latter was conducted under the auspices of the Museo del Hombre Panameño (Museum of Panamanian Man). Both organizations were staffed by numerous graduates from the INIDEF in Caracas. Panamanian folklorist Julio Arosemena Moreno undertook studies in anthropology and folklore in Ecuador and Mexico before teaching folklore at the Universidad de Panamá (University of Panama). He worked as a consultant for the UNESCO Action Committee on Handicrafts and the Ministerio de Cultura y Juventud de Costa Rica (Costa Rican Ministry of Culture and Youth). Given that Arosemena's training was more anthropological, it is not unexpected that his publications demonstrate a broad interest in folklore, and not just musical folklore.[132]

Finally, the Honduran composer and ethnomusicologist Rafael Manzanares Aguilar (1918–1999) began his professional career in Tegucigalpa in the 1940s as a teacher and marimba player with the Orquesta Tropical de Antonio Medina (Antonio Medina's Tropical Orchestra). Manzanares Aguilar's research was concerned with the origins of Honduran music and dance, and his investigations, which took him to numerous regions of Honduras, were the inspiration for his efforts in the founding of the Cuadro de Danzas Folklóricas (Folkloric Dance Scenes, a kind of cultural promotion group).[133] Manzanares Aguilar later took on the directorship of the Oficinas del Folklore Nacional (Offices of National Folklore) under the auspices of the Ministry of Education. In addition to his numerous publications on Honduran folklore, Manzanares Aguilar is perhaps best remembered in his native Honduras as a song composer, and many of his romantic titles have been recorded and disseminated throughout Central America.

## ELSEWHERE IN SOUTH AMERICA

Colombia's most active music scholar in the mid-twentieth century, Andrés Pardo Tovar (1911–1972), was a true polymath: trained in law and political science, teaching music at the Conservatorio Nacional de Música until 1964 and then sociology at the Facultad de Educación y Ciencia (Faculty of Education and Science), both at the Universidad Nacional de Colombia (National University of Colombia).[134] In 1959, while at the conservatory, Pardo Tovar organized the Centro de Estudios Folclóricos y Musicales (CEDEFIM, Center for Folkloric and Musical Studies), Colombia's first ethnomusicological research institution. Two prominent studies of fieldwork undertaken in the Chocó province were published soon after, followed by a study on the stringed instruments found in the Andean town of Chiquinquirá.[135] His main oeuvre, *La cultura musical en Colombia*, appeared after he became the founding director of the Instituto Colombiano de Etnomusicología y Folclore (INCODEFOL, Colombian Institute of Ethnomusicology and Folklore) at the Universidad de América (University of America) in 1964. Jesús Bermúdez Silva (1884–1969) and Luis Carlos Espinosa (1919–1990) continued on at CEDEFIM. The latter had earlier been affiliated with the Departamento de Investigaciones Folklóricas (Department of Folkloric Research, founded in 1960), part of the Instituto Popular de Cultura in Cali.[136] He and Enrique Buenaventura, the institute's first director, took two fieldwork trips to the Cauca Valley region on

Colombia's Pacific coast, where Espinosa later recorded the music of indigenous groups. In a joint venture with CEDEFIM in 1963–64, the institute carried out fieldwork in the port of Gaupi, Cauca.[137]

By the end of the 1960s, the Instituto Colombiano de Antropología (ICA, Colombian Institute of Anthropology, Bogotá) was home to the largest collection of recordings of Colombian traditional music, due in no small part to the work of its early curator, Carlos Garibello Aldana, who also undertook a great deal of fieldwork in generating the recordings, particularly among Colombia's Amerindian populations.[138] Also noteworthy is a joint fourteen-month recording study (1960–61) undertaken with the participation of British ethnographers Brian Moser and Donald Tayler and staff members of the ICA, particularly Nestór Uscátegui Mendoza, who had received a Guggenheim fellowship in 1957. Moser and Tayler later published a report on the fieldwork in the Piraparaná River area, and Espinosa and Pinzón, while with CEDEFIM, published a study on the ICA archival recordings made of the Cuna Amerindian groups in Chocó.[139] The ICA was also responsible for the publication of the *Revista Colombiana de Folclor*, which regularly contained research of ethnomusicological interest. In 1964 the Junta Nacional de Folclor (JNF, National Meeting of Folklorists) was instituted as a coordinating body for the various Colombian institutions working in folklore.[140]

Professional music scholarship was also advanced in smaller countries such as Ecuador, Bolivia, and Uruguay. In the case of the first, the Instituto Ecuatoriano de Folklore (Ecuadorian Institute of Folklore), attached at first to the Casa de la Cultura Ecuatoriana (CCE, House of Ecuadoran Culture, Quito), was particularly active in the late 1960s, under the leadership of the Brazilian folklorist Paulo de Carvalho Neto (1923–2003) and artists and intellectuals such as Oswaldo Guayasamín, Oswaldo Viteri, and Leonardo Tejada.[141] Also connected to the Casa was the Museo de Instrumentos Musicales Pedro Pablo Traversari (Pedro Pablo Traversari Museum of Musical Instruments), with its reputable collection of musical instruments and artifacts from Ecuador and elsewhere in the world, and named for Pedro Pablo Traversari (1874–1956), an early researcher of Ecuadorian folk music. The Departamento de Etnomusicología y Folklore (Ethnomusicology and Folklore Department) within the Instituto Otavaleño de Antropología (IOA, Otavaloan Institute of Anthropology) begun under the directorship of Carlos A. Coba Andrade, another scholar trained at the INIDEF in Caracas, who had undertaken extensive research in Afro-Ecuadorian regions, Ecuadorian musical instruments, and Andean music.[142]

In Bolivia, two particularly important figures in Bolivia music research are Antonio Paredes Candía (1923–2004) and Julia Elena Fortún (b. 1929). Paredes was a noted folklorist whose work included a survey of mestizo music and dance traditions and the study of a number of regional fiestas.[143] Fortún, who holds degrees in music, anthropology, and history, has published a number of studies on indigenous and mestizo music and dance throughout her career.[144] She was also instrumental in the creation of a number of institutions for the study and promotion of expressive culture, most importantly among them the Departamento del Folklore (Folklore Department) of the Ministry of Education (1954), which by 1975 she helped to expand into the Departamento de Etnomusicología y Folklore (Ethnomusicology and Folklore Department) at the Instituto Nacional de Antropología (National Institute of Anthropology). More recently, another prolific scholar, Walter Sánchez, has published regional studies on various types of folk and traditional music, many of them under the auspice of the Fundación Simón I. Patiño (Simón I. Patiño Foundation) in Cochabamba.[145]

Research in Uruguay has demonstrated intellectual and institutional connections within and beyond its national borders, best demonstrated by the work of pioneer musicologist Lauro Ayestarán (1913–1966).[146] Affiliated with the Instituto de Estudios Superiores (Institute of Advanced Studies) under the German Uruguayan musicologist Francisco Curt Lange (1903–1997), Ayestarán joined forces with Aretz in 1943, then Vega's assistant, to launch a survey of traditional music in his own country. He would eventually collect and compile more than four thousand field recordings from throughout Uruguay. He also contributed to the *Cancionero popular americano*, coordinated by Charles Seeger; he taught musicology at the Pontificia Universidad Católica Argentina (Pontifical Catholic University of Argentina) at the invitation of the composer Alberto Ginastera, and participated in many international conferences, including the First Inter-American Conference on Musicology, held in 1963 in Washington, D.C., and the Second Inter-American Conference on Ethnomusicology at Indiana University in 1965. The Centro Nacional de Documentación Musical Lauro Ayestarán (Lauro Ayestarán National Center for Musical Documentation) was founded in 2009 to house his vast personal collection of books, scores, and recordings, some of which have been digitalized and are publicly accessible.[147]

Also notable is the work of Coriún Aharonián (b. 1940), a student of Vega and Ayestarán. Though much of Aharonián's work has been in the composition of new music, he has continuously published on musicological issues outside the world of contemporary concert music, focusing on the music of Uruguay, music education, and the ideas of his former teacher, Carlos Vega.[148] In addition to assuming various roles in the cultural and musical life of Uruguay, he is found at the center of many institutional initiatives there, such as the establishment of the Cursos Latinoamericanos de Música Contemporánea, or abroad, such as with the International Society for Contemporary Music and the International Association for the Study of Popular Music (IASPM).

### THE SPANISH-SPEAKING CARIBBEAN

While interhemispheric contact generally intensified throughout the second half of the twentieth century, the Cuban-U.S. schism has led to an insularity in the theory and methods of Cuban musicology since the Cuban Revolution in 1959, eschewing any connection to or overlap with U.S. perspectives over the past fifty years and suffering a paucity of academic and financial resources effected by both the U.S. trade embargo and Cuban isolationism. The effects of both the revolution and the legacy of Ortiz in terms of the intellectual orientation of Cuban music research remained intrinsic to the constructed arch through which musicology has officially been validated on the island. It is no wonder then that the recurring themes of the musical and sociopolitical intersection with the United States and "correctives" to historical narratives of the same remain foregrounded in Cuban musicology. Certainly, there are both examples of scholarly contact that have connected Cuban and U.S. scholars,[149] as well as some emblematic studies demonstrating an atypically broad scholarly appetite, such as Natalio Galán's monumental study of the Cuban *son* (popular music and dance genre).[150] Nonetheless, these examples remain peripheral to the core of Cuban musicology, which since the 1960s has been decidedly shaped by two prominent scholars, Argeliers León (1918–1991) and María Teresa Linares (b. 1920). This husband-and-wife team remained staunch supporters of Cuba's revolutionary ideologies and continued the scientific approaches of Fernando Ortiz, León's former teacher.

Argeliers León, in addition to his formal studies of music and pedagogy, took summer courses at the Universidad de Havana (University of Havana) in ethnology and folklore with Fernando Ortiz, and analysis with the Spanish-born pianist María Muñoz de Quevedo.[151] León would later teach analogous summer courses at the university, create a chair in African Art and Black Culture in Cuba, and found the Departamento de Musicología (Department of Musicology) in the Instituto Superior de Arte (ISA, University of Arts of Cuba) and its degree program in musicology, which has graduated well over a hundred musicologists. León was, however, best known for his work as the director of the Department of Folklore at the Teatro Nacional de Cuba (National Theater of Cuba), which acted as a research arm of this institution to investigate the ethnically diverse source materials used in their theatrical productions. The productions at the theater were presented in a fashion that was somewhat antithetical to the style and scope of performances by the Conjunto Folklórico Nacional (Cuban National Folkloric Company).[152] León later founded the Instituto Nacional de Etnología y Folklore (National Institute of Ethnology and Folklore, 1961) in the Academía de Ciencias de Cuba (Cuban Academy of Sciences) and the Department of Music in the Casa de las Américas. Along with his editorial work with the journals *Boletín Música* and *Actas del Folklore* and his efforts in the restoration of the musicology award,

León's published monographs remain a testament to his intellectual legacy.[153] Among his more prominent students were the Cuban researchers Miguel Barnet, Rogelio Martínez Furé, and Rafael López Valdés.

Born in 1920 in Havana, María Teresa Linares has an academic résumé that connects her to numerous musical and research institutions in Havana: a professor at the Conservatorio Amadeo Roldán (Amadeo Roldán Conservatory) and the Universidad de Havana, a board member of the Instituto Nacional de Etnología y Folklore; director of the Conjunto Folklórico Nacional (National Folkloric Ensemble); director of the Museo Nacional de Música (1984–97, National Museum of Music), then linked with the Centro de Investigación y Desarrollo de la Música Cubana (CIDMUC, Center for Research and Development of Cuban Music); producer at EGREM (Empresa de Grabaciones y Ediciones Musicales), Cuba's national recording and music publishing company.

Linares's research interests differed from those of her husband, even though the first volume in the LP recording series, *Antología de la Música Afrocubana*, featured many of the early field recordings made by León and Linares of Afro-Cuban musicians.[154] She continued as the general producer of this recording series, but her real interests were squarely set on European-derived vernacular genres of Cuba.[155] Linares persisted with this agenda in the midst of the more prevalent attention lent to Afro-Cuban traditions by most Cuban musicologists and ethnologists—the latter being part of the continuing legacy of Ortiz's work. She worked for the most part on predominantly Euro-Cuban musical forms from the Cuban countryside, and particularly with *décimas* (song form based on ten-line stanzas) singers and practitioners of the accompanying string band tradition of the Cuban *punto*.[156] She was awarded the Premio Nacional de la Música and is a member of the Order of Félix Varela, Cuba's highest honor for artistic and cultural contribution.[157]

Of the many research institutions that arose in Latin America after 1960, the aforementioned Centro de Investigación y Desarrollo de la Música Cubana deserves particular attention. The center was founded in 1978 with Olavo Alén Rodríguez as its director. CIDMUC emerged under the auspices of the Cuban Ministry of Culture as one of its academic units. Though the main objective of the unit was to further research and archival work on Cuban music, the center was also committed to "taking into account its diverse cultural roots and the relation it has maintained at all times with the musical cultures of other people."[158] Though its scope and influence could not parallel that of INIDEF, it did demonstrate a musicological approach that looked beyond Cuba's borders, despite the seemingly insular focus of the center's title. CIDMUC also licensed parts of its archives to foreign recording companies as a means of both disseminating Cuban music and funding the archives of the center. The CIDMUC archives are a resource open to Cuban as well as international scholars, such that networks of exchange, both of resources and ideas, remain of benefit to Cuban and international scholarship alike. Finally, it is noteworthy that the CIDMUC staff boasts a wide variety of research expertise, incorporating within its musicological approach the expertise of psychologists, sociologists, acousticians, and computer and data management specialists who bring more "systematic" methods to the musical research undertaken through the center.

Just as the Cuban Revolution marked a crucial turning point in the social and intellectual history of twentieth-century Cuba, so too did the end of Trujillo's regime shape the second wave of Dominican musicology. In addition to a concern for the effects of the Trujillo years on the production of Dominican popular music, scholarship since 1961 has been occupied with the recurring themes of the history and unclear origins of merengue (and popular music as a whole), the status of Afro-Dominican music and its connection to Haiti, and the links between Dominican musics and the larger Caribbean basin.

Among the most prominent contributions of the time are Julio Hernández's study of traditional Dominican music, Emilio Rodríguez Demorizi's on merengue, and Bernarda Jorge's on art and salon music.[159] The scholarship in the 1970s took on a far more inclusive scope than in previous decades, notably incorporating the intersection of music and dance, as well as lending much needed attention to Afro-Dominican music. Fradique Lizardo (1930–1997) emerged as a preeminent voice of this period, and his work also lent special attention to Dominican dance, reflecting his work as director of Ballet Folklórico Dominicano.[160] The bulk of his publications, emerging in the 1970s, also coincided with the rigorous and extensive fieldwork that was being undertaken by Martha Ellen Davis.[161] Over the course of the past two decades, Dominican musicology has continued to benefit from both local and U.S. scholarship.[162]

Dominican musicology has historically lacked any regularly published national scholarly periodical. The *Boletín del Folklore Dominicano* (begun in 1946), the *Revista Dominicana de Cultura* (1955–56, edited by Rodríguez Demorizi), and the *Revista Dominicana de Folklore* (begun by Lizardo in 1975) were either short-lived or irregular in their delivery, or both. Nonetheless, increased institutional support in various forms has materialized over the past two decades, which has included the belated embracing of Afro-Dominican musics. The *Boletín del Museo del Hombre Dominicano*, a regularly published venue open to contributions on Dominican music scholarship, and the conference proceedings from the Centro Cultural Eduardo León Jimenes have been two examples of the work proceeding from this increased support.

The Instituto de Cultura Puertorriqueña (ICP, Institute for Puerto Rican Culture) was founded in 1955 with the mandate to promote Puerto Rican cultural values. Located in San Juan, the organization has supported numerous artistic, archeological, and ethnohistorical endeavors, in addition to providing institutional support to various archives, museums, cultural centers, and the Biblioteca Nacional de Puerto Rico (Puerto Rico National Library). The ICP also manages a publishing branch for both monographs and periodicals. In 1973 the Center for Puerto Rican Studies was established at Hunter College (CUNY) with mandates to collect, preserve, and provide access to archival and library resources documenting the history and culture of Puerto Ricans; to produce, facilitate, and disseminate interdisciplinary research about the diasporic experiences of Puerto Ricans; and to link this scholarly inquiry to social action and policy debates. In 1987, this interdisciplinary institution began publishing *CENTRO, Journal for the Center for Puerto Rican Studies*, an interdisciplinary periodical focusing on the humanities, social sciences, and natural sciences.[163]

Puerto Rican music studies have been taken up with decided fervor by many nonmusic specialists over the last thirty years, shifting much of the research to the sociology of music or to cultural studies. Nonetheless, some commendable historical studies on the music of Puerto Rico, particularly those of Pedro Malavet Vega and Peter Manuel's treatment of Puerto Rican danza, have lent much-needed attention to the historical record on Puerto Rican musics.[164] Afro–Puerto Rican music and dance genres, such as *bomba* and *plena*, have emerged as central themes in contemporary scholarship, a corrective to a longstanding gap in the literature, as have concerns over commodified popular musics (e.g., rap, rock, and reggaeton), their transnational movements, and their effects on Puerto Rican culture.[165] Given the untidy lines of demarcation that are part and parcel of the history of salsa, issues of identity and ownership have been foregrounded as a prominent theme in Puerto Rican musicology, taken up by local and foreign scholars alike, particularly addressing connections to Cuban musical culture and the Newyorican community. Considerable attention has also appeared from among sociologists and nonmusic specialists interested in the intersections of music, popular culture, and Puerto Rican identity.

## BRAZIL

The nationalist orientation that characterized the Estado Novo and the military dictatorships that followed (1964–85) continued to constrain scholarly work in Brazil even after their demise. The Brazilian State had already participated as cultural mediator for popular music in the early 1900s; its national policy toward culture intensified in the 1970s. Despite state repression, a number of thorough musical studies appeared in those years, such as the historiographies of Brazilian music by José Ramos Tinhorão, Vasco Mariz, and José Maria Neves.[166] Brazilian scholars—and non-Brazilian scholars alike—Suzel Ana Reily observed, "frequently projected their own nationalist preoccupation into the past," thereby creating a particular type of Brazilian music histories. "This process of nationalization has been represented through a chronological succession of styles, which came to acquire canonical statues, defining what constitutes 'authentic' Brazilian national music."[167]

An interest in studying urban popular music was kindled by innovating trends such as bossa nova and *tropicália*, an artistic movement that aimed to incorporate some of rock's modern aesthetics and technological possibilities with traditional Brazilian sounds. By the 1960s, the term "Brazilian popular music" had taken on a different meaning from that of Oneyda Alvarenga's 1950 *Música popular brasileira*, where only 20 of its 374 pages were devoted to urban popular music.[168] Ary Vasconcelos's 1964 panorama of Brazilian popular music, for example, is a compilation of biographical data on urban popular musicians, and José Eduardo Homem de Mello's 1976 published survey of popular Brazilian music includes firsthand information on contemporary popular music.[169] Mello had started out as a professional jazz bassist and journalist before he traveled to New York to study musicology at the Juilliard School. Back in Brazil, he worked many years for TV Record (Rede Record de Televisão), contracting international artists such as Sammy Davis Jr. and Sarah Vaughn, and serving as sound engineer in MPB programs and music festivals organized by the station—MPB is the acronym for Música Popular Brasileira, the musical-sociocultural movement that has dominated the artistic scene in Brazil since the mid-1960s. Other thorough studies of popular music, from a more sociological point of view, were Tinhorão's several books published in the 1970s that focus on the subject of MPB and on the role of modern technology—the record industry, radio, and television—in the production of popular music.[170]

A major contribution to the regional tradition of popular music in Brazil was the pioneering undertaking by Marcus Pereira, a lawyer, journalist and co-owner of a nightclub in São Paulo, who had developed a passion for the music of the northeast. "His long-held ambition to bring this music to a wider audience was realized in 1972 when he commissioned a team of researchers . . . to roam the Northeast recording aspects of popular music and culture." A music collector, Pereira had no folkloric or musicological intentions: rather, his personal interest in the musics of "the real Brazil," carried out largely at his own expense, led to this massive project, resulting in a series of commercially available recordings titled *Música Popular do Brasil*. According to Sean Stroud, the recordings "gave a major boost to the awareness of regional diversity, and encouraged many artists working in the field of popular music to experiment with regional styles in their own compositions."[171]

State projects such as the series of 45rpm recordings of regional folk music released by the Fundação Nacional de Artes (FUNARTE, est. 1975, National Art Foundation) and the Campanha de Defesa do Folclore Brasileiro (Campaign for the Defense of Brazilian Folklore), in contrast, received little publicity. FUNARTE also published a series of books on popular music. An interest in outstanding musical personalities led to biographies on songwriter and radio and television talent-show host Ary Barroso (1903–1964), choro composer and musicians Pixinguinha (1897–1973), and on the samba singer, Broadway actor and film star Carmen Miranda (1909–1955).[172] During the same period, a series of writings about urban samba, samba schools, and carnival music more general appeared as well.[173] Augusto de Campos edited a critical anthology of modern popular Brazilian music that contained in-depth studies of the bossa nova, *jovem guarda* (young guard), and *tropicália* movements of the 1960s and 1970s.[174]

Many of these studies written by folklorists, sociologists, historians, literary critics, and journalists were well documented but lacked the insights a trained ethnomusicologist could have provided. The discipline of ethnomusicology was still in its infancy—the pioneer graduate courses dated only from the 1980s and the graduate programs from the 1990s—but anthropological studies such as Rafael José de Menezes Bastos's on Kamayurá music and culture, Elisabeth Travassos's on music and shamanism among the Kayabi, or José Jorge de Carvalho's dissertation on the Sango cults of Recife paved the way for future research in Amerindian and Afro-Brazilian musical traditions.[175]

With the return of democracy, the ways in which music had been implicated in the construction of a national identity came under scrutiny, in particular how dominant narratives had marginalized Brazil's multiple musical identities.[176] In the process of the nation rediscovering its cultural heritage, the discipline of ethnomusicology grew more important.[177] The consolidation of ethnomusicological studies as a scientific discipline in Brazil is evidenced by the emergence of graduate courses during the 1990s and the creation of the Associação Brasileira de Etnomusicologia (ABET, Brazilian Association of Ethnomusicology) in 2001, whose mission it is to foster the study of ethnomusicology in Brazil, to promote systematic interchanges between all researchers of Brazilian topics, and to serve as mediator for communicated perspectives through the formulation of public policies concerning traditional musics.

## International Institutions, Research Centers, and Their Publications

The idea of Latin Americanist scholarship and scholarly exchange as central to the project of pan-Americanism had become prominent in the 1930s, influenced by the Good Neighbor Policy initiative, a reevaluation of U.S. policy toward Latin America during Franklin D. Roosevelt's presidency. The bilateral and multilateral relations among neighbors were further fostered to secure access to raw materials and the hemisphere as part of the U.S. war effort. The establishment of an interdisciplinary field of Latin American Studies was not only of academic interest. In fact, "the [U.S.] State Department enlisted Irving Leonard, then the Latin American specialist in the Humanities Division of the Rockefeller Foundation, to survey U.S. campuses to identify 'specialists to perform missions to Latin America,' and programs that were training experts who might be useful to the war effort."[178]

Due to this strong pan-American concern, the number of institutions, research centers, and international cooperative efforts between governmental culture branches increased markedly during the postwar era. Most prominent among the latter were a variety of initiatives in conjunction with UNESCO and the OAS, an involvement that is readily apparent from the list of publications, conference proceedings, and working papers on musicology and folklore of the Americas.[179] The two organizations also came to be linked to music scholarship in Latin America, if not the study of its expressive culture as a whole, through some of their program affiliates: the Coordinación Educativa y Cultural Centroamericana (CECC, Central American Educational and Cultural Coordination Organization), an affiliate of UNESCO; the Venezuelan FUNDEF, linked to the OAS Regional Cultural Development Program; the Inter-American Culture Policy Observatory (ICPO; Observatorio Interamericano de Políticas Culturales, OIPC), operated under the auspices of the OAS Inter-American Committee on Culture (CIC) and with the assistance of the OAS Unidad de Desarrollo Social y Educación (UDSE, Unit for Social Development and Education). It should then come as no surprise that in perusing the publications of Latin American musicology in the second half of the twentieth century, we find chains of institutional acronyms butted up against one another in the citation of many publications.

To illustrate the pervasiveness of institutional structuring in Latin America during this period, we would suggest a closer look at the institutional history of the aforementioned Fundación de Etnomusicología y Folklore (FUNDEF). The institutional progeny of Venezuela's INIDEF, the FUNDEF was instituted in 1988 and was a branch of the Venezuelan Institute for Scientific Research, which was under the auspices of the Venezuelan Consejo Nacional de Cultura (CONAC, National Council of Culture).[180] The FUNDEF was also linked to the Centro Interamericano de Etnomusicología y Folklore (CIDEF, Inter-American Center for Ethnomusicology and Folklore), which was part of the Regional Cultural Development Program of the OAS and was a National Commission of the Instituto Andino de Artes Populares (IADAP, Andean Institute of Popular Arts), under the auspices of the Andrés Bello Convention.[181] In 2006, FUNDEF was officially renamed the Centro de la Diversidad Cultural (CDC, Center for Cultural Diversity), now under the auspices of the Venezuela's Ministerio del Poder Popular para la Cultura (MPPC, Ministry of the People's Power for Culture). Members of the Center have represented Venezuela at the UNESCO General Conventions on Cultural Diversity (31st Session, Paris, 2001) and the Protection and Promotion of the Diversity of Cultural Expressions (33rd Session, Paris, 2005).[182] Some of these members also served on the board of the FUNDEF between the years 2003–5, leading up to the reconfiguration of FUNDEF as a center for "cultural diversity," in lieu of ethnomusicology and folklore. The institutional interconnectedness, or overlap, was pervasive.

Multitiered institutional funding was crucial not only to the establishment of research centers in Latin America, but also to the congregation of scholars from all parts of the Americas. To illustrate, though the First Inter-American Conference on Ethnomusicology, in 1963 in Washington, D.C., was sponsored by the Library of Congress, it was organized by the Inter-American Institute for Musical Research, based at Tulane University (New Orleans, Louisiana), under the directorship of the music historian Gilbert Chase (1906–1992), with financial support from the American Council of Learned Societies and the Social Science Research Council. Subsequently, the proceedings of the conference were published by the Pan American Union, General Secretariat of the OAS. Also represented at the conference were the following institutions, either among invited guests or from among the advisory board members of the Inter-American Institute for Musical Research: the Museo Históríco Nacional del Uruguay (National Historical Museum of Uruguay), Department of Cultural Affairs (UNESCO, Paris), Instituto Interamericano de Musicología (Inter-American Institute of Musicology, Montevideo), Library of Congress (Music Division), Museum of Music (Scarsdale, N.Y.), Music Library Association, Journal of the Society for Ethnomusicology, International Folk Music Council (U.S. National Committee), and the International Inventory of Musical Sources (Répertoire International des Sources Musicales, U.S. Committee). Representatives from these institutions were present in addition to a number of scholars from academic programs or research institutes within U.S. or Latin American universities.

Let's not forget, however, that the emergence of these pan-American initiatives in the context of asymmetrical power relations in the hemisphere not only created a problem of epistemological categories, they also depended on funding controlled by a U.S. federal government that pursued an imperialistic foreign policy. The establishment of the Pan American Union in 1910, the subsequent establishment of the OAS in 1948, the reconfiguration of the Pan American Union as the General Secretariat of the OAS in 1951, and the Consejo Interamericano de Música (CIDEM) accord in 1968 are all connected. These are not only links in a chain of successive developments within what is recognized today as the OAS, but they emerged from seminal ideas already present at the Congress of Panama organized by Simón Bolívar in 1826. Institutions have histories and intellectual lineages, and as such they merit close attention in understanding our own history of ideas.[183]

## Dialogues, Intersections, and Points of Departure

At this juncture it is worth reiterating that ethnomusicological practices in Latin America had begun on their own trajectory well before the term "ethno(-)musicology" had even coalesced among U.S. scholars. Certainly the use of the term emerged in no small part due to the social and intellectual shifts affected by World War II; a reassessment of musical scholarship, which had been linked to earlier comparative frameworks, was moved into a new light. It is also worth reiterating that the 1920s and 1930s marked a heightened awareness in Europe and the Americas of diasporic cultural expressions, creole musics, and the presence of African culture in the Americas. It was a trend that was impelled by a seemingly diverse set of cultural forces that, upon closer examination, demonstrates connections with U.S. ethnomusicology: a certain reactionary origin in response to the violence and social upheaval brought about by an antecedent war.

Although inter-American musical links existed before 1939,[184] two crucial events pertinent to Latin American studies happened in this momentous year: the Hispanic Division of the Library of Congress was established with the historian Lewis Hanke (1905–1993) as its first chief. The division was initiated to serve as a center for studies in Spanish, Portuguese, and Latin American culture and provide information to the U.S. Congress, the U.S. civil service, and those interested in the dissemination of the division's resources, namely academics, universities, and the general public. The division also helped to maintain the extensive Hispanic holdings of the Library of Congress and prepare ancillary materials for efficient access of the collection (e.g., bibliographies, manuscript manuals, and reference tools). The selection of Hanke as chief of the division was undoubtedly linked to the 1935 publication of the *Handbook of Latin American Studies*, an annotated bibliography that in the meantime includes thousands of citations taken from monographs, scholarly periodicals, collected editions, and conference proceedings.[185]

The second event was the seminal meeting of Gilbert Chase, Charles Seeger (1886–1979), and the German Uruguayan musicologist Francisco Curt Lange (1903–1997) at the International Congress of the American Musicological Society (AMS) in September 1939 in New York. The Latin American presence at the conference was thin to say the least, but at this meeting Seeger proposed to Chase that a council be established to promote a musicological interchange between the Americas. (Incidentally, both Chase and Seeger were born in Latin America.) The plan however was held in abeyance following the news that the

Division of Cultural Relations, a branch of the U.S. State Department, planned to host a conference on inter-American musical relations, which was to be held at the Library of Congress only a month later.[186]

From 1940 to 1943, Chase worked as the Latin American specialist in the Music Division of the Library of Congress, while in 1941 Seeger took over the directorship of the Division of Music at the Pan American Union (PAU). Seeger's tenure marked the beginning of a series of seminal publishing efforts by the PAU in Latin American musicology, as well as other inter-American initiatives until his departure in 1953.[187] The transition from the PAU to the General Secretariat of the OAS was completed in 1951, and in 1958 the Inter-American Music Council (CIDEM) was established by the General Secretariat, pursuant to resolution 9 of the first CIDEM meeting.[188] The council mandated the creation of an inter-American musical organization that would function with a permanent character, centralize inter-American musical activities and work closely with the International Music Council of UNESCO. The *Boletín del Consejo Interamericano de Música* became the principal publication of the CIDEM. In 1968, the council of the OAS and CIDEM adopted an accord of cooperation centralizing all the musical activities and initiatives sanctioned by the OAS through the institute.

In 1961 the Inter-American Institute for Musical Research was established at Tulane University in New Orleans under the directorship of Chase. The institute's advisory board was a truly international affair, including leading music scholars from eight Latin American countries and the United States.[189] The institute's organ, the *Anuario/Yearbook*, was edited by Chase with assistant editor James Downey. It first appeared in 1965 and accepted submissions in English, Spanish, Portuguese, and French.

Also in 1961, the Latin American Music Center was established at Indiana University with support from the Rockefeller Foundation. The center was a division of the university's School of Music aimed at "the promotion of Latin American music through performance, research, and study."[190] Juan Orrego-Salas, the center's founding director, remained in that position until his retirement in 1987.

In 1963, the Primera Conferencia Interamericana de Etnomusicología (First Inter-American Conference on Ethnomusicology) was held in Cartagena, Colombia. The meeting was jointly held with the Third General Assembly of the CIDEM and sponsored by the Colombian Ministry of Education, the Secretary of Public Education (Department of Bolívar), the CIDEM, and PAU. The proceedings of the conference were published by the PAU in 1965 and included thirteen papers in total—eight in Spanish and five in English. Among the contributors were Seeger, Hood, Leach, Ayestarán, Pardo Tovar, and Vega.

That same year, the Inter-American Institute for Musical Research, under Chase's directorship, organized the First Inter-American Conference on Musicology, held in Washington, D.C., and sponsored by the Library of Congress,

Music Division, under the directorship of Harold Spivacke. The conference was restricted to the advisory board members of the institute and invited guests. Three of the papers presented at the conference—by Lange, Ayestarán, and Vega—appeared in the first volume of the *Anuario/Yearbook*.

A persistent concern among musicologists working in Latin America at that time was the difficulties encountered with access to bibliographic sources. Various motions were put forward at this first meeting to enlist the help of the representatives of *MLA/Notes* and cooperation with RISM in strengthening the interchange of bibliographic resources and documentation among scholars and institutions, both in terms of cataloging and the microfilming of manuscripts. It was proposed that the Inter-American Institute for Musical Research take over the publication of a third edition of the *Guide to the Music of Latin America*, enhanced with the input of the other proposed bibliographic measures at the conference, and "cooperate in the preparation of materials for the music section of the *Handbook of Latin American Studies*."[191]

In 1965, Indiana University hosted the Second Inter-American Conference on Ethnomusicology, jointly held with the First Inter-American Composers' Roundtable and the Fourth General Assembly of the CIDEM. There were a total of twenty-seven papers, of which thirteen were on ethnomusicology and twelve on composition, and Seeger and Luis Sandi each presented at a joint session. Sixteen of the twenty-seven papers were delivered in Spanish, an indication of the strong Latin American presence at the conference, which was in part effected by the travel funds provided by the Council on Leaders and Specialists (U.S. State Department) for a number of Latin American participants. During the preparation of the conference proceedings, news had reached the editors of the deaths of three major pioneers of Latin American music scholarship: Vicente T. Mendoza, Lauro Ayestarán, and Carlos Vega. The proceedings, edited by List and Orrego-Salas, were published in 1967 as *Music in the Americas*.

Of the many recommendations that emerged from the 1961 meeting in the U.S. capital was a recommendation by Bruno Nettl, then editor of *Ethnomusicology*, "that a special issue of *Ethnomusicology* . . . , devoted to Latin American studies, be prepared in cooperation with the Inter-American Institute for Musical Research."[192] In 1966, *Ethnomusicology* published a "Latin American Special Edition" with Chase as guest editor. The volume provided scholarly contributions, translations, regional reports, and reviews by scholars from the United States and Latin America.[193]

These were heady times, and yet by the 1970s the winds had begun to subside to some degree. The proposed second meeting of the Inter-American Conference on Ethnomusicology, which was to be hosted in 1965 or 1966 by the Inter-American Institute for Musical Research at Tulane University, did not take place. Chase left Tulane, moving on to the University of Oklahoma and eventually taking a visiting position at University of Texas at Austin that he held from 1975 until his retirement in 1979. By 1970, the Inter-American Institute for Musical Research had been dissolved, though the *Anuario/Yearbook* continued as an autonomous publication under the sponsorship of the University of Texas at Austin. It was renamed the *Anuario Interamericano de Investigación Musical*.[194] Chase remained the editor of the new series, with Béhague and Stanford as the associate editors, but by 1975 the series had been suspended.

On the bright side, the appearance of the *Inter-American Music Review* (*IAMR*) in 1978, edited by Stevenson, filled in the void left by the *Anuario*. The *IAMR* accepted submissions in English, Spanish, and Portuguese and remained active for three decades due to the tireless work of Stevenson, providing an especially important publishing venue for Latin American music scholars, particularly those focused on historical musicology and Western art music traditions in the Americas (which had received lesser attention in the *Anuario*). One finds valuable research on plainchant, early polyphony, and colonial music making in the Americas, as well as helpful bibliographies and reviews of historical sources in Latin American and Caribbean music.[195]

The year 1980 marked five years since the dissolution of the *Anuário* and one year after the death of Charles Seeger. Both figured prominently in the first publication of the *Latin American Music Review/Revista de Música Latinoamericana* (*LAMR*) in 1980. Its founding editor, Gerard Béhague, clearly conceived of *LAMR* as a successor to the *Anuario*, though he distinguished the new journal from its predecessor by its broader scope, as he asserted in his editorial notes in the first issue: "LAMR is designed to fill a long-felt need for a periodical that focuses exclusively on all of Latin America's varied oral and written musical traditions" with an interest in contributions from "historical, musicological, and ethnomusicological studies."[196]

Béhague purported a very broad reading of what could be included within "Latin American music"—likely inherited from his teacher Chase, who shared the notion with Seeger. Béhague defined the scope of the journal as encompassing "studies on all aspects of Latin American and Caribbean music . . . , including the music of Mexican Americans, Puerto Ricans, Cubans, Spaniards, and Portuguese in the United States and Canada."[197] Béhague's open invitation to scholarship on not only the music from the Spanish- and Portuguese-speaking nations of the Americas but also the music of their diasporas and the wider Caribbean is a notable shift from much of the thinking, both then and now, on what constitutes Latin American music. It is worth noting that *LAMR* accepted submissions in English, Spanish, Portuguese, and French. The latter was no stretch for Béhague, whose first language was French, but it did recognize the need to invite Francophone America into the fold of Latin America.

Béhague's editorial notes also seem to be the first time that Canada was so prominently mentioned in a hemispheric view of Latin American musicology, a fulfillment of this notion of a truly pan-American musicology on the mind of Seeger as far back as the 1939 AMS meeting.[198] Not only would Béhague have been well aware of the sizeable Latin American community in Canada by 1980, but two of his former students from the University of Illinois, Robert Witmer and Stephen Blum, had already been working at York University in Toronto for some time, and by 1980 they had established a graduate program in ethnomusicology, from which eventually numerous scholars emerged with interests in Latin America and the Caribbean. Furthermore, the inclusion of French Caribbean and Latin Canadian music within the purview of Latin American musicology was rather prescient given that a substantial swath of scholarship on the music of the French Caribbean and its diaspora has subsequently come from French Canadian scholars. Béhague would also have been familiar with the work of Charles Boilès on Mexican music and Ramón Pelinski on Argentine tango; both men were on faculty at the Université de Montréal (University of Montreal) at the time.

Also in 1980 appeared the first issue of the *Black Music Research Journal* (*BMRJ*), edited by Sam Floyd. Affiliated with the Center for Black Music Research at Columbia College Chicago, the *BMRJ* accepts scholarly submissions on a wide range of musical topics connected to black music. Although this journal does not focus specifically on the music of Latin America, numerous essays over the years have dealt with Afro-Latin musical forms, and the journal has been one of the principal chroniclers of the pervasive influence of Latin American musics on U.S. styles, as well as issues of stylistic and aesthetic commonalties among African American musical expressions throughout the Americas. The *BMRJ* remains a vital source for Afro-Latin scholarship.[199]

During the politically charged atmosphere of the 1980s, the interdisciplinary field of Latin American Studies established itself on numerous U.S. campuses and enjoyed great popularity among students who questioned the U.S. foreign policy of the Reagan administration and sought knowledge about Latin America. The growth of Latin American Studies programs prompted an upsurge of scholarly activity in the region. On the other hand, the Cold War era also marked numerous shifts in the relationship between scholars in the United States and those in Latin America that complicated the idea that a growing intimacy among scholars of and in the Americas might continue in a linear progression.

## Diversification, Disjunctions, and Potentialities

The 1980s marked a time of introspection in the humanities, recasting our understandings of the relationships of power and reciprocity among scholars, their informants, the academy, and the field of study. Bronislaw Malinowski's controversial diaries had been published, Paul Rabinow's introspective challenges had been made to the ethnographic enterprise, anthropological subjectivity and intersubjectivity were pervasively on the minds of ethnographers, and anthropology found itself in the throes of internal challenges to its established order. The ideas of the Birmingham School had also taken hold in U.S. academies by this time, foregrounding reciprocity in the construction of "culture" texts and undermining the once relatively stable notions of class agency and the distinction between production and consumption in the field. The result was that "cultural theory" was in full swing as the 1980s unfolded, with an emphasis on popular culture, media studies, subcultures, and subaltern subjectivities. Furthermore, Latin Americans in the United States and Canada were graduating from institutions of higher learning in ever greater numbers: their perspectives on Inter-American relations were reshaping U.S. and Canadian inquiries into the same. The crumbling of the pan-American scholarly community that had thrived during the "heady times" of the 1960s, thus, was effected by some rather disjointed streams of communication, partly resulting from inequalities of power and resources, partly from a general dissatisfaction mapped onto music scholarship with a certain zeal during the zeitgeist of the self-critical 1980s in the social sciences and humanities.

Latin American scholars have been especially attuned to the growing problem—palpable at the first Annual Meeting of the Society for Ethnomusicology (SEM) in Mexico City in 2009, but maybe less so at the International Conference for Musicology organized by CENIDIM and the International Musicological Society (IMS) in that same city the following year—and adept at drawing attention to the elephant in the room. In particular scholars relying on ethnographic work have yet to resolve a number of issues about how the hemispheric community should proceed in addressing the imbalances that are not only inherent to most of the ethnographic work, but also parallel to our practices within our scholarly communities. As Raúl Romero had earlier remarked so pointedly: "The weakness of the local [scholarship] is the failure in establishing effective channels of dialog with hegemonic scholarships. The weakness of the foreign [scholarship] is the failure to see that doing ethnography with real people should serve higher purposes than merely scientific inquiry."[200]

It is telling that Romero foregrounds the *place* of scholarship here. It is an important reminder of the propinquity of "the field" for researchers living in Latin America. "Local" scholarship has characteristically been deeply imbued with a sense of the immediacy of the music, its environs, the stewardship of its transmission, the sociopolitical worlds in which it is allowed to emerge (or not), and endeavors that might further musical dissemination or ameliorate the lives of music makers. This is not however to suggest that only "local" scholarship would be attuned to such concerns.

The demands of any conscientious academic endeavor are multiple and at times overwhelming; however, the difficulties of communication to which Romero refers emerge from a veritable disjuncture among our scholarly communities. They are certainly not imagined. For "local" scholars, their experience vis-à-vis the scholarship from Anglo-American sources tends all too frequently to be best characterized as condescension from without, seeing their work "dismissed as trivial, outdated, or unsophisticated."[201] The degree to which this perception accords with reality is not so easily set aside. These impressions have become pervasive among Latin American scholars with respect to their relationships to Anglo-American scholars and scholarship, and it should come as no surprise that the effects of such an overwhelming perception may overtake the tone of some of the works we have included in this anthology.

The fact is that scholarship remains uneven irrespective of the locale where the scholar might principally reside. Béhague was perhaps the most persistent in his criticism of the "unevenness" in Latin American music scholarship—although this is first and foremost due to the fact that he was arguably the most prolific in terms of the publication of overview essays and assessments of the same. Most adamant was his critique of descriptive or historical research to the negation of approaches that might contribute to theoretical issues of interest to the larger community of scholars. In terms of area studies, Béhague was also critical of the lack of attention to the Amerindian music of Brazil and to the ways in which U.S. musics have shaped music making in Latin American. Many of these lacunae are now fewer. "Local" scholars in no small part have since the 1980s contributed to a more comprehensive and differentiated understanding of Latin American musical life.

Particularly since the mid-1980s, Latin American ethnomusicology has produced, or reproduced, an ever-increasing number of multilingual publications and translations—efforts to redress the linguistic barriers that permeate much of our scholarly community, and some of the mistrust that has arguably resulted from the same. Various collected editions have been mounted to highlight important essays in the history, theory, and methods of English-language ethnomusicology for a Spanish-reading audience.[202] Some important monographs in ethnomusicology are now available in English and Spanish.[203] At present, there are so many historical studies, collected editions, journal articles, book chapters, and textbooks published in Spanish, as well as in Portuguese, that it is impossible to draw attention to any sizeable sample of these texts here.[204] In addition, some English-language editions have in turn included the work of a number of Spanish- or Portuguese-speaking authors translated into English.

The availability of Spanish- and Portuguese-language scholarship through online journals is growing, as well. These sources have been crucial to the dissemination of research across regional, institutional, and linguistic borders that would have escaped the purview of scholars only a couple of decades ago given the obstacles presented by the relatively slow interchange of print media, its restricted dissemination, and the financial inability of many institutions to maintain numerous subscriptions in their holdings. Online journals, such as *Redes Música*, *Revista Eletrônica de Musicologia*, *Música e Cultura*, *A Contratiempo*, and *Revista Transcultural de Música* (*TRANS*), have become core sites for scholars keeping abreast of timely scholarship published in Spanish or Portuguese and salient English-language articles or book chapters translated into Spanish. For those interested in popular music, the proceedings from the biannual IASPM Latin American branch conferences, posted on its website since 2000, is an excellent source of information.[205]

It remains to be seen to what degree the increasing convenience in scholarly approaches to Latin American music across the divides are due to a new generation of more cosmopolitan musicologists or to a compression in the distances and obstacles, both real and imagined, that have historically separated us, or to some combination of both these factors. In either regard, greater mobility among scholars over the past thirty years—in their fieldwork, theoretical orientations, academic formations, dissemination of scholarly work, place of residence—has been an increasingly prevalent condition year by year that will hopefully continue to bear fruit not only in Latin American popular music studies, where such convenience is intense, but also in all areas of a veritable "musicology of the Americas" envisioned by some of those pioneering figures of the twentieth century.[206]

In the end, whatever may have been included among the features that have historically distinguished popular music studies among English-, Spanish-, or Portuguese-language publications, there is now much more to be said of their commonalties in terms of their theoretical and methodological concerns. Yet, no defined canon or "school" has been developed; no dominant discourses, hegemonies, or ideologies have come to govern Latin American music scholarship. The continent in all its diversity has prevented a monolithic perspective to emerge and, thus, preserved the complexity and multivocality of music scholarship.

In his recent book, *Pensar la música desde América Latina*, Juan Pablo González encourages us to think (and rethink) music from a Latin American perspective.[207] His brief survey of the history of Latin American musicology, similar to ours, examines the development of the field as a pan-American intellectual endeavor. We are convinced that familiarizing ourselves with musical studies from a different vantage point will lead to a greater dynamics of discussions across disciplinary, subdisciplinary, national, hemispheric, institutional, and language boundaries. It is therefore our sincere hope that the few selected articles translated for this anthology become building blocks to bridge these gaps, by acquainting English-language readers with some of the very issues, concerns, assessments, and knowledges of Latin American musical scholarship.

## Notes

This introduction is a revised, rewritten, reorganized, and expanded rendering of Michael Marcuzzi's unfinished manuscript. His broad knowledge of Latin American music scholarship and deep passion for the subject were manifest on every single page. I tried to follow suit. Any errors or oversights, however, are mine.

1. Bruno Nettl, *Nettl's Elephant: On the History of Ethnomusicology* (Urbana: University of Illinois Press, 2010), 26.

2. Gerard Béhague, "Bridging South America and the United States in Black Music Research," *Black Music Research Journal* 22, no. 1 (2002), 1–11, p. 1.

3. Gerard Béhague, "Boundaries and Borders in the Study of Music in Latin America: A Conceptual Re-Mapping," *Latin American Music Review* 21, no. 1 (2000), 16–30.

4. Walter A. Clark, "Preface: What Makes Latin American Music 'Latin'? Some Personal Reflections," *Musical Quarterly* 92, no. 3–4 (2009), 167–76, and the articles compiled in this issue dedicated to Latin American music.

5. Sarah Hamilton-Tyrell, "Mário de Andrade, Mentor: Modernism and Musical Aesthetics in Brazil, 1920–1945," *Musical Quarterly* 88, no. 1 (2005), 7–34, p. 7.

6. Gerard Béhague, "Latin America," in *Ethnomusicology: Historical and Regional Studies*, ed. Helen Myers (New York: Norton, 1993), 472–94, p. 472.

7. Gerard Béhague, "Ecuadorian, Peruvian, and Brazilian Ethnomusicology: A General View," *Latin American Music Review* 3, no. 1 (1982), 17–35; Stephan Palmié, "Fernando Ortiz and the Cooking of History," *Ibero-Amerikanisches Archiv* 24, no. 3–4 (1998), 353–73.

8. This interest is apparent in Carlos Vega, "La flauta de pan andina" and "Escalas con semitonos en la música de los antiguos peruanos" (La Plata: XXV Congreso Internacional de Americanistas, 1932).

9. Carlos Vega, *Los instrumentos musicales aborígenes y criollos de la Argentina* (Buenos Aires: Ediciones Centurión, 1946).

10. Fernando Ortiz, *Los instrumentos de la música afrocubana* (Havana: Dirección de Cultura del Ministerio de Educación, 1952); Isabel Aretz, *Instrumentos musicales de Venezuela* (Cumaná: Universidad de Oriente, 1967); Josafat Roel Pineda, Fernando García, Alida Salazar, and César Bolaños, *Mapa de los instrumentos musicales de uso popular en el Perú: clasificación y ubicación geográfica* (Lima: Instituto Nacional de Cultura, Oficina de Música y Danza, 1978); Roberto Rivera y Rivera, *Los instrumentos musicales de los Mayas* (Mexico City: Instituto Nacional de Antropología e Historia, 1980); Ernesto Cavour Aramayo, *Los instrumentos musicales de Bolivia* (La Paz: Editorial Cima, 1994).

11. Isabel Aretz, "Carlos Vega, 1898–1966," *Ethnomusicology* 10, no. 3 (1966), 318–21.

12. Carlos Vega, *Fraseología: proposición de un nuevo método para la escritura y análisis de las ideas musicales y su aplicación al canto popular* (Buenos Aires: Imprenta de la Universidad de Buenos Aires, 1941); *Panorama de la música popular argentina con un ensayo sobre la ciencia del folklore* (Buenos Aires: Losada, 1944); "La zamacueca: cueca, zamba, chilena, marinera," in *Las danzas populares argentinas*, vol. 2 (Buenos Aires: Instituto Nacional de Musicología "Carlos Vega," 1986 [1952]).

13. "Acculturation and Musical Traditions in South America" was published posthumously in George List and Juan Orrego-Salas, ed., *Music in the Americas*, Inter-American

Music Monograph Series, vol. 1 (Bloomington: Indiana University Research Center in Anthropology, Folklore, and Linguistics–CIDEM–Pan American Union–National Music Council of the United States, 1967). Carlos Vega, "Mesomusic: An Essay on the Music of the Masses," *Ethnomusicology* 10, no. 1 (1966), 1–18.

14. Béhague, "Ecuadorian, Peruvian, and Brazilian Ethnomusicology," 19.

15. Hamilton-Tyrell, "Mário de Andrade," 8.

16. Along with Mário de Andrade, the group included Oswald de Andrade, Menotti del Picchia, Tarsíla do Amaral, and Anita Malfatti.

17. The *Manifesto* begins: "Only Cannibalism unites us. Socially. Economically. Philosophically. The unique law of the world. The disguised expression of all individualisms, all collectivisms. Of all religions. Of all peace treaties. Tupi or not Tupi: that is the question." (All translations are ours unless otherwise noted.) The play on the Hamlet quote, itself a literary cannibalism of sorts, is in reference to the Tupi, a Brazilian Amerindian group, purported to have cannibalized warriors captured in battle. The claim being that the Brazilian history of cannibalizing the Other is one of its greatest assets. See Gerard Béhague, *Heitor Villa-Lobos: The Search for Brazil's Musical Soul* (Austin: Institute of Latin American Studies, University of Texas at Austin, 1994).

18. Mário de Andrade, *Ensaio sobre a música brasileira* (São Paolo: I. Chiarato, 1928); *Macunaíma, o herói sem nenhum caráter* (São Paulo: Livraria Martins Editora, 1965 [1928]).

19. For examples of musical subjects, see Fernando Ortiz, *La fiesta afrocubana del "Día de reyes"* (Havana: Siglo XX, 1925); "La religión en la poesía mulata," *Estudios Afrocubanos* 1 (1937), 15–62; "La música sagrado de los negros yoruba en Cuba," *Ultra* 3, no. 13 (1937), 77–86; *La africanía de la música folclórica cubana* (Havana: Letras Cubanas, 2001 [1950]); *Los bailes y el teatro de los negros en el folklore de Cuba* (Havana: Letras Cubanas, 1985 [1951]); *La música afrocubana* (Madrid: Ediciones Jucar, 1974). See Jane G. Rubin, ed., *Miscellanea II of studies dedicated to Fernando Ortiz (1881–1969)* (New York: InterAmericas, Society of Arts and Letters of the Americas, 1998), 82–141.

20. Among others, the Sociedad Cubana del Folklore (1923), the Institución Hispano-Cubano de Cultura (1926), and the Sociedad de Estudios Afro-Cubanos (1937). He also served as president of the Junta Nacional de Arqueología y Etnografía and the Sociedad Económica de Amigos del País. The journals include *Surco: Cultura Contemporánea* (1930), *Archivo del Folklore Cubano* (1924), *Revista Bimestre Cubana* (1936), *Ultra: Cultura Contemporánea* (1936), and *Estudios Afro-Cubanos* (1937).

21. Robin Moore, "Representations of Afrocuban Expressive Culture in the Writings of Fernando Ortiz," *Latin American Music Review* 15, no. 1 (1994), 32–54, p. 32.

22. Fernando Ortiz, *Los instrumentos de la música afrocubana* (Madrid: Música Mundana, 1996 [1952, vol. 1–2]; Havana: Ministerio de Educación, Dirección de Cultura [1952, vol. 1–3]; Havana: Cárdenas [1954–55, vol. 4–5]). Though difficult to find as a complete set, together the five volumes represent one of the most sought-after resources on Cuban music. Fernando Ortiz, *Contrapunteo cubano del tabaco y el azúcar: advertencias de sus contrastes agrarios, económicos, históricos y sociales, su etnografía y su transculturación* (Madrid: Cátedra, 2002 [1940]), with an introduction by Bronisław Malinowski; *Cuban Counterpoint: Tobacco and Sugar*, trans. Harriet de Onís (New York: Alfred A. Knopf, 1947).

23. Margaret Kartomi, "The Processes and Results of Musical Culture Contact: A Discussion of Terminology and Concepts," *Ethnomusicology* 25, no. 2 (1981), 227–49, p. 232.

24. See Robert Parker, *Carlos Chávez: A Guide to Research* (New York: Routledge, 1998); Leonora Saavedra, ed., *Carlos Chávez and His World* (Princeton, N.J.: Princeton University Press, 2015).

25. Robert Stevenson, *Music in Aztec and Inca Territory* (Berkeley: University of California Press, 1968), 16–17.

26. Leonora Saavedra, "Carlos Chávez y la construcción de una alteridad estratégica," in *Diálogo de resplandores: Carlos Chávez y Silvestre Revueltas*, ed. Yael Bitrán and Ricardo Miranda (Mexico City: Instituto Nacional de Bellas Artes, 2002), 125–36.

27. Carlos Chávez, *Toward a New Music: Music and Electricity*, trans. Herbert Weinstock (New York: W. W. Norton, 1937).

28. Carlos Chávez, *Musical Thought* (Cambridge, Mass.: Harvard University Press, 1961).

29. Rubén M. Campos, *El folklore y la música mexicana: investigación acerca de la cultura musical en México (1525–1925)* (Mexico City: Secretaría de Educación Pública, 1928); *El folklore musical de las ciudades: investigación acerca de la musica mexicana para bailar y cantar. Obra integrada con 85 composiciones para piano, cuyas melodías están intactas* (Mexico City: Secretaría de Educación Pública, 1930); Higinio Vázquez Santa Ana, *Historia de la canción mexicana, canciones, cantares y corridos coleccionados y comentados* (Mexico City: Talleres Gráficos de La Nación, 1931); Gabriel Saldívar and Elisa Osorio Bolio, *Historia de la música en México (épocas precortesiana y colonial)* (Mexico City: Secretaría de Educación Pública, 1934).

30. Also working at the Musical Research Section were Baltasar Samper, who headed the folklore subsection; Jesús Bal y Gay, who took on the art music subsection; Luis Herrera de la Fuente as the folklore archivist; Julián Zúñiga, who served as the transcriber and Braulio Muñoz as the engraver and copyist; and Raúl Hellmer as the folklorist.

31. Oscar Somoza, "Mendoza," in *Dictionary of Mexican Literature*, ed. Eladio Córtes (Westport, Conn.: Greenwood Press, 1992), 424–26.

32. Also included among the early Mexican folklorists would be María Luisa de la Torre Otero, author of *El folklore en México: el arte popular y el folklore aplicados a la educación* (Mexico City: n.p., 1933).

33. Vicente T. Mendoza, *El romance español y el corrido mexicano: Estudio comparativo* (Mexico City: Ediciones de la Universidad Nacional Autónoma, 1939).

34. Vicente T. Mendoza, *El corrido mexicano* (Letras mexicanas, no. 15) (Mexico City: Fondo de Cultura Económica, 1954); *El corrido de la revolución mexicana* (Mexico City: Biblioteca del Instituto Nacional de Estudios Históricos de la Revolución Mexicana, 1956); *Lírica narrativa de México: El corrido* (Mexico City: Instituto de Investigaciones Estéticas, Universidad Nacional Autónoma de México, 1964).

35. Clara Meierovich, *Vicente T. Mendoza, artista y primer folclorólogo musical* (Mexico City: Universidad Nacional Autónoma de México, 1995).

36. Other influential monographs by Mendoza include *Panorama de la música tradicional de México* (Mexico City: Imprenta Universitaria, 1956); *La canción mexicana: ensayo de clasificación y antología* (Mexico City: Fondo de Cultura Económica, 1982 [1961]); and

with Virginia Rodríguez Rivera de Mendoza, *Estudio y clasificación de la música tradicional hispánica de Nuevo México: estudios de folklore, 5* (Mexico City: Universidad Nacional Autónoma de México, 1986).

37. Daniel Castañeda and Vicente T. Mendoza, *Instrumental precortesiano: investigaciones de la Academia de Música Mexicana del Conservatorio Nacional de Música* (Mexico City: Secretaría de la Educación Pública, Publicaciones del Museo Nacional, 1933).

38. Otto Mayer-Serra, *Música y músicos de Latinoamérica* (Mexico City: Editorial Atlante, 1947).

39. María Baratta and Jeremías Mendoza, *Cuzcatlán típico: ensayo sobre etnofonía de El Salvador, folklore, folkwisa y folkway* (San Salvador: Ministerio de Cultura, 1951).

40. Edited by Myron Schaeffer and published by the Universidad Interamericana in Panama City, Méndez wrote a foreword to the first of these studies: *Boletín del Instituto de Investigaciones Folklóricas* 1, no. 1 (1944). Though the first study was published in Spanish, a four-page insert of English text was provided, summarizing the volume. The second issue was in Spanish and English, published under the titles "La mejorana, canción típica panameña"—"The Majorana [*sic*], a Typical Song of Panama," *Boletín del Instituto de Investigaciones Folklóricas* 1, no. 2 (1944).

41. Agapito Rey, review, "*Boletín del Instituto de Investigaciones Folklóricas* by Myron Schaeffer," *California Folklore Quarterly* 4, no. 4 (1945), 436–38.

42. George List, "Ethnomusicology in Ecuador," *Ethnomusicology* 10, no. 1 (1966), 83–86, p. 83. See also Charles Sigmund, "Segundo Luis Moreno (1882–1972): Ecuador's Pioneer Musicologist," *Anuario Interamericano de Investigación Musical* 8 (1972), 71–104.

43. Segundo Luis Moreno Andrade, *La música en la provincia de Imbabura (apuntes para la historia de la música en el Ecuador)* (Quito: Escuela Tipográfica Salesiana, 1923); "La música en el Ecuador," in *El Ecuador en cien años de independencia*, ed. Orellana J. Gonzalo (Quito: Imprenta de la Escuela de Artes Oficios, 1930), 187–276; and the bilingual *Música y danzas autóctonas del Ecuador—Indigenous Music and Dances of Ecuador* (Quito: Edición Fray Jodoco Ricke, 1949).

44. José Varallanos, *El cóndor pasa: vida y obra de Daniel Alomía Robles, músico, compositor y folklorista peruano* (Lima: Talleres Gráficos, 1988). On the Peruvian scholars mentioned in this section, see individual entries in Alberto Tauro, *Enciclopedia ilustrada del Perú: síntesis del conocimiento integral del Perú, desde sus orígenes hasta la actualidad*, 17 vols., 3rd ed. (Lima: PEISA, 2001).

45. Fernando Rios, "*La Flûte Indienne*: The Early History of Andean Folkloric-Popular Music in France and Its Impact on *Nueva Canción*," *Latin American Music Review* 29, no. 2 (2008), 145–81.

46. Enrique Pinilla, "Informe sobre la música en el Perú," in *Historia del Perú: procesos e instituciones* (Lima: Editorial Juan Mejía Baca, 1981), 400.

47. See also Segundo Luis Moreno, *La música de los Incas: rectificación de la obra intitulada "La musique des Incas" et ses survivances por Raúl y Margarita d'Harcourt* (Quito: Editorial Casa de la Cultura Ecuatoriana, 1957) for a subsequent amendment to the work of the d'Harcourts, and Paulo de Carvalho Neto, *Diccionario del folklore ecuatoriano* (Quito: Casa de la Cultura Ecuatoriana, 2001 [1964]) for an example of how the d'Harcourt tran-

scriptions continued to be considered important documents in Andean music scholarship for decades to come.

48. Aretz, "Carlos Vega," 318.

49. Gilbert Chase, "Andrés Sas (1900–1967)," *Anuario* 3 (1967), 75–76.

50. Andrés Sas, "La música culta en América: consideraciones sobre su estado actual," *Revista Musical Chilena* 2, no. 11 (1946), 15–24, and no. 12 (1946), 15–22.

51. Andrés Sas, "Ensayo sobre la música inca," *Boletín Latinoamericano de Música* 1 (1935), 71; "La formación del folklore peruano," *Boletín Latinoamericano de Música* 2 (1936), 97; "Ensayo sobre la música nazca," *Boletín Latinoamericano de Música* 4 (1938), 221–33.

52. Rodolfo Holzmann, "Aporte para la emancipación de la música peruana," *Revista de Estudios Musicales* 1, no. 1 (1949), 61–80.

53. Rodolfo Holzmann, *Panorama de la música tradicional peruana* (Lima: Casa Mozart, 1964); "De la trifonía a la heptafonía en la música tradicional peruana," *Revista San Marcos* 8 (1968), 5–51; *Q'ero, pueblo y música: un estudio etnomusicológico basado en 33 piezas del repertorio vocal e instrumental de los q'eros* (Lima: Patronato Popular y Porvenir, Pro Música Clásica, 1986).

54. Josafat Roel Pineda, "El wayno del Cuzco," *Folklore Americano* 6–7 (1959), 129–246. See also Vega, *Fraseología.*

55. Raúl R. Romero, *Debating the Past: Music, Memory, and Identity in the Andes* (New York: Oxford University Press, 2001), 91–102.

56. José María Arguedas, *Canto kechwa* (Lima: Ediciones Club del Libro Peruano, 1938); *Canciones y cuentos del pueblo quechua* (Lima: Editorial Huascarán, 1949); *Señores e indios: acerca de la cultura quechua* (Montevideo: Calicanto, 1976); *Nuestra música popular y sus intérpretes* (Lima: Mosca Azul y Horizonte Editores, 1977). The last two books were published posthumously.

57. Manuel Rigoberto Paredes, *El arte en la altiplanicie* (La Paz: Gamarra, 1913); later republished in an expanded and corrected version as *El arte folklórico de Bolivia* (Gamarra, 1949); *Mitos, supersticiones y supervivencias populares de Bolivia* (La Paz: Arno Hermanos, 1920).

58. Antonio González Bravo, "Kenas, pincollos y tarkas," *Boletín Latino-Americano de Música* 3 (1937), 25–32; "Clasificación de los sicus aimaras," *Revista de Estudios Musicales* 1, no. 1 (1949), 92–101.

59. Juan Max Boettner, *Música y músicos del Paraguay* (Asunción: Edición de Autores Paraguayos Asociados, 1956).

60. Eugenio Pereira Salas, *Los orígenes del arte musical en Chile* (Santiago: Universidad de Chile, 1941).

61. A good overview of Pereira's work can be found in Gilbert Chase, *A Guide to the Music of Latin America: A Joint Publication of the Pan American Union and the Library of Congress*, 2nd ed. revised and enlarged (Washington, D.C.: Pan American Union and Library of Congress, 1962).

62. Carlos Isamitt, "Los instrumentos araucanos," *Boletín Latino-Americano de Música* 4 (1938), 305–12; "La danza entre los araucanos," *Boletín Latino-Americano de Música* 5 (1941), 601–6.

63. Carlos Lavín, "El ravel y los instrumentos chilenos," *Revista Musical Chilena* 10, no. 48 (1955), 15–27; "La tirana: fiesta ritual de la provincia de Tarapacá," *Revista Musical Chilena* 6, no. 37 (1950), 12–36; "Nuestra Señora de las Peñas: fiesta ritual del norte de Chile," *Revista Musical Chilena* 4, no. 31 (1948), 9–20, and no. 32 (1948–49), 27–40.

64. Béhague, "Latin America," 481.

65. Dan Bendrups, "Easter Island Music and the Voice of Kiko Pate: A Biographical History of Sound Recording," *World of Music* 49, no. 1 (2007), 125–41, p. 132.

66. Margot Loyola, *Bailes de tierra en Chile* (Valparaíso: Ediciones Universitarias de Valparaíso, 1980); *La tonoda: testimonios para el futuro* (Valparaíso: Pontificia Universidad Católica de Valparaíso, 2007); Margot Loyola and Osvaldo Cádiz, *La cueca: danza de la vida y de la muerte* (Valparaíso: Ediciones Universitarias de Valparaíso, 2010).

67. Emirto de Lima, "La chanson populaire en Colombie," *Acta Musicologica* 4, no. 3 (1932), 28–29; *Folklore colombiano* (Barranquilla: Lit. Barranquilla, 1942).

68. Quotation is by Egberto Bermúdez, "From Colombian 'National' Song to 'Colombian Song': 1860–1960," *Lied und populäre Kultur/Songs and Popular Culture: Jahrbuch des Deutschen Volksliedarchivs* 53 (2008), 167–261, p. 168. Other antecedent studies include Santos Cifuentes, "Hacia el americanismo musical: la música en Colombia," *El Correo Musical Sudamericano* (Sept. 22, 1915), 4–10; and Victor J. Rosales, "La música en Colombia y sus cultivadores," *Boletín de la Unión Panamericana* (1927), 454–57.

69. Guillermo Uribe Holguín, "Sobre la música nacional" in *Vida de un músico colombiano* (Bogotá: Librería Voluntad, 1942), 127–42. For more on the distinction made in Colombia between *música nacional* and *música colombiana*, see Bermúdez, "From Colombian 'National' Song to 'Colombian Song.'"

70. Daniel Zamudio, *El folklore musical en Colombia* (Bogotá: n.p., 1938). The studies by Santos Cifuentes (1915), Rosales (1927), and Zamudio (1949) were all republished in *Textos sobre música y folklore*, 2 vol., ed. Hjalmar de Greiff and David Feferbaum (Bogotá: Instituto Colombiano de Cultura, 1978).

71. Gabriel María Rubio Navarro, *Música y escritura en Alejo Carpentier* (Alicante: Universidad de Alicante, 1999).

72. Alejo Carpentier, *La música en Cuba* (Mexico City: Fondo de Cultura Económica, 1946). Published as *Music in Cuba*, trans. Alan West-Durán, ed. Timothy Brennan (Minneapolis: University of Minnesota Press, 2001). Alejo Carpentier, "América Latina en la confluencia de coordenadas históricas y su repercusión en la música," in *América Latina en su música*, ed. Isabel Aretz (Mexico City: UNESCO-Siglo Veintiuno, 1985 [1977]), 7–19.

73. Edna M. Ródriguez-Mangual, *Lydia Cabrera and the Construction of an Afro-Cuban Cultural Identity* (Chapel Hill: University of North Carolina Press, 2004).

74. Lydia Cabrera, *Cuentos negros de Cuba* (Havana: La Verónica, 1940); *¿Por qué? . . . Cuentos negros de Cuba* (Havana: Ediciones C.R., 1948).

75. Lydia Cabrera, *El monte, igbo finda, ewe orisha, vititinfinda: notas sobre las religiones, la magia, las supersticiones y el folklore de los negros criollos y del pueblo de Cuba* (Havana: Ediciones C.R., 1954). Cataloging formed an integral part of Cabrera's ethnographic output, including tomes on religious lexica and ritual symbology. See Lydia Cabrera, *Anaforuana: ritual y símbolos de la iniciación en la sociedad secreta Abakuá* (Madrid: Ediciones R., 1975).

76. Lydia Cabrera and Josefina Tarafa, *Havana, Cuba, ca. 1957: Rhythms and Songs for the Orishas* (Smithsonian Folkways Recording SFW40489, 2001); *Matanzas, Cuba, ca. 1957: Afro-Cuban Sacred Music from the Countryside* (SFW40490, 2001); *Havana & Matanzas, Cuba, ca. 1957: Batá, Bembé, and Palo Songs from the Historic Recordings of Lydia Cabrera and Josefina Tarafa* (SFW40434, 2003); Michael Marcuzzi, review of *Havana & Matanzas, Cuba, ca. 1957: Batá, Bembé and Palo Songs* by Lydia Cabrera, Josefina Tarafa, *Latin American Music Review* 29, no. 1 (2008), 112–15, p. 112.

77. Díaz-Ayala Collection, Special Collections and University Archives, Florida International University, http://specialcollections.fiu.edu, accessed May 15, 2015.

78. Cristóbal Díaz Ayala, *Música cubana del areíto a la nueva trova* (Miami: Ediciones Universal, 1981); *Cuando salí de la Habana: 1898–1997: cien años de música cubana por el mundo* (San Juan, P.R.: Fundación Musicalia, 1998); *Cuba canta y baila: discografía de la música cubana, 1898–1925* (San Juan, P.R.: Fundación Musicalia, 1994); *Cuba canta y baila: discografía de la música cubana, 1925 al presente* (Miami: Ediciones Universal, 2001), among others.

79. *Costumbrismo* (adj. *costumbrista*) was principally a nineteenth-century movement in literature and the visual arts that focused on the quotidian manners, or "customs," of Hispanic life. In writing, authors tended to provide quaint "folkloric" details of traditional ways, a response to the realities of what was perceived to be a rapidly changing, nineteenth-century world. Though at times satirical, *costumbrista* writing characteristically attended to detail rather than offered substantive insight into what tended to be a meticulous representation of traditional life. The result often projected a decidedly romantic rendering of emblematic figures or settings, such as the noble peasant or the idyllic pastoral scene.

80. Alejandro Tapia y Rivera, *Obras completas* (San Juan: Instituto de Cultura Puertorriqueña, 1968); Manuel A. Alonso, *El gíbaro: cuadro de costumbres de la isla de Puerto Rico* (San Juan: Instituto de Cultura Puertorriqueña, 1849 [1974]).

81. Salvador Brau, "La danza puertorriqueña," in *Ensayos (disquisiciones sociológicas)* (Río Piedras: Editorial Edil, 1972 [1885]); Braulio Dueño Colón, "Estudio sobre la danza puertorriqueña," in *Ensayos sobre la danza puertorriqueña*, ed. Marisa Rosado (San Juan: Instituto de Cultura Puertorriqueña, 1977 [1914]), 14–22. For more on Dueño Colón, see Manuel Dueño Colón, *Braulio Dueño Colón, estudio biográfico* (New York: n.p., 1951).

82. Fernando Callejo Ferrer, *Música y músicos puertorriqueños* (San Juan: Editorial Coquí, 1971 [1915]).

83. Julio Arzeño, *Del folk-lore musical dominicano* (Santo Domingo: Roques Roman, 1927).

84. See Peter Manuel, *Creolizing Contradance in the Caribbean* (Philadelphia: Temple University Press, 2010), 45; see also Julio Alberto Hernández, *Música tradicional dominicana* (Santo Domingo: Minsterio de Cultura, 2010 [1969]).

85. Jacob M. Coopersmith, "Music and Musicians of the Dominican Republic: A Survey—Part I," *Musical Quarterly* 31, no. 1 (1945), 71–88; "Music and Musicians of the Dominican Republic: A Survey—Part II," *Musical Quarterly* 31, no. 2 (1945), 212–26; *Music and Musicians of the Dominican Republic* (Washington, D.C.: Division of Music and Visual Arts, Dept. of Cultural Affairs, Pan American Union, 1949).

86. Flérida Lamarche de Nolasco, *La música en Santo Domingo y otros ensayos* (Ciudad Trujillo: Editora Montalvo, 1939); *Grandes momentos de la historia de la música* (Ciudad

Trujillo: Editora del Caribe, 1957), which was awarded the Premio Nacional Luisa Ercina Chevalier for didactic works in 1957.

87. Edna Garrido de Boggs, *Panorama del folklore dominicano* (Coral Gables, Fla.: University of Miami Press, 1961); *Reseña histórica del folklore dominicano* (Santo Domingo: Secretaría de Estado de Cultura, Dirección Nacional de Folklore, 2006); Edgar Valenzuela, Martha E. Davis, Xiomarita Pérez, ed., *Más allá del sur dominicano: textos folklóricos de Edna Garrido de Boggs* (Santo Domingo: Dirección General de la Feria del Libro, 2007).

88. Based on a felt urgency to register popular manifestations of rural culture before it was too late, the mission of this research team was to study all aspects of folklore, with particular emphasis on popular music, dance, and costume. The collected materials consisted of 20 notebooks of songs, 168 78rpm records containing 1,500 songs, 1,066 photographs, 9 16 mm films, and 775 objects. See Flávia Camarga Toni et al., *Missão de Pesquisas Folclóricas* (São Paulo: Associação Amigos do Centro Cultural São Paulo, 2010). A six-CD set (and program notes in three booklets) with de Andrade's field recordings from 1937 and 1938 was released in 2006, *Mário de Andrade, Missão de Pesquisas Folclóricas: Música tradicional do norte e nordeste* (CDSS005/06 Serviço Social do Comércio, São Paulo, 2006).

89. Sá Pereira was director of the Escola de Música da Universidade Federal do Rio de Janeiro (National School of Music of the University of Rio de Janeiro) and also represented Brazil at the 1942 gathering of Latin American music specialists in Washington, D.C., hosted by the Pan American Union, Music Division, during Charles Seeger's tenure as chief.

90. Suzel Ana Reily, "Introduction: Brazilian Musics, Brazilian Identities," *British Journal of Ethnomusicology* 9, no. 1 (2000), 1–10, p. 5.

91. The term "Western" is employed here in a geographic sense, meaning scholars from Europe and Anglo-America, as opposed to scholars from Latin America.

92. Javier León, "Peruvian Musical Scholarship and the Construction of an Academic Other," *Latin American Music Review* 20, no. 2 (1999), 168–83, p. 173.

93. Theodor Koch-Grünberg's first report was published in two volumes (1909–10) and later revised and reissued in one volume as *Zwei Jahre bei den Indianern Nordwest-Brasiliens* (Stuttgart: Strecker und Schröder, 1923).

94. Theodor Koch-Grünberg, *Vom Roroima zum Orinoco: Ergebnisse einer Reise in Nordbrasilien und Venezuela in den Jahren 1911–1913*, 5 vols., appendix to 3rd vol. by Erich von Hornbostel, 307–440 (Berlin: D. Reimer, 1917–28), reissued by Cambridge Library Collection, 2009–10.

95. An excerpt can be viewed at "Klänge und Bilder der Tropen: Ein Multimedia-Visionär im Urwald," Miradas Alemanas Hacia América Latina, Ibero-Amerikanisches Institut, www.miradas-alemanas.de, accessed April 9, 2014.

96. Federica de Ritter translated Koch-Grünberg's vols. 1 to 3 (*Del Roraima al Orinoco* [Caracas: Banco Central de Venezuela, 1970]), including Hornbostel's appendix, "La música de los Makuschi, Taulipáng y Yekuaná"; the piece was also published in *Archivos Venezolanos de Folklore* 3, no. 1 (1955–56).

97. Fritz Bose, *Die Musik der Uitoto* (*Zeitschrift für Vergleichende Musikwissenschaft* 1) (Burg: A. Hopfer, 1934). The Preuss recordings were deposited in the Berlin Phonogramm-Archiv.

98. The Mason recordings were first deposited in the Field Colombian Museum of Natural History (now the Chicago Natural History Museum) before being transferred to Indiana Archives.

99. Karl G. Izikowitz, *Musical and Other Sound Instruments of the South American Indians: A Comparative Ethnographical Study* (East Ardsley, U.K.: S. R. Publisher, 1970 [1935]).

100. Another prominent example of European scholarship outside the dominant West European presence are the recordings and study by Finnish anthropologist Rafael Karsten (1879–1956), *The Head-Hunters of Western Amazonas: The Life and Culture of the Jibaro Indians of Eastern Ecuador and Peru* (Helsinki: Societas Scientiarum Fennica, 1935).

101. Raoul d'Harcourt and Marguerite d'Harcourt, *La musique des Aymara sur les hauts plateaux boliviens* (Paris: Société des Américanistes, 1959); see also *La musique des Incas et ses survivances* (Paris: Librairie Orientaliste Paul Geuthner, 1925).

102. Béhague, "Latin America," 472.

103. Ronald R. Smith, "A Discussion of Central America and Northern South America," *Latin American Music Review* 3, no. 1 (1982), 1–16, p. 2.

104. The Inter-American conference of 1948 in Bogotá, Colombia, organized by the Pan American Union, led to the creation of the Organization of American States (OAS). In 1951 the Pan American Union was renamed the Secretariat of the OAS.

105. Formerly the *Pan American Bulletin*, the *Inter-American Music Bulletin* was another OAS-sponsored publication that addressed musical subjects in addition to a wide range of other cultural themes.

106. It was formerly known as the *Revista de Folklore* (1947–51), then the *Revista Colombiana de Folklore* (1952–59), the *Revista Colombiana de Folclor* (1960–86), and now the *Nueva Revista Colombiana de Folklore*.

107. María Ester Grebe, "Generative Models, Symbolic Structures, and Acculturation in the Panpipe Music of the Aymara of Tarapaca, Chile" (PhD diss., Queen's University Belfast, 1980).

108. Most notable for Chilean musicology are the links between this repertory and the Chilean *guitarrón* tradition (*canto a lo poeta* [*a lo divino*]). See María Ester Grebe, "Modality in Spanish Vihuela Music and Archaic Chilean Folksongs: A Comparative Study," *Ethnomusicology* 11, no. 3 (1967), 326–42; "Modality in the Spanish Vihuela Music of the Sixteenth Century and Its Incidence in Latin-American Music," *Anuário Musical* 26 (1971), 29–59.

109. María Ester Grebe, "Clasificación de instrumentos musicales," *Revista Musical Chilena* 25, no. 113–14 (1971), 18–34; "Instrumentos musicales precolombinos de Chile," *Revista Musical Chilena* 28, no. 128 (1974), 5–55; "El kultrún, un microcosmos simbólico," *Revista Musical Chilena* 27, no. 123–124 (1973), 3–42; "Meli–Witran–Mapu: construcción simbólica de la tierra en la cultura mapuche," in *Pekuntun: Instituto de Estudios Indígenas* (Temuco, Chile: Universidad de la Frontera, 1994).

110. Interview by Rodrigo Moulian T. and Yanko González C., "María Ester Grebe: caminando con los Ngen," *Revista Austral de Ciencias Sociales* 9 (2005), 39–48, http://redalyc.org/, accessed Oct. 21, 2015.

111. María Ester Grebe (with Joaquín Fernández and Carlos Fiedler), "Mitos, creencias y concepto de enfermedad en la cultural mapuche," *Acta Psiquiátrica y Psicológica de*

*América Latina* 17, no. 3 (1971), 180–93; "Psiquiatría folklórica de Chile: estudio antropológico de sus enfermedades vigentes," *Acta Psiquiátrica y Psicológica de América Latina* 20 (1974), 307–82; "Taxonomía de enfermedades mapuche," *Nueva Época* 2 (1975), 27–39; "Relevancia sociocultural y médica de la terapéutica y profilaxis simbólica en las culturas tradicionales de Chile," in *Ciencias Sociales y Medicina* (Santiago: Universitaria, 1992); "El subsistema ngem en la religiosidad mapuche," *Revista Chilena de Antropología* 12 (1993–94), 45–64.

112. José Jorge de Carvalho, "Music of African Origin in Brazil," in *Africa in Latin America: Essays on History, Culture, and Socialization*, ed. Manuel M. Fraginals, trans. Leonor Blum (New York: Holmes and Meier, 1984), 227–50; with Rita L. Segato, *Shango Cult in Recife, Brazil* (Caracas: FUNDEF, CONAC, 1992); *Cantos sagrados do xangô do Recife* (Brasilia: Fundação Cultural Palmares, 1993); *The Multiplicity of Black Identities in Brazilian Popular Music* (Brasilia: Universidade de Brasilia, 1994); "Black Music of All Colors: The Construction of Black Ethnicity in Ritual and Popular Genres of Afro-Brazilian Music," in *Music and Black Ethnicity: The Caribbean and South America*, ed. Gerard Béhague (Miami: University of Miami, 1994), 187–206; "La etnomusicología en tiempos de canibalismo musical: una reflexión a partir de las tradiciones musicales afroamericanas," *Revista Transcultural de Música/Transcultural Music Review* 7 (2003), available at www.sibetrans.com/trans; "Yorùbá Sacred Songs in the New World," in *Òrìṣà Devotion as World Religion: The Globalization of Yorùbá Religious Culture*, ed. Jacob K. Olupona and Terry Rey (Madison: University of Wisconsin Press, 2008), 416–47.

113. J. Arturo Chamorro Escalante, "Uso y función del teponaztli en el medio rural tlaxcalteca," *Folklore Americano*, 28 (1979), 69–83; "Chirimías: sondeo histórico de un modelo islámico en América hispana," *Latin American Music Review* 3, no. 3 (1982), 165–87; *La música popular en Tlaxcala* (Mexico City: Premiá Editora, 1983); *Los instrumentos de percusión de México* (Mexico City: El Colegio de Michoacán, Conacyt, 1984); *Sones de la guerra: rivalidad y emoción en la práctica de la música p'urhépecha* (Zamora: El Colegio de Michoacán, 1994); *Mariachi antiguo, jarabe y son: símbolos compartidos y tradición musical en las identidades jaliscienses* (Zapopan: El Colegio de Jalisco, 2000); *Guía etnográfica: para la investigación de la música y la danza tradicionales* (Guadalajara: Universidad de Guadalajara, 2003); ed., *El bolero: historia musical, estructura y discursos performativos, en homenaje a César Portillo de la Luz y Vicente Garrido* (Guadalajara: Universidad de Guadalajara, 2005); *La cultura expresiva wixárika: reflexiones y abstracciones del mundo indígena del norte de Jalisco* (Guadalajara, Jalisco: Universidad de Guadalajara, 2008).

The musicologists Arturo Salinas and Leticia Varela are two other Mexican scholars with prominent institutional connections outside of Mexico. Salinas, distinguished visiting composer in residence at Mills College (Oakland, Calif.) and the Walden School's 2002 composer-in-residence, also taught at Princeton. Varela received her doctorate from the University of Cologne and taught at the University of Hermosilla, Sonora. Her dissertation on Yaqui music was later published in Spanish language (Leticia R. Varela, *La música en la vida de los Yaquis* [Hermosillo: Secretaría de Fomento Educativo y Cultura, Gobierno del Estado de Sonora, 1986]).

Sergio Navarrete Pellicer earned a master of music degree from the University of Maryland and a doctorate in anthropology from the University College London. Navarrete Pellicer's work focuses on marimba music of Guatemala, Mexican brass bands, and cathedral music. He is author of *Maya Achi Marimba Music in Guatemala* (Philadelphia: Temple University Press, 2005), coauthor and editor of *Ritual sonoro en catedral y parroquias* (Mexico: Centro de Investigaciones y Estudios Superiores en Antropología Social, 2013), and general coordinator of the five-volume *Ritual sonoro catedralicio* (Mexico City: CIESAS, UdeG, ColJal, BUAP, CENIDIM, INBA, 2013).

114. Raúl R. Romero, "La investigación musical en América del Sur," *Letras: Revista de la Universidad Nacional Mayor de San Marcos, Lima* 90 (1986), 71–92; "Música urbana en un contexto campesino: Tradición y modernidad en Paccha (Junín)," *Antropológica* 7 (1989), 121–33; "Preservation, the Mass Media and Dissemination of Traditional Musics: The Case of the Peruvian Andes," in *World Music, Musics of the World: Aspects of Documenation, Mass Media, and Acculturation*, ed. Max Peter Baumann (Wilhelmshaven: Florian Noetzel Verlag, 1992), 191–210; *Música, danzas y máscaras en los Andes* (Lima: Pontificia Universidad Católica del Perú, Instituto Riva-Agüero, 1993); "Black Music and Identity in Peru: Reconstruction and Revival of Afro-Peruvian Musical Traditions," in *Music and Black Ethnicity: The Caribbean and South America*, ed. Gerard Béhague (New Brunswick, N.J.: Transaction Publishers, 1994), 307–30; *Debating the Past*; *Sonidos andinos: una antología de la música campesina del Perú* (Lima: Pontificia Universidad Católica del Perú, 2002); *Identidades múltiples: memoria, modernidad y cultura popular en el Valle del Mantaro* (Lima: Fondo Editorial del Congreso del Perú, 2004); *Andinos y tropicales: la cumbia peruana en la ciudad global* (Lima: Pontificia Universidad Católica del Perú, 2007, with DVD).

115. Raúl R. Romero, "Tragedies and Celebrations: Imagining Foreign and Local Scholarships," *Latin American Music Review* 22, no. 1 (2001), 48–62.

116. Juan Pablo González (with José Miguel Varas), *En busca de la música chilena: crónica y antología sonora* (Santiago de Chile: Editorial Catalonia, 2005); "Nostalgia, renovación y ruptura en la música chilena para piano de comienzos del siglo XX," in *Arte, identidad y cultura chilena (1900–1930)*, ed. Fidel Sepúlveda (Santiago de Chile: Pontificia Universidad Católica de Chile, 2006), 287–335; "Un siglo de música en Chile," in *100 años de cultura en Chile: 1905–2005*, ed. Juan Andrés Piña (Santiago de Chile: Editorial Zig-Zag, 2006), 201–51; with Claudio Rolle and Oscar Ohlsen, *Historia social de la música popular en Chile, 1950–1970*, 2 vols. (Santiago de Chile: Universidad Católica de Chile, Casa de las Américas, 2005, 2009).

117. For a bibliography of the earlier works of Luis Felipe Ramón y Rivera and Isabel Aretz, see Chase, *Guide to the Music of Latin America*, 378–82. Aretz began a larger project that included a comprehensive study of Venezuelan organology.

118. Ramón also founded the National Traditional Orchestra ("Típica") in that same year to revive Venezuelan traditional music.

119. Smith, "Discussion of Central America," 2. There are important publications affiliated with the team of Aretz–Ramón y Rivera and their students, in particular the *Revista Venezolana de Folklor*, a semiannual published from 1968 to 1975 and edited by Ramón y Rivera, which later became the *Revista INIDEF* (1975–83).

120. Rosa Elena Vázquez Rodríguez, *La práctica musical de la población negra en el Perú: la danza de negritos del Carmen* (Havana: Casa de las Américas, 1982).

121. José Manuel Juárez Toledo, "Aportes para el estudio de la etnomusicología guatemalteca," *Tradiciones de Guatemala* 8 (1977), 141–85; *La música en los rituales dedicados al maíz* (Guatemala City: National Commission of the 3rd Central American Corn Festival; Ministry of Culture and Sport, 1988).

122. Roberto Díaz Castillo, *Artes y artesanías populares de Sacatepéquez* (Guatemala City: Universidad de San Carlos de Guatemala, Centro de Estudios Folklóricos, 1976); *Folklore y artes populares* (Guatemala City: Centro de Estudios Folklóricos, Universidad de San Carlos de Guatemala, 1968). Celso A. Lara Figueroa, *Contribución del folklore al estudio de la historia* (Guatemala City: Editorial Universitaria, 1977); *Leyendas y casos de la tradición oral de la ciudad de Guatemala* (Guatemala City: Editorial Universitaria, 1973).

123. Both journals publish on a variety of folklore-related subjects (see, for example, Matthias Stöckli, "La música del baile de la conquista: aspectos conceptuales," *La Tradición Popular* 171 [2007], 1–16).

124. Gerard Béhague, "Reflections on the Ideological History of Latin American Ethnomusicology," in *Comparative Musicology and Anthropology of Music: Essays on the History of Ethnomusicology*, ed. Bruno Nettl and Philip V. Bohlman (Chicago: University of Chicago Press, 1991), 56–68, p. 61.

125. For more on the institutions and societies of Mexican musicology, see Steven Loza, "Contemporary Ethnomusicology in Mexico," *Latin American Music Review* 11, no. 2 (1990), 201–50.

126. For example, Guillermo Contreras Arias (along with Hiram Dordelly Núñez), one of the principle ethnomusicologists at the CENIDIM, is known for his study and collection of Mexican musical instruments as well as his performing career in traditional music ensembles (*Atlas cultural de México: música* [Mexico City: Secretaría de Educación Pública, 1988]). Dordelly Núñez has published didactic materials drawn from his field research on Mexican traditional musics (*Cancionero del Cuarteto Coculense* [Mexico City: Centro Nacional de Investigación, Documentación e Información Músical "Carlos Chávez," 2004]).

127. Loza, "Contemporary Ethnomusicology in Mexico."

128. Robert Stevenson, *Latin American Colonial Music Anthology* (Washington, D.C.: Organization of American States, 1975); *Seventeenth-Century Villancicos, from a Puebla Convent Archive, Transcribed with Optimal Added Parts for Ministriles* (Lima: Ediciones Cultura, 1974); ed., *Christmas Music from Baroque Mexico* (Berkeley: University of California Press, 1974); *Foundations of New World Opera* (Lima: Ediciones Cultura, 1973); "Latin America," in *Music in the Modern Age*, ed. F. W. Sternfeld (London: Weidenfeld and Nicolson, 1973), 407–32; "Written Sources for Indian Music until 1882," *Ethnomusicology* 7, no. 1 (1973), 1–40; "The First New World Composers: Fresh Data from Peninsular Archives," *Journal of the American Musicological Society* 23, no. 1 (1970), 95–106; *Music in El Paso, 1919–1939* (El Paso: University of Texas at El Paso, 1970); *Renaissance and Baroque Musical Sources in the Americas* (Washington, D.C.: Organization of American States, 1970); *Mexico City Cathedral Music, 1600–1750* (Washington, D.C.: Academy of American Franciscan History, 1964); "Comienzos de la ópera en el Nuevo Mundo," *Boletín Interamericano de*

*Música* 40 (1962), 3–19; *Music in Mexico: A Historical Survey* (New York: Crowell, 1952); and the aforementioned *Music in Aztec and Inca Territory*, among many more.

129. E. Thomas Stanford, *Catálogo de los acervos musicales de las catedrales metropolitanas de México y Puebla de la Biblioteca Nacional de Antropología e Historia y otras colecciones menores* (Mexico City: Instituto Nacional de Antropología e Historia, 2002); *El son mexicano* (Mexico City: Fondo de Cultura Económica, 1984); "La etnomusicología y el rescate de una riqueza que se pierde," in *Indigenísmo, pueblo y cultura*, ed. Jas Reuter (Mexico City: Consejo Nacional Técnico de la Educación, 1983), 97–106; *El villancico y el corrido mexicano* (Mexico City: Instituto Nacional de Antropología e Historia, 1974); "The Mexican Son," *Yearbook of the International Folk Music Council* 4 (1972), 66–86; *Catálogo de grabaciónes del laboratorio de sonido del Museo Nacional de Antropología* (Mexico City: Instituto Nacional de Antropología e Historia, 1968); *Archivo de música sacra de la Catedral de Puebla, Puebla* (Mexico City: Biblioteca Nacional de Antropología e Historia, 1967); *Archivo de música sacra, Catedral Metropolitana, Ciudad de México* (Mexico City: Biblioteca Nacional de Antropología e Historia, 1966); "A Linguistic Analysis of Music and Dance Terms from Three Sixteenth-Century Dictionaries of Mexican Indian Languages," *Yearbook/Anuario of the Inter-American Institute for Musical Research* 2 (1966), 101–59; "La lirica popular de la costa michoacana," *Anales del Instituto Nacional de Antropología e Historia* 16, no. 45 (1964), 231–82. He coedited *La música de México* (Mexico City: Instituto de Investigaciones Estéticas, Universidad Nacional Autónoma de México, 1987), the first volume (*Período virreinal*) with Miguel Alcázar and Jesús Estrada, and the second (*Período de la independencia a la revolución*) with Gloria Carmona and Velia Nieto.

130. Stanford was crucial to the establishment of the ethnomusicology curriculum and research lab at the Escuela Nacional de Antropología e Historia (ENAH, National School of Anthropology and History). On Stevenson's service, see Walter A. Clark, "Remembrances: Robert Murrell Stevenson, 1916–2012," *Bulletin of the Society for American Music* 39, no. 2 (2013), 36–37.

131. See Smith, "Discussion of Central America."

132. Julio Arosemena Moreno, *La mejorana, instrumento folklórico panameño* (Panama City: n.p., 1983); *Danzas folklóricas en la villa de Los Santos* (San Salvador: Ministerio de Educación, 1977).

133. Rafael Manzanares Aguilar, *El folklore en Honduras: concepto* (Tegucigalpa: Editorial Ministerio de Educación, 1974); *La danza folklórica hondureña* (Tegucigalpa: Partido Nacional de Honduras, 1972); *Instrumentos musicales tradicionales de Honduras* (Washington, D.C.: Organización de los Estados Americanos, 1969); *Canciones de Honduras/Songs of Honduras* (Washington, D.C.: Secretaría General, Unión Panamericana, Organización de los Estados Americanos, 1960).

134. See Egberto Bermúdez, "Andrés Pardo Tovar (1911–72) y la tradición musicológica en Colombia," *Ensayos: Historia y Teoría del Arte* 23 (2012), 115–33.

135. Andrés Pardo Tovar, *Los cantares tradicionales del Baudó* (Bogotá: Universidad Nacional de Colombia, 1960); with Jesús Pinzón Urrea, *Rítmica y melódica del folclor chocoano* (Bogotá: Universidad Nacional de Colombia, 1961); with Jesús Bermúdez Silva, *La guitarrería popular de Chiquinquirá* (Bogotá: Universidad Nacional de Colombia, 1963).

136. The IPC also oversaw the publication of *Páginas de Cultura* (Culture pages), which frequently offered studies pertinent to the interests of ethnomusicology.

137. The documentation produced in the study also includes numerous photographs as well as three 16 mm rolls of ethnographic footage, featuring dance and the construction of musical instruments. See Octavio Marulanda, ed., "Investigación folklórica," *Páginas de Cultura* 1 (1964), 1, 7.

138. George List, "Ethnomusicology in Colombia," *Ethnomusicology* 10, no. 1 (1966), 70–76.

139. Brian Moser and Donald Tayler, "Tribes of the Piraparaná," *Geographical Journal* 129, no. 4 (1963), 437–39; *Rio Piraparaná* (London: Royal Geographical Society, 1963). Luis Carlos Espinosa and Jesús Pinzón Urrea, "La heterofonía en la música de los indios Cunas del Darién," *First Inter-American Ethnomusicology Conference* (Washington, D.C.: Pan American Union, 1965), 119–29.

140. In 1965, the JNF published a review of their activities in the *Anales de la Junta Nacional de Folclor*; see Guillermo Abadía, *La música folclórica colombiana* (Bogotá: Universidad Nacional de Colombia, Dirección de Divulgación Cultural, 1965).

141. Paulo de Carvalho Neto's studies contributed to the larger theoretical questions surrounding folklore research and interregional concerns in Latin America: "Folklore of the Black Struggle in Latin America," *Latin American Perspectives* 5, no. 2 (1978), 53–88; *The Concept of Folklore*, trans. Jacques Marcel Patrick Wilson (Coral Gables, Fla.: University of Miami Press, 1971); "The Candombe, a Dramatic Dance from Afro-Uruguayan Folklore," *Ethnomusicology* 6, no. 3 (1962), 164–74; *Folklore del Paraguay* (Quito: Editorial Universitaria, 1961); *Diccionario del folklore ecuatoriano*.

142. Carlos Alberto Coba Andrade, *Instrumentos musicales populares registrados en el Ecuador* (Otavalo: Instituto Otavaleño de Antropología, 1981); *Persistencias etnoculturales en la Fiesta del Inti Raymi, conocida como la de San Juan en Otavalo* (Quito: Casa de la Cultura Ecuatoriana "Benjamín Carrión," 2001); with Hernán Jaramillo Cisneros, *Ecuador indígena: sincretismo e identidad en las culturas nativas de la Sierra Norte* (Quito: Ediciones Abya-Yala, 1991).

143. Antonio Paredes Candía, *La danza folklórica en Bolivia* (La Paz: Ediciones Isla, 1966); *Fiestas populares de Bolivia* (La Paz: Ediciones Isla, 1977); *La serenata y el añorado "pasacalle"* (La Paz: Ediciones Isla, 2000).

144. Julia Elena Fortún, *Las fiestas de Navidad en Bolivia: música, danzas, costumbres* (Madrid: Instituto Bernardino de Sahagún, 1952); *La danza de los diablos* (La Paz: Ministerio de Educación y Bellas Artes, 1961); *Festividad del Gran Poder* (La Paz: Ediciones Casa de la Cultura, 1992).

145. Walter Sánchez C., *Yagua Tairari: música y cantores de los Guaraní* (La Paz: Centro Cultural y Pedagógico Simón I. Patiño, 1997); *El tambor mayor: música y canto de las comunidades negras de Bolivia* (La Paz: Centro Cultural y Pedagógico Simón I. Patiño, 1998); *El festival Luz Mila Patiño: 30 años de encuentros interculturales a través de la música* (Geneva: Fundación Simón I. Patiño, 2001); ed., *La música en Bolivia: de la prehistoria a la actualidad* (Cochabamba: Fundación Simón I. Patiño, 2002); ed., *El violín en Bolivia* (Cochabamba: Fundación Simón I. Patiño, 2011).

146. Lauro Ayestarán, *La música en el Uruguay* (Montevideo: Sodre, 1953); "El barroco musical hispanoamericano: los manuscritos de la Iglesia de San Felipe Neri (Sucre, Bolivia) existentes en el Museo Histórico Nacional del Uruguay," *Yearbook/Anuário* 1 (1965), 55–93; *El folklore musical uruguayo* (Montevideo: Arca, 1967), among others.

147. Centro Nacional de Documentación Musical Lauro Ayestarán (CDM), www.cdm.gub.uy, accessed May 15, 2015, with digital archive of recordings by Ayestarán.

148. Coriún Aharonián, *Músicas populares del Uruguay* (Montevideo: Escuela Universitaria de Música, Universidad de la República, 2007); *Educación, arte, música* (Montevideo: Ediciones Tacuabé, 2004); "Carlos Vega y la teoría de la música popular: un enfoque latinoamericano en un ensayo pionero," *Revista Musical Chilena* 51, no. 188 (1997), 61–74; *Conversaciones sobre música, cultura e identidad* (Montevideo: Ombú, 1992); with Carlos Vega, *Estudios para los orígenes del tango argentino* (Buenos Aires: Editorial de la Universidad Católica Argentina, 2007).

149. For example, Peter Manuel, *Essays on Cuban Music: North American and Cuban Perspectives* (Lanham, Md.: University Press of America, 1991); and some Cuban research published in the *Latin American Music Review.*

150. Natalio Galán, *Cuba y sus sones* (Valencia: Pre-Textos, 1983).

151. He also studied composition with José Ardévol (Havana) and Nadia Boulanger (Paris).

152. See Katherine J. Hagedorn, *Divine Utterances: The Performance of Afro-Cuban Santería* (Washington, D.C.: Smithsonian Institution Press, 2000), 148–53.

153. Argeliers León, *Música folklore: Yoruba, Bantú, Abakuá* (Havana: Ediciones del C.N.C., 1964); *Del canto y el tiempo* (Havana: Editorial Pueblo y Educación, 1974); "Of the Axle and the Hinge: Nationalism, Afro-Cubanism and Music in Pre-Revolutionary Cuba," in *Essays on Cuban Music: North American and Cuban Perspectives*, ed. Peter Manuel (Lanham, Md.: University Press of America, 1991), 267–82; *Tras las huellas de las civilizaciones negras en América* (Havana: Fundación Fernando Ortiz, 2001). Some of his early field recordings (1948–67) can be heard on the volume *Antología de la música cubana: viejos cantos afrocubanos* (Linares 1970–79, 2006).

154. Linares is credited as the general producer of these volumes as well as the producer of various individual recordings in the series, director of selected in situ recordings, and author of the liner notes. Most recently EGREM has reissued the collection in a ten-CD box set (2006) with the original liner notes. The first LP in the series, which included field recordings made by Linares and A. León, has also appeared as *Viejos cantos afrocubanos* and *Música afrocubana.*

155. Her earlier essay, "Ensayo sobre la influencia española en la musica cubana" (in *Música guajira*, Argeliers León and María Teresa Linares [Havana: Ediciones del Consejo Nacional de Cultura, 1955]) marked a beginning of this career-spanning attention to "musical Spain in Cuba."

156. María Teresa Linares, *El punto cubano* (Santiago de Cuba: Editorial Oriente, 1999); *La música entre Cuba y España* (Madrid: Fundación Autor, 1998–99); *La música y el pueblo* (Havana: Instituto Cubano del Libro, Editorial Pueblo y Educación, 1974); *La música popular* (Havana: Instituto del Libro, 1970).

157. For more on A. León and Linares, see Hagedorn, *Divine Utterances*, 143–72.

158. Olavo Alén Rodríguez, "The Music Archives at the CIDMUC and their Influence on the Musical Culture of Cuba," in *Archives for the Future: Global Perspectives on Audiovisual Archives*, ed. Anthony Seeger (Shubha Chaudhuri: Seagull Books, 2004), 130–42, p. 130, available at www.seagullindia.com/.

159. Hernández, *Música tradicional dominicana*; Emilio Rodríguez Demorizi, *Música y baile en Santo Domingo* (Santo Domingo: Librería Hispaniola, 1971); Bernarda Jorge, *La música dominicana, siglos XIX–XX* (Santo Domingo: Universidad Autónoma de Santo Domingo, 1982).

160. See José G. Guerrero, *Fradique Lizardo: Cultura y folklore en la República Dominicana* (Santo Domingo: Editora Universitaria, Ciudad Universitaria, 2005).

161. Fradique Lizardo, *Instrumentos musicales folklóricos dominicanos* (Santo Domingo: UNESCO, 1988); *Apuntes: Investigación de campo para el montaje del espectáculo: religiosidad popular dominicana* (Santo Domingo: Dirección General de Bellas Artes, 1982); *Cultura africana en Santo Domingo* (Santo Domingo: Taller, 1979); *Instrumentos musicales indígenas dominicanos* (Santo Domingo: Alfa y Omega, 1976); *Danzas y bailes folklóricos dominicanos* (Santo Domingo: Fundación García-Arévalo, 1975); "Danzas y bailes folklóricos dominicanos," *Folklore Series*, no. 1/4 (Santo Domingo: Museo del Hombre Dominicano, 1974); with Victoria Muñoz, *Fiestas patronales y juegos populares dominicanos* (Santo Domingo: Ediciones Fundación García-Arévalo, 1979).

162. For example, José G. Guerrero, *Cotuí: villa, carnaval, cofradía y palos. Un estudio etnohistórico* (Santo Domingo: Editora Universitaria, 2005); *Carnaval, cuaresma y fechas patrias* (Santo Domingo: Editora De Revistas, 2003); Miguel Holguín-Veras, *Canciones antiguas dominicanas: análisis acerca de su autoría* (Santo Domingo: Academia de Ciencias de la República Dominicana, 2001); *Eduardo Brito: Antonio Mesa y cuatro artículos sobre la música en República Dominicana* (Santo Domingo: Ediciones Holedi, 1988); Cataña Pérez de Cuello, *Sinfonía de ideas en 4 movimientos* (Santo Domingo: Banco Central de le República Dominicana, 2006); *El merengue: Música y baile de la República Dominicana* (Santo Domingo: Codetel, 2003); *El universo de la música: apreciación, teoría e historia de la música occidental y dominicana* (Santo Domingo: Taller, 1993).

163. *Centro Journal*, http://centropr.hunter.cuny.edu/centro-journal, accessed June 16, 2014. Also available in print format.

164. Pedro Malavet Vega, *De las bandas al Trío Borinquen (1900–1927)* (Ponce: Ediciones Lorena, 2002); *Historia de la canción popular en Puerto Rico (1493–1898)* (Ponce: Editora Corripio, 1992); *Del bolero a la nueva canción: la música popular en Puerto Rico de los años '50 al presente* (Ponce: Editora Corripio, 1988); *Navidad que vuelve: la tradición y el cantar navideño en Puerto Rico* (Ponce: P. Malavet Vega, 1987).

165. Correctives in the literature gap include, for example, María Luisa Muñoz, *La música en Puerto Rico* (Sharon, Conn.: Troutman Press, 1966), Ramón López, *Los bembeteos de la plena puertorriqueña* (San Juan: Huracán, 2008); J. Emanuel Dufrasne-González, ed., *Puerto Rico también tiene—tambó!: recopilación de artículos sobre la plena y la bomba* (Rio Grande: Paracumbé, 1994); Lydia Milagros González García, *Elogio de la bomba: Homenaje a la tradición de Loíza* (Loíza: La Mano Poderosa, 2004).

166. José Ramos Tinhorão, *Pequena história da música popular*, 7th ed. (São Paulo: Editora 34, 2013 [1975]); Vasco Mariz, *História da música no Brasil* (Rio de Janeiro: Civilização Brasileira, 1983 [1981]); José Maria Neves, *Música contemporânea brasileira* (São Paulo: Ricordi, 1981).

167. Reily, "Introduction," 6.

168. Oneyda Alvarenga, *Música popular brasileira* (Rio de Janeiro: Editôra Globo, 1950).

169. Ary Vasconcelos, *Panorama da música popular brasileira*, 2 vols. (São Paulo: Livraria Martins, 1964); José Eduardo Homem de Mello, *Música popular brasileira* (São Paulo: Edições Melhoramentos, 1976).

170. José Ramos Tinhorão, *Música popular: de índios, negros e mestiços* (Petrópolis: Editora Vozes, 1972); *Música popular: do gramofone ao radio e TV* (São Paulo: Editora Ática, 1982). For a comprehensive source of relevant publications up to the mid-1980s, see Charles A. Perrone, "An Annotated Interdisciplinary Bibliography and Discography of Brazilian Popular Music," *Latin American Music Review* 7, no. 2 (1986), 302–40.

171. Sean Stroud, "Marcus Pereira's *Música Popular do Brasil*: Beyond Folklore?" *Popular Music* 25, no. 2 (2006), 303–18, 306, 315.

172. Mário de Moraes, *Recordações de Ary Barroso* (Rio de Janeiro: FUNARTE, 1979); Sérgio Cabral, *Pixinguinha: vida e obra* (Rio de Janeiro: FUNARTE, 1978); Marilioa T. Barboza da Silva and Arthur de Oliveira Filho, *Filho de Ogum Bexiguento* (Rio de Janeiro: FUNARTE, 1979); Abel Cardoso Júnior, *Carmen Miranda: a cantora do Brasil* (São Paulo: author's edition, 1978).

173. See, for example, Sérgio Cabral, *As escolas de samba* (Rio de Janeiro: Editorial Fontana, 1974); Edigar de Alencar, *O carnaval carioca através da música*, 2 vols. (Rio de Janeiro: Livraria Freitas Bastos, 1965); Eneida de Morais, *História do carnaval carioca* (Rio de Janeiro: Editora Civilização Brasileira, 1958).

174. Augusto de Campos et al., *Balanço da bossa: antologia crítica da moderna música popular brasileira* (São Paulo: Editora Perspectiva, 1974).

175. Rafael José de Menezes Bastos, *A musicológica Kamayurá: para uma antropologia de comunicação no Alto-Xingu* (Brasília: Fundação Nacional do Índio, 1978); "Música, cultura e sociedade no Alto-Xingu: a teoria musical dos índios Kamayrá," *Latin American Music Review* 7, no. 1 (1986), 51–80; Elisabeth Travassos, *Xamanismo e música entre os Kayabi do Parque do Xingu* (Rio de Janeiro: Museo Nacional, Universidade Federal do Rio de Janeiro, 1984); José Jorge de Carvalho, "Ritual and Music of the Sango Cults of Recife" (PhD diss., Queen's University of Belfast, 1984).

176. See Rafael José de Menezes Bastos, "The 'Origin of Samba' as the Invention of Brazil (Why Do Songs Have Music?)," *British Journal of Ethnomusicology* 6 (1999), 67–96; Mareia Quintero-Rivera, *A cor e o som da nação: a idéia de mestiçagem na crítica musical do Caribe hispânico e do Brasil (1928–1948)* (São Paulo: Annablume and FAPESP, 2000).

177. Samuel Araújo and José Alberto Salgado e Silva, "Musical Knowledge, Transmission, and Worldviews: Ethnomusicological Perspectives from Rio de Janeiro, Brazil," *World of Music* 5, no. 3 (2009), 93–110, mention Rosa Maria Barbosa Zamith's association with Anthony Seeger as catalyst of ethnomusicological studies at the conservatory of Rio de Janeiro.

178. Jesse Hoffnung-Garskof, "Latin American Studies and United States Foreign Policy," *International Institute Journal* 2, no. 1 (2012), available at http://hdl.handle.net/2027/spo.11645653.0002.103, accessed June 20, 2014.

179. For example, Isabel Aretz "Ethnic Music of the Guianas, Venezuela and Colombia," prepared for the Meeting of Experts on Musical Traditions in Latin America, Caracas (UNESCO, 1971); ed., *América Latina en su música* (Mexico City: Siglo XXI, 1977); *Historia de la etnomusicología en América Latina: desde la época precolombina hasta nuestros días* (Caracas: Ediciones FUNDEF-CONAC-OEA, 1991); Chase, *Guide*; Espinosa and Pinzón Urrea, "La heterofonía"; Argeliers León, *Música popular de orígen africano en América Latina* (Paris: UNESCO, 1968); Lizardo, *Instrumentos musicales*; Manzanares Aguilar, *Instrumentos musicales.*

180. CONAC was formed in 1975. In 1999 the council came under the auspices of the newly created Ministerio de Educación, Cultura y Deportes (Ministry of Education, Culture and Sports).

181. The Organización del Convenio Andrés Bello is an international and intergubernatorial organization working toward the integration of education, culture, the sciences, and technology within the signatory states. It was founded in 1970 with the creation of the treatise in Bogotá, which was then revised in 1990. Member states include Bolivia, Chile, Colombia, Cuba, the Dominican Republic, Ecuador, Mexico, Panama, Paraguay, Peru, Spain, and Venezuela.

182. UNESCO, "Convention on the Protection and Promotion of the Diversity of Cultural Expressions 2005," http://portal.unesco.org, accessed June 11, 2014.

183. From even a perfunctory look at a sample of U.N. cultural themes since the mid-twentieth century, it is not difficult to trace the origins of Venezuela's Centro de la Diversidad Cultural (CDC, Center for Cultural Diversity) in 2006: one need only look to the themes of the General Conventions on Cultural Diversity (31st Session, Paris, 2001), the Safeguarding of Intangible Cultural Heritage (32nd Session, Paris, 2003), and the Protection and Promotion of the Diversity of Cultural Expressions (33rd Session, Paris, 2005). The international links are both unambiguous and longstanding.

184. See Eugenio Pereira Salas, *Notes on the History of Music Exchange between the Americas before 1940* (Washington, D.C.: Pan American Union, 1943).

185. Since 1964, the annual *Handbook of Latin American Studies* volumes alternate focus on the sciences and the humanities, and include coverage in the following disciplines: anthropology (including archaeology and ethnology), art, economics, digital media (beginning in 1995), geography, government and politics, international relations, literature, music, philosophy, and sociology. Today, the *Handbook* is available either in print or online at nearly every university library in Asia, Europe, Canada, and the United States where Latin American studies are programmed. Through its exchange program, the Library of Congress also makes the *Handbook* available to most Latin American institutions unable to afford the subscription.

186. One of the important outcomes of the conference was a special issue of the *Boletín Latino-Americano de Música* (vol. 5, 1942), coedited by Lange and Seeger, which was dedicated to U.S. music. The issue came with a supplementary musical publication,

a feature that was repeated in 1946 (vol. 6) with a focus on Brazilian musical compositions. The *Boletín* was published by the Instituto Interamericano de Musicología in Montevideo.

187. Among PAU's efforts in Latin American musicology are Gilbert Chase, *Partial List of Latin American Music Obtainable in the United States: With a Supplementary List of Books and Phonograph Records* (Washington, D.C.: Pan American Union, Music Division, 1941 and 1942); Gustavo Duran, *Recordings of Latin American Songs and Dances: An Annotated List of Popular and Folk Music* (Washington, D.C.: Pan American Union, 1942); Pereira Salas, *Notes on the History.*

188. The council was later renamed the Inter-American Council for Education, Science and Culture, in line with UNESCO, further buttressing the aforementioned overlapping activities of both organizations in the post-1960 period of Latin American music scholarship.

189. Lauro Ayestarán (Uruguay), Juan Bautista Plaza (Venezuela), Luiz Heitor Corrêa de Azevedo (Brazil), Francisco Curt Lange (Uruguay), Vicente Mendoza (Mexico), Eugenio Pereira Salas (Chile), Andrés Sas (Peru), and Carlos Vega (Argentina), Gilbert Chase, Irving Lowens, Albert Luper, Charles Seeger, Carleton Sprague Smith, and Robert Stevenson (U.S.A.). Isabel Aretz de Ramón y Rivera, Luis Ramón y Rivera (Venezuela), Jesús Bal y Gay (Spain), Andrés Pardo Tovar (Colombia), Mantle Hood, Alan Merriam, and Lota M. Spell (U.S.A.) also appear as Advisory Board Members of the Inter-American Institute of Musical Research in the first edition of the *Anuario/Yearbook* (1965), though they were not on the role of the 1961 Inter-American Conference on Musicology (Washington, D.C.), sponsored by the Library of Congress, Music Division.

190. List and Orrego-Salas, *Music in the Americas*, 2.

191. Irvin Lowens, "The First Inter-American Conference on Musicology: A Brief Report," *Notes* 20, no. 2 (1963), 215.

192. *Anuario/Yearbook* 1 (1965), 150.

193. *Ethnomusicology* 10, no. 1 (1966); including contributions by Chase, Vega, John Chappell, Ramón y Rivera, Gertrude P. Kurath, Arthur M. Jones, Orrego-Salas, Stanford, List, Aretz, Zdenka Fischmann, Daniel Crowley, Robert Black, Béhague, Juana de Laban, and Henrietta Yurchenco.

194. *Anuario/Yearbook* (1965–69, vols. 1–5); *Yearbook for Inter-American Musical Research/Anuario Interamericano de Investigación Musical/Anuário Interamericano de Pesquisa Musical* (1970–75, vols. 6–11).

195. Walter A. Clark, "Robert M. Stevenson's Inter-American Music Review: Thirty Years of Landmark Publishing," paper presented at the Latin American Music Center's 50th Anniversary Conference "Cultural Counterpoints: Examining the Musical Interactions between the U.S. and Latin America," Indiana University, Bloomington, 2011.

196. Gerard Béhague, "Editorial Note," *Latin American Music Review* 1, no. 1 (1980), 1.

197. Ibid.

198. The earliest formal Canadian musicological presence as part of any Inter-American initiative seems to be connected to CIDEM. Arnold Walter was a founding member and later served as its president (1969–72). As well, the Fifth General Assembly of CIDEM

was held in Toronto in 1967. The Canadian representation, however, was mostly focused on Western art music, pedagogy, and curriculum in the public education systems.

199. Béhague, "Bridging South America."

200. Romero, "Tragedies and Celebrations," 58–59. For more on this, see Francisco Cruces and Raquel Pérez, "Un lugar de descanso—y perplejidad: conversación con Bruno Nettl y José Jorge de Carvalho," *Revista Transcultural de Música/Transcultural Music Review* 7 (2003), available at www.sibetrans.com/trans.

201. J. León, "Peruvian Musical Scholarship," 170.

202. Francisco Cruces et al., *Las culturas musicales: lecturas de etnomusicología* (Madrid: Editorial Trotta, 2001); Enrique Cámara de Landa, *Etnomusicología* (Madrid: Instituto Complutense de Ciencias Musicales, 2003), a student manual in Spanish on theory and methods that is being adopted in graduate and undergraduate programs throughout Latin America and Spain.

203. See, for example, Robin Moore, *Nationalizing Blackness: Afrocubanismo and Artistic Revolution in Havana, 1920–1940* (Pittsburgh: University of Pittsburgh Press, 1997); *Música y mestizaje: revolución artística y cambio social en La Habana, 1920–1940* (Madrid: Colibrí, 2002); Helena Simonett, *Banda: Mexican Musical Life across Borders* (Middletown, Conn.: Wesleyan Univerisity Press, 2001; *En Sinaloa nací: historia de la música de banda* (Mazatlán: Asociación de Gestores del Patrimonio Histórico y Cultural de Mazatlán, 2004); Zoila Mendoza, *Shaping Society through Dance: Mestizo Ritual Performance in the Peruvian Andes* (Chicago: University of Chicago Press, 2000); *Al son de la danza: identidad y comparsas en el Cuzco* (Lima: Pontificia Universidad Católica del Perú, 2001); *Crear y sentir lo nuestro: folclor, identidad regional y nacional en el Cuzco, siglo XX* (Lima: Pontificia Universidad Católica del Perú, 2006); *Creating Our Own: Folklore, Performance, and Identity in Cuzco, Peru* (Durham, N.C.: Duke University Press, 2008); Heidi Feldman, *Black Rhythms of Peru: Reviving African Musical Heritage in the Black Pacific* (Middletown, Conn.: Wesleyan University Press, 2006); *Ritmos negros del Perú: reconstruyendo la herencia musical africana* (Lima: Pontificia Universidad Católica del Perú, 2009); Manuel Moreno Fraginals, ed., *L'Afrique en Amérique Latine* (Paris: UNESCO, 1984); *Africa in Latin America*, trans. Leonor Blum (New York: Holmes and Meier, 1984); *África en América Latina* (Mexico City: Siglo XXI, 1987); Ramón Pelinski, ed., *El tango nómade: ensayos sobre la diáspora del tango* (Buenos Aires: Corregidor, 2000), also appeared in French.

204. However, we must mention the bilingual volume by Max Peter Baumann, ed., *Cosmología y música en los Andes* (Frankfurt and Madrid: Vervuert and Iberoamericana, 1996), and the bilingual anthologies by Matthias Stöckli and Arnd Adje Booth, ed., *Flower World: Music Archaeology of the Americas/Mundo florido: arqueomusicología de las Américas*, 3 vols. (Berlin: Ekho Verlag, 2012–14); Albert Recasens and Christian Spencer Espinoza, ed., *A tres bandas: mestizaje, sincretism e hibridación en el espacio sonoro iberoamericano* (Madrid: Sociedad Estatal para la Acción Cultural Exterior, 2010); Consuelo Carredano and Victoria Eli, ed., *Historia de la música en España e Hispanoamérica* (Madrid: Fondo de Cultura Económica, 2010); and the monumental *Diccionario de la música española e hispanoamericana*, 10 vols. (Madrid: Sociedad General de Autores y Editores, Instituto Nacional de las Artes Escénicas y de la Música, Instituto Complutense

de Ciencias Musicales, 1999–2000), directed by Emilio Casares Rodicio (unfortunately, the music of Brazil and Portugal has not been included in this compendium of over 24,000 entries).

205. The IASPM is at http://iaspmal.net.

206. See the critical writings on this topic by Juan Pablo González, "Musicología popular en América Latina: síntesis de sus logros, problemas y desafíos," *Revista Musical Chilena* 55, no. 195 (2001), 38–64; "Los estudios de música popular y la renovación de la musicología en América Latina ¿La gallina o el huevo?," *Revista Transcultural de Música/Transcultural Music Review* 12 (2008), available at www.sibetrans.com/trans; "Musicología y América Latina: una relación posible," *Revista Argentina de Musicología* 10 (2009), 43–72.

207. Juan Pablo González, *Pensar la música desde América Latina: problemas e interrogantes* (Santiago de Chile: Universidad Alberto Hurtado, 2013).

# PART ONE

# Academic Lineages, Disciplinary Canons, and Historiographies

The history of Latin American music research has been characterized by the intertwining of methodologies, intellectual genealogies, and theoretical perspectives. A number of research projects from the latter nineteenth century and early twentieth century paralleled those of European comparative musicology. Self-taught and formally trained composers with a background in Western art music figured prominently in these musicological endeavors, collecting and documenting various forms of local music and dance that subsequently informed their own creative work. Theories borrowed from folklore and ethnology also played an important role in some of the first attempts at systematic theories and methodologies regarding the study of music in Latin America. Later studies benefited from contributions of both locally and internationally trained scholars with backgrounds in historical musicology, anthropology, ethnomusicology, sociology, and linguistics, and more recently of specialists on media, popular culture, gender, cultural, and postcolonial studies. This variety has led to competing ways of defining the scope of Latin American music research. In some instances, any kind of music-related research is likely to simply be identified as musicology, without attention to disciplinary distinctions such as music history or ethnomusicology. In others, however, it is not uncommon for scholars to observe a type of division of labor in regard to different types of music. Musical practices associated with relatively geographically isolated indigenous or Afro-descendant communities have historically been associated with the domain of anthropologists. Studies of folk and vernacular mestizo and creole traditions, particularly those linked to national imaginaries, have been connected to the work of folklorists, some of whom conducted their work under the auspices of state-sponsored programs and institutions. Colonial and early republican-era musical forms as well as urban popular genres are associated with musicology. While these distinctions bear some similarity to Anglo-American and European research traditions, the specific way in which the relationship between these domains is conceived, articulated, and contested are the product of a different intellectual history.

The readings in this part 1 seek to provide a better understanding of this shifting landscape of disciplinary boundaries and definitions by focusing on both the legacy of particular academic lineages as well as their more recent contestation. This collection begins with Raúl Romero's examination of the accomplishments and significance of South American music scholars during the first half of the twentieth century (chapter 1). Like their contemporary counterparts in Europe and the United States, these scholars were invested in establishing a baseline of musical knowledge, compiling general histories, and elaborating various types of taxonomies (about musical instruments, scales, genres). Romero in particular points to the 1930s as an important moment for the development of Latin American music research, one that was characterized by the emergence of the first institutions and systematic studies devoted to the research of local musics, as well as regionally based conferences and periodical publications that kept individuals in different countries abreast of one another's research. He also highlights the self-taught backgrounds of some of those researchers, which brought together an eclectic combination of Western music theory and composition, positivist historical analysis, theories about cultural survivals and diffusionism, and an interest in various taxonomic schemes. Romero argues that such approaches, and their accompanying assumptions regarding musical phenomena, were not completely displaced by more theoretically rigorous studies and methodologies that emerged during the second half of the twentieth century. Instead, traditionalist and contemporary approaches have continued to coexist, making for a more epistemologically diverse music research tradition.

The relationship between older and more contemporary approaches to the study of Latin American music is also an underlying concern of Carlos Miñana Blasco's overview of the development of folk and vernacular music studies in Colombia during the latter part of the twentieth century (chapter 2). For Miñana Blasco, this relationship is more contested. He regards ethnomusicology as a more recent field of study that has helped to decenter more essentialist notions about music and tradition that have tended to predominate in Colombia. Miñana Blasco argues that these outmoded paradigms have remained influential because of the resonance that they have had with nationalist ideologies that also seek to idealize the Colombian past in specific ways, not only influencing and legitimizing a particular type of scholarly inquiry, but also shaping perceptions about music and music making on the part of institutions, folk music festivals, educational programs, and listeners themselves. In this setting, he sees ethnomusicology as a field capable of still speaking to older research concerns regarding music structure and genre classification while at the same time also reorienting research toward sociocultural context and the role music has in structuring contemporary social relationships. He further suggests that scholars' more recent interest in urban, mass-mediated, popular music has contributed to this further decentering by locating Colombia within regional and global transnational networks of production, consumption and exchange.

This growing emphasis that Latin American music scholars have placed on popular music is the subject of Juan Pablo González's essay (chapter 3). Latin American popular music research among Anglo-American and European scholars has largely been conducted by ethnomusicologists, many of whom have supported a broader definition of "popular music" that is more consistent with the Spanish usage of the term (*música popular*, music of the people) but that also tends to go beyond the general scope and focus that most popular music scholars place on urban, mass-mediated musical forms. González's piece can be read as a reaction to this tendency, one that advocates for Latin American scholars to adopt instead a narrower definition of popular music closer to that used by their Anglo-American and European counterparts. His motivation behind this call stems partly from a desire to better differentiate the various types of academic inquiry that are often subsumed under the single umbrella term of "musicology" in Latin America (historical musicology, folklore, ethnomusicology, popular music studies, etc.). It also speaks to his concern that some scholars (whether from the region or elsewhere) working with Latin American music have had a tendency to dismiss urban, mass-mediated forms of music for distorting or supplanting other local forms of music making, rather than approaching them as legitimate objects of study. In the process, González also shifts the vantage point of his discussion, focusing more on the unique contributions that Latin American scholars can make to the study of popular music beyond just the Latin American region.

Beyond the critical mapping out of these different intellectual genealogies, Latin American music scholars have been increasingly concerned with the epistemological and theoretical implications of their legacy. Julio Mendívil's study on the contested history of the *charango* (a small lute) in Peru offers a useful starting point in this regard (chapter 4). His project rests on the juxtaposition of theories by local musicians and lay researchers from Ayacucho about the origins of the *charango* against those offered by a number of well-known Latin American scholars. While acknowledging that the former theories are short on documentary evidence and tend to replicate local indigenist ideologies, Mendívil also questions the legitimacy of the latter ones. He argues that choices made by Carlos Vega and other scholars also tend to reflect a tendency to interpret the significance of key documentary evidence in ways that support a particular grand narrative regarding the development of the instrument, one that is contradicted by ethnohistorical and contemporary ethnographic data. Rather than just offering a potential corrective to academic theories regarding the *charango*, Mendívil makes a case for the need to understand both sets of theories as interrelated attempts at reinventing the past in specific ways: one that invokes historical documents as an objective measure of the "real" historical facts, and another that purposely adopts an ahistorical position that privileges myth and vernacular beliefs as a means of delegitimizing the hegemonic narratives of academics.

Alejandro Vera expands on Mendívil's archaeology of canonical disciplinary texts, focusing on the unacknowledged role that late nineteenth- and early twentieth-century nationalist ideologies have had in the shaping of Chilean music historiography (chapter 5). He is concerned with the authority that has been imparted to the work of key figures such as historian Eugenio Pereira Salas, whose monumental history of Chilean music from pre-Columbian times to the nineteenth century he deems instrumental in establishing certain conventional wisdom regarding the development of music in Chile.[1] In particular, Vera examines the generally accepted notion that pre-independence Chile was musically impoverished and underdeveloped, with the latter part of the eighteenth century constituting a precursor stage to the radical transformation that Chilean music would undergo at the start of the nineteenth century. Resorting to archival documents and scholarship available only since 2000, he challenges this particular interpretation of the Chilean musical past, arguing that Pereira Salas and other scholars of the time were invested in legitimizing a nationalist project that regarded the emergence of the republic in 1810 as break between a stagnant Spanish past and a modern and cosmopolitan Chilean nation. Vera also advocates for a more conscious acknowledgment of the endurance of these nationalist perspectives into the late twentieth and early twenty-first centuries, suggesting that more recent narratives regarding Chilean popular music and its ability to subsume foreign musical influences bear a certain ideological resemblance.

Finally, Carolina Santamaría-Delgado (chapter 6) offers an important reflection regarding disciplinary boundaries in Latin America (what Juan Pablo González in his article refers to as multiple "musicologies"). Echoing some aspects of Mendívil and Vera's work, Santamaría-Delgado suggests that the demarcation between musicology, ethnomusicology, folklore, and popular music studies has grown out of a type of epistemological revisionism, one informed by Eurocentric notions about music and the inability of scholars or institutions to convincingly situate various Latin American genres within the domain of any one of these disciplines. Drawing on Latin American postcolonial studies, she argues that genres like the *bambuco* constitute a type of hybrid musical knowledge that is only partially accessible to the above-mentioned disciplinary epistemes, leading to struggles over the interpretation, appropriation, and transformation of the genre that tend to reproduce an underlying colonial structure of power. Santamaría-Delgado's account of the ongoing struggles by musicians, academics, critics, and institutions to understand the *bambuco* vis-à-vis European art music, and later commercially recorded music, shows many of the pitfalls of such approaches, prompting her to call on Latin American music scholars to draw on more hybrid methodologies and theoretical approaches as a means of decentering the privileging of certain forms of musical knowledge.

Javier F. León

## Note

1. Eugenio Pereira Salas, *Los orígenes del arte musical en Chile* (Santiago de Chile: Imprenta Universitaria, 1941).

# 1

# Music Research in South America

RAÚL R. ROMERO

The goal of this article is to present a brief and condensed history of music research in South America, specifically with regard to works concerning traditional music. At the beginning of the twentieth century, the first systematic studies of traditional music began to appear in different South American countries. The growth in ethnomusicological research was already quite evident in the 1930s, intensified by the prolific work of Carlos Vega and the appearance of a journal that centralized many otherwise isolated efforts, the *Boletín Latinoamericano de Música* (Latin American music bulletin). Until the 1960s, these efforts shared a common theoretical and methodological perspective on traditional music. This homogeneity confirms the idea that those years (1930–60) can be understood as a period in which "traditionalist" points of view prevailed. The appearance of modern perspectives in the 1960s led to the end of that prevalence. Since that moment, "traditional" ethnomusicology has coexisted with these newer currents.

In this article, emphasis is placed on the period that I have called "traditional," although there will be constant references to previous and recent ethnomusicological practices. Nonetheless, a few clarifications are in order. First, for historical and cultural reasons, I exclude Brazilian scholarship from this evaluation, limiting myself to Hispanic South America. Second, one should bear in mind that this work addresses South American ethnomusicology, not ethnomusicology in South America. In other words, I exclude the contributions of foreign scholars in order to emphasize the development of native scholarship, and only in a few

Originally published by Raúl R. Romero as "La investigación musical en América del Sur," *Letras* (Universidad Nacional Mayor de San Marcos, Lima-Perú) 90 (1986), 71–92. Translated by Jonathan Ritter with permission.

cases, of European researchers who have made a country in South America their new home.

Reasons for this exclusion are self-evident. While the works of foreign ethnomusicologists—who have come to this part of the world for only a limited period of time—have contributed to the global knowledge of South American traditional music, they reflect the academic interests of their respective countries of origin. Consequently, they do not adequately represent the autochthonous currents followed by South American researchers.

## Predecessors in the Colonial Period

Together with the humanists of the Renaissance and the rationalists of the eighteenth century, such as Jean Jacques Rousseau, the Spanish chroniclers of the early colonial period may also be considered some of the first predecessors of ethnomusicology.[1] Their writings cover a wide variety of topics regarding life in the Inca Empire, with music meriting special recognition as an important part of Inca civilization. Felipe Guamán Poma de Ayala, for example, dedicated a considerable number of pages of his vast work to the description of musical activities.[2] Many of his well-known drawings of pre-Columbian daily life show musical instruments and their performers. In addition to Guamán Poma de Ayala, other Spanish chroniclers of the sixteenth and seventeenth centuries, such as Pedro de Cieza de León, Bernabé Cobo, and Garcilaso de la Vega, offered interesting descriptions of a variety of musical aspects that have still not been systematically examined.[3] With the exception of Robert Stevenson's attempt to outline Inca attitudes toward music, no other source exists to evaluate their musical merits.[4] In the majority of cases, ethnohistorical references have been presented by ethnomusicologists only to confirm the pre-Hispanic origins of a particular phenomenon.

The most useful and suggestive musical references from this early literature can be grouped into the following areas: 1) regional and ethnic diversity; 2) music and social structure; 3) musical genres; and 4) musical instruments and performance aspects.

### REGIONAL AND ETHNIC DIVERSITY

Despite that fact that the Andean world has been seen, at least in ethnomusicological literature, as a homogenous musical area, early chroniclers emphasized the musical differences between diverse regions and ethnic groups. Bernabé Cobo captured this phenomenon clearly: "Every province of the Inca Empire had its own way of dancing, whose dances never changed; although now every nation, in church fiestas, imitates and mimics the dances of other provinces."[5] Guamán Poma de Ayala corroborated the impressions of Cobo, noting the ethnic factor in this process: "In this manner, the four parts of Tawantinsuyo [the Inca Empire] had their respective verses and *takis* [songs]. The Quichuas, Aymarays [Aymaras], Collas, Soras, and some of the Condes peoples, had their own special verses."[6] His observations regarding the richness and variety of musical styles grew in importance considering that contemporary Andean society is equally characterized by musical differentiation. Musical diversity, therefore, is a cultural trait that has pre-Columbian antecedents, a reality that should be taken into consideration in any current study of Andean music.

### MUSIC AND SOCIAL STRUCTURE

The existence of a "folkloric" music in opposition to an "official" music was clearly documented by the chroniclers. As has been said in the lines above, Andean music has been considered as a whole, without taking into consideration that in a stratified society, music tends to reflect social and cultural differentiation. In pre-Columbian times, certain types of music were associated with the nobility and were reserved for special rituals. This was music not considered apt for popular consumption and was reserved for the elite. This probably explains its disappearance after the Spanish conquest and the disintegration of the Inca hierarchy, while popular music continued to thrive.[7] Cobo describes a case in which only the members of the hierarchy could participate: "The proper dance of the Incas was called *guayyaya*; only those with Inca lineage and royal blood performed, and they carried before them the king's standard, with a *champi* that bore the royal insignia. Dancing to the sound of a large drum, carried on the back of a plebian or villainous Indian, and played by a woman. . . . At times, in important fiestas, the Inca himself entered into the dance."[8] Cobo also mentions another dance in which the Inca himself danced with women, with the music of an *araui*, and Poma de Ayala describes the *uaricza araui*, a song performed by the Inca and a chorus of young maidens.[9]

Epic singers were also part of this tradition. Cieza de León explains with certain detail the function of these songs as similar to Spanish *romances* and *villancicos* [poetic-musical forms]. According to Cieza de León, these songs were a historical recounting of past glories and achievements of the Inca emperors. Just a few were selected to memorize these songs, which contained in their lyrics many years of history. They were performed only on special occasions and always in the presence of the nobility and the Inca.[10]

Stevenson mentioned the case of the much-appreciated conch shell, which was used in the Inca Empire as a musical instrument.[11] Conches were used for ritual propitiations related to the *huacas* or Inca deities, and were in addition a symbol of power and prestige. Authorities were buried with conch shells as a sign of their status. These instruments were acquired through commerce, in exchange for other valuable goods such as ornaments of silver and gold. For that reason, it was not considered a common instrument and, as Stevenson argues, always remained an aristocratic symbol.

These few examples corroborate the existence of a popular music opposed to a restricted musical activity of and for the high levels of Inca society. Taking into account that the empire was a stratified society, it should not come as a surprise that music reflected that social reality.

## MUSICAL GENRES

Regional and ethnic diversity had to be accompanied by a process of musical differentiation that resulted in a rich variety of dances and songs. Cobo excitedly commented that "it is worth seeing the many and diverse dances performed in the procession of the Holy Sacrament and in other large fiestas. Finding myself once in the town of Collao at the procession of Corpus Christi, I counted forty dances, each different from the next, all imitating in their dress, song, and mode of dancing the Indian nations to which they pertained."[12]

Unfortunately, the characterizations of music and dances elaborated by the chroniclers were made on the basis of song texts, leaving aside properly musical features. For that reason, the greater part of their references pertain to the dominion of literary verses, and this information does not permit an adequate understanding of the works that are described in terms of their musical structure. In general, references to musical genres consequently tend to be merely nominative or defined in relation to their "character." Poma de Ayala, for example, mentions various musical genres, indicating their general character and offering a transcription of their texts. Among them, the *haraui* (a nostalgic song of love), the *cachiua* (happy song), and the *uanca* (also a type of love song) were apparently the most important.[13] Cobo corroborates the references of Poma de Ayala in relation to the *haylli*, a harvest song that according to Poma de Ayala was sung by women and accompanied by *pingollos*, or flutes played by men.[14]

Colonial dictionaries also contain valuable information regarding musical genres.[15] Josafat Roel Pineda, for example, utilized González Holguín's 1608 published dictionary of the Quechua language in his reconstruction of the *wayno*, based on the observation that the term *taqui* referred to both the song and the dance.[16]

## MUSICAL INSTRUMENTS AND PERFORMANCE ASPECTS

References to and descriptions of musical instruments are abundant in the chronicles, and are an indication of their ample and varied use in daily life. Nonetheless, other sources exist that also offer useful data about pre-Hispanic musical instruments. These are, among others, archeological remains of instruments themselves, and designs contained on pre-Columbian ceramics and textiles. The chroniclers, nonetheless, confirmed the existence of many types of drums, idiophones, flutes, and trumpets in the Inca Empire, as well as the nonexistence of stringed instruments. We can also find information about the function of certain instruments, such as the already mentioned case of the conch shell and the *qeppas* (trumpets), the latter used on solemn occasions associated with warfare. Stevenson and Jiménez Borja compiled numerous references from the chronicles regarding musical instruments in studies that should serve as basic guides for readers interested in this branch of research.[17]

On a related subject, references to aspects of musical performance are scarce, but constitute the only technical descriptions we have of specific pre-Columbian practices. One of the most detailed descriptions of musical performance is that of Garcilaso de la Vega regarding panpipe groups: "When an Indian played a *cañuto* [one tube of a panpipe], the other responded with the consonance of a fifth or some other, followed by the other in a different consonance, and the other with another, at times rising to high points and at others lowering to the bass, always in time." In relation to the musical scale, Garcilaso noted the presence of the use of large intervals in place of small ones, writing that "they did not know how to vary their melodies with small-value notes, but always stuck with whole notes."[18]

Poma de Ayala mentions the musical accompaniment played on the *pingullo* and *quena-quena* in various dances and songs, and also points out two cases of antiphonal song between women and men. The first of these, the *uaricza araui*, was sung for the Inca with the help of a llama.[19] The song imitated the soft cry of the animal, which was repeated again and again until approximating the shrill sound emitted by the llama.

According to Carlos Vega, Garcilaso may have tried to describe the anhemitonal pentatonic scale, *anhemitonal* meaning "without semitones," supposedly that of widest use in the Inca Empire, or at least, one of the most recurrent among those that existed. The scale was "intoned simultaneously for the Inca, who said 'Yn' various times, retaining an appropriate rhythm and tone, frequently interrupted by responding verses from the Coyas and Ñustas, who first sang in a high voice, then lowered little by little, until arriving at a soft tone that distinguished the *uaricza* and the *araui*."[20] The second case of antiphonal song was called *saynata*, with an ironic theme in which a man responded to a chorus of women.[21]

Despite these brief descriptions of musical techniques, demonstrating chroniclers' interest in music itself, they did not leave a single musical transcription. The first attempt to document folk music in South America in written form occurred much later in the colonial period with Bishop Baltazar Martínez y Compañón's nine-volume work on life and the natural environment in Trujillo, the city in which he was appointed. Written in the second half of the eighteenth century, his work attempted to provide a general ethnography of the region by describing various aspects of provincial life in Trujillo, including customs and behavior, flora and fauna, and history. Twenty pages of volume 2 are dedicated to music, and include seventeen songs and three instrumental dances, all collected around Trujillo.[22] Among similar contributions is the collection [of the Franciscan] Gregorio de Zuola, who included seventeen pieces of music of anonymous origin as part of his nearly five-hundred-page encyclopedia, written in the last years of the seventeenth century. Nonetheless, this collection, like others of less importance, presented transcriptions of a marked Hispanic European origin, with minimal indigenous characteristics.[23]

Early Spanish chroniclers were responsible for the first attempts to document and communicate the indigenous music of South America to a foreign audience. The chroniclers were the first ethnomusicologists, not only because they were the first writers to pay attention to music, but because in treating it, they considered it an integral part of the social and cultural worlds they were attempting to describe.

At the conclusion of colonial domination in South America, the new republics had to reorganize their economic and political structures. The nineteenth century was a period in which there was little activity that might be referred to as musical research. The recollection of autochthonous melodies became the dominant activity, followed by a few composers and musicians who were exploring a different world, anticipating the beginning of modern academicism in the first decades of the twentieth century.

## The Beginnings of Academicism

Music research in the nineteenth century consisted primarily of collecting traditional melodies. The notion that autochthonous melodies needed to be preserved and presented to the urban public, arranged according to the rules of [Western] "art," was widespread in this era. One example of this practice was the collection by Marcos Jiménez de la Espada's 1881 *Colección de cantos y bailes indios de yaravíes quiteños* (Collection of Indian yaraví songs and dances from Quito), which included twenty *yaravíes* and four dances, the majority arranged for piano.[24] Other important collections were those of Ventura R. Lynch and of Daniel Alomía Robles. Both tirelessly collected Andean melodies during the last years of the nineteenth century and the beginning of the twentieth.[25] Robles collected and transcribed more than a thousand indigenous melodies, and enriched his notation with commentary about the occasions in which these melodies were performed. Robles's collection constitutes one of the more important contributions to the preservation of Andean musical patrimony, but remained unpublished [until 1990].[26]

The desire to arrange traditional melodies in accordance with the demands of Western aesthetics was also the principal motivation behind Claudio Rebagliati's collection of South American dances and popular songs published in 1870.[27] Rebagliati, born in Italy but later a resident of Peru, included in his collection twenty-two Andean and Creole songs arranged for piano. Conscious that his intent was to adapt the collected melodies for European tastes, he wrote in the preface to the work: "This collection consists of popular airs, unpublished and anonymous, known in South America only by [oral] tradition and, for that same reason, performed in various ways and always incorrectly. My intention has been to subject them to the rules of Art, taking care at the same time not to make them lose any of their peculiar color."[28]

Rebagliati's justification exemplifies the mentality of the nineteenth-century collectors of traditional music. While the act of collecting reflected an important interest in traditional music, colonial prejudices and ethnocentric perspectives still prevailed. Indigenous melodies could not have been presented such as they were, perhaps because they represented the primitivism of the rural population or the urban poor. Arranged for the piano—the characteristic instrument of European music—or for a small orchestra, they could presume an acceptable [musical] level that justified their preservation.

Despite the ethnocentrism manifested in these arrangements, the interest shown in collecting and transcribing traditional melodies for publication reveals that autochthonous music was beginning to be considered an object of serious attention. The first signs of sincere interest in the systematic study of traditional music appeared in Cuzco at the beginning of the twentieth century. These efforts were primarily dedicated to the debate over the use of the pentatonic scale in Andean music. José Castro, a pianist and composer from Cuzco, was the first to call attention to the use of this scale with a monograph on the pentatonic system in the indigenous music of precolonial Peru, published in 1898.[29] Castro, by his own admission, came to recognize the use of pentatonicism while playing the black keys on a piano. He analyzed the pentatonic scales used in twenty-four songs, obtained from diverse collectors from Cuzco, and elaborated their structural characteristics and differences with the Western diatonic scale. Years later, Leandro Alviña, a student at the Universidad Nacional de San Antonio Abad del Cusco (National University of Saint Anthony the Abbot in Cuzco) and also a composer in his own right, wrote a thesis on Inca music in 1908, centered on the use of pentatonicism.[30] Around the same time, Daniel Alomía Robles noted the importance of pentatonicism in Andean music, which he collected during his travels in the countryside. His thoughts on this material, although not published [during his lifetime], were summarized and presented by Alberto Villalba Muñoz in an influential conference at the Universidad Nacional Mayor de San Marcos (National University of San Marcos) in Lima.[31]

The debate over the use of pentatonic scales was the first manifestation of a growing interest in the analysis of musical structures that later would be continued by diverse authors.[32] Despite the fact that this discussion was centered in Cuzco, and that Alviña was the first university student to demonstrate that music could be an object of academic study, that was not where the first nucleus of ethnomusicological activity was formed. It was not until the 1930s that systematic studies began to spread throughout South America. The most important center of study was created around the figure of Carlos Vega in Argentina. Vega, a self-taught musicologist, began working in 1926 at the Museo Argentino de Ciencias Naturales (MACN, Museum of Natural Sciences), where he created the Gabinete de Musicología Indígena (Office of Indigenous Musicology), and in 1931 founded and directed the Instituto de Musicología (Musicology Institute) in the Ministry of Education. Under the auspices of these institutions, Vega began an intense period of research and publication, not limiting himself to Argentine music, but also including other countries in South America. From the beginning of the 1930s, Vega traveled to Chile, Peru, Bolivia, and Paraguay, collecting hundreds of melodies and data for his future works. From that point until his death in 1966, Vega published constantly, gathering talented disciples around him, and becoming the most influential and creative author among his South American colleagues.

In the 1930s, Vega anticipated some of his future projects through a number of articles published in *La Prensa* in Buenos Aires. In this newspaper, Vega wrote about a variety of Argentine songs and dances, revealing a special interest in the problem of origins and applying [English anthropologist E. B.] Tylor's theory of survivals to Latin American folklore.[33] Vega's first major publication in that decade was a monograph on the music in a seventeenth-century colonial codex,[34] in which he presented transcriptions from the de Zuola manuscript, a colonial collection of popular music of that epoch. Nonetheless, the properly ethnomusicological work of Vega was inaugurated by two presentations that he delivered at the 25th International Congress of Americanists (25° Congreso Internacional de Americanistas) in La Plata in 1932. The first of these was a monograph on the Andean pan flute of which Vega dedicated the greater part to an analysis demonstrating the Polynesian origin of the instrument. His analysis was based on the postulations of the German anthropological school of "cultural circles" (*Kulturkreis*), which Vega had learned and adopted since beginning his work at the Museum of Natural Sciences.[35] In the second paper, he speculated about the use of pentatonicism in Andean music, and argued against the idea that was in general use in the pre-Columbian era, asserting instead that other tonal systems were also employed in ancient Peru.

Far from Vega's circle, the 1930s also witnessed a surge in ethnomusicological activity in other countries. The coincidence of individual initiatives in Chile, Ecuador, Peru, and Colombia suggests a common environment favorable to research.

The appearance of numerous general overviews characterizes much of the relevant scholarship of these years. In 1930, Segundo Luis Moreno Andrade published a historical account of Ecuadorian music, which endeavored to introduce the reader to the variety of musical traditions in that country.[36] Similar works and objectives followed with Carlos Raygada in Peru, José Ignacio Pardomo Escobar in Colombia, and Eugenio Pereira Salas in Chile.[37] The holistic perspective of these works explains the simultaneous inclusion of academic and oral traditions as integral parts of national musical heritage. In addition, the breadth of these works was a consequence of the scarcity of previous studies, which obligated these scholars to write in general and all-encompassing terms as a way of covering all of the existing material that otherwise remained unknown.

During this decade, and in a similar fashion, the first more specific works appeared. The articles by Carlos Isamitt about Araucanian musical instruments launched the study of organology in Chile.[38] In Peru, the Belgian Peruvian composer Andrés Sas published a series of articles about traditional Peruvian music. His essay on Nazca music offered important evidence in favor of the hypothesis that pentatonicism was not the only scale utilized in pre-Hispanic times. In previous articles, Sas had analyzed Andean harmonic patterns and the historical formation of Peruvian folklore.[39] Also in Peru, Teodoro Valcárcel, an important composer related to the nationalist currents of the time, attempted to begin serious and institutionally backed research through the Department of Folklore at the Conservatorio Nacional de Música (National Conservatory of Music).[40] His ambitious project, which included the collection, classification, and analysis of traditional Peruvian music, however, was never realized.[41]

Essential for the development of research in the 1930s was the appearance of the *Boletín Latino-Americano de Música* in 1935, founded and directed by the German Uruguayan musicologist Francisco Curt Lange. Under the auspices of the Instituto de Estudios Superiores (Institute of Advanced Studies) in Montevideo, Lange created the *Boletín* in response to his hope for the autonomous development of American music, despite the predominance of European tastes in the cultural sphere of South American elites. The *Boletín* served this ideal by becoming the showcase for the work and scholarship of researchers of traditional and academic American music. The publication and distribution of these works was the first stage in the development of "musical Americanism," as Lange himself referred to this movement.[42]

In this context, research on traditional music played a basic role: that of showing to the vast inter-American community, through systematic analysis, the elements of autochthonous music that could serve as the foundation for the autonomous development of academic American music. Many of the best contributions to South American ethnomusicology were published in this *Boletín*. Among them, the series of papers by Isamitt on Chilean organology and by Sas on traditional

Peruvian music, and the national overviews by Raygada and Pardomo Escobar, are the most representative.[43] The *Boletín* coincided with the growth in musical research in those years and served as a vehicle for its diffusion at an inter-American level. It also reoriented individual research projects toward common objectives.

The following two decades were marked by the maturation of previous currents. The nucleus formed by Vega in Argentina continued to play a central role due to his prodigious publications and the work of his disciples, who by the 1940s were already disposed to continue his legacy. While in the prior decade Vega had been researching and writing about a variety of subjects, it was in the 1940s that he definitively structured his principal theories and methods. His proposal for the analysis of the structure of musical phrases, his division of South America into musical areas that he termed *cancioneros* [corpus of songs], and his treatment of organology, in which he introduced the classificatory system of Hornbostel-Sachs for the first time [in South America], are considered his most important contributions during this period.[44]

Equally important regarding Vega was his great capacity for training disciples. Isabel Aretz, his most prominent and prolific student, continued many of the lines of research initiated by her teacher. In her first book on Argentine music, Aretz presented an overview of the traditional music of Tucumán, both past and present, while her second one accomplished the same for songs and dances of Argentina more generally.[45] In these two important contributions, Aretz followed Vega's theories, citing and applying his method for the structural analysis of musical phrases, called *fraseología* [phraseology], as well as the theory of *cancioneros*, accepting it as a general framework for her work. In the 1950s, Aretz moved to Venezuela and dedicated the greater part of her research to traditional Venezuelan music. Her publications on the *tonos de velorio* [wake songs], the *mare-mare* [indigenous dance genre], and the *polo* [song genre]are examples of her research in this new period.[46]

Luis Felipe Ramón y Rivera, a musicologist who became acquainted with Vega and his theories while living in Argentina, was a central figure in Venezuelan ethnomusicology. His monographs on popular polyphony and work songs are distinguished examples of his research.[47] His book on the *joropo* [music and dance genre] is representative for this type of work and one of the best structural descriptions of a specific South American genre.[48] In this monograph, Ramón y Rivera presents a history of the *joropo*, classifying its diverse variants, making reference to social aspects that surround its performance, and anticipated the use of a particular method of analysis that he would later come to call *fenomenología* [phenomenology].[49]

The Uruguayan Lauro Ayestarán, a close collaborator of Carlos Vega, as well, dedicated an important part of his work to the study of academic music in his country. In 1943, Ayestarán also began a systematic collection of Uruguayan traditional music under the auspices of the Department of Musicology at the Museo Histórico Nacional (National Museum of History) in Montevideo, adding to the valuable recordings of its already ample collection.[50] Although Ayestarán did not write extensive treatises on traditional music, he did publish short articles about popular songs and dances in *El Día*, one of the principal newspapers in Uruguay.[51]

The active role that Curt Lange played in bringing together isolated efforts of independent ethnomusicologists in South America came to an abrupt end in 1947 with the sixth edition of *Boletín Latinoamericano de Música*. The shortage of funds and institutional support forced Lange to put an end to this Americanist venture. Lange reestablished himself in Mendoza, Argentina, editing the *Revista de Estudios Musicales* (Journal of musical studies) from 1949 to 1953. This journal did not succeed, unfortunately, in fulfilling the same objectives that the *Boletín* had in the 1930s. The *Revista Musical Chilena*, founded in 1945 in the Department of Music at the Universidad de Chile (University of Chile), would not play this role either. While the *Boletín* emphasized inter-Americanism and awarded equal space to all Latin American authors, the *Revista* obeyed a different set of rules, remaining principally but not exclusively a vehicle for the work of Chilean researchers.

Perhaps as a result of the absence of the *Boletín* within the South American music scene, ethnomusicological activities were scarce between 1940 and 1960, with the already-mentioned exception of the circle surrounding Vega. In Ecuador, Moreno Andrade continued with his solitary efforts and published two monographs on autochthonous music and dance of Ecuador and on the music of the Incas, the latter a critique of the d'Harcourts' [Raoul and Marguerite] classic 1925 book on Andean music.[52] Eugenio Pereira Salas addressed specific themes in traditional Chilean music after his general overview appeared in 1941, with a series of articles in the *Revista Musical Chilena*.[53] Finally, among the most important contributions of this period is the study by Arturo Jiménez Borja on pre-Columbian and contemporary organology in the Andean region.[54]

Those thirty years from 1930 to 1960 constituted a period in South America in which a common theoretical and methodological perspective was adopted for research on traditional music. It was an era of self-taught pioneers who, without the guide of prior models for their research or regular institutional support, explored for the first time areas that no one had previously studied, with the academic means then available to them.

## Current Approaches

Since the 1960s, South American ethnomusicology has coexisted with new currents and perspectives practiced by a new generation of ethnomusicologists. These scholars have introduced a more rigorous methodology as well as the theoretical influence of modern anthropological schools of thought.

Among the most important contributions of traditional ethnomusicologists in these years are the studies of Vega on archaisms in traditional Latin American music and on mesomusic.[55] His most distinguished followers, Aretz and Ramón y Rivera, continued their studies in Venezuela. Aretz's major work was her treatise on Venezuelan organology, and Ramón y Rivera wrote on folk music of his country, including Afro-Venezuelan music.[56] The most important project of these two scholars was the founding of the Instituto Interamericano de Etnomusicología y Folklore (INIDEF, Inter-American Institute of Ethnomusicology and Folklore) in 1970 in Caracas. With the solid financial backing of the Venezuelan government and the Organization of American States, INIDEF, under the direction of Aretz, became the most dynamic center of ethnomusicological research in the region. Beginning in 1971, INIDEF organized advanced courses in ethnomusicology for scholars from different American countries, and in 1973 began sponsoring periodic fieldwork projects, in which the collection of ethnographic material was the principal goal. The recordings and materials obtained from these projects are deposited in the archives of folkloric music at INIDEF.[57]

New directions in South American ethnomusicology are found in the works of scholars who began their work in the 1960s. In Peru, an important initiative that bore results was the attempt by Josafat Roel Pineda to found a department of ethnomusicology within the Conservatorio Nacional de Música. Under the leadership of Roel Pineda, several important monographs were written on traditional Peruvian music, such as that of Félix Villareal Vara on carnival and the marking of cattle, Consuelo Pagaza Galdo on the *yaraví* [song genre]. Roel Pineda himself wrote a historical and musical analysis of the *wayno*, the most popular dance in Peru.[58]

In Chile, the existence of a department of music in the Universidad de Chile and of a regularly published journal favored the development of research and the unification of efforts. Among those associated with the university and the *Revista Musical Chilena*, María Ester Grebe was the most prolific author, with the most solid methodology, of her generation. Grebe's contributions are numerous, from publications concerning theory and methodology in ethnomusicology, to specific studies on traditional Chilean music with attention to social context.[59] Manuel Dannemann and Raquel Barros have also made important contributions to Chilean ethnomusicology.[60]

These works display a clear difference from those that I have called "traditional" perspectives toward the study of traditional music in South America. Since the 1960s, the impact of the structural-functionalist school has emphasized the notion of interaction between music and its cultural context, introducing more rigorous methods and techniques in both fieldwork and analysis. More specific units of analysis were preferred over the holistic perspective implied in the practice of panoramic overviews previously mentioned, and little by little the speculation based on evolutionist and diffusionist dogmas has disappeared.

## Research Areas

It is possible to distinguish five fundamental areas of research that have been frequently emphasized by South American authors: general overviews; organological studies; monographs on musical genres; analysis of the structure of musical scales; and the collection and transcription of traditional melodies.

As already mentioned, panoramic essays were the preferred mode of publication by South American scholars beginning in the 1930s. The majority of these works consisted principally of presenting the most important songs and dances of a given territorial unit—a region or a country—with a description of their musical characteristics. The justification for this type of publication was related to the absence of serious studies on traditional music prior to the 1930s, and the desire to collect and preserve everything possible. Almost all of the publications of this type in Argentina, Peru, Ecuador, Venezuela, Colombia, and Chile were based on these motivations.[61]

These overview essays were strictly limited to musical materials, and in a few cases were equivalent to an illustrated list of existing songs and dances within a country or region. The sociocultural context of the music and the role and function of performers remained outside the scope of these studies. Aretz's take on traditional Argentine music in 1952 is one of the most important works of this type and serves as a model for this mode of research. The information presented consists of a brief description of musical instruments, followed by a section—more than half of the book—dedicated to songs and dances. Brief historical considerations and musical transcriptions are offered as part of an introduction to the analytical description of genres in terms of their harmonic, melodic, and rhythmic aspects. The presentation of this type of material has not been, however, always the same. Raygada, Pereira Salas, Pardomo Escobar, and Moreno Andrade were among the authors who included all musical styles in their treatises—including academic music—dedicating only a small part of their works to traditional music. Nevertheless, these were the first important studies of traditional music to be published in their respective countries.

Organological studies in South America have followed a similar trajectory. Vega's book on Argentine musical instruments was the first important work to be published in this vein. Vega created a model that can be considered representative of this kind of work. Special attention was paid to the system of instrument classification, introducing the Hornbostel-Sachs system, the geographic distribution of the instrument, aspects of its construction, performance techniques, tuning systems, and brief references to the musical styles associated with the instrument. Vega's perspective was expansive, including not only the instruments of his home country in Argentina, but also those in popular use in northeast Argentina that were characteristic of Andean countries, among them Peru, Chile, and Bolivia.

Vega's emphasis on classification, to which he dedicated the first chapter of his book, led to the widespread acceptance and predominance of the Hornbostel-Sachs system in South America. Its use by Vega and his disciples arose from the need for an organized system of classification with which to confront the study of a great variety of instruments. The authors mentioned here held in common a desire to include in their treatises the totality of existing instruments in their respective countries, in a practice similar to their panoramic views of songs and dances. One exception to this case was the work of Jiménez Borja on Peruvian organology, which did not utilize the Hornbostel-Sachs classificatory system. That work was fundamentally a historical study of pre-Columbian musical instruments, based on a reading of chroniclers' and travelers' accounts. Jiménez Borja made frequent references, nonetheless, to contemporary instruments. Although he consistently utilized a division of idiophones, membranophones, and aerophones (chordophones did not exist in pre-Columbian Peru), he made no further subdivisions in these categories. Other works on more specific aspects of organology also emphasized strictly musical aspects of the instruments under study.[62] The symbolic and social significance of many South American instruments remained outside the scope of these works, sidelined in favor of more empirical aspects.

In a similar fashion, the writing of monographs on musical genres has been a favorite theme among South American ethnomusicologists. In these works, musical analysis in terms of melodic, harmonic, and rhythmic considerations has been the primary emphasis. *El joropo* by Ramón y Rivera is an outstanding example of this type of study, in which the author introduces a particular style of analysis that he would later call "phenomenology." Aretz, Vega, Roel Pineda, Villarreal Vara, and Pagaza Galdo have written similarly important works on musical genres, all having in common a special interest in formal musical aspects.[63] The monographic character of these studies favored intensive research on the chosen genre, emphasizing historical information and choreographic description (if necessary), but above all an exhaustive musical analysis.

Structural analysis of musical scales has been a recurrent theme, although in a special manner in the Andean region. The debate over the use of pentatonicism, the most popular theme in this area of research since the beginning of the century, is the principal cause for this abundance of research. In addition to the historical issues under discussion, the study of the Andean pentatonic scale also included its abstract structural organization. For example, the principal difference between Castro's arguments and those of Alviña was that while the first affirmed that the order was do-re-mi-sol-la, the latter argued for the series la-do-re-mi-sol, thus altering the fundamental note. A more elaborate version was proposed by Raoul and Marguerite d'Harcourt, who, based on materials obtained in situ, classified Andean pentatonicism into five modes: mode A (la-sol-mi-re-do); mode B (sol-mi-re-do-la); mode C (mi-re-do-la-sol); mode D (re-do-la-sol-mi); and mode E (do-la-sol-mi-re). Other studies have gone beyond the strict discussion of pentatonicism, including that of Rodolfo Holzmann on the use of different musical scales in Peruvian music.[64] The author presents examples that range from three up to seven notes, and he analyzes them in terms of their formal structure. Finally, the activity of collecting and publishing transcriptions without an adjoining study of the material thus presented, has been intense since the end of the nineteenth century. Guzmán, Holzmann, and Pagaza Galdo have published their collections with the goal of popularizing traditional songs and dances.[65]

A quick review of these areas of study reveals an interest in form over content, as well as an interest in description over interpretation. The relationship between music and society has never been the subject of study, and the context of the music studies has not been adequately described in the majority of cases. One should remember, however, that this characteristic is shared with other ethnomusicological traditions in other parts of the world. Alan Merriam mentions that ethnomusicology in Europe and the United States also favored descriptive studies in the past.[66] The same characterization can be applied to South American ethnomusicology between 1930 and 1960.[67]

It is thus not coincidental that two of the most important contributions of South American ethnomusicologists consist of methods for formal analysis. The methods of Carlos Vega (phraseology) and of Luis Felipe Ramón y Rivera (phenomenology) were a response to the need for scientific criteria and original techniques to be applied to strictly musical analysis. Description being a fundamental goal, and musical analysis a common and unavoidable practice, South American researchers directed their creative efforts in that direction.

## Notes

1. Bruno Nettl, *Theory and Method in Ethnomusicology* (New York: Free Press, 1964), 13.

2. Felipe Guamán Poma de Ayala, *Nueva corónica y buen gobierno*, ed. Luis Bustíos Gálvez (Lima: Ministerio de Educación, 1956 [1615]).

3. Pedro de Cieza de León, *El señorio de los Incas* (Lima: Instituto de Estudios Peruanos, 1967 [1533]); Bernabé Cobo, *Historia del nuevo mundo*, vol. 3. In *Obras del P. Bernabé Cobo*, vol. 2, ed. P. Francisco Mateos (Madrid: Ediciones Atlas, 1956 [1653]); Garcilaso de la Vega, *Comentarios reales de los incas*, vol. 1 (Lima: Universidad Nacional Mayor de San Marcos, 1959 [1609]).

4. Robert Stevenson, *The Music of Peru: Aboriginal and Viceroyal Epochs* (Washington, D.C.: Organization of American States, 1960).

5. Cobo, *Historia*, 270.

6. Poma de Ayala, *Nueva corónica*, 242.

7. An idea suggested by Robert Stevenson, *Music in Aztec and Inca Territory* (Berkeley: University of California Press, 1968), 145.

8. Cobo, *Historia*, 271.

9. Ibid., 271; Poma de Ayala, *Nueva corónica*, 235.

10. Cieza de León, *El señorio*, 30–32.

11. Stevenson, *Music of Peru*, 24–25.

12. Cobo, *Historia*, 270–71.

13. Poma de Ayala, *Nueva corónica*, 233–35.

14. Ibid., 233; Cobo, *Historia*, 271.

15. Diego González Holguín, *Vocabulario de la lengua general de todo el Perú llamada lengua qquichua, o lengua del inca*, ed. Raúl Porras Barrenechea (Lima: Universidad Nacional Mayor de San Marcos, 1952); Ludovico Bertonio, *Vocabulario de la lengua aymara* (La Paz: Litografía Don Bosco, 1956).

16. Josafat Roel Pineda, "El wayno del Cuzco," *Folklore Americano* 6–7 (1959), 129–245.

17. Stevenson, *Music of Peru*; Arturo Jiménez Borja, "Instrumentos musicales peruanos," *Revista del Museo Nacional* 19–20 (1951), 37–80.

18. De la Vega, *Comentarios reales*, 201. [Translator's note: De la Vega's language regarding musical specifics is somewhat opaque in this passage ("no supieron echar glosa con puntos disminuidos; todos eran enteros de un compas"). Consequently, some translators of de la Vega's text have interpreted this sentence as referring to rhythmic value, others to note intervals. The language quoted here, which refers to "note values" within the context of a melody, is taken from Stevenson's translation in *Music of Peru*, 42.]

19. Poma de Ayala, *Nueva corónica*, 233, 236.

20. Carlos Vega, "La flauta de pan andina" (La Plata: XXV Congreso Internacional de Americanistas, 1932), 350.

21. Poma de Ayala, *Nueva corónica*, 242.

22. Carlos Vega, "La obra del Obispo Martínez Compañón," *Revista del Instituto de Investigación Musicológica Carlos Vega* 2, no. 2 (1978), 12.

23. Stevenson, *Music of Peru*, 151–54.

24. Marcos Jiménez de la Espada, *Colección de cantos y bailes indios de yaravíes quiteños* (Madrid: IV Congreso Anual de Americanistas, 1881).

25. Ventura R. Lynch, *La provincia de Buenos Aires hasta la definición de la cuestión capital de la República* (Buenos Aires: Imprenta de La Patria Argentina, 1883).

26. Translator's note: Robles's work was collected, edited, and published posthumously by his family; see Armando Robles Godoy, ed., *Himno al sol: la obra folkórica y musical de Daniel Alomía Robles*, 3 vols. (Lima: Consejo Nacional de Ciencia y Tecnología, 1990).

27. Claudio Rebagliati, *Album sudamericano: colección de bailes y cantos populares* (Milan: Stabilimento de Edoardo Sonzogno, 1870).

28. Claudio Rebagliati quoted in Carlos Raygada, "Guía musical del Perú," *Fénix* 14 (1964), 64.

29. José Castro, "Sistema pentafónico en la música indígena pre-colonial del Perú," *Boletín Latino-Americano de Música* 4 (1938), 835–41 (reprint).

30. Leandro Alviña, *La música incaica* (Lima: Universidad del Cuzco, 1908). Alviña's thesis was not limited to this topic. He also attempted to reconstruct the history of Peruvian music throughout the ages, dividing his study into pre-Columbian music, the age of conquest, independence, and the republican period.

31. Alberto Villalba Muñoz, *Conferencia literario musical* (Lima: E. Rosay, 1910).

32. The use of pentatonic scales has been a favored topic of discussion in South America. After Castro and Alvinã, many renowned scholars wrote on this subject. See, for example, Carlos Vega, "Escalas con semitonos en la música de los antiguos peruanos" (La Plata: XXV Congreso Internacional de Americanistas, 1932); Teodoro Valcárcel, "Síntesis del plan de trabajo del departamento de folklore," *Boletín Latino Americano de Música* 2 (1936), 458–59; Andrés Sas, "Ensayo sobre la música nazca," *Boletín Latino Americano de Música* 4 (1938), 221–23; and Isabel Aretz, "Músicas pentatónicas en sudamérica," *Archivos Venezolanos de Folklore* 1, no. 2 (1952), 283–309. The classification of pentatonic modes by Raoul d'Harcourt and Marguerite d'Harcourt, *La musique des Incas et ses survivances* (Paris: Paul Geuthner, 1925), has been one of the most influential hypotheses on this issue.

33. Some years later, Carlos Vega synthesized his thoughts on this material in *Danzas y canciones argentinas* (Buenos Aires: Ricordi, 1936).

34. Carlos Vega, *La música de un códice colonial del siglo XVII* (Buenos Aires: Imprenta de la Universidad, 1931).

35. According to Pola Suárez Urtubey, the first contact that Vega had with anthropology occurred when he became associated with the Museum of Natural Sciences. See the prologue to the *Revista del Instituto de Investigación Musicológica Carlos Vega* 1, no. 1 (1977), 5.

36. Segundo Luis Moreno Andrade, "La música en el Ecuador," in *El Ecuador en cien años de independencia*, ed. Orellana J. Gonzalo (Quito: Imprenta de la Escuela de Artes Oficios, 1930). See Charles Sigmund, "Segundo Luis Moreno (1882–1972): Ecuador's Pioneer Musicologist," *Yearbook for Inter-American Musical Research* 8 (1972), 71–104.

37. Carlos Raygada, "Panorama musical del Perú," *Boletín Latino-Americano de Música* 2 (1936), 169–214; José Ignacio Pardomo Escobar, "Esbozo histórico sobre la música colombiana," *Boletín Latino-Americano de Música* 4 (1938), 387–570; Eugenio Pereira Salas, *Los orígenes del arte musical en Chile* (Santiago: Universidad de Chile, 1941). Though the work of Pereira Salas appeared in 1941, and thus not strictly in the 1930s, it pertains stylistically to the aforementioned group. The division of decades presented in this section should be understood as flexible and approximate.

38. Carlos Isamitt, "Un instrumento araucano: la trutruka," *Boletín Latino-Americano de Música* 1 (1935), 43–46; "Cuatro instrumentos musicales araucanos," *Boletín Latino-Americano de Música* 3 (1937), 55–66; "Los instrumentos araucanos," *Boletín Latino-Americano de Música* 4 (1938), 305–12.

39. Andrés Sas, "Ensayo sobre la música inca," *Boletín Latino-Americano de Música* 1 (1935), 71–77; "La formación del folklore peruano," *Boletín Latino-Americano de Música* 2 (1936), 97–103.

40. Teodoro Valcárcel, "¿Fue exclusivamente de 5 sonidos la escala musical de los incas?," *Revista del Museo Nacional* 1, no. 1 (1932), 115–21.

41. Valcárcel, "Síntesis del plan de trabajo," 458–59.

42. Francisco Curt Lange, "Arte musical latino americano: raza y asimilación," *Boletín Latino-Americano de Música* 1 (1935), 13–28; "Tres conferencias en la Universidad Mayor de San Marcos de Lima: americanismo musical," *Boletín Latino Americano de Música* 2 (1936), 117–56.

43. See notes above.

44. Carlos Vega, *Panorama de la música popular argentina* (Buenos Aires: Editorial Losada, 1944); *La música popular argentina: fraseología* (Buenos Aires: Imprenta de la Universidad, 1941); *Los instrumentos musicales aborígenes y criollos de Argentina* (Argentina: Ediciones Centurión, 1946).

45. Isabel Aretz, *Música tradicional argentina: Tucumán, historia y folklore* (Tucumán: Universidad Nacional de Tucumán, 1946); *El folklore musical argentino* (Buenos Aires: Ricordi Americana, 1952).

46. Isabel Aretz, "Música de los estados Aragua y Guarico: los tonos de velorio," *Revista Venezolana de Folklore* 1, no. 2 (1948), 47–78; "El maremare como expresión musical y coreográfica," *Boletín del Instituto de Folklore* 3, no. 2 (1958), 45–108; "El polo," *Boletín del Instituto de Folklore* 3, no. 6 (1959), 227–73; *Instrumentos musicales de Venezuela* (Universidad de Oriente, Venezuela, 1967).

47. Luis Felipe Ramón y Rivera, "La polifonía popular de Venezuela," *Revista del Instituto Nacional de la Tradición* 1 (1949), 83–92; *Cantos de trabajo del pueblo venezolano* (Caracas: Fundación Eugenio Mendoza, 1955).

48. Luis Felipe Ramón y Rivera, *El joropo: baile nacional de Venezuela* (Caracas: Ministerio de Educación, 1953).

49. Luis Felipe Ramón y Rivera, *Fenomenología de la etnomúsica del área latino americana* (Caracas: Consejo Nacional de la Cultura, 1980).

50. Editors' note: Ayestarán collected and compiled over four thousand field recordings of Uruguayan folk songs that have been incorporated into the Lauro Ayestarán Center for Musican Documentation (Centro Nacional de Documentación Musical Lauro Ayestarán), founded in Montevideo in 2009. www.cdm.gub.uy, accessed May 15, 2015.

51. These articles were published in Lauro Ayestarán, *El folklore musical uruguayo* (Montevideo: Arca, 1971).

52. Segundo Luis Moreno Andrade, *Música y danzas autóctonas del Ecuador—Indigenous Music and Dances of Ecuador* (Quito: Editorial Fray Jodoco Ricke, 1949); *La música de los incas* (Quito: Casa de Cultura Ecuatoriana, 1957). Consuelo Pagaza Galdo, "El yaraví," *Folklore Americano* 8–9 (1961), 75–141.

53. Eugenio Pereira Salas, "Los estudios folklóricos y el folklore musical de Chile," *Revista Musical Chilena* 1, no. 1 (1945), 4–12; "Los villancicos chilenos," *Revista Musical Chilena* 9, no. 15 (1955), 37–48; "Consideraciones sobre el folklore en Chile," *Revista Musical Chilena* 13, no. 68 (1959), 83–92.

54. Jiménez Borja, "Instrumentos musicales peruanos."

55. Carlos Vega, "Una cadencia medieval en América," *Yearbook of the Inter-American Institute for Musical Research* 1 (1965), 94–111; "Mesomusic," *Ethnomusicology* 10, no. 1 (1966), 1–17.

56. Aretz, *Instrumentos musicales de Venezuela*; Luis Felipe Ramón y Rivera, *La música folkórica de Venezuela* (Caracas: Universidad Central de Venezuela, 1969); *Música afrovenezolana* (Caracas: Universidad Central de Venezuela, 1971).

57. Editors' note: INIDEF was reorganized in 1987 as a Venezuelan government entity, Fundación de Etnomusicología y Folklore (FUNDEF, Foundation for Ethnomusicology and Folklore), which still exists.

58. Félix Villareal Vara, "El carnaval y la marcación de ganado en Jesús," *Folklore Americano* (1959), 6–7; Pagaza Galdo, "El Yaraví"; Roel Pineda, "El wayno del Cuzco."

59. María Ester Grebe, "Objeto, métodos y técnicas de investigación en etnomusicología: algunos problemas básicos," *Revista Musical Chilena* 30, no. 133 (1976), 5–27; "Antropología de la música: nuevas orientaciones y aportes teóricos en la investigación musical," *Revista Musical Chilena* 35, no. 153–55 (1981), 52–74; *The Chilean Verso: A Study in Musical Archaism* (Los Angeles: University of California, Los Angeles, 1967); "El Kultrún mapuche: un microcosmo simbólico," *Revista Musical Chilena* 27, no. 123–24 (1973), 3–42; "La trifonía atacameña y sus perspectivas inter-culturales," *Revista Musical Chilena* 28, no. 126–27 (1974), 21–46; "Presencia del dualismo en la cultura y música mapuche," *Revista Musical Chilena* 28, no. 126–27 (1974), 47–79; "La música alacalufe: aculturación y cambio estilístico," *Revista Musical Chilena* 28, no. 126–27 (1974), 80–111.

60. Manuel Dannemann and Raquel Barros, "Los problemas de la investigación del folklore musical chileno," *Revista Musical Chilena* 14, no. 71 (1960), 82–100; "El guitarrón en el departamento de Puente Alto," *Revista Musical Chilena* 14, no. 74 (1960), 7–45; "Introducción al estudio de la tonada," *Revista Musical Chilena* 18, no. 89 (1964), 105–116; *El romancero chileno* (Santiago: Universidad de Chile, 1970).

61. Vega, *Danzas y canciones argentinas*; Aretz, *Música tradicional argentina* and *El folklore musical argentino*; Raygada, "Panorama musical del Perú"; Moreno Andrade, "La música en el Ecuador" and *Música y danzas autóctonas del Ecuador*; Ramón y Rivera, *La música folkórica de Venezuela* and *Música afro-venezolana*; Pardomo Escobar, "Esbozo histórico sobre la música colombiana"; Pereira Salas, *Los orígenes del arte musical en Chile*.

62. Sas, "Ensayo sobre la música nazca"; Vega, "La flauta de pan andina"; Antonio González Bravo, "Kenas, pincollos y tarkas," *Boletín Latino-Americano de Música* 3 (1937), 25–32; "Trompeta, flauta traversa, tambor y charango," *Boletín Latino-Americano de Música* 4 (1938), 167–75; "Clasificación de los sicus aymaras," *Revista de Estudios Musicales* 1 (1949), 92–101; Josafat Roel Pineda, "Un instrumento musical de paracas y q'ero," *Boletín del Conservatorio Nacional de Música* 30 (1961), 18–29.

63. Aretz, "El polo"; Vega, *Los instrumentos musicales*; Roel Pineda, "El wayno del Cuzco"; Villareal Vara, "El carnaval"; Pagaza Galdo, "El yaraví."

64. Rodolfo Holzmann, "De la trifonía la heptafonía en la música tradicional peruana," *Revista San Marcos* 8 (1968), 5–51.

65. Victor Guzmán, *Cancionero incaico* (Buenos Aires: Imprenta de la Universidad, 1929); Rodolfo Holzmann, *Panorama de la música tradicional del Perú* (Lima: Casa Mozart, 1966); Consuelo Pagaza Galdo, *Cancionero andino sur* (Lima: Casa Mozart, 1967).

66. Alan Merriam, *The Anthropology of Music* (Evanston, Ill.: Northwestern University Press, 1964), 38.

67. Signs of a growing interest in studying music in its sociocultural context are seen, for example, in Grebe, "El Kultrún mapuche" and "Presencia del dualismo." She applied the principles of cognitive anthropology in her works, especially with reference to the problem of cultural dualism in the musical life of the Mapuche.

# 2

# Between Folklore and Ethnomusicology

## *Sixty Years of Folk and Vernacular Music Studies in Colombia*

CARLOS MIÑANA BLASCO

This article aims to offer a balanced perspective on the study of folk and vernacular music in Colombia.[1] It does not pretend to be exhaustive, but rather to present a broad panorama to orient those who wish to delve into the small maze that is the field of musicological studies in the country.[2]

### "A Very Folkloric Country"

Studies of folk and vernacular music in Colombia, as in other parts of the world, have been marked by the concept of "folklore," a term introduced in 1846 by William J. Thoms's field of studies focused on "antiquities," a line of inquiry that was in fashion as early as the eighteenth century. The concept is interpreted differently depending on author, era, and trends, and it has had difficulty defining its area of study as "science"—as Argentine musicologist Carlos Vegas would have liked—among literary studies, music studies, archeology, sociology, and anthropology.[3]

One constant among folklorists, despite their differences, is the apocalyptic vision of folk and vernacular culture in the face of modernization: traditions are steamrolled by the relentless engine of progress, and so they must be collected, photographed, filmed, and recorded. Folk and vernacular culture is not contemporary but rather a "survivor" from the past, a type of living fossil that must be protected and displayed in "cultural zoos" such as folk festivals, museums, and libraries.[4]

Originally published by Carlos Miñana Blasco as "Entre el folklore y la etnomusicología: 60 años de estudios sobre la música popular tradicional en Colombia," *A Contratiempo: Revista de Música en la Cultura* 11 (2000), 36–49. Translated by Juan C. Agudelo and published with permission of Carlos Miñana Blasco, Professor, Universidad Nacional de Colombia.

Tied to collection and conservation is also classification, whose final product of synthesis and effort to overcome anecdotal description is taxonomy. Works within the folklore paradigm, therefore, tend to be ambitious and, from a quantitative perspective, pretentiously exhaustive—possible only if the conception of culture is static, self-contained and closed—encapsulated in terms of long lists and works of encyclopedic character such as "general compendia," dictionaries, lexicons, and handbooks. The folklorist is more interested in pursuing the forgotten melody missing from his or her collection than in understanding musical practices and transformation in a sociocultural context. He or she prefers to carefully accumulate and catalog information instead of risking interpretation.

From the beginning, folklore projects were linked to nationalist projects. In folklore, national identity lies in the idealized past embalmed and consecrated by folklorists' authority. Folk and vernacular culture becomes a thing, objectified in museums or in books. Identity lies in "the" *cumbia*, not just any *cumbia* but "that" *cumbia* that meets the conditions and requirements determined by folklorists. Folkloric *cumbia* or folkloric *bambuco* are ultimately the product of folklorists, just as is the "traditional costume for the sanjuanero." This opens the door for a case study enumeration of "authentic features," the basis for folk festivals and competitions whose goal is to preserve the "purity" of "folk expressions." In the Colombian case, these notions continue to be so strong that the very concept of folklore becomes untouchable. To question it, and the work of folklorists on traditional culture, is to harm the mainstream sensibilities, to negate Colombia's cultural identity, roots, and values, to renounce the state, which in certain contexts is cause for public disciplining or, at least, exclusion.

Folklore organizations and societies have emerged as a result of this perception of folk and vernacular culture as rescue missions and collector clubs. Already by 1881 there was a folklore society in Spain, directed by Antonio Machado, and another in the United States. In Latin America, folk studies begin to appear at around this time, especially focusing on literature.[5] It is not until the 1950s, however, that a work of some significance in the field of musical studies is published in Colombia, and not until 1959 that this notion of folk and vernacular culture becomes fixed in the Centro de Estudios Folklóricos y Musicales (CEDEFIM, Center for Folkloric and Musical Studies).[6] At around the same time we find the earliest recordings of folk and vernacular music, especially of indigenous communities and Afro-descendant and mestizo communities of the north coast.[7]

Nevertheless, in the 1930s and 1940s there are pioneering works such as Emirto de Lima's series about melodies from the north coast, Daniel Zamudio's supposedly national panorama, Father Francisco de Igualada's volume on Amazonian indigenous music, José Ignacio Perdomo Escobar's glossary of folkloric terms, and Gnecco Rangel Pava's book on tunes from the municipality of Guamal.[8] Otto Mayer-Serra's monumental *Música y músicos de Latinoamérica*

(Music and musicians of Latin America) compiles the contributions of these pioneers, for the most part.[9] Although incipient, these works have great musicological value since their authors were mostly professional musicians or at least had basic formal musical education. They present different and sometimes contradictory assessments of folk and vernacular music, but they all coincide in attributing to it the essence of nationhood, warning of the risks of its loss in the avalanche of modernization and recommending its study and conservation.[10] [Zamudio, for instance, declares], "We stress that it is necessary to collect as much as possible in this subject; to make compilations of the melodies . . . Perhaps it is not too late, since undoubtedly, all this will disappear at the hands of mechanical society."[11]

This folklorist notion, although arriving late in comparison to other countries, has had a profound impact on the country. Soon thereafter, centers for folkloric studies and folklore academies appear throughout the nation. There were university departments devoted to the subject, and the publication of "general compendia," manuals, and dictionaries such as those by Guillermo Abadía Morales, Octavio Marulanda, Javier Ocampo, and Harry C. Davidson were truly best sellers.[12] Other more local studies, such as those of Compae Goyo (Guillermo Valencia Salgado), William Fortich, Consuelo Araújo, Miguel Angel Martín, Blanca Álvarez, and Misael Devia Morales, achieve greater depth and a more lively and affective tone due to their tighter focus and the greater engagement of the authors in the field.[13] They are organized and systematized records of personal memories and experiences.

All of these texts, the general as well as the local, tend to be large works of collection, the fruits of lifelong labor, and are characterized by inadequate and uncritical use of second- and third-hand sources, a reliance on scant or unsystematic fieldwork, an accumulation and juxtaposition of extensive information, and the near absence of a critical lens in their folklorist focus. They tend not to incorporate musical transcriptions; but where they do, they can be dismissed since the authors, as a rule, were not musicians and, from a strictly musical perspective, [their transcriptions] are not used to illustrate anything. Musical analysis as such is absent, and imprecise commentaries and evaluations abound, erroneous and without evidence. They also tend to not include a discography.[14]

These texts have carried out, and continue to carry out, a fundamental role in the creation of both a "Colombian folk music" imaginary and for that matter of "Colombian culture." Proof of this are their numerous editions, the extent to which they are consulted in libraries, and their use as required reading both at the university level and in general education. In light of the absence of better quality sources, they have served to demonstrate the diversity of Colombian people, to display and praise some manifestations of folk and vernacular culture, even if only within a rigid schema. Motivated by them, some young readers from the cities carried out fieldwork, recorded, experienced, and learned traditional music. Festivals and folk competitions were organized on the basis of these folklore manuals. In other words, living musical traditions and folk and vernacular practices were evaluated on the basis of deficient investigations that did not account for the complexity of the processes of folk and vernacular music in the country. Expressions including "typical" dress, choreography, and instrumentation were regulated; "official" versions of anonymous melodies were adopted; and lively debates (that continue to this day) took place over the greater "authenticity" of one version over another. This generated a process of uniformity of vernacular culture throughout the country, sanitizing its creativity, and condemning and rejecting its diversity and dynamism.[15] The omnipresence of these texts is almost total, not only for the above-mentioned reasons, but also because they continue to feed off each other, reinforcing, copying, and reproducing themselves in an increasingly broad spiral.

## Musicians as Researchers

Professional musicians with formal schooling have shown relatively little interest regarding folk and vernacular music and research. This has contributed to Colombia's lagging progress in this field in comparison with other countries in the Andean region (Peru, Bolivia, Ecuador), and the Caribbean (Venezuela), and decades behind countries like Mexico, Brazil, Argentina, and Cuba.[16]

After the above-mentioned pioneering studies by Emirto de Lima and Daniel Zamudio, the first people to write about music based on fieldwork, recordings, transcriptions, and musicological analysis were members of CEDEFIM, which was part of the Conservatorio Nacional de Música (National Conservatory of Music) in Bogotá, and who began conducting research in 1959. Of this handful of short publications—which were at times overly descriptive, superficial, and based on small, unrepresentative samples—the one by Andrés Pardo Tovar and Jesús Pinzón Urrea stands out.[17] From the same period we find works by Father Andrés Rosa about a traditional genre (*rajaleña*) in the Department of Huila in the southwest of the country; keen writings on Andean urban and peasant music by Pinzón Urrea and Luis Torres Zuleta about urban *bambuco*; and a study by Blas Emilio Atehortúa about the San Pascual Bailón feast at the Tota Lake in the Department of Boyacá, which includes transcriptions but no musicological analysis.[18] A pioneering work on dance practices in Mompós was published in Medellín.[19] Some of the members of this research project (Alberto Londoño, Oscar Vahos) went on to lead additional investigative and pedagogical efforts in connection to the Escuela Popular de Arte (EPA, Popular School of Art) and the Centro de Estudios Folclóricos (CEF, Center for Folkloric Studies). In the Department of Valle, Lubín Mazuera published a musical analysis of *bambuco*, although this was not based on field research.[20] Carmen Ortega Ricaurte compiled the first bibliography of music in Colombia in 1973.[21] A few years later, Jorge Morales Gómez published a bibliography of Colombian folklore in which music plays a significant role.[22]

Academic musicians from this period wished to nourish from the fountain of folk and vernacular music for their compositions. Motivated by the work of folklorists, even at times working alongside them—as was the case with Guillermo Abadía Morales at CEDEFIM in Bogotá—and thanks to the success of "nationalist" musical movements in South America, Colombian musicians traveled throughout the country collecting and transcribing indigenous, peasant, and Afro-Colombian melodies. Many of the publications from this period feature only one or two transcribed melodies with some commentary, melodies that would subsequently appear, transformed, into symphonic or chamber works. Just as earlier transcriptions from the 1940s and 1950s, these later transcriptions of the 1960s and 1970s are "packaged" somewhat mechanically into the academic patterns of European music. Most of them would not withstand comparison to field recordings, except those of Pinzón Urrea (and perhaps Atehortúa), who undoubtedly achieved with Western musical notation the closest approximation to the "wild" and different sounds of indigenous and folk and vernacular music. Many of these works continue to circulate under, and ultimately supporting, the folklore paradigm by adding "musical illustrations" to the existing work of folklorists.[23]

## Anthropologists, Sociologists, and Linguists as Musicians

Studies carried out by professionals from the social sciences have tended to focus less on music as a sonic phenomenon and more on the contexts and spaces where music happens and its mediating role in social relations. The first works of this type focused on Afro-Colombian and indigenous contexts.[24]

Although we can trace several references to music by anthropologists and sociologists (e.g., texts by Aquiles Escalante or Rogerio Velásquez, and generally all ethnographies of Colombian indigenous groups), the masterful works of Norman E. Whitten Jr. on musical contexts in the Pacific lowlands of Ecuador and Colombia stand out.[25] Other notable works from an anthropological perspective include those of Benjamín Yépez and more recently of Peter Wade on Afro-Colombian urban contexts.[26] In 1989, the Universidad de Antioquia (University of Antioquia) published a commendable anthropological and musicological monograph by Sergio Iván Carmona Maya about the Kuna tribe on the Panamanian border, clearly influenced by the structuralism of [Claude] Lévi-Strauss.[27]

Many anthropological studies of music, until recently, have also been influenced by the folklore paradigm. For example, the 6º Congreso de Antropología en Colombia (6th Conference of Anthropology in Colombia) in 1992 featured a panel titled "Folklore in the Construction of the Americas" with twenty papers.[28]

With respect to linguistic and literary studies, I already mentioned published collections of sung couplets and songbooks. Although works of this type continue to be published, since the 1970s researchers have taken other approaches focusing on social characteristics (violence, gender, social class). The Instituto Caro y Cuervo (Caro and Cuervo Institute) is the organization that has most consistently developed work in this area from a perspective of linguistics.[29]

Studies on *vallenato* music have always been unique and difficult to categorize, beginning with Araújo's *Vallenatología*. Nevertheless, all of them agree on placing a fundamental emphasis on song texts—even when the research is not explicitly literary—due to the narrative force, local flavor, and variety of song verses. It is thus difficult to avoid the commitment to contextualization that each song requires. Among the best published works in this area are those of Ciro Quiroz Otero and Rito Llerena Villalobos.[30] A proper musicological study about *vallenato* and the profound, recent transformations that have made it one of the best-selling and internationally influential genres has yet to be written.[31]

Two very different works, both between the literary and biographical, deserve special mention: Arturo Escobar Uribe's book on musician-singer Salvo Ruiz [1878–1961] and Jorge Villegas and Hernando Grisales's on musician-composer Crescencio Salcedo Monroy [1913–1976].[32]

## Approaching Ethnomusicology

If the relationship between musicology, folklore studies, and anthropology can be traced back to the nineteenth century, ethnomusicology as a distinct discipline with some recognition from both musicology and anthropology only emerges in the 1950s, linked to the emergence of the Society for Ethnomusicology and to the work of Alan Merriam. This is a modern discipline based on fieldwork and the methods of cultural anthropology and musicology, whose goal is to examine music as a cultural product in its cultural context: an anthropology of music that does not ignore technical musical analysis, just as ethno-linguistics cannot ignore phonological, morphological, and syntactic features.[33]

We consider that in Colombia there have only been a few ethnomusicological studies in the strictest sense of the discipline. This is understandable given the absence of institutions to train ethnomusicologists, training that belongs at the postgraduate level [graduate school in the United States]. Only recently have some scholars who completed their formal training in this field abroad returned to Colombia.

These caveats in mind, in the 1970s there begin to appear studies approaching "classic" ethnomusicology, that is, based on relatively extensive fieldwork and relying on rigorous ethnographic techniques of observation, recording, transcription and analysis. In 1977 we see the first work of some significance in this vein, Dirk Koorn's *Folk Music of the Colombian Andes* about the *guabina veleña* [a capella lyrical lament] and the *torbellino* [instrumental counterpart of the *guabina*], based on fieldwork in several towns in the Department of Santander (Vélez, Guavatá, Barbosa, Bolívar, and Puente Nacional). In 1983, George List, a researcher from Indiana University in Bloomington, published his six-hundred-page research analyzing music from the small town of Evitar on Colombia's north coast. List completed his research in the late 1970s. Incidentally, both Koorn's and List's works were doctoral dissertations for U.S. universities, both were published in English, both have a very local scope, and neither had extensive distribution within Colombia.[34]

In 1987, I completed a project on flute and *chirimía* [a type of shawm] music in Popayán, which combined the study of documentary sources from a diachronic perspective with fieldwork, and linked these to festival contexts, musical practices, and musicological analysis.[35] Along similar lines of investigation and with the financial support from the Centro de Documentación Musical (Center of Musical Documentation) at the Instituto Colombiano de Cultura (COLCULTURA, Colombian Culture Institute), I wrote a manuscript on flute and drum music of the peasants in Cauca and Huila, in southwestern Colombia.[36] Following brief fieldwork in Guapi and Buenaventura as well as examining marimbas in organology museums in Bogotá, I wrote an article on the interpretation of marimba tuning based on interval analysis and performance practice.[37] In 1994, the Instituto Colombiano de Antropología (Colombian Anthropology Institute) published a monograph about Nasa [indigenous group from the southwestern highlands, also know as the Páez] feasts and music, also carried out with financial support from COLCULTURA.[38]

Musician María Eugenia Londoño, anthropologist Silvio Aristizábal, and psychologist Ana María Arango carried out a novel interdisciplinary work combining the study of musical features, games, child socialization, and formal schooling toward a model of bilingual and bicultural education among the Embera-Chamí people of Cristianía, Antioquia. Londoño, with collaboration from Jorge Franco, presented a version of this project with more emphasis on musical aspects, which won the 1993 Premio Casa de las Américas (House of the Americas Prize) for musical investigation.[39]

In 1985, the Universidad Nacional de Colombia (National University of Colombia) attempted to update its research trajectory established in the 1970s by advancing an academic perspective at the Instituto de Investigaciones Estéticas

(Institute of Aesthetic Research) counter to folklorist tradition. It published the *Revista Colombiana de Investigación Musical*, but unfortunately this effort failed after the first issues, which focused on classification of musical instruments. The Universidad Nacional de Colombia later published a book on this same topic by Egberto Bermúdez.[40] Bermúdez, who holds an advanced degree in musicology from the United Kingdom, has steadily continued his research and promoted the circulation of valuable recordings. His earliest publications offered a profound critique toward established Colombian musicology, both against folklorists (such as Abadía Morales) as well as historians (such as Father Perdomo and Pardo Tovar).[41] Afterward, Bermúdez assumed a productive position offering new approaches to topics that had already been examined. His work covers a wide gamut: colonial music, unpublished historical studies of folk and vernacular music, organology, and contemporary popular and ethnic musical practices (in particular in the areas of San Andrés y Providencia and the Wayúu tribe). He has also advanced the distribution of records, by directing discographic projects on folk and vernacular music and television series.[42]

In the Department of Tolima, center-west of the country, linked to a musical performance project with the group Cantatierra, Humberto Galindo has published a series of musicological and biographic studies about *caña* [regional dance genre] and the musician-composer Cantalicio Rojas González [1897–1974]. In the Llanos region, we have a compilation of writings about the oral traditions and music from the plains, including the work of renowned harpist Carlos Rojas Hernández, however, without proper musicological analysis.[43] Alfonso Dávila Riveiro published about urban popular music of the Amazon.[44]

Toward the end of the 1980s and early 1990s we see new paths of significant research including graduate theses, monographs, and research from Colombian universities that represent an acceptable and noteworthy academic level that breaks new ground in the field. Although these projects focus on the musical, they do so with different framings and perspectives: some more oriented to description and analysis of musical sounds; others offering context along the lines of anthropology or sociology; and finally others, perhaps most interesting, carried out by students with interdisciplinary backgrounds in both social sciences and music, many deserving of publication.

## The Role of "Cultural Promotion" Groups and Other Institutions

In the 1970s, many Colombian urban musicians outside commercial circuits, as well as many music students and music lovers in general, considered themselves "researchers." Going to the field or to a folk festival with a tape recorder and photo camera to capture sound and sight meant to be a researcher. From the folklore perspective, researching meant collecting what was about to be lost.

Some went further: they studied the melodies or drum rhythms that they recorded, bought instruments (sometimes leaving peasant or indigenous musicians without instruments for their own use), and formed musical ensembles that attempted to imitate groups belonging to "the grassroots."[45] In these cases, research was not just recording but also studying music to perform it faithfully. Some imitations were so good that folklorists saw the need to distinguish between "authentic" and "staged" folklore, the latter being organized by people in the city for distribution in commercial and cultural circuits different from traditional ones. The sphere of Colombian music, which had up to that point been monopolized by *estudiantinas* [ensembles consisting of a variety of plucked and strummed string instruments] and several varieties of groups styled after Garzón y Collazos [a vocal-instrumental duet (1938–77) that became a veritable paradigm of "Colombian music" from the Andes], was suddenly broadened to include other ignored styles labeled "music of the people." This approximation to folk and vernacular musical cultures took on overtones of political engagement and militancy. In the "staging" there was a selection and re-elaboration of the researched subjects. Folklore had to be distilled, finding those expressions of "class" and filtering out "ideological" expressions introduced among the people by the elite and the dominant classes.[46]

Finally, some—I include myself in this group—with formal musical education who found it difficult to imitate traditional musicians "by ear" saw the need to analyze and transcribe in order to study their music. Many of these transcriptions from the 1970s and 1980s—almost entirely unpublished—were not intended primarily for research but rather as teaching aids, and frequently they were produced in academic contexts. They were transcriptions without a musicological goal: guides, mnemonic strategies, or schematics for performance instead of analysis.

In this context, centers dedicated to the research and teaching of regional music such as the Instituto Popular de Cultura (IPC, Popular Institute of Culture) in Cali and the EPA in Medellín, and the Instituto de Cultura y Bellas Artes de Boyacá (ICBA, Institute of Culture and Fine Arts of Boyacá) in the city of Tunja, have made progress on rigorous investigation continuing to this day. They, as well as the Centro de Documentación Musical at COLCULTURA, today part of the Ministry of Culture, maintain archives with valuable recordings from fieldwork, but analysis remains at an early stage.[47]

For many years the CEF, made up of professors from the EPA, published a newsletter with transcriptions and short articles under the leadership of Gustavo López. Some of these professors have published collections of dances, children's games, with musical illustrations and recordings, but without emphasis on musicological analysis.[48] Similarly, in the shadow of stage folklore dance groups, numerous works with substantial research components have been carried out in various parts of the country, many of them unpublished.[49]

A volume on music, region, and pedagogy, with articles about the regionalization of traditional music in Colombia and about methodological and pedagogical aspects in folk and vernacular music was published by the ICBA (also with some problems in the transcription and musical analysis).[50] This work was in large part led by a team of professors linked to the Fundación Nueva Cultura (New Culture Foundation) and the Plan Piloto for the study of Hispanic Caribbean music; the latter now the music school of the Academia Superior de Artes de Bogotá (ASAB, School of Arts in Bogotá), a novel and controversial institution that grants degrees in higher education. They have produced various educational materials, historical studies, and transcriptions of regional musics, materials intended for pedagogy that remain largely unpublished. Among these I highlight the work of the late Samuel Bedoya Sánchez on composition of folk and vernacular music (*Conducción de líneas*), on music from the Plains region (unpublished), on the regionalization of music in Colombia, and ten modules for band directors, edited by COLCULTURA in 1990. Other professors involved with the project have produced articles published in the journal *A Contratiempo*, including Jorge Sossa's about the *cuatro* [guitar-like instrument] in *joropo* music and Néstor Lambuley's about percussion in *cumbia*. The works of this group are visibly influenced by the structuralist framings of musical analysis.[51]

## Events and Publications

Events from conferences, seminars, and meetings, as well as specialized publications, are intimately tied to the building and consolidation of academic and disciplinary communities. The panorama in this regard is worrisome and revealing, for it confirms the weaknesses and separation that I have identified throughout this article. Of the five conferences organized by the Consejo Interamericano de Música (CIDEM, Inter-American Music Council), only the first, which took place in Cartagena in 1963, included the participation of Colombian panelists.[52] The events that followed in Colombia would abandon the term "ethnomusicology" and center instead on folklore until the mid-1980s, when there was a turn toward the term "popular." Nevertheless, festivals and "folklore" meetings continue to be dominant to the present.

The Junta Nacional de Folclor (National Meeting of Folklorists) was a large event that took place in Medellín in 1981, organized by the Pilot Public Library and the EPA. Today, in hindsight, we perceive it as the culminating moment of the folklorist paradigm in Colombia and as the beginning of its downfall. The 1[er] Foro-Taller

Nacional de Música y Danza Campesinas de Boyacá y Áreas de Interinfluencia: Joropo-Torbellino (1st National Forum-Workshop on Peasant Music and Dance from Boyacá and Nearby Areas: Joropo-Torbellino), which took place in Tunja in 1985, signaled another break for the folklorists but from a different perspective. The event was organized by a group from the Fundación Nueva Cultura and Samuel Bedoya Sánchez, who were emerging as proponents of a new paradigm in the study of folk and vernacular music. The 5° Taller Latinoamericano de Música Popular (5th Workshop of Latin American Popular Music) took place in Bogotá in 1988, also organized by the Fundación Nueva Cultura, differed from earlier meetings in the inclusion of folk and vernacular musicians from Argentina and Uruguay in the organizing committee. These musicians brought a fresh, creative, and irreverent perspective of folk and vernacular music—less academic and stale.

In the past decade, there have been relatively few large-scale events explicitly devoted for meeting and exchanging ideas with researchers about folk and vernacular music. There have been a few periodic gatherings by the Forum for Latin American Music and the Caribbean (Tribuna Musical de América Latina y el Caribe, TRIMALCA), part of UNESCO's Council on International Music, as well as two International Meetings of Popular Music Researchers (actually binational, between Ecuador and Colombia), organized by the Instituto Andino de Artes Populares (IADAP, Andean Institute of Popular Arts) in Quito. These events have been formal, increasingly bureaucratic, poorly attended, and with few in-depth debates.

Faced with, and perhaps due to, the scarcity of academic events, music festivals and contests—such as Mono Núñez, Aguadas, and the Festival del Porro—have created small spaces for discussion in between the sound of *tiples* [small guitar-like instrument], guitars, and trumpets, but ultimately also marginal spaces. Debates about folk and vernacular music have become decentralized and democratized, and they occur in the streets, in the amphitheaters, or in bars on festival days, but we doubt that this will help consolidate an academic community on the matter. Sometimes in anthropology conferences there may be an isolated presentation, but there are rarely panels or symposia.

COLCULTURA has awarded scholarships since 1987 to support cultural research, and dedicates funds annually explicitly for musical research. However, publication of award recipients' research has been neglected, as has the formation of an academic community.

Journal publications are a good mirror of the panorama sketched thus far. For more than fifty years, the dominant folklore paradigm has always had its own publications, often promoted from within anthropology.[53] The *Revista del Instituto Etnológico Nacional* has adopted a more anthropological perspective, which featured an outstanding work by Gerardo Reichel-Dolmatoff regarding musical practices of the Kogi [indigenous ethnic group]. Also along these lines is the

*Revista Colombiana de Antropología*, which replaced the *Revista Colombiana de Folclor* as the official publication of the Instituto Colombiano de Antropología e Historia (Colombian Institute of Anthropology and History). This name change may indicate a symbolic expulsion of folklore studies from the academic sphere of anthropology. In fact, only occasionally do articles about music appear in journals of anthropology (e.g., those of the Universidad Nacional de Colombia and the Universidad de Antioquia).

The EPA, the IPC, and prominent regional organizations of folk and vernacular culture have sporadically published small newsletters on folklore with some musical studies; noteworthy among these is the *Boletín del Centro de Estudios Folclóricos* in Medellín. *Emberá: Revista de Folclor* was launched at the 1981 Junta Nacional de Folklore in Medellín, but only two issues were ever published. Several other journals of a literary bent and folklorist perspective have also emerged from Bogotá and other areas.[54] Folk festivals and contests also publish newsletters and pamphlets with some frequency, some of which include articles of interest for regional studies.

Directed by Egberto Bermúdez and edited by the Instituto de Investigaciones Estéticas at the Universidad Nacional de Colombia, the *Revista Colombiana de Investigación Musical* was launched in 1985 as an attempt to break with the folklore paradigm; but only one issue was ever published. Two years later, in the same vein but without academic pretensions, I initiated *A Contratiempo: Música y Danza*, edited by the Fundación Dimensión Educativa and with correspondents in more than ten cities. Although operating without institutional support, we published eight issues between 1987 and 1992 with about a thousand total pages. Conceived as an open and pluralist space, it included a broad—perhaps excessively so—variety of subjects and themes. Nevertheless, the biggest focus, perhaps more than 30 percent, were studies of a musicological nature devoted to folk and vernacular music, and therefore of indisputable value to the field in discussion. In 1992 *A Contratiempo* came under the direction of the Centro de Documentación Musical at COLCULTURA. This second period was academically oriented and focused more on music.[55]

Finally, it is necessary to mention that field recordings have an educational impact. Aimed at a broad public, they usually include commentaries from nonspecialists.[56] Similarly, journalistic writings on music frequently appear in the national and regional press, in particular in magazines and supplements as well as on the radio.[57]

## The Emergence of a New Paradigm

If we look at the themes proposed at the 1997 conference "The Rhythms of Culture: Dancing to Las Américas—An International Research Conference on Popular

Musics in Latin(o) America," organized by the University of Michigan, it is evident that ethnomusicological inquiries at an international level had for some time been moving in different directions [focusing on topics such as]: music in the diaspora; race, ethnicity, class, and gender; transnational flows in music; dance and the politics of performance; music and memory; folklore, ritual, and popular musics; popular music and mass media; popular music and social movements; nationalism and music; orality, history and identity; exploring methodology; and music and globalization. This list reflects the emergence of perspectives from postmodern studies, interdisciplinary approaches, and in general from the field known as cultural studies. In Colombia, these avenues of research have become popular through the works of Néstor García Canclini and Jesús Martín Barbero, but their impact on musicology is still nascent.

Another trend at the time came from sociology and anthropology. Ana María Ochoa, from her position at the Ministry of Culture, was leading an important effort in this new model of ethnomusicology and cultural studies. This intellectual project needed a new publication forum. Ochoa proposed to take up the initiative of *A Contratiempo: Música y Danza*, which had ceased circulation in 1992, as mentioned above. The journal's title became *A Contratiempo: Música en la Cultura*, an indication for its new orientation: with excellent editing, stronger critical standards, a selection of articles current and contemporary for academia were published under her leadership from 1992 to 1997. Ochoa also advanced a series of musicological research projects in the context of cultural studies, proposed new avenues, and re-situated research in the field, as elucidated in her article "¿Qué cultura va a tener? Un paseo musical y literario por los estudios culturales" (What culture will it be? A musical and literary journey through cultural studies).[58]

However, Colombia is neither the United States nor Europe. In the 1940s, when pioneering works were just beginning to tell the story of folk and vernacular music in our country, in other places there was no longer any "traditional" music left to transcribe and analyze since most of it had already been compiled in hundreds of songbooks, records, and musicological studies that led to the development of texts for schools and universities, comparative studies, macro-musicological analysis, and so forth.[59] What is needed [in Colombia] are thorough fieldwork, high-quality field recordings that meet ethnomusicological standards within ethnomusicology, with rigorous collection of data, songbooks, transcriptions, analysis, educational texts, historical studies, and also studies that investigate the transformation of folk and vernacular music in the context of globalization. It is impossible today to attempt to write a general panorama like those done during the time of folklore manuals. To approach a broader perspective, we first need many local and regional in-depth studies, small building blocks that will allow us to slowly assemble the mirror—cracked as it may be—of Colombia, so that we may look and recognize ourselves and project ourselves into the future.

The overview presented here shows that, despite often not being able to count on official or institutional backing, a substantial group of researchers and students have been taken by the richness, diversity, and vitality of folk and vernacular music in Colombia. All of their work—even those that leave something to be desired on account of inadequate focus, methodological practices, or lack of rigor—deserve some merit for having set the foundation for the consolidation of a field of studies and an academic community.

## Notes

Translator's note: During the translation process, the author revised and updated references to recent editions of unpublished works or publications up to 2012.

1. Even though the concepts of *popular tradicional* [popular traditional] or *música colombiana* [Colombian music] and their boundaries are questionable and arbitrary, this essay intentionally leaves out popular music of the salon and urban realm that was disseminated not by oral tradition but through sheet music and recordings. For studies of recorded music, see Egberto Bermúdez "From Colombian 'National' Song to 'Colombian Song': 1860–1960," *Lied und populäre Kultur/Song and Popular Culture* 53 (2008), 167–259, and "Cien años de grabaciones comerciales de música colombiana: los discos de 'Pelón y Marín' (1908) y su contexto," *Ensayos: Historia y Teoría del Arte* 17 (2009), 86–134. The boundaries are given to a certain degree by the authors themselves, who put the music in categories such as "folklore," "traditional music," or "Colombian music." Nevertheless, the majority of the music referred to in this essay circulates outside the music industry; only until recently has some of it been recorded for documentary, rather than commercial, purpose. Excluded as well is indigenous music, which I treated in other articles; see Carlos Miñana Blasco, "Investigación sobre músicas indígenas en Colombia. Primera parte: un panorama regional," *A Contratiempo* 13 (2009), and "Investigación sobre músicas indígenas en Colombia. Segunda parte: campos disciplinares, institucionalización e investigación aplicada," *A Contratiempo* 14 (2009), available at http://acontratiempo.bibliotecanacional.gov.co.

Editor's note: The distinctions made by the author above can be further complicated by translation of the word "popular" into English, where usage tends to denote exactly the type of urban, mass-mediated and commodified musical forms that he is omitting from this article. For the purposes of this article, the term *traditional popular* will be translated as "folk and vernacular" to avoid confusion with the English usage.

2. Since this is primarily a descriptive and bibliographic work, I include numerous citations accompanied by brief commentary in the text or in the notes.

3. Carlos Vega, *La ciencia del folklore* (Buenos Aires: Nova, 1960). Claude Lévi-Strauss, *Antropología estructural* (Buenos Aires: Eudeba, 1968 [1958]), 323, proposed that "folklore studies belong, either because of their subjects or methods (and doubtless for both reasons

simultaneously) within anthropology." Currently it would not make sense even to argue for it as a "field" or subdiscipline within it. An excellent analysis of the problematic of folklore in Latin America appears in Néstor García Canclini's "The Staging of the Popular," in *Hybrid Cultures: Strategies for Entering and Leaving Modernity* (Minneapolis: University of Minnesota Press, 1995), where he argues that folklore studies could be absorbed within cultural studies from a more interdisciplinary perspective, and more in accord with current thinking on science. [García Canclini's *Hybrid Cultures* was originally published as *Culturas híbridas: estrategias para entrar y salir de la modernidad* (Mexico City: Grijalbo, 1990).]

4. The collecting drive of folklorists had been so strong that musicologist Carlos Vega, one of its biggest proponents in Latin America and perhaps worldwide, stated that "in a way, the death of folkloric things is secondary once they have been documented, since it is not common that one would encounter them again" (*La ciencia del folklore*, 124).

5. See Félix Coluccio, *Folkloristas e instituciones folklóricas del mundo* (Buenos Aires: El Ateneo, 1951). A brief panorama of popular music and literature in Colombia from that period is offered by José María Vergara y Vergara, "Poesía popular, carácter nacional, conclusión," in *Historia de la literatura en Nueva Granada* (Bogotá: Banco Popular, 1974 [1867]), 2:205–20. Some time later, the compilation of folk and vernacular literature would also become significant. For those interested in musicological studies, it is worth mentioning here some *coplerios* [couplet books] that have enjoyed certain diffusion in editions prior to the 1970s. These include Antonio José Restrepo, *De la tierra colombiana: el cancionero de Antioquia* (1930); Juan de Dios Arias, *Folklore santandereano*, 2nd ed. (1943); Benigno Gutiérrez, *De todo el maíz* (1944); Sergio Elías Ortiz, *Cantares del Departamento de Nariño* (1946); Octavio Quiñones Pardo, *Interpretación de la poesía popular* (1947); Joaquín Medina, *Cantas del Valle de Tenza* (1949); José Antonio León Rey, *Espíritu de mi Oriente: cancionero popular* (1951); Lucio Pabón Núñez, *Muestras folklóricas del norte de Santander* (1952); Jaime Exbrayat, *Cantares de vaquería del folclor cordobés y bolivarense* (1959); Ricardo Sabio Labay, *Corridos y coplas: llanos orientales de Colombia* (1963); and the overarching synthesis by Andrés Pardo Tovar, *La poesía popular colombiana y sus orígenes españoles* (1966). Incidentally, on Gutiérrez's songbook, see Carlos Miñana Blasco, "La música antioqueña en el cancionero de Benigno A. Gutiérrez: análisis musical y comentarios pedagógicos e históricos de 27 tonadas" (unpublished, 1982).

6. The CEDEFIM depended on the Conservatorio Nacional de Música (National Conservatory of Music) at the Universidad Nacional de Colombia. Directed by the lawyer Andrés Pardo Tovar, the advisory council included Fabio González Zuleta (director of the conservatory), Jesús Bermúdez Silva, and Luis Duque Gómez; see Egberto Bérmudez, "La Universidad Nacional y la investigación musical en Colombia: tres momentos," in *Miradas a la Universidad Nacional de Colombia*, ed. Juan Manuel Roca (Bogotá: Universidad Nacional de Colombia, 2006), 7–83, for a history of the fundamental role of the university in musicological studies in Colombia and for a history of the CEDEFIM. See also Egberto Bermúdez, "Panamericanismo a contratiempo: musicología en Colombia, 1950–70," in *Música/Musicología y colonialismo*, ed. Coriún Aharonián (Montevideo: Centro Nacional de Documentación Lauro Ayestarán, 2011), 101–58. Both of these texts

situate the transformation of Colombian musicology in a broader context of national and international sociopolitical and cultural changes.

7. For a rather complete outline of the "missions," expeditions, and recordings that took place between the 1940s and 1980s in Colombia, see Isabel Aretz, *Historia de la etnomusicología en América Latina: desde la época precolombina hasta nuestros días* (Caracas: FUNDEF, CONAC, OEA, 1991), 245–49.

8. Emirto de Lima, *Folklore colombiano* (Barranquilla: La Iguana Ciega, 1942), one of the first musicological works of its breadth on folk and vernacular music in Colombia (although some portions had been previously published in *Boletín Latino-Americano de Música* 4 [1938], 95–98; 635–48), is a compilation of various lectures in which he illustrated musical examples with the piano: songs of street vendors, *gaita* tunes, *caña de millo* melodies, and so forth. The book includes transcriptions that functioned as guides for playing these musical examples on piano. Daniel Zamudio's 1936 lecture, "El folklore musical en Colombia," *Revista de las Indias* (Bogotá, 1949; reissued in *Boletín de la Radiodifusora Nacional* 200–203 [April–June 1961]); Francisco de Igualada, "Musicología indígena de la amazonia colombiana," *Boletín Latino-Americano de Música* 4 (1938), 675–708; José Ignacio Perdomo Escobar, "Glosario Folklórico de términos relativos a danzas, cantares e instrumentos típicos de Colombia," in *Historia de la música en Colombia* (Bogotá: Ministerio de Educación, 1945), but published earlier as an extended article in the *Boletín Latinoamericano de Música* (1938), 387–570; Gnecco Rangel Pava, *Aires guamalenses* (Bogotá: Kelly, 1948) includes a series of musical transcriptions, very likely executed and "musicalized" by composer Andrés C. Rojas. It is also worth mentioning the excellent work of Narciso Garay, *Tradiciones y cantares de Panamá: ensayo folklórico* (Brussels: Ediciones de L'Expansion Belge, 1930), since it includes various musical expressions shared between Panamá and the Colombian Caribbean region. It is worth noting that political boundaries do not always, or rather almost never, correspond to cultural regions, and that borders function less as divisions and more as points of contact. The Venezuela musicological bibliography is fundamental for the study of the plains music of Colombia, for the music of the Wayú community, and even for *vaquería* songs (Isabel Aretz, *Historia de la etnomusicología en América Latina* [Caracas: FUNDEF, CONAC, OEA, 1991], 252–61); the same could be said for Ecuadorian research on Afro-Esmeraldan music.

9. Otto Mayer-Serra, *Música y músicos de Latinoamérica*, 2 vols. (Mexico City: Editorial Atlante, 1947).

10. For example, faced with the positive assessment of music from the Caribbean coast by Emirto de Lima (who lived in Barranquilla), Zamudio trumpets his *cachaco* (from Bogotá) perspective by saying that: "They [the blacks] came with their music, which was mixed with that of the Spanish and has given us a hybrid and damaging product. It is necessary to impose a purification" ("El folklore musical," 405). Rangel Pava, *Aires guamalenses*, 24, suggests that the roots of Caribbean music from his region are indigenous and Spanish, but does not consider the contributions of black people.

11. Zamudio, "El folklore musical."

12. Guillermo Abadía Morales published a few brief articles in the popular magazine *Cromos* beginning in 1943, but his massive production began in the 1960s, in particular

via radio programs published by the *Boletín de Programas de la Radiodifusora Nacional de Colombia*. In 1973, a first synthesis came out under the title *La música folklórica colombiana* (Bogotá: Universidad Nacional). He would later produce several books, but the emblematic summary of his work is the *Compendio general del folklore colombiano* (Bogotá: Instituto Colombiano de Cultura, 1977), a work that has been reedited a few times and which Abadía Morales wrote for the elective courses he taught at the conservatory at the Universidad Nacional de Colombia. Octavio Marulanda worked primarily in the Valle del Cauca, as professor and researcher at the IPC of Cali and at FUNMÚSICA, organizer of the Mono Núñez Contest of Colombian Andean Music in Ginebra. In addition to numerous articles about music in the department of Valle, his most influential works include *El folclor de Colombia: práctica de la identidad cultural* (Bogotá: Artestudio, 1984) and another work on children's games. He follows, almost to the letter, Adabía Morales's works, but his publications have been less widely distributed. Javier Ocampo López, history professor at the Universidad Pedagógica y Tecnológica de Colombia (Pedagogical and Technological University of Colombia) in Tunja, has centered his studies in Boyacá. His books about folklore suffer from a lack of fieldwork, but they incorporate valuable information from his use of historical sources, although paradoxically the information struggles in the context of the static rigidity of folklorism. He began to publish on the topic beginning in 1970, and his best-known works, actual best sellers, break from the encyclopedic character and clunky, dense writing of Abadía Morales and Marulanda. These include *El folclor y los bailes típicos colombianos* (Manizales: Talleres de la Imprenta Departamental, 1981), *Música y folclor de Colombia* (Bogotá: Plaza y Janés, 1984), and *Las fiestas y el folclor en Colombia* (Bogotá: El Áncora, 1985). These three books are actually different versions of the same work with small modifications. Harry C. Davidson, *Diccionario folklórico de Colombia: música, instrumentos y danzas*, 3 vols. (Bogotá: Banco de la República, 1970), has important value as a collection of historical documentary sources, although it is neither very rigorous nor critical.

13. Guillermo Valencia Salgado, *Córdoba: su gente, su folclor* (Montería: Editorial Mocari, 1994 [1987]); William Fortich Díaz, *Fandango cantado en el Sinú Medio* (Montería, 1985), and *Con bombos y platillos* (Montería: Domus Libri, 1994); Consuelo Araújo de Molina, *Vallenatología: orígenes y fundamentos de la música vallenata* (Bogotá: Tercer Mundo, 1973); Miguel Angel Martín, *Del folclor llanero* (Villavicencio: Lit. Juan XXIII, 1986 [1979]); Blanca Álvarez, *Raíces de mi terruño: enciclopedia folklórica del tolimense*, 2nd ed. (Ibagué: Ministerio de Gobierno, 1985); Misael Devia, "Folclor tolimense," in *Revista Colombiana de Folclor* (Bogotá, 1962), republished recently in *Nueva Revista Colombiana de Folclor*. Manuel Zapata Olivella published in the *Boletín Cultural y Bibliográfico* of the Banco de la República a series of brief articles where he emphasized the idea of *mestizaje* in traditional music, but which is not too distant from the essentialism of folklorists (the first, "Razones del mestizaje folclórico colombiano," appears in vol. 3, no. 3 [1960], 163–65; the last, "Aculturación del arte popular colombiano," appears in vol. 7, no. 9 [1964], 1660–62). His sister, Delia, went on to take an important leadership role in the configuration of folkloric Afro-Colombian dance in the country.

14. I do not go into details in the wide-ranging criticism of these texts. For examples, one can look at Egberto Bermúdez's detailed and devastating critique of the classification

of musical instruments by Abadía Morales and subsequent authors (in *Revista Colombiana de Investigación Musical* 1, no. 1 [1985]); Carlos Miñana Blasco's critique of the use of sources, in *Kuvi: música de flautas entre los Paeces* (Revista Informes Antropológicos, no. 8) (Bogotá: Instituto Colombiano de Antropología, 1994); and Ana María Ochoa's critique over folklorist and sexist trends, in "Tradición, género y nación en el bambuco," *A Contratiempo* 9 (1997).

15. For a case study on music contests and their impact in regional musical processes, see Carlos Miñana Blasco, *De fastos a fiestas: Navidad y chirimías en Popayán* (Bogotá: Ministerio de Cultura, 1997), 47–60. A team from the Universidad de Antioquia, led by María Eugenia Londoño, carried out a series of studies (that remain unpublished) about various music contests and festivals in Colombia. Ana María Ochoa dealt with the Mono Núñez festival in her doctoral dissertation, "Plotting Musical Territories" (Indiana University, 1996).

16. The traditional music of these countries was studied closely beginning at the end of the nineteenth century, and especially noteworthy are the works of the d'Harcourt husband-and-wife team in 1925 as well as Louis Girault's records from the 1950s. From the 1970s, we find the studies by Luis Segundo Moreno in Ecuador, as well as the exceptional organological work of Carlos Coba. More recently, I highlighted the work of Max Peter Baumann and the IADAP under the Convenio Andrés Bello, carried out with Patricio Mantilla and Patricio Sandoval. The journal *Opus* by the Central Bank of Ecuador (Banco Central de Ecuador) is also worth mentioning for its important work bringing light to research and compositional projects. Even though the pioneering studies in Venezuela have been recent (until 1950), they have found important support in the leadership of Luis Felipe Ramón y Rivera and Isabel Aretz. The Instituto Interamericano de Etnomusicología y Folklore (INIDEF, Inter-American Institute of Ethnomusicology and Folklore), funded by the Organization of American States (OAS) and the Venezuelan government, played a crucial role.

17. Andrés Pardo Tovar and Jesús Pinzón Urrea, *Rítmica y melódica del folclor chocoano* (Bogotá: Universidad Nacional de Colombia, 1961).

18. Andrés Rosa, "Esencia, estilo y presencia rajaleña," *Thesaurus: Boletín del Instituto Caro y Cuervo* 19, no. 3 (1964), 510–42; Jesús Pinzón Urrea, "La música vernácula del altiplano de Bogotá," *Boletín Interamericano de Música*, no. 77 (1970); Luis Torres Zuleta (unpublished, 1974); Lilia Montaña de Silva Célis, "Fiesta de San Pascual Bailón," in *Mitos, leyendas, tradiciones y folclor del Lago de Tota* (Tunja: Universidad Pedagógica y Tecnológica de Colombia, 1970), 407–28, musical transcriptions by Blas Emilio Atehortúa.

19. Ramiro Alvarez López, *Tres danzas de Mompós* (Medellín: Centro de Investigaciones y Promociones Folclóricas, 1970).

20. Lubín Mazuera, *Orígenes históricos del bambuco* (Cali: Imprenta Departamental, 1972).

21. Carmen Ortega Ricaurte, "Contribución a la bibliografía de la música en Colombia," *Revista de la Dirección de Divulgación Cultural de la Universidad Nacional de Colombia* 12 (1973).

22. Jorge Morales Gómez, *Contribución a la bibliografía del folclor colombiano* (Bogotá: Centro Don Bosco, 1978); it includes publications only up to 1973.

23. For a much more detailed study of the relationships between professional musicians and traditional music, see the recent works mentioned by Bermúdez, "La Universidad Nacional." These works cover the introduction of the term "ethnomusicology" in the country, mostly by Andrés Pardo Tovar in the 1960s ("Musicología, etnomusicología y folklore," *Boletín Interamericano de Música* 32 [1962], 3–11), under the influences of a musical pan-Americanism and U.S. academia. Nevertheless, as Bermúdez mentions, the folklorist position led by Abadía Morales would be the one to triumph in Colombia against the concept of ethnomusicology.

24. Aquiles Escalante, *El negro en Colombia* (Bogotá: Universidad Nacional, 1964); see Egberto Bermúdez, "Música indígena colombiana," *Maguaré*, no. 5 (1987), 85–98, for an overview of indigenous music studies; see also the bibliography compiled by Blaz Telban for ethnographies, *Grupos étnicos de Colombia* (Quito: Abya-Yala, 1988).

25. Works published by Norman E. Whitten Jr. since 1967 include "Música y relaciones sociales en las tierras bajas colombianas y ecuatorianas del Pacífico," *América Indígena* 27, no. 4 (1967), 635–66; and especially *Pioneros negros: la cultura afro-latinoamericana del Ecuador y de Colombia* (Quito: Centro Cultural Afro-Ecuatoriano, 1992; original in English [*Black Frontiersmen: A South American Case*, Cambridge, Mass.: Schenkman Publishing, 1974]).

26. Benjamín Yépez Chamorro, *La música de los guahibo, sikuani-cuiba* (Bogotá: Fundación de Investigaciones Arqueológicas Nacionales, Banco de la República, 1984), cassette included; "La música de los murui-muinane," *Boletín de Antropología* 6, no. 21 (1987), 199–210; and the recording *Música de los huitotos* (Bogotá: FINARCO, 1981). See also Peter Wade, "Black Music and Cultural Syncretism in Colombia," in *Slavery and Beyond: The African Impact on Latin America and the Caribbean*, ed. Darién J. Davis (Wilmington, Del.: Scholarly Resources, 1995), 121–46; and "Entre la homogeneidad y la diversidad: la identidad nacional y la música costeña en Colombia," in *Antropología en la modernidad: identidades, etnicidades y movimientos sociales en Colombia*, ed. María Victoria Uribe and Eduardo Restrepo (Bogotá: Instituto Colombiano de Antropología, 1997), 61–91.

27. Sergio Iván Carmona Maya, *La música: un fenómeno cosmogónico en la cultura Kuna* (Medellín: Editorial Universidad de Antioquia, 1989). Curiously, Carmona ignores the pioneering work of Narciso Garay, *Tradiciones y cantares de Panamá*. It would have been interesting to compare the contemporary transcriptions of the *kantule* song of the Kuna from those of sixty years earlier.

28. Eugenia Villa and Jorge Morales, ed., *El folclor en la construcción de las Américas: memorias del VI Congreso de Antropología en Colombia* (Bogotá: Universidad de los Andes, 1992), which includes an introduction by Guillermo Abadía Morales, who states: "Anthropologists, sociologists, and historians cannot discount or underestimate the ethnographic work of dozens of researchers in the field, without whose work at the local, regional, and even national levels it would be impossible to recover the many folkloric materials." (One might ask: is collecting folkloric materials the same as ethnography?) "Although their written contributions may not have the bibliographic rigor required in some cases, we consider them contributions toward the knowledge of our own creole ways within the formative processes of the Americas" (11).

29. In the context of the *Atlas lingüístico-etnográfico de Colombia* (Bogotá, 1983), the institute released two records and published a supplement to vol. 3, written by María Luisa Rodríguez de Montes, compiling musical examples of field songs, although—as before—the transcriptions present some problems. In an almost exhaustive study about the *romance* in Colombia written by Gisela Beutler and also published by the institute, there were several musical transcriptions without analysis (*Studien zum spanischen Romancero in Kolumbien in seiner schriftlichen und mündlichen Überlieferung von der Zeit der Eroberung bis zur Gegenwart* [Heidelberg: C. Winter, 1969]. It was translated in 1977 as *Estudios sobe el romancero español en Colombia en su tradición escrita y oral desde la época de la Conquista hasta la actualidad* [Bogotá: Instituto Caro y Cuervo, 1977]). Other researchers who have continued to study the *romancero* form include Germán de Granda, *Estudios sobre un area dialectal hispanoamericana de población negra: las tierras bajas occidentales de Colombia* (Bogotá: Instituto Caro y Cuervo, 1977), and Susana Friedmann Altmann from the Instituto de Investigaciones Estéticas at the Universidad Nacional de Colombia, "Estrategias orales y la transmisión musical del romance en las tierras bajas de Colombia," in *El folclor en la construcción de las Américas*, ed. Eugenia Villa and Jorge Morales (Bogotá: Universidad de los Andes, 1992), 103–18. Friedmann also published *Las fiestas de junio en el Nuevo Reino* (Bogotá: Instituto Caro y Cuervo, Patronato Colombiano de Artes y Ciencias, 1982), a historical book that attempts to make a comparison to contemporary feast day celebrations. According to the author, after her fieldwork failed to reveal certain expected practices, she became "unmotivated" and was less than thorough in completing her project. For those of us familiar with the region it is clear that the scant transcriptions do not accurately represent the music of the grassroots communities of Tolima Grande. Studies on couplet and songbooks after the 1970s are characterized by a sociological or anthropological framing and by a thematic treatment in an attempt to overcome folklorist taxonomies. A recently published work in this line is Pablo Mora Calderón's "Contribuciones al cancionero infame de Colombia," *A Contratiempo* 10 (1998), 23–25. Finally, I highlight the excellent work of Armin Schwegler, which although focused on linguistics also addresses the musical practices in *lumbalú* rites in San Basilio de Palenque; *"Chi ma nkongo": lengua y rito ancestrales en El Palenque de San Basilio (Colombia)*, 2 vols. (Frankfurt: Vervuert, 1996).

30. Ciro Quiroz Otero, *Vallenato, hombre y canto* (Bogotá: Icaro, 1983); Rito Llerena Villalobos, ed., *Memoria cultural en el vallenato: un modelo de textualidad en la canción folclórica colombiana* (Medellín: Universidad de Antioquia, 1985); and another work focused on the literary, Consuelo Posada, *Canción vallenato y tradición oral* (Medellín: Universidad de Antioquia, 1986).

31. María Eugenia Londoño, "Introducción al vallenato como fenómeno musical," in *Memoria cultural en el vallenato*, ed. Rito Llerena Villalobos (Medellín: Universidad de Antioquia, 1985), 125–34, abounds with generalities and musical analysis reduced to noting different tempi, instrumentation, and time signatures of "musical types that make up the vallenato genre." On the other hand, a new musicological study about *vallenato* by guitarist and composer Héctor González, *Vallenato, tradición y comercio* (Cali: Universidad del Valle, 2007), will be difficult to top. It includes an audio CD (including MIDI versions of

transcriptions, since the original recordings of the transcriptions are easily obtained in the commercial market) and numerous transcriptions of vocal and instrumental parts. Also, it is necessary to include among the literary studies the work of the late Hispanist scholar Jacques Gilard (see Egberto Bermúdez, "Jacques Gilard y la música popular colombiana," *Caravelle* 93 [2009], 14–40).

32. Arturo Escobar Uribe, *Salvo Ruiz, el último juglar* (Bogotá: Editorial Presencia, 1964), and Jorge Villegas and Hernando Grisales, *Crescencio Salcedo, mi vida* (Bogotá: Ediciones Hombre Nuevo, 1976).

33. The consolidation of anthropology of music, or ethnomusicology, is today a fact. Some proof of this are international journals like *Ethnomusicology*; or texts that trace the development of the field such as Bruno Nettl and Phillip V. Bohlman, ed., *Comparative Musicology and Anthropology of Music: Essays on the History of Ethnomusicology* (Chicago: University of Chicago Press, 1991); or in Spanish, José Antonio Martín Herrero, *Manual de antropología de la música* (Salamanca: Amaru, 1997); or contemporary perspectives and post-modern perspectives on fieldwork such as Gregory F. Barz and Timothy J. Cooley, ed., *Shadows in the Field: New Perspectives for Fieldwork in Ethnomusicology* (Oxford University Press, 1997).

34. In its journal, INIDEF in Caracas published an excerpt of Dirk Koorn's dissertation, "Folk Music of the Colombian Andes" (University of Washington, 1977), translated into Spanish (no. 3, 1978). Eleven years after its first writing, the Patronato de Artes y Ciencias translated George List's *Music and Poetry in a Colombian Village* (Bloomington: Indiana University Press, 1983) as *Música y poesía en un pueblo colombiano: una herencia tricultural* (Bogotá: Colegio Máximo de las Academias Colombianas, 1994). With regards to the excellent work by List, which was executed with the best technology of the time for musical transcription, it is necessary to highlight an "error" in his assessment—if that is the proper term—from the inability to distinguish between metric and structural accents: he transcribed the *llamador* drum in *cumbia* as being on the beat instead of on the upbeat, letting himself be led by the force of the structural accents in the percussion without considering their relationship to the singing or the overall metric sensibility. Curiously, List does not include in his extensive bibliography the earlier work of Emirto de Lima. List had been publishing articles abroad on his research since 1966, including "The Musical Bow at Palenque," *Journal of the International Folk Music Council* 18 (1966), 36–49; "The Mbira in Cartagena," *Journal of the International Folk Music Council* 20 (1968), 54–58; and "El conjunto the gaitas de Colombia: la herencia de tres culturas," *Revista Musical Chilena* 27, no. 123–24 (1973), 43–54. He also released the record *Cantos Costeños: Folksongs of the Atlantic Coast, a Region of Colombia* (Ethnosound Records, 1973). The article "Colombia II: Folk Music" that appeared in the first edition of the *New Grove Dictionary of Music and Musicians* ed. Stanley Sadie (1980), 4:570–81, was also written by George List. As I mention elsewhere in this article, it is worrisome that most international publications about Colombia neither are done by nor do they cite recognized Colombian researchers, not so much as a chauvinist argument, but rather because foreign researchers have spent very little time in the country and done only very focused research.

35. Carlos Miñana Blasco, *Música de flautas y chirimías en Popayán* (Bogotá: Ministerio de Cultura, 1987). The book received an award from the Institute of Ibero-American

Cooperation (Instituto de Cooperación Iberoamericana) in Madrid, and was published by the Ministry of Culture as *De fastos a fiestas: Navidad y chirimías en Popayán* (Bogotá: Centro de Documentación Musical, Dirección General de Artes, Ministerio de Cultura, 1997).

36. Carlos Miñana Blasco, "Música campesina de flautas y tambores en el Cauca y sur del Huila" (unpublished, 1989).

37. This article, expanded and with a new analytical perspective, was republished as "Afinación de las marimbas en la costa pacífica colombiana: ¿un ejemplo de la memoria interválica africana en Colombia?," in *Músicas y prácticas sonoras en el Pacífico afrocolombiano*, ed. Juan Sebastián Ochoa, Carolina Santamaría, and Manuel Sevilla (Bogotá: Editorial Pontifica Universidad Javeriana, 2010), 287–346. Likewise, analysis on issues of musical memory in this case study appear in Carlos Miñana Blasco, "Los problemas de la memoria musical en la conexión África-Colombia: el caso de las marimbas de la Costa Pacífica colombo-ecuatoriana," in *Memoria del saber hacer*, XI Encuentro para la Promoción y Difusión del Patrimonio Inmaterial de Países Iberoamericanos (Santa Cruz de Mompox, 2011), 49–73.

38. Miñana Blasco, *Kuvi: música de flauta entre los paeces* (Bogotá: Gente Nueva, 1994); in 1998, the Ministry of Culture and the Fundación De Mvsica released *Nasa Kuv': fiestas, flautas y tambores nasa*, a CD with field recordings that complemented this investigation, including 36 pages of liner notes. See also Carlos Miñana Blasco, "Los caminos del bambuco en el siglo XIX," *A Contratiempo* 9 (1997), 7–11. I am also interested in the study of urban musical phenomena and for pedagogy, hoping that musicological investigations do not just live in libraries but that they impact the valuation and transformation of popular and traditional music; see, for example, *Küc'h yuuya' u'hwectha'w: de correría con los "negritos,"* which includes a 120-page book for teachers, a 60-page workbook for students, a cassette, and a documentary film (Popayán: Programa de Educación Bilingüe del CRIC y UPN, 1996 and 1997), and *Culturas musicales juveniles y escuela* (Bogotá, 1997).

39. Part of this work was published in *A Contratiempo* 7 (1990), 13–21. The award-winning work was María Eugenia Londoño, *La música en la comunidad indigena emberá-chamí de Cristianía: descripción de su sistema musical y aporte metodológico para el aprovechamiento de la música en los procesos de reapropiación cultural y desarrollo etnoeducativo*. As a result of this work, a cassette tape has been released (*Música indígena emberá-chamí, Cristianía, Colombia*) and a CD (*Cantos emberá-chamí: comunidad indígena de Cristianía, Colombia*), accompanied by a 12-page booklet (1998). A working group has coalesced, led by Londoño, and including Alejandro Tobón, Jorge Franco, Jesús Zapata, Luis Fernando Franco, and Fernando Mora. The group has advanced different research projects and distribution of folk and vernacular music, among these a compilation and adaptation of transcriptions of roots music (104 pieces) with a pedagogical aim (*Valores musicales regionales y educación musical en Colombia: subproyecto N. 1: región andina Colombiana*, 3 vols. and 1 cassette, unpublished). Within this project (*Valores musicales regionales*), the workgroup wrote a fourth volume, also unpublished, where they analyze in detail four festivals and contests of folk and vernacular music in the Andean region (*Vélez, Ginebra, Aguadas, and Antioquia le canta a Colombia*). In 1996, and by initiative of this group, the Fondo de Investigación y Documentación de Músicas Regionales (Fund for the Research

and Documentation of Regional Musics) was created under the auspices of the Facultad de Artes (Department of Arts) and the Instituto de Estudios Regionales (Institute for Regional Studies) at the Universidad de Antioquia. The group's more recent publications can be found at www.udea.edu.co/portal/page/portal/Programas/GruposInvestigacion/Grupos/Artes/ValoresMusicalesRegionales.

40. Egberto Bermúdez, *Los instrumentos musicales en Colombia* (Bogotá: Universidad Nacional de Colombia, 1985).

41. Egberto Bermúdez, "Historia de la música vs. Historia de los músicos," *Revista Universidad Nacional de Colombia* 3 (1985), 5–17.

42. Egberto Bermúdez, *La música en Colombia: siglos XVI al XVII* (Bogotá, 1994, unpublished); *Catálogo colección de instrumentos musicales "José Ignacio Perdomo Escobar"* (Bogotá: Banco de la República, 1986); *La música en el arte colonial en Colombia* (Bogotá: Fundación De Mvsica, 1994, includes a CD titled *Música del periodo colonial en América Hispánica*, performed by the group Canto and directed by Egberto Bermúdez); *Las Iglesias de madera de San Andrés y Providencia: arquitectura y música* (Bogotá: Fundación De Mvsica, 1998), 65–93, includes a CD titled *Praise Him* and a 36-page booklet); also about the San Andrés island, the CD *Nobody's Business But My Own* (1996, with a 32-page booklet).

43. This publication is introduced by María Eugenia Romero and David Puerta Zuluaga, *Cantan los alcaravanes* (Bogotá: Empresa Colombiana de Petróleos; Occidental de Colombia; Compañía Shell de Colombia, 1990, cassette tape included) and sponsored by the Asociación Cravo Norte–Occidental de Colombia. Romero has carried long-term research on the culture of the Llano.

44. Alfonso Dávila Riveiro, "La cuenca amazónica: músicas populares urbanas," *A Contratiempo* 5 (1988), 24–37.

45. Editors' note: The term used by the author is *de base*, or "belonging to the base" in the Marxist sense of the term—of the people. We have interpreted this as "the grassroots."

46. The perspective from the Left helps differentiate and contextualize the debate about popular culture and folklore. Folklore was backward-glancing, behind the times, because it was imbued with the aristocratic and bourgeois culture, with the myth (keep in mind Paulo Freire's negative conception of the myth), with rites and alienating religion. Popular culture is proletarian, the new culture of conscious masses and vanguards linked and led by organized parties. Antonio Gramsci's hypothesis, as well as case studies by Italian anthropologist Luigi Maria Lombardi-Satriani (on port workers in Italy), explored these two concepts showing how popular culture cannot be divorced from the everyday life of the popular class, whereas folklore obscures a series of contests against elite or hegemonic culture. In Latin America, it is Brazilian folklorist Paulo de Carvalho Neto, who, perhaps more than anyone else, shows how popular culture—in his case poetry and oral literature—has this counter-hegemonic ability. García Canclini, *Hybrid Cultures*, would take this to its limit, beginning by elaborating subtle distinctions (culture of the elite, of the masses, popular culture, traditional culture, hegemonic culture, etc.) and practically erasing the boundaries between these in the end of his analysis. García Canclini places emphasis not on boundaries but on relations, the mediations and the "flows" through which "products" undergo permanent re-significations and relocations in social praxis.

47. See Carlos Miñana Blasco, "Escuelas y experiencias pedagógicas de música popular: estado actual y perspectivas en Colombia," *A Contratiempo* 8 (1991), 43–52. The IPC in Cali was founded in 1947. It has a good collection of unpublished transcriptions and notes on fieldwork of expeditions organized by the Department of Folkloric Investigations, founded in 1960. The EPA (which emerged from the old IPC in Medellín) was created by law in 1970, although it had been conducting pedagogical activities with support from the city government since 1963 and conducting research since 1969. Near Cali, in Ginebra (Valle del Cauca), site of the annual Mono Núñez Contest/Festival of Regional Andean music, there is also the Centro de Documentación Musical Hernán Restrepo Duque (Hernán Restrepo Duque Center for Musical Documentation), which Octavio Marulanda led for a number of years. It is also worth mentioning the documentation work carried out by sociologist Álvaro Pareja at the Centro de Documentación e Investigaciones Musicales del Quindío (Center for Musical Documentation and Investigations of Quindío) in Armenia. The Centro de Documentación Musical at COLCULTURA—which is the most important one in Colombia due to its large holdings of transcriptions (of both art and popular music), books (including, for example, the personal collection of Abadía Morales), recordings and videos—has played an indisputable and important role in the collection of traditional music. Unfortunately it has also suffered from several problems: bureaucratic mishandlings, personal politics, lack of professionalism, mismanagement in the organization of information, reduced budgets, and little impact or promotion of its holdings. With the transformation of COLCULTURA into the Ministerio de Cultura (Ministry of Culture), some changes toward more professional management are evident. Unfortunately, the handling of cultural politics by government agencies at the level of the state does not guarantee the continuity of the work or the funding for projects for the long term.

48. For example, Oscar Vahos, *Juguemos: cultura para la paz* (Medellín: Litoroca, 1998); Alberto Londoño, *Danzas colombianas* (Medellín: Universidad de Antioquia, 1988); and *Baila Colombia* (Medellín: Universidad de Antioquia, 1995).

49. A typical example of this focus, in addition to the book by Londoño, is the important effort by the dance group at the Universidad Tecnológica del Magdalena (Technological University of Magdalena), under the guidance of Ibsen Díaz (see *A Contratiempo* 5 [1988], 50–68).

50. *Música, región y pedagogía* (Tunja: Instituto de Cultura y Bellas Artes de Boyacá, 1989).

51. The group Nueva Cultura has played an important, invigorating, and long-term role for folk and vernacular music, attempting to integrate research, dissemination (several aesthetic recording projects that had great impact at a national level), and pedagogy (the pilot project at the Academia Musical Luis A. Calvo (Luis A. Calvo Music Academy); then at the ICBA in Tunja; and later at the Escuela de Música (School of Music) at the School of Arts at the Universidad Distrital Francisco José de Caldas (District University of Bogotá), both the youth, young adult, and university level). However, the least visible part of the project has been the research. Some institutions at the international level are worth mentioning. INIDEF, founded in 1970 in Venezuela, and more recently the IADAP in Ecuador, funded by the Convenio Andrés Bello, have played key roles in training Colombian

researchers (among these María Eugenía Londoño and Benjamín Yépez) and developing methodology for fieldwork and collection. INIDEF, along with the collection at Indiana University in the United States, is the most important archive on the continent for folk and vernacular music of Latin America. However, of 33 field research projects lasting at least three months and carried out in nearly all Latin American countries, only one was in Colombia, specifically in the Sierra Nevada in the Santa Marta region, producing 144 magnetic tapes, 750 slides, and 384 photographs (Aretz, *Historia de la etnomusicología*, 248, 354).

52. This conference included participants from many countries, including U.S. scholars such as Charles Seeger, Mantle Hood, Willard Rhodes, and George List, and was called the First Iberoamerican Ethnomusicology Conference. Expanded commentary on this conference appears in Bermúdez, "La Universidad Nacional," 57.

53. The *Revista de Folklore de Colombia: Órgano de la Comisión Nacional de Folklore del Instituto Etnológico y de Arqueología, Ministerio de Educación Nacional* (Bogotá: Ministerio de Educación Nacional, 1946–1951); its second incarnation, the *Revista Colombiana de Folclor: Órgano del Instituto Colombiano de Antropología* (Bogotá: Ministerio de Educación Nacional, 1953, 1959–1966, 1969); and finally, the *Nueva Revista Colombiana de Folclor* (Bogotá: Patronato Colombiano de Artes y Ciencias, 1986–2008). Today, it continues key work in disseminating folk and vernacular culture, but it has not yet published any rigorous musicological studies, with the exception of reprinting the 1964 work cited by Rosa, "Esencia, estilo y presencia rajaleña."

54. The one with the largest distribution is, without a doubt, the literary journal *El Aleph* from Manizales, as well as *El Túnel* from Montería and *La Corocora* from the Llanos. A cultural journal exceptional for its time (1947) was *Hojas de Cultura Popular Colombiana*, with articles about popular and highbrow music. Continuing with this same focus on distribution, although much more editorially modest, is *Boletín de Programas del Instituto Nacional de Radio y Televisión*. This was the medium through which the works of Abadía Morales and Perdomo Escobar began to circulate. A selection of the music and folk texts from the *Boletín* was published in two volumes by COLCULTURA in 1978.

55. *A Contratiempo: Música en la Cultura* (issues 9 to 12 between 1997 and 2002) with Ana María Ochoa as editor. In the third period it went digital (2009–12). All issues are available at http://acontratiempo.bibliotecanacional.gov.co.

56. Among these works we must include Joaquín Piñeros Corpas, *Introducción al Cancionero Noble de Colombia* (Bogotá: Universidad de los Andes, 1963), as well as various series edited by COLCULTURA under the directorship of Octavio Marulanda (*Costa Pacífica de Colombia*, 1979) and Benjamín Yepes (*Antología de la música popular y tradicional de Colombia*, 1985, which does not include liner notes). The most ambitious and widely disseminated project, but still unfinished, is the series edited by PROCULTURA under the direction of Egberto Bermúdez (*Música tradicional y popular colombiana*, 1987). The Fundación De Mvsica, also under Bermúdez's leadership, currently profiles its collection Mvsica Americana as the largest producer of field recordings, with rigorous liner notes of some length (30 pages). We do not account for records released abroad, in particular about indigenous music and music from the Atlantic and Pacific coasts (see

Aretz, *Historia de la etnomusicología*). We also do not include releases from commercial or independent recording companies, which have been fundamental for the analysis of *llanera* music, *vallenato*, concert or wind band music, and music of *caña de millo* and *gaitas*, to name a few.

57. This is the case of José Arteaga, who published *Música del Caribe* (Bogotá: Voluntad, 1994) or José Portaccio Fontalvo, *Colombia y su música* (Bogotá: N.p., 1994–95). The latter, although still sharing many traces of the folklorism, has a more respectful treatment of written sources and refers regularly to commercial recordings. Pablo Mora currently produces a series of programs from an anthropological perspective and with contemporary radio language, some of them published. As far as field video recordings, the most significant has been the monumental series *Yuruparí*, directed by Gloria Triana and produced by Audiovisuales in the 1980s. The rise of regional television has proliferated the production of local programs about traditional music.

58. Ana María Ochoa, "¿Qué cultura va a tener? Un paseo musical y literario por los estudios culturales," *Nomadas* 8 (1998), 179–89.

59. For example, a study like that of Miguel Palacio Garoz, *Introducción a la música popular castellana y leonesa* (Castilla y León: Consejería de Educación y Cultura, 1984) does not mention fieldwork, but instead uses statistical methods to compare 1,700 recorded and transcribed melodies dating back to 1869 in a region of Spain the equivalent size of the state of Antioquia [approx. 94,000 square kilometers or 58,400 square miles], against another sampling of 2,181 melodies for a different region.

# 3

# Popular Musicology in Latin America

## *Synthesis of Its Accomplishments, Problems, and Challenges*

JUAN PABLO GONZÁLEZ

## Fundamentals of a New Field

At the eighth annual conference of the Asociación Argentina de Musicología (Argentine Musicology Association) in Mendoza in 1994, dedicated to the theme of analytical procedures in musicology, Gerard Béhague suggested that one of the greatest difficulties facing popular music studies is the lack of consensus on what exactly is or should be understood as "popular music."[1] In fact, it refers to the following: music that is in fashion, although fashion trends can also affect other forms of artistic expression; mass-mediated music, although folk music is also becoming increasingly mediatized [mass mediated]; music having mass circulation, although Chopin today is similarly enjoyed by millions of listeners; or urban music, although any symphony performance would also fall into this category. What, then, is popular music? Although many scholars have stopped asking this question, I will not sidestep the basic problem of the delimitation of our field of study, for it is preferable to risk a definition than to skip over it.[2]

I take the term "urban popular music" to refer to a music that is a mass-mediated, a mass-culture phenomenon, and an agent of modernization. It is mass mediated in the sense that the music industry and technology structure the relationships between musicians and publics, as well as those between music and musicians, who receive their art primarily by listening to recordings. It is mass circulated because it reaches millions of people simultaneously, globaliz-

---

Originally published by Juan Pablo González as "Musicología popular en América Latina: síntesis de sus logros, problemas y desafíos," *Revista Musical Chilena* 55, no. 195 (2001), 38–64. Available at www.revistamusicalchilena.uchile.cl. Translated by Gregory Robinson and published with permission of *Revista Musical Chilena*.

ing local sensibilities and creating trans-social and transnational alliances. It is modern because of its symbiotic relation with the culture industry, technology, and communication, from which it develops its capacity to express the present, a fundamental historical moment for the young audience that sustains it.

From a more anthropological perspective, it is undeniable that there are urban popular musical practices that are not mass culture phenomena, but are rather centered on specific local communities. They are not mass mediated, but rather their musical events are self-produced by communities. And, they are not modern, since within them the values of tradition prevail. Nevertheless, the majority of these cases, because they exist in urban contexts, possess a latent potential for mass circulation, since such communities are growing and changing. There is some degree of mass mediation in the form in which musicians have learned their art; and traditional values can mix with attachment to the memory of a modern past. It is possible to find cases like this in the musical practices of immigrant groups, in rock concerts of the so-called urban tribes, and among street musicians. Even without any of these, we would still see expressions of urban folklore, like the *cueca chilena* [Chilean cueca, a folk music and dance genre] or the practices of organ grinders in Santiago de Chile and Valparaíso.[3]

In Latin America, then, the field of study of popular music is traversed by other unmediated, local, traditional, and highbrow musics. It is a field that seems to resist classification and that will continually defy the frameworks we attempt to apply to it. José Antonio Robles has warned us about the rate of change in popular music that its continual movement "would impede us from taking a good photo."[4] Ana María Ochoa, for her part, reminds us that this is a field continually being defined by the different representational practices that people employ to inhabit it, manage it, and use it.[5] In this way, interested parties from commercial, political, and academic perspectives vie for a field that is in permanent motion.

There is no doubt that the mass mediation of music radically changed the way in which we have practiced and used music in the twentieth century. While musical practice is no longer a face-to-face event for most people living in cities, new genres, styles, and audiences have been created by the mass media.[6] Although we might well lament the banalization, simplification, and standardization produced by mediation, we also must recognize that this mediation has played important musical and cultural roles, not just by influencing the creation of new genres, but by transforming itself into a vehicle for memory, contributing to the construction of national identities, and broadening the transmission of tradition. Carlos Rojas has argued that we are witnessing both the final positioning of recorded sound as a vehicle of communication and the redefinition of the musical tradition.[7]

Multitrack recording allows for the weaving and unraveling of musical fabric, with the resulting analytic and performative implications that this carries for the aural or collective creation of musical works, or both. Thus, technological mediation, at the same time that it becomes a substitute for musical notation when it comes to the dissemination and preservation of musical works, also replaces [older] analytical strategies and compositional processes. This, in great part, allowed the type of musical development that popular music experienced since 1967, the year in which the Beatles began using the recording studio as a creative space, taking seven hundred hours to record their LP *Sgt. Pepper's Lonely Hearts Club Band*.[8]

The mass mediation of recorded sound has also produced new aesthetic parameters for listening, which have come to influence all "live" musical performances. As Simon Frith noted, since the 1960s, recordings rather than concerts have come to define the quality of sound in popular music—and we could well make the same observation about Western art music.[9] As a result, musicians must make their live performances resemble their recordings as closely as possible. The appearance of the microgroove vinyl record [33⅓ rpm] and the concept of high fidelity in the late 1940s influenced the hierarchy in which recorded sound came to occupy a position above sound in its natural state.[10]

Despite the radical changes that the industrialization and mass mediation of music have brought to our musical life, the academy has taken longer than expected in accounting for this new state of things. How to take seriously, academics wonder, that which was conceived as entertainment? Why treat as important a music that appeals only to the body? The first strategy for academically validating our field of study was to establish links between popular music and Western art music: the great composers also wrote popular music, performed today in concert halls; the songs of the Beatles are equivalent to Schubert's *Lieder*, and Cole Porter's harmony is similar to that of Debussy. Later, inspired by postmodernism, we spoke of the "classics" of popular music, discovering in the heavy-metal guitarist the improvising virtuoso of our art music past, and we used Schenkerian methods to analyze songs by John Lennon.[11]

Nevertheless, already in 1982, Philip Tagg set out to justify the academic study of popular music without a comparison to Western art music.[12] Tagg highlighted the large quantity of time and money invested in this music; its role in forging youth identity; the mass mediation of orally transmitted music; the new roles for music created by audiovisual media; the universalization of African American popular music genres; the lack of a "present" for concert music in general; and the emergence of scholar-fans, who, motivated by their experiences with popular music as young people, decided to pursue it as their legitimate object of study.

In the twentieth century, Western art music yielded a considerable amount of space to popular music. On the one hand, contemporary Western art music composition, in an attempt to push toward the future, outpaced the aesthetic competencies of the public of the present, and on the other, musical institutions and the culture industry looked to the past, perennially harvesting what had already been grown. This lack of a musical present for the greater public has been filled by mass-mediated popular music, thus justly earning the label of "modern music" since the 1950s [as opposed to the modernist style of Western art music composition by the same name, which remained inaccessible to most audiences].

Dave Russell argues that it is necessary to study that which is really important to people and not that which the academy thinks should be important to them.[13] Social relevance, aesthetic value, and the demand for a critical perspective fully justify the study of popular music. The social relevance of a music through which millions of listeners simultaneously construct their senses of reality—articulating in the listener ways of feeling, thinking, dreaming, acting, seeing the world, and experiencing one's self—the aesthetic value of a repertoire within which the countries of Latin America have made fundamental contributions to Western music, and the need to construct an informed and critical perspective to deal with the torrent of sound that surrounds us have urgently demanded the creation of a musicology of that music within our society that is the most abundant, the most beloved, and the one that we can come to despise the most.

## The Latin American Contribution

The musicological study of popular music began simultaneously in Latin America, the United States, and Great Britain in the late 1970s, although in Latin America the subsequent development was slower.[14] Twenty years later, popular music had gained a secure position within Latin American musicology, as demonstrated by three interdisciplinary conferences on popular music (Havana, 1994; Santiago, 1997; Bogotá, 2000),[15] as well as the presence of this field of study in the annual conferences of the Asociación Argentina de Musicología and the Simposio Latinoamericano de Musicología (Latin American Musicology Symposium), held in Curitiba since 1997, and in publications like the *Latin American Music Review* and the *Revista Musical Chilena* (Chilean Music Review).

Popular musicology in Latin America has taken a different path from its counterpart in the northern hemisphere. This difference consists not only of differing epistemological approaches, which in turn are derived from the study of distinct realities, but also in the characteristics of the individuals who cultivate these studies and the function that musicology itself fulfills in our society. In a certain way, the Latin American musicologist plays what Gabriel Zaid has called "the social function of the intellectual."[16] This is not only a matter of developing the discipline or broadening knowledge, but also of capturing a vision of reality that becomes a mirror by which society can contemplate, critique, and comprehend itself.

The intellectual, then, would be the person "who opines on matters of public interest with moral authority among the elites."[17] Nonetheless, it is more the reception of the discourse than the discourse itself that makes the intellectual. When the intellectual's vision of the realities or dreams of a group attracts the attention of that group, Zaid maintains, the intellectual comes to be regarded as such. Zaid argues that intellectuals have more gravitas in Roman Catholic societies than in Protestant ones because, in the latter, every faithful person is his or her own moral authority. By contrast, in the Catholic world there is more tension between popular belief and official ideology, putting the intellectual in a unique position to bring together the free and individual conscience of the Protestant laity with the pastoral role of the Catholic priesthood.[18]

The aesthetic tendencies and epistemological decisions of Latin American musicologists are often connected to this pastoral consciousness of the intellectual. On the one hand, there has been resistance to the entry into the Latin American academy of notions about music that label it as commercial, inconsequential, lacking in authenticity, unsophisticated, and of the body [as opposed to the intellect].[19] On the other hand, [Latin American academics] have privileged the study of popular music that may be regarded as "interesting": music that is cutting-edge, off-center, appropriately politically engaged, or socially relevant. Northern [European and Anglo American] musicologists, by contrast, more easily choose to focus on the anonymous, the musically unremarkable, or the "politically incorrect." When this happens among us [Latin American scholars], as Omar Corrado shows, it is more often with the irreverent intent of *épater le bourgeois* [shocking the respectable middle class] than with the simple intention of delimiting an object of study.[20]

The relationship of the scholar with the music that he or she studies involves different levels of affective, aesthetic, and ideological affiliations. In the case of scholar-fans, for example, the researcher's personal context figures heavily in the repertoire he or she ultimately decides to study. In any case, in an ongoing search for meaning, scholars will always ascribe value to what they are studying, in line with their own capabilities and inclinations. In the same way that we construct senses of reality and models of individual and collective identity through our emphases and methods of study, we use our aesthetic preferences to construct our own senses of belonging and affiliation. For each scholar, these affiliations, articulated, imposed and shared through popular music, form important contextual reference points.[21]

The mass circulation and hybridization of Afro-Bahian music, for example, has permitted Brazilians of African descent to engage in processes of social identification in accordance with the phenomenon of Pan-Africanism, in vogue since the 1970s.[22] Something similar occurs in Colombia, where the Afro-descendant population has expanded and diversified its musical practices, re-Africanizing Colombian popular music and incorporating foreign African-influenced genres, like Cuban *son* [music and dance genre], Jamaican reggae, and Nigerian *jùjú* [popular music genre]. Through this mass circulation and pluralization of musical Africanness, Colombians and Brazilians alike negotiate and define an emerging sense of black identity.[23] In the case of Peru, the reconstruction of Afro-Peruvian genres of the past and the formation of groups with a folkloric orientation have offered the black population a model of identification and a renewed pride in their own traditions.[24] This occurs even though the reconstructions are based on secondary sources, products of research and extrapolation, like those produced by the music and dance company Cuadrilla Morena de Pancho Fierro (Pancho Fierro Black Ensemble, 1956) and the writings and recordings of Nicomedes Santa Cruz. On the other hand, *chicha*, or *cumbia andina* [Andean cumbia]—a hybrid genre that Andean migrants developed in Lima and that was successfully disseminated in the capital and in other coastal cities—has come to constitute the urban expression of a new Andean cultural identity. This identity transcends the regional and has attained national significance, allowing children of migrants to articulate values of both tradition and modernity.[25] Margaret Bullen showed how migrants construct bifurcated and transitional cultural identities through the discourse of *chicha*, in both the songs themselves and in the ways of talking about the genre.[26] The European-descended society of Arequipa, which rejected indigenous migration and the music that accompanied it, denied *chicha*'s cultural value and looked disdainfully on those who practiced it in a clear act of power. *Chicha* itself responded to this act, creating an alternative discourse of resistance and a model of identity for those who were deemed not to have one. Thus, popular music helps to rearticulate and democratize Latin American society, and in a certain way a musicology dedicated to these repertoires also contributes to this process.

## Ethnomusicological Aspects

Ethnomusicology's emphasis on the distant and pure and its negative view of the transforming influence of modernity on traditional culture have kept some of [Latin American] ethnomusicologists and many [Latin American] folklorists away from phenomena that involve mediation and urban culture. This divide is reinforced by the micro-level perspective of ethnographic study, its emphasis on closed communities, and cultural anthropology's delay in engaging in the study of Western culture. Nonetheless, ethnomusicology increasingly keeps bumping up against popular music, to the point that it can no longer avoid mentioning it. We consider a few examples in greater detail.

## MEDIATION OF TRADITION

The successive waves of migration from rural to urban areas that took place throughout Latin America during the twentieth century have also moved the geographic and demographic focus of the ethnomusicologist, who has finally been brought to the city by the same communities that he or she studies. In this way, ethnomusicology has begun to consider one of the urban musics most vehemently rejected by [Latin American] intellectuals: the music of people from rural areas who have migrated to the city. This music, as Suzel Reily argues, stands as a symbol of reconciliation between urban economic mobility and the ethos of noncompetitive rural sociability.[27] Through their music, immigrants construct a symbolic universe in which they manage to reconcile the contradictory experiences of rural and urban living, creating a positive image of themselves.

Before arriving in the city, the ethnomusicologist had already confronted the mediated acculturation produced in rural areas by the influence of recordings, radio, film, and television, and the adoption of media as a vehicle of memory by the folkloric community itself. In many cases, ethnomusicologists have observed these acts with concern. Henry Stobart, for example, lamented the fact that Bolivian indigenous communities began devaluing their own traditional music with the arrival of Western music, which enjoyed greater prestige.[28] At the same time, the increased quantity of cassette recorders in these communities led to greater standardization of melodies and less emphasis on their constant reinvention, and even to the replacement of live music with recorded music in ritual contexts. In a similar fashion, Daniel Sheehy described with concern the effects that the growth of national radio, recording, and cinema industries had on Mexican musical life in the 1930s.[29] These changes caused the migration of regional musicians, the professionalization of popular musicians, the development of folk-derived popular styles, the growth of a "star system," and the homogenization of musical tastes.

Government support for the development of folkloric festivals, whether it be for policies of cultural unification or diversification, like those implemented in Bolivia in the 1950s and Colombia in the 1980s, respectively, have constituted another mechanism for the mediation of tradition. These festivals have contributed to the segregation of musicians and audiences, the separation of musical practices from their traditional occasions and functions, and a stronger emphasis on instrumental virtuosity.[30] Although all of this has ultimately led to the development of new musical forms and meanings, none of it has been considered "ethnomusicologically correct." These are processes of urbanization of rural repertoires that have been taking place in Latin American since the end of the twentieth century. In the case of Argentina, this urbanization has been the result of folkloric collection and documentation itself; the activities of theaters, circuses, and *payadores* [popular musician-poets]; the development of *peñas* [meeting places for musicians and other artists]; and the influence of nationalist ideologies.[31] In this way, the phenomenon of folkloristic performance (*proyección folklórica* [folk-inspired performances aimed at the professional stage]) has emerged, linked to the construction of hegemonic notions of national identity, and to the development of the tourism industry, in other words, to different forms of mediation of folklore.[32] Enrique Cámara reminds us that the concept of folkloristic performance goes back to [the Argentine scholars] Carlos Vega and Augusto Raúl Cortazar.[33] Vega did not directly recognize the mediated nature of folkloristic performance, although he did ascribe political, ethical, and aesthetic interests to it. Cortazar, by contrast, highlighted the presence of premeditated and institutionalized agendas within it.[34] Cámara suggests broadening the concept of folkloric performance to include all possible forms of transcultural communication. Almost 80 percent of the cases of transculturation as defined by Cámara in his study of the *baguala* [a lyric song form of northern Argentina and Bolivia] involve some form of mediation—whether it be productive, institutional, technological, or artistic—that serves to resemanticize the original cultural product.

The incorporation of oral music in education curricula and in notated transcription also constitutes forms of mediation of folklore, as was the case with Colombian *bambuco* and *pasillo* [dance-music genres]. Chilean dances already in decline among local communities in the 1930s maintained a mediated presence in elementary schools and later in folkloric groups linked to businesses and trade unions.[35] In Venezuela, the majority of school children in Caracas are encouraged to learn the *cuatro* [four-stringed small guitar] and the *joropo* [courtship dance style of the Llanos, eastern Colombia and southwestern Venezuela], reflecting a new pride among urban listeners for their country's rural folklore.[36] In countries where traditions are heavily regionalized such as Mexico, governments have strived to promote a common folkloric canon. The Mexican public school curriculum includes a limited repertoire of traditional songs and dances, especially the *jarabe tapatío* or *jarabe nacional* [folk dance from the Mexican state of Jalisco], because it is a collection of regional *son* [a generic term for rural music, song, and dance] styles strung together into a single composition.[37]

Finally, the recent globalization of local repertoires under the rubric of world music and its fascination with sonic re-spatialization, has emerged from the discovery and promotion of Third World music by global rock and pop stars who have reinvented their own musical styles and opened a new market. This mediation paradoxically reaffirms the regional style within transnational rather than national spaces, as has typically occurred with folkloric performance.[38] The multiple mediations to which oral tradition is subjected by both exogenous and endogenous forces and the resemanticization that these mediations produce constitute a problem that ethnomusicological studies of popular music in Latin America have not yet been able to address.

## URBAN ETHNOGRAPHY

The city offers vast fields of ethnographic study that have not yet been sufficiently explored by [Latin American] ethnomusicology. The rock concert, the folkloric *peña*, and social dance spaces constitute principal areas of focus for the event-based ethnography practiced within Latin American popular ethnomusicology. Rehearsals, processes of recording and mixing, activities of the disc jockey and street musicians, and the nonprofessional activities at schools, clubs, or the campfire have also earned some attention.[39] Indeed, bars, nightclubs, and brothels have been places of steady employment for musicians and have fostered the creation and development of important genres within [Latin American] popular music. Throughout the [twentieth] century, places like the Colombian *piqueteadero* (café or general store), the Chilean *casa de canto* [song house], the Peruvian *coliseo* [coliseum], the Argentine *tanguería* [tango club], the *peña* [music club or private gathering], the migrant club, and the tourist restaurant have harbored diverse musical practices, contributing in many cases to the very survival of genres and performance practices.[40]

In the study of popular music, then, the ethnographic perspective is essential because it permits us to construct the meaning of a work according to spaces, events, practices, and forms of consumption of specific groups within networks of social relationships at particular historical moments. Musical consumption is one of the most methodologically problematic areas for the study of popular music, because it is the space of greatest individual and collective freedom from the intentions and motives of the industry. Within the history of popular music, aspects of use or consumption have helped to define notions of musical genres themselves. These aspects allow us to determine, for example, whether we are listening to domestic music or concert music.

Present-day musical consumption involves large spaces within which listeners can exercise their wills, extending all the way to the creative, performative field. The twentieth-century listener's ability to modify the dynamic contrast, the volume, the equalization, the spatiality, and the temporality of music, together with the freedom to rearrange the narrative order of a disc, opens a broad set of questions on the transformation of the work by the consumer. For instance, patrons in the *viejotecas* [from the word "discotheque," "old-theques," playing old recordings of dance music] of Cali increased the speed of salsa LPs [to accommodate their tastes and needs].[41] Our identities are constructed in our forms of consumption, as Mario Rey remarked.[42] Musical experience and the meanings people construct around or through music are intimately linked to the ways in which they use it. This underscores the importance of adopting a holistic perspective in the study of music and its function in the lives of individuals, cultures, and societies.[43] Dave Russell, meanwhile, proposes the interpretation of ethnographic study through the lens of social history, linking empirical work to a broader vision of the dynamic social factors of the twentieth century, such as secularization, consumerism, migration, and deindustrialization. He believes that this approach would produce a more complete vision of the patterns of change in popular musical life.[44] In taking on the study of small communities in urban contexts, we must not forget that they are participating in global processes of which they are often not even conscious.

## Musicological Aspects

When Latin American musicologists began to systematically address popular music, following Carlos Vega's concept of mesomusic, they realized that the analytical tools and theoretical assumptions of traditional musicology were insufficient for a deep understanding of this music.[45] A group of scholars that worked on the second volume of an anthology of the tango in the Río de la Plata area avoided some of the pitfalls they faced by adopting broader and more integrated approaches, combining methods from ethnomusicology and historical musicology.[46] In this way, musicology of the popular took on the thrilling task of developing new forms of knowledge by creating a field of study linked to the mass mediation of a musical sensibility of the present. I now examine the ways in which musicologists have approached the study of popular music, considering three basic aspects of the discipline: analysis, historiography, and documentation.

### ANALYSIS

According to Béhague, the question of analysis is the one that has most concerned scholars of popular music, although the principle disciplines involved, sociology and musicology, have not offered theoretical approaches sufficiently elaborate to tackle them.[47] Nevertheless, since the early 1980s, popular musicology has developed a number of approaches to the issue of analysis.

The proliferation of songbooks and sheet music for popular music, published from the end of the seventeenth century, permit an analytical approach based exclusively on their literary or musical texts, and drawing as much on methods from literary studies as historical musicology; this trend is continued by scholars in Latin America today.[48] Charles Perrone, for example, underscored the importance of the analysis of song discourse within the study of Brazilian popular music, whether these analyses focus on social attitudes, political protest, artistic subcurrents, or historical development.[49] Similarly, in Argentina, where an emphasis on literary approaches to the study of tango and *lunfardo* [slang associated with lower classes in Buenos Aires] was nurtured by publications of tango texts from the "golden age" in the 1960s by Editorial Freeland.[50] Likewise, the abundance of transcriptions of rock repertoire, or "rock scores," along with transcriptions of electric-guitar solos enabled extensive formal analysis of musical scores with few references to the semantic dimensions of music in its social context.[51]

The analytical limitations of sheet music stem from the fact that this medium does not accurately register any recorded version of a song. In many cases, popular music composers do not read or write music and hence must rely on others to transcribe their compositions, never having the opportunity to review what they have written.[52] These scores are for domestic rather than professional use and thus are rhythmically and harmonically simplified and lack full instrumentation. Adela Pineda, when studying the evolution of *bolero* [romantic, cosmopolitan genre of Cuba and Mexico] in the work of Agustín Lara, for example, had to leave aside the analysis of sheet music because the written notation did not coincide with versions of the same works recorded by Lara and other performers, causing the author to conclude that Lara's *boleros* should be studied by ear.[53]

In any case, it is necessary to remember that mediatized popular music constitutes a plurality of texts, where lyrics, music, interpretation, visual narrative, arrangement, recording, mix, and editing converge. Analysis, then, must consider at least some of these texts and the semantic relationships produced within a specific convergence among them. Popular musicologist Stan Hawkins proposed to highlight the relationships between musical structure, connotations of the text, and visual and performative narratives within a specific cultural context.[54] This focus is akin to the theory of social homology developed by ethnomusicology in the 1960s, which, according to Béhague, could be useful in the study of urban popular music despite its slightly overreaching claims of cultural absolutism.[55]

British scholars like Wilfrid Meller, Simon Frith, Richard Middleton, and Stan Hawkins have privileged the analysis of recorded performances as text, considering the levels of meaning that song lyrics acquire when they are sung, taking into account factors such as timbre, expression, breath, gesture, and "grain," along with the rhythmic, melodic, harmonic, and coloristic transformations songs undergo when interpreted and mixed in a recording studio.[56] In this way, that which is heard has surpassed that which is read in overall importance.

Middleton advanced a new analytic perspective for popular musicology, suggesting to look "to Lévi-Strauss's theory of 'correspondences' between musical and somatic structures, to Blacking's idea that musical processes are linked to somatic states and rhythms, to Barthes' proposal that they trace the operation of 'figures of the body' or 'somathemes.'"[57] The analyst thus should draw on his or her own somatic responses to music, taking on the perspective of the informant. In fact, Susan McClary distinguishes music's "ability to make us experience our bodies in accordance with its gestures and rhythms."[58] It is as if music, by not materializing in an object, does so through our bodies, Ochoa adds.[59]

The use of semiotics in the study of popular music has permitted the advancement from descriptive analysis of the "sonic organism," belonging to the conservatory tradition, toward hermeneutic analysis more appropriate to the poststructuralist conception of current musicology.[60] In searching for a semantic dimension of the musical text, Middleton suggests reusing the Baroque theories of mimesis—which relate compositional theory with expressive effect—together with theories of classical rhetoric, both of which show how to generate and drive emotions in an audience. These analytical models are applicable to repertoires with strong semantic conventions, as are both Baroque and popular music.[61]

The use of musical styles and processes external to the language of a particular song, a practice that has been common since the Beatles and which can be observed in infinite examples within Latin America, is an important way in which songwriters ascribe meanings in popular music. The existence of this phenomenon allows for a partial resolution of the problem in which musicology must use words to explain a non-denotative art. References to other processes, genres, styles, or songs allow scholars to analytically construct the meaning of a song. As Peter Winkler argues, the meanings that a song articulates spring not so much from the simple identification of external elements in the work, but rather from the relationships of association or differentiation that the external elements generate within the song.[62] Corrado properly applies this principle in his analysis of the decentering strategies in the music of the Argentine singer and philosophy professor Liliana Herrero.[63]

Popular musicology seeks to reach a deeper understanding of the meaning of a song's text by considering the meanings imbued individually and collectively to recorded sound. Philip Tagg approaches these meanings pragmatically with his concept of "museme," or minimal unit of musical meaning. Musemes arise from fields of extramusical association generated in an audience by certain features of musical repertoires produced by the industry, especially those from film and television. Furthermore, musematic meaning is present in all music through associations generated by the historical and social contexts within which it has been practiced, borrowings between genres, and the conventions of language. The different musemes that a song can contain establish relationships between themselves, generating mixes and tensions that escalate the possible levels of meaning within the musical work.[64] Tagg and Guilherme de Alencar Pinto masterfully applied musematic analysis to Chico Buarque's song "Deus lhe pague" [1971; God bless you] by examining the relations between the sarcasm of the text, the monotony of the melody, the harmonic tension, the constricted vocal style, and the instrumentation, grouped into three juxtaposed musematic nuclei: music reminiscent of the soundtrack to police drama, rural music from the northeast, and Afro-Brazilian percussion.[65] These elements are woven together to create a specific meaning for particular listeners in a determined historical moment, with the first nucleus referencing corruption and oppression and the other two referencing ethnicity, marginality, and poverty.[66]

In general terms, the analysis conducted by Latin American popular musicology has tended more toward the identification of specific aspects of song, like its ambiguity, oppressiveness, directionality, or spatiality, without necessarily establishing relations with fields of extramusical associations. It is in the case of Cuban musicology, and especially in the work of Danilo Orozco, that we find a stronger linking between structural and expressive elements of music with idiosyncratic elements of the social contexts in which this music is practiced.[67]

Various Latin American scholars of popular music also work on contemporary art music repertoires, with the result that their analytical tools are well suited to take on the problems of modernity in music, appropriate for the study of the more vanguardist strains of popular music.[68] The problem with this approach arises, as Coriún Aharonián notes, when one takes on a style that is not conceived within the parameters of notated music.[69] Traditional musicology, which lacks a theory of rhythm as intricate as the ones it has for harmony and form, tends to reduce rhythmic phenomena linked to performance, such as anticipation of attack, additive rhythm, metric irregularity, and corporeal polyrhythm. For the analysis of music as a performative phenomenon, the analytic tools of popular musicology are more useful.[70] This new kind of analysis cannot fully replace traditional methods, for it must be used in accordance with the nature of the music under consideration and with the available resources. A song from the beginning of the [twentieth] century preserved in sheet music, for example, would require a more traditional approach than a hip-hop song full of samples and recorded on forty-eight tracks.

Latin American popular music is more than the rock and pop that is disseminated by the music industry: it includes many genres as well as their crossings, crystallizations, derivations, and tensions.[71] Vega justified his and other contemporary musicologists' work on the assumption that "music manifests itself through genres." The challenge of studying musical genre today involves moving beyond the evolutionist perspective from which it was first approached and which centers on processes of complication and simplification, which often correspond with specific implicit or explicit value judgments. To the compilation and edition of songbooks, taxonomies, and "genre-ologies," Latin American popular musicology has added the study of the concept of genre itself and a consideration of the performative, compositional, and social aspects that shape it. Deborah Pacini Hernandez, for example, traced five recent transnational genres of Latin American popular music to their respective local traditions, considering the social, political, and market conditions that permitted their development.[72]

Orozco, meanwhile, developed a concept of genre in Cuban music, based both on levels of functionality and on interactions between genres. In this way, the author established a particularly effective way of defining genre for a scenario with an exceptional level of coexistence between old and new repertoires.[73] By tying the concept of genre to historical processes and features of Cuban social identity, Orozco is able to distinguish genres and subgenres, matrices of relationships and synthesis. In his analysis of Argentine accordionist and *chamamé* [folk music genre from the northeastern part of the country] composer Chango Spasiuk, Corrado proposes a vision of genre that considers aesthetic issues.[74] According to Corrado, generic transformations, the loss of key genre characteristics, as well as intergeneric and performative dialogues reveal aesthetic-productive strategies and relationships between the center and the periphery. However, what is missing in Latin American popular musicology is a reflection about genre itself and the extramusical aspects that help to define and outline it. Genres express something more than music; it is the social and cultural contexts that gather, link, and order them and make them meaningful.

### HISTORIOGRAPHY

The large quantity of salon music edited and produced to accommodate the demands of the rising bourgeoisie [in the late nineteenth century], as well as the wealth of written information published by the media to promote musical consumption, constitute apt primary sources for historical musicological studies. The existence of these written documents, although they may have been incomplete, allowed popular music at first to fit with a certain level of comfort within the field of musicology. In turn, this written tradition made it easier to validate popular music by tracing similarities with art music. Moreover, there is a great quantity of published commentaries on the consumption of popular music in a vast array of printed sources, both specialized and general. Thus, the historiography of popular music challenges us to sort out, prioritize, and interpret the various mediations.

Sarah Thornton defines four criteria by which we habitually define the historical importance of a mass-mediated cultural event: level of consumption, level of mediation, biographical interest, and critical acclaim.[75] The strategies for ordering the past—quantify, mediate, personalize, and canonize—are at the root of any historical research on popular music that considers sales, media, the artist, or the "classical" repertoire as sources, respectively. I consider the characteristics of and problems presented by each of these four strategies.

**QUANTIFY.** When using sales figures as a resource, we should bear in mind that the industry creates needs to satisfy them. As with pop charts, cultural products not only reveal values and attitudes of the social groups that produce and consume them, as Russell points out, but they also help to generate them.[76] Simply put, people consume songs because they are consistently offered to them. This is the logic behind the practice of "payola," developed in the United States in the 1950s, in which record companies paid commissions to disc jockeys so that they would play their new records a specified number of times.[77]

Nonetheless, popular trends can be quite ephemeral. As shown in González and Rolle's research on musical memory in Chile, certain songs that were at the top of the pop charts fifty years ago have disappeared altogether, while, by contrast, some repertoires that received much less media attention have persisted to the present.[78] This also points to the circulation of certain Latin American popular styles outside of major media channels.

**MEDIATE.** The music industry and the traces it has left in its efforts to strengthen consumption have served as privileged sources for the reconstruction of sociomusical contexts in which specific styles, genres, and repertoires were practiced.[79] Nevertheless, when considering the media and the music industry as resources, it is important to remember the institutional interests behind the dissemination of information. In fact, the majority of the information on popular music published in Chilean periodicals from the mid-twentieth century takes the form of advertisements, often camouflaged as news by their formatting and wording.[80]

Thornton reminds us that the difference between journalistic and academic writings lies in the fact that the first pretends to tell the truth, feigning that the world speaks for itself.[81] Academic writings, by contrast, make evident their own methods and approaches, openly adopting perspectives from which they observe and account for the world.

**PERSONALIZE.** The vast majority of mediated information on popular music has centered on stardom. First comes the singer, followed by the genre and then the repertoire. The Chilean press of the 1940s and 1950s usually emphasized the international level of the star: Jorge Negrete is the "ídolo de América" (Idol of the Americas), Pedro Vargas "el gran señor de América" (Great Gentleman of the Americas), Mario Clavel "el chansonnier de América" (Chanson-Singer of the Americas), Eduardo Farrel "el trovador de América" (Troubadour of the Americas), and Libertad Lamarque "la novia de América" (Sweetheart of the Americas).[82] The star also has qualities that make him or her shine. These could be vocal attributes, like Juan Arvizu's "voice of silk and velvet"; physical attributes, like Tongolele's status as a "Caribbean cyclone"; personal attributes like the grace and risqué humor of Ester Soré; or social rank like Alfonso Ortiz Tirado's role as a doctor and philanthropist, or Margarita Lecuona's role as a "sophisticated lady of society."

**CANONIZE.** When invoking the notion of the "classic," one enters the realm of canonization, a somewhat delayed aspect of popular music research due to the fact that most research on this music treats it as a social and cultural phenomenon. Nonetheless, popular music scholars' constant usage of aesthetic and value judgment bear the danger of ethnocentrism and hegemony.

An interesting discussion about canonization in popular music developed in 1997 among the members of the International Association for the Study of Popular Music.[83] Some argued for canonization [of the popular music repertoire], while others warned that the creation of a canon is always an act of power. In my own experience as coeditor of two volumes of the "classics" of Chilean popular music, I can attest that the latter is true, as conflicts of interest arose as soon as we attempted to define central aspects of the memory of a people.[84]

Frith insists on the necessity of knowing how musical value judgments are made and how these judgments inform our listening experiences.[85] Corrado, on the other hand, warns that our value judgments might "legitimize the operations of the cultural industry in the name of cultural studies or the democratization of consumption," but he nevertheless finds such judgments necessary to advance the aesthetic assessment of the repertoires we study—although in this ultimate task we may still be a bit blind.[86]

Thornton's proposed four strategies for ordering the mediatized cultural past are useful if we maintain a critical relationship with the resources—which are both reflections and part of history—and if we pay attention to the discourses printed in the periodicals of the era. The historian's concern should be the study of representations more than the history of that which is supposedly represented.[87]

Social history and ethnohistory prove especially useful when creating a history of popular music. English social historiography, for example, has dealt effectively with the study of folk song and of the music hall in Great Britain, and the consequences of social and technological change in Victorian and post-Victorian musical life. It has done this in an effort to privilege the perspectives and experiences of subordinate groups, assuming that cultural products reveal the values and attitudes of those who produce and consume them.[88] At the same time, ethnohistory helps reinforce our understanding of historical documents, as Béhague argues.[89] In effect, the testimonies provided by the multiple actors involved in the processes of creation, interpretation, production, diffusion, and promotion of popular music, added to those of the current and past public, allow for the multiplication of the singular narrative thread of conventional historiography, offering us an emic and plural reconstruction of history.

## DOCUMENTATION

Because we are dealing with a music that has taken so long to gain serious consideration in academic circles, publications—such as bibliographies, discographies, and reference works that would provide us with complete and accurate information on Latin American popular music—have been slow to appear. There are few complete discographies on Latin American musicians, even though discography is fundamental in the study of mediated repertoires that are only partially edited in sheet music. Valuable biographical studies, such as that of Ernesto Lecuona and Lucho Gatica, lack a discography. Those of Ari Barroso, Fito Páez, Atahualpa Yupanqui, and León Gieco include discographies, but they are missing crucial information.[90]

The discographies of Violeta Parra, Víctor Jara, Lucho Bermúdez, Carlos Gardel, Astor Piazzolla, and Bola de Nieve are outstanding.[91] Thorough discographies have been published on tango, *nueva canción* [lit. new song, Andean-inspired protest music], Chilean popular music on 78rpm discs, and Brazilian music.[92] It is also necessary to mention the eight-hundred-page discography of Spanish-language songs recorded in the United States between 1893 and 1945 completed by Richard Spottswood in his monumental discography on U.S. "ethnic" recordings.[93] Additionally, the proliferation of web pages on popular musicians, created by their publishers or their fans, offers a new and complete source of discographic information in a constant state of growth.

The vast bibliographies on popular music published in printed or electronic form include those compiled by John Shepherd as part of the *Encyclopedia of Popular Music of the World*, and by Peter Wicke at the Research Center for Popular Music at Humboldt University in Berlin.[94] Both have sections dedicated to Latin America, the first with studies by Latin American scholars and the second with publications about Latin American genres with international repercussions or local importance, but written by Anglo-American and European scholars. Nevertheless, there has not yet been published a great bibliography on Latin American popular music, as there has for Latin American music in general or for the *nueva canción* in particular.[95]

In reference works published in Latin America up to the 1980s, the presence of popular musicians is uneven. In Rodolfo Arizaga's encyclopedia of Argentine music, a musician as little-known outside of Argentina as Luis Gianneo occupies three pages, while Carlos Gardel [the most famous tango singer] has only eighteen lines.[96] While it includes Astor Piazzolla, it omits other great tango artists such as Roberto Firpo, Osvaldo Pugliese, and Aníbal Troilo. Marcos Antonio Marcondes's encyclopedia of Brazilian music represents the polar opposite of Arizaga's work since, of the six composers to whom he gives the most space, four are popular: Wilson Batista, Vinicius de Morais, Ari Barroso, and Ataulfo Alves.[97] Helio Orovio's dictionary of Cuban music appears to be the most balanced, with concert musicians and popular musicians receiving similar treatment.[98]

Diverse reference works edited in the late 1990s and early 2000s substantially improved the specialized information on Latin American popular music, leaving popular musicology better documented for the twenty-first century. The *Diccionario de la música española e hispanoamericana* (Dictionary of Spanish and Hispanic American music), under general editor Emilio Casares, constitutes the most complete reference work on mediatized popular music of Spanish-speaking America.[99] This dictionary, while offering historical, ethnographic, biographical, and discographic information on a large proportion of Latin American popular music, facilitates greater depth in local studies and a broader perspective in regional investigations, strengthening both temporal and spatial contextualization.

The *Bloomsbury Encyclopedia of Popular Music of the World* (EPMOW) devotes a respectable amount of space to Latin American music.[100] This multivolume work has the virtue of broadening its biographical perspective, approaching musicians, groups, producers, recording engineers, and industry personalities. At the same time, it gives more attention to genres and styles, to the music industry, to performative practices, and to the places and contexts in which they are carried out.

The 1998 *Garland Encyclopedia of World Music*, the world's first encyclopedia of music based in oral tradition, has a thousand-page volume dedicated to Latin America, edited by Dale Olsen and Daniel Sheehy.[101] Written by both Latin American and foreign scholars, this volume includes entries on mediatized popular music in Latin America. These articles consider the influence of technology and mediation on oral musical traditions, mediatized popular genres and their performance contexts, transnational and transcultural influences, folklore movements, and rural/urban relationships, in addition to the construction and negotiation of identities through popular music.

## Conclusion

Based on the usual division of various musicologies according to their fields of study and epistemological approaches, we can define popular musicology as that which studies mass-disseminated, mediated, and modern music based on an interdisciplinary, holistic, and interpretive approach.

Mass-mediated popular music produces a broader confluence of disciplinary interests than any other style, which has caused popular musicology to develop with a high degree of interdisciplinarity. Entering into a field of study already occupied by sociology and anthropology, literary and cultural studies, social history, semiotics, and gender studies has offered popular musicology the advantage of getting to know multidisciplinarily, and the challenge of entering into the broad realm of the humanities and social sciences. Even the definition of a musical field as mediatized, mass produced, and modern contributes to the confluence of disciplinary perspectives. The definition of an area of study will always be a function of our objectives and interests and, in our case, of the dialogue that we wish to establish within and outside music and the academy.

At the Third Latin American Conference of the International Association of the Study of Popular Music (IASPM-AL), held in Bogotá in 2000, a third of the participants came from fields in the social sciences and humanities, most notably sociology, anthropology, history, journalism, and literary studies. Participants from all of these fields entered into dialogue with discourses from musicology, ethnomusicology, and music education, helping to create a rich, multidisciplinary network around music.

At the same time, mass-mediated popular music constitutes a privileged meeting ground for these various musicologies because it has been the area of greatest confluence among the three aspects of our discipline: the historical, the ethnographic, and the systematic. This confluence, already supported during the symposium on the theoretical unity of musicology, held during the third annual conference of the Asociación Argentina de Musicología in Buenos Aires in 1989, arises from the existence of a field of study that, for years, was no one's territory and now seems to be everyone's territory.[102]

Popular musicology opens the path to a critical and interpretive approach that leaves behind the empirical positivism of traditional musicology.[103] Even more importantly, maintaining an attitude corresponding to the libertarian, rebellious, and critical spirit of a great part of popular music, prominent academic representatives of popular musicology like Middleton and Tagg see in the practice of this discipline a way to free ourselves from an atomized bourgeois subjectivity, moving forward in the reintegration of the body, mind, and spirit.[104] From this position, popular musicology helps deconstruct the hegemonic and Eurocentric vision from which the history of Western music has been written and through which the sonic plurality that surrounds us in Latin America has been hierarchically organized.

## Notes

1. Gerard Béhague, "Hacia un enfoque etnomusicológico para el análisis de la música popular," in *Actas de las IX Jornadas Argentinas de Musicología y VIII Conferencia Anual de la Asociación Argentina de Musicología*, ed. Irma Ruiz, Alejandra Cragnolini, and Elizabeth Roig (Buenos Aires: Instituto Nacional de Musicología Carlos Vega, 1998), 306.

2. The second meeting of IASPM (International Association for the Study of Popular Music), held in Reggio Emilia, Italy, in 1983, with the title, "What Is Popular Music?," took on the definition of this field of study as its central theme.

3. Agustín Ruiz, "Organilleros de Chile: de la marginalidad al patrimonio. Apuntes para la historia social del oficio," *Resonancias* 9 (2001), 55–86, offers interesting background on the practice of the barrel-organ player in Chile.

4. José Antonio Robles, "La historia de las músicas populares en América Latina y el Caribe," *Actas del III Congreso IASPM-AL* (Bogotá, 2000), available at www.iaspmal.net.

5. Ana María Ochoa, "Interacciones entre lo global y local," *Actas del III Congreso IASPM-AL.*

6. Anthony Seeger, "Musical Genres and Contexts," in *South America, Mexico, Central America, and the Caribbean*, ed. Dale Olsen and Daniel Sheehy (New York: Garland Publishing, 1998), vol. 2 of *Garland Encyclopedia of World Music*, 51.

7. Carlos Rojas, "El joropo en el siglo XX: la redefinición de un lenguaje," *Actas del III Congreso IASPM-AL.*

8. See George Martin and William Pearson, *El verano del amor: así grabaron Los Beatles el álbum Sgt. Pepper*, trans. Ricardo Gil Salinas (Zaragoza: Milenio, 1997). Originally published as *With a Little Help from My Friends: The Making of Sgt. Pepper* (Boston: Little, Brown, 1994).

9. Simon Frith, *Music for Pleasure* (New York: Routledge, 1988), 20.

10. For a study on the effects of commercial recording on the uses and meanings conferred on the voice, see Juan Pablo González, "El canto mediatizado: breve historia de la llegada del cantante a nuestra casa," *Revista Musical Chilena* 65, no. 194 (2000), 26–40.

11. In the 1960s in Chile, popular song had been elevated to the category of *cantata*.

12. Philip Tagg, "Analysing Popular Music: Theory, Method and Practice," *Popular Music* 2 (1982), 37–67.

13. Dave Russell, "The 'Social History' of Popular Music: A Label without a Cause?," *Popular Music* 12, no. 2 (1993), 139–54, 153.

14. Undoubtedly the cultural and educational policies imposed by the military governments that prevailed in the region during this period helped to delay this study.

15. These were the first three conferences held in Latin America connected to the International Association for the Study of Popular Music.

16. Gabriel Zaid, "Intelectuales," *El Mercurio, Artes y Letras* (Oct. 25, 1998), E8–E9.

17. Ibid., E8. This function would be seen for the first time with Emile Zola's public entry into discussions of political or military issues with his open letter to the president of the republic ("J'Accuse. . . !," *L'Aurore*, Jan. 13, 1898: 1).

18. Zaid, "Intelectuales," E9.

19. Omar Corrado, "Estrategias de descentramiento: la música de Liliana Herrero," in *Música popular en América Latina: actas del II Congreso Latinoamericano IASPM*, ed. Rodrigo Torres (Santiago: Rama Latinoamericana IASPM, 1999), 415, points out that in Argentina, "the relationship between intellectuals and anything popular has historically been traumatic, belligerent, elusive," a relationship that can be extended to the case of Chile.

20. Corrado, "Estrategias de descentramiento."

21. These can be national affiliations as with *cueca*, regional affiliations as with *chamamé*, affiliations of class as with *bossa nova*, of race as with *axé*, or of ideology as with *nueva canción*; see Deborah Pacini Hernandez, "Popular Music of the Spanish-Speaking Regions," in Olsen and Sheehy, *South America, Mexico, Central America, and the Caribbean*, 104.

22. Charles Perrone, "Popular Music of Brazil," in Olsen and Sheehy, *South America, Mexico, Central America, and the Caribbean*, 110.

23. Lawrence App, "Afro-Colombian Traditions," in Olsen and Sheehy, *South America, Mexico, Central America, and the Caribbean*, 409. The massification of Colombian Africanness went through a process of whitening, as in the case of *vallenato* performed by Carlos Vives. A somewhat similar process occurred with the *cumbia* in the hands of Lucho Bermúdez in the 1940s. For *vallenato*, see Ana María Ochoa, "El multiculturalismo en la globalización de las músicas regionales colombianas," in *Cultura, medios y sociedad*, ed. Jesús Martín Barbero and Fabio López de la Roche (Bogotá: Universidad Nacional de Colombia, 1998), 101–13.

24. William David Tompkins, "Afro-Peruvian Tradition," in Olsen and Sheehy, *South America, Mexico, Central America, and the Caribbean*, 502.

25. Raúl Romero, "Peru," in Olsen and Sheehy, *South America, Mexico, Central America, and the Caribbean*, 485.

26. Margaret Bullen, "Chicha in the Shanty Towns of Arequipa, Peru," *Popular Music* 12, no. 3 (1993), 230.

27. Suzel Ana Reily, "Brazil: Central and Southern Areas," in Olsen and Sheehy, *South America, Mexico, Central America, and the Caribbean*, 320. The various processes of rural-urban migration that have occurred in Latin America in the twentieth century have produced a series of mediatized popular genres like the *canción ranchera* in Mexico City, *música sertaneja* in São Paulo, *chicha* in Lima, and the *bailanta* in Buenos Aires.

28. Henry Stobart, "Bolivia," in Olsen and Sheehy, *South America, Mexico, Central America, and the Caribbean*, 297.

29. Daniel Sheehy, "Mexico," in Olsen and Sheehy, *South America, Mexico, Central America, and the Caribbean*, 619–20.

30. For more background on the case of Bolivia, see Stobart, "Bolivia," 297.

31. Ercilia Moreno Chá, "Argentina," in Olsen and Sheehy, *South America, Mexico, Central America, and the Caribbean*, 262.

32. Folkloristic performance today arises from the mediated transmission of elements of traditional culture, often collected, preserved, and learned through mass media.

33. Enrique Cámara, "Folclore musical y música popular urbana: ¿proyecciones?," in Torres, *Música popular en América Latina*, 329–40. See also Coriún Aharonián, "Carlos Vega y la teoría de la música popular: un enfoque latinoamericano en un ensayo pionero," *Revista Musical Chilena* 51, no. 188 (1997), 61–74.

34. Cámara, "Folclore musical y música popular urbana," 329n1.

35. These dances primarily consist of the *rin*, the *pericona*, the *sirilla*, the *refalosa*, the *cachimbo*, and the *trote*. See Juan Pablo González, "Música popular chilena de raíz folclórica," in *Clásicos de la música popular chilena: 1960–1973 raíz folclórica*, ed. Luis Advis, Eduardo Cáceres, Fernando García, and Juan Pablo González (Santiago: Ediciones Universidad Católica de Chile y Sociedad Chilena del Derecho de Autor, 1998), 2:8–27.

36. Max Brandt, "Venezuela," in Olsen and Sheehy, *South America, Mexico, Central America, and the Caribbean*, 523.

37. Sheehy, "Mexico," 619.

38. Ochoa, "El multiculturalismo en la globalización," 103.

39. Ruth Finnegan, *The Hidden Musicians: Music-Making in an English Town* (Cambridge: Cambridge University Press, 1989) has demonstrated the value of the ethnographic

study of amateur musical practice, tracing musical histories of individuals, families, and institutions.

40. It is also necessary to mention Colombian *bailaderos* [dance halls], linked to *vallenato*, Peruvian *chichódromos* [chichadromes, places to dance chicha music], and Chilean *salsotecas* [salsa-theques]. At the same time, streets, plazas, buses, and subway stations have frequently served as stages for street musicians and Andean groups in the Americas and Europe.

41. Lise Waxer, "'Hay una discusión en el barrio': el fenómeno de las viejotecas en Cali, Colombia," *Actas del III Congreso IASPM-AL.*

42. Mario Rey, "Creando confines socio-musicales: la música popular y la subculturización de la juventud cubana," *Actas del III Congreso IASPM-AL.*

43. Sara Cohen, "Ethnography and Popular Music Studies," *Popular Music* 12, no. 2 (1993), 135.

44. Russell, "'Social History' of Popular Music," 147.

45. Chilean historian Eugenio Pereira Salas, *Historia de la música en Chile (1850–1900)* (Santiago: Publicaciones de la Universidad de Chile, 1957), 362–63, had already traced the outlines of the field of popular music in 1957 when he pointed out that "for some critics, the appearance of the popular in the realm of music can be considered a schism that began during the Romantic era, a struggle between the creators of pure genres for the elite and an intermediate type [of music] directed, mechanized, and standardized for massive public consumption." See also Carlos Vega, "Mesomúsica," *Polifonía* (1966), 131–32; Carlos Vega, "Mesomúsica: un ensayo sobre la música de todos," *Revista Musical Chilena* 51, no. 188 (1997), 75–96.

46. Pablo Kohan, "Comentarios sobre la unificación teórica de la musicología según las propuestas de Irma Ruiz y Leonardo Waisman," *Revista Musical Chilena* 43, no. 172 (1989), 33–40. Only the first volume of this anthology was published: Jorge Novarti and Irma Ruiz, *Antología del tango rioplatense* (Buenos Aires: Instituto Nacional de Musicología, 1980).

47. Béhague, "Hacia un enfoque etnomusicológico," 305.

48. On examples of literary analysis of popular music, see Peatman in Frith, *Music for Pleasure*, 106. On traditional musicological analysis, see Alec Wilder, *American Popular Song: The Great Innovators, 1900–1950* (Oxford: Oxford University Press, 1972).

49. Perrone, "Popular Music of Brazil," 107.

50. Moreno, "Argentina," 264.

51. Allan Moore, "The So-Called 'Flattened Seventh' in Rock," *Popular Music* 14, no. 2 (1995), 185–201.

52. The Chilean composer Clara Solovera (1909–1992), for example, used to dictate the melodies of her *tonadas* to the composer José Goles (1917–1993) over the telephone, so that he could write and harmonize them.

53. Adela Pineda, "La evolución del bolero urbano en Agustín Lara," *Heterofonía* 102–3 (1990), 10.

54. Stan Hawkins, "Prince: Harmonic Analysis of 'Anna Stesia,'" *Popular Music* 11, no. 3 (1992), 325–35.

55. Béhague, "Hacia un enfoque etnomusicológico."

56. Wilfrid Meller, *A Darker Shade of Pale: A Backdrop to Bob Dylan* (London: Oxford University Press, 1985); Frith, *Music for Pleasure*; Richard Middleton, *Studying Popular Music* (Milton Keynes, U.K.: Open University Press, 1990); Stan Hawkins, "Perspectives in Popular Musicology: Music, Lennox, and Meaning in 1990s Pop," *Popular Music* 15, no. 1 (1996), 17–36; Hawkins, "Prince."

57. Richard Middleton, "Popular Music Analysis and Musicology: Bridging the Gap," *Popular Music* 12, no. 2, (1993), 177–90, p. 177–78.

58. Susan McClary, *Feminine Endings: Music, Gender, and Sexuality* (Minneapolis: University of Minnesota Press, 1991), 23.

59. Ochoa, "El multiculturalismo en la globalización."

60. Tagg, "Analysing Popular Music"; Middleton, *Studying Popular Music.*

61. For a study of the analytical application of musical rhetoric in the present, see Gustavo Becerra, "La posibilidad de una retórica musical hoy," *Revista Musical Chilena* 52, no. 189 (1998), 37–52.

62. Peter Winkler, "Randy Newman's Americana," *Popular Music* 7, no. 1 (1987), 4.

63. Omar Corrado, "Migraciones y permanencias: El Chango Spasiuk," *Actas del III Congreso IASPM-AL.*

64. Tagg isolated elements that a group of listeners recognizes as musemes through the systematic substitution of the diverse musical parameters of a song.

65. As demonstrated at the *12th Latin American Course on Contemporary Music* (*XII Curso Latinoamericano de Música Contemporánea*), held in 1984 in Brazil. See Guilherme de Alencar Pinto, "Análisis: Deus lhe pague," *La del Taller* 4 (1985), 19–26.

66. The song's arrangement, which contains a great part of its musematic content, is by Rogerio Duprat (1932), a Brazilian composer and disciple of Cualdio Santoro who, since the mid-1960s, has linked himself to MPB (Música Popular Brasileira; Brazilian popular music).

67. Danilo Orozco, "Perfil sicocultural y modo son en la cultura cubana," *Actas del I Congreso IASPM-AL* (Havana, 1994).

68. Coriún Aharonián, "Desafíos para un análisis de las vanguardias en la música popular uruguaya," in Torres, *Música popular en América Latina*, 418–30; Corrado, "Estrategias de descentramiento"; Damián Rodríguez Kees, "'Jóia,' necesidad y factibilidad del análisis de la música popular," in Torres, *Música popular en América Latina*, 399–409.

69. Aharoinán, "Desafíos para un análisis," 421.

70. Ibid., 424–25.

71. Orozco in Agustín Ruiz, "Aquí Macondo: conversación con Danilo Orozco," *Revista Musical Chilena* 51, no. 188 (1997), 40–60; Corrado, "Estrategias de descentramiento"; Juan Pablo González, "Cristalización genérica en la música popular chilena de los años sesenta," in Torres, *Música popular en América Latina*, 365–74; Fabián Pínola, "Retoques (El 'tango' y el 'folclore' en el 'Rock nacional argentino')," in Torres, *Música popular en América Latina*, 256–69.

72. Pacini Hernandez, "Popular Music of the Spanish-Speaking Regions," 102–4.

73. Orozco, "Perfil sicocultural." In Cuba, urban popular music, or "professional" music, as some have called it, has developed and institutionalized multiple instrumental formats

that endow it with its rich variety and distinctive character. See Olavo Alén, "Cuba," in Olsen and Sheehy, *South America, Mexico, Central America, and the Caribbean*, 834–36. Alén distinguishes among *dúo, trío, cuarteto, sexteto de son, septeto, conjunto, charanga típica, piquete típico, órgano oriental, estudiantina, coro de clave, grupo de guagancó, comparsa*, and *gran combo* or *gran orquesta*.

74. Corrado, "Migraciones y permanencias."

75. Sarah Thornton, "Strategies for Reconstructing the Popular Past," *Popular Music* 9, no. 1 (1990), 87–95.

76. Russell, "'Social History' of Popular Music."

77. More information on payola can be found in Pekka Growno and Ilpo Saunio, *An International History of the Recording Industry*, trans. Christopher Moseley (London: Cassell, 1998), 106.

78. Juan Pablo González and Claudio Rolle, "Recordando lo no vivido: música popular urbana como vehículo de la memoria," in *Memoria para un nuevo siglo, Actas del Seminario* (Santiago: Universidad de Santiago, 1999).

79. The products and services generated by the industry, such as sheet music, songbooks, phonograms, films, radio programming, promotional materials, catalogs, and sound reproduction equipment, have constituted a first-rate resource for the study of urban popular music.

80. The three basic ingredients necessary to sell music in Santiago during the 1940s were joy, romanticism, and social distinction. *Rumbas, congas*, and swing dances offered joy; *tangos* and *boleros* offered romanticism; salons and dance schools offered social distinction.

81. Thornton, "Strategies for Reconstructing," 91–92, drawing on White's distinction between "narrativizing" and "narrating."

82. Editors' note: The author's usage of the term "America" in the original Spanish text does not mean the United States but rather what in English would be referred to as "the Americas."

83. On the International Association for the Study of Popular Music Listserv, iaspm-list@info.comm.uic.edu.

84. Luis Advis and Juan Pablo González, *Clásicos de la música popular chilena, 1900–1960* (Santiago: Ediciones Universidad Católica de Chile y Sociedad Chilena del Derecho de Autor, 1994).

85. Simon Frith, "Towards an Aesthetic of Popular Music," in *Music and Society: The Politics of Composition, Performance and Reception*, ed. Richard Leppert and Susan McClary (Cambridge: Cambridge University Press, 1987), 133–202.

86. Omar Corrado to the author, email December 17, 1999.

87. Stedman Jones, cited in Russell, "'Social History' of Popular Music," 149.

88. Ibid.

89. Béhague, "Hacia un enfoque etnomusicológico," 312.

90. Carmella de León, *Ernesto Lecuona* (Havana: Editorial Letras Cubanas, 1996); Gonzalo Rojas Donoso, *Contigo en la distancia: Lucho Gatica, el Rey del Bolero* (Santiago: Ediciones Cerro Huelén, 1992); Sérgio Cabral, *No tempo de Ari Barroso* (Rio de Janeiro:

Lumiar Editora, 1992); Horacio Vargas, *Fito Páez (la biografía): la vida después de la vida* (Rosario: Ediciones Homo Sapiens, 1994); Félix Luna, *Atahualpa Yupanqui* (Madrid: Ediciones Júcar, 1974); Oscar Finkelstein, *León Gieco: crónica de un sueño* (Buenos Aires: Editora AC, 1994).

91. Isabel Parra, *El libro mayor de Violeta Parra* (Madrid: Ediciones Michay, 1985); Claudio Acevedo et al., *Víctor Jara: obra musical completa* (Santiago: Ocho Libros Editores y Fundación Víctor Jara, 1996); José Portaccio Fontalvo, *Carmen tierra mía: Lucho Bermúdez* (Bogotá: Disformas Triviño, 1997); Miguel Ángel Morena, *Historia artística de Carlos Gardel* (Buenos Aires: Corregidor, 1990); Natalio Gorin (ed.), *Astor Piazzolla: a manera de memorias* (Buenos Aires: Editorial Atlántida, 1990); Miguelito Ojeda, *Bola de Nieve* (Havana: Editorial Letras Cubanas, 1998).

92. Roberto Gutiérrez Miglio, *El tango y sus intérpretes: vida y discografía de los cantores y cancionistas del tango*, 4 vols. (Buenos Aires: Corregidor, 1994); Stefano Gavagnin, "A proposito dei complessi cileni: note sul linguaggio e sulla discografia dei gruppi della 'Nueva Canción Chilena,'" *Rivista Italiana di Musicolologia* 21, no. 2 (1986), 300–335; Clara Díaz Pérez, *Una historia de la nueva trova cubana* (Havana: Editorial Letras Cubanas, 1994); Juan Astica, Carlos Martínez, and Paulina Sanhueza, *Los discos 78 rpm de música popular chilena: breve reseña histórica y discográfica* (Santiago: FONDART, 1997); Jairo Severiano and Zuza Homen de Mello, *A canção no tempo: 85 anos de músicas brasileiras*, vol. 1, *1901–1957* (São Paulo: Editora 34, 1997).

93. Richard Spottswood, *Ethnic Music on Records: A Discography of Ethnic Recordings in the United States, 1893–1942* (Urbana: University of Illinois Press, 1990), 7 vols.

94. John Shepherd et al., *Continuum Encyclopedia of Popular Music of the World* (London: Continuum, 2003–12) and *Bloomsbury Encyclopedia of Popular Music of the World* (New York: Bloomsbury Academic, 2015–). See also Institut für Musikwissenschaft und Medienwissenschaft, Humboldt-Universität zu Berlin (Research Center for Popular Music, Humboldt University of Berlin), at www.musikundmedien.hu-berlin.de/de.

95. The bibliography compiled by Gerardo Huseby and appearing in *Revista Musical Chilena* 177 (1992), 178 (1992), and 181 (1994), includes in the ethnomusicology section an entry on "urban popular music," an area in which there has been a large increase in interest and in material published; see also Gerardo Huseby, "La bibliografía musicológica latinoamericana," *Revista Musical Chilena* 47, no. 180 (1993), 63; Jan Fairley, "Annotated Bibliography of Latin-American Popular Music with Particular Reference to Chile and to Nueva Canción," *Popular Music* 5 (1985), 305–56.

96. Rodolfo Arizaga, *Enciclopedia de la música argentina* (Buenos Aires: Fondo Nacional de las Artes, 1971).

97. Marcos Antonio Marcondes, *Enciclopedia da música brasileira erudita, folclórica, popular* (São Paulo: Art Editora, 1977).

98. Helio Orovio, Diccionario de la música cubana: biográfico y técnico (Havana: Letras Cubanas, 1981).

99. Emilio Casares Rodicio, gen. ed., *Diccionario de la música española e hispanoamericana*, 10 vols. (Madrid: Sociedad General de Autores y Compositores, 1999–2002).

100. John Shepherd, gen. ed., *Genres: Caribbean and Latin America*, vol. 9 of *Bloomsbury Encyclopedia of Popular Music of the World* (2014).

101. Dale Olsen and Daniel Sheehy, ed., *South America, Mexico, Central America, and the Caribbean* (New York: Garland Publishing, 1998), vol. 2 of *Garland Encyclopedia of World Music.*

102. The presentations given at this symposium are published in the *Revista Musical Chilena* 43, no. 172 (1989), 5–46.

103. Béhague, "Hacia un enfoque etnomusicológico."

104. Philip Tagg, review of *Music and Culture Theory* by John Shepherd et al. (Cambridge: Polity Press, 1997), *Popular Music* 17, no. 3 (1998), 331–48.

# 4

# The Construction of History

## *The* Charango *in the Collective Memory of Mestizo Ayacucho*

JULIO MENDÍVIL

In Peru it is widely contended that the *charango*, that small chordophone associated with the armadillo and bearing five double courses of strings, arose as a result of indigenous people making fun of the Spanish musical practice of guitar playing. Although few works have been published on the elusive "history" of this instrument, a few basic notions, grounded in "demonstrable historical facts," are all that is needed to refute such an assertion. Based on data obtained from *charango* players and the public on the one hand, and from musicological material on the other, I show how collective memory differs from a historically based viewpoint in terms of how the "history" of the *charango* is understood and transmitted, and how the Andean mestizo population, through its conceptualization of the instrument, strives to reinforce its cultural identity in response to official Peruvian culture, which is promulgated by academic researchers.

## The *Charango* in Mestizo Collective Memory

According to Andean collective memory, the *charango* arose as a means of ridiculing the guitar, the instrument of colonial secular society par excellence, a process whereby the Indian shrank it down to the size of a mere ornamental object, only later investing it with musical qualities through a long creative process. I have heard this assertion made by [both] young and distinguished mestizo musicians at innumerable concerts, and even by certain scholars of Andean folklore.[1] I have

Originally published by Julio Mendívil as "La construcción de la historia: el charango en la memoria colectiva mestiza ayacuchana," *Revista Musical Chilena* 56, no. 198 (2002), 63–78. Available at www.revistamusicalchilena.uchile.cl. Translated by Mona-Lynn Courteau and published with permission of *Revista Musical Chilena*.

also been able to confirm that the idea that the *charango*'s small size is due to its origin as a satire of the guitar prevails among audiences at Andean music concerts, although no one is able to defend this claim, nor even attempts to. I refer to this assumption as the collective memory theory. This theory aims to explain the origin as well as the indigenous character of the instrument on material and conceptual levels, and even the names used to refer to it, as we shall see below.

A brief excursion into myth is necessary before delving into the task at hand. I am grateful to José Castro Pozo for providing me with a previously unpublished version of a myth on the origin of the *charango*, collected by his father, Hildebrando Castro Pozo. Here is a summary of this myth:

> An Indian left his native village on the high plateau in search of a better life, and became a tenant farmer in the mountainous lands. Tired of being abused, he decided to return to his village, taking with him his pet, a small armadillo. They lost their way and had to endure many trials, but ever the animal consoled the Indian by singing him beautiful melodies. After many days without food, the armadillo died of starvation, begging the man to save himself by eating his flesh. The Indian was so grateful to his pet for its sacrifice that he took its shell and fashioned it into an instrument so that he might continue to sing with his friend.

With all possible respect to the author, I regard this myth as "suspicious," not only because its provenance is unspecified and it adheres to existing myth complexes concerning the *charango* that fail to refer to the instrument's origin, but also because of its very structure: it is more akin to a children's story than a creation myth, more suggestive of the literary imagination of an indigenist author—such as that of Castro Pozo—than to Andean oral tradition. Nonetheless, as I demonstrate, this story is inscribed within the collective memory theory, functioning, or claiming to function, as a means of legitimizing the instrument.

The collective memory theory also features an attempt at assigning the etymology of the instrument's name to the language of the Incas. Based on information imparted by two Peruvian teachers, a group of schoolchildren from the Río de la Plata [borderland region between Argentina and Uruguay] noted in a college essay that "the word charango comes from the Quechua culture whose language, *runa simi* [*runasimi*], refers to this instrument as *chawaqku*, which means joyful and noisy, like Carnival."[2] This word does not appear in Quechua dictionaries, nor are my Quechua informants convinced of its existence, let alone its etymological origin. It is interesting to note that neither of these teachers, who gave this information to their pupils without providing any bibliographical references, is familiar with the Quechua language. In short, from a historical point of view this claim is unsupported.

From the outset we may note a paradox within the collective memory theory: an instrument intended to ridicule the other would not go on to be adopted as a means of expressing deep sentiments such as solitude, sadness, and, most importantly, joy. I have also always found paradoxical the assumption that indigenous people resorted to the armadillo shell due to a scarcity of materials for the construction of stringed instruments, since the shell was only sought as a substitute for the resonator, whereas the other parts of the instrument continued to be made of wood. The average person does not perceive these as paradoxes, not even if they are familiar with what we will refer to as the historical theory. It is quite the opposite for defenders of the historical theory, who instead consistently point to the lack of objectivity and of scientific methodology that characterize the "theories" sustained by collective memory. At the Congreso Nacional de Folklore (National Folklore Congress) held in 1985 in Lima, I mentioned the findings of my probing into the history of the *charango* to Peruvian ethnomusicologist Josafat Roel Pineda; after pronouncing the statements of my informants as unfounded and fanciful, he steered me onto "a good lead": a European guitar with five double courses from the Renaissance period. Since then, I have followed the *charango*'s "historical tracks."

## The *Charango* According to Peruvian Historical Musicology

The *charango*'s European origin was contested until the middle of the [twentieth] century.[3] In 1937, Héctor Gallac put an end to the debate, basing his arguments on the writings of "scholars" such as Andrés Sas and the d'Harcourts [Raoul and Marguerite], who had shown that there were no stringed instruments in ancient Peru. For Gallac, the instrument arose as a reproduction of the Spanish guitar, "a wholesale substitution of the instrument with the primitive and crude *charango*, as dictated by circumstances of Indian indigence."[4] Thus, for this Argentine scholar, any attempt to confer upon the *charango* an "autochthonous genealogy" was to be discounted as untenable.

It is well-known that Peru's lute family of instruments originated on the [Iberian] peninsula. Antonio Corona Alcalde writes: "The importing of stringed instruments began virtually at the moment of discovery [of the Americas], when in 1496 and 1497 Ferdinand the Catholic ordered that the necessary measures be taken to send musical instruments to Hispaniola (Santo Domingo) [Dominican Republic] to provide a pastime for those who remained there. Subsequently, those with musical inclinations brought their own instruments, such as Rui González, a clerk who came with Diego Colón's fleet in 1509 and brought along "a vihuela and strings."[5]

There was a certain preference for chordophones. José Torre Revello has published an interesting list of music books that were brought to Peru at the dawn of the colonial period, including vihuela books.[6] There are also accounts of stringed-instrument players arriving in the Americas early on, some of whom founded music schools.[7] This set into motion a second stage of assimilation for chordophones, that of the natives coming under the spell of Apollo's lyre.[8]

As it had in Mexico, this stage began very early in Peru. José Carlos Campos and Robert Stevenson noted the presence of vihuelists there in 1546 and 1553.[9] One of these, Juan de la Peña Madrid, opened a music school in 1568 together with the mulatto Hernán García, suggesting that cultural intermixing began early in Peru.[10] Nor was there any delay in the rise of indigenous enthusiasm for chordophones. This is nicely illustrated on folio 857 of Guamán Poma [de Ayala]'s *Nueva crónica*. Under the provocative title "Indios criollos y criollas indias" (Male Creole Indians and female Indian Creoles) Guamán Poma shows an Indian playing a chordophone with a handle and singing a song, ostensibly indigenous as it is in Quechua, the text of which appears beside the image (fig. 4.1). Even if we suppose that the chronicler's illustration of the instrument was not an exact reproduction, it is important to note that, already in the early seventeenth century,

Fig. 4.1 Illustration appearing in Guamán Poma de Ayala's *Nueva corónica y buen gobierno*

evidence of musical hybridization involving stringed instruments was recorded in a "historical" document.[11]

The first "historical" mention of a *charango* was gathered by Carlos Vega and dates to an 1814 report by a cleric from Tupiza [Potosí, Bolivia], who stated that the Indians "demonstrated equal liking for small guitars of their own, which here they call *charangos*."[12] Thomas Turino, for his part, has documented depictions of sirens playing instruments that may be *charangos* in some mid-eighteenth-century colonial churches on the high Andean plateau of Peru and Bolivia, which suggests that the instrument has an earlier origin.[13] Vega pins its immediate historical precursor to a European five-course guitar mentioned by Marin Mersenne in his *Harmonie universelle* (publ. 1636), noting that both instruments feature reentrant and pentatonic tuning (fig. 4.2).[14]

The instrument's name, like the instrument itself, also seems to have an Old World origin. An Uruguayan publication from 1823 refers to a chordophone, the "*changango*, for singing and sorrow."[15] Lauro Ayestarán, who uncovered the source, remarks: "Note one important detail: the first verse mentions the changango, which in Argentina at the moment is one of the terms used to refer to the *charango*, that small guitar with five double courses and an armadillo shell for a

Fig. 4.2 Five-course guitar, as illustrated in volume 3 of Marin Mersenne's *Harmonie universelle*

resonator. Nonetheless, more than a hundred years ago, the term *changango* was applied to the Creole guitar. [Poet] Hilario Ascasubi, in a footnote in his work *Paulino Lucero*—a gaucho recounting tales of the Great War [Uruguayan Civil War, 1839–51]—provides an authoritative description of the instrument: 'changango: an old and poorly constructed guitar.'"[16] We know of two variants of the term that denote types of guitar: *charanga*, in reference to a handle lute with a box—or, in Colombia, to one whose resonator is made of an armadillo shell—and *charranga*, a Guatemalan guitar.[17] All these terms are, apparently, onomatopoeic renderings of the act of strumming a chordophone.

None of these sources, however, suggest that the instrument was a satire of the guitar—quite the opposite, in fact. Mexican accounts refer to great skill on the part of the indigenous people in the manufacture of stringed instruments. Bernal Díaz del Castillo said that the Indians "made very good vihuelas."[18] One famous anecdote concerns [friar Bartolomé] de las Casas and a slave with three "large and very good vigüelas"; in this story, the slave-made instruments are so perfectly constructed that the bishop mistakes them for "vigüelas de Castilla" [Castilian vihuelas], later affirming that the Indians fashioned European instruments without having received any expert training in how to do so.[19] Nor does Juan de Torquemada skimp on praise for indigenous artisans: "The first Musical instruments, which they made, and used, were Flutes: later, *Chirimías* [a type of shawm]: then Crumhorns: and after those, Bowed Vihuelas . . . all in all there is no type of Musical instrument in use within God's church that the Indians do not possess, and use in all the Main Settlements and even the Minor ones: and they make them all, such that there is no longer any need to import them from Spain." He adds: "the Indians make all their own instruments for their own uses and purposes, and they play them in our convents. The other instruments, which are used by Secular Persons for comfort and rejoicing, the Indians also fashion; and they play them: Rebecs, Guitars, Discants [higher pitched instruments], Vihuelas, Harps, and Monochords; and so we can conclude that there is nothing they cannot make."[20]

Guamán Poma takes a similar approach in a reference to the evangelization of the natives in Peru: "And so the Indians of this kingdom serve his Majesty as his vassals, just as do the Castilian Spanish. They know and practice every type of occupation, artistic endeavor, manual labor, and are great singers of organum and plainsong and players of the vihuela, *flauta*, *chirimía*, trumpet, cornet, and bowed vihuela, organ."[21]

Apart from this snippet from Guamán Poma, I know of no other direct sources in reference to the Andean region. However, if we take into account that Mexican Indians and mestizos played an active role in the musical scene in early colonial times, we can assume that a similar process also unfolded in the Peruvian cities. According to Campos, in 1569 there were already Indian vihuelists in Peru, whom, he affirmed, "began to construct vihuelas that over time would become the *charango*."[22] Although Campos does not disclose his sources, the data I have gathered appear to corroborate his claim.

At this point, let me summarize the historical theory: the indigenous people quickly accepted European stringed instruments; they were made to or wished to learn to play them and applied themselves devotedly to the task, very soon mastering their use and their construction. With the passage of time, a chordophone with a handle and double courses originating in Europe was transformed into the *charango* as we know it today. I have demonstrated that the word *charango*, far from stemming from some Quechua word, is in fact an archaism of [Latin] American Spanish. And so I agree with Gallac, if only on this point, in denying the *charango* "any autochthonous genealogy—if we abide by its dictionary definition of *that which originates in the same country in which it lives, acts or works*" (emphasis added)—and also with Roel Pineda.[23]

## The Fabrication of the *Charango*'s History

At first, the scholarly point of view's authority in the debate over the *charango*'s history may appear irrefutable, given that, contrary to collective memory, it is based in concrete data. I now engage in a critical review of my own explanation above in order to lay out a problem in Latin American musicology that, I believe, tends to be overlooked: that of "historical vision." As Derrida pointed out, any text is limited to a particular textual system.[24] As such, writings on historical events tend to make use of concepts that do not fit into strict categories. It is therefore necessary to review those categories. I have been deliberate in describing my investigations in the language of a detective novel, characterizing my sources as "clues" and the evidence as "tracks," as such is the approach I have taken in my critique of musicological historiography: to seek out the truth and origin of the matter, as though the work of the musical historian consisted in filling in the gaps that separate us from the past. As such, it will not be difficult to establish a link between an early text like Gallac's, which places science before the "pure empiricism of popular esteem" in order to reach the conclusion that the researcher, in resolving historical problems, ought to avoid placing stock in folk traditions or opinions which may be confusing and contradictory; and a later one such as Corona Alcalde's article, in which the author is willing to make concessions to "intelligent speculation" until new information—that is, concrete evidence—comes to light to take its place, as though the existence of a single isolated example of a certain instrument were sufficient to supplant an entire process of great complexity.[25] On the contrary: what I propose in this essay—adopting Foucault's terminology—is an archaeological discourse analysis of the word *charango* to allow us to reexamine the criteria that have informed the writing of the instrument's history thus far.[26]

Lévi-Strauss, defending the historicity of myths, has reminded us that despite being rife with ambiguities and generalizations, the historical view is accepted as legitimate.[27] Let us examine some of these ambiguities in the case of the *charango*. What do we know of the *charango*? From a systematic perspective, the *charango* can be classified as a composite chordophone: a handle lute with a neck and a concave resonator.[28] According to Vega, the *charango* is distinct from the European guitar because of its armadillo-shell resonator, a viewpoint shared by Antonio Gonzáles Bravo, who refers to the instrument as "a small guitar around 55 centimeters long and 17 cm wide . . . with a box made of an armadillo shell."[29] However, one only needs to examine the *Mapa de los instrumentos musicales de uso popular en el Perú* (Map of folk musical instruments in Peru) to appreciate that the word *charango* refers to various lutes with box-shaped or concave resonators, with three, four, five, or six single or double courses, plucked with the fingers or a plectrum.[30] There is no reason to believe that this was not also the case in the past. Thus, we must ask ourselves: Which *charango* are we talking about when we refer to the history of the *charango*? The one referred to by the Tupiza cleric in 1814, did it have a concave resonator made of an armadillo shell? No historical evidence exists to confirm this. Quite the opposite, in fact: I find strange the idea that such a feature would have escaped the Tupiza priest's watchful eye. Even Turino was careful to point out that the *charangos* held by the sculpted mermaids could just as well have been vihuelas or guitars with concave resonators.[31] However, before divorcing the *charango* from its European predecessors, we ought to consider whether the indigenous or mestizo population of the eighteenth century made such a distinction—which seems highly unlikely given the number of stringed instruments referred to as *charangos* until the nineteenth century. A good example of the potential to be misled by "historical" data can be found in the book *Música y músicos de Latinoamérica* (Music and musicians of Latin America) by Otto Mayer-Serra.[32] Misled by Hilario Ascasubi's use of the term *changango* for guitar, Mayer-Serra ascribed the instrument to the Argentine gauchos of the nineteenth century.

The most common tuning applied to the instrument is the one I have reproduced in fig. 4.3 and which, in Peru, because of the sound resulting from the set of intervals produced by the strings when they are played undamped in ascending order, is known as "Santo Domingo" [using its solfège syllables][33]; it may be transposed down a fourth or up a fifth depending on the size of the instrument.[34]

Fig. 4.3 "Santo Domingo" *charango* tuning (the pitches represent the open strings of the instrument)

Fig. 4.4 Mersenne five-string guitar tuning

It is certain that this tuning has European antecedents, but on a formal level only, not in its sound design. According to Juan Bermudo's 1555 publication, various small chordophones featured courses tuned at octaves.[35] Many of these tunings could have influenced the sound of today's *charango*. Why, then, restrict ourselves to Mersenne's guitar, with its reentrant pentatonic tuning (fig. 4.4)?[36] I believe that the similarity established by Vega between the two instruments is completely arbitrary and stems from his diffusionist stance, which prefers the hypothesis of a transplant over a possible independent invention to explain a likeness.[37] Note how this "archaic European Guitar" is tuned. Vega was doubtless impressed by the reentrant tuning [tuning where open strings are not ordered from lowest to highest pitch], as can be deduced from the following: "Nowadays, the reentrant tuning is rare indeed; however, there is no doubt that in Europe, until 1600, there existed types of guitars that featured such an *anomaly*. Father Marin Mersenne, who published his *Harmonie Universelle* in 1636, mentions a type of guitar with five double courses, like a *charango*" (emphasis added). He continues: "As can be observed, the general contour of this archaic European [guitar]'s tuning is the same as that of our *Charango*: rising from the fifth to the fourth course; descending to the third course; then again rising through to the first course. As for the intervals, they only differ in the sounding of the thirds and firsts."[38]

Vega, like his contemporaries, believed in the survival in the Americas of early anomalies in European music. That was why he did not hesitate in drawing a link between the *charango*'s pentatonicism and that of Mersenne's guitar.[39] Today that contention is not tenable. Hortense Panum, unaware of the debate over the *charango*'s origins, has demonstrated that the reentrant tuning published by Mersenne was not as he described, instead corresponding to that of the five-course vihuela documented by Vicente Espinel, though without octave tuning, as can be seen in figure 4.5.[40] Indeed, if Espinel's guitar was tuned at octaves, the result would be Mersenne's tuning, without the reentrant tuning (fig. 4.6). It is

Fig. 4.5 Espinel five-course guitar tuning

Fig. 4.6 Five-course guitar tuning (with octave)

thus necessary to look to new sources and possibilities: the chordophone with four or five double courses mentioned by Praetorius, the small four-string *mandola* and the *chitarrino diuerso*, a small five-string guitar, that appear in Filippo Bonanni's *Gabinetto Armonico* (publ. 1723), or the Spanish guitars referred to by Gonzáles Bravo, among others.[41]

Some may take issue with the fact that we have not been focusing on the "authentic" *charango*, the one with five courses and an armadillo shell. In reality, it is not possible to do so. Even in 1940 José M. Arguedas referred to the Ayacuchan *charango* as a four-stringed instrument.[42] In addition, as already pointed out, the *charango* has many variants, as much in the shape of the table as of the resonator (fig. 4.7).[43]

This fluctuation between lutes with or without ribs [i.e., one-piece resonators], typical of the *charango* as well as of other Latin American chordophones such as the mandolin and the *mandola*[44] and other instruments beyond Peru,[45] beckons us to focus no longer on a single history of the *charango*, but on the possible histories of the various *charangos* and their connections with their European predecessors, the *bandurrias*, *guitarras*, *citoles*, and vihuelas. Indeed, the histories of these instruments, like those of their Andean successors, were not linear but fluctuated between lutes with or without ribs, as any study of medieval or Renaissance iconography will reveal.[46] The question now arises: was the armadillo shell really adopted because of a lack of materials, or was it inspired by European chordophones with concave resonators? As I have already noted, the Spanish themselves held chordophones built at the hands of indigenous artisans in high esteem, deeming them perfectly executed. Was it these same Indians who, unable to reproduce European guitars, created the crude *charango*, as dictated—in Gallac's terms—by their indigence? Or did they modify the instrument according to their own creative musical genius?

Fig. 4.7 *Charango* table shapes as illustrated in *Mapa de los instrumentos musicales de uso popular en el Perú*

We know that various terms are presently used to denote different varieties of *charangos*, among them *walaycho*, *ayquileño*, *kirki*, *maulincho*, *chillador*, and *qonqota*. As long as typological work has not been carried out on these varieties and we remain ignorant as to whether these terms are based in some taxonomical principle, it is very difficult to refer to the history of the instrument as a single process. In order to render discernible the first steps toward an archaeological discourse analysis of the *charango*, it will be necessary to review both playing and lute construction techniques, as well as *performance* characteristics in Europe, such as that seen in Guamán Poma's drawing—does it not hark back, in some ways, to European troubadour traditions?—to compare these with ethnohistorical and musicological material, not only to establish similarities, but also rifts, since the history of the *charango* can only be what it always has been: "a garden of forking paths."[47]

## Conclusion

I have expanded my argument in order to show that, within the historical view, the *charango*'s process of consolidation has been simplified to explain its contemporary manifestation, establishing half-truths as absolutes; but is it not true that this same method seems to drive the collective memory theory? I have found that the collective memory, rather than acknowledging a historical theory, prefers a thesis that lacks historicity—which is quite troubling to academics. Why would this be? I propose two reasons.

First, there exists a way of perceiving history that is different from that of the West, which, like the latter, tries to make sense of its present through the application of cognitive tools borne of its own cultural environment, such as oral traditions based on myth, rumor, and a vernacular etymology. In comparison with historical literature, oral tradition functions perfectly and adequately as a coding system for understanding and transmitting knowledge.

Second, there is a lack of faith in a coding system that stems from a tendency to discredit any other coding system that is not history-based, yet one that cannot arrive at a definition of history that avoids laying bare its own inherent contradictions, which are then covered up using a variety of "unhistorical" tactics: for example, the Tupiza *charango* is a historical bit of information but does not actually reveal any truths about the instrument that it purports to represent.

The question is not so much the veracity of the guitar satire theory, but what this theory conveys. The answer is not difficult to find: while the discourse of collective memory emphasizes the *charango*'s autochthonous character, the historical theory plays it down or even denies it. Today's *charangos* were constructed, both materially and conceptually, in Andean lands. How can we avoid calling the *charango* autochthonous, in the sense of *that which originated in the same country in which it exists, acts or is put to use*? If the term "charango" were of European origin, why would the collective memory not have adopted an indigenous term to make the instrument appear more *autochthonous*?[48]

Mestizo collective memory makes no bones in its assessment of the situation: the *charango* can only be explained as the transformation of a defeat, a musical conquest, into a messianic victory that positions the Indian at the center of cultural syncretism in the Andes in the present day. In this interpretation, the *charango* is seen as a symbol of cultural *mestizaje* [mixing], as a symbolic overemphasizing of the contribution of Europe to its consolidation. It is evident that the armadillo theory emphasizes the creativity of the indigene by highlighting his inventiveness in the face of scarcity. In this sense we can also understand the origin myth, which, as with the musical conquest story, also features the theme of overcoming adversity, made possible by the actions of an outside person (from the mountain), and represents the start of a new era. In its own way, we might say, we are dealing with a historical truth, if our idea of history includes the positionalities and beliefs of those that construct it.

I conclude with food for thought from Jeremy Beckett, writing in reference to Aboriginal Australians: "Nations are not made out of archeological remains, half-forgotten languages or folk traditions: these 'dead' elements only come alive in the course of political, social and cultural conflict, which is then represented as a realization of a destiny prefigured in that past."[49] Similarly, Ayacuchan collective memory reinvents its past, in a way that is different from our own means of restructuring our own past, to propel itself into a future that it aspires to. A move toward this way of constructing musical concepts, of understanding and transmitting them for the musical act—not to put its veracity to the test or to call it into question but to embrace it in all its historical dimensions—is the work of musicology at the start of the new millennium.

## Notes

1. I decided to keep interview sources anonymous. In general, however, information is owed to mestizo musicians, students, and immigrants from Ayacucho residing in Lima or outside the country, and to children of Ayacuchan immigrants who are interested in, or consume, Andean music. As did Thomas Turino, "The Urban-Mestizo Charango Tradition in Southern Peru: A Statement of Shifting Identity," *Ethnomusicology* 18, no. 2 (1984), 253–70, I have noted among these groups an ambiguous stance toward indigenousness: while on the one hand they tend to highlight their Andean identity, on the other, they take care to present themselves as different, and superior, to the indigenous.

2. J. Esain, P. Fernández, and R. Echarte, *El charango*, based on information by Fernando Paucar and Alberto Maqui, typed manuscript (Mar del Plata, 1987), 2.

3. In this section I focus on the work not only of Peruvian scholars but also of foreign ones. In including the latter, I do not wish to imply that they have shaped the Peruvian musicological perspective, but rather that they have formed a basis for this Peruvian perspective, having been accepted as valid.

4. Héctor Gallac, "El origen del charango," *Boletín Latino-Americano de Música* 3, no. 3 (1937), 73–75, p. 75.

5. Antonio Corona Alcalde, "La vihuela, el laúd y la guitarra en el Nuevo Mundo," (Actas del XV Congreso de la Sociedad Internacional de Musicología "Culturas musicales del Mediterráneo y sus ramificaciones" [Madrid, June 3–14, 1992]), *Revista de Musicología* 16, no. 3 (1993), 1360–72, p. 1363.

6. José Torre Revello, "Algunos libros de música traídos a América en el siglo XVI," in *Textos sobre música y folklore* (Bogotá: Instituto Colombiano de Cultura, 1978), 1:69–75.

7. Alejo Carpentier, *La música en Cuba* (Havana: Editorial Letras Cubanas, 1988), 18; Bernal Díaz del Castillo, "Verdadera historia de los sucesos de la conquista de la Nueva-España," in *Historiadores primitivos de Indias* (Madrid: Atlas, 1947 [1568]), 2:1–317, p. 306.

8. Corona Alcalde, "La vihuela," 1364–65.

9. José Carlos Campos, "Los primeros músicos españoles llegados al Perú y los siguientes mestizajes musicales producidos en el Perú," *Revista Musical de Venezuela* 10, no. 28 (1989), 127–48, p. 128; Robert Stevenson, *Music in Aztec and Inca Territory* (Berkeley: University of California Press, 1968), 289.

10. Robert Stevenson, *The Music of Peru: Aboriginal and Viceroyal Epochs* (Washington, D.C.: Pan American Union, 1960), 181.

11. Felipe Guamán Poma de Ayala, *Nueva corónica y buen gobierno* (Mexico: Siglo XXI, 1988 [1613]), 2:802–3.

12. Carlos Vega, *Los instrumentos musicales aborígenes y criollos de la Argentina* (Buenos Aires: Ediciones Centurión, 1946), 151.

13. Thomas Turino, "The Charango and the *Sirena*: Music, Magic and the Power of Love," *Latin American Music Review* 4, no. 1 (1983), 81–119, p. 109.

14. Vega, *Los instrumentos*, 151. I got this lead from Roel Pineda.

15. Lauro Ayestarán, *El folklore musical uruguayo* (Montevideo: Arca Editorial, 1977), 117.

16. Ibid. Ayestarán is referring to Hilario Ascasubi, *Paulino Lucero, o los gauchos del Río de la Plata cantando y combatiendo contra los tiranos de las Repúblicas Argentina y Oriental del Uruguay 1839 a 1851* (Paris: Paul Dupont, 1872).

17. José Díaz Gaínza, *Historia musical de Bolivia* (La Paz: Editorial Puerta del Sol, 1988), 173; Egberto Bermúdez, *Los instrumentos musicales en Colombia* (Bogotá: Universidad de Colombia, 1985), 32; Sybil Marcuse, *Musical Instruments: A Comprehensive Dictionary* (New York: Doubleday, 1964), 90.

18. Díaz del Castillo, "Verdadera historia," 311.

19. Bartolomé de las Casas, *Apologética historia sumaria* (Madrid: Alianza Editorial, 1992 [1555–57]), 1:596.

20. Juan de Torquemada, *Monarquía indiana* (Mexico: Editorial Porrúa, 1975 [1615]), 3:214.

21. Guamán Poma de Ayala, *Nueva corónica*, 764.

22. Campos, "Los primeros músicos españoles," 135, 144.

23. Gallac, "El origen del charango," 75.

24. Jacques Derrida, *De la grammatologie* (Frankfurt: Suhrkamp, 1998 [original in French, 1967]), 276.

25. Gallac, "El origen del charango," 74–75. Corona Alcalde, "La vihuela," 1363.

26. Michel Foucault, *Archäologie des Wissens* (Frankfurt: Suhrkamp, 1997 [original in French, 1969]), 198.

27. Claude Lévi-Strauss, *Mitológicas* (Mexico: Fondo de Cultura Económica, 1986 [original in French, 1964]), 1:122.

28. In this translation of the Hornbostel-Sachs classification system I adopt the phrase "with a concave resonator" as proposed by Egberto Bermúdez, "Las clasificaciones de instrumentos musicales y su uso en Colombia: un ensayo explicativo," *Revista Colombiana de Investigación Musical* 1, no. 1 (1985), 3–78, p. 60, as it seems more appropriate to me than Vega's term, "shell" (Vega, *Los instrumentos*, 150). Equally acceptable to me is the term "bowl-shaped" proposed by Argentine organologist Yolanda Velo (personal communication).

29. Vega, *Los instrumentos*, 150 and 152. Antonio Gonzáles Bravo, "Trompeta, flauta travesera, tambor y charango," *Boletín Latinoamericano de Música* 4, no. 4 (1938), 167–75, p. 174.

30. Instituto Nacional de Cultura, *Mapa de los instrumentos musicales de uso popular en el Perú* (Lima: Oficina de Música y Danza, 1978), 136–41.

31. Turino, "The Charango," 110.

32. Otto Mayer-Serra, *Música y músicos de Latinoamérica* (Mexico: Editorial Atlanta, 1947), 276.

33. To tune the *charango*, the player sings the interval sequence with help of these solfège syllables: "san" (high E), "to" (A), "do" (low E), "min" (C), "go" (G).

34. Héctor Luis Goyena, "El charango en el departamento de Chuquisaca (Bolivia)," *Temas de Etnomusicología* 2 (1986), 6–28, p. 19–22, has documented this same procedure in Bolivia, referring to other sequences of intervals only in the case of the Pascua [Easter] tuning.

35. Juan Bermudo, *[El libro llamado] Declaración de instrumentos musicales*, facsimile (Kassel: Bärenreiter, 1957 [1555]), xxix.

36. Marin Mersenne, *Harmonie universelle* (Paris: Éditions du Centre National de la Recherche Scientifique, 1963 [1636]), 3:191.

37. Carlos Vega, "Clasificación de la música," *Musicología en Latinoamérica*, ed. Zoila Gómez García (Havana: Editorial Arte y Literatura, 1985), 164–83, p. 178.

38. Vega, *Los instrumentos*, 153, 153–54.

39. Ibid., 154.

40. Hortense Panum, *The Stringed Instruments of the Middle Ages: Their Evolution and Development* (London: William Reeves, 1971), 453.

41. Michael Praetorius, *Syntagma musicum* (Kassel: Bärenreiter, 1985 [1619]), 2:54–55; Filippo Bonanni, *Antique Musical Instruments and Their Players. 152 Plates from Bonanni's 18th-Century "Gabinetto Armonico"* (New York: Dover, 1964 [1723]), 53–54; Gonzáles Bravo, "Trompeta," 174–75.

42. José María Arguedas, "El charango," in *Indios, mestizos y señores* (Lima: Editorial Horizonte, 1985), 53–57, p. 54.

43. Instituto Nacional de Cultura, *Mapa de los instrumentos musicales*, 138.

44. Ibid., 133–35.

45. See Raoul d'Harcourt and Marguerite d'Harcourt, *La música de los incas y sus supervivencias*, trans. Roberto Miró Quesada, Mari-Blanca Gregori de Pinto, and Jaime Campodónico (Lima: Oxy, 1990 [original in French, 1925]), 83; Egberto Bermúdez, *Colección de instrumentos musicales José Ignacio Perdomo Escobar* (Bogotá: Banco de la República, 1986), 48.

46. Sebastian Virdung, *Musica getutscht und ausgezogen* (Kassel: Bärenreiter, 1970 [1511]); Curt Sachs, *Handbuch der Musikinstrumentenkunde* (Hildesheim: Editorial Georg Olms, 1967 [1930]), 205–35; Panum, *Stringed Instruments*, 407–71.

47. Editors' note: "a garden of forking paths" is an allusion to Jorge Luis Borges's short story, "El Jardín de senderos que se bifurcan" (1941). His vision of "forking paths" is often cited as inspiration by scholars.

48. Is another term for the *charango*, *maulinche*, in fact a poor reflection of Aymara etymology, being, according to Aymara informants, derived from *malincha*, meaning "a lively child," "happy" and "lively"?

49. Jeremy Beckett, "The Past in the Present; the Present in the Past: Constructing a National Aboriginality," in *Past and Present: The Construction of Aboriginality*, ed. Jeremy Beckett (Canberra: Australian Institute of Applied Sciences, 1988), 191–217, p. 212.

# 5

# Decline or Progress?

## *Eighteenth-Century Music and Nineteenth-Century Nationalism*

ALEJANDRO VERA

A study of the influence of nineteenth-century nationalism on musical history is not novel in and of itself. Its role in the formation of national styles and repertoires, whether in highbrow or oral traditional music, is a well-known fact on which numerous works of interest have already been written in the Hispano-American context.[1] In general terms, these works have examined the influence of nationalism on the music of their own time, principally in the nineteenth and early twentieth centuries, which has allowed for the study of the output of important composers who were immersed in the search for national identity. In addition, one can relate this tendency to the historicist principle, according to which each music should be judged according to the aesthetic and ideological criteria of its time. In this way, the category of nationalism would serve to study the music of the period in which it was born and developed as such, but not that of later eras, nor, much less, those preceding its appearance.[2]

In spite of the logic of this contention, in this article I propose adopting a different perspective: focusing on the Chilean case, I study the impact of nineteenth-century nationalism on the constructions of the musical history of the preceding century, that is to say, on the discourses (histories, chronicles, etc.) about eighteenth-century music that emerged along with independence.[3] In doing this, I base myself on the hypothesis that the current opinions and judgments about pre-republican music, many of them accepted as absolute truths, come in great

---

Originally published by Alejandro Vera as "¿Decadencia o progreso? La música del siglo XVIII y el nacionalismo decimonónico," *Latin American Music Review* 31, no. 1 (2010), 1–39.  Translated by Sydney Hutchinson with permission.

measure from the aspirations, tastes, and ideologies of those who wrote about it in the nineteenth and twentieth centuries. I have discussed this topic in a previous article, where I argue that the exaggerations about the precariousness of colonial music in "traditional" historiography,[4] represented by historian Eugenio Pereira Salas and musicologist Samuel Claro Valdés, can be explained in great part by the influence of the nationalist intellectual project initiated around 1840 by José Victorino Lastarria and others.[5] However, here I attempt to demonstrate that the impact of nationalism on the image of the eighteenth century was more complex—and even contradictory—than for the earlier colonial period.

A proposition such as this one is justified by the well-known influence that modern nationalism—or rather nationalist ideology, whose principal objectives were to achieve autonomy, unity, and national identity—had on the makeup and development of history as a discipline.[6] As is known, the role of the latter consisted of giving each country a past and an identity, which explains the tendency of historiography of the nineteenth century and first half of the twentieth to concentrate on great people, institutions, and events in national history—what we know as "grand history"—as well as its largely political character, and above all its difficulty in achieving the objective character to which its authors aspired.[7] This had important consequences for the image of the past the historians projected; for we have long known that the past is related not only to the characteristics of the historical period being treated, but also to the historian's present.[8]

The hypothesis that an ideology emerging in the nineteenth century should determine the current image of the eighteenth century coincides with some points of view that consider history as a synchronic fabric in which one event can affect another independently from its placement in time. In reality, this occurs in the discursive (or textual) plane of history, or rather in the stories and interpretations made from it. An article, chronicle, or commemorative poem about a prior historical event influences it, not because it really modifies it, but because it changes our way of interpreting it; the same can be said of a musical text.[9] From this, one can deduce that colonial history cannot be adequately studied without also knowing the evolution of later eras.

In this article, however, I consider that the discursive dimension of history is just one of its parts, which must be put in tension with its factual (or real) dimension.[10] This implies going beyond the dichotomy between interpretation and documentary work that is still so common in our discipline. And this is no easy job because, in general terms, this dichotomy is characteristic both of traditional musicology and of the so-called new musicology.[11] In broad strokes, we could say that, for the former, the role of the musicologist consisted of describing and chronologically ordering objective historical works and deeds in order to interpret them later, once a "sufficient" quantity of information was amassed.[12]

The latter, although it recognized the role of the musicologist in the construction of historical facts,[13] also considered the process of description and ordering as a stage prior to, and thus different from, the interpretation or criticism of the same, which constituted its fundamental objective.[14] Of course, this last point implied a contradiction: on the one hand, it was said that there were no objective facts that would be spontaneously delivered to the scholar, since all were mediated by interpretations (i.e., they were discursively constructed); and on the other hand, one conceived of an initial stage in musicological research that consisted of the objective description of facts (without interpretation).

This disassociation, and the superior level attributed to interpretation, perhaps explains why new musicology has in certain measure left out the "empirical evidence" that could support its hypotheses,[15] as well as the fact that it is highly critical of the interpretations or points of view of traditional musicology but, at the same time, quite uncritical of the documentary data it has provided. This does not only concern the musicological field: in his recent history of the seventeenth century, Alfredo Jocelyn-Holt Letelier assumes, based on the testimony of Pereira Salas, that Chile had to wait until 1707 to know the harpsichord (*clavicordio*),[16] which joined to other data would demonstrate that Chile was "outside of all the [main] networks [of cultural exchange]."[17] As was to be expected, more recent musicological research has demonstrated that this instrument was found in Chile as early as the sixteenth century.[18] And although in the case of a general history, it is understandable that the author cannot verify the truth of specific data on music, the same passive attitude toward the statements of Pereira Salas can be noted in some specifically musicological works, as we see later.

Confronted with this supposed dichotomy between description and interpretation, it is worth mentioning that the chronological ordering of facts, although it seems at first glance a neutral operation, really entails assessment, since it is based on the principle that there is an evolutionary and thus hierarchical relationship between them—"what *is* is an improvement over what *was*" [original emphasis].[19] Thus, in a strict sense, it is practically impossible not to interpret, especially considering that the historiography of recent decades has made evident the textual (interpretative) nature of the sources with which the historian works.[20] From this point of view, even the document goes from being an inert object with just one meaning to an active component in the process of interpretation that also challenges the scholar, since, just like any text, it has within itself the ideological battles, dialogues, and tensions that characterize language in society.[21]

Thus, in this article I contrast historiographical works on the eighteenth century not only with the ideological determinants of the period in which they were written, but also with new, recently discovered documentary evidence about the music of that era, without forgetting its textual nature, but paying attention to what it tells us about the past. In this way, I attempt to join archival research with historiographic criticism, avoiding the aforementioned dichotomy between the two. In fact, these same documents will help prove the distance between the interpretations of traditional historiography and the musical past it tried to reflect, and allow us to think about the musicology of the present, as we see in the final part of the article.

But before moving on to the principal topic, I make a brief aside to examine the influence that nationalism had on the image of eighteenth-century music in Spain, not only because of the need to study Latin American music in the global context into which it was inserted at the time,[22] but also because it provides interesting food for thought for the Chilean case, especially due to the differences between it and the Spanish one.

## The Eighteenth Century and Spanish Musical Historiography

According to the traditional studies by Mariano Soriano Fuertes, Felipe Pedrell, and others, Felipe V's assumption of the throne in 1700 caused the introduction of foreign music to Madrid. If in the beginning mainly French dances came, soon the Italian style began to impose itself, principally after the 1703 arrival of the Trufaldines opera company, with its first production of Cesti's *Il pomo d'oro*, and that of Queen Isabel of Farnesio in 1717. Little by little, Italian composers displaced Spaniards from the top positions, not without the natural resistance of the latter, who fought to maintain their style. Likewise, traditional Spanish genres such as the *villancico* would end up losing their essence, as the recitative-aria pair replaced the classic *estribillo-coplas* [refrain-stanzas] structure. Naturally, all of this would have brought with it a loss of national identity and the consequent decline of Spanish music.[23]

In a more recent era, a number of studies have demonstrated various aspects of the inexactitude of this report. First, the process of reopening toward foreign music began before the dynastic change: Felipe IV had already put on several operatic shows and had in his service important persons who favored the introduction of recitative in the court theater.[24] Some years later, beginning around 1677, there was a reform advanced by Juan José of Austria as prime minister that "musically defined the use of Italian pieces and of instrumental groups related to the trio sonata."[25] Second, the introduction of Italian opera occurred later than previously thought, since the Trufaldines were not really an opera company but a comedic one. Thus, the lasting performance of operas sung in Italian, by artists of that nationality, began in 1738 with the debut of Francesco Corselli's *Alessandro nelle Indie* (Alexander in India).[26] Third, and this is even more relevant, the introduction of foreign genres did not imply the disappearance of local genres, nor a fight to the death between them, but a relatively peaceful coexistence that gave rise to certain forms of hybridity; for instance, the *zarzuela Viento es la dicha de amor* (Wind is the joy of love) by José de Nebra demonstrates the coexistence of recitative and aria with some four-part choruses, a seguidilla, and some *coplas* [couplets] proper to the Spanish stage tradition.[27] Likewise, its aria "Teme aleve fementido" (Fear treacherous perfidy), preserved in Montevideo, begins with an instrumental ritornello in Italian style, divided in two parts, which helps to structure the entire work.[28] This fact points to a radical contradiction with the traditional ideas about Nebra as a defender of Spanish style. If Emilio Cotarelo y Mori and Anglés considered him "the Lope de Vega of Spanish music" and a "Hispanicist to the bone,"[29] respectively, his own preserved pieces show that Italianized procedures and forms were part of his compositional language.

So where, then, did the myth of the Italian invasion and the heroic but unfruitful resistance of some Spanish composers come from? The explanation, at least in part, seems to be that such a story was a good fit for the nationalist ideology in vogue at the moment that Francisco Barbieri, Pedrell, Cotarelo y Mori, and others began to historicize the musical past; above all, because in the Spanish case the rejection of any foreign influence as a constitutive part of national identity was especially virulent, something which, although it seems paradoxical, was largely a product of the desire to incorporate Spanish musical history into the European discourse.[30] At the same time, the idea shared among all of them—that a moment of recuperation of lost musical traditions was beginning in the late nineteenth century—was also related to the aforementioned ideology.[31]

But this narrative was not a disinterested one. In the case of the composer and bibliophile Francisco Barbieri, for example, his hypothesis about the existence of an autochthonous school born in the sixteenth century, which disappeared under the hegemony of Italian opera and was restored in the late nineteenth century, was nothing but a defense of his own activity as a *zarzuela* composer at a moment in which international competition was intense and was putting the success of the genre at risk.[32] Hence was also born the topic—initiated by another *zarzuela* composer, Soriano Fuertes—of the supposed simplicity and expressivity of the Spanish musical school of the sixteenth century,[33] which constituted a means of vindicating the simplicity these composers attributed to their own works.[34]

Although a summary like this one is excessively brief and does not do justice to the substantial contributions of traditional Spanish historiography, it does allow us to affirm that nationalism pervaded a great deal of its postulates, and it presents various ideas that will be important when we get into the Chilean case. The first is that nineteenth-century nationalism affected not only the image of the eighteenth century but also that of the sixteenth and seventeenth centuries; the latter had been practically ignored until Barbieri took an interest in the later song collections—he was planning to edit that of Sablonara (1625)[35]—which he saw as a continuation of the *Cancionero musical de palacio* collection. Likewise, Pedrell began to edit this repertoire because he considered it representative of a particularly Spanish music.[36] It is therefore difficult for us to understand narratives about the eighteenth century without considering discourses about earlier centuries. Second, the postulates of Soriano and Barbieri largely constituted a defense of the music they themselves cultivated, in a clear relationship between past and present. Third, one of the fundamental problems in Spanish historiography was the difficulty of integrating the foreign presence into its own identity. This led it to fit musical processes to certain dates and political events to which a specific meaning had been attributed from the nationalist point of view—the paradigmatic one being the arrival of a "foreign" dynasty around 1700 as the beginning of the supposed loss of Hispanic musical identity. In the view of its earliest scholars, the Spanish eighteenth century represented decline because in this era music had become de-Hispanified.[37]

## The Chilean Case

One of the first obstacles a critical work on traditional historiography will come up against is, paradoxically, one of the critiques most commonly made of it: that of being essentially descriptive and limiting itself to ordering facts in a chronological sequence. This entails the supposition that the "hard data" such historiography offers do not deserve to be questioned further. As I mentioned in the beginning, such a reading supposes an important contradiction with the revisionist works of recent years, which have demonstrated that traditional studies were strongly influenced by ideologies and personal aspirations, and thus were far from the objectivity they championed.[38]

I have also indicated that although more recent musicology has been interested in the influence of ideology on the construction of history, one of its principal claims was always that of getting beyond the "descriptivism" of traditional musicology,[39] a claim that is also found in Chilean musicological production.[40] However, in the case at hand, the conception of Pereira Salas's work as descriptive comes from his own prologue to the essential book *Los orígenes del arte musical en Chile* (The origins of musical art in Chile), published in 1941: "The present work is based on a detailed study carried out in archives, libraries, and private papers, which gives the book a distinctly historical, and in part musical archaeological, character. Here there are more facts than doctrines. The author has preferred to allow the documents to speak rather than to fill the spaces with rhetoric and imagination."[41]

This interpretation of his own work was accepted almost without reservation by the specialists of his time and afterward. Charles Seeger considered it an excellent example of the "scientific and objective type of historiography,"[42] and Luis Merino did nearly the same some years later.[43] It was thought, then, that *Los orígenes del arte musical en Chile* was an objective book largely because its author had described it as such, by which I do not mean to say that Pereira Salas deliberately falsified the character of his work, but rather that his intent to be descriptive did not guarantee the achievement of his purpose. And we frequently pay too much attention to the intentions of the subjects we study, forgetting the unintentional effects of their actions when they come up against a certain context, social or ideological.[44]

A closer look at the Pereira Salas book allows one to notice its fundamentally interpretive character. The numerous thematic and temporal holes are covered with a priori judgments like the following:

> This monastery [San Agustín] seems to have stood out as far as music was concerned, since besides having Baltasar de los Reyes in its order, it had a music teacher, Don Pedro Aranguiz Colodio, who gave organ lessons from 1608 to 1609 for a salary of forty *patacones*.
>
> The primacy of San Agustín lessened a bit after 1652, the year in which the Santa Iglesia cathedral was inaugurated.[45]

As we see, the author assumes that the San Agustín monastery was the preeminent one and that it was displaced by the cathedral forty years later, without giving further support. We could attribute a positivist character to this statement: without information about other religious institutions, one assumes that there was no significant musical activity in them. However, Pereira Salas's statements entail a deeper interpretation: that the Santiago of the seventeenth century could not have more than one musically well-off religious institution because of colonial Chile's endemic poverty. In effect, the general image of the colony that Pereira Salas presents is that of a dark age characterized by isolation and uninteresting musical activity, especially in comparison with the republican era. The author even indicates that during colonial days "music was played by ear, and children learned to sing like birds." In addition, he situates the beginning of "musical art" in Chile in 1819, the year in which a Danish trader, Carlos Drewetcke, brought a few "symphonies and quartets by Haydn, Mozart, Beethoven, and Cromer."[46] The fact that both statements, especially the first, contradict the data this same historian offers in other parts of the book,[47] implies that they are conditioned less by the era under examination than by the cultural and ideological context in which he was immersed. And given that this context cannot be reduced to a single topic, I am obliged to consider other aspects before moving on to the one that lies at the center of this study.

At first glance, behind the supposed superiority of the Republic lies the classic vision of history as progress, present in Chilean historiography since the nineteenth century.[48] The following statement by another author exemplifies the thought expressed by the majority of historians, even up to the present day: "The supply of objects necessary for well-being . . . passed through different stages in the Capitanía General [colonial government], from a miserable level to a high one. . . . In the later years of Spanish domination, Chile's Capitanía General was properly established."[49] But the hypotheses of Pereira Salas are also based on the traditional idea about the autonomy of art: the progress that had occurred around 1819 was due to the fact that before that year music had been "a mere social diversion, a frivolous way of killing time, or a liturgical or civic accompaniment for religious and political life."[50] With this statement, the author means to bring attention to the establishment of private and public concerts in a modern sense, especially after the arrival of [Spanish artist and composer] Isidora Zegers and the development of the so-called philharmonic societies,[51] activities that seem rather contemplative and distant from any specific social function. However, Pereira Salas omits at least two fundamental aspects here: first, the activity developed by Zegers and others in the 1820s presents clear analogies with the salons [*tertulias*] the Spaniard María Luisa de Esterripa, wife of the governor Luis Muñoz de Guzmán, and some intellectuals developed in the later years of the colonial period,[52] in turn clearly related to others from earlier periods that I analyze later, which denotes the arbitrary character of his naming 1819 as the beginning of "artistic" activity. Second, the historian forgets the important social function these events had, since both Zegers and Esterripa represented an educated elite that was trying to legitimate itself through the adoption of practices different from those of common people, and the novel repertoires gave them an exclusive connotation that contributed to the success of their purposes. In fact, the political use of autonomous art has been subject to sound criticism in recent decades,[53] and, if one may use analogies with the present, it does not seem forced to exemplify it with a brief fragment of the cultural policy of the Chilean military dictatorship in 1975, evidently meant to justify the disappearance of the leftist musical movement: "Art can no longer be committed to political ideologies, but only to the truth of the one who created it."[54]

But the supposed break of 1819 was not really an original idea of Pereira Salas. Rather, it came from the famous *Recuerdos de treinta años* (Memories of thirty years), published in 1872–74 by the musician José Zapiola. It was he who affirmed that in that year Drewetcke had brought the aforementioned pieces by Haydn and others and that "he brought the musicians together, not without difficulty, certain days each week to execute some of these compositions, playing the violoncello part and giving out advice on the art, which was unknown until that time."[55] In addition, he indicated that the arrival of Zegers in 1822 meant a true "musical revolution," because she brought Rossini opera scores, among other things. These ideas appear repeatedly in the Chilean musicological literature,[56] which demonstrates the enormous influence Zapiola had on the construction of colonial and republican history. Nevertheless, and in spite of his importance as a source, his data must be put into perspective because of the very nature of the text. As Ángel Rama explains, during a time (1870–1900) in which the city [Santiago] was undergoing dramatic growth and transformation that threatened the control of the intellectual elite, discourses about the "past city" did not constitute an objective narrative about the earlier era—although they were dressed up with "the plausible discourse of nineteenth-century realism"—but rather a means of maintaining that control and setting up the cultural bases for a new era. For the same reason, it is imprudent to say that the references have a rigorous character.[57]

In fact, Zapiola's statements are far from being disinterested given that, immediately afterward, he recalls that around 1819 he was carrying out his "first musical studies."[58] In other words, what Zapiola indicates is that true musical art in Chile began with him, and this constitutes a powerful reason for which to doubt his statements.

As significant as the three aspects examined (historical progress, the autonomy of art, and Zapiola's influence) seem, in my opinion, nationalist ideology was a determining factor in the negative image of the colonial period,[59] given that the colonial past represented Spanish domination, and thus a foreign incursion into national history.[60] Although this can be observed at least since the beginning of the independence process around 1810, in the historiographic field, the initiator of the anticolonial paradigm is José Victorino Lastarria, with his essay "Investigaciones sobre la influencia social de la conquista" (Inquiry on the social influence of the conquest [of Chile]), published in 1844.[61] As Bernardo Subercaseaux states, the central idea of this piece is that progress would only be achieved if Chile would de-Hispanify, thus recuperating its lost identity.[62] Although some of Lastarria's ideas—especially about the means of making history—were questioned in later historiography, the rejection of the Spanish presence during the colonial period was an idea common to all Chilean historians of the nineteenth century.[63]

Pereira Salas's statements about the unprecedented musical growth in the republican era and the very poor prior conditions, as well as some inconsistencies he falls into through his determination to maintain this idea, can be better understood in light of the aforementioned ideological context. It seems not accidental that the chapter in *Los orígenes del arte musical en Chile* dedicated to "the first national composers" begins with Manuel Robles, a musician active in the first decades of the nineteenth century who the author believes "deserves a preferential place" for having written "our first national song."[64] At this point, it is important to remember that we are referring to one of the historians most interested in the colony, to which he dedicated invaluable contributions in music as well as in other spheres.[65] Consequently, I am arguing not that he disregarded the period, but rather that the influence of nationalism caused him to argue for the great superiority of the republican period, a fact that may explain some contradictory opinions in his work, which run from even a Hispanic character to the exaltation of independence.[66] In any case, we can imagine the way in which his ideas were seized upon by specialists who, unlike him, did not feel appreciation or particular interest in the colonial period.[67]

However, we are not speaking only of a historiographic nationalism related to the past, but of one that is strongly linked to the present of the author. Around the time of the publication of *Los orígenes del arte musical en Chile*, Pereira Salas was already immersed in the recovery of Chilean musical traditions, a task that would occupy an important part of his professional life. Just two years after he published that book, a commission made up of him and six others created the Instituto de Investigaciones Folklóricas (Institute of Folkloric Research), whose principal objectives were the systematic registry, study, and diffusion of national folklore through concerts. When in 1944 the institute came to belong officially to the Facultad de Bellas Artes de la Universidad de Chile (Fine Arts Department of the University of Chile), Pereira Salas was named its head, and at the end of the year he published, together with Jorge Urrutia Blondel, a collection of traditional and folk Chilean airs.[68] In turn, a commission constituted of him and others granted the 1945 Premio Nacional de Arte (National Art Prize) to Pedro Humberto Allende, considering that his work demonstrated an "exaltation of the national" with a language of indisputable musical value. It is significant that this was the first time such a distinction was awarded to a musician, as is the fact that Allende had a close friendship with Felipe Pedrell, whose role in the development of Spanish musical nationalism has already been noted.[69] Within this context, the account of Pereira Salas, with regard to independence as an awakening of artistic-musical duty, acquires a clearer meaning.

Because of all of this, it is noteworthy that the image of the eighteenth century shown by traditional historiography is a little different from that of previous centuries. In comparison with the republican era, this is a period deemed as having neither a consolidated written tradition nor a rigorous musical pedagogy, to the point that importing a harpsichord treatise at the end of that century constituted a "notable exception," and the musical text of "bargain" compositions was "of such harmonic and melodic poverty that it is not worth the trouble of even the most summary analysis."[70] Compared with the prior era, however, this is a century of progress in all aspects of musical life: the presence of instruments, the religious processions, cathedral music, and inaugural ceremonies or royal wakes. Pereira Salas even alludes to the "intellectual progress of the woman" that "helped to raise the tenor of salon life."[71] Predictably, these ideas are also gathered in the book on the history of music in Chile by Claro Valdés and Urrutia Blondel.[72]

There is no doubt that the evolutionary paradigm of history already noted is present in these interpretations. However, this fact does not explain why the quantitative and qualitative leap assigned to the eighteenth century should be considerably greater than that attributed to the seventeenth century: although Pereira Salas and Claro Valdés assume that, beginning in 1600, dedication to war is not exclusive and this permits an incipient development of musical life, at the same time—and in a contradictory way—the latter affirms that "the Chile of the seventeenth century did not reflect European cultural advancement, occupied as it was with war and colonization. . . . Nothing was known of the great European advances and the Chilean colonists dedicated themselves to minor tasks, full of terror faced with natural phenomena and submissively obedient to the royal decrees that came to them from across the sea."[73] The paradigm of history as progress is insufficient, then, for understanding the meaning of these statements. However, the introductory paragraphs to the chapter on the eighteenth century in *Los orígenes del arte musical en Chile* can shed light on this point:

> The eighteenth century represents the sovereignty of the French spirit in the world. . . . Rigid Spain adopts the Gallic smile and not far from the wastelands of El Escorial we see the emergence of French roses in the gardens of La Granja. . . . In the shadow of concealed official protection, the ship owners and merchants of Britannia arrived, and with them the various manufactured products and advances of civilization. The contagion was immediate in the colonies. The Governors wanted to demonstrate their power with carriages and livery; billiards helped the creole playboys to kill time elegantly; carpets and tapestries covered their daises; vases, urns, and panes of glass replaced the copper cauldrons and the simple national pottery.[74]

Subsequently, Pereira Salas substitutes musical instruments for these household objects: in 1707 the "first" harpsichord appeared on the dais of President Ibáñez y Peralta, an occurrence "eclipsed" a few years later by the "novelties" introduced by Governor Cano de Aponte, who brought in his baggage a harpsichord, four violins, a harp, and several tambourines.[75] Additionally, Claro Valdés affirms: "in this era, culture has a unique flowering and the country of Chile, in a period of stable peace due to the end of the war of Arauco [a long-running conflict between colonial Spaniards and the Mapuche people], enters a stage of accelerated development."[76]

For them, as well as for the historians they cite, the introduction of French taste and "sociability" in Spain and its colonies, with the support of a French king, constitutes a sign of progress.[77] Apart from the questionable fact that all these positive changes are attributed exclusively to high culture, Pereira Salas and Claro Valdés's interpretation of the dynastic change is the opposite of that of traditional Spanish historiography: if, as we saw, the latter demonized foreign music, attributing the beginning of the decline of national music to it, Chilean historiography characterized it as a positive influence for the country. However—and this is a central idea in the present work—both points of view are influenced by the same nationalist ideology that emerged in the nineteenth century, given that when one considers that "rigid Spain adopts the Gallic smile," as Pereira Salas states, or that the arrival of French influence allowed "a unique flowering" of culture, as Claro Valdés claims, what is basically being argued is that Chile progressed because it de-Hispanified. And this is clearly related to the anticolonial model initiated by Lastarria and others, which brought them to look precisely to France in the search for optimal models for the construction of the new nation. What is interesting here is that it shows us how the same ideology can produce very different and even opposing historiographic constructions, depending on the cultural context into which it is inserted. Thus, the Chilean tale is a kind of inverse canon of Spanish historiographic discourse: both share the difficulty of incorporating the foreign presence—Italian in one case, Spanish in the other—into the history of the nation, and they therefore reflect the nationalist ideas of their time. Both also coincide in the interpretation of 1700 as the year in which the Spanish empire begins to de-Hispanify. The difference is in the negative and positive connotation they respectively assign to this fact, although it depends, in the end, on a very similar way of conceiving history.

## Eighteenth-Century Music Revisited: The Private Sphere

With the previous proposals, I do not mean to state that no aspects of musical life developed in the eighteenth century. What I do say is rather that the identification of this nationalist component in traditional writings makes one suspect that many of the "advances" and "novelties" attributed to this century could really be a continuation of processes previously begun, and the same could be true of the supposed republican break. But to find this out it will be necessary to revisit the eighteenth century from a different perspective, comparing it with previous eras and, above all, paying more attention to the diverse sources that bear witness to the colonial past. Since it is impossible to formulate a global synthesis in the space allowed, I limit myself to examining an aspect that has scarcely been studied, even by more recent historiography: the cultivation of music in the private sphere.

Considering Zapiola's statements about the supposed opening process experienced in 1819, it will be interesting to begin with a glance at musical importation in the previous period.[78] A look through the entries registered in the Archivo Nacional de Chile (National Archives of Chile) has allowed me to inventory fifty musical objects—instruments, scores, and others—that arrived in the port of Valparaíso between 1769 and 1799.[79] One of the first conclusions that arise from the inventory (appendix 1) is not especially new: almost all of the objects came from the port of Callao, Lima, which demonstrates the influence that the capital of the viceroyalty had even at the end of the eighteenth century.[80] However, that port also acted as an intermediary, so that some of the objects originally came from Spain and other places, such as the noteworthy musical clock that arrived in 1790.

Among the instruments, the *clave* [harpsichord], is predominant and appears in 35 of the 50 objects inventoried. However, in 1791 a "clave o forte peano" [harpsichord or forte piano] arrived, which suggests that the term *clave* was ambiguous in this period. A proper "forte piano" also appears in 1785,[81] demonstrating the importance keyboard instruments had in the second half of the eighteenth century, although this does not mean that these were used exclusively, since the same inventory shows the importation of four psalteries, one violin, and even some sleigh bells (*cascabeles*).

On the other hand, in the entries registered from the Andean mountain region, which unfortunately have been preserved in only a fragmentary way, we find some flutes, a psaltery, and a violin, besides the obligatory harpsichord that Antonio de Segovia brought in 1776 (appendix 2). The fact that the mountain region was a route for the importation of musical instruments, which were brought in carts that had to pass over heights that sometimes easily surpassed 3,000 meters, demonstrates that ideas about musical isolation based on the geographic characteristics of Chile must be further elucidated.[82]

There is no doubt that the registered entries reflect only a small part of the musical instruments and objects that arrived in Chile in the eighteenth century. The fact that guitars and harps are not included is proof of this, since they were instruments much used at the time, as notarized documents confirm. For instance, in Ignacio Hurtado's 1774 inventory we find a harp and a guitar, and in that of Francisco Javier Ureta we find a harp and a harpsichord.[83] "Large guitars" are found in the inventory of Ambrosio Regoy, originally from Galicia, in 1763, and that of Gaspar Flores in 1793.[84] In addition, "a red guitar from China" whose characteristics are unfamiliar to me appear in 1723 in the will of María Josefa del Solar.[85] It is possible to imagine at least two explanations for this omission: first, the guitar and the harp were surely manufactured in Chile[86] so that their importation was unnecessary; second, both instruments had been popularized in the eighteenth century, so it is possible that around 1770 they did not yet have the exclusive connotations the Santiago elite was looking for.

Some of the instruments were destined for religious institutions in other cities. The "little organ" of 1792 and the 1796 harpsichord were for the Dominican monastery in Valparaíso, and the 1797 organ for the monastery of the same order in Coquimbo. In addition, a crate of church music papers had the final destination of the cathedral of Córdoba in Tucumán [now in Argentina] (appendix 1 [at 1799]), which demonstrates that Chile could also be an intermediate point between Callao and other destinations. These cases lie a bit outside the private sphere, but their nature is the same as that of the goods destined for homes: they are mainly concrete orders placed from Chile and paid for by the addressees.

The musical papers for the Cathedral of Córdoba bring us to an interesting topic, not mentioned until now: the importation and reception of scores. Although the registered entries are very brief on this, it is evident that, just as in the case of the instruments, they only contain the suggestions of a practice that was much more common.[87] Disregarding the musical books documented in religious institutions,[88] in the 1775 inventory of goods of the *maestro de campo* (field marshal) Andrés de Rojas y Lamadris (or Lamadrid) we find an "art of music" in Portuguese[89] that could match the one Antonio Fernandes published in Lisbon in 1626.[90] Also, in the 1798 inventory of José Cabrera, a canon in the Santiago cathedral, we find a book of plainchant by "Roel" and the well-known treatise on modulation by Antonio Soler, published in Madrid in 1762.[91] This last is very interesting because, if the other treatises found in Chile could be described as traditional, Soler's proposals for modulating from one key to another were novel and generated quite a bit of controversy in their time.[92] We have also known for some years of the existence of the "Sixth Book" (*Libro sesto*) of María Antonia Palacios, a manuscript that dates to the end of the eighteenth century and mainly contains music for keyboard instruments.[93] To this can be added a new manuscript by the Spanish guitarist Santiago de Murcia, dating to 1722 and recently found in Chile by the author. Although this source was doubtlessly copied in Spain, the content of the prologue and other data make one think that it could have arrived in Chile—or at least in Latin America—in the eighteenth century. Its music includes principally pieces of the Hispanic tradition, French suites and dances that reveal the African influence in the Iberoamerican sphere, such as *zarambeques* and *cumbés* [colonial dance genres possibly associated with communities of African descent].[94]

Although the identities and familial links of the recipients are beyond the scope of the present work, I cannot leave out María Josefa Morandé, who received some musical papers in 1790 (appendix 1). According to the available information, she was the daughter of Juan de la Morandé and Juana del Solar, and sister of María Ignacia and Francisca Javiera.[95] The first carried a viola in his baggage when he left the port of Cádiz for Buenos Aires in late 1722, which, as far as I know, amounts to the first known reference to this instrument in Chile.[96] María Ignacia entered the ancient establishment of the convent of Santa Clara and, in her 1743 renunciation, she indicated that her parents had given her a "harpsichord made in Paris."[97] [Her sister] Francisca Javiera married Francisco García Huidobro, marquis of Casa Real, in 1737, which is relevant because in the appraisal of the latter's goods carried out in 1775, "a song with the accompaniment of two violins, viola, for bass, by Mr. David Pérez, called Didone" was found.[98] Thus, the possession of musical objects was sometimes a part of longstanding family traditions warranting future study.[99]

The newly assembled information documents interesting musical activity in the private sphere in the second half of the eighteenth century. It seems clear that the cultivation of music of the written tradition in homes, as well as in religious institutions, was not a phenomenon limited to "notable exceptions" before the republic, as Pereira Salas claimed, which supports the hypothesis that the origin of these ideas may be found more in nineteenth-century nationalism and its validity around 1940 than in actual colonial sources. The reception of these foreign musical objects in Chile also helps to dismantle—or at least to put into perspective—the myth established by Zapiola about 1819 being a revolutionary year in the musical sphere. Otherwise, I have noted that this myth seems to be, above all, an egocentric postulate by which Zapiola aims to situate himself as a precursor of musical "art."[100]

One question that emerges here is why scores have not been preserved that would account for the repertoire employed in the private sphere, besides a few exceptions, among which we can enumerate the aforementioned manuscripts of María Antonia Palacios and Santiago de Murcia. I know of a few historical references to dances cultivated in colonial Chile, principally through Pereira Salas, who mentioned among the creole ones "El más vivo" (The cleverest one) and the "Sandoval"; among the "Spanish" ones of popular character, the fandango, seguidilla, *bolera*, *tirana*, and zapateado; and among the aristocratic dances, the contra dance and the minuet. But musical examples are scarce.[101] In fact, apart from the zapateado, the earliest dances that appear in Pereira Salas's own Chilean musical inventory date from the end of the nineteenth century.[102]

This has been a determining fact in the idea that such a tradition was practically nonexistent, just as it has been in the characterization of the cathedral of Santiago as the most important musical institution of the colony, which we owe to Claro Valdés.[103] This last proceeds not only from a Eurocentric vision of history, nor from the scarcity of research in other archives and institutions, as I have stated,[104] but above all to the fact that the only musical archive known until now to contain colonial scores is preserved there. Nonetheless, this argument conceals a positivist assumption—there were no scores in other places because we don't have tangible evidence of their existence—that is disputable. Even current experience shows us, in spite of a relative revalorization of historical patrimony, that the common tendency is to throw out the musical materials that are no longer useful to us (our old harmony books, the first youthful attempts at composition, and so forth). In this sense, perhaps the proper question is not why certain scores have been lost—this is what one would expect—but why the ones that have come down to us were preserved. This also disguises a greater interest insofar as it implies examining the historical and institutional context of the repertoire studied, as well as the continuity of certain pieces over time. Then again, the cathedral archive itself demonstrates that the preservation of scores is not necessarily related to the musical activity of a period, for which reason its pieces date to the second half of the eighteenth century, despite the fact that a documented musical practice had previously existed. The argument that earlier scores perished in the fire of 1769 is baseless, since a report by the majordomo of the cathedral sent to the king indicates that, in terms of musical objects, only two organs and four books of music were burnt.[105] Thus, the causes of the tardy preservation of the cathedral repertoire must be found in other aspects, among which the process of reform of sacred music that began in the nineteenth century—which caused new copies of the ancient repertoire to be made—probably plays a role, as I hope to show elsewhere.

This reflection on the archive of the cathedral is pertinent because small samples of the repertoire we are concerned with have also been preserved there, including one unknown until now.[106] In folder 83, which contains an anonymous *trisagio* (litany of saints), there is a "Minué del Día 11 de Marzo de 1767 en el que canta un Compadre la felisidad de su suerte" (Minuet from 11 March 1767 in which a friend sings of his good luck) (fig. 5.1).[107] Apparently, the last folio of the second flute part of the *trisagio* had been originally left blank, and it was used to copy the minuet, as well as a short "amen" found on the reverse.

The finding of this score is significant because it contributes a dance from a period of which nothing had previously been known. Although one cannot be sure that the indicated date corresponds to the day of its composition or performance, the characteristics of both the copy and the music fit well within the third quarter of the eighteenth century: the irregular distribution of the phrases in periods of very different duration and the greater length of each part (twelve measures) are common for these later minuets;[108] in addition, the relative slowness of the harmonic rhythm (measures 5–6), the use of mode change and of ornaments all situate this piece in the latter years of the baroque style, although this means taking a term from European musical history whose relevance in colonial America is at least arguable. The main melody has an evidently instrumental character, so that it could be an arrangement of a piece for a keyboard or other instrument: the incoherencies in the placement of the text in relation to the arrangement of the eighth notes and the complexity of the vocal execution make this possible.[109]

On the other hand, the fact that it is a sung minuet as well as the format used for its notation—the bass parts and the song only—seem to relate this piece to the repertoire of theatrical *tonadillas* (*tonadillas escénicas*),[110] as also occurs with

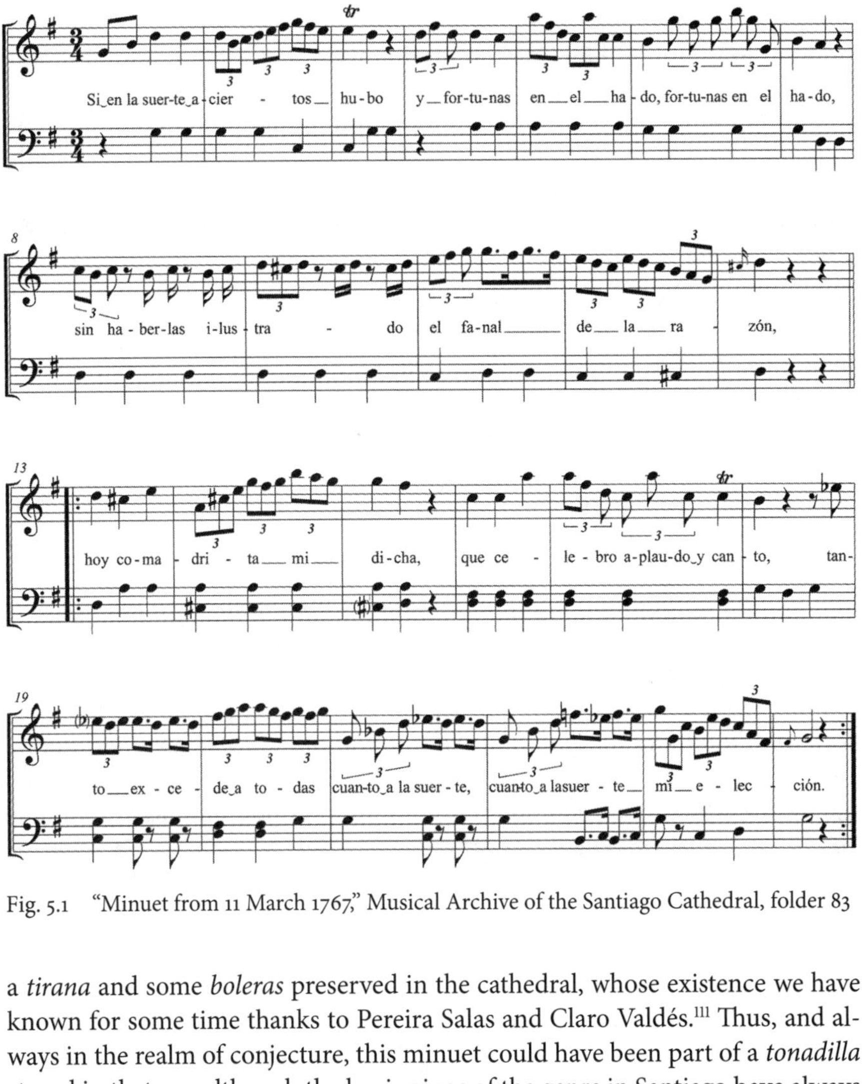


Fig. 5.1 "Minuet from 11 March 1767," Musical Archive of the Santiago Cathedral, folder 83

a *tirana* and some *boleras* preserved in the cathedral, whose existence we have known for some time thanks to Pereira Salas and Claro Valdés.[111] Thus, and always in the realm of conjecture, this minuet could have been part of a *tonadilla* staged in that era, although the beginnings of the genre in Santiago have always been dated to a decade later (1777).[112] In any case, the possible relation to the theater does not impede us relating this piece with the private context: one of the characteristics of *tonadillas* was precisely their rapid diffusion from theaters to the home sphere; similarly, they gathered together the dances that were most fashionable in the places in which they were performed.[113]

But if all of this allows us to question the myth of the republic as [coinciding with] an absolute change in secular musical practice, it would seem that the ideas about progress in the eighteenth century have been confirmed: practically all the data offered dates from the second half of this century. But once again, this judgment is hasty. The fact that we only have information about the entry of instruments beginning in the 1760s is due to the fact that they began to be registered in this period, at least according to the sources that I have been able to view in the National Archives. At the same time, although there is growth in imports as the nineteenth century nears, this could be related to the number of sources preserved: only since the 1780s have I found an entry for each year, and beginning in the 1790s it is very common to find more than one.[114] Therefore, where there seems to be growth, first of all, is in the tendency to register port entries in document form.[115] This fact is important, because if there was a difference between the Hapsburg and Bourbon dynasties, it is that the latter was more systematic in creating specific documents for the different spheres of its government.[116]

The proof that the impression given by entry registries could be deceptive is that other sources give information about the importation of instruments in earlier periods: I have already mentioned the Paris harpsichord that María Ignacia Morandé possessed in 1743, and we also know of diverse goods that were brought from Lima: strings for the Jesuits' harpsichord in 1742, organs in 1683 and 1695 for the Mercedarians, and a harpsichord around 1597 for the Augustines.[117]

However, perhaps it could be in the notarized documentation that one could find clearer proof that this musical activity in the private sphere did not begin in 1700. In the late sixteenth century it was common for private individuals or merchants living in Santiago to buy vihuela strings, like the four packages Francisco Navarro acquired in 1590.[118] Thus, it is not surprising that in 1587 the mulatto Antón de Guzmán should possess a vihuela that had been pawned by Jerónimo Bermúdez for ten gold pesos, nor that Francisco de Saucedo, in his 1605 will, should indicate having a "large viguela" held by Father Joan Cano de Araya.[119]

Moving to a later era, in 1679 the *licenciado* (lawyer) Francisco Millán had a vihuela he left to his natural son of the same name;[120] in the inventory of Cavalier Domingo Pérez de Riobó, carried out in 1680, we find a "new guitar" and "a manuscript with harp bass strings [*bordones de arpa*]";[121] in 1682 we find two "big harps" in the matrimonial dowries of María Campusano and Ana María de la Vega, valued at the large sums of 30 and 20 pesos, respectively; in 1689 there is a harp valued at 12 pesos in the dowry of Inés de Olivera;[122] in 1689 the Indian Andrés Samaya, originally from the northern locality of Huasco, declares in his will that he possesses a guitar;[123] and another dowry, that of Josepha Velasco, shows a harp and a vihuela jointly valued at 40 pesos in 1691.[124]

It is clear that the cited goods demonstrate a musical activity in homes similar to what we have seen in the eighteenth century, which speaks to a relative continuity rather than the rupture commonly asserted. From this point of view, the almost unique importance traditional historiography accords to the salon (*tertulia*) as a phenomenon begun in that century seems arguable. Pereira Salas states that in 1707, in the house of Governor Ibáñez y Peralta, "the first French-style musical salon, the first simulation of Versailles in the noble and faithful Santiago del Nuevo Extremo" took place.[125] It is clear that the instruments cited before 1700 must have carried out some function in the houses in which they were found. Thus, if the concept of salon defines a private meeting in which music plays a significant role, its exclusive application to the eighteenth and later centuries seems more a product of the nationalist ideas examined in the previous section than of a factual description. And it is here that knowledge of the sixteenth and seventeenth centuries becomes important: our interpretation of the century that concerns us also depends on them.

We might say that what we have seen in this section allows us to question both sides of the coin of the Chilean eighteenth century. On the one hand, the obscurantist image of this period in comparison with the republic is not justified: the information provided demonstrates a very clear relationship between the supposed novelties that have been attributed to independence, particularly since 1819, and certain practices that were well established before 1800. On the other, although it is possible that musical commerce grew through the eighteenth century, it is arbitrary to attribute total isolation to the previous centuries, and above all, to suppose that the year 1700 marked a radical change in terms of the cultivation of music in the private sphere.

## The Eighteenth Century as a Mirror of the Present

Instead of ending with conclusions in the conventional mode—some of which I have presented in each section—I prefer to end by briefly interrogating myself about the relationship between the eighteenth century and the present, which has been one of the threads running through this work, no longer basing myself on the present of Pereira Salas, whom I have cited so recurrently, but on our own. Although the previous pages are dedicated to that century, it is evident that we are not dealing only with historiographic or musical problems, but with an attitude of negation of the past that seems to have been decisive in the formation of Chilean identity. When considering this attitude, it is easier to understand, for example, traditional Chilean indifference toward its historical patrimony.[126] In addition, the persistent gaze toward Europe (excluding Spain) that begins with the republic, which aims to substitute local (Spanish colonial) traditions with new ones, can partially explain the special facility contemporary Chile has for assimilating foreign styles and genres as its own, as has happened, for example, in the realm of popular music.[127]

On the other hand, nationalist ideology, although it originates with the arrival of the republic, seems to be present up to our time, since even in works about later eras we find the myth repeated in which a sizable vacuum is filled by the abrupt arrival of a cluster of foreign music or composers, as we see in Zapiola's statements about 1819; and it is no coincidence that these moments of progress or growth are made to coincide with important dates in national history.[128] Reflecting on these problems is even more necessary in the current context, because the commemoration of two hundred years of independence in 2010—in Chile as well as in other Latin American countries—brings with it the danger of exacerbating old anticolonial ideas with consequences that are difficult to predict, but which probably would include the consolidation of a national identity in a certain ahistorical mode, constructed to begin in a period that seems to emerge spontaneously, with no connection to the past. The search for alternatives requires one to become conscious of these problems, which implies, among other things, a revision of the descriptive character commonly attributed to traditional historiography and a profound questioning of the decline-progress dichotomy as a basis for the construction of history (both musical and political); a dichotomy that, as we have seen, is simply the result of the greater or lesser adaptation of each period to the nationalist paradigm.

Another important problem, which has occasionally come to the foreground here, is the Eurocentric character of traditional historiography and the inattention to the indigenous and African-origin population that this has meant.[129] On the one hand, this attitude can be related to the same period sources that, being created by the dominant groups, tend to preserve their history exclusively, or to offer a derogatory vision of subaltern groups.[130] However, it is clearly possible to find data of interest, as proved by the studies of mission music carried out since 1997, for example, so that the problem seems to be rather the insufficient attention to the topic in traditional studies and, above all, their view of indigenous and African cultures as primitive.[131] The natural reaction to this has been the about-face of recent historiography toward these cultures, which has crystallized into the development of the indigenist current or so-called postcolonial studies.[132]

But here there is also, without doubt, a close relationship to the present that is not avoided but rather reclaimed by the representatives of these currents. The numerous conflicts in the Arauco region in the present decade, as well as the various marches undertaken by indigenous communities,[133] denote the multiple unresolved problems related to Chilean identity and, especially, its inability to integrate ethnic minorities. And this is no surprise given that even in the "academic" production of Chilean political historiography we occasionally find clearly racist statements.[134] Thus, defending the indigenous people of the colony, or of the eighteenth century, equates to defending them today.

The question is to what point these demands of our present time can bring us to reinvent the eighteenth century without paying enough attention to the testimonies of the past, an attitude that would not be different from that we have been attributing to, and criticizing in, traditional historiography, however much we might hope otherwise. This statement is not capricious, since that seems to have occurred on more than one occasion: Marcelo Hazan has recently shown us that the image of the composer José Maurício Nunes Garcia, a mulatto and Kapellmeister of the imperial court, as a victim of the imperial court's intrigues and of racial prejudices was constructed under the influence of anticolonial nationalism and ignoring any data that could clarify it, like the fact that Nunes Garcia occupied the most important position for a Brazilian musician of the time and, especially, that he himself had a slave in his service.[135] In the case of Chile, it is possible that a similar example could be found in the hypothesis that María Antonia Palacios, owner of the aforementioned "Sixth book," was a black slave of the late eighteenth century, as Guillermo Marchant has proposed. His principal argument lies in not having found another person with this name in the Santiago documents other than a slave belonging to Juan Antonio Palacios. In such a state, this idea, although plausible, can be no more than conjecture, as the author recognizes in his early works.[136] In spite of this, the passage from a speculative tone to a totally convinced one in recent years can only be explained by a desire to find direct testimonies to the music practiced by slaves in colonial Chile, given that the evidence continues to be just as scarce.[137]

On the other hand, it is easy, after years of oblivion, for ethnic vindication to be exacerbated to the point that practices that appear more European are left out. In fact, the only generally proposed alternative to the path begun by Pereira Salas and Claro Valdés seems to be the study of oral traditional music.[138] The need to restudy the same fields they worked on from a new perspective and with the support of other sources, as presented in this study, is rarely mentioned. In our efforts to overcome traditional Eurocentrism we run the risk of concentrating only on what makes us different from Europe, thus confusing what is ours with what is exclusive. But what is most relevant is that this posture is no different from nineteenth century nationalism in its classic aspect: the search for identity in a remote past—in this case the pre-Columbian period—in which one might find contained the authentic, unique characteristics of the nation.[139] And this seems reason enough to argue that historiographic nationalism has not been abandoned,[140] but only replaced by another, different one, which perhaps is often hidden under the wider umbrella of Americanism.[141]

It seems, then, that we have come to a point at which the eighteenth century tends to be confused with other eras in musical history. On the one hand, the image of this century depends in great part on the nineteenth and twentieth centuries, because it is there that the history of the colony was modeled. However, our knowledge of the sixteenth and seventeenth centuries also plays a role here, not only because they can provide historical background or the causes of processes that occurred in the eighteenth century,[142] but also because the interpretation we make of the latter is conditioned by that of prior centuries. Yet perhaps the most interesting thing is to affirm how the study of past music can help us to be conscious of problems concerning the musicology of the present day, which is essential if we consider that it is already constructing a new history of music in Latin America.

## Notes

This work was written as a part of FONDECYT (National Fund for Scientific and Technological Development) grant 1071121, "Tradición y renovación en la música del Chile colonial" (Tradition and renovation in the music of colonial Chile), in which Victor Rondón participated as a coresearcher. During the first phase of the project, I enjoyed the enthusiastic collaboration of assistants Jaime Canto and Laura Jordán.

1. See, for instance, Malena Kuss, "Nacionalismo, identificación y Latinoamérica," *Cuadernos de Música Iberoamericana* 6 (1998), 133–49; Bernardo Illari, "Zuola, criollismo, nacionalismo y musicología," *Resonancias* 7 (2000), 59–95; Bernardo Illari, "Etica, estética, nación: las canciones de Juan Pedro Esnaola," *Cuadernos de Música Iberoamericana* 10 (2005), 137–223. Aurelio Tello, "Aires nacionales en la música de América Latina como respuesta a la búsqueda de identidad," *Hueso Húmero* 44 (2004), 210–37.

2. Illari, "Etica, estética, nación," 142.

3. Among the cited texts, this view is similar to the section where Illari analyzes the form in which Hispanicist nationalism affected the image of the Zuola Codex, a colonial manuscript of Peruvian origin. Illari, "Zuola, criollismo," 61 and onward.

4. My use of quotation marks here is intentional and is owing to the fact that it is questionable to speak of traditional historiography in a country that has not really had a tradition of studies on the music of the colonial period. Despite this problem, I use the term to differentiate the studies of Pereira Salas and Claro Valdés from those that would follow thirty years later, to which I refer further below.

5. Alejandro Vera, "Musicología, historia y nacionalismo: escritos tradicionales y nuevas perspectivas sobre la música del Chile colonial," *Acta Musicologica* 78, no. 2 (2006), 139–58.

6. I follow the definition of Anthony D. Smith, *Nacionalismo: teoría, ideología, historia* (Madrid: Alianza Editorial, 2004), 23, 116–20. Originally published as *Nationalism: Theory, Ideology, History* (2001).

7. Julio Aróstegui, *La investigación histórica: teoría y método* (Barcelona: Crítica, 2001), 76–78.

8. Leo Treitler, *Music and the Historical Imagination* (Cambridge, Mass.: Harvard University Press, 1989), 1–5, 37, 42.

9. Michael L. Klein, *Intertextuality in Western Art Music* (Bloomington: Indiana University Press, 2005), 8; see also Treitler, *Music and the Historical Imagination*, 43.

10. See Linda Hutcheon, *A Poetics of Postmodernism: History, Theory, Fiction* (New York: Routledge, 1988), 16, 128, 143.

11. Perhaps it would be more correct to call it postmodern musicology. The arguments for this idea are discussed in Pilar Ramos, *Feminismo y música: introducción crítica* (Madrid: Narcea, 2003), 36–41.

12. See the critique in Treitler, *Music and the Historical Imagination*, 114, 314–15. Another matter, as we will see, is that the school of thought described should be consistent with this proposal.

13. Gary Tomlinson, "The Web of Culture: A Context for Musicology," *19th-Century Music* 7, no. 3 (1984), 350–62, p. 357. In the field of history, see Hayden White's classic "Interpretation in History," *New Literary History* 4, no. 2 (1973), 281–314, p. 287–88.

14. See, for example, the summary in stages that Joseph Kerman makes in his own study of a Byrd motet (analysis, concordances with other sources, historical context, critique of the work). Joseph Kerman, *Contemplating Music: Challenges to Musicology* (Cambridge, Mass.: Harvard University Press, 1985), 125.

15. Stephen Miles, "Critical Musicology and the Problem of Mediation," *Notes* 53, no. 3 (1997), 722–50.

16. Editors' note: The Spanish terms *clavicordio* and *clave* were used historically to designate the harpsichord; the clavichord, for its part, was referred to as *monocordio*. See Beryl Kenyon de Pascual, "*Clavicordios* and Clavichords in 16th-Century Spain," *Early Music* 20, no. 4 (1992), 611–30.

17. Alfredo Jocelyn-Holt Letelier, *Historia general de Chile: los césares perdidos* (Santiago de Chile: Editorial Sudamericana, 2004), 2:282.

18. Alejandro Vera, "A propósito de la recepción de música y músicos extranjeros en el Chile colonial," *Cuadernos de Música Iberoamericana* 10 (2005), 7–33, p. 27.

19. Treitler, *Music and the Historical Imagination*, 92; see also Ramos, *Feminismo y música*, 36.

20. Hutcheon, *Poetics of Postmodernism*, 125, 143.

21. One of the fundamental postulates of intertextual theory; see Graham Allen, *Intertextuality* (London: Routledge, 2000), 36.

22. See Hugo Quintana, "Música europea y música latinoamericana del siglo XVIII," *Revista de La Sociedad Venezolana de Musicología* 2, no. 2 (2002), 45–78.

23. A critical summary of this focus is found in Juan José Carreras, "De Literes a Nebra: la música dramática entre la tradición y la modernidad," in *La música en España en el siglo XVIII*, ed. Malcolm Boyd, Juan José Carreras, and José Maximo Leza (Cambridge, Mass.: Cambridge University Press, 2000 [original in English, 1998]), 19–28. The traditional focus is represented especially by the important work by Emilio Cotarelo y Mori, *Orígenes y establecimiento de la ópera en España hasta 1800* (Madrid: Tipografía de la Revista de Archivos, Bibliotecas y Museos, 1917).

24. Louise K. Stein, *Songs of Mortals, Dialogues of the Gods: Music and Theatre in Seventeenth Century Spain* (Oxford: Clarendon Press, 1993), 130 and onward.

25. Pablo L. Rodríguez, "Música, poder y devoción: la Capilla Real de Carlos II (1665–1700)" (PhD diss., Universidad de Zaragoza, Spain, 2003), 4.

26. Carreras, "De Literes a Nebra," 22–23, 27. The supposed opera *Il pomo d'oro* was really a comedy with the same name as the Cesti opera, which caused Cotarelo's confusion.

27. José Máximo Leza, "La zarzuela *Viento es la dicha de amor*: producciones en los teatros públicos madrileños en el siglo XVIII," *Música y literatura en la Península Ibérica: 1600–1750*, ed. Carmelo Caballero Fernández-Rufete, Germán Vega, and María Antonia Virgili Blanquet (Valladolid: Junta de Castilla y León, 1997), 393–99.

28. Samuel Claro Valdés, *Antología de la música colonial en América del Sur* (Santiago de Chile: Universidad de Chile, 1974), 137–43.

29. Cited in ibid., xxix.

30. Juan José Carreras, "Hijos de Pedrell: la historiografía musical española y sus orígenes nacionalistas (1780–1980)," *Il Saggiatore Musicale* 8, no. 1 (2001), 121–69, pp. 131, 134, 136, 151.

31. For nationalism, both the distant past and destiny represent something glorious because they embody the authenticity time has taken away from the nation (Smith, *Nacionalismo*, 45, 47).

32. Carreras, "Hijos de Pedrell," 138–44.

33. See a critique of this idea in Pilar Ramos, "The Construction of the Myth of Spanish Renaissance Music as a Golden Age," in *Early Music-Context and Ideas* (Krakow: University of Krakow, 2003), 1–2.

34. Carreras, "Hijos de Pedrell," 159.

35. ["That of Sablonara" refers to the *Cancionero de la Sablonara*, work of the court copyist Claudio de la Sablonara.] On this frustrated project, see Luis Robledo, *Juan Blas de Castro (ca. 1561–1631): vida y obra musical* (Zaragoza: Institución Fernando el Católico, Diputación Provincial, 1989), 12.

36. First of all, Felipe Pedrell, *Teatro lírico español anterior al siglo XIX*, vols. 3 and 4 (La Coruña: Canuto Berea y Compañía, 1897–1898).

37. This doubtless also was influenced by many other factors not touched upon here; for example, the secularization of the eighteenth century, given that the Spanish musicology of the early twentieth century was essentially Catholic (Ramos, "Construction of the Myth," 4).

38. In the area of Chilean history, see Allen L. Woll, *A Functional Past: The Uses of History in Nineteenth Century Chile* (Baton Rouge: Louisiana State University Press, 1982).

39. "Musicology is perceived as dealing essentially with the factual, the documentary, the verifiable, the analyzable, the *positivistic*. Musicologists are respected for the facts they know about music" (Kerman, *Contemplating Music*, 12).

40. Víctor Rondón, "El archivo musical colonial como memoria del poder: el caso chileno," *Anais III Simposio Latino-Americano de Musicología*, ed. E. Seraphim Prosser (Curitiba: Fundação Cultural de Curitiba, 2000), 57–69, p. 62, states about studies of scores and prior diachronic analyses: "I think that toward the end of this millennium, it is now possible to add to this eminently descriptive occupation a new phase, one which revises or proposes a critical and interpretative vision."

41. Eugenio Pereira Salas, *Los orígenes del arte musical en Chile* (Santiago de Chile: Imprenta Universitaria, 1941), xviii.

42. Charles Seeger, "*Los orígenes del arte musical en Chile.* By Eugenio Pereira Salas," *Hispanic American Historical Review* 22 (1942), 171–73, p. 172.

43. Luis Merino, "Don Eugenio Pereira Salas (1904–1979), fundador de la historiografía musical en Chile," *Revista Musical Chilena* 33, no. 148 (1979), 66–87, p. 66.

44. See Rolf G. Foerster, *Jesuitas y mapuches, 1593–1767* (Santiago de Chile: Editorial Universitaria, 1996), 19.

45. Pereira Salas, *Los orígenes*, 26.

46. Ibid., 75, 155.

47. For example, the absence of a written tradition that can be deduced from his words contradicts the existence of the musical archive of the cathedral referred to on *Los orígenes*, p. 52. It is worth mentioning that the idea that this supposed lack connotes a musical inferiority is clearly Eurocentric; but it is also true that in institutions like ecclesiastical ones, which aimed to reproduce Spanish or Liman models, one would expect that their musical practices would also be reproduced.

48. Bernardo Subercaseaux, *Historia de las ideas y de la cultura en Chile: sociedad y cultura liberal en el siglo XIX: J. V. Lastarria* (Santiago de Chile: Editorial Universitaria, 1997), 1:52–53.

49. Domingo Amunátegui Solar, *Formación de la nacionalidad chilena* (Santiago de Chile: Ediciones de la Universidad de Chile, 1943), 66, 76.

50. Pereira Salas, *Los orígenes*, 75.

51. Luis Merino, "La sociedad filarmónica de 1826 y los inicios de la actividad de conciertos públicos en la sociedad civil de Chile hacia 1830," *Revista Musical Chilena* 60, no. 206 (2006), 5–27.

52. This has been documented by Pereira Salas, *Los orígenes*, 48–49.

53. A summary can be found in Ramos, *Feminismo y música*, 115–37, who sums up the feminist critique of the concept.

54. Quoted in Laura Jordán, "Clandestinidades en la música de resistencia" (thesis, Pontificia Universidad Católica de Chile, 2007), 13.

55. José Zapiola, *Recuerdos de treinta años (1810–1840)* (Buenos Aires and Santiago de Chile: Editorial Francisco de Aguirre, 1974), 44.

56. Aside from Pereira Salas see, among others, Samuel Claro Valdés and Jorge Urrutia Blondel, *Historia de la música en Chile* (Santiago de Chile: Editorial Orbe, 1973), 86; and Merino, "La sociedad filarmónica," 11. Conversely, a more critical view of the Zapiola text can be found in Jaime Canto, "Música y sociedad en las tres primeras décadas del siglo XIX en Santiago de Chile" (thesis, Pontificia Universidad Católica de Chile, 2007), introduction.

57. Ángel Rama, *La ciudad letrada* (Santiago de Chile: Tajamar Editores, 2004 [1984]), 126–27.

58. Zapiola, *Recuerdos de treinta años*, 44.

59. Of course, nationalism can be related to the other three factors. Below, I examine its relationship to the idea of progress or decline in history. Its links to the autonomy of art remain to be explored in a future work.

60. Vera, "Musicología, historia y nacionalismo."

61. José Victorino Lastarria, *Investigaciones sobre la influencia social de la conquista y del sistema colonial de los españoles en Chile* (Santiago de Chile: Imprenta del Siglo, 1844).

62. Subercaseaux, *Historia de las ideas*, 43.

63. Woll, *A Functional Past*, 63.

64. Pereira Salas, *Los orígenes*, 90.

65. Eugenio Pereira Salas, *Juegos y alegrías coloniales en Chile* (Santiago de Chile: Zig-zag, 1947); *Historia del arte en el reino de Chile* (Santiago de Chile: Universidad de Chile, 1965); *Historia del teatro en Chile desde sus orígenes a la muerte de Juan Casacuberta 1849* (Santiago de Chile: Ediciones de la Universidad de Chile, 1974).

66. For example, Pereira Salas, *Los orígenes*, 52, indicates that "these two influences, the Spanish and the Peruvian, contributed to the awakening of written music in our country." However, this statement implies the idea that during the colony there were no Chilean composers, which allows him to situate the beginning of "national" composition in the nineteenth century.

67. Roberto Escobar, *Músicos sin pasado: composición y compositores de Chile* (Santiago de Chile: Editorial Pomaire, Universidad Católica de Chile, 1971), 88, for instance, indicates that the cittern, harp, and guitar were the favorite instruments of the eighteenth century in Chile because "they were the only ones that could be obtained."

68. See Raquel Barros and Manuel Dannemann, "Los problemas de la investigación del folklore musical chileno," *Revista Musical Chilena* 56, suppl. espec. (2002), 105–19; Rodrigo Torres Alvarado, ed., *Aires tradicionales y folklóricos de Chile* (Santiago de Chile: Universidad de Chile, 2005 [1944]).

69. Raquel Bustos, "Allende Sarón, Pedro Humberto," in *Diccionario de la Música Española e Hispanoamericana*, ed. Emilio Casares (Madrid: Sociedad General de Autores y Editores, 1999), 1:290–93.

70. Pereira Salas, *Los orígenes*, 51, 54, 155.

71. Ibid., 28, 30, 32–34, 40. The exception would be military music (49).

72. Claro Valdés and Urrutia Blondel, *Historia de la música en Chile*, 46, 53, 56.

73. Ibid., 45.

74. Pereira Salas, *Los orígenes*, 28.

75. Ibid., 28–29. About the error of considering this harpsichord the first, see my note 18.

76. Claro Valdés and Urrutia Blondel, *Historia de la música en Chile*, 46.

77. This is made even clearer by Vicente Grez: "ideas have progressed too much. Many French families had established themselves in the capital and they were changing the customs. They lived less in the church and more in the salons" (cited in Pereira Salas, *Los orígenes*, 29).

78. More information on this is in Vera, "A propósito."

79. The topic of exportation remains for a future work. The scarce information found so far refers to guitar strings.

80. About Lima's musical influence, see Pereira Salas, *Los orígenes*, 34, 213; Juan Carlos Estenssoro, *Música y sociedad coloniales: Lima 1680–1830* (Lima: Colmillo Blanco, 1989), 110 and onward; and Vera, "A propósito," 26 and onward.

81. This allows us to move up a bit the arrival of this instrument in relation to Pereira Salas, *Los orígenes*, 41, although there is no reason to claim it was the first.

82. I would like to rectify an error in my article (Vera, "A propósito," 29). I state there that the 1783 harpsichord for María Plaza (appendix 1) arrived through the Cordillera mountain range. However, it entered through the port of Valparaíso.

83. Archivo Nacional de Chile (National Archives of Chile, hereafter AN), Escribanos de Santiago (Scribes of Santiago, hereafter ES), vol. 719, 404 and 408v.

84. AN, ES, vol. 772, 14v, and vol. 856, 195.

85. Ibid, vol. 522, 237.

86. Pereira Salas, *Los orígenes*, 30, 226.

87. The registered entries from Valparaíso include only the mentioned shipment to Córdoba and the "music papers" that María Josefa Morandé received in 1790, while in those from the Cordillera mountains we find only a small box of music in 1776 (appendices 1 and 2).

88. See Vera, "A propósito," 29, 31.

89. AN, ES, vol. 720, 281v.

90. I refer to the *Arte de musica de canto dorgam, e canto cham* (Lisboa, 1626). There is evidence that this treatise circulated in Brazil; see Fernando Pereira Binder and Paulo Castagna, "Teoria musical no Brasil: 173–1854," *Revista Eletrônica de Musicologia* 1, no. 2 (1996), www.rem.ufpr.br (accessed December 3, 2007).

91. AN, ES, vol. 946, 236v. The former could be the *Institución harmónica, o doctrina musical, teórica, y práctica, que trata del canto llano, y de órgano* (Madrid, 1748) by Antonio Roel del Río.

92. Frederick Marvin, "Soler, Antonio," *Grove Music Online*, ed. L. Macy. www.grovemusic.com (accessed December 3, 2007).

93. See Guillermo Marchant, "El Libro Sesto de María Antonia Palacios, c. 1790: un manuscrito musical chileno," *Revista Musical Chilena* 53, no. 192 (1999), 27–46; I refer to this source again later.

94. Alejandro Vera, "Santiago de Murcia's *Cifras Selectas de Guitarra* (1722): A New Source for the Baroque Guitar," *Early Music* 35, no. 2 (2007), 251–69. On Murcia and his contact with Latin America, see Alejandro Vera, "Santiago de Murcia (1673–1739): New Contributions on His Life and Work," *Early Music* 36, no. 4 (2008), 597–608.

95. José Rafael Reyes, "Morandé: un linaje bretón en Chile," *Revista de Estudios Históricos* (Instituto Chileno de Investigaciones Genealógicas), 35 (1990), 69–103.

96. Archivo General de Indias, Contratación 1700, "Registro del navío nombrado de San Raphael, y Santo Domingo."

97. AN, Real Audiencia, vol. 773, 145v. I owe this document to historian Javiera Ruiz Valdés.

98. From Pereira Salas, *Los orígenes*, 42, but originally in Elías García Huidobro, "Una casa colonial a mediados del siglo XVIII," *Revista Chilena de Historia y Geografía* 14, no. 18 (1915), 354.

99. Note that María Josefa del Solar, mentioned earlier as owner of a red guitar from China, was the sister of Juana del Solar.

100. About the importance of myth in the writing of history, see White, "Interpretation in History," 288–89, 292–93.

101. Pereira Salas, *Los orígenes*, 207–13. Frézier included the transcription of a *zapateo* in his recounting of the travels undertaken in the Southern Cone, which Pereira reproduced (328). We also have reference to the "La Bandera" dance (Gabriel Guarda, "Arte y evangelización en Chile: siglos XVI–XVIII," *Boletín de la Academia Chilena de la Historia* 116 [2007], 79). The "Sixth book" contains, among other works, twenty-three minuets and six variations on a minuet (Marchant, "El Libro Sesto," 37–45). The Murcia manuscript contains sixteen minuets (Vera, "Santiago de Murcia's *Cifras*," 257).

102. Eugenio Pereira Salas, *Biobibliografía musical de Chile desde los orígenes a 1886* (Santiago de Chile: Ediciones de la Universidad de Chile, 1978). Pereira Salas does not include the "Sixth book" among the works cited, despite the fact that its existence was known at the time (it is mentioned in Claro Valdés and Urrutia Blondel, *Historia de la música*, 60).

103. Claro Valdés and Urrutia Blondel, *Historia de la música*, 60.

104. Maximiliano Salinas Campos, "¡Toquen flautas y tambores! Una historia social de la música desde las culturas populares en Chile, siglos XVI–XX," *Revista Musical Chilena* 54, no. 193 (2000), 45–86; see Alejandro Vera, "Music in the Monastery of La Merced, Santiago de Chile, in the Colonial Period," *Early Music* 32, no. 3 (2004), 369–82.

105. On the 1769 fire: Samuel Claro Valdés, "Chile: época colonial," in *Diccionario de la música española e hispanoamericana*, ed. Emilio Casares (Madrid: Sociedad General de Autores y Editores, 1999), 3:626. On the majordomo's report: Archivo Histórico del Arzobispado de Santiago (Historical Archive of the Archbishopry of Santiago), Gobierno, vol. 7, part 8, unpaginated.

106. This is not exceptional. In relation to America and Spain, see Bernardo Illari, "Metastasio nell'Indie: de óperas ausentes y arias presentes en América colonial," in *La ópera en España e Hispanoamérica*, ed. Emilio Casares and Alvaro Torrente (Madrid: Instituto Complutense de Ciencias Musicales, 2001), 1:343–74, and Miguel Ángel Marín, *Music on the Margin: Urban Musical Life in Eighteenth-century Jaca (Spain)* (Kassel: Reichenberger, 2002), 278 and onward.

107. This minuet does not figure in Samuel Claro Valdés, *Catálogo del Archivo Musical de la Catedral de Santiago de Chile* (Santiago de Chile: Universidad de Chile, 1974), nor in the foundational work of Robert Stevenson, *Renaissance and Baroque Musical Sources in the Americas* (Washington, D.C.: Organization of American States, 1970).

108. See, for example, Craig H. Russell, ed., *Santiago de Murcia's "Códice Saldívar No.4": A Treasury of Secular Guitar Music from Baroque Mexico* (Urbana: University of Illinois Press, 1995), 1:109.

109. Also noteworthy is the quaternary form that the piece adopts, in a transitory way, in measure 4.

110. The typical format of the *tonadilla* is described in Begoña Lolo, "La tonadilla escénica, ese género maldito," *Revista de Musicología* 25, no. 2 (2002), 440 n4.

111. Pereira Salas, *Los orígenes*, 210–11, 325–26, and Claro Valdés, *Catálogo del Archivo*, 18–20. Claro Valdés includes the transcriptions. Pereira Salas attributes them to Antonio Aranaz.

112. Pereira Salas, *Historia del teatro*, 44, 53.

113. Lolo, "La tonadilla."

114. One object in the 1760s, six in the 1770s, fifteen in the 1780s, and thirty-three in the 1790s (appendices 1 and 2).

115. However, it could be argued that this greater control on the part of the authorities was due precisely to a growth in maritime commerce in Chile.

116. In the Archivo del Palacio Real de Madrid (Archive of the Royal Palace of Madrid), for example, the name of the copyists begins to be specified; compare Rodríguez, "Música, poder y devoción," 208–9, with Alvaro Torrente, *Fiesta de navidad en la Capilla Real de Felipe V* (Madrid: Editorial Alpuerto, 2002), 49–51.

117. Vera, "A propósito," 27.

118. AN, ES, vol. 5, 268v. Also see vol. 7, 399v, and vol. 8, 242, 282v, 312, and 339v. With the exception of the first two volumes, the rest begins in 1586, which shows the difficulty of investigating musical information in this century.

119. Ibid., vol. 3, 396v, and vol. 35bis, 159.

120. Ibid., vol. 350, 189.

121. Ibid., vol. 351, 617v–618.

122. Ibid., vol. 370, 139 and 233; vol. 374, 110v.

123. Julio Retamal Ávila, *Testamentos de "indios" en Chile colonial, 1564–1801* (Santiago de Chile: Universidad Nacional Andrés Bello, Red Internacional del Libro, 2000), 219.

124. AN, ES, vol. 375, 61v. See other data on the presence of harps in inventories in Laura Fahrenkrog, "El arpa en Santiago de Chile durante la Colonia" (thesis, Pontificia Universidad Católica de Chile, 2006), section titled "La actividad musical doméstica" (Domestic musical activity).

125. Pereira Salas, *Los orígenes*, 29, 40–43.

126. This opinion differs from that of Emma de Ramón, *Obra y fe: la catedral de Santiago 1541–1769* (Santiago de Chile: Dirección de Bibliotecas, Archivos y Museos, Centro de Investigaciones Diego Barros Arana, LOM Ediciones, 2002), 168, who situates its origin around 1730.

127. This tendency is noted in Juan Pablo González and Claudio Rolle, *Historia social de la música popular en Chile, 1890–1950* (Santiago de Chile: Universidad Católica de Chile, Casa de las Américas, 2005), 41–44.

128. Juan Pablo González, "Música: de la partitura al disco," in *100 años de cultura chilena 1905–2005*, ed. Cristian Gazmuri (Santiago de Chile: Zig-Zag, 2006), 201–52, p. 205, for example, indicates that with Pedro Humberto Allende (1885–1959), "Chilean music is properly situated for the *first time* in the 'sphere of action' of Western music. . . . The *few foreigners who have come to these distant lands* have made an important contribution to the updating of Chilean musicians during the twentieth century" (emphasis added). Later he adds: "In this way, in the 1910s [the centennial of independence] began the updating of musicians, and of the Chilean public, with the European musical scene."

129. See Salinas Campos, "¡Toquen flautas y tambores!"

130. A fact that Chilean musicology has been warned against by Rondón, "El archivo musical."

131. Among the post-1997 studies are Victor Rondón, "Música jesuita en Chile en los siglos XVII y XVIII: primera aproximación," *Revista Musical Chilena* 51, no. 188 (1997),

7–39; *19 canciones misionales en mapudúngún contenidas en el Chilidúgú (1777) del misionero jesuita en la Araucanía Bernardo de Havestadt (1714–1781)* (Santiago de Chile: Universidad de Chile, Revista Musical Chilena, FONDART, 1997).

132. For a summary of this current, see Gustavo Verdesio, "Colonialism Now and Then: Colonial Latin American Studies in the Light of the Predicament of Latin Americanism," in *Colonialism Past and Present: Reading and Writing about Colonial Latin America Today*, ed. Alvaro Félix Bolaños and Gustavo Verdesio (New York: State University of New York Press, 2002), 1–17, p. 3.

133. One among many is that carried out by the community of Temu Cui Cui on October 15, 2007, in Santiago, in which five thousand people participated. The objective was to demand legal recognition of indigenous peoples by the Chilean state.

134. Especially surprising is the following statement by Amunátegui Solar, *Formación de la nacionalidad chilena*, 79: "Our America offers serious problems. . . . I refer to the coexistence of races that among us are found at different levels of culture. For example, until only a few years ago, the Fuegoans lived in the Republic, occupying one of the lowest extremes of the human scale."

135. Marcelo Hazan, "José Mauricio Nunes García (1767–1830): Exploring the Making of a Brazilian Myth," paper presented at the 18th Conference of the International Musicological Society (Zurich, 2007). I thank the author for having allowed me to consult his work.

136. Guillermo Marchant, "El Libro Sesto de María Antonia Palacios" (abstract of master's thesis), *Revista Musical Chilena* 52, no. 189 (1998), 108–9, describes this slave as a "possible user of the *repertorio*."

137. See Marchant, "El libro sesto" (1999 article), 36, in which the author considers his hypothesis as "almost undeniable." Also see Guillermo Marchant, "Una negra llamada María Antonia," in *Mujeres, negros y niños en la música y sociedad colonial iberoamericana*, ed. Víctor Rondón (Santa Cruz de Bolivia: Asociación Pro Arte y Cultura, 2002), 83. In spite of that, the idea began to enjoy a certain acceptance among specialists in other disciplines; see Paulina Barrenechea Vergara, "María Antonia, esclava y músico: la traza de un rostro borrado por/para la literatura chilena," *Atenea* 491 (2005), 87–98, p. 87–88.

138. According to Salinas Campos, "¡Toquen flautas y tambores!," 73: "At the end of the century, Samuel Claro Valdés became interested in the Arab-Andalusian traces in the *cueca*. . . . The *canto a lo divino* [a vocal-poetic genre focused on sacred themes], among other popular artistic and musical expressions, can also send us in that direction."

139. Smith, *Nacionalismo*, 46.

140. The idea is opposite to that of Richard Taruskin, "Nationalism," *New Grove Dictionary of Music and Musicians*, ed. Stanley Sadie and John Tyrrell (London: Macmillan, 2001), 703.

141. Kuss, "Nacionalismo, identificación," 138, argues that Inter-Americanism is a kind of identification that, like nationalism, has also had important repercussions among twentieth-century composers. We may, thus, understand it as a variant of nationalism (how many times have we heard the metaphor of the Americas as a [single] great nation?). Tello, "Aires nacionales," 232–34, also refers to the Inter-Americanism promoted by Curt Lange in the 1930s.

142. It would, in effect, be exaggerated to deny the existence of causal relationships in history. In this sense, the claim by Leonard B. Meyer in *El estilo en la música: teoría musical, historia e ideología* (Madrid: Ediciones Pirámide, 2000 [1989]), 229, that "history is not the result of a causal past but of a selective present" is too radical. Nonetheless, his interest lies in clearly defining the importance of the present in historical narration.

## Appendix 1. List of musical objects that appear in the entry registries of Valparaíso (1769–99)

| Year | Object | Addressee* | National Archives of Chile Source |
|---|---|---|---|
| 1769 | Harpsichord | not specified | Capitanía General, vol. 360 |
| 1771 | Harpsichord | Joseph Prieto | Capitanía General, vol. 360 |
| 1771 | Harpsichord | Joseph Antonio Sierra | Capitanía General, vol. 360 |
| 1773 | Harpsichord | Joseph Perfecto de Salas | Contaduría Mayor, 2nd series, vol. 733 |
| 1781 | Harpsichord | Nicolás Odria? | Contaduría Mayor, 2nd series, vol. 2271 |
| 1783 | Harpsichord | María Plaza | Contaduría Mayor, 1st series, vol. 1773, and 2nd series, vol. 2278 |
| 1783 | Harpsichord | Agustín Tagle | Contaduría Mayor, 2nd series, vol. 2278 |
| 1783 | Harpsichord | Antonio Ugarte | Contaduría Mayor, 2nd series, vol. 1795 |
| 1783 | Organ | Fr. José Cruz (prior of the Dominican Recoleta) | Contaduría Mayor, 1st series, vol. 1795, and 2nd series, vols. 2278 and 2279 |
| 1783 | Psaltery | Domingo Díaz Muñoz | Contaduría Mayor, 1st series, vol. 1795 and 2nd series, vol. 2278 |
| 1783 | Guitar strings | Miguel Terán | Contaduría Mayor, 1st series, vol. 1795 |
| 1784 | Harpsichord | María Concepción de Elso | Contaduría Mayor, 2nd series, vol. 2281 |
| 1784 | Harpsichord | Rafael Landa | Contaduría Mayor, 2nd series, vol. 2281 |
| 1785 | "Forte-piano" | not specified | Contaduría Mayor, 2nd series, vol. 2283 |
| 1788 | Harpsichord | José Ignacio Alcalde | Contaduría Mayor, 2nd series, vol. 2294 |
| 1788 | Harpsichord | Manuel Pérez Cotapos | Contaduría Mayor, 2nd series, vol. 2294 |
| 1788 | Harpsichord | Joaquín Bezanilla | Contaduría Mayor, 2nd series, vol. 2294 |
| 1789 | Harpsichord | Julián Villeruelo | Contaduría Mayor, 2nd series, vol. 2294 |
| 1790 | Harpsichord | Narcisa Ximénez | Contaduría Mayor, 2nd series, vol. 2297 |
| 1790 | Harpsichord | Vicente de Larriba? | Contaduría Mayor, 2nd series, vol. 2298 |
| 1790 | Harpsichord | Juana Josefa Santibáñez | Contaduría Mayor, 2nd series, vol. 2299 |

| | | | |
|---|---|---|---|
| 1790 | Harpsichord | María Mercedes Contador | Contaduría Mayor, 2nd series, vols. 2297 and 3693 |
| 1790 | "Music papers" | María Josefa Morandé | Contaduría Mayor, 2nd series, vols. 2297 and 3693 |
| 1790 | "Wooden clock with music made in Spain" | Jaime Beltrán? | Contaduría Mayor, 2nd series, vol. 2298 |
| 1791 | "1 harpsichord or forte piano" | Carmen Errázuriz | Contaduría Mayor, 2nd series, vol. 2299 |
| 1791 | Harpsichord | Manuela Zañartu | Contaduría Mayor, 2nd series, vol. 2299 |
| 1791 | Harpsichord | Juan José Moreno | Contaduría Mayor, 2nd series, vol. 2302 |
| 1792 | Jingle bells (*cascabeles*) | Victorio Priego? | Contaduría Mayor, 2nd series, vol. 2301 |
| 1792 | "Little organ" | Church of Santo Domingo de Valparaíso | Contaduría Mayor, 2nd series, vols. 2301, 2302, and 2303 |
| 1792 | Harpsichord | Lorenzo Pérez de Arce | Contaduría Mayor, 2nd series, vol. 2302 |
| 1792 | Harpsichord | Juan Manuel de la Cruz | Contaduría Mayor, 2nd series, vol. 2302 |
| 1793 | Violin | Juan Antonio Uriarte | Contaduría Mayor, 2nd series, vols. 2304, 2305, and 2309 |
| 1793 | Harpsichord | María de la Luz Valdivieso | Contaduría Mayor, 2nd series, vols. 2306 and 2307 |
| 1794 | Harpsichord | Modesto Novajas y Solano | Contaduría Mayor, 2nd series, vols. 2306 and 2308 |
| 1794 | Psaltery | Francisco Vélez | Contaduría Mayor, 2nd series, vols. 2307 and 2308 |
| 1795 | Harpsichord | Carmelite nuns of Santiago | Contaduría Mayor, 2nd series, vol. 2311 |
| 1795 | Harpsichord | Gregorio de Andía y Varela | Contaduría Mayor, 2nd series, vols. 2313 and 2314 |
| 1795 | Harpsichord | Atanasio Muñoz | Contaduría Mayor, 2nd series, vols. 2313 and 2314 |
| 1795 | Guitar strings | Manuel Muñoz? | Contaduría Mayor, 2nd series, vol. 2312 |
| 1796 | Harpsichord | Fr. Antonio Galiano (prior of Santo Domingo de Valparaíso) | Contaduría Mayor, 2nd series, vols. 2313 and 2314 |
| 1796 | Harpsichord | José Prieto (the same as in 1771?) | Contaduría Mayor, 2nd series, vol. 2315 |
| 1796 | 2 psalteries | José de la Concha | Contaduría Mayor, 2nd series, vol. 2318 |
| 1797 | Harpsichord | Joaquín Malo | Contaduría Mayor, 2nd series, vols. 2316, 2317 and 2318 |
| 1797 | Harpsichord | José Antonio González** | Contaduría Mayor, 2nd series, vols. 2317 and 2318 |
| 1797 | Harpsichord | María Cruz Arcaya | Contaduría Mayor, 2nd series, vol. 2318 |
| 1797 | Harpsichord | Salvador Trucios | Contaduría Mayor, 2nd series, vol. 2318 |

| | | | |
|---|---|---|---|
| 1797 | Harpsichord | Rafael de Beltrán | Contaduría Mayor, 2nd series, vol. 2319 |
| 1797 | Organ | Monastery of Santo Domingo de Coquimbo | Contaduría Mayor, 2nd series, vol. 2318 |
| 1799 | "1 little crate with church music papers" | Cathedral of Córdoba of Tucumán | Contaduría Mayor, 2nd series, vol. 2324 |
| 1799 | Harpsichord | Cristóbal Valdés | Contaduría Mayor, 2nd series, vol. 2324 |

* On some occasions, the address is difficult to determine. The person "documented" as the addressee does not always correspond to the user. For example, a 1790 harpsichord appears as "addressed to and paid for" by Francisco Antonio Sánchez but for the use of Narcisa Ximénez. We can then assume that there are other similar instances. In those cases I note the uncertainty [with a question mark after the name].

** This is not the organist—and subsequent *maestro de capilla* (chapel master)—of the same name, but, as the document later mentioned, the captain of the naval ship *La Piedad*.

## Appendix 2. List of musical objects entering via the Cordillera de los Andes (1776–90)

| Year | Object | Addressee | National Archives of Chile Source |
|---|---|---|---|
| 1776 | Harpsichord | Antonio de Segovia | Contaduría Mayor, 2nd series, vols. 644 and 651 |
| 1776 | "1 little box with music" | not specified | Contaduría Mayor, 2nd series, vols. 651 and 652 |
| 1776 | "Some flutes" | not specified | Contaduría Mayor, 2nd series, vols. 651 and 652 |
| 1781 | Psaltery | Francisco Tadeo Diez de Medina | Contaduría Mayor, 2nd series, vol. 658 |
| 1790 | Violin | Pedro Domingo de Larrea | Contaduría Mayor, 2nd series, vol. 3693 |

# 6

# The *Bambuco*, Hybrid Knowledges, and the Academy

## *A Historical Analysis of the Persistence of Coloniality in Latin American Musical Studies*

CAROLINA SANTAMARÍA-DELGADO

For the last twenty-five years, discussions have taken place in the social sciences about the erosion of disciplinary boundaries between areas of knowledge, such as anthropology, sociology, and psychoanalysis, the scope of which had previously been clearly differentiated. Currents of thought that emerged in the 1960s through the 1980s, such as feminism, cultural studies, and postcolonial studies, began to seriously question the ways in which disciplines and the discourses generated from within articulated inequalities of power that had been a constitutive part and parcel of Western culture. As the Enlightenment-era ideal of absolute purity of scientific objectivity has disintegrated, old paradigms of cultural analysis have had to be newly reimagined. These changes have not gone unnoticed in music studies, where we have recognized the musicologist as having a subject position. That is to say, we recognize a musicologist as someone who analyzes musical expressions from a particular social point of view, that is, in keeping with his or her own historical moment, gender, and ethnic and social class identity. Abandoning the notion of the musicologist as scientific observer, a neutral and objective being, has become an issue not only for researchers facing fieldwork and ethnographic methods, but also for those researchers who work with and interpret scores and historical documents.

---

Originally published by Carolina Santamaría Delgado as "El bambuco, los saberes mestizos y la academia: un análisis histórico de la persistencia de la colonialidad en los estudios musicales latinoamericanos," *Latin American Music Review* 28, no. 1 (2007), 1–23.  Translated by Michael O'Brien with permission.

Since musicologists and ethnomusicologists have come to face basically the same problems in trying to understand that which is musical from within a specific cultural framework and from a particular subject position, they have started to converge in many topics, such that the conventional boundaries between historical musicology and ethnomusicology have blurred. Although there has been no small amount of resistance to the emergence within musicology of new perspectives such as feminism,[1] and despite the still-substantial ideological differences between some members of each guild, we are gradually coming to the conclusion that historical musicology and ethnomusicology are in fact two sides of the same coin. This is reflected in the purpose seen in some U.S. and Canadian universities, in which both disciplines are combined into a single academic unit and students are trained in the use of methodological tools developed by each discipline. This transformation has been the result of an attitude critical of the academy's Eurocentrism, and has attempted to call into question the hegemonic position of bourgeois European culture vis-à-vis other musical cultures. Why has the prefix "ethno" been valid for nearly all of the world's music except European art music? Why do the majority of music schools in the United States and the rest of the Americas continue to focus nearly exclusively on teaching the Western canon? The critique of the hegemony of European perspectives in musicology had among its pioneers respected African musicologists who had been trained in British schools, such as Kwabena Nketia and Akin Euba.[2] One of the more recent chapters in the self-critique from within U.S.-based disciplines of musical scholarship led to an animated exchange of emails on the Society for Ethnomusicology (SEM) Listserv, in which members passionately debated about the ethnocentrism and insularity of the U.S. and Canadian academies with respect to the presence and publications of similar disciplinary societies from outside of the English-speaking world.

It seems strange that this topic has not generated a greater degree of attention and continuous reflection from within the community of Latin American musicologists and ethnomusicologists. It is true that North/South academic inequality has generated important critical responses, such as those by Javier León and Raúl Romero,[3] and that a certain spirit of independence from First World academic centers has inspired the creation and spectacular growth of the Latin American branch of the International Association for the Study of Popular Music (IASPM-LA) in recent years. Nonetheless, these have been critical positions "directed outwardly," generally toward examining the hegemonic position of the U.S. and Canadian academies in the production of knowledge about music in Latin America. There does not yet seem to have been articulated an "inward" critical position that explores the way that discourses of power have historically been constructed within the disciplines of musical research in our countries.[4] In no way do I think that this is due to a lack of awareness of the problem; rather

I think it is due to the lack of a clear theoretical and conceptual framework that would allow us to explore the issue in depth.

From my point of view, Latin American postcolonial studies provide the appropriate theoretical framework for critically deconstructing the ways in which music studies and musicological, folkloric, and ethnomusicological knowledge in Latin America have been constructed. Reflections on the nature of Latin American colonialism by authors such as Enrique Dussel, Aníbal Quijano, Walter Mignolo, and Santiago Castro-Gómez offer critical guidance for analyzing the aesthetic and epistemological problems that confronted musicians and researchers of the nineteenth and twentieth centuries who collected, composed, or analyzed music in Spanish- and Portuguese-speaking countries.[5] The purpose of this attempt at a revisionist history of the development of music research disciplines is, ultimately, to reveal the way we conceive of musical knowledge, and to call into question the persistence of boundaries between historical musicology, ethnomusicology, folklore, and popular music studies—boundaries that remain today, or even continue to be formed—within our academic institutions.

Recognizing the significance of the construction of local histories,[6] I use my own work on the relationship between social class and musical practice in urban centers of Andean Colombia in the first half of the twentieth century as a source in order to reconstruct the history of the *bambuco* [see note][7] and its conflicted relationship with the world of academia.[8] These reflections on the evolution and development of discourse surrounding the Colombian *bambuco*, from the mid-nineteenth through the mid-twentieth century, will serve to illustrate what I call the problem of epistemic inaccessibility of hybrid knowledges (*saberes mestizos*).[9] This problem refers to the obstacles that faced local institutions and local music scholars, especially those with academic training, when dealing with musical traditions of uncertain ethnic origin.[10] I begin with the hypothesis that, notwithstanding racial prejudices, attempts to "whiten" this musical tradition were the result of colonialists' inability to access epistemes that were not entirely European; "mestizo" musics such as the *bambuco* embodied a combination of European forms of musical knowledge with others that were indigenous or African, resulting in forms of knowledge that simply "did not fit" within parameters that were recognized as absolute, objective, and scientific. In the case of the *bambuco*, we see below how this problem delayed by decades the systematic and deep study of the genre and its repertoire. At the same time, the absence of clear epistemic boundaries between musical forms of knowledge practically paralyzed the establishment and disciplinary development of music studies at the local level. Before discussing the strictly musical material, I briefly outline the theoretical tools that I use for this analysis.

## Coloniality and Knowledge

Although not appropriate here to carry out a detailed analysis of the emergence of Latin American postcolonial studies, or its relationship with the work of thinkers like Michel Foucault or Edward Said,[11] it is worth remembering the implications of Aníbal Quijano and Walter Mignolo's work, expanding the geopolitical and temporal boundaries of the origins of modernity.[12] According to First World thinkers such as Immanuel Wallerstein (and by representatives of the Third World, like Edward Said), modernity's beginnings are to be found in the eighteenth and nineteenth centuries, with the Industrial Revolution and the birth of capitalism. Modernity, thus, was the result of strictly intra-European phenomena, such as the Enlightenment and the French Revolution. Mignolo and Quijano argue, however, that this vision of a world-system, in Wallerstein's terms, does not account for the formation of the first worldwide commercial circuit, nor the creation of the idea of "the West," which emerged toward the end of the fifteenth century with the discovery of the Americas. This is a key issue when it comes to understanding the colonial experience as a constitutive rather than a derivative element of modernity. One can then understand the continued relevance of concepts such as "colonial difference" and "the coloniality of power." Colonial difference is a notion that emerges from the concept of "race," an idea created in the sixteenth century in order to classify the world's population and to define the division of labor; the coloniality of power, on the other hand, is a concept that describes the mechanisms that produce and reproduce colonial difference. In other words, being described as "Indian," "white," or "black" served as a way to define an individual's position within the framework of the social division of labor. Racial or colonial difference was maintained and has been maintained—although it has been rearticulated through other terms and other discourses—due to social mechanisms that perpetuate this division. The point is that, notwithstanding the socioeconomic basis of the idea, "race" remains an epistemic category for controlling knowledge and intersubjectivity: the coloniality of power not only classifies human beings on a scale from inferior to superior according to race, but also brings order to the knowledges and forms of knowing created by those being classified. Thus, knowledge produced by white men is generally regarded as "scientific," "objective," and "rational," while that produced by men of color (or women) is "magical," "subjective," and "irrational." In this way, despite the fact that concrete manifestations of colonialism have become a thing of the past (or at least, we hope that they have), coloniality persists as an important component of the modern and postmodern being. Coloniality is, in Mignolo's terms, the dark side of modernity.

Along with the concepts of colonial difference and the coloniality of power, I also use the idea of "purity of blood" to analyze the means through which it was possible (at least theoretically) to breach racial boundaries within the Spanish imperial system, which had its own ways of rationalizing and controlling a population born of the ethnic mix of indigenous, European, and African peoples. "Purity of blood" refers to the taxonomic system for classifying ethnicities that cataloged the place that each person held within colonial social structures depending on the amount of "white" Spanish blood in that person's heritage. According to this logic, a person classified as a mestizo (son of a Spanish father and an indigenous mother) could clean their impure bloodline after a few generations if he were able to get his sons and daughters to intermarry exclusively with Spaniards. For those individuals belonging to lesser castes, however, this process of purification could take much longer, or in the case of Negroes and mulattos, this ascent in social status would be completely impossible.[13] This same mechanism was also used during the nineteenth century to symbolically "purify" social practices, including music, which were associated with different ethnic groups.

My analysis of the history of the Colombian *bambuco*, and the processes of racial "purification" that took place through discourse about that genre from the mid-nineteenth to the mid-twentieth century, examines the struggles for power which surrounded this traditional Andean genre, identified as a national symbol by the elites around the 1850s. As we will see, the *bambuco*'s indefinite classification as either a folk, popular, or art music corresponds with the lack of certainty among scholars concerning the music's epistemic status and the nature of its form of hybrid knowledge: Is *bambuco* truly "studyable"? And if so, who, or what discipline, ought to study it? With what methods, and in order to ask what questions? We will also see how social transformations during this period changed the terms through which colonial difference was marked or articulated and how a preoccupation with "race" in the nineteenth century gave way to notions of "class" in the following century.

## The *Bambuco*'s Racial Origins (1867–1900)

The *bambuco* is a traditional musical genre that was transmitted orally, and for which we have no documentary evidence prior to the nineteenth century. Probably, though, it originated in the wind and percussion ensembles played by indigenous and black musicians in the southern province of Gran Cauca.[14] By the end of the nineteenth century, the *bambuco* had gained entrance to the aristocratic circles of Bogotá as a genre of salon dance music, or as a part of collections of short piano pieces for use in the home. At the same time, an urban type of *bambuco*, a song form accompanied by string instruments, became popular among the working class in Bogotá and Medellín. During this period, texts by poets and intellectuals such as José María Samper and Rafael Pombo helped make the genre into a symbol of the young nation of Colombia. Around 1900, Pedro Morales Pino [1863–1926] established a new instrumental ensemble of winds and strings (known as *lira*, but sometimes also called *estudiantina* [generic term for string ensembles in Latin America], or *orquesta colombiana* [lit. Colombian orchestra]) which combined instruments from the European symphony, such as violins, cellos, and flutes, with string instruments original to Colombia, such as the tiple and the *bandola* [a six double-stringed instrument similar to a mandolin]. The members of Morales Pino's group, La Lira Colombiana, were mainly tailors and shoemakers by trade, and were the same musicians who played, alongside the poets and intellectuals of the literary circle called La Gruta Simbólica (the Symbolic Grotto), in literary social gatherings and the bohemian nightlife of fin-de-siècle Bogotá. Morales Pino's most important contribution, however, was not so much the creation of the instrumental format of the *lira* itself, but rather his bringing of Andean genres from the oral tradition into a written tradition. La Lira Colombiana toured several Central American nations around the turn of the century, and a few years later other similar groups would travel as far as Mexico and the United States in order to record the first albums of *bambucos*, *pasillos*, *torbellinos* [dance genre from the Colombian Andean region], and danzas.

Nonetheless, this process of refinement and elevation of the *bambuco* as national symbol did not happen as calmly as my above description may suggest. In fact, some aspects of the *bambuco*'s social and ethnic status had become the topic of heated debates between intellectuals, especially after Jorge Isaacs [1837–1895] insinuated in his famous 1867 novel *María* that the *bambuco* was originally a musical practice of black slaves. Several authors fervently opposed Isaacs's idea, which was seen as a perverse attack on the *bambuco*'s good reputation, and they proceeded to highlight a number of musical and textual characteristics that would reinforce the genre's Spanish origins.[15] Their interest in defending the *bambuco*'s European origins was clear: to transform the *bambuco* into a national music, it had to become creolized.[16] That is, it needed to pass through a process of purification that would allow it to represent the ideal of the citizen of the new republic: male, white, and literate. The *bambuco* had already completed a good part of that journey by gaining entry to the salons of the aristocracy and by beginning to be translated and established as a written tradition. Thus, Isaacs's observation was dangerous, since affirming any kind of connection with Africanness would have frustrated any potential for the *bambuco* to "purify" its ethnic stigma. No one seemed to bother that Isaacs—the son of landed gentry from the Cauca region who had gained their riches through the work of enslaved blacks working in mines and sugar plantations—most likely simply described a musical practice that he had seen and heard as a child.[17] Not to mention how problematic the ethnic origin of the novelist himself was, with a father of English descent, a convert from Judaism to Christianity, and hailing from Jamaica. As if that weren't enough, Isaacs's own political opinions were rather controversial, given that his ideals had led him to political activism; first as a moderate conservative and later as a radical liberal, and to participate actively in the numerous civil wars which rocked the country at mid-century. Despite all this, Isaacs enjoyed immense prestige as an intellectual and his words carried great weight. This led writers to enter the fray in order to discredit Isaacs's observations. His opponents drew upon a wide range of arguments in order to claim that the *bambuco* was an entirely white genre, ranging from etymological explorations of the term "bambuco" itself to audacious colonial prejudice articulated in a rather arbitrary fashion, such as the argument that the *bambuco* is too civilized to have evolved from indigenous musics, which "suffer from melodic and rhythmic inferiority."[18]

## The *Bambuco* and the National Academy (1900–1910)

It would seem that, after what Morales Pino accomplished at the beginning of the twentieth century, the *bambuco* would have attained a higher status after having been turned into a written musical tradition, which is a fundamental step in becoming a form of civilized knowledge. Nonetheless, the practice of *bambuco*, and of other Andean musical genres, encountered tremendous opposition from within the still-nascent world of Colombian academia. Toward the end of the nineteenth century, the Academia Nacional de Música (National Academy of Music) in Bogotá was the only formal institution for musical education in the country, where Morales Pino and other musicians committed to the development of a national musical repertory were educated.[19] Founded in 1882 by Jorge Price, the son of an English businessman who was an aficionado of music and active member of Bogotá's cultural scene, the academy formalized musical instruction that had previously only been offered privately by nonprofessional teachers. Despite its relative success, the academy suffered serious financial ups and downs and was forced to interrupt its activities in 1899 due to the Thousand Days' War (1899–1902). The academy reopened in 1905, and five years later was put in the hands of Guillermo Uribe Holguín, a musician from an aristocratic family who had just finished his studies in the Schola Cantorum in Paris. The new director changed the institution's name to the Conservatorio Nacional de Colombia (National Conservatory of Colombia), restructured and reinforced its operations, and imposed a new curriculum based on the French conservatory model. One of the consequences of these reforms was the exclusion of all kinds of nonacademic music within the school, including the *bambuco*.

Uribe Holguín's resolution caused tremendous discontent among the musicians and provoked an immediate reaction from the outgoing director, who argued that it was absurd to inhibit the practice of a national repertoire just at the time when a great number of young performers and new *estudiantina* ensembles were emerging. Despite these protests, the new director went forward with his conservative reforms, and all those musicians who performed *bambuco* and other traditional genres were virtually excluded from the school.[20] One could interpret Uribe Holguín's reforms, which guided the institution for a quarter century, as a reaction by the affluent class against the social advancement of the underclass and their music. Although there is much truth to this interpretation, it does leave out one critical point, which is that the academic model from the French conservatory system which Uribe Holguín was following simply did not imagine the study of musics other than the art music of the European bourgeoisie; it did not even include the study of French folk or traditional musics. As Castro-Gómez points out, a school is one of the legitimizing instruments of the state where the ideal citizen is formed in accordance with a civil society's canons, and one of its functions is to define what knowledge is scientific and what knowledge is not.[21] In this case, the French conservatory model established a clear aesthetic difference between arts and crafts (*arte y artesanía*), and the *bambuco* was, without any doubt, dismissed as belonging to the latter category. However "purified" the musical tradition and its performers may have been, the *bambuco* remained a hybrid form of knowledge (or at least not a white, bourgeois, European form of knowledge) that had no place in the Conservatorio Nacional's classrooms. Alternatively, the collection of oral and traditional repertoires, an approach associated with folklore studies that could well have been the appropriate environment for the study of *bambuco* within the academy, did not fall within the interests of a French-style conservatory program, either. Uribe Holguín's many opponents saw his position as a rejection of the *bambuco*'s value, an assertion that was not necessarily entirely true, since later in his life Uribe Holguín would come to use elements of folk music within his own art music compositions. In any case, the director of the most important musical institution of the country had sent an absolutely clear message: traditional music belonged outside of the artistic, aesthetic, and intellectual objectives of the academy.

## Ambiguities with Mechanical Reproduction (1920s–1930s)

The Conservatorio Nacional's reforms effectively split the local musical scene in two: on one side were those who made art music belonging to the urban, European, and hegemonic population, and on the other were those who made traditional music that supposedly belonged to rural, subaltern, and mixed-race [mestizo] populations.[22] Nonetheless, the emergence of recording technology began to subvert this apparently clear division of musical practices and knowledges. At almost the same time that the director of the conservatory fought, against time and tide, to maintain these borders, numerous *duetos* [performing duos] and *liras* had gained access to recording studios in Mexico and the United States. Emilio Murillo's *estudiantina* was one of the first ensembles to record *bambucos* in the Columbia Records studios in New York (1910). Murillo was a pianist and composer from Bogotá's middle class, a student at the old academy, and a pupil of Morales Pino. An original member of La Lira Colombiana, he was a fervent advocate for the creation of a popular style of national music. In other words, Murillo was the complete antithesis of Uribe Holguín.

Once back in Bogotá after his U.S. travels, Murillo became the prime antagonist of the Conservatorio Nacional's Europeanizing policies, offering his opinions in whatever article or journalistic commentary he could manage to publish and looking for support among local politicians and businessmen for his project. Furthermore, he was an active participant in initiatives such as the publication of sheet music of national popular genres in the newspaper *Mundo al Día*.[23] Murillo's nationalist aspirations seemed to be on the right track; between the mid-1910s and the mid-1920s, the *bambuco* recordings that Murillo and others had made sold like hotcakes in the local market. Columbia and RCA Victor established distribution networks with local representatives, and performances by *estudiantinas* began to flourish in the theaters of Bogotá and Medellín. Despite this success in the growing urban cultural market in the early twentieth century, the polemical debate over this new music's value and status grew more aggressive in tone than ever. In order to demonstrate how these arguments evolved, I here introduce another of Murillo's antagonists who took part in the arguments surrounding *bambuco*: Gonzalo Vidal, a composer from Popayán (Cauca Province) who lived in Medellín.

In 1928, Murillo and Vidal were engaged in a savage debate that took place in letters published in various periodicals in Bogotá and Medellín. Murillo was attempting to convince some Medellín politicians to join his crusade in favor of the institutionalization of a national popular music. After Vidal learned of this matter practically by accident, he furiously attacked Murillo's idea in a ruthless critique of phonographic recordings, which, he argued, had come to serve as "carriers of contagion."[24] For Vidal, recordings of nonart music were no more than a convenient way to justify the existence of lazy musicians who did not want to improve themselves through the difficult practice and performance of European art music. Vidal lamented the fact that a foreign public might have access to records of *bambuco* and other national popular genres because "abroad, they will perceive this music as something derived from Indians, aboriginals, from the Chibchas, as something naive, primitive, and jungle-like."[25] For Vidal it was unthinkable that this music could be national music, as this term could, in his way of thinking, only apply to a style of art music.

What is most striking in Vidal's argument is the fact that he recognizes a new category of urban popular music, even though he does so in a rather negative tone. In his writings, Vidal differentiates between three types of music: art music, popular music (*música popular*, "music that comes from the popular classes: guabinas, *pasillos*, *bambucos*, etc."), and music that he considers to be an urban imitation of the latter, an artificially created popular music that "ought to be labeled 'vulgar music' (*música populachera*)," a term that, of course, carries the connotation of populist, unrefined, and cheap music. These arguments are key to understanding how newer and older categories of social stratification began to overlap in the 1920s. On one hand, Vidal articulates his disregard for *bambuco* records using terms of ethnic prejudice deriving from colonial difference: *bambuco* music is not good enough because it is still indigenous and primitive. On the other hand, Vidal criticizes the artificiality and low standards of the music produced for mass consumption by the new urban working class. Both critiques originate in prejudices founded within the coloniality of power, but they are articulated in different ways given the overlapping of the old caste system and the new notion of a modern, class-based society. Another important detail is Vidal's use of the term "música popular," which is radically different in meaning than the English term "popular music" as it is used in the English-speaking academic world. Popular music, in the latter sense, necessarily means a mass-mediated music that is the product of the culture industry and that is distributed and consumed on a large scale. In Spanish, on the other hand, the term música popular refers to "the people's music," which is not necessarily the same as traditional folk music, and as a result the term can have affective as well as political implications. In fact, Vidal uses the term *música popular* to describe an authentic traditional music of rural origin, in contrast with urban music of mass consumption, which he calls vulgar and artificial.

Vidal's observations further complicate our view of the national music scene of that period: according to him, the *bambuco* as performed by the artisans in Bogotá and Medellín who managed to record albums is neither art music nor traditional, but rather belongs to a third and disreputable category, that of the "vulgar" *bambuco*. While the traditional *bambuco* might well be an object of collection and study by folklorists—a discipline that, incidentally, had no institutional history in the country at that point—Vidal takes away the value of authenticity from the urban *bambuco*, it loses even the status of a musical knowledge that deserves, at the very least, to be collected as a part of a folklore anthology. Vidal's argument that practicing vulgar music was no more than an excuse for lazy musicians was, of course, a personal attack on Murillo and his colleagues, but it also had the immediate consequence of delegitimizing the early fieldwork they were doing to collect folkloric materials.[26] Although there's no doubt that Vidal's opinion is prejudicial, it is interesting to note that Murillo's reaction to these attacks was also articulated from a perspective of colonial difference and the coloniality of power. Murillo tried to defend his own position by arguing, once again, that the *bambuco*'s value laid in its supposed European origins. We know of this episode because of a couple of caricatures (although here I refer to only one of them) published in *El Tiempo*, the most influential liberal newspaper in Bogotá, in 1930.

Ricardo Rendón, who was at that time the most respected caricaturist in the country, overheard a conversation between Murillo and the young composer Antonio María Valencia, in which they were discussing the European origins of various local practices, including the *bambuco* and the game of *turmequé* [see note].[27] Rendón mocked these comments in a memorable scene that takes place in front of Bogotá's emblematic "guardian" mountain peaks of Monserrate and Guadalupe (fig. 6.1): in the foreground we see Beethoven, who has just set aside a bottle of beer to pick up a guitar or tiple and sing "Tiplecito de mi vida," a

**Escena chibcha.**

Fig. 6.1 "Escena chibcha" (Chibcha scene), caricature by Ricardo Rendón *bambuco* then much in fashion.[28] The explanation is to be found in the footnote at the bottom: "In Beethoven's scherzo we find the same rhythmic sense as in the *bambuco*: Antonio María Valencia." Behind the great German composer we see a similarly unlikely scene: a group of Athenian spectators watch a muscular athlete prepare to throw the discus, but Rendón subtly informs us that we are not seeing a classical Greek athletic event, but rather a simple and vulgar game of *turmequé*. The caption refers to Murillo: "They are searching for an Athenian precedent for the game of *turmequé*, perhaps from the century of Pericles." This caricature makes evident the persistence of colonial prejudices, but more importantly it demonstrates that the struggles between popular and academic musicians had not remained only within the halls of the Conservatorio Nacional but rather resonated significantly in Bogotá's public opinion. The joke also suggests that, even among intellectuals themselves, arguments that defended the racial purity of musical practices were beginning to become obsolete, given that it had become evident that there was additionally a class-based conflict at work.

## The Not-Entirely-"Civilized" Urban *Bambuco* (1940–50)

By the end of the 1940s, various groups had appropriated the *bambuco*, generating important transformations in the way that it was perceived and categorized. By 1940, the prejudices that had inspired Vidal's aversion to mass-mediated music had nearly entirely disappeared, due to wide social acceptance of forms of mass media, such as the radio. Radio had become an important source of employment for musicians, and nearly any performer who wanted to make a living in the new market economy was obliged to participate in recordings and live radio programs. Repertoire by duos called *duetos bambuqueros* had become a part of regular radio programming; thus we can say that the urban *bambuco* had finally become a genre of "popular music" in the English sense. Another sign of the *bambuco*'s favorable reception among the professional middle class of the time is that radio personalities (journalists who covered performances and record reviewers, such as Camilo Correa and Hernán Restrepo Duque) took the lead in promoting national popular music. One ought to mention as well that the nation's first active music researcher, the self-taught musicologist Andrés Pardo Tovar, began to develop his own work within the world of radio, rather than within the academy.

Quite a few things related to *bambuco* took place during this time period, but here I refer to only one: the controversy that arose over the musical transcription of the *bambuco*. I mentioned above that at the beginning of the twentieth century, Morales Pino had translated several traditional Andean genres to paper. Nonetheless, the rhythm of the *bambuco* did not seem to fit well within any particular meter; apparently, the rebellious *bambuco* resisted attempts to be affixed to the page. This was a serious problem, given that orchestral arrangements for radio performances were only done through written music, but above all because records of Colombian national popular music were still being recorded abroad due to the lack of a local recording industry. The only way to record a *bambuco* was to send the score to Argentina or Mexico so that studio musicians in those places could perform them. But how to achieve that, if *bambuco* does not sound the way that it is written? In 1943, Luis Miguel de Zulátegui, a composer and music critic for the Medellín radio magazine *Micro*, committed himself to the difficult task of solving this problem. Through the pages of that magazine, Zulátegui invited musicians to participate in a survey, through which they could send their own proposals for how to transcribe the *bambuco*. Once an agreement had been reached, Zulátegui argued, the government ought to establish a standard by decree. Despite Zulátegui's willingness to open the debate, in the course of an entire year only one musician, the art music composer Jesús Bermúdez Silva, had sent a commentary on the matter.

At first glance, and setting aside for the moment the absurd notion of a government decree, the lack of participation in Zulátegui's survey may seem to demonstrate apathy and neglect on the part of musicians. Nonetheless, there is far more depth to the issue. First, the problem lies in the fact that Zulátegui's initial question had been badly formulated. Given the way that the survey was articulated, using a complicated nine-point questionnaire full of specialized terminology, it would have been quite difficult for those musicians without a solid academic background to understand. How could *bambuco* musicians have such a background when they still faced difficulties in getting the Conservatory to accept them as students? Second, the questions required a response for which there was simply no epistemological frame of reference. By way of illustrating this problem, I draw on musical transcription, using as an example Morales Pino's classic *bambuco* "Cuatro preguntas" (Four questions).

The *bambuco*'s rhythm is characterized by the use of sesquialtera, a common feature of Latin American rhythmic patterns, which can be notated equally in 3/4 or 6/8 meter. But unlike similar rhythmic patterns such as *son jarocho* [regional style of Mexican folk music], the problem in transcribing *bambuco* rhythms cannot be resolved simply by alternating between these meters. The difficulty arises from the coexistence of both meters' senses of accentuation. This is evident in the ends of phrases and in the melodic articulations (which coincide with the textual accents in the case of sung *bambuco*) which only rarely coincide with the accents in the bass and the harmonic changes. This can be seen clearly in figure 6.2, in which we have Morales Pino's own original transcription for piano of his famous *bambuco* from the early twentieth century, and in which the left hand of the piano imitates the pattern played on the tiple. At first glance it may seem unclear why the composer chose to notate it in 3/4 meter; the vocal accents

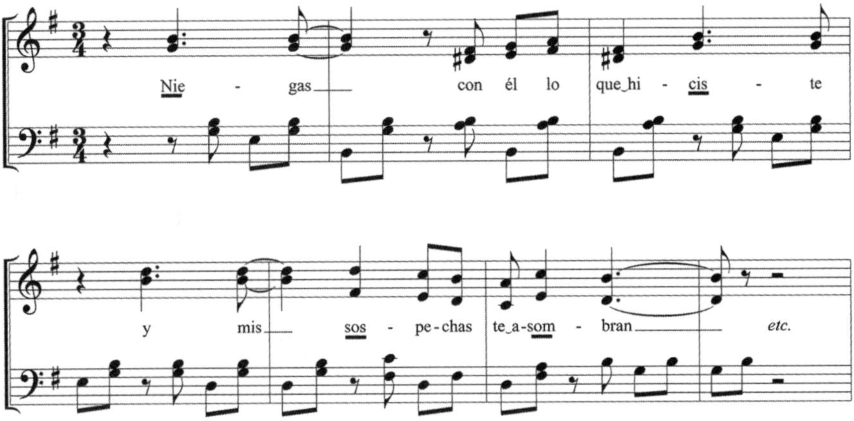


Fig. 6.2 Example from Morales Pino's "Cuatro preguntas" as notated by the composer

(underlined) do not fall on the first beat of the measure, and the harmonic change happens halfway between the measures. The logic behind this transcription lies in placing the accent in the bass line on the first eighth note of each measure. This way of writing is counterintuitive and quite difficult to read for musicians unfamiliar with the oral tradition. The same musical excerpt is much easier to read when transcribed into 6/8 with the downbeat shifted, as shown in figure 6.3.

In figure 6.3, the textual accents fall on the strong beats of measures 1, 3, and 5, and the harmonic changes are contained within each measure. Nonetheless, the bass never lands on a strong beat, which can make the rhythm feel a little

Fig. 6.3 Example of Morales Pino's "Cuatro preguntas" notated in 6/8 and with the downbeat shifted to fit the melodic phrasing

"wobbly" given that it never produces a clear feeling of being anchored. It is up to the performer to learn how to feel the space that is left on the first beat, and the bottled-up energy that the chords played on weak beats produce, which is what I call "settling into the syncopation." As Manuel Bernal explains, during performance it is common for both metric accentuations to coexist; at times the 3/4 meter is marked by the guitar, which indicates the important beats in executing the dance step.[29] Furthermore, in the middle of the performance the musicians may leap from one metric accentuation to the other, given that going in and out of these changes without "falling off" is part of the game of skill in maintaining the syncopated rhythm. As Bernal says, there is not one way of accentuating that is better, or more correct than the other, but rather that some *bambucos* simply "sound" better in 3/4, and others sound better in 6/8. There is no single formula for *bambuco*; rather there are "many *bambucos*."

I will attempt to explain why it is possible for Bernal to reach this conclusion in the beginning of the twenty-first century while it was not possible for Zulátegui and his contemporaries half a century before. Bernal's interpretation is arguing against Enlightenment science's claim to be able to reach a single objective truth that is demonstrable in all cases. The conclusion that would be reached by such an Enlightenment-style scientific approach would seem to be that if the *bambuco* does not fit within a single mold, it is because the *bambuco* itself is wrong. But what happens if we change our point of enunciation? What happens if we call into question the epistemological apparatus that says that the *bambuco* does not fit? First, since the problem seems to lie in the placement of accents, let us examine carefully the European concept of meter. Meter is used to mark a regular period of time, and categorizes hierarchically some beats as strong and others as weak; each one of those beats is subdivided in a regular fashion, replicating that same hierarchy. Meter in European music works within symmetrical time periods, within what Ángel Quintero Rivera calls a Newtonian worldview, which clashes with other asymmetrical ways of counting and subdividing time like the claves of African-derived tropical musics.[30] Trying not to fall back on the endless controversies over the possible ethnic origins of the *bambuco*, it is still possible to affirm that its metric logic is rather analogous to the layering of different rhythmic levels that is characteristic of many African musical traditions.

Let us turn now to the very problem of transcribing an oral tradition within the European notational system. Since the 1960s, ethnomusicologists have observed that transcription, particularly in the case of non-European musics, is always a subjective description of a musical event. We also recognize that there are different ways to transcribe depending on the function that one wishes the notation to serve. There are descriptive transcriptions, which describe in great detail one particular musical event, and other that are prescriptive, serving as guidelines for future performances.[31] In other words, transcription is a useful tool for analysis and performance, but it has its limits and is never completely objective. This observation leads me finally to indicate the two aspects of a Eurocentric perspective that seem most limiting: the hegemony of written forms of knowledge over oral ones, and the low regard in which it holds the body as a vehicle for attaining knowledge. Any musician knows that a fundamental part of learning to play an instrument is observing and imitating one's teacher. For a good musician, it is obvious that not all that is essential for performance is written clearly in the score: in Baroque music the ornaments are left out; so is the way a pianist might expressively change tempo in a rubato when playing the music of Chopin. The academicism of the nineteenth century sought to fix absolutely everything on paper, but music is a performative art that is nourished by the oral transmission from teacher to pupil. This brings me to my last point, which is the exclusion of bodily experience as a valid medium for knowing and acquiring knowledge. When musicians learn to feel the way to settle into the syncopation of the *bambuco*, they do so through the sensations that they experience in their body when playing or singing. For all of these reasons (and probably others that escape me), the fact that the *bambuco* does not fit within the scientific paradigm lies in the paradigm itself that is insufficient, limited, and imperfect.

Half a century ago, questioning this paradigm was not feasible, nor was it desirable for those who maintained control over [musical] knowledge. As my analysis shows, academic knowledge at that time was unable to access other local forms of knowledge associated with the *bambuco* and demonstrates not only the political dimension but also the epistemological dimension of colonial difference. It is interesting to note that the debate over how to transcribe the *bambuco* has been a constant in all of the musicological literature about this genre published in the last fifty years. Bernal's reflection is an attempt to bring to a conclusion a debate that, having gone on for so long, has become utterly tedious. The debate's longevity demonstrates the profound hold that coloniality continues to have on our forms of knowing, understanding, and assimilating those musical traditions that do not entirely correspond to European musical parameters.

## Postcolonial Critique

During the first half of the twentieth century, the rigidity of colonial difference kept the Colombian academic establishment from being able to access the *bambuco* as a hybrid form of knowledge. Of course, colonial difference was not a problem that plagued the Colombian musical establishment exclusively. Researchers in other Latin American nations faced the same dilemma, and some of them found solutions that allowed them to study so-called "impure" musics.

In Argentina, for example, Carlos Vega defined folklore as a science, basing his work on the supposed lack of ethnic miscegenation (*mestizaje*) in Argentine society.[32] His model, in keeping with his historical moment, consisted of tracing backward the "survivals" that he found in folk music, starting from the assumption that only the upper classes in a society are capable of creating cultural works (the lower classes, according to Vega's argument, only mimic the upper classes). Thus, folklore as a science would serve as a way to reconstruct the history of the musical evolution of the upper (white and European-descended) classes, since it was considered impossible for musical survivals to originate in the lower classes or in ethnic minorities. In Cuba, by contrast, the social and political climate, a result of resisting U.S. hegemony, allowed researchers to confront this problem differently. The 1920s and 1930s saw the emergence of Afrocubanismo (Afro-Cubanism), a political and intellectual movement that celebrated the importance of African traditions in Cuba's national culture.[33] This attitude opened up a new political and epistemological space for the work of researchers like Fernando Ortiz and Alejo Carpentier.

Clearly, reinterpreting history in order to identify the underlying coloniality is one way of questioning the basis of the disciplinary boundaries between musicology, folklore, and ethnomusicology in Latin America. Nonetheless, my analysis ought not to be restricted to simply providing evidence of the prejudices on which the disciplines of musical research have been constructed. The most important challenge lies in making the critique of colonial difference go further than merely its political dimensions, and for it to begin to truly affect the ways that music schools face the teaching and research of music other than European art music. In other words, how should we approach the systems of thought that belong to musical traditions other than our own? How might we apprehend processes of teaching and learning based on oral transmission and bodily language? How can we teach our students that the score is merely an incomplete representation of the musical event, and that what we call "music" is a process that is far more rich and complex? How can we get the academic complex to embrace and integrate other forms of knowledge? There are no simple answers to these and other questions that emerge from recognizing colonial difference. Nonetheless, I believe that we can find new methodological paths if we take into account Mignolo's proposal regarding the production of border knowledge. Thinking from the border means reflecting and constructing from within an awareness of our own intermediate position between an academic Eurocentrism and popular or traditional cultures. The exercise I carried out above, and through which I deconstructed the problem of transcribing the *bambuco*, is one example of border thinking. In order to be productive on an immediate and practical level, this analysis intends to motivate a series of reflections on how to approach, learn, teach, and transmit the *bambuco* within academic spaces. Of course, popular and traditional musics like the *bambuco* have been produced and reproduced outside of academic structures, but I think that in many cases there was also a fervent opposition from within those structures. It is worth asking whether the exclusion of these musics in our conservatory curricula today is due to incompatibilities of an aesthetic nature or rather to epistemological inflexibility in the structures of academic musical thinking.

The main benefit of thinking about local musics from the border lies in the possibilities that this type of thinking can open within the academic world in general—a world that continues to be dominated by assumptions such as the hegemony of the written word over oral tradition and the separation between body and mind in the development of cognitive processes. Music and the other performative arts could have much to contribute to other disciplines regarding their experience in these environments. On a more practical level, the challenge of designing methods of instruction for non-European musics is one way to incorporate within academic discourse that which traditional musicians have been doing intuitively for a long time.[34] Some ethnomusicologists, who have had experience teaching and learning non-European musics in academic contexts, have produced interesting reflections, such as the volume edited by Ted Solís.[35] Nonetheless, this collection of essays is restricted to thinking about the "Otherness" of musical knowledge that is foreign to U.S. culture. It is up to us, the Latin American musicologists, ethnomusicologists, and music theorists, who live every day surrounded by the incredible vitality of these traditional and popular musics, to take the challenge of thinking and creating new ways of approaching our own musical knowledges.

## Notes

The reflections presented in this article are part of a larger work concerning the relationship between the academy and coloniality, which is being carried out in coordination with researchers from the Instituto de Estudios Sociales y Culturales Pensar (Thought Institute for Social and Cultural Studies) at the Pontificia Universidad Javeriana (Pontificial Xaverian University) in Bogotá. An adapted version of this text appears in Santiago Castro-Gómez and Ramón Grosfoguel, *El giro decolonial: reflexiones para una diversidad epistémica más allá del capitalismo global* (Bogotá: Siglo del Hombre, 2007).

1. For an example of this confrontation, see the exchange of opinions between Pieter Van den Toorn, "Politics, Feminism, and Contemporary Music Theory," *Journal of Musicology* 9 (1991), 275–99, and Ruth Solie, "What Do Feminists Want? A Reply to Pieter van den Toorn," *Journal of Musicology* 9 (1991), 399–410.

2. Kwabena Nketia, "The Problem of Meaning in African Music," *Ethnomusicology* 6, no. 1 (1962), 1–7; Akin Euba, "Towards an African Pianism: Keyboard Music of Africa and Its Diaspora," unpublished symposium proceedings (Music Department, University of Pittsburgh, 1999).

3. Javier León, "Peruvian Musical Scholarship and the Construction of an Academic Other," *Latin American Music Review* 20, no. 2 (1999), 168–83, and Raúl Romero, "Tragedies

and Celebrations: Imagining Foreign and Local Scholarships," *Latin American Music Review* 22, no. 1 (2001), 48–62.

4. There are important exceptions to this rule, such as Ana María Ochoa's work on the historiography of the *vallenato* [folk musical genre from the Caribbean coast of Colombia] and her in-process work on the ways that sound and musical knowledge in Latin America were constructed in the mid-twentieth century (personal communication). See Ana María Ochoa, "Garcia Márquez, Macondismo, and the Soundscapes of Vallenato," *Popular Music* 24, no. 2 (2005), 207–22.

5. For an introduction to the relationship between power and knowledge in Latin America, see Edgardo Lander, ed., *La colonialidad del saber: eurocentrismo y ciencias sociales. Perspectivas latinoamericanas* (Buenos Aires: Clacso, 2000).

6. Walter D. Mignolo, *Historias locales/diseños globales: colonialidad, conocimientos subalternos y pensamiento fronterizo* (Madrid: Ediciones Akal, 2003).

7. Editors' note: The *bambuco* is a musical genre from the Andean region of Colombia. It is considered by many to be one of Colombia's national musics and, as the author discusses in this article, exists in a variety of interrelated incarnations that cut across social class and cultural background, ranging from folk and popular versions to those more strongly associated with the Colombian art music tradition.

8. Carolina Santamaría, "Bambuco, Tango, and Bolero: Music, Identity, and Class Struggles in Medellín, Colombia, 1930–1953" (PhD diss., University of Pittsburgh, 2006).

9. Translator's note: The original Spanish term *saberes mestizos* has been rendered here as "hybrid knowledges" in consultation with the author, who wishes to avoid the strictly racial or ethnic senses of hybridity suggested by *mestizo* in English in favor of a broader sense of cultural hybridity following Néstor García Canclini, *Hybrid Cultures: Strategies for Entering and Leaving Modernity*, trans. Christopher L. Chiappari and Silvia L. López (Minneapolis: University of Minnesota Press, 2005).

10. Editors' note: By "academic training," the author is referring to individuals with an in-depth formal musical education in Western music theory and composition.

11. For a short and pleasant introduction to this topic, see Santiago Castro-Gómez, *La poscolonialidad explicada a los niños* (Popayán: Universidad del Cauca, 2006).

12. Aníbal Quijano, "Colonialiadad del poder, eurocentrismo y América Latina," in *La colonialidad del saber: eurocentrismo y ciencias sociales. Perspectivas latinoamericanas*, ed. Edgardo Lander (Buenos Aires: Clacso, 2000), 201–46; Walter D. Mignolo, *The Darker Side of the Renaissance: Literacy, Territoriality and Colonization* (Ann Arbor: University of Michigan Press, 1995), and *Historias locales/diseños globales.*

13. Santiago Castro-Gómez, *La hybris del punto cero: ciencia, raza e ilustración en la Nueva Granada (1750–1816)* (Bogotá: Editorial Pontificia Universidad Javeriana, 2005).

14. Carlos Miñana, "Los caminos del bambuco en el siglo XIX," *A Contratiempo* 9 (1997), 7–11.

15. Hernán Restrepo Duque, *A mí cánteme un bambuco* (Medellín: Ediciones Autores Antioqueños, 1986), and Harry C. Davidson, *Diccionario folklórico de Colombia: música, instrumentosy danzas*, vols. 1–3 (Bogotá: Banco de la República, 1970), cover the better part of these arguments and the authors who took part in this debate.

16. Ana María Ochoa, "Género, tradición y nación en el bambuco," *A Contratiempo* 9 (1997), 35–44. Editors' note: The English and French usage of the term "creole" tends to imply the adoption or appropriation of European cultural traits by mixed populations that oftentimes remain racially coded wholly or partially as "black," particularly within the history of race politics in the United States. The author's usage here reflects the Spanish language and Latin American sense of the term, which is tied to the concept of "purity of blood" that she introduces earlier. In this context, and especially during the nineteenth- and early twentieth-century period with which she deals, criollos are people who regarded themselves as being ethnically and culturally predominantly of European descent (at least seven-eighths according to the older colonial caste system established by the Spanish), but who over time had also adopted or appropriated African or indigenous cultural traits, or both. Creolization then implies a process of subordinating these non-European traits as means of rooting, differentiating from (and in the case of some nationalist ideologies improving upon) European cultural heritage.

17. Although there are no extant studies of the musical practices of slaveholding haciendas of the Gran Cauca during the nineteenth century, we can assume that some duties like instrumental performance would have been relegated to nonwhite individuals, as happened in Brazil and other societies based on plantation economies.

18. Bravo Marquez, cited in Restrepo Duque, *A mí cánteme un bambuco*, 7.

19. Ellie Anne Duque, "Instituciones musicales," in *Historia de la música en Santafé y Bogotá, 1538–1938* (Bogotá: Fundación de Música, 2000), 125–48.

20. Ibid.; Jaime Cortes, "La polémica sobre lo nacional en la música popular colombiana," *Actas del III Congreso IASPM-AL*, Bogotá, 2000, www.iaspmal.net/ (accessed Oct. 16, 2013).

21. Santiago Castro-Gómez, "Ciencias sociales, violencia epistemica y el problema de la 'invención del otro,'" in *La colonialidad del saber: eurocentrismo y ciencias sociales. Perspectivas latinoamericanas*, ed. Edgardo Lander (Buenos Aires: Clacso, 2000), 145–61.

22. "Art music" and "traditional music" are terms I use here to differentiate between musical environments, but which do not correspond to the contemporary usage in this historical context. In fact, a great part of the conflict that these musicians faced originated in the fact that performers of traditional Andean genres were not willing to recognize any differentiation between these two musical practices.

23. Jaime Cortes, *La música nacional popular colombiana en la colección Mundo al Día (1924–1938)* (Bogotá: Universidad Nacional de Colombia, Facultad de Artes, 2004).

24. Gonzalo Vidal, "Música nacional," *Progreso* 2, no. 36 (1928), 568.

25. Gonzalo Vidal, "Música nacional," *El Heraldo de Antioquia (Medellín)* (July 11, 1928), 8.

26. Nonetheless, one ought to mention that Murillo's collection of traditional, anonymous songs could be called nonscientific given that it was absolutely unsystematic, and was not designed with the ultimate end of publishing an anthology of folk songs like those of Béla Bartók in Hungary or Felipe Pedrell in Spain. Furthermore, the appearance of some of those songs on phonographic recordings, under Murillo's own name, raised quite a few suspicions (which today we would call messes over copyrights, although at

that time they would have had no economic implications as there was no legislation that regulated them).

27. *Turmequé*, also known as *tejo*, is a game that was inherited from the Chibcha people, an indigenous group native to the high plateau around Bogotá. The game consists of trying to explode a small gunpowder charge that is placed atop a clay box. In order to do this, players stand back a given distance and throw a *tejo*, a heavy metal disc. The winner, of course, is the one who manages to blow up the most charges, while the loser generally pays for all of the beer consumed during the game.

28. It is worth noting that Alejandro Wills, the composer of "Tiplecito," did not call it a *bambuco* but rather a *torbellino*. The term "torbellino" is often used in Colombia to designate pieces in a fast tempo, although there is a traditional genre by this name in the region of Vélez (Santander) which has specific characteristics.

29. Manuel Bernal, "De el bambuco a los bambucos," *Anais do V Congresso IASPM-AL*, Rio de Janeiro, 2004, www.iaspmal.net/ (accessed Oct. 16, 2013).

30. Ángel G. Quintero Rivera, *Salsa, sabor y control: sociología de la música tropical* (Mexico: Siglo Veintiuno, 1998).

31. Charles Seeger, "Prescriptive and Descriptive Music Writing," in *Studies in Musicology 1935–1975* (Berkeley: University of California, 1977), 168–81.

32. Carlos Vega, *Panorama de la música popular argentina, con un ensayo sobre la ciencia del folklore* (Buenos Aires: Instituto Nacional de Musicologia Carlos Vega, 1998, [1944]).

33. Robin Moore, *Nationalizing Blackness: Afrocubanismo and Artistic Revolution in Havana, 1920–1940* (Pittsburgh, Pa.: University of Pittsburgh Press, 1997).

34. It bears mentioning that there are already examples of border methods of teaching—although their authors may not call them such—for instance, Leonor Convers and Juan Sebastián Ochoa, *Gaiteros y tamboleros: material para abordar el studio de la música de gaitas de San Jacinto, Bolívar (Colombia)* (Bogotá: Pontificia Universidad Javeriana, 2007), a book on *gaita* [vertical flute] music of the Caribbean coast of Colombia.

35. Ted Solís, ed., *Performing Ethnomusicology: Teaching and Representation in World Music Ensembles* (Berkeley: University of California Press, 2004).

# PART TWO

# Popular Music, Style, and the Social Construction of Genre

Genre has been one of the central organizing categories associated with the study of various forms of Latin American and Caribbean music. Much of this concern with genre has been tied to the regional circulation of various music and dance forms, going back to the colonial period, which in postindependence contexts led scholars in different countries to both trace common influences as well as demarcate local particularities. In Mexico, for example, folklorist Vicente Mendoza's comparative studies sought to map out both continuities and differences between Mexico, Europe, and other parts of Latin America, as is the case with his attempts to link the *corrido* and the Spanish *romance*, and his exploration of the migration of the Chilean *cueca* into Southern Mexico.[1] Similarly, Carlos Vega documented the spread of multiple versions of the *cueca* throughout South America, contributing to the subsequent stylistic codification of these variants by folklore schools and folkloric dance troupes in Argentina, Bolivia, Chile, and Peru.[2] It also provided an early model for various regional taxonomies of genre elsewhere in South America.[3] This tracing of stylistic variants and genealogies has been a particularly important project of a number of Caribbean scholars, as the crisscrossing of nineteenth-century music and dance genres throughout the islands has generally been regarded as having sparked the genesis of a number of twentieth-century national genres, perhaps most notable among them the Dominican merengue, the better known of a number of "cousins" that also flourished in Haiti, Puerto Rico, and the Caribbean coastal regions of Colombia and Venezuela.[4] They have also been influential in the elaboration of musical histories, with the endurance of specific stylistic features or the transformation from one genre into another serving as signposts for the larger interactions between different social or ethnic groups, as has tended to be the case in various accounts of the development of Brazilian popular music.[5]

Similarly, Latin American and Caribbean music scholarship continues to be concerned with genre, although in recent decades the primary interest has been to examine the various ways in which genre is musically, discursively, and socially constructed, not only by practitioners themselves, but also by listeners, music critics, and academics. Rubén López-Cano's contribution to the ongoing debates regarding the development of the mambo (chapter 7) offers a good example of how these studies have taken on an increasingly reflexive position regarding the historical construction of genre and the need to negotiate a number of competing voices within those debates. In this regard, he echoes and expands on scholarship critical of the conceptualization of popular music genres in terms of a unilinear evolution of style propelled by actions of visionary "great men."[6] López-Cano relies on the growing availability of historical recordings to trace a number of stylistic features associated with mambo to multiple precursors, not only in Cuba but also in New York City. While recordings made in one locality may not have circulated in the other, he argues that this stylistic tracing can help track the movements of musicians as they traveled back and forth between the two countries, undoubtedly borrowing ideas from other musicians and bands that they encountered. In the process, he makes a persuasive case for mambo having coalesced out of the cross-pollination of multiple experimental trends by artists both in Cuba and New York, rather than having been invented single-handedly by any one individual. Furthermore, he calls for a more in-depth historiography of mambo as a means of putting into better perspective the various ideological motivations that have led to the championing of one particular "great man" over another.

If the musical analysis of historical recordings provides López-Cano with a way of reexamining and better understanding the development of a genre, Carlos Sandroni's analysis of *samba carioca* in 1920s and 1930s Rio de Janeiro shows some of the limits and challenges that historical recordings can present for music scholars (chapter 8). As Sandroni explains, scholars, critics, and musicians agree that during that time period, key musicians and composers from the neighborhood of Estácio de Sá introduced rhythmic innovations that redefined *samba carioca* into what is still considered one of the more iconic styles of samba in Brazil. Yet, there seems to be little to no recorded evidence of this. The very percussion instruments that are associated with these innovations are omitted from audio recordings made during that time period, with more representative recordings of the style not appearing until decades later. In order to bridge this gap, Sandroni follows a novel approach inspired by Cuban musicologist Alejo Carpentier's discussion of *clave*, a rhythmic ostinato that plays a central organizing role in various Cuban genres. Positing that the *tamborim* (a small frame drum) in *samba carioca* plays a role similar to that of *clave*, he finds evidence of this type of structuring in the improvised vocal melodies of these early recordings, establishing a continuity of practice.

Rodrigo Torres Alvarado's study of the music of Chilean singer, composer, and folklorist Violeta Parra (chapter 9) expands on the notion of genre beyond its conceptualization as a stylistic paradigm. Instead, Torres Alvarado suggests that Parra and her music must be understood within the larger framework of Chilean folk and popular music in the twentieth century and the role that these had in the Chilean national imaginary. From this perspective, he argues that Parra's stylistic, performative, and aesthetic innovations constitute reactions to earlier musical models that used static notions of "the people" as a means of promoting a particular brand of national integration. Rather than conceiving of folk and vernacular music as practices that should exist outside of modernity, Torres Alvarado suggests that Parra's own musical activity in these realms was tied to the progressive modernization of rural areas during the mid-twentieth century. As such, Parra's construction of what he regards as an alternative musicality was a way of reimagining popular song, not as a museum piece or a commodified form of entertainment, but as a dynamic contemporary practice that could more effectively speak truth to power and challenge older musical, national, and gender models.

Staying on the folk and vernacular vein, Claudio Díaz's work on the emergence of the *nuevo cancionero argentino* (new Argentine songbook) movement, examines the construction of musical genre as a larger social practice (chapter 10). Drawing on the work of French sociologist Pierre Bourdieu, Díaz conceives of the folk-popular music realm in Argentina as a field of cultural production. Within this field, he argues, the notion of tradition operates as a socially motivated discursive construct that enforces specific parameters of inclusion and exclusion through the gradual establishment of specific aesthetic, ideological, and ethical codes. Díaz emphasizes the ongoing processes of transformation that take place within the field, showing how the emergence of the *nuevo cancionero* movement out of an older "classic paradigm" was the result of the decentering of one set of codes and standards in favor of another. As such, many of the features associated with the *nuevo cancionero* movement, such as its links to the political left and to vanguardist artistic movements, were not entirely new developments as much as latent tendencies that the new paradigm was able to capitalize on in order to establish a new sense of tradition and continuity.

Iñigo Sánchez Fuarros (chapter 11) also emphasizes the importance of continuity in his discussion of *timba*, a genre that came to symbolize for many Cubans the ethos of the Special Period (*período especial*, the decade-long economic crisis that was largely prompted by the collapse of the Soviet Union, one of Cuba's principal trade partners). Sánchez Fuarros seeks to draw a distinction between different kinds of appropriation associated with the construction of musical genre, arguing that power relations between the various stakeholders should be a factor in how genre is conceptualized. In particular, he takes issue with how these differences in power led to the promotion of Cuban *son* and a nostalgia for prerevolutionary Cuba in the international music arena (through the success of projects like the Buena Vista Social Club), in the process silencing the voice of *timba*, a contemporary genre that spoke more directly to the realities many Cubans were experiencing at that time. As a means of understanding the social relevance of *timba* in Cuba, Sánchez Fuarros advocates for an analysis of the genre as part of the larger history of Cuban popular dance, arguing that during the Special Period *timba* musicians did not just borrow stylistic and aesthetic elements from Afro-Cuban *rumba*. More importantly, they also managed to appropriate the social role previously ascribed to *rumba* as a musical and social practice capable of social commentary, giving Cubans a way of voicing their discontent.

Finally, Rodrigo Cantos Savelli Gomes and Maria Ignêz Cruz Mello (chapter 12) offer an analysis of how social constructions of genre often interact with other social constructs—in this particular case, gender. Playing on the fact that the Portuguese terms for "genre" and "gender" are homonyms (*gênero*), the authors explore how discourses about music and musical practice can reveal particular gendered perspectives that in turn influence how music and musical practice are enacted. Their study attempts to remedy the comparative lack of attention that they feel issues of gender have garnered in the ethnomusicological study of popular music. Gomes and Mello seek to bring an ethnographic perspective that focuses on discursive practices rather than on the analysis of lyrics and musical texts. After surveying different types of popular music in Brazil, the authors settle on a more in-depth study of multiple bands in the area of Florianópolis, observing that while women participate in a variety of popular music genres ranging from transnational genres like hip-hop to local ones like *pagodge* (a variant or substyle of samba), their presence is markedly more pronounced in rock. Yet, despite this more visible participation, women's activities and contributions to this musical realm continued to be understood as interventions into what is still discursively constructed as a male musical genre. Gomes and Mello use interview data to show how female performers are held to a number of double standards regarding their musicianship skills, the "authenticity" of their sound, their ability to resist commodification, and so on. They argue that this discursive structuring leads to a gendered genre compartmentalization in which "women's rock" becomes a subcategory of the main musical practice, prompting the authors to call for further study and a more systematic theorizing of this type of dynamic.

Javier F. León

## Notes

1. Vicente T. Mendoza, *El romance español y el corrido mexicano: estudio comparativo* (Mexico City: Universidad Nacional Autónoma de México, 1939); *La canción chilena en México* (Santiago de Chile: Instituto de Investigaciones Musicales, Universidad de Chile, 1948).

2. Carlos Vega, *La zamacueca (cueca, zamba, chilena, marinera): la zamba antigua* (Buenos Aires: Julio Korn, 1953). For a discussion of the regional musical circuit that made this dissemination possible, see Carmen Gutiérrez de Arrojo, "La música en Mendoza," *Mendoza, cultura y economía*, eds. Arturo Roig, Pablo Lacoste, and María Cristina Satiari (Mendoza: Caviar Bleu, 2004), 401–10.

3. Luis Felipe Ramón y Rivera, *El joropo: baile nacional de Venezuela* (Caracas: Ministerio de Educación, 1953); Fernando O. Assunção, *Orígenes de los bailes tradicionales en el Uruguay* (Montevideo: Impresora Rex, 1968); Lubín E. Mazuera, *Orígenes históricos del bambuco, teoría musical y cronología de autores y compositores colombianos* (Cali: Imprenta Departamental, 1972).

4. Emilio Rodríguez Demorizi, *Música y baile en Santo Domingo* (Santo Domingo: Colección Pensamiento, 1971); Jean Fouchard, *La meringue, danse nationale d'Haïti* (Montréal: Leméac, 1973); María Cadilla de Martínez, "La historia de la danza puertorriqueña en el siglo XVI y sus evoluciones," *Revista Musical Chilena* 6, no. 37 (1950), 43–77; Cristóbal Soto, "No se ha caído el merengue caraqueño," *Revista de la Fundación Bigot* 27 (1993), 36–45; Ciro Quiroz Otero, *Vallenato: hombre y canto* (Bogotá: Icaro, 1983), 213–21.

5. See for example Mario de Andrade, *Ensaio sobre a música brasileira*, 2nd ed. (São Paulo: Martins, 1962); Ary Vasconcelos, *Panorama da música popular brasileira* (São Paulo: Martins, 1972); José Ramos Tinhorão, *Pequena história da música popular: da modinha à canção do protesto* (São Paulo: Circulo do Livro, 1980).

6. For a now-classic and influential study, see Scott DeVeaux, "Constructing the Jazz Tradition: Jazz Historiography," *Black American Literature Forum* 25, no. 3 (1991), 525–60. Similar arguments to those followed by López-Cano have also been explored more recently in reference to the interrelationships between early jazz and Caribbean musical genres; see Alejandro L. Madrid and Robin Moore, *Danzón: Circum-Caribbean Dialogues in Music and Dance* (New York: Oxford University Press, 2013).

# 7

# Notes for a Prehistory of Mambo

RUBÉN LÓPEZ-CANO

## Who "Invented" the Mambo?

When the question arises regarding who originated the mambo, the well-known fragment that Benny Moré (1919–1963) used to sing is often cited: "Who invented the mambo that suffocates me? Who invented the mambo that drives women crazy? . . . Who invented that crazy thing? . . . A *chaparrito* [shorty] with a seal's face!,"[1] obviously referring to [Cuban bandleader] Dámaso Pérez Prado (1917–1989).[2] However, between 1949 and 1951, Tito Puente's orchestra, with the voice of Cuban Vicentico Valdés, recorded in New York "Mambo en blues," a number that offers its own opinion on the matter: "They say that it was born in New York, Mexico also accepted it, it drove Borinquen [Puerto Rico] crazy, and in Havana it was a sensation."[3]

The problem of mambo's origin has been highly debated by those who study the genre. It seems that nobody denies that it was born in Cuba. However, the question about the composer who created it continues to be one of the iciest polemics in "mambology": was it an original creation by Pérez Prado, or is he merely the most famous figure of a music that has other "inventors"? According to [writer and music critic] Leonardo Acosta, the discussion started in the 1950s, when [Cuban musician, composer and bandleader] Arsenio Rodríguez claimed that he introduced the

Originally published by Rubén López-Cano as "Apuntes para una prehistoria del mambo," *Latin American Music Review* 30, no. 2 (2009), 213–42.  Translated by Marysol Quevedo.

*diablito* (the name given to the mambo's characteristic syncopated ostinato melody) in the *son* ensembles.[4] In the 1960s, [Cuban musicologists] Odilio Urfé and María Teresa Linares agreed that the *danzón* [an earlier dance genre] "Mambo" by Orestes López was the originator of the *guajeos* [general term of ostinato accompaniment patterns] and of the genre.[5] In a later interview, Pérez Prado proclaimed himself as the sole inventor and claimed that the term had no musical connotations before him. Orestes López and Antonio Arcaño, angered, countered immediately.[6] In more recent times, Bebo Valdés fed the polemic claiming that the style was the legacy of many Cuban musicians from the 1940s.[7]

Although Acosta had argued since 1989 that the mambo was something that "was in the air" of the music scene toward the late 1940s, he also pointed out that there were competing notions of what was the mambo, one as rhythm and another as genre.[8] On the other hand, even though no one seems to question Pérez Prado's leading role,[9] the list of musicians who possibly intervened in the formation of the genre continues to grow. To Pérez Prado, Orestes López, and Arsenio Rodríguez have been added pianist Réne Hernández, Julio Cueva, Israel "Cachao" López, Bebo Valdés, and the *tres* [six-string, three-course guitar-like instrument] player and arranger Andrés Echevarría (Niño Rivera) and, more recently, Estanislao Serviá, a little-studied *danzonero* who seems to have included syncopated *guajeos* in the *danzón* before Orestes López.[10]

Among the Cuban musicians who worked in New York and collaborated in the development of the style in that city, the individuals cited most often are Frank Grillo "Machito" and Mario Bauzá. While only some U.S. authors have given importance in the development of New York mambo to Marcelio Guerra and José Curbelo,[11] the contributions of Anselmo Sacasas and Pupi Campo have barely been mentioned.[12] In this article I propose to reconsider the Havana–New York connections in the formation of the style, revising the roles played by Miguelito Valdés, José Curbelo, and Anselmo Sacasas in the musical practices related to the mambo, and their contributions to the process of construction and dissemination of the genre. I focus on events in Havana and New York around 1946, a crucial year for mambo's development. To this end I analyze recently rereleased recordings of these musicians as well as information offered in the 2002 *Enciclopedia discográfica de la música cubana* (Encyclopedic discography of Cuban music), volume 2, *1925–1960*, by Cristóbal Díaz Ayala.

My objective is not to revisit the arguments regarding the place of origin of the mambo or of its creator, but rather offer information that invites us to question the pertinence and productivity of these research questions. I focus on the need to propose new paths for study that will aid in clarifying the nature of the discussion.

## "Mambo No. 5": The Mambo's Stylistic Types

A strategy for understanding the stylistic development of the mambo is to define some stylistic main types associated with the genre.[13] Toward this goal I propose that we use as the prototype "Mambo No. 5" of Pérez Prado that along with "Qué rico el mambo" were numbers that established the worldwide success and fundamental traits of the mambo.[14]

Classified as "mambo-kaen," "Mambo No. 5" is predominantly instrumental.[15] It is in rondo form: A–B–A'–C–A''–D–coda. Each section is framed by a strong rhythmic cadence *a tutti* that we will call "block" (b). At a specific moment, a bongo solo appears (which Pérez Prado omitted in later recordings): ${}_{b1}A_{b1'}–B_{bi\ \text{bongo solo}}–A'_{b2}–C_{b3}–A''_{b4}$–D–coda. The blocks recall the cadences of *rumba* and have total silences that, despite their short durations, stress the listener's expectations. The A section presents a highly syncopated and articulated riff that repeats as an ostinato in the saxophones over which the trumpets develop different melodies (fig. 7.1).

The trumpets' melody is simple and with rough gestures always in the high register. When the section repeats for the first time (A'), the trumpets perform a characteristic effect of the mambo known as shake or *chiva*: playing in the extreme high register in sforzato with forte dynamics or louder, with trill at a step, half-step, or microtone.[16] The effect is electrifying. In A'' the trumpet's melody is high, very articulated, and punched on the final downbeat of each phrase. The B section is another riff similar in character to the previous one, but with a different melody (fig. 7.2).

After two riff measures in the saxophones, the trumpets join, repeating at an octave higher for two additional measures. The gradual accumulation of brass instruments in instrumental interludes is called *chambola*. The C section is a chorus that repeats "Sí, sí, sí, yo quiero mambo, mambo" (Yes, yes, yes, I want mambo,

Figure 7.1 First riff of "Mambo No. 5" by Dámaso Pérez Prado

Figure 7.2 Second riff of "Mambo No. 5" by Dámaso Pérez Prado

Figure 7.3 Third riff of "Mambo No. 5" by Dámaso Pérez Prado

mambo). It vaguely resembles a similar chorus from the *danzón* "Mambo" by Orestes López. The last section (D) is again built over a chromatic, syncopated riff (fig. 7.3).

The trumpets enliven the tempo by superimposing this riff with another one with a lot of swing in which they play a small descending glissando at the end of each phrase. At all times the bass plays on the third and fourth beat of each measure, reminiscent of the *tumbao* [ostinato pattern played by the bass] of the *danzón de "nuevo ritmo"* ("new-rhythm" *danzón*).[17] It concludes with a jazz-altered chord.

In summary, the main stylistic types of "Mambo No. 5" by Pérez Prado are as follows: (1) syncopated riffs that repeat as ostinatos in the saxophones, that function as main melodies; (2) melodies developed by trumpets in the high registers; (3) shakes or *chivas* in the trumpets; (4) vigorous rhythmic cadences with inserted stressing silences; (5) bass *tumbao* following the *danzón de "nuevo ritmo"*; (6) *chambolas* or gradual superimposition of brass instruments; and (7) characteristic chorus. These stylistic types appear time and time again, in a more or less literal way, or in diverse realizations or variations, in mambo pieces by Pérez Prado and other composers. It is worthwhile to look for traits of this type in some Cuban music performed by jazz-format orchestras in Havana and New York during the 1940s.

## In the Beginning There Was the *Danzón*

The most extensive and plausible hypothesis affirms that the ostinato syncopated riffs originated in the *guajeos* of the *danzón de "nuevo ritmo."* Toward the end of the 1930s, groups such as Orquesta Arcaño y Sus Maravillas (Arcaño and His Wonders Orchestra) introduced in the last section of the *danzón* syncopated motives played by string ostinato, allegedly inspired by the motives used by *treseros* [*tres* players] from the Oriente [Eastern Cuba] to begin their *sones* [plural of the Cuban *son*].[18] Over the ostinato, flute improvisations (rhythmically repeating individual notes, without articulating melodies), piano, and *tumbadoras* [conga drums] were played. They called the ostinato *guajeo*, and one of the first *danzones* composed with this technique was precisely titled "Mambo" (ca. 1937 and 1939) by Orestes "Macho" López (1908–1991), cellist for the Orquesta Arcaño y Sus Maravillas (fig. 7.4).

Figure 7.4 *Guajeo* in the strings in the last section of the *danzón* "Mambo" by Orestes López

The success of the jazz big bands during the 1930s in the United States favored their dissemination through Havana.[19] They could play a wider variety of genres than other types of ensembles (such as the *charangas* [flute, string, and piano ensembles]), and by 1945, when Havana became a mainstream tourist destination, they assumed an important role in the tourism and music industries.[20] The jazz big bands appropriated the *guajeo* technique, mostly in their performances of *guarachas* [fast-tempo Cuban dance genre]. The first part of this genre used to be more strophic, while the second part, also called the *montuno* section, had a livelier and more danceable character.[21] The syncopated ostinato *guajeos* appeared in this section, played by saxophones over which the trumpets would articulate riffs and main melodies. The most common story insists that the *guarachas* with *guajeo* sections were the point of origin of Pérez Prado's mambo.

One of the earliest extant recordings of these *guarachas*, played by a jazz band with an air of mambo, is "Figurina del solar" by Chapotín and Pérez Cánova. According to Díaz Ayala's catalog, it was recorded on February 24, 1944, by Julio Cueva's Orchestra (Orquesta de Julio Cueva) and with the voice of "Cascarita" (Orlando Guerra, 1920–1973).[22] After two introductory strophes the *montuno* begins, presenting a variant of the *guajeo* seen in the *danzón* "Mambo," chromatically melodized (fig. 7.5).

All the action has the sonority of "mambofied" *guarachas* that Pérez Prado would record throughout the following years.[23] Who made the arrangement of this number? During this period, René Hernández (1916–1977) was the pianist and arranger of Cueva's orchestra. However, this does not guarantee that this "mambofied" arrangement was of his authorship. We know that Pérez Prado used to be Cascarita's favorite arranger. Even if the piano solo in the recording completely lacks Pérez Prado's style, making it very likely that it was performed by Hernández himself, the arrangement could have been an original by Pérez Prado and purchased by Cueva. It was quite common for arrangers and composers to sell their arrangements to other orchestras, even when they worked exclusively

Figure 7.5 *Guajeo* in "Figurina del solar" by Julio Cueva's Orchestra

for one ensemble. This complicates the establishment of personal styles among composers, arrangers, and orchestras. It is possible to hear Pérez Prado's style in many numbers recorded by Cascarita with different orchestras from this era, during which the former was the "official" pianist and arranger of the Casino de la Playa Orchestra (Orquesta Casino de la Playa). On the other hand, some *guaracha* and mambo numbers that found success in New York were purchased in Havana for a couple of dollars, which contributed to the dissemination of the "mambofied" style in the United States.

A discussion about the author of the arrangement for "Figurina del solar" is relevant as long as Hernández is considered as another of the "inventors" of the mambo. In effect, in December 1945 he would leave Julio Cueva's Orchestra to substitute for Joe Loco at the piano in Machito's Afro-Cubans in New York,[24] introducing in this way "the mambo to Machito's orchestra, with his arrangements and his pianistic style."[25]

## *Guajeo* Evolution Theories

During the first half of the 1940s, the term "mambo" was used by musicians in *charangas* and jazz bands to designate the composition "mambo" by Orestes López, the last section of the *danzón de "nuevo ritmo,"* or the corresponding section of the "mambofied" *guarachas*. Perhaps around that time the concept began to be used in the jazz *descargas* [a section in a composition or a stand-alone piece featuring a series of improvised solos] in which they would request that an accompaniment instrument (piano or saxophones) play as a foundation a syncopated *guajeo*, or for the bass or piano to play a *tumbao*, similar to the ones used in the *danzón de "nuevo ritmo"* over which they would improvise.

It is possible to imagine a linear development from the syncopated motives of the *treseros* from Oriente, to the *guajeo* in the mambo, passing through the *danzón de "nuevo ritmo"* and the "mambofied" guarachas from the jazz bands (fig. 7.6).

However, Enrique Jorrín, creator of the *cha-cha-chá* dance genre, was said to have been "somewhat upset by the notion" that Pérez Prado (or any big-band arranger) could have imported it directly from the *son* without passing through the *danzón* (fig. 7.7).[26]

After all, it is possible to hear these syncopated motives in many jazz band numbers unrelated to the *guarachas* or the mambo, that were surely copied from the accompaniment motives in the *son*. See, for example, the *guajira* "Sopa de pichón" that Machito recorded between 1941 and 1942 in New York (i.e., chronologically and especially distanced from the musics related to the mambo) (fig. 7.8).

But not every syncopated motive generated the effect of the *guajeos* in the mambo. Furthermore, the *guajeos* of *danzón de "nuevo ritmo"* certainly con-

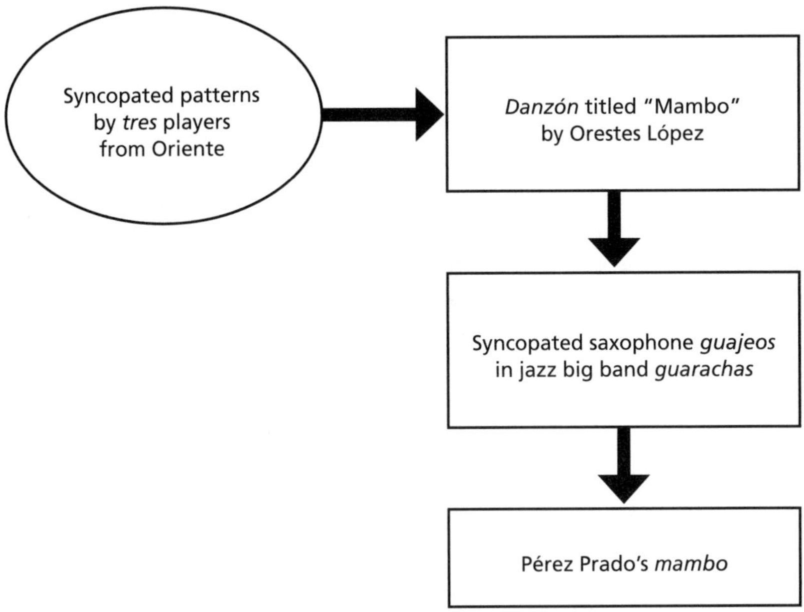


Figure 7.6 Unidirectional model of the "evolution" of the *guajeo* from the *son* to the mambo

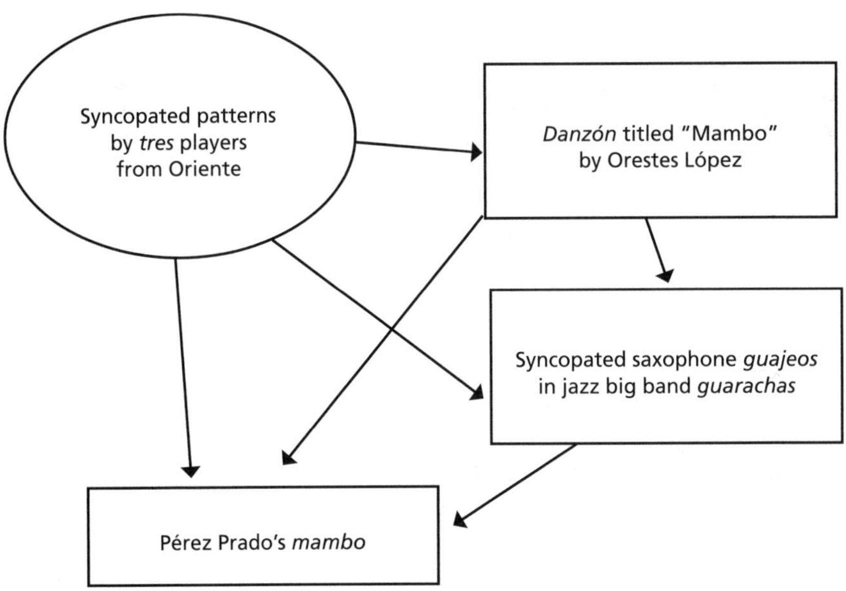


Figure 7.7 Multidirectional model of the development of the mambo's *guajeo*

Figure 7.8 Syncopated riff in "Sopa de pichón" by Machito

tributed much more than a few syncopations. Arcaño himself said that this innovation was motivated by the dancers' needs.[27] The *danzón* is one of the most formal dances of the Caribbean, and its etiquette is to be followed strictly. [According to López de Padura,] "When I started playing in 1926, the *danzón* was still a very formal salon dance, very traditional, with a very rigid scheme."[28] The "mambofied" section of the *danzón* was inserted at the end, after each number fulfilled the other demands of the musical form. This meant that it occupied a specific moment within a narrative plot of an emotion-kinetic-gestural nature. Its incisive and piercing rhythm was tested by dancers as a form of liberation and through its constant progression would lead them to a sort of a dancer's ecstasy. Regarding this trait of the "mambofied" *danzón*, we have the testimony by Manuel Cuellar Vizcaíno, published in the magazine *Bohemia* in 1948:

> For some time we have been observing something completely new in the dancers' atmosphere. . . . It is a new style of dancing the *danzón* in its last section, imposed . . . by a new way of playing . . . [the] fourth step that the dancer doesn't even mark with their foot, but with a full-body shake/tremble, as though they are shaking off something that starts tickling their back around the kidney area and starts to creep up to the shoulders. In the midst of the dance's frenzy the members of the couple tend to separate and shake each on their own, liberally enjoying the music's bewitchment. . . . The dancers . . . have the need to exhale screams like explosions from escape valves. What has been described in part or jointly, received the name of mambo.[29]

But, as with any new dance style that provokes ecstasy, the mambo had its detractors: "The enemies of the mambo claim that with it the elegance and grace of the *danzón* disappear . . . they argue that "that" came from the Americans as an aggression to our national dance, introducing with it the prosaic movements and gestures that have nothing to do with our customs."[30]

Before it was used by dance orchestras, the term "mambo" referred to Afro-Cuban ritual and musical practices, mostly of the Congo or Bantú cultures.[31] But in the realm of the virtuosic and acrobatic style of the *rumba columbia*, it was an aesthetic category that expressed "efficiency, demand, approval."[32] I find this point quite relevant: in my opinion, the term "mambo" remits to this effect of

Figure 7.9 Anticipated *guajeo* of "Coge pa' la cola" by Cascarita and Pérez Prado

Figure 7.10 Main *guajeo* of "Coge pa' la cola"

efficiently achieving ecstasy and the total surrender of the body, reached by the dancers of the *columbia*. In some way, the ecstatic dancing was lived on in the new section of the *danzones*, and it was one of the motivations of the jazz bands to incorporate *guajeos* in the "mambofied" *montunos* of their *guarachas*. This can be seen in the next example.

On November 27, 1945, Cascarita and Pérez Prado, the latter now as a member of the Casino de la Playa Orchestra, recorded the *guaracha* "Coge pa' la cola."[33] From the first stanza in the first section there is already a part featuring a *guajeo* that is a rhetorical anticipation or flash-forward of what the *montuno* will be. It is as though ecstasy hastens, as though the climax is reached for before it is possible (fig. 7.9).

But the theme's culminating point is reached in the second part, through the repetition of a chromatic *guajeo* (fig. 7.10).

The piano solo is full of clusters, tense silences, virtuosic outbursts, and double-sharp notes, struck as if it were a rumba drum and not a keyboard: that was Pérez Prado's pianistic style. In the culminating measures, Cascarita observes the level of ecstasy achieved in the music by repeating the *guajeo*, and he exclaims: "¡Oye el mambo!, ¡el mambo está botao! . . . ¡oye!, ¡cómo está, cómo está el mambo!" (Listen to the mambo! The mambo is off the hook! . . . Listen! How is, how is that mambo!) That was the spirit of the "mambo" in the *guarachas* of the jazz bands and the function of their *guajeo*.[34]

## The *Guaracha* and the Mambo

During the 1940s, at least three types of *guarachas* coexisted that contributed—to a greater or lesser extent—to the development of the *guajeos* of the mambo. These were *guarachas* with ostinato and without *guajeo*, slow *guarachas* with syncopated ostinato, and "mambofied" *guarachas*. I cite examples recorded before and including 1945.

### *GUARACHAS* WITH OSTINATO AND WITHOUT *GUAJEO*

These are *guarachas* that present small motives that repeat in ostinato in the saxophones but that do not possess the type of syncopation typical of the *guajeo*. To this category belong *guarachas* such as "En tiempo de mangos," "No tengo tambó," "Ya' tá," "Castillos en el aire" (classified as *son guajiro*), "El cuento del sapo," and "Dice mi gallo," all recorded by Julio Cueva's Orchestra. The Casino de la Playa Orchestra, with the voice of Cascarita and Pérez Prado's arrangements, recorded "Azúcar pa' un amargo." The Palau Brothers' Orchestra (Hermanos Palau Orquesta) also recorded "Apriétame más" with Cascarita.[35]

### SLOW *GUARACHAS* WITH SYNCOPATED OSTINATO

These slow and heavy-tempo *guarachas* have a certain "familiar air" in the number "Me voy pa'l pueblo," which we could consider a prototype of this category and which Benny Moré recorded in Mexico City around 1948 with Mariano Mercerón's Orchestra (Orquesta Mariano Mercerón). In this category the ostinati show strong syncopation, although not at the speed or the swing of the "mambofied" *guajeos*. To this category belong numbers such as "Sacando boniato," recorded by Julio Cueva; and "Yo pico un pan" and the marvelous number "Esto es lo último,"[36] both recorded by the Casino de la Playa Orchestra, with Cascarita and Pérez Prado. Also within this style are "Baltasar tiene un pollo" and the classic "Puntillita" as recorded by the Palau Brothers' Orchestra (also with Cascarita).[37]

### "MAMBOFIED" *GUARACHAS*

These are *guarachas* that present in their *montuno* variants of the type of *guajeo* we have already seen. Their syncopation and swing relate them with what will become the mambo. Besides the numbers already mentioned, to this style also belong "¿Por qué llora la vaquita?" and "¿Que no le tiraron?," both recorded by Julio Cueva's Orchestra.[38]

I have mentioned only examples of *guarachas* recorded up to 1945 because, as we will see, around 1946 there were a series of events of great importance to the development of the mambo as an independent genre. Curiously, these occurred differently in New York and in Havana, as a result of musicians who resided in one place or traveled between them. It is these connections and interconnections that we should analyze.

## The Pérez Prado Connection (or Dámaso in Freezeland)

Several sources agree that Pérez Prado traveled to New York toward the beginning of 1946.[39] John "Big Daddy" Rodríguez, a famous bongo player who performed with the main Latin bands of New York, remembers meeting him at La Salle cafeteria, the emblematic meeting point of Hispanic musicians. Rodríguez helped him find a coat to survive the harsh winter. Pérez Prado was trying to sell his big band arrangements for two dollars each. Rodríguez, at the time Xavier Cugat's bongo player, remembered that Cugat recorded at least once a month, and that he always needed new numbers. Although "during those times it was easier to have a hearing with the Pope than with Cugat," Rodríguez was able to convince him to buy some of the arrangements . . . and it seems that he bought several.[40]

But in the period that Pérez Prado was in New York, important Cuban musicians who had settled in that city visited the island. In actuality, they never lost contact and continuously traveled to Havana for family or professional matters. They habitually noted down musicians and singers, in addition to purchasing arrangements and print music at stores or directly from composers or arrangers.

Machito as much as Tito Puente and other Latin band directors residing in New York frequently hired musicians who lived in Havana. A well-known link for those directors was Armando Romeu, who for more than twenty years as the head of the Tropicana's Orchestra received frequent visits from his colleagues in New York who came to him for advice, in the same way that in New York they went to Mario Bauzá.[41]

## The Miguelito Valdés Connection

One of the established musicians in New York who was most active and professionally recognized in Cuba, was Miguelito Valdés (1912–1978). Between December 1645 and January 1946 he apparently visited Havana to receive "a medical treatment to overcome a serious affliction of the vocal chords."[42] During that trip he was hailed as popular as if he were a national hero, even receiving an official medal.[43] Between late 1946 and early 1947, he made a series of recordings in Havana "with authentic Cuban musicians" for his company Musicraft.[44] Of the eight numbers recorded, "Algo nuevo" stands out and is attributed to Valdés himself.[45] Although it is classified as a *rumba*, "Algo nuevo" sounds more like a *son* (or a *son guajiro* [a hybrid between a son and a guajira]). Distanced from the typical sonority of the music recorded in Havana during those times, the song develops the main melody through chromatically descending sequences and accompanies the following text:

| | |
|---|---|
| Algo nuevo | Something new |
| para la rumba | for the rumba |
| que le faltaba | that it missed |
| pa' completar, | to complete |
| no son timbales | it is not timbales |
| ni las maracas, | nor the maracas |

| | |
|---|---|
| tampoco el güiro | neither is it the guiro |
| ni el tumbador | nor the tumbador (congas) |
| . . . y es el mambo . . . | . . . and it is the mambo . . . |

The song does not specify the characteristics of the mambo that it announces. During the first part, the bass *tumbao* plays on the third and fourth beats of the measure, similar to the *danzón de "nuevo ritmo."* In the refrain, the bass changes playing something similar to a *guajira*, and in the second part it introduces on the third beat the style of the anticipated bass of the *son*.[46] At the end of two large sections, the instruments intone a long riff broken by silences and syncopations (fig. 7.11).

It is not an ostinato, and its resemblance to the *guajeos* in the "mambofied" *guarachas* is slight. Apart from the two subtle traits already mentioned, the song presents no other element similar to the mambo of the *danzón* nor to the "mambofied" *guarachas*. Perhaps it is one of the first examples of what Gustavo Pérez Firmat called *metamambos* or *mamboids*: numbers that, without being mambos, nonetheless sing about and celebrate it.[47] What can be affirmed is that the song shows us the importance that musicians in New York gave to "that new thing" that caused frenzy in Cuba around 1946. Several numbers like this spread the news of the rhythm, genre, or practice, to the Latinos who resided in the Big Apple.

But there is another more intriguing example. In 1946 Valdés presumptively recorded, with his sextet for the same company, an interesting *descarga* [jam] called "Mambo No. 2" that takes place over a "mambofied" *guajeo* divided among various instruments in the manner of a hocket (fig. 7.12).

The only information on this number [title and genre type in parenthesis] is offered by the recording label on which it finally appeared in 2001.[48] Díaz Ayala does

Figure 7.11 Riff for the last sections of "Algo nuevo" by Musicraft

Figure 7.12 Main *guajeo* of Miguelito Valdés's "Mambo No. 2"

not provide information regarding its origin. Could it be a premature relative of the *descargas* of Peruchín or of Chico O'Farril, of the "mambofied" *guajeos* that they would develop years later? Stylistically, the number seems closer to the *descargas* than the instrumental group of Miguelito Valdés, featuring René Hernández, which around 1949 recorded for Gabriel Oller's SMC in New York, and which includes numbers such as "Gandinga" or "Harlem Special," arranged by Valdés and Hernández themselves.[49] Here we have another mystery for mambology.

Let us return to Pérez Prado for a moment. Revising Díaz Ayala's records of recordings, we find that in a period spanning from mid-March to early July 1946 he ceases to record in Havana. It is possible that during this period he traveled to New York. On March 15, Cascarita had a session [in Cuba] with the Palau Brothers' Orchestra, with which he recorded "Baltasar tiene un pollo." The sound of some of the saxophone riffs is very similar to the style of Pérez Prado, who more than likely was the author of the arrangement. But, since the piece does not have a piano solo, we do not know if Pérez Prado participated in the recording. However, he surely must have participated in the March 4 session in which, with the Pérez Prado Ensemble (Conjunto Pérez Prado), he recorded, among other numbers, "El tumbaito." It is curious that, during this same period, this *guaracha* was also recorded in Havana by Miguelito Valdés during the previously mentioned sessions and by Anselmo Sacasas in New York, only four days before the Pérez Prado [March 4] recording. But there are more interesting things about Sacasas and this recording session. So let us review [what we know of] the Sacasas connection.

## The Anselmo Sacasas Connection

Anselmo Sacasas (1912–1998) arrived in New York with Miguelito Valdés in 1940, after a brilliant career with the Casino de la Playa Orchestra in Havana. His frequent trips to Cuba include one in 1942, when he visited his ailing father, and one in 1945 when he was searching for a singer. On the latter trip (it was difficult to find singers in New York who could sing in the Cuban style), he found Rubén González in Havana.[50] Then the singer for the Niagara Ensemble (Conjunto Niágara), González would travel with Valdés to New York, where the two would record some of Valdés's most important numbers.[51] Sacasas introduced in his arrangements many of the musical trends and tendencies from Havana, particularly those related to the *danzón*.[52] It is not strange, then, that in the beginning he worked with orchestras in the *charanga* style and always proclaimed "to be proud to be a Charanguero."[53] In numbers such as "Pa' lo pollo maí" and "Vamos a gozar" he introduced in the *montuno* section *tumbaos* reminiscent of the *tumbaos* of the *danzón de "nuevo ritmo."* A separate mention should be given precisely to his version of "El tumbaito,"[54] in which he occasionally inserted fragments of the *tumbao* of the celebrated *danzón* "Almendra" by composer Adalberto Valdés, with whom he worked in Tata Periera's Charanga during the 1930s.[55] Over this characteristic *tumbao*, Sacasas introduced in the trumpets the shake or *chiva* effect (fig. 7.13). This recording is one of the first where this effect appears; it is also the oldest of the group of recordings studied and reviewed in the Díaz Ayala discography.

Even more interesting is a *guaracha* recorded in the same session, simply titled "Mambo" (written by C. Valencia and Sacasas). Although the number was reedited in 1996,[56] it has not received the attention of mambology, and it is mentioned only indirectly by Pérez Firmat.[57] In many aspects, this song repeats some of the stylistic traits of the *guarachas* by Sacasas from this period, such as modulations between sections, introductions and interludes that resemble music from Broadway, and strict melodic phrases that develop melodies in the Tin Pan Alley style. However, they also present some highly innovative elements that I have not found in earlier numbers from either Havana or New York in the studied recordings. The *guaracha* has nine sections.

1. Introduction. The trumpets intone a melody in Sacasas's style, for eight bars, followed by a short interlude with the bass and piano in unison.

2. Instrumental version of song. The main melody is played in succession by the trumpets, piano, and strings. The song has a first part (A). The second part (B) modulates to the subdominant (here the main melody played by the trumpets is very articulated and syncopated, and it sings over the syncopated rhythms played by the saxophones, which do not resemble "mambofied" *guajeos*), and lastly, a refrain. [It returns from the modulation.]

Figure 7.13 Reference to the *tumbao* of "Almendra" in Anselmo Sacasas's "El tumbaíto"

3. The song repeats, but this time with lyrics, which is a long narrative:[58] (A). "En mi Cuba (ideal), el país sin igual no se baila ya más la rumba. / Ni tampoco el buen son, siempre muy sabrosón (eso sí ya tú ves) le zumba. / Nuevo ritmo salió ya era hora por Dios este cambio me alegra tanto. / Si tú quieres gozar y aprenderlo a bailar, ven y escucha lo que te canto." (In my ideal Cuba, a country without equal the rumba is no longer danced. / Nor does the good *son*, always very flavorful [and that is, you see], resonate. / A new rhythm came out already, and now for God's sake, this change makes me happy. / If you want to fun and to learn how to dance it, come and listen what I sing.) (B) (modulates to the subdominant): "Tienes que bailarlo suave, tienes que bailarlo bien. / Echa un pie y no te trabes, ya verás qué fácil es. / Vamo' a empezarlo a bailar." (You have to dance it slow, you have to dance it well. / Put one foot, and don't get stuck, you will see how easy it is. / Let's start dancing it.) Refrain: Chorus: "Mambo"; Soloist: "Yo quiero bailar" (I want to dance); Chorus: "Mambo" etc. (Short rhythmic cadence.)

4. Instrumental interlude 1.

5. Refrain: Chorus: "Mambo"; Soloist: "Yo quiero bailar," etc. (Short rhythmic cadence. Return from modulation.)

6. B section of the song in instrumental version (the main melody is played by the saxophones).

7. Instrumental interlude 2. (Modulation to the subtonic.)

8. B section of the song repeats in instrumental version (now the main melody is played by the trumpets, higher and doing crescendo, in comparison to 6.).

9. Instrumental interlude 3 and finale (return from the modulation).

In the same way that "Algo nuevo" by Valdés did, the *guaracha* "Mambo" spreads the news in New York of a new rhythm (or practice) that is shaking up Cuba, the symbolic and effective cradle of the dance music vanguard of the Caribbean. The refrain, where the solo and chorus alternate, resembles the similar chorus of the *danzón* "Mambo" by Orestes López and the chorus of "Mambo No. 5" by Pérez Prado. But most interesting are the interludes. Interlude 1 is a strange or inverted variant of a "mambofied" *guajeo*: the *guajeo* for accompaniment is developed by the trumpets, while the saxophones perform a repeated note with trills and ornaments. Perhaps this picture is inspired by the flute interventions of Arcaño in the last section of the *danzón de "nuevo ritmo,"* where one note is repeated insistently with diverse rhythms and occasionally would add trills and other ornamentations (fig. 7.14).

Interlude 2 presents a *guajeo* in its "natural voice," the saxophones, over which the trumpets perform the shake (fig. 7.15).

In interlude 3, once more the trumpets perform the *guajeos*, while the saxophones develop fast motives (fig. 7.16).

Despite its singularity, the performances in interludes 1 and 3 can also be understood as variant (even if somewhat strange) of the stylistic type of the

Figure 7.14 Stylistic type of the *guajeo* of the mambo in “Mambo” by Anslemo Sacasas

Figure 7.15 Stylistic type of the mambo in interlude 2 in “Mambo” by Anslemo Sacasas

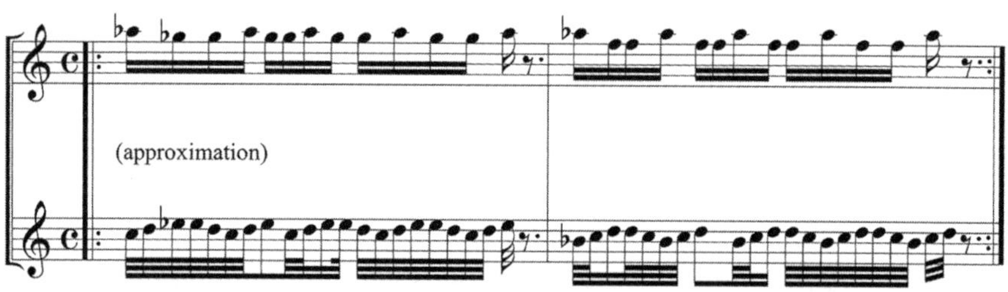


Figure 7.16 Stylistic type of the mambo in interlude 3 in “Mambo” by Anslemo Sacasas

“mambofied” *guajeo*. It is very likely that the instrumental versions, in coherence with the lyrics, are presenting the new music practice from Havana to a New York audience. In spite of its importance, this *guaracha* has remained unnoticed by most who study the mambo. It is one of the first numbers (if not the first) that has as its title the word “Mambo” outside of the realm of the *danzón de “nuevo ritmo,”* which constitutes an important step in the process of conceptualizing the mambo as an independent genre or practice. We do not know whether or not this number was played in Havana, since the only other recording of it is from 1947, when Antonio Machín recorded it in Spain, classifying it as a *rumba* and attributing its authorship to Sacasas.

Sacasas recorded a few "mambofied" *guarachas.* In 1945 he recorded "Si tú me llevas, te llevo," which presents several syncopated riffs, but no ostinato. He also recorded an arrangement of "Capullito de alelí," with a "mambofied" riff in a couple of measures without a main melody (minute 1:26). In 1946 Sacasas recorded "La bodega del Ñato," which presents the shake effect of the inverted *guajeo* (in the trumpets) while the saxophones play chromatic lines similar to the *guaracha* "Mambo" (2:04). The songs "Lengua mala" (1:40), "Soltando chispas" (1:52), and "Me deja solito" (1:59), present sections of "mambofied" *guajeos* in the saxophones that accompany the trumpets in the high register in the indicated timings. "Me deja solito" has, additionally, passages in the style of the New York mambo (2:30).[59] In 1947 we have "Paquete no" and "A-E-I-O-U," with shake effects; "Dale, Pepe," with several guajeos; and "Cantando y riendo," which is one of the first New York numbers classified as mambo. Already in 1949, during the height of the mambo, he recorded the classics "Chupa, chupa," "Vamos, prietita," "New York rumba," "Maíz," "Guararé," "Opus 13," "B Flat mambo," and the stupendous "El salon del rey del mambo,"[60] this last based on "In the Hall of the Mountain King" from the *Peer Gynt Suite* by Edvard Grieg.[61]

## Pérez Prado Lands in Havana

In an interview conducted by Enrique C. Betancourt and published in the August 1946 issue of *Radio Magazine*, Pérez Prado revealed details of his trip to New York.[62] His stay lasted only three months. Although he apparently had the intention of remaining longer, the U.S. Musicians Union forced him to remain inactive for six months before he could register and work, which led him to cease this pursuit. Through Diosa Costello, Puerto Rican starlet and wife of Pupi Campo, he met at La Salle cafeteria the singer Luis Campo and the bongo player "Ñico," at that time a member of Xavier Cugat's orchestra.[63] In the end he prepared (or sold) arrangements to Cugat (among them one on the song "Dice mi gallo"), Miguelito Valdés ("Negro soy" by Eliseo Grenet), and Desi Arnaz ("Juan Pescao" and "El caimán").[64] But the most interesting was his announcement of his future release of a new "musical style": "I am preparing a new musical style that I think people are going to like very much: the 'son mambo.' I will title the first number 'Pavolla.' I only need to go through the piano part one more time, and perhaps, some corrections. The label 'Vda. De Humara y Lastra' is waiting for it as a good thing to record and release to the market. Let's see what comes out of it. I trust in the public's enthusiasm through the warm reception given by the musicians."[65]

This is the first news we know of Pérez Prado's intention to innovate with a new style in which the term "mambo" appears. We know absolutely nothing about his alleged first number, "Pavolla." We know, however, that on July 2 he returned to the recording studio [in Havana] with the Casino de la Playa Orchestra and Cascarita. Some of the numbers from this session point to some possible influence from his recent trip: in the introduction to "Ten jabón," a slow *guaracha*, he inserted a short bass solo in a very jazzy style; and the *tumbao* toward the end of the session resembles the New York interpretation of the *tumbaos* of the *danzón de "nuevo ritmo."* The final *montuno* of "El pollo" resembles the *montunos* of New York mambos: agitated tempo, persistence of a single chord in which the *tumbao* stands out (in this case the *guajeo* in the saxophones) over which he develops different interventions by the voice, brass, piano, and percussion, all with a very particular swing. But the most interesting are the instrumental parts featured in the introductions and codas for "Ronco" and the slow *guaracha* "Estoy acabando," also recorded in this session. In them he incorporated elements from Broadway themes similar to the ones used by Latin orchestras in New York in their *guarachas*. "Estoy acabando" is highly stylized and begins with Cascarita's exclamations: "¡Hey man! ¡Okay!" Even though some themes from Tin Pan Alley were already used by the *charangas* playing *danzón*, especially by Arcaño y Sus Maravillas, it is no less curious that they appeared in Pérez Prado as soon as he returned from his trip, and in a manner very similar to how his New York colleagues used them. Regardless, shortly after, Pérez Prado stopped using these introductions while at the same time assimilating influences from jazz bands and swing.

But Pérez Prado was not the only one to have made firm strides in the construction of mambo in Havana.

## The Bebo Valdés Connection

On October 29, 1946, Julio Cueva (with Cascarita on vocals) recorded "Rareza del siglo" by Bebo Valdés (1918–2013), at that time pianist and arranger for the orchestra. The number was originally classified as a *montuno* beguine, but it is built almost in its entirety over a highly interesting and experimental "mambofied" *guajeo* in which the interval of the augmented fourth is highlighted (fig. 7.17).[66]

Figure 7.17 *Guajeo* in Bebo Valdés's "Rareza del siglo"

The song alludes to a new innovative musical style, and it is conscious of its own complexity:

| | |
|---|---|
| Rareza del siglo<br>que van a escuchar.<br>La que un día todos<br>podrán comprender.<br>La que algún día les agradará,<br>la que un día tendrán que cantar,<br>la que un día tendrán que apreciar,<br>disfrutar y bailar con gran placer. | Rarity of the century<br>that they will hear.<br>That one that one day<br>everyone will understand.<br>The one that one day they'll like,<br>that one day you will have to sing,<br>that one day they will have to<br>appreciate, enjoy and dance with<br>pleasure. |

But on November 20, Pérez Prado returned to the recording studios with the goal of innovating with a style linked to the mambo. Among the numbers that he recorded, "Llora" and "Suavecito pollito" stand out, both slow *guarachas* with very "mambofied" ostinato *guajeos*. He presented the second one as a main theme at the end of each stanza, and both are very similar to "Figurina del solar." In the last instrumental, he introduced the shake effect in the trumpets and saxophones ("Suavecito pollito" is one of Pérez Prado's first recordings where they appear). He also recorded the "mambofied" *guaracha* "Son los bobitos," which already has many of the typical traits of the sung mambos that he would record with Benny Moré some years later in Mexico City. But for us the most interesting are the two instrumental numbers. The first is "Rumbambó," based on the orchestral *rumba* in the New York style, whose title refers to the mambo for the first time in Pérez Prado. The second is "Trompetiana," which as far as we know was the first piece by Pérez Prado (and the dance orchestra in Havana and New York) to be classified generically as mambo.[67] Unfortunately, this last number is lost, and we do not know if it is related to the promised "Pavolla" or if it served as a foundation for some of his later recordings in New York or Mexico City. Meanwhile, interesting things continued to happen in the city of skyscrapers.

## The José Curbelo Connection

José Curbelo (1919–2012) arrived in New York in 1939. Around 1942 his orchestra replicated Cugat's strategies and offered "toned-down" music for U.S. tastes. However, when the style of Machito and his Afro-Cubans began to impose itself, and mostly when he began to share the billboard with him [Machito] in the Conga club around 1945, his sound changed toward a "fiercer rumba" that won him prestige among Latin American and U.S. audiences, critics, and musicians.[68] In polls gathered by the newspapers *La Prensa* and *Revista Teatral* during 1944 and 1947, Curbelo's orchestra was valued by the audience as the best Latin Music orchestra, above even Machito's.[69] For U.S. critics, Curbelo was one of the main figures in the consolidation of the Latin sound in New York, and in the creation of the mambo.[70]

Toward the end of 1946 in New York City he had several performances in the jazz salon the China Doll (previously the Conga club) that were broadcasted through radio. Among the members of his orchestra, two young Puerto Ricans stood out: the singer Tito Rodríguez and the *timbalero* Tito Puente. In an October broadcast they performed "Botamos la pelota,"[71] a *conga* by Silvio Contreras that he recorded in 1940 with his *charanga* Contreras Brothers' Orchestra (Orquesta Hermanos Contreras). In his arrangements, Curbelo eliminated the conga rhythm, classified it as a *guaracha*, and introduced several elements that would become part of the characteristic style of New York mambo. After a brief six-measure instrumental introduction, a sung part bursts out, parodying the original lyrics:

| | |
|---|---|
| Pero botamos la pelota en el '39, | But we knocked the ball out of the park in '39, |
| botaremos la pelota en el '46, | we will knock it out of the park in '46, |
| con la orquesta de José Curbelo, | with José Curbelo's orchestra, |
| veni, venimos arrollando | we come, we come to roll over (everyone)[72] |

After a musical interlude, the main melody repeats in the trumpets first, and later in the piano, followed by a repetition of the introductory bars, and finally the "mambofied" part begins: a *tumbao* in the piano and another in the bass that keep in the same chord a very lively tempo, and over which the singer improvises alternating with the chorus "arrollando, arrollando" (rolling over, rolling over). Then the percussion increases with the *cáscara* [accompaniment pattern played on the body or shell of a drum] in the *timbales* by Puente, and, finally, the *guajeos* in the saxophones appear which repeat in ostinato and over them, after a few measures, the trumpets play shakes and different ornaments (fig. 7.18).

This section is followed by a brilliant piano solo (with a lot of New York flavor), more interventions by Rodríguez and the chorus, and the final coda.

On November 29, Curbelo again performed at the China Doll (with the same stellar billing as main singer and in the *timbales*) and from there they rebroadcasted over the radio "El rey del mambo," a *guaracha* by Félix Cárdenas Hernández, composer from Matanzas, also the author of the celebrated *son* "Puntillita" and other numbers that were recorded in both Havana and New York by musicians such as Pérez Prado or Machito. This important number has received only simple commentary from Roberts and Pérez Firmat and is not mentioned by Cuban mambologists. It begins with an introduction in which the saxophones play a syncopated riff that is not a *guajeo* (fig. 7.19).

Figure 7.18 Saxophone and trumpet *guajeos* in "Botamos la pelota" (measures 76–83)

Figure 7.19 Initial riff in "El rey del mambo" by Félix Cárdenas Hernández

After a very jazzy harmonic digression in the trumpets, the sung section begins:

| | |
|---|---|
| Yo soy el rey del mambo sí señor (repeat) | I am the king of the mambo, yes sir (repeat) |
| Porque lo llevo en la sangre como es | Because it is in my blood |
| (syncopated motive in the trumpets) (repeat) | (syncopated motive in the trumpets) (repeat) |
| A gozar con mi mambo | To have fun with the mambo |
| (high register intervention by the trumpets) | (high register intervention by the trumpets) |
| a bailar con mi tambor | dance with my drum |
| (short fast *chambola*) | (short fast *chambola*) |
| (repeat) | (repeat) |
| Refrain: Rico mambo, mambo . . . | Refrain: Tasty mambo, mambo . . . |

The instrumental interludes include short *chambolas* played by the saxophones, which accompany the trumpets that play very high, repetitive, and short chromatic gestures. The treatment of the brass differs from other *guarachas* recorded by Curbelo during this period. In this piece brass has a more prominent role, showing great virtuosity and developed in higher registers. The theme continues with Curbelo's characteristic piano solo and a section where chorus and soloist alternate.

The piece informs us that, toward the end of 1946, the expression "El rey del mambo" was already in use in New York. This is the first instance of the ongoing (and useless) debate of who should rightfully "occupy the throne." We do not have any information on whether the number was recorded (or known) in Havana. We know only of a couple of recordings by Machito where the composition remains unusually arranged. On March 29, 1949, during the height of mambo in New York, Machito performed it in a radio program. Although his arrangement includes more stylistic traits of the mambo (the beginning riff is "mambofied," and in the interlude the trumpets keep playing high, short gestures, but over an accompaniment that consists clearly of a *guajeo* in the saxophones), the result sounds foreign compared with the stylistic standards of the late 1940s. Machito's version is closer to a *rumba* style and substitutes the piano solo for a percussion solo.

Curbelo also recorded other "mambofied" numbers: In 1946 he recorded "Llora," a *guaracha* that repeats the chromatic motives in the *guajeos* as found in "Figurina del solar" that we saw in Pérez Prado's version (see the preceding section), over a *tumbao* in the bass that accents beats 3 and 4, similar to the *danzón de "nuevo ritmo."* In 1947 he recorded "Rumba bomba," a number with lyrics sung partly in Spanish and partly in English, and the famous *rumba* "La ruñidera."[73] Both develop shake effects in the trumpets. In 1952 he recorded two of his most successful mambos: "Paula" and his arrangement of the famous "El jibarito" by Rafael Hernández. Between 1952 and 1953 he recorded the mambo "La familia" and the number "La la la," the latter classified as a mambo, although it already had the sound of the salsa that Fania would disseminate almost twenty years later.

## Conclusions

During the 1940s, "mambo" was understood as a series of different musical practices among which stood out the peculiar way of playing the *montuno* section in the big-band *guarachas*. The mambo, understood as the musical genre that made Pérez Prado famous, emerged from these disparate practices. However, historically it was not the only set of musical practice that went by that name. It is very likely that Bebo Valdés, Anselmo Sacasas, and other Cuban musicians based in New York knew of these new tendencies from their travels to Havana (the historic and symbolic capital of Caribbean dance music) and hurried to introduce them in New York. In this process they created very personal interpretations of the formal, rhythmic, orchestral, and probably dance models of the island. By celebrating the "mambofied" *guarachas* and *danzones* that were successful in Havana and by imitating their style, they may have contributed to the conceptualization of these sections as a stand-alone genre. Perhaps Pérez Prado, one of the leading figures of this practice, became aware of the phenomenon during his 1946 trip to New York and, noticing its musical potential and popularity, hastened to put forward an independent style based on these "mambofied" practices. This is a plausible hypothesis, despite the possibility of errors in the dates in Díaz Ayala's discography,[74] and despite the moment in which each number is deemed to have been influential: it is likely that by the time that a number was recorded, it would have already been played in the dance halls, otherwise it would not have been widely known until much later, after being recorded.

Be that as it may, the information provided in this article highlights the need to reconsider the ways in which we habitually think of the relationships between Cuban musicians on the island and in New York, and begin a more systematic study regarding their possible influences and contacts. It is true that during the 1940s Cuba was a musical powerhouse that exported genres, pieces, and musics to the rest of Latin America and the United States. However, it is also true that, although the music by Cuban bands in New York was not heard in Havana, the leaders of these bands could have influenced in various ways the leading Havana musicians with whom they maintained contact. On the other hand, more than a mere copy of trends in Havana, the Cuban music that developed in New York had its own personality, and was influenced in no small part by other (non-Cuban) Caribbean and U.S. musicians who participated in these bands, eventually appropriating the music. We are, then, faced with a case of reterritorialization of a musical culture, and it has to be studied as such.

Likewise, this history of connections reminds us how complex it is to tell a linear history of the mambo. Each new piece of information complicates this task further. Perhaps the mambo is one of those phenomena that lack simple and direct causes. Told linearly, its history perhaps exists only in the discourse and not in the events, whose articulation escapes all logic of narrative history. Is it really possible to discern with clarity who "invented" the mambo? And furthermore, is that question pertinent? Are popular culture forms of expression, however sophisticated they may be, invented, or are they more like stages of more complex processes that are informed by the talent of brilliant individuals? On the other hand, are those inventors needed? Are Pérez Prado, Bebo Valdés, or Machito not brilliant artists with unique styles and personalities that deserve our respect and merit a study, rather than submitting them to competitions to see who occupies a symbolic throne? Is it not an honor for musicians of the caliber of Tito Puente, Tito Rodríguez, or Noro Morlales to influence the music of any country?

In my opinion, it would be more productive to ask ourselves what are the motives for this type of debate, analyze the roots and motivations that promote one or another version, and discern how the mambo, a "simple" dance for entertainment and escape, can insert itself into overarching disputes about identity, the recuperation and appropriation of historical heritage, or the legitimation of a musical tradition, a social group, and even, a political orientation. More than asking ourselves "who invented the mambo," we would have to focus on the "inventors" of each "inventor of the mambo."

## Notes

In this article I retrieve and develop information offered in the "Mambo" entry I wrote for the *Bloomsbury Encyclopedia of Popular Music of the World*, vol. 9, ed. John Shepherd and David Horn (London: Bloomsbury Publishing, 2014).

1. "Locas por el mambo," number recorded by Benny Moré and Pérez Prado's orchestra in Mexico City on June 3, 1950 (Cristóbal Díaz Ayala, *Enciclopedia discográfica de la música cubana 1925–1960* [2002], entry 121). http://latinpop.fiu.edu/, accessed April 2, 2006.

2. For a biography on Pérez Prado see Carlos J. Sierra, *Pérez Prado y el mambo* (Mexico City: La Muralla, 1995); for Benny Moré see Raúl Martínez Rodríguez, *Benny Moré* (Havana: Letras Cubanas, 1993).

3. Tito Puente, "Mambo en Blue," *Mambo Macoco: Tito Puente and His Orchestra*, TCD 018 (Tumbao Records, 2004).

4. Leonardo Acosta, *Elige tú que canto yo* (Havana: Letras Cubanas, 1993), 268–69. The *son* is a Cuban music and dance genre that gained international notoriety in the 1930s.

5. Odilio Urfé, "Danzón, mambo y cha-cha-cha," *Revolución y cultura* 77 (1979), 54–57. María Teresa Linares, *La música y el pueblo* (Havana: Editorial Pueblo y Educación, 1974).

6. Erena Hernández, *La música en persona* (Havana: Letras Cubanas, 1986), 17, 28, 59–60.

7. Sergio Burstein, "Bebo Valdés: el pianista eterno," November 2005, https://es.groups.yahoo.com/neo/groups/herencialatina/conversations/messages/4935, accessed April 2, 2006; Diego Salazar, "Bebo de Cuba: entrevista con Bebo," *ClubCultura* (March 3, 2005), www.clubcultura.com, accessed April 2, 2006; Pablo Larraguibel, "Bebo Valdés: la memoria del sabor" (interview, n.d.), *Anapapaya Jazz Latino y música caribeña*, http://anapapaya.com/, accessed April 2, 2006.

8. Leonardo Acosta, *Otra visión de la música popular cubana* (Havana: Letras Cubanas, 2004), 90. In reality, the different musical meanings of the term "mambo" that engage in the polemic include: 1) a rhythm based on the syncopated *guajeo*; 2) a section of the *danzón de "nuevo ritmo"* and the *guarachas* of the jazz bands where this *guajeo* can be found; 3) the practice of improvising over this *guajeo* in the *descargas* [jam sessions], and 4) an autonomous genre. In addition, the word "mambo" also alluded to the phrases of brass interludes, diverse musical practices of Bantú origin, and many other extramusical meanings; see Olavo Alén, "Pérez Prado, Dámaso," in *Diccionario de la música española e*

*hispanoamericana*, ed. Emilio Casares (Madrid: Sociedad General de Autores y Editores, 2001), 8:670–71, and Ana Casanova, "Mambo," in *Diccionario de la música española e hispanoamericana*, ed. Emilio Casares (Madrid: Sociedad General de Autores y Editores, 2000), 7:79–80.

9. Acosta, *Elige tú que canto yo*, 29.

10. Acosta, *Otra visión de la música popular cubana*, 91.

11. John S. Roberts, *The Latin Tinge* (New York: Oxford University Press, 1999), 123–24; John S. Roberts, *Latin Jazz* (New York: Schirmer, 1999), 71.

12. Apparently, in Los Angeles there also developed a mambo scene prior to Pérez Prado's success; see Luc Delannoy, *¡Caliente! Una historia del jazz latino* (Mexico City: Fondo de Cultura Económica, 2001), 199–201.

13. In other works I have introduced the concept of the cognitive stylistic type (indebted to the notion of Eco's cognitive type), as analytical category to study some listening strategies; see Rubén López-Cano, "From Rhetoric Musical Figures to Cognitive Types: An Italian *Lamento* Strolling along the Streets of Madrid," paper presented at the *Ninth International Doctoral and Postdoctoral Seminar on Musical Semiotics* (University of Helsinki, Nov. 13–17, 2002), and "De la retórica a las ciencias cognitivas: un estudio intersemiótico de los tonos humanos de José Marín" (PhD diss., University of Valladolid), both texts are available at www.lopezcano.net. The stylistic types to which I refer in this work are not cognitive types. They deal, simply, with formal patterns with a wide range of possibilities of occurrence.

14. According to Díaz Ayala, the number was recorded on March 7, 1950 (*Enciclopedia discográfica*, entry 2033). However, many sources indicate that it was already a hit in 1949.

15. Pérez Prado conceived of two types of mambos that he named "Mambo Kaen" (slower) and "Mambo Batiri" (fast and vigorous).

16. Daniel Duarte, "Al grito de: ¡mambo! Aportes de instrumentación y orquestación en la música de Dámaso Pérez Prado," *Arte e investigación* 10, no. 2 (2006), 27.

17. Editors' note: *Tumbao* is one of multiple terms that refer to the basic rhythmic and melodic ostinato patterns used to accompany various Afro-Cuban genres. The term can be used somewhat interchangeably with terms like *guajeo* and *montuno*, which can lead to some confusion. *Tumbao* is used in reference to bass patterns, and to a lesser degree, to conga drum and piano accompaniment patterns. The term *guajeo* is a little more inclusive, used also to refer to patterns played by other melodic instruments like the *tres* [guitar-like instrument with three courses of double strings], the violin, and the saxophone, although it is not commonly used to refer to patterns associated with percussion instruments. Both *tumbao* and *guajeo* are used throughout this article in the manner described above.

18. Urfé, "Danzón, mambo y cha-cha-cha," 57.

19. Acosta, *Otra visión de la música popular cubana*, 182.

20. Leonardo Acosta, *Descarga cubana: el jazz en Cuba 1900–1950* (Havana: Ediciones Unión, 2000), 136.

21. Editors' note: The term *montuno* has multiple meanings. As used in this article, it refers to the final section of some Afro-Cuban compositions. However, this is also a term used to refer to piano ostinato accompaniment patterns (see note 17). To avoid confusion between the two usages, this translation uses the modified term "*montuno* section."

22. Díaz Ayala, *Enciclopedia discográfica*, entry 630. For a biography on Cueva, see Dulcila Cañizares, *Julio Cueva: el rescate de su música* (Havana: Letras Cubanas, 1991).

23. This *guajeo* can be heard in some sections of the previously cited "Locas por el mambo."

24. Max Salazar, *Mambo Kingdom: Latin Music in New York* (New York: Schirmer, 2002).

25. Acosta, *Elige tú que canto yo*, 31. His place in Julio Cueva's would be filled by Bebo Valdés, another of the "creators" of the mambo. Valdés remained with Julio Cueva until 1947 (Díaz Ayala, *Enciclopedia discográfica*, entry 2609).

26. Maya Roy, *Músicas cubanas* (Madrid: Akal, 2003), 101.

27. See the documentary *Arcaño y sus maravillas* (1974), dir. Óscar Valdés.

28. Israel "Cachao" López, *Yo soy, del son a la salsa* (New York: RMM Filmworks, 1997), dir. Rigoberto López and Leonardo Padura.

29. Manuel Cuéllar Vizcaíno, "La revolución del mambo," *Bohemia* (May 30, 1948), reprinted in Radamés Giró, ed., *El mambo* (Havana: Letras Cubanas, 1993), 23–24.

30. Ibid., 24. The creation of the *danzón de "nuevo ritmo,"* and particularly the mambo section, can be seen in an article that replicates the quote from Cuéllar Vizcaíno from Odilio Urfé, "La verdad sobre el mambo," *Inventario: Mensuario Polémico de Arte y Literatura* 1, no. 3 (1948), reprinted in Giró, *El mambo*, 31–35. In time, Urfé would become a defender of this style. It is curious that the discussion that developed in 1948 focused only in the realm of the *danzón*, and practically did not mention the "mambofied" *guarachas* nor the different mambos that were played by the jazz bands.

31. Ibid., 31; Casanova, "Mambo," 79; Radamés Giró, *Panorama de la música popular cubana* (Havana: Letras Cubanas, 1998), 211; Fernando Ortiz, *Los bailes y el teatro de los negros en el folklore de Cuba* (Madrid: Música Mundana, 1998), 144–45. Among the nonmusical meaning of the term "mambo" we have valorization of the socioeconomic situation, "If the mambo was hard it meant the situation was bad" (Pérez Prado quoted in Hernández, *La música en persona*, 17), and "the unique, the relevant, the unheard of" (Argelio Santiesteban, *El habla popular cubana de hoy* [Havana: Editorial de Ciencias Sociales, 1995], 3003–4).

32. Urfé, "La verdad sobre el mambo," 31; Ortiz, *Los bailes y el teatro de los negros*, 151.

33. Díaz Ayala, *Enciclopedia discográfica*, entry 436A.

34. Machito would later (ca. 1950–51) develop a version in which the *guajeo* in the second section was replaced by the classic *tumba* of New York mambo, with a more animated tempo over the same chord all the time, and with its particular swing. Some current *timba* singers still introduce in the guides or improvised *sones* the refrain "los que son, son y los que no son pa' la cola" (those who are, are, and those who are not, to the end of the line).

35. Precise recording dates: "En tiempo de mangos," "No tengo tambó," "Ya' tá," and "Castillos en el aire" (Feb. 24, 1944); "El cuento del sapo" and "Dice mi gallo" (May 31, 1945) (Díaz Ayala, *Enciclopedia discográfica*, entry 630). "Azúcar pa' un amargo" (Nov. 16, 1945) (ibid., 436A) and "Apriétame más" (Jan. 7, 1946) (ibid., 1240).

36. This number enjoyed great success and was recorded several times in Havana as well as in New York by the Machito and Pupi Campo's orchestra, among others, and by

Vicentico Valdés in Mexico City. This version by Pérez Prado already reflects the style of the sung mambos that he would record with Benny Moré in Mexico City around 1949.

37. The arrangement sounds very much in the style of Pérez Prado. Precise recording dates: "Sacando boniato" (July 21, 1944) (Díaz Ayala, *Enciclopedia discográfica*, entry 630); "Yo pico un pan" (Nov. 16, 1945), "Esto es lo último" (Nov. 27, 1945) (ibid., 436A); "Baltasar tiene un pollo" and "Puntillita" (March 15, 1946) (ibid., 1240).

38. When the first was recorded, René Hernández was still the orchestra's arranger and pianist; when the second was recorded, Bebo Valdés was already the orchestra's pianist and arranger. Precise recording dates: "¿Por qué llora la vaquita?" (July 21, 1944) and "¿Qué no le tiraron?" (May 31, 1945) (Díaz Ayala, *Enciclopedia discográfica*, entry 630).

39. Freezeland is the name that Cuban musicians, such as Machito or Arsenio Rodríguez, occasionally used to refer to New York or other cities in the United States in songs.

40. Salazar, *Mambo Kingdom*, 107.

41. Acosta, *Descarga cubana*, 190–91.

42. Jordi Pujol, CD liner notes, *Algo nuevo: Mambo and Rumba Sessions. Miguelito Valdés [and] His Orchestra and Sextet* (2000, Tumbao TCD 104).

43. Salazar, *Mambo Kingdom*, 45.

44. Pujol, *Algo nuevo*.

45. Although Salazar and Pujol coincide in Valdés's trip at the end of 1945, Salazar does not acknowledge the trip in the end of 1946, and in his biographical report it appears that all his recordings for Musicraft took place in New York. Díaz Ayala, however, registered the master number (5573) of the 78rpm disc of the recording, which would indicate that he recorded in Cuba (Díaz Ayala, *Enciclopedia discográfica*, entry 2620).

46. Peter Manuel, "The Anticipated Bass in Cuban Popular Music," *Latin American Music Review* 6, no. 2 (1985), 249.

47. Gustavo Pérez Firmat, *Vidas en vilo: la cultura cubanoamericano* (Madrid: Colibrí, 2000), 105.

48. Miguelito Valdés, *Algo nuevo: Mambo and Rumba Sessions* (2001, Tumbao TCD 104).

49. Salazar, *Mambo Kingdom*, 47.

50. He had to turn to his main *tumbador*, the Cuban Octavio "Cuso," to do the main voice. This Rubén González is not to be confused with the famous pianist of the Buena Vista Social Club pianist of the same name.

51. Jordi Pujol, CD liner notes, *Poco loco: Anselmo Sacasas y su orquesta* (1995, Tumbao TCD 057) and for the CD *Sol tropical. Anselmo Sacasas y su orquesta* (1996, Tumbao TCD 079).

52. Another Havana trend introduced in the repertoire by Latin orchestras in New York was the "Botecito," recorded by Machito around 1947.

53. Salazar, *Mambo Kingdom*, 60.

54. Precise composition dates: "Pa' lo pollo maí" (March 16, 1945); "Vamos a gozar" (May 9, 1945); "El tumbaito" (March 8, 1946—only four days after the recording of this number by Pérez Prado) (Díaz Ayala, *Enciclopedia discográfica*, entry 2332).

55. Like many numbers from this period, especially those recorded by Julio Cueva, "El tumbaito" refers to the shortage of certain items: "Como no hay jabón ¿qué vamos a hacer? / Se acabó el jabón no hay na' que perder / . . . yo tengo un truquito que nadie lo sabe, con mi tumbaito yo lavo la ropa" (Since there is no soap, what are we going to do? / The soap ran out and there is nothing to lose / . . . I have a little trick that nobody knows, I wash my clothes with my tumbaito). It seems to take a snapshot of Cuban reality of more recent times. Miguelito Valdés's version uses repeatedly the *tumbao* of the bass of the *danzón* "Mambo."

56. Anselmo Sacasas and His Orchestra, *Sol tropical* (1996, Tumbao TCD 079).

57. Pérez Firmat, *Vidas en vilo*, 101.

58. Lyric fragments that are unclear are printed in parentheses.

59. Machito recorded this number around 1951 using a style closer to the *cha-cha-chá* and including shake effects in the trumpets.

60. Between 1948 and 1949 Machito recorded a version of the number with a lot of swing.

61. Precise recording dates: "Si tú me llevas te llevo" (May 9, 1945); "Capullito de alelí" (May 13, 1945); "La bodega del Ñato" (May 23, 1946); "Lengua mala," "Soltando chispas," and "Me deja solito" (Dec. 5, 1946); "Paquete no" (April 11, 1947) and "A-E-I-O-U" (Dec. 1, 1947); "Dale Pepe" and "Cantando y riendo" (Nov. 10, 1947); "Chupa, chupa," "Vamos, prietita," "New York rumba," and "Maíz" (June 1, 1949); "Guararé," "Opus 13," "B.Flat mambo," and "El salón del rey del mambo" (Oct. 5, 1949) (Díaz Ayala, *Enciclopedia discográfica*, entry 2332).

62. The interview now appears in an autobiographical book published by the author in Puerto Rico in 1986. It is possible that some of the parts were rewritten afterward.

63. Ñico was possibly John "Big Daddy" Rodríguez, also nicknamed by Mario Bauzá as "La Vaca" (the Cow) due to his large size.

64. Enrique Betancourt, *Apuntes para la historia* (San Juan, P.R.: Ramallo, 1986), 111–21.

65. Ibid., 112–13.

66. Years later, Celia Cruz would record in Venezuela with Luis Alfonso Larrain's Orchestra, a version in which the dissonances diminish since the *guajeo* is played by the bass in the foreground and at a faster pace.

67. Díaz Ayala, *Enciclopedia discográfica*.

68. Jordi Pujol, CD liner notes, *Rumba Gallega: José Curbelo and His Orchestra* (1994, Tumbao TCD 042) and for the CD *Live at the China Doll New York (1946): José Curbelo and His Orchestra* (1995, Tumbao TCD 074); Salazar, *Mambo Kingdom*, 98.

69. Pujol, *Live at the China Doll New York*.

70. Roberts, *Latin Jazz*, 71.

71. The information comes from the CD notes. No record exists for radio broadcast.

72. The song's original lyrics state: "Botamos la pelota en el año 40, con la orquesta Hermanos Contreras vení a rumbear" (We knocked the ball out of the park in 1940, with the Hermanos Contreras' orchestra come to *rumbear* [party]).

73. Recording dates: "Rumba bomba" (Jan. 29, 1947); "La ruñidera" (Nov. 26, 1947) (Díaz Ayala, *Enciclopedia discográfica*, entry 639).

74. In Pérez Prado's case (always polemic), Díaz Ayala points out the inconsistencies in some of the dates of recording supposedly "done in Cuba" with dates for April, June, and September 1949, when Pérez Prado was already in Mexico. As a possible explanation he suggests that they could be recordings done previously, and that the dates in the records of the Victor recording company reflect the "impression to release the album" (Díaz Ayala, *Enciclopedia discográfica*, entry 2003). It is not plausible that during this period Pérez Prado would record in both countries.

# 8

## "I Got Phrasing"

### *Changes in Samba's Melodic Rhythm, 1917–1933*

CARLOS SANDRONI

In *The Mystery of Samba*, Hermano Vianna convincingly demonstrates that Rio de Janeiro's samba, or *samba carioca*, is the result of a complex process of social construction.[1] In this essay, I address a moment of this construction process, one which the literature continues to regard as crucial. I deal with the period between the 1920s and 1930s, when a group of composers from the Estácio de Sá neighborhood in Rio de Janeiro successfully imposed itself on the city's music scene. This group, known as the Estácio Bambas [loosely, Hustlers from Estácio de Sá], was led by Ismael Silva (1905–1978), who shared the limelight with Nilton Bastos (1899–1931), "Bide" Alcebíades Barcelos (1902–75), and "Brancura" Sílvio Fernandes (1908–1935), among others. The importance of the Estácio Bambas in the history of samba can be traced to a set of factors, two of which I would like to stress here. The first is the creation of the Deixa Falar carnival group, or *bloco*, founded in 1928 under the leadership of the Estácio Bambas, and which would become the prototype for the future samba schools. The second factor is the fact that Francisco Alves (1889–1952), the most well-known Brazilian popular singer of the late 1920s and early 1930s, recorded a number of Estácio sambas beginning in 1928: from 1931 to 1933 Alves had an "exclusivity contract" with Ismael Silva, the main Estácio composer. Indeed, no other singer could record Silva's compositions without Alves's authorization.

The first samba recorded by a composer of the Estácio group was "A malandragem" (Hustling) by Bide. The singer on the 1928 recording was Francisco

---

Originally published by Carlos Sandroni as "Ritmo melódico nos bambas do Estácio," in *Ao encontro da palavra cantada—poesia, música e voz*, ed. Cláudia Neiva de Matos, Elizabeth Travassos, and Fernanda Teixeira de Medeiros (Rio de Janeiro: 7Letras, 2001), 53–60. Translated by Michael Iyanaga with permission.

Alves, who, as was a common practice at the time, listed himself as co-composer. The most famous samba composer of this era was Sinhô (José Barbosa da Silva, 1888–1930), also known as the Samba King, whose compositions were characteristic of a musical and lyrical style that had been popular at least since 1917, when "Donga" Ernesto dos Santos (1889–1974) released "Pelo telefone" (By telephone), the first really successful samba song to be recorded.

The samba style practiced by Donga and Sinhô was very close rhythmically to *maxixes* [fast, syncopated dance music form] and Brazilian *tangos*, two of the most prominent genres of Brazilian popular music during the late nineteenth century. Elsewhere I have referred to this earlier rhythmic style as the "tresillo paradigm," a term coined by Cubans for the sequence of two dotted eighth notes followed by an eighth note.[2] This pattern is the simplest version of a wide range of possible variations, and Brazil's most common version might have been what Mário de Andrade called the "characteristic syncopation" [or eighth note, quarter note; eighth note, quarter note; quarter note]. The paradigm's first documented appearances in Brazilian music come from the late eighteenth century, in the *modinha* [sentimental song genre] scores housed in Lisbon's Ajuda Library, which were studied by Gerard Béhague.[3] Later, in the nineteenth century, the paradigm is found in scored *lundus* [song type], *cateretês* [social dance form] and *maxixes*, and was ushered into the twentieth century in the guitar accompaniments of the pioneers of recorded music, among them Eduardo das Neves, Cadete, and Baiano. Baiano sang "Pelo telefone" on the 1917 recording, where we once again hear a guitar reproducing the characteristic syncopation. And the same type of rhythm prevailed on the 1920s samba recordings, in the accompaniments of the small brass and woodwind orchestras popular at that time.

The recorded Estácio sambas, on the other hand, which begin with "A malandragem," would come to be characterized by a significantly different rhythmic style. To begin, the Estácio percussionists would eventually introduce the emblematic instruments of the nascent samba schools: *surdos* [bass drums], *cuícas* [friction drums], and *tamborins* [small frame drums, singular form is *tamborim*]. More than this, however, these percussionists would innovate a way of employing these instruments in song, of blending them in a percussion section, the *batucada*, which would prove to be influential in Brazilian popular music throughout the twentieth century. I have elsewhere described these rhythmic peculiarities as the "Estácio paradigm."[4]

Attributing so many innovations to the Estácio Bambas is nothing new: critics and journalists have written on the topic, and samba musicians themselves have spoken about it widely. As such, we might be led to believe that the first Estácio samba recordings—such as "A malandragem" and the innumerable other recordings made by Francisco Alves between 1928 and the early 1930s—would already demonstrate the characteristic rhythmic innovations quite clearly. Yet listening to this material belies such an assumption. This is primarily due to the fact that recordings from this period do not include percussion instruments. The *ritmistas*, as percussionists–turned–music professionals were then called, did not begin to appear regularly in the recording studios prior to 1933. Thus, the participation of a few *ritmistas* from Rio's Salgueiro neighborhood in the 1930 recording of "Na Pavuna" was clearly an exception to a more general rule. And even on this recording, the samba's *batucada* is closer to the *tresillo* paradigm (i.e., the rhythm heard on "Pelo telefone") than to the percussion recorded on many sambas from 1934 onward.[5]

Still, when the first Estácio sambas appear, it is within a musical context entirely dominated by the previous style. Until well into the 1930s, arrangers treated these sambas as they had Sinhô's: with the same accents in the lower wind registers (in the *choro* [dance genre] "baixaria," or bass lines, style), and with the same basic *tresillo* paradigm accompaniment style, quite audible in certain parts of the piano or the *cavaquinho* [small, four-stringed guitar] lines. It is only little by little, in a learning curve traceable on consecutive recording dates, that professional studio musicians changed the style of their work.

Such a situation is problematic for samba historians. Everyone is willing to agree that the Estácio Bambas remodeled *samba carioca*, creating a stylistic paradigm that, if not still dominant today, was at least dominant until around the 1960s, that is, until Paulinho da Viola's generation. However, the testimony of a crucial player in this story, the sound recording, seems to belie this narrative. In other words, the performances on the discs of the era suggest that the Estácio sambas were rhythmically identical to the sambas of Donga and Sinhô, flagrantly contradicting the apparent consensus in samba scholarship.

A symptom of this paradox is the fact that, for the reasons already noted, my description of the Estácio paradigm was not based on the Estácio Bambas's recordings themselves, but rather on later recordings by Paulinho da Viola, Cartola, and Nelson Cavaquinho, where *tamborins*, *surdos*, and *cuícas* are finally heard in all their glory.[6] In fact, one can even question the name I gave the paradigm, unless it were possible to find hints, at the very least, of the paradigm on the recordings made by the bambas themselves.

My attempt to resolve this problem is inspired in an observation made by Alejo Carpentier in 1979 that points to the direct relationship that exists between the sung word and the general musical structure. In his book on Cuban music, Carpentier affirms that "the rhythm of the claves, as Emilio Grenet so keenly noted, *is the only thing that can always adapt itself, without variation, to all types of Cuban melodies*, constituting therefore a type of constancy in the phrasing [una especie de constante escansional]" (original emphasis).[7]

It is important to note that in Cuban music the claves have a musical function analogous to that of the *tamborins* in Brazilian *batucadas*, that of being "time-line" instruments as studied in African music by Nketia, among many others.[8] I considered this when I appropriated the idea of "constancy in the phrasing," but in its inversion. Rather than begin with a given clave to test different melodies, I decided to verify whether the melodies of the Estácio Bambas could teach me something about the rhythmic patterns of the subjacent accompaniments. Put otherwise, I sought to discover if the "clave" missing in these recordings could be reconstructed from these melodies. The strategy turned out to be quite fruitful. For this experiment I transcribed a large number of samba melodies recorded between 1927 and 1933. While I focused primarily on sambas written by Estácio composers or by composers who were manifestly influenced by the Estácio style, I also analyzed and compared sambas by the older generation, and arrived at the conclusions I present here.

The melodies of the Estácio Bambas were structured in two parts, called the *primeira* and *segunda* [first and second]. The *primeira* is fixed and choral. This means, first of all, that both the melody and the lyrics remain constant throughout every repetition of the samba, and secondly, that the melody would be sung primarily by a group. The *segunda* is variable and solo, that is, each repetition of the song is reproduced with new lyrics (although the melody remains unchanged), and always by a solo voice. This two-part structure corresponds with firsthand descriptions of the street samba practiced in Rio de Janeiro at the time. The samba school parades in particular were, until the 1940s, conducted to the sound of sambas with this structure. Yet it is important to note that in this street samba, contrary to that which took place in the recording studio, the *segunda* was improvised.

In the *primeiras* of the sambas I analyzed, I could not at first detect anything close to the "constancy in the phrasing" mentioned by Carpentier. But in the *segundas*, the recurrence of specific rhythmic patterns was easily recognizable. The fact is, the second parts of the melodies of a great number of the sambas written by Ismael Silva and his friends during the period under investigation have a rhythmic organization in which three basic patterns predominate. These appear in figure 8.1.

This is the case of songs such as "A malandragem" (1928, Hustling) by Bide and Francisco Alves; "Me faz carinhos" (1928, Give me affection) and "Não é isso que eu procuro" (1928, This isn't what I'm looking for) by Ismael Silva and Alves; "Se você jurar" (1931, If you swear) by Silva, Nilton Bastos, and Alves; "O que será de mim" (1931, What will become of me), by Silva, Bastos, and Alves; "Para me livrar do mal" (1932, To rid myself of harm) by Noel Rosa and Silva, among other hits.

The second parts of these sambas demonstrate metric similarities (in the literary sense) that make them particularly apt to certain rhythmic standardizations.

Fig. 8.1 Musical examples a–c

Their verses always comprise two heptasyllabic quatrains. The accents generally fall on the third and seventh syllables. This common meter also allows the melodic rhythms of the second parts to constitute a set of identifiable patterns. Indeed, each of the eight verses occupies a rhythmic cycle of two measures, 2/4. If we consider each second part, comprising eight cycles of two measures, as a syntagmatic chain, we see that each of the three identified rhythmic types can appear in any of the eight positions defined above. These position variations occur not only in juxtapositions of different sambas, but also in comparisons of the second parts within the same samba. It is as though the singer chooses from among the alternatives within the small repertoire of stylistically equivalent rhythmic variations—but only these.

For my investigation, however, the most significant issue is that this repertoire of variations adhered to the rhythmic pattern of the Estácio paradigm, which I had identified on recordings of *tamborins* and *cuícas* made nearly a half century later. It was in fact the singers, and in particular Francisco Alves, who first made apparent on record the rhythmic patterns that would better characterize *samba carioca* in the following decades. Carpentier actually was not alone in offering a clue to my conclusion. In their magnificent biography of Noel Rosa, João Máximo and Carlos Didier relate an episode that clearly illustrates the near-ethnographic zeal with which Francisco Alves sought out hit sambas. This story narrates a moment at Café Trianon, when the singer encountered a group that happened to be singing "É bom parar" (You'd better stop), a samba by Rubens Soares:

> Francisco Alves indeed [got] excited. "Repeat that refrain, Rubens. And with that same *bossa* that the guys put on it. I want to learn exactly how you did it." Rubens repeated it. One, two, several times, until Francisco Alves memorized the lyrics and assimilated the refrain's so-called *bossa*.[9]

What might be this so-called "bossa" that moves an already successful singer to spend hours learning with "the guys" at Café Trianon? It is difficult to know with certainty, but to anyone familiar with *samba carioca*, it would be hard to believe that this "bossa" did not have something to do with rhythm. Soares's testimony indicates that Alves, and perhaps other singers of the time, was close to the "sources"—as one might put it—making a difference in performance when compared to other professionals, such as arrangers and orchestra musicians, who were also involved in the production of samba recordings but had less contact with these same "sources."

Another testimony relevant to the issue at hand is that of Paulo Tapajós:

> Radamés [Gnattali] really used to enjoy talking about the particularities of Brazilian rhythm, notably samba rhythm, and it is important to say here that it was [drummer] Luciano Perrone who suggested to Radamés that he write his samba arrangements with the rhythmic division of the tamborins. This happened at a time when samba had a style of instrumentation that was unsuited for the division done by singers. They weren't musicians, but their intuition led them to a rhythm with a much more flavorful accentuation than what was on paper. Song and orchestra seemed to fight. Radamés composed, with Luciano, "Ritmo de samba na cidade" (Rhythm of samba in the city), which stood as a grand dividing moment of the formulas adopted until then, such that samba orchestration came to be defined as being either before or after "Ritmo de samba na cidade."[10]

Tapajós employs the term "division" (*divisão*) which is utilized in popular Brazilian music to designate the variations of rhythmic-melodic articulation employed in songs. In this way, Tapajós suggests the existence of a rhythmic articulation typical of *tamborins* ("the rhythmic division of the tamborins"), which would be adopted by the singers but not by the orchestra or in sheet music. *Tamborins* and singers stood in opposition to both the orchestra and sheet music (they "seemed to fight"); the former [tamborins and singers], pertaining to the sphere of oral tradition (for he claims the singers "weren't musicians"), the latter [orchestra and sheet music], to that of the written tradition. In oral tradition, rhythm was articulated in a way that was aesthetically valued by Tapajós as "much more flavorful."

I fear that the story was not quite as simple as Tapajós suggested: the adoption of the new rhythmic division by all of those involved in the recordings was the result not of a single recording but rather of a learning process—a creative process, to be sure—that took years.[11] At any rate, what I emphasize here is that on the path traversed by samba recordings toward a rhythmic enunciation coherent with that of the *tamborins*, singers preceded the accompaniment. Indeed, Tapajós also seems to indicate that if we wish to know something about the *tamborins* absent from the popular Brazilian music recordings of the 1930s, we should look to the melodic rhythm performed by the singers.

To conclude, I return briefly to a question I have left unanswered: why is the constancy in the phrasing recognizable only in the second parts of the Estácio sambas? First, I should note that subsequent analyses did in fact reveal the Estácio melodic rhythm, though less overtly, in the first parts of the sambas, as well. But this finding does not resolve the problem, for there is a pronounced and uniform difference in the way the constancy in the phrasing appears in the first part of the analyzed sambas compared with the second part, and this difference is marked enough to be considered significant. As such, I believe this divergence can be best explained by noting the difference in context to which I have already alluded: the second parts were originally improvised by the soloists. Indeed, in Brazilian music there are many different styles of improvised song. The freedom of poetic invention in these songs is commonly restricted by certain standardized musical contours. This is the case, for example, in sung duels in northeastern Brazil, known as *desafio* or *repente*, which utilize melodic formulas to structure the singing. This is also the case—closer to the topic at hand—with the improvisation found in other styles of *samba carioca*, such as *partido-alto*. It is hardly true that new melodies could not be invented in these situations, but verbal improvisation within a fixed meter takes precedent over musical variation, leading singers to adopt stereotypical melodic-rhythmic formulas. It seems to me that the high degree of melodic-rhythmic standardization in the second parts of the Estácio Bambas's sambas, as compared with their first parts, could reasonably be linked to these factors. Initially, then, the second parts would be composed in a manner very close to the improvisational practices of the period, only later adopting a greater freedom of melodic-rhythmic invention.

## Notes

"I Got Phrasing," or "Arranjei um fraseado," is the title of a 1933 samba by Noel Rosa. This article was first presented as a paper at the conference "I Encontro de Estudos da Palavra Cantada" (First Conference on the Study of the Sung Word), held in Rio de Janeiro in September 2000, organized by Cláudia Neiva de Matos, Elizabeth Travassos, and Fernanda Teixeira de Medeiros, the Universidade Federal Fluminense (Federal Fluminense University) and the Universidade do Estado do Rio de Janeiro (Rio de Janeiro State University).

1. Hermano Vianna, *The Mystery of Samba: Popular Music and National Identity in Brazil* (Chapel Hill: University of North Carolina Press, 1999; originally published as *O mistério do samba* [Rio de Janeiro: Zahar, 1995]).

2. Carlos Sandroni, *Feitiço decente: transformações do samba no Rio de Janeiro, 1917–1933* (Rio de Janeiro: Zahar, 2012 [2001]), 28–32; "Le *tresillo*: rythme et 'métissage' dans la

musique populaire imprimée latino-américaine du XIXème siècle," *Cahiers de Musiques Traditionnelles* 13 (2000), 55–64.

3. Gerard Béhague, "Biblioteca da Ajuda (Lisbon) Mss. 1595/1596: Two Eighteenth-century Anonymous Collections of Modinhas," *Anuário do Instituto Interamericano de Pesquisa Musical* 4 (1968), 44–81.

4. Sandroni, *Feitiço decente*, 32–37; see also Carlos Sandroni, "La samba à Rio de Janeiro et le paradigme de l'Estácio," *Cahiers de Musiques Traditionnelles* 10 (1997), 153–68.

5. Carlos Sandroni, "Dois sambas de 1930 e a constituição do gênero: *Na Pavuna* e *Vou te abandonar*," *Cadernos do Colóquio* 4, no. 1 (2001), 8–21.

6. On the Estácio paradigm, see Sandroni, *Feitiço decente*, 32–37.

7. Alejo Carpentier, *La música en Cuba* (Havana: Letras Cubanas, 1979), 55–56.

8. J. H. Kwabena Nketia, *The Music of Africa* (London: Victor Gollanz, 1975), 131–32.

9. João Máximo and Carlos Didier, *Noel Rosa: uma biografia* (Brasília: Universidade de Brasília, 1990), 410.

10. Paulo Tapajós, liner notes for the LP *Radamés Gnattali Sexteto* (Rio de Janeiro: Odeon, 1975).

11. A similar and equally questionable story is told by Sérgio Cabral, *No tempo de Ari Barroso* (Rio de Janeiro: Lumiar, 1992), 182, who insists that the first arrangement "to show the wind section playing in the samba rhythm" was in Ari Barroso's "Aquarela do Brasil," known in the United States as "Brazil," from 1939.

# 9

# Singing Difference

## *Violeta Parra and Chilean Song*

RODRIGO TORRES ALVARADO

"Violeta, you are a poet, a composer, and weave tapestries and paint. If you had to choose one medium of expression, which one would you keep?"
"I would choose to stick with the people."
—Published interview with Violeta Parra

In the 1950s, at the height of the modernizing process, the collective practice of traditional song burst on Chilean urban society as a factor that was unexpectedly efficient in the renovation of stories of identity, establishing itself as a vital space of coexistence and friction between different narratives and representations of the vernacular world.[1]

In this article, I explore this phenomenon, focusing on the emergence of a different mode of reworking traditional song, one that was an alternative to the one institutionalized by the culture industry at the time. To this end, I consider the case of Violeta Parra, an artist recognized today as a major figure in popular Latin American song and one of the prominent women in Chilean culture.

After her suicide on February 5, 1967, she acquired the quality of a martyred artist and entered the realm of myth. Pablo Neruda would call her a "saint of pure clay."[2] And wrapped up in the myth, her work would continue to represent, even today, an excess symbolic of a difficult consensus, of contradictory validity. Currently, she is as much an official icon of national popular culture as she is "a song of cultural difference," denied by that same nation.

---

Originally published by Rodrigo Torres Alvarado as "Cantar la diferencia: Violeta Parra y la canción chilena," *Revista Musical Chilena* 58, no. 201 (2004), 53–73. Available at www.revistamusicalchilena.uchile.cl. Translated by Juan Eduardo Wolf with permission of *Revista Musical Chilena*.

What and how was it that she sang, given that her song still endures as a difficult and obstinate memory? In short, I propose that Violeta Parra and her songs are as much an emblem as a driving force for the process of installing a new imaginary for traditional vernacular culture into Chilean society. This process can be summarized as the displacement of the notion of vernacular tradition as a "non-space" for modernity to its affirmation as the basis for a local contemporary art, and furthermore, as a model for social change: the utopian dream of the people, of the "interior" Other.

## Song, Nation, and the Vernacular World

Diverse studies have signaled the importance of popular song in making up "universes of recognition" in contemporary societies.[3] In the case of Violeta Parra's songs, it seems inevitable to reference the complex link between power and the construction of collective identities and, particularly, representations of the vernacular world.

The histories of Latin America's republics are full of numerous, if also fruitless, attempts to have "the people not be represented but to have them present themselves." Yet the mediated representation by external forces has prevailed without rebuttal. What normally is labeled as folklore is one of mediation, an external mechanism of representation that establishes the editing and symbolizing, usually of an essentialist nature, of the vernacular or traditional cultures represented, a process that Néstor García Canclini describes as the "melancholy invention of traditions."[4]

In the 1930s and 1940s, the so-called national folklore had a strategic encounter with the new media of mass communication. In the space of the media triad of radio–records–sound cinema, stereotyped expressions of oral-vernacular cultures from different Latin American regions were placed on the stage, being projected from urban centers to the entire territory with a reach more efficient than that of academically institutionalized folklore. This alliance meant a mass encounter between states and their population, in which communication technology was an effective promotional resource for nation-building projects that, once consolidated, transformed "the idea of nation into a feeling and the stuff of daily life."[5]

The elevation of the vernacular world via the mechanisms of representation of the culture industry is a phenomenon directly related to this discussion: the (concentrated) effort of the state and the culture industry to "modernize" so-called folklore, converting it into the foundation of a symbolic universe representative of the entire nation. In various countries, this was the privileged orientation for building macro-narratives of identity, useful in unifying behaviors and legitimizing a state's cultural policy.[6]

One of the central tropes of the resulting national symbolic prototypes is that of "representative" musical genres. These musical—as well as choreographic—prototypes make up a constellation of "typical musics" of the continent. In Chile, they were the rural *tonada* [folk ballad genre] and the *cueca* [regional dance genre]; just as in Mexico they were the northern *corrido* and the *son* from Jalisco, in Cuba the *son*, in Argentina the *tango* from the Río de la Plata region and the *zamba* from Cuyo, in Brazil the samba from Rio, in Colombia the Andean *bambuco* , in Peru the *vals criollo*, and so forth.

In terms of the Chilean popular song of the time, one can distinguish three simultaneous processes, relatively interrelated, that sought recourse in different traditions, repertoires and pathways. They would constitute the warp on which Violeta Parra would weave her own song style.

## "REPRESENTATIVE" CULTURE AND MUSIC IN CHILE

Throughout the twentieth century, the agrarian-rural tradition was the foundation and rationale behind Chilean "representative culture," whose central symbolic prototype was modeled on the hacienda, establishing an imaginary anchored in an idealized rural world that was increasingly out of step with the booming industrial society.[7] In the realm of music, it primarily expresses itself in the previously mentioned Chilean typical music (*tonadas* and *cuecas*) that were interpreted and created by urban ensembles and that were legitimized and popularized through mass media between 1930 and 1950.

In the 1960s and 1970s, a period of important restructuring and change on the continent, there was a considerable, if not definitive, reduction in the usefulness of this agro-nationalist narrative and, correspondingly, in the representational value of the "typical musics" of each country. For example, in Colombia, the Andean *bambuco* was no longer one of the most popular genres; the same thing happened with typical Chilean creole music, which was displaced by other "modernizing" expressions of folklore.[8]

## POPULAR SONG AND POLITICS

Beginning in the 1920s, within the political arena, the emergence of an organized, leftist movement would manifest itself: the labor movement. From within its bosom—and consistent with a predetermined political orientation and historical project—a new symbolic prototype of "the people" with its corresponding "universe of identification" would be constructed. [Emerging] from this environment, politically engaged songs would effectively participate in a new ritualization of social conflict, in which signs of struggle would be the distinctive marker, associated with the image of a mobilized and organized people. Their songs would constitute one of the principal sources of a symbolic repertoire that would crystallize in a new, long-standing epic narrative of the "vernacular subject." For decades, storytelling and epics would be the foundations of the bond between art and politics, as well as the basis of the most important Chilean artistic movement during these years.

In 1970, after various attempts, this political movement finally triumphed in the presidential elections. The government of [socialist] president Salvador Allende (1970–73) would make the repertoire of images and symbols that had accumulated over the years its own. Thus, as the affective potential of this repertoire unfurled itself within the new context, these songs would not only become historical icons of the labor movement's struggle, but also as the basis for the construction of a national and popular identity.[9] Within this frame, [three years after her death] Violeta Parra's songs and the Chilean New Song (Nueva Canción Chilena) movement would rework this legacy, projecting it into the imaginary of all of society.

### POPULAR SONG AND THE RELIGIOSITY OF THE OPPRESSED

A third process of popular song is one associated with ancient traditional culture, fundamentally rural and peasant, sustained by a Christian worldview and yet profoundly distant from the [Roman Catholic] church. It has been called vernacular religion or the religion of the oppressed. This narrative of popular song and religiosity that constitutes one of the axes upon which Latin American mestizo culture turns is a field problematically interdependent with the processes previously described. At its essence, the tradition of *canto a lo divino* [sacred song, a type of sung poetry with religious themes] encompasses this important dimension of Chilean popular song: "Starting from the poetic and peasant experience of *canto a lo divino*, one would have to note that this spirituality is nurtured by a minstrel tradition of medieval origin, that, rescuing popular carnival culture, and, simultaneously, a Franciscan-based Christianity, for centuries has sustained a resistance (and even a symbolic inversion) of religiosities of 'power' (that were so important in Hispanic American Christianity)."[10]

The staging and reworking of this tradition within urban [popular] song would build a repertoire in which humanist values based in Christianity, in tune with this "vernacular spirituality," were essential.[11] From this perspective, Violeta Parra's songs present a case of strong commitment to "vernacular Christianity," although staged in contexts and ways that were different from traditional songs. Furthermore, one can argue that this religiosity makes up part of the deep structure of her worldview and the whole of her artistic body of work.

## Violeta Parra's "Song of Difference"

### THE PATH OF A POPULAR ARTIST

The fact that she was a woman with peasant roots is a fundamental aspect of understanding Parra's artistic mission and her apparatus within Chilean society.

She was born in 1917 in San Carlos, Chillán, a small town in southern Chile, at the precise moment when the expanding industrial society began to deconstruct the old order of rural life (displacing the hacienda and replacing it with the factory). The culture that industrial society introduced would strip the migrant masses of peasants of their ancestral identity, leaving them to wander the cities in search of integration into this new setting.[12]

The experience of this wave of migration to the great capital, which Violeta Parra and her family painfully lived through, would dominate in all her art. It would be associated with the notions of loss of origin, of unwanted upheaval and dispersion of a community that had a common destiny: itinerancy. Similarly, the "cold" industrial society would be associated with a constant bitterness, with loss and abandonment. And, as opposed to the evils of "this modern world"—to use her phrase—this lost world would embody the idea of a paradise or memory needing to be recovered, a utopian model for a future society, of harmonic unity between secular and sacred, between society and nature.[13] Her word would be hard and condemning on the one hand, and tender and sweet on the other: the rebellion of an accusing gesture and the tenderness of a reconciling gesture—the two poles of her songs.

After Violeta Parra moved to Santiago in 1932 with her sisters and brothers, she dedicated herself to singing in nightspots in the working-class neighborhoods. For years, she was an interpreter of the latest repertoire broadcast on radios and songs that patrons requested, including Chilean, Latin American, and Spanish popular genres. Beginning in 1947, she and her older sister Hilda formed the Parra sisters duo (Las Hermanas Parra), becoming professional "folkloric" artists (playing the so-called "typical music") within the circuit of nightclubs, radio, and recordings. In 1953, she made a radical turn in her work, renouncing the passive reproduction of the rural stereotype that had been established in urban settings.

In this new process she assumed the traditional *performative* model of the rural songstress that she would gradually strain to the point of transgression. She would dedicate herself completely to collecting material in the field—to "unearth folklore" as she put it—and to learn the vernacular poets' trade. And she did it precisely when the rural world faced the definitive pressure of modernizing change (urbanization and industrialization).

This was probably the most decisive moment of her artistic career. From then on, she would restlessly engage in the three-way role of researcher, performer, and creator. She would produce her own criteria for collecting in the field; she would develop a vast plan of promoting traditional music through radio programs, recording records conceived as didactic, and monographic works, perform in different settings, and initiate her prolific personal creative work.

## SONG SOURCES

The legacy of the vernacular poets is probably the seminal marker of Violeta Parra's New Song. Transmitted through oral tradition since colonial times, the *canto a lo poeta* [lit. poet's song, a sung poetry genre] and *la paya* [another sung poetry genre featuring improvised poetry] are verbal art forms that consist in singing verses, memorized or improvised, based on a proposed theme (known as the *fundamento* [foundation]). Its performance is executed via the use of an inherited repertoire of melody types (intonations) and of diverse forms of accompaniment (called *toquíos*) on the guitar or *guitarrón* [large guitar]; in the case of the guitar, there exist a wide variety of tunings.[14] In this difficult mission of saying something through song, the vernacular poets recite, using the *décima* form, within two fundamental thematic fields:[15] the *canto a lo divino*, in which they comment on different topics from the Old Testament, and the *canto a lo humano* (secular song), which provides an ample range of subjects from verses to ponder: verses about the world turned upside down, greetings, toasts, and chronicles of local and world events.[16] Itinerant artists in service to the community, circulating among local communities in different regions and cities of the country, the *payadores* and *cantores a lo poeta* [performers of the *paya* and of *canto a lo poeta*] are chroniclers and spokespeople of their communities, of their memories and their conditions. They make up a hereditary lineage, almost exclusively male, with notable exceptions.[17] In her pilgrimage through the world of the peasant and his or her culture, probably the most fertile experience and revelation that Violeta Parra had was her exposure to the wise masters of the *lira popular* [vernacular poetry, see note], from whom she learned directly.[18] This explains the centrality of the *décima* in her poetry as well as the clear presence in her songs of melodic turns from this ancient repertoire; and it also explains the fact that she has been considered part of the lineage of vernacular poets.[19]

As a poetic and musical practice on the one hand and as an option for community communication on the other, the *cantor a lo poeta* would constitute a model for Violeta Parra's artistic strategy. To this model she would integrate that of the rural songstress, the model upon which she would base her persona as performer. Both figures, central to peasant music practice, would be the basis for her personal mode of questioning the society of her time (fig. 9.1).

The melody of "La carta" (The letter) is in the style of the melody types (intonations) of the *canto a lo poeta*, as is the guitar accompaniment (*toquío*), based on two chords—tonic and seventh degree—in the mixolydian mode range. The melody is rhythmically strained by the narrative in an obvious manner.

(Text: "They sent me a letter by mail this morning. In this letter they tell me my brother was jailed. And withouth pity, with shackles, they dragged him through the streets, yes!")

Fig. 9.1 Excerpt (verse 1) of "La carta"

## Violeta Parra's Poetic Art: "Everyone's Song Is My Own Song"

Song, composition, poetry, painting, tapestry, ceramics—multiple were the expressive domains that Violeta Parra's creative spirit explored. Underlying the whole of her work are two attitudes that stand out as decisive and that, furthermore, signal an interesting perspective for analysis. One is the central value she placed on orality and vernacular traditions, with all that is implied in terms of artistic creation. The other is the capacity to transit between different expressive domains, linking them to a common imaginary, a dynamic of intertextuality emerging from the need to express herself with an unprejudiced openness to mixture, to risk a gesture beyond the conventional. Both elements—and probably many others—would redefine, from another perspective, her practice of popular song, which in this case considered here on three complementary levels: performance, texts [and worldview], and music.

### PERFORMANCE

In Violeta Parra's work, the central and overarching field of performance appears, above all, as the need for effective communication with the public—or rather with *her* public. The issue can be generalized to apply to the new movement of song that began to emerge during those years, in which song creation was sustained by a performance style that, in contrast to conventional performances of the time, revisited a major challenge: the search for a new meaning well summarized in the lyric "everyone's song is my own song."[20] Thus, the very space of artistic performance transformed itself into a space for the recognition—or even the modeling—of identities and of social practices that questioned their place and meaning within the tapestry of power relations of modern society.

I believe this is the foundation that sustains the creation of a new type of song. And in that process, Violeta Parra would become a catalyst that would support what can be called an emic style of performance. "Emic" in the sense of a deep and empathetic record of the vernacular world and its representation in the heart of the city and its artistic circuit.[21]

This enterprise would require the invention of a strategy that would neutralize the markers and rituals of the established modes of artistic communication. That is why I believe that a more accurate way of analyzing her work is to conceive of it as the construction (and socialization) of an alternate musicality, in which the execution of another style of performance and communication with the audience is of equal or greater importance than the creation of works. In the space of her artistic work, Violeta Parra would attempt to close the breach between the stage and audience and between art and reality. She would conceive of it as a space without borders, where the artist is an artist of a communicated collective. Her words to this end are an eloquent testimony:

> I do not see the difference between the artist and the audience: it is the miracle of the encounter. I believe that I am closer to my public than the public is to me, because I sing for them, not for me. To have a public is the natural result of my work. We have to justify our existence and I am sure that the whole world is able to do the same as I am. For me, it is about an obligation.
>
> I believe that all artists should aspire to have as a goal to ground themselves, to ground their work, in direct contact with the audience. I am very content to have arrived at a point in my work in which I no longer even want to make tapestries, painting, poetry, just like that, detached. I'm satisfied with running *La Carpa* [The Tent, see note] and working with living elements for now, with the public very close to me—one that I can feel, touch, speak to, and incorporate into my soul.[22]

On recordings, radio, concerts, itinerant tours, *peñas* [social events with musical performance], and *carpas* [large tents setup as impromptu cultural centers], the artist produced a practical performance style geared toward a direct and "spontaneous" communication with the audience that would become the basis for a liturgy of event-song that turned on the figure of the singer (singer-songwriter or urban minstrel). With an austere style, purged as much as possible of all artifice, she liberated herself on stage from the feminine stereotype that perpetually required women to play a sensual, seductive role. Violeta Parra herself constructed a new representation of the common woman. This mode, enriched by her experience singing in the small nightclubs in Paris's Latin Quarter (1955–56; 1961–65), would be the basis of a new type of event and musical performance that probably was the most characteristic and important in the evolution of the Chilean New Song movement: the *peñas*. At these performance events, a new ritual in which the singer communed with the audience crystallized, negating the distance that had separated them in the nightclub format.

From a poetic viewpoint, the emphasis on a narrative with a testimonial tone and on a temporality that references the ancient traditions of vernacular poetry breaks the conventional format of the urban song. This tone and temporality would establish an alternative to the stereotypical lyricism predominant in the typical folk genre (mainly in *tonadas*), one that would constitute the basis of a new epic song for the turbulent years of the 1960s.

The usefulness of the music to a strategic narrative approximates the temporality of the vernacular poets, indicating the recuperation of the tale in song: singing to be heard by an attentive listener, in liturgies "of religious silence."[23] On the other hand, this restricts the possibility of playful improvisation and of sonorous display for its own sake: this song would distance itself from dance and from the festive dimension.

The use of the voice and the guitar also signals an emphasis on the expression. In this type of supremacy of the simple—averse to artifices and virtuosities—we find a conceptual nucleus for the construction of a new authenticity, one that would be a source of friction with the aesthetic of the prevailing folk music. Thus, for example, certain singers of the time would consider Violeta's voice, her timbre and her way of using it, as foreign compared to what was "artistically correct."

Furthermore, not just her work but her very image should be valued; an image that Violeta Parra certainly constructed in close relationship to the identity of the "popular Other," such that her life and work would be confused with theirs. It would be a self-centered and testimonial body of work, fashioned from her position as woman–mother–head of household–artist (the mark of gender is evident here). Through her personal symbolic universe, she would make the world of the outcast, with whom she profoundly identified, visible and tangible. She would speak the language of the people, her voice would be the same as theirs, her song would be "everyone's song." In short, a new paradigm for the popular artist and the standard of a "new authenticity."

## TEXTS AND WORLDVIEW

The breadth, diversity, and depth of the thematic catalog of her songs made Violeta Parra an exceptional case within Chilean context at the time. It surpassed the purely recreational or frivolously amorous function of popular song; from its status as minor art, she would reposition it to the rank of a powerful expressive genre of existential experience.

Considering her songs as a whole, there appear clear axes of her worldview that can be schematically structured as opposing pairs relative to social, cultural, political, religious, and existential phenomena. As a way of offering a brief glimpse in this vein, I examine three thematic axes of her songbook: the world, the secular, and the sacred.

**THE WORLD.** This theme principally references her experience of Chilean society, condensed into a dualistic representation of opposing pairs: landowner/laborers, rich/poor. Injustice and poverty appear as the backdrop of social life, considered to be directly derived from the power structure as symbolized [in one of her songs] by the figure of the president of the [Chilean] Republic. She critiques him as the person responsible for the oppressive, exploitative, deceptive, and repressive situations that the people experience:

| | |
|---|---|
| Cuando vi de los mineros | When I saw how the miners |
| Dentro de su habitación | Lived inside their quarters |
| Me dije: mejor habita | I said to myself: the refined thief |
| En su concha de caracol | Lives better whether |
| O a la sombra de las leyes | Inside his snail's shell |
| El refinado ladrón. | Or under the shadow of law. |
| ¡Y arriba, quemando el sol! | And from above, the sun burns! |

Excerpt from "Y arriba quemando el sol" (And from above, the sun burns):

| | |
|---|---|
| No es vida la del chilote, | The Chilote has no life, |
| No tiene letra ni pleito, | Cannot read or file a lawsuit, |
| Tamango llevan sus pies, | Has sandals on his feet, |
| Milcao y ají su cuerpo, | Potato pancakes and hot peppers in his body, |
| Pellín para calentarse, | Beachwood to heat himself |
| Del frio de los gobiernos, | From the coldness of the government, |
| llorando estoy, | I am crying, |
| Que le quebrantan los huesos, | They shatter his bones, I am leaving, |
| me voy, me voy. | I am leaving. |

Excerpt from "Según el favor del viento" (At the will of the wind)

| | |
|---|---|
| Arauco tiene una pena | The Araucanian has a sorrow |
| Más negra que su chamal, | Darker than his wrappings, |
| Ya no son los españoles | It is no longer the Spaniards |
| Los que les hacen llorar, | Who makes them cry, |
| Hoy son los propios chilenos | Today it is the very same Chileans |

| | |
|---|---|
| Los que les quitan el pan. | Who take away their bread. |
| ¡Levántate, Pailahuán! | Rise up, Pailahuán! [name for a Mapuche leader] |

Excerpt from "Arauco tiene una pena" (The Araucanian has one sorrow)

She would unmask the power structure and its institutions (elections, the justice and educational systems, civic and military ceremonies):

| | |
|---|---|
| Miren como sonríen los presidentes | Look at the smiles of the presidents |
| Cuando le hacen promesas al inocente. | When they make promises to the innocent. |
| Miren como le ofrecen al sindicato | Look how they offer the labor union |
| Este mundo y el otro los candidatos. | This World and the other, these candidates. |
| Miren como redoblan los juramentos | Look how they double down on their promises |
| Pero después del voto doble tormento. | But after the election double the torment. |

Excerpt from "Miren como sonríen" (Look how they smile)

She denounced the repressive mechanism exercised by the engine of power:

| | |
|---|---|
| Yo que me encuentro tan lejos, | I, who find myself so far away, |
| Esperando una noticia, | Awaiting some news, |
| Me viene a decir la carta | A letter comes to tell me |
| Que en mi patria no hay justicia. | That in my homeland there is no justice. |
| Los hambrientos piden pan, | The hungry ask for bread, |
| Plomo les da la milicia. ¡Ay sí! | The military gives them lead. Oh, yes! |

Excerpt from "La carta" (The letter)

On the other hand, she would proclaim the value of liberty, she would idealize the rural world as a utopia, and she would exalt the forces of social change (students, leaders, and folk heroes):

| | |
|---|---|
| ¡Que vivan los estudiantes | Long live the students |
| Que rugen como los vientos | Who roar like the wind |
| Cuando meten al oído | When cassocks and regiments |
| Sotanas y regimientos! | Fill their ears! |
| Pajarillos libertarios, | Libertarian little birds |
| Igual que los elementos. | Just like the elements |
| Caramba y zamba la cosa | Good heavens and zamba and all that |
| ¡Que vivan los experimentos! | Long live experiments! |

Excerpts from "Que vivan los estudiantes" (Long live the students)

**THE SECULAR.** The human condition and its most transcendent matters have a dramatic register within the life-death continuum. Most likely it is within these bounds that the deepest and most personal level of her songs resides. Love, particularly the experience of being in a relationship as a couple, is the human dimension that Violeta Parra would sing about using the largest number of frameworks: from love/pain to love as a redemptive force.

| | |
|---|---|
| Maldigo luna y paisaje, | I curse moon and landscape, |
| Los valles y los desiertos, | The valleys and the deserts, |
| Maldigo muerto por muerto | I curse the dead for being dead, |
| Y al vivo de rey a paje; | And the living from king to pageboy; |
| El ave con su plumaje | The bird with its plumage, |
| Yo la maldigo a porfía, | I curse it obstinately, |
| Las aulas, la sacristía, | The classrooms, the sacristy, |
| Porque me aflige un dolor; | Because it causes me pain; |
| Maldigo el vocablo amor, | I curse the word "love" |
| Con toda su porquería. | With all its filth. |
| ¡Cuánto será mi dolor! | How much pain will I have? |

Excerpt from "Maldigo del alto cielo" (I curse the high heavens)

| | |
|---|---|
| El amor es torbellino | Love is a whirlwind |
| Ee pureza original, | Of original purity, |
| Hasta el feroz animal | Even the fierce animal |
| Susurra su dulce trino. | whispers its sweet song. |
| Detiene a los peregrinos, | It detains pilgrims, |
| Libera a los prisioneros, | It frees prisoners, |
| El amor con sus esmeros | Love with its troubles |
| Al viejo lo vuelve niño | Turns the old young again. |
| Y al malo sólo el cariño | And only affection turns the evil one |
| Lo vuelve puro y sincero. | Pure and sincere again. |

Excerpt from "Volver a los diecisiete" (To be seventeen again)

As a contrast to love/life, death is another dimension underlying her work (with clear autobiographical references). The religious conception of death, threshold of the superhuman to the profound mysteries of existence, emerges as powerful:

| | |
|---|---|
| Cuando la carne se muere | When the flesh dies |
| El alma busca en la altura | The soul searches the heights |
| La explicación de su vida | For the explanation of its life |
| Cortada con tal premura, | Cut down in such haste, |
| La explicación de su muerte | For the explanation of its death, |
| Prisionera de su tumba. | The prisoner of its tomb. |
| Cuando se muere la carne | When the flesh dies |

| | |
|---|---|
| El alma se queda a oscuras. | The soul remains in darkness. |

Excerpt from "Rin del angelito" (*Rin* [dance] of the little angel)

Faced with experiencing death, she questions existence and the meaning of life (and also, of song):

| | |
|---|---|
| ¿Qué es lo que canta?, digo yo | I say, what do you sing? |
| No lo consigue responder, | I cannot get an answer from him, |
| Vana es la abeja sin su miel, | The bee without its honey is in vain, |
| Vana la hoz sin segador. | The sickle without sower is in vain. |
| ¿Es el dinero alguna luz | Is money some type of light |
| Para los ojos que no ven? | To those eyes that do not see? |
| Treinta denarios y una cruz | Thirty dinars and a cross |
| Responde el eco de Israel. | Responds the echo of Israel. |
| ¿De dónde viene tu mentir | Where does your falsehood come from |
| Y adónde empieza tu verdad? | And where does your truth begin? |
| Parece broma tu mirar, | Your gaze appears to be a joke, |
| Llanto parece tu reír. | Your laughter appears to be weeping. |

Excerpt from "Cantores que reflexionan" (Singers who reflect)

Between the tension of life and death, in all its range of unrefined contingency, is where she would bring up the radical questions of humanity and its meaning, which gather full resonance in her song, "Gracias a la vida" (Thanks be to life), her existential farewell and testament:

| | |
|---|---|
| Gracias a la vida que me ha dado tanto | Thanks be to life, which has given me so much |
| Me dio el corazón que agita su marco | It gave me a heart that beats within its frame |
| Cuando miro el fruto del cerebro humano, | When I see the fruits of the human mind, |
| Cuando miro al bueno tan lejos del malo, | When I see good so far from evil, |
| Cuando miro el fondo de tus ojos claros. | When I see the depth of your fair eyes. |

**THE SACRED.** The dichotomy already indicated between the secular individual and power in society has an equivalence in the religious plane, as an opposition between the sacred and the [Roman Catholic] church. The dichotomy distinguishes between the church (the representatives and administrators of the official religion) and the sacred as a transcendent attitude (purity and goodness associated with the religion of the oppressed, as previously mentioned). It is a critical point of view that denounces the effect of "the opium of the people" and unmasks the alliance between the church and power structures:

| | |
|---|---|
| Porque los pobres no tienen | Because the poor do not have |
| En este mundo esperanza | Hope in this world |
| Se amparan en la otra vida | They seek refuge in the next life |
| Como una justa balanza. | Like a set of just scales. |
| Por eso las procesiones, | That explains the processions, |
| Las velas y alabanzas . . . | The candles and shouts of praise . . . |
| | |
| De tiempos inmemoriales | From time immemorial |
| Que se ha inventado el infierno | Hell was invented |
| Para asustar a los pobres | To scare the poor |
| Con sus castigos eternos, | With its eternal punishments, |
| Y el pobre que es inocente | And the poor who are innocent |
| Con su inocencia creyendo . . . | With their innocence believing . . . |
| | |
| El cielo tiene la rienda, | Heaven has the reins, |
| La tierra y el capital, | The land and the capital, |
| Y a los soldados del Papa | And the soldiers of the Pope |
| Les llenan bien el morral. | Have their backpack filled well. |
| Y al que trabaja le meten | And upon he who works, they force |
| La Gloria como un bozal . . . | The Gloria like a muzzle . . . |

Excerpt from "Porque los pobres no tienen" (Because the poor don't have)

In the face of the injustice of the powerful, she questions "the Holy Father who lives in Rome," protesting the situation of the poor:

| | |
|---|---|
| Miren como nos hablan de libertad | See how they speak to us of liberty |
| Cuando de ella nos privan en realidad. | When they deprive us of it in reality |
| Miren como pregonan tranquilidad | See how they cry for tranquility |
| Cuando nos atormenta la autoridad. | When we are tormented by authority. |
| ¿Qué dirá el Santo Padre que vive en Roma, | What would the Holy Father who lives in Rome say |
| Que le están degollando a su paloma? | To their slaughtering of his dove? |

Excerpt from "¿Qué dirá el Santo Padre?" (What would the Holy Father say?)

And against the obscurantist manipulation of the truth, she espouses the demystifying glance of science:

| | |
|---|---|
| Me gustan los estudiantes | I like the students |
| Que van al laboratorio | Who go to the laboratory |

| | |
|---|---|
| Y descubren lo que se esconde | And discover what is hidden |
| Al fondo del confesionario. | In the depths of the confessional. |

Excerpt from "Que vivan los estudiantes" (Long live the students)

| | |
|---|---|
| ¿Qué vamos a hacer con tanto | What will we do with so many |
| Tratado del alto cielo? | Treatises about Heaven on high? |
| Ayúdame, Valentina, | Help me, Valentina, |
| Ya que tú volaste tan lejos. | Seeing as how you flew so far. |
| Dime de una vez por todas | Tell me once and for all |
| Que arriba no hay tal mansión: | That up there, there is no such mansion: |
| Mañana la ha de fundar | Tomorrow man will establish it |
| El hombre con su razón. | With his reason. |

Excerpt from "Ayúdame, Valentina" (Help me, Valentina)

## MUSIC: THE VIOLETA PARRA SONGBOOK

Parra's songs would cover a trajectory from a song rooted in rural musical tradition to composed song, with a musical catalog that would become more varied and personal with each addition, gradually integrating elements from other musical traditions. In this way, she would combine her role as a token singer—an interpreter and promoter of the traditional songbook—with her role as multidisciplinary creative artist.

From a perspective of musical genre or style, her songs do not align themselves exactly within traditional categories (folk songs) nor do they fit within popular ones (the so-called commercial song). They could be considered part of that intermediate space that Charles Keil called "people's music." And as far as "people's music" is concerned, there exists an interesting parallel in the development of Chilean urban song—and the significance of Violeta Parra's songs to it—with the modulation of one stereotype to another, as Keil signals happened with urban blues and polka in the United States. Keil makes a distinction between the first appearance of both genres on record, around 1928, in a "clean, modern, and authentic form," and later, approaching 1952, the emergence in Chicago of a dirty blues and honky-tonk style of polka, that would change the established norms in both genres.[24] He further specifies that both moments coincide with changes in the economy and forms of communication—specifically, the arrival of new forms of mass communication after World War I, and the diversification of that media following World War II.

For the most part, Violeta Parra represents the emergence of a new version of the genre "Chilean popular song with folkloric roots" within the circuit of the local music industry.[25] In its early stages, her basic approach would be the negotiation, by way of contrast, with the *música típica* [lit. typical music, early popular versions of traditional Chilean folk music] that at the time represented the stylistic framework dominant on the popular song circuit (performance techniques, vocal and instrumental arrangement styles, repertoire). The championing of a concealed authenticity would be the antonym of an aesthetic of the imaginary and the "pretty," in which formal values were preponderant. This renovation of the genre would represent itself as the construction of a new authenticity that would consolidate its own aesthetic.

Central aspects of this poetics of song are present in "Yo canto la diferencia" (I sing difference). It is a *tonada* in the style of Chillán, her birthplace, composed in 1960 for the celebrations commemorating the sesquicentennial of Chile's independence. It constitutes, in a way, the public declaration of her artistic manifesto, a singer assuming a stance toward society.

On the musical plane, the new style's markers are signaled in the use of the structures and elements of traditional peasant song, giving the connotation of an attitude of return to the simple and austere. The rhythmic-melodic figure of the song and its accompaniment—fluctuating between 6/8 and 3/4—are characteristics of the traditional *tonada*. Similarly, the recurrence of sonorities and harmonic gesture characteristic of the *canto a lo poeta*—such as certain modal inflections: tonic chord–major II chord. Its structure is of the type of song without refrain, consisting of a single pattern repeated as many times as needed to conform to the verses of the text: a seventeen-measure cycle, organized in the sequence of 4+(1)+4+4+2+(2). Interestingly, within this frame, its internal dynamic is flexible to the flow of the words and its character is epic-narrative, as is also the effect of its last verse, which functions as a sentence or conclusion in the manner of a condensed refrain (fig. 9.2).[26]

The championing and reworking of a concealed authenticity implicitly brings with it the notion of founding traditions that are outside of the official prototype of the Chileanness (based on the model of the hacienda).[27] Concretely, this is the case of indigenous and peasant musics from other regions. One song that illustrates this integrating process well is "Y arriba quemando el sol" [1960, And from above the sun burns] (fig. 9.3).

Here a radical contrast is established with the stereotype of a festive folk, grittily exploring the dramatic living conditions of the miners in the Chilean north. She calls it a "northern" style, and it is based on a dance rhythm from that Andean region. The austerity of the elements is particularly evident in this song. It is constructed on the basis of one "rhythmic" note, repeated insistently, that descends through the tonic chord (G–(F)–D–B–G); here F natural is an important step since it reveals the use of tools from a different modality (mixolydian). When the sequence arrives to the tonic (G), it jumps an octave to finish the verse with the sentence-refrain: "And from above the sun burns!" A gesture of synthesis and certainly of dramatic effect. In the version recorded in Paris (1963), the traditional harmonic accompaniment (guitar) is not present; the song accompaniment consists instead of a rhythmic pattern executed on vernacular percussion

(Text: "I sing in the Chillán style when I have something to say, and I don't take the guitar seeking applause. I sing the difference that lies between truth and falsehood, otherwise I don't sing")

Fig. 9.2 Excerpt (verse 1) of "Yo canto la diferencia"

(Text: "When I went to the plains I carried my heart full of joy, like a yellow finch. But it died there. First I lost the feathers, and then the voice. And overhead the sun burned!")

Fig. 9.3 Excerpt (verse 1) of "Y arriba quemando el sol"

instruments (*bombo, caja, matraca* [bass drum, snare drum, rachet]) as well as the use of the *quena* [Andean end-blown flute], clear references to the musical traditions of the Andean highlands, assimilated early on and that would later become the central stylistic marker of Chilean [new] song.

## Conclusion

The conclusion is simple: the championing of difference, that of the "popular Other" and her own, is a fixture of Violeta Parra's music. Her musical legacy remits to a social practice of song that flourished in the 1950s, and that powerfully crystallized in the imaginary of Chilean society between the 1960s and early 1970s as a space for the epic affirmation of a sense of having previously been deemed worthless or irrelevant. In this context, Violeta Parra would constitute a morality of song: a model of interaction between the rural and the urban, of the recycling of vernacular traditions within the process of artistic creation; a testament to the supreme exercise of her autonomy and to the vernacular world's ability to resist in the face of a problematic modernization. From this perspective, she will be often claimed as the soul of the Chilean New Song movement. Furthermore and above all, her song of difference opened a space sensitive to the recognition of the multiple identities that make up the country of Chile.

### Notes

In November 1999 I was invited to participate in the "Symposium in Honour of Robert Pring-Mill" organized by the Institute of Popular Music at the University of Liverpool. With this work, the fruit of those days' labor, I also offer tribute to the beloved teacher Robert Pring-Mill and his dedication to and sensitive work with Latin American song and poetry. I also express my sincere gratitude to my friends at the Institute of Popular Music.

The epigraph is excerpted from a 1965 interview with Violeta Parra in Geneva, published in Isabel Parra, *El Libro Mayor de Violeta Parra* (Madrid: Ediciones Michay, 1985), 147.

Translator's note: In the main title as well as some subtitles, the author quotes Violeta Parra's lyrics.

1. Editors' note: The author uses the term "popular" in Spanish to denote two types of musical and cultural practices that in English can be identified by different terms. For the purpose of clarity, this translation will use the term "vernacular" when referring to musical, poetic and cultural practices associated with everyday life in rural areas of Chile. These are the practices that, as the author discusses, informed Violeta Parra's own artistic work. The urban, regional, national, or mass mediated practices that use these vernacular expressions as departure point or source inspiration, including Parra's own music, are denoted by the term "popular."

2. Pablo Neruda, "Elegía para cantar," in Violeta Parra, *Décimas: Autobiografía en verso*, 2nd ed. (Buenos Aires: Editorial Sudamericana, 1998), 9.

3. "Universes of recognition" is Marc Augé's phrase, cited in Denis-Constant Martin, *Cartes d'identité: comment dit-on "nous" en politique?* (Paris: Presses de la Fondation Nationale des Sciences Politiques, 1994), 26. Among the studies, see, for example, Paul Austerlitz, *Merengue: Dominican Music and Dominican Identity* (Philadelphia: Temple University Press, 1995); Gage Averill, *A Day for the Hunter, a Day for the Pray: Popular Music and Power in Haiti* (Chicago: University of Chicago Press, 1997); Yvonne Daniel, *Rumba: Dance and Social Change in Contemporary Cuba* (Bloomington: Indiana University Press, 1995); Jorge Duany, "Ethnicity, Identity and Music: An Anthropological Analysis of the Dominican Merengue," in *Music and Black Ethnicity: The Caribbean and South America*, ed. Gerard Béhague (New Brunswick, N.J.: Transaction, 1994), 65–90; Jocelyn Guilbault, *Zouk: World Music in the West Indies* (Chicago: University of Chicago Press, 1993); Deborah Pacini Hernández, *Bachata: A Social History of a Dominican Popular Music* (Philadelphia: Temple University Press, 1995); Manuel Peña, "From Ranchero to Jaitón: Ethnicity and Class in Texas-Mexican Music (Two Styles in the Form of a Pair)," *Ethnomusicology* 29, no. 1 (1985), 29–55; Suzel Ana Reily, "*Música sertaneja* and Migrant Identity: The Stylistic Development of a Brazilian Genre," *Popular Music* 11, no. 3 (1992), 337–57; Thomas Turino, "'Somos el Perú': Cumbia Andina and the Children of Andean Migrants in Lima," *Studies in Latin American Popular Culture* 9 (1990), 15–37; Alejandro Ulloa, *La salsa en Cali* (Cali: Ediciones Universidad del Valle, 1992); Christopher A. Waterman, *Jùjú: A Social History and Ethnography of an African Popular Music* (Chicago: University of Chicago Press, 1990).

4. Néstor García Canclini, *Culturas híbridas: estrategias para entrar y salir de la modernidad* (Mexico City: Grijalbo, 1990), 248, 193.

5. Ibid., 238.

6. This is what Josep Martí i Pérez calls "representative culture," configured by the cultural elements selected according to criteria appropriate to the rhetorical narratives of the moment. The author classifies all the elements observed within the territory of a region or a country into three groups: elements with representative value, neutral elements, and rejected elements. Clearly, representative culture constitutes only one small part of the total cultural legacy. See Josep Martí i Pérez, "Culturas en *Contacto* en nuestra sociedad actual: algunas reflexiones sobre pluriculturalidad a través del fenómeno musical," *Actas del Primer Coloquio de Antropología y Música*. Diálogos 1, *Música Oral del Sur* 3 (1998), 135.

7. A paradigmatic symbol of the landowner's power, the hacienda or *latifundio*, a large rural property, is the epicenter of an ideal representation of the past, like a world devoid of social conflicts. *Música típica* [early popular versions of traditional Chilean folk music] groups, in their onstage paraphernalia, represented the landowner and his festive attire.

8. A number of works by Chilean researchers deal with the "modernization" of folklore. See, for example, Eduardo Carrasco, *La Nueva Canción Chilena en América Latina* (Santiago de Chile: Centro de Indagación y Expresión Cultural y Artística, 1982), and *La revolución y las estrellas* (Santiago de Chile: Ediciones del Ornitorrinco, 1988); Osvaldo Rodríguez, *Cantores que reflexionan* (Madrid: Ediciones Lar, 1984); Rodolfo Parada-Lillo, "L'articulation entre tradition et modernité dans la culture: la nouvelle chanson chilienne, 1960–1975" (PhD diss., Université de la Sorbonne Nouvelle, Paris, 1992); Juan Pablo González, "Evocación, modernización y reivindicación del folclore en la música popular chilena: el papel de la performance," *Revista Musical Chilena* 50, no. 185 (1996), 25–37, and "Música popular chilena de raíz folcló-

rica," in *Clásicos de la música popular chilena, 1960–1973. Raíz folclórica*, ed. Luis Advis et al. (Santiago de Chile: SCD–Ediciones Universidad Católica de Chile, 1998), 2:10–27.

9. A constellation of historical figures and facts relevant to this trajectory of struggle would be cemented as a "universe of recognition." Among these are the massacre of thousands of miners and their families at the School of Santa María in Iquique (1907); the death of Luis Emilio Recabarren, founding leader of the labor movement; the [memory of] the miners of the northern Pampas [1920s]; the massacre of rebel peasants in Ránquil (1934); the assassination by the police of a worker, Ramona Parra (1944); the settlement of Herminda de la Victoria, the first collective occupation of urban spaces by the homeless (1957); [the legacy and deaths of] the popular singers Violeta Parra [1917–1967] and Víctor Jara [193–1973], president Salvador Allende [1908–1973], and the poet Pablo Neruda [1904–1973]; and on the international plane: the Bolshevik (1905) and Mexican (1910) Revolutions; the Spanish Civil War [1936–1939]; the Cuban Revolution (1959); the activism of Ernesto "Ché" Guevara [1928–1967]; Ho Chi Minh and the Vietnam War [1955–1969]; university students and their protests [in Latin America, Europe, and the United States, 1960s and 1970s].

10. Maximiliano Salinas Campos, *Canto a lo divino y religión del oprimido en Chile* (Santiago de Chile: Rehue, 1992), 42.

11. Eduardo Carrasco, "Canción popular y política," in *Música popular en América Latina*, ed. Rodrigo Torres (Santiago de Chile: FONDART/ IASPM, 1998), 63–70, p. 69.

12. In South America, and probably in all of Latin America, references to this migratory phenomenon appear in popular song: in Brazil with Luiz Gonzaga and the *música sertaneja* [country music] and also in songs from the *tropicália* movement; in Argentina with Atahualpa Yupanqui; and so forth.

13. Editors' note: The author is making reference to Parra's song "En este mundo moderno" (In this modern world), which is a critique of bourgeois society and its disconnect from plight of the Chilean underclass.

14. Scholars have come to recognize the use, even today, of more than forty tunings of the peasant guitar in Chile's central zone. See Raúl Díaz Acevedo, *Finares campesinos* (Temuco: FONDART, 1994). [Translator's note: The Chilean *guitarrón* referred to here is an instrument of the same shape, although deeper and not as wide, as a guitar. It usually has twenty-five strings, twenty-one of which are mounted from the headstock and arranged into five orders. The remaining four drone strings, known as *diablitos* (little devils), are mounted from the region where the neck meets the body. The instrument is almost exclusively the domain of the troubadours referred to in this article as "vernacular poets."]

15. The *décima* is an ancient metric form of Spanish renaissance poetry, also called the Décima Espinela in honor of its creator, Vicente Espinel. It is one of the most widespread traditional metric forms in Latin America. Each *décima* is constructed of ten eight-syllable lines, and the complete verse consists of four *décimas*.

16. Editors' note: *Canto a lo divino* and *canto a lo humano* are the two subtypes that make up *canto a lo poeta*, which is the umbrella term for a variety of sung poetic genres.

17. One such exception is Rosa Araneda, an important member of the brotherhood of vernacular poets at the end of the nineteenth century. See Micaela Navarrete, *Aunque no soy literaria. Rosa Araneda en la poesía popular del siglo XIX* (Santiago de Chile: Ediciones Biblioteca Nacional, 1998).

18. Editors' note: *Lira popular* (lit. poetry of the people), is the Chilean term for what in other countries is known as Cordel literature. This is the term used to refer to numerous loose-leaf, mass-produced printed publications that circulated in Chile's main urban centers between the end of the nineteenth century and the first decades of the twentieth century. Vernacular poets—mostly men of rural origin who had migrated to the city—used this medium to publish their verses, commenting on the affairs of the day by means of poetic forms and imagery associated with oral literature.

19. Magdalena Vicuña, "Violeta Parra: hermana mayor de los poetas populares," *Revista Musical Chilena* 12, no. 60 (1958), 71–77.

20. Last verse of "Gracias a la vida" (Thanks be to life), one of her last songs (1966).

21. I functionally use the concept of "vernacular world" as a generic reference to the "internal Other" or the so-called "peasantry" consisting of a numerous group of indigenous and mestizo people in the country.

22. Parra, *El libro mayor*, 46, 140. [Translator's note: La Carpa de la Reina was a large circus-like tent that Violeta Parra erected in 1965 within a public park in the municipality of La Reina. It was dedicated to performance and teaching of folkloric music, dance, and art. For more information, see Juan Pablo González et al., *Historia social de la música popular en Chile, 1950–1970* (Santiago de Chile: Ediciones Universidad Católica de Chile, 2009), 235].

23. Nicanor Parra's expression in his poem "Defensa de Violeta Parra" (In defense of Violeta Parra), 1964: "Lo que tiene que hacer el auditor / es guardar un silencio religioso / porque tu canto sabe adónde va / perfectamente" (What the listener must do / is to keep a religious silence / because your song knows where it goes / perfectly).

24. Charles Keil, "People's Music Comparatively: Style and Stereotype, Class and Hegemony," in *Music Grooves*, Steven Feld and Charles Keil (Chicago: University of Chicago Press, 1994), 197–217. Keil insists on the need for a more complex consideration of the historic processes of the style of "people's music" in the twentieth century, stating eight related hypotheses that suggest fruitful paths of analysis.

25. This denomination is what is presently used in Chile to define the borders of a vast and varied repertoire. Luis Advis et al., *Clásicos de la música popular chilena, 1960–1973. Raíz folclórica*, vol. 2 (Santiagode Chile: SCD–Ediciones Universidad Católica de Chile, 1998).

26. This same procedure exists in "La carta" (see fig. 9.3), which has a cycle of 12 measures: 2+2+3+3+(2); and in "Y arriba quemando el sol" (see fig. 9.5), with a 16-measure cycle: 4+4+4+3+(1).

27. In an interview in the first edition of the magazine *Juventud* (Santiago, July 1977), 29, Los Huasos Quincheros, the representative group for this official Chileanness, summarized the origin, function, and meaning of this genre like this: "We play music from the Central Valley because that is where Chile was born. That is where its independence was forged, and that is where our ancestors nurtured patriotism. . . . We have succeeded in imposing a style, a form, and a spirit on the national folklore milieu. We also export our music to all the world, and, more importantly, we teach people to love what is Chilean and her traditional values. . . . We offer the tradition of a glorious past that should serve us now and in the future."

# 10

# The *Nuevo Cancionero* Movement

## *A Change of Paradigm in Argentine Folklore*

CLAUDIO F. DÍAZ

Since the mid-twentieth century, a field of cultural production was gradually established in Argentina. It grew out of the more general evolution of the mass communications media and mass culture, and controversially came to be called folklore in the social imaginary. Quite a number of scholars have shown the difference between this type of musical expression, which pertains to mass culture, and authentically "folkloric" phenomena—no matter how they are defined. Despite these issues, the type of "folklore" connected to the recording industry and large Argentine festivals like Cosquín and Jesús María has continued to evolve, is still called "folklore," and is an important type of popular music in Argentina.

As I have mentioned elsewhere, I propose that Argentine folklore be studied as a specific field of cultural production—in other words, as a system of social relations having its own rules of production and canonization.[1] Because this field of discursive production is part of the cultural industry's overall production of popular music, its game rules are very different from those found in the sociocultural areas where the musical genres comprising the larger field of popular music originated. However, like all fields of discursive cultural production, folklore operates according to the principle of competition for legitimacy, which evolved according to specific rules and is based on specific ideals regarding canonization. These rules are not arbitrary; instead, they were gradually constructed in the course of the battles that impacted the field's formative process from the 1920s

A longer version of this work was originally published by Claudio F. Díaz as "El Nuevo Cancionero: un cambio de paradigma en el folklore argentino," in *Lugares del decir 2: competencia social y estrategias discursivas*, ed. Ricardo L. Costa and Danuta T. Mozejo (Rosario: Editorial Homo Sapiens, 2007), 203–47. Translated by Jane L. Florine with permission.

on. This is how the "classic" paradigm of production—as I call it—specific to the field of folklore was constructed.

By "paradigm," I mean the set of assumptions, convictions, and agreements that was generally shared by the social agents who made up the field—not taking into account existing differences of opinion and fights for legitimacy. These shared beliefs were the ones that made it possible to clearly recognize which creations belonged to the field of folklore: in other words, to be able to say that these works were "folklore" as opposed to those that were not.

During the field of folklore's process of development, the classic paradigm that was constructed came to be made up of a set of rules (thematic, compositional, performative, rhetorical, lexical, etc.) that determined the correct way of producing its musical works and therefore created criteria for inclusion and exclusion—the basis of the classic paradigm's identity.[2] Thought of in this way, social agents internalized the paradigm. Not only that, the field itself made sure that it would be spread and passed down to future generations through a variety of means (from schools that taught folklore to didactic articles found in specialized magazines).

The classic paradigm of folklore had already been formed by the middle of the twentieth century. During the late 1950s and early 1960s, this field of production experienced a period of expansion and consolidation called the "folklore boom." Then, around the mid-1960s, a number of musical phenomena appeared that brought tension to the field because their aesthetic and ideological approaches challenged key aspects of the dominant paradigm of production. This chapter analyzes some of the characteristics of these new aesthetic concepts and proposes an explanatory hypothesis about their appearance. Before addressing the main elements of these aesthetic concepts that arose in the mid-1960s, however, it is first necessary to provide precise details about the classic paradigm of folklore.

## "Tradition" in the Classic Paradigm

If anything characterized the dominant paradigm in folklore in the late 1950s, it was the central place of the concept of tradition. This concept, however, is a particularly ambiguous one that has multiple meanings. For many scholars, tradition—the continuation of the past into the present—is one of the basic components of "what is truly folk."[3] As Gabriel Ábalos has shown, however, the term "tradition" is used in many ways that are often contradictory.[4] For the purposes of this chapter, however, instead of "tradition" being an essence or a visible continuity with the past, I take it to be more of a discursive construct whose function is to legitimate aesthetic, ethical, or ideological concepts that prevail in the present.[5]

It can therefore be said that the tradition discussed in folklore is a "selective tradition," a conscious way of building a true connection with the past by means of a selection process that involves placing emphasis on certain things, omitting others, and silencing yet others. This selective tradition, which had become dominant in the field by the 1950s, was genealogically connected to cultural nationalism—and to what cultural nationalism would later be deemed to be—beginning in the Centennial Era and including the important contributions of Peronism.[6] As part of this selective tradition, a set of characteristics was established that would gradually become the norm for judging authenticity of folk songs. Without attempting to be exhaustive, I list some of these traits below.

A. The nationalization of genres: in a long and complex process, the various musical genres from different regions of Argentina came to be recognized and ontologically defined as distinct expressions of the same "national being." Musics that were distinctly regional or local began to be known through ample discourse production that legitimated them in magazines, radio programs, and so on, with emphasis placed on a given genre's place and region within the realm of "national folklore." This particular phenomenon was observed in various ways. For example, specialized folklore programs on some radio stations began to devote nights or specific time slots to each province or region.

Accompanying the spread of these regional genres was a legitimating strategy that tried to show the authenticity of the different musical styles by saying that they were rooted in popular customs and ways of life from various parts of the nation.

In this nationalization process, Augusto Raúl Cortazar, Carlos Vega, and Félix Coluccio—along with other intellectuals who in one way or another were part of the field—played an important part.[7] These intellectuals, in fact, used the symbolic capital they had accumulated while doing research and participating in academic life to contribute their knowledge to specialized magazines and other publications, thereby sharing information about the history of the various musical genres they had studied as well as popular fiestas, traditional ceremonies, and customs from the corresponding regions.

A general result of this process was that musical genres that had developed independently, or had been unknown to each other because they were from different sociocultural areas, began to be seen as part of the same system and to be governed by the same rules. Processes of hybridization as well as the use of various kinds of music by performers who had initially specialized only in regional genres also began in this same fashion.

Along with the desire to disseminate knowledge about these genres, the use of a variety of musics and hybridization tended to legitimate these same types of music by showing that they were different ways of expressing the "same nation."

This concept came to be a key part of the classic paradigm and its particular manner of creating tradition.

B. The nation portrayed in different regional musics was based on an origin myth.[8] According to this myth, there was a former way of life that had virtues and values that needed to be rescued and honored. This way of life that had existed before the advent of modernity led to an idealized view of rural life and at times to a negative vision of urban space. Located in the interior, that idealized rural world was a place where national essence was preserved. In addition, this place was inhabited by a prototypical persona who was also idealized: the countryman, the man from the provinces, the man from the interior, and—even more symbolically—the gaucho [cowboy].

Rural areas, the interior of the country, and the gaucho—along with his customs, dress, and musical instruments—were therefore expressions of the national soul and of authentic Argentine popular art. This idealized image became established as modernization, industrialization, and urbanization came into play and drastically transformed the Argentine social map. During the first part of the twentieth century, the rapid development of the forces of production involved massive internal migration, new forms of exploitation, and new social identities in addition to the waves of European immigration that had occurred since the end of the nineteenth century. In this particular social context, the insistence on connecting the values that defined nationality with a type of human being, an idealized past, and an idealized image of "the native land" or "the interior" became especially important, as well. Claudio Monti and Adrián Javier Weissberg have analyzed the process through which this idealized and positive image of the gaucho was constructed, as well as the values associated with him: honesty, generosity, valor, love of country (understood as fighting against foreign invaders or Indians), respect for family and religion, and so on.[9]

In the discipline of folklore, which developed as modernization and internal migration occurred, this led to a special rhetoric as well as one of the most recurrent special topics found in the classic paradigm: the *pago*,[10] an idealized place exuberantly conceived as retaining otherwise-lost values and nostalgically described from an urban, dysphoric perspective. In an extreme sense, this loss of values and virtues was a loss of identity, which could be recuperated only by singing. In addition to its aesthetic component, folkloric song therefore acquired an ethical and ideological facet linked not only to provincialism, but also to nationality—where song, the Argentine people, the *pago*, and nationality were united in tradition.

C. The song of the people, which expressed the nation authentically, used a particular language. This language addressed the various regional ways of life and included all types of provincial speech. In the same way that genres and customs were valued as expressions of nationality, so were regional accents and different idiomatic expressions. These possible combinations, which were highly varied, became even more complex with the introduction of words taken from indigenous languages—which in some cases reflected different regional cultural layers and in others were a sign of bilingualism. It was therefore quite common to find Quechua expressions in the music of Santiago del Estero or Guaraní ones in the music of the Littoral region.[11] The language of folklore, however, was for the most part based on a literary model: gaucho literature that was reconverted, reinterpreted, and adapted to reflect regional ways of speaking. In this sense, Hernández's *Martín Fierro*, which was recovered by Lugones and positioned in the literary canon, was paradigmatic.[12] On one hand, it was a model that created narrative and ideological concepts, but on the other, it reinforced a type of language that eventually became established as "traditional."

D. This concept, expressed through traditional language and focused on the *pago* and on the Argentine people, used landscapes, customs, popular fiestas, and ceremonies of each region as its subject matter. Dances and music, as well as food and dress, appeared repeatedly in the songs. In many of them, the notable precision with which customs were referred to and places were described made it clear that their purpose was didactic. This didacticism was also found in and stimulated by magazines and specialized publications, a type of teaching emphasis that well suited what was discussed earlier because spreading knowledge about local customs was part of the nationalization process. Listeners, after all, had to become familiar with objects, customs, and musics they did not know about—yet could possibly adopt—because they were all just different facets of the same nation expressed in folklore. Consequently, the language of folklore had to be taught.

E. Perhaps the most important characteristic of the "tradition" I analyze in this chapter was the special expressive strategy constructed in the songs. The language of folklore, the surrounding scenery, places, and customs, the idealized *pago* connected to the original values of the nation, and nationalized musical genres and song itself made up the symbolic space from which a *provinciano* [man from the interior]—in other words, a criollo or a gaucho—spoke. In this tradition, however, the interior provinces, their customs, and their musics were synonymous with the nation. When a man from the interior spoke through song, it was an Argentine who did so. More precisely put, the "I" from the provinces was part of a "we" that expressed authentic *argentinidad* [Argentine national sentiment] and its essence.

On the other hand, this expressive strategy was not purely discursive; instead, it was also subject to the compositional and performance rules of the different genres that were in themselves expressions of the nation's popular soul. Because of this, the compositional styles, manner of arranging voices, selection of suitable musical instruments for each genre, typical traits of the accompaniment, and so forth, tended to become standardized. As part of this process, the influence of "pioneers," "masters," and "models" in the areas of composition, arranging, and/or performance corresponding to the different genres involved became stronger (Buenaventura Luna, Ernesto Montiel, Los Hermanos Ábalos, Atahualpa Yupanqui, and others). Respect for stylistic rules—that is, the "tradition" I analyze here—therefore became a sign of authenticity in folk song. Around the early 1960s, these criteria connected to authenticity had already become "naturalized", so by then it was possible to talk about a completely established classic paradigm.

## Crisis of the Classic Paradigm

The establishment of the big folklore festivals (such as Cosquín, Jesús María, and Baradero) in the early 1960s showed that the field of production had become established and had developed in three ways. For one, measurable growth had occurred in both production and consumption. This phenomenon, known as the folklore boom, was evident in sales statistics, the interest shown in folklore by recording companies, the great number of folklore radio programs, the presence of canonic folklore artists on television, and the attention paid to folklore by the press. The mere fact that festivals were successful showed the existence of an audience interested in folklore. In addition, however, it reflected the interest of different market sectors, such as the recording industry, radio and television sponsors, and even the state, in establishing folklore as a field of cultural production. On the other hand, because the classic paradigm had become firmly rooted, criteria had been developed to judge the legitimacy of musical works and whether or not they belonged to the field. Among other things, this resulted in an abundance of new artists at the beginning of the decade [the 1960s] whose output fit within the dominant aesthetics. In addition, typical avenues—such as *Folklore* magazine, which first appeared in July 1961, and the many cultural associations, traditionalist centers, *peñas* [restaurants with live music], and radio and television programs that developed at the start of the 1950s—were created and established to promote and reproduce these rules.

However, a third element pertaining to the development of the field must be considered: the growth and establishment of what I have discussed above produced the conditions necessary for folklore to be thought of as a separate realm of cultural production within Argentina. During the entire time the field of folklore was developing, it was relatively homogeneous. Although the field's greatest source of diversity was the regional origin of its various musical styles, this difference, as I have already pointed out, tended to be nullified through legitimating strategies that nationalized these musics and made them part of the same selective tradition. In the 1960s, difference began to be introduced by another type of process, as well. For one, the compositions of musicians like Ariel Ramírez, Eduardo Falú, and Gustavo Leguizamón (to name just a few) expanded the dictates of the classic paradigm. Without challenging any of the classic paradigm's fundamental beliefs, these individuals added "art" music elements to it, thereby creating a new type of folklore sound. Both their success and the positive response of critics created a context ripe for innovation and the search for new musical languages. In addition, the relative general success of folklore and its mass dissemination led many young musicians, some from other fields of production (e.g., choral music, music literature, and "young people's" music), to develop an interest in folk music and to attempt to enter the field. As new arrivals, these musicians had to come up with ways to get their own aesthetic creations recognized. In some cases, they imitated successful models, thus following the rules of the reigning paradigm. In other cases, however, they developed differentiating strategies that provoked a crisis in the reigning norms of production—the classic paradigm—in more than just one way. To be more exact, this crisis had to do with the appearance of the *nuevo cancionero* [Argentine new song] movement, its followers, and the tensions it created in the field of folklore.

## A Folklore Manifesto

The first thing to point out about the appearance of the *nuevo cancionero* movement is how it was introduced to the public: by means of a "manifesto." Signed by Tito Francia, Oscar Matus, Armando Tejada Gómez, and Mercedes Sosa, among others, the manifesto, which became known in 1963, marked the public appearance of these artists who wanted both a place in the field of folklore and a new identity.[13] This was neither a group of artists dedicated to regional musics nor a "company" like the one Ariel Ramírez had founded; instead, it was a "collective." In other words, it was a purposeful banding together of artists who promoted an aesthetic, ethical, and political ideal that they shared and publically expressed as a united front, thus transcending their individual works.[14] Although it is true that all branches of modern art, especially the avant-garde, have typically published manifestos corresponding to schools or movements, speaking publically through this kind of discursive vehicle was a new approach for taking on a position in the field of folklore, which until this time did not have much internal differentiation. To be exact, what was radically new about this action was that manifestos generally showed a genealogy and presented a project. The *nuevo cancionero* movement's genealogy and aim stirred up major areas of conflict without entirely severing ties with the classic paradigm of folklore. I address these facets of the movement below.

## GENEALOGY

As opposed to how tradition was understood in the classic paradigm, the *nuevo cancionero* movement emphasized renovation and what was new without rejecting these roots. For this reason, instead of showing its origin as a tradition connected to an idealized, premodern past that held foundational values, *nuevo cancionero* glorified as "textual fathers" [whose songwriting skills should be imitated] two people in the field who had great legitimacy: Buenaventura Luna and Atahualpa Yupanqui. Although the movement also recognized the work of other agents who had made valuable contributions by collecting and circulating vernacular songs, the manifesto clarified that merely compiling music led only to stagnation: "The obsession with [song collecting] degenerated into *postcard folklorism* that we are still suffering from today. For *men who had built the country and whose reality changed from day to day*, it was lifeless and had no meaning. Buenaventura Luna, as for song lyrics, and Atahualpa Yupanqui, as for both lyrics and music, began a *renewal movement* that expanded folklore's content without eliminating its native roots" (original emphasis).[15]

According to the manifesto, in order to remain in this traditionalist and collecting stage, folklore had supposedly degenerated into folklorism. As the quotation above shows, the classic paradigm's concept of tradition was presented somewhat dysphorically and as the opposite of what could be accomplished through renovation. Renovation was depicted as pitting the past and the present against each other, and the present was shown to be the result of man's [mankind's] transformations of reality instead of the degeneration and/or loss of original values. Far from being a fixed vision that bound values to the past and considered all types of transformation to be a threat, man was now presented as an active subject who constructed and modified reality. This change, which was positive, was to be carried out along with aesthetic renewal.

The present, therefore, was idealistically depicted as being a time of renovated native popular music in which the new generations were central figures. This type of representation was part of a discursive strategy that also targeted the meaning of the folklore boom and positioned the *nuevo cancionero* movement as a legitimate part of it: "There are people who tend to believe that this growth of interest in folklore is a passing fad. . . . We believe that this native popular music boom is not circumstantial but [instead] is an indication of a *heightening of awareness of the Argentine people*" (original emphasis).[16]

The "Argentine people," then (per the manifesto), was the subject of a long search in which popular artists had participated and that had gone through ups and downs. One of the discoveries made during this collective artistic search was tango. The discovery of tango and its commercial success, however, had supposedly paved the way for conflict because the interior and its music had been pushed aside and tango had been emptied of content by anti-subjects that fed dark interests.[17] True popular artists, then, faced two enemies: on one hand, an asphyxiating past ("tradition") that did not acknowledge the transformations that man had produced as part of his reality, and on the other, marketeers who condemned music to a stereotype that fit their commercial interests (in other words, to traditionalist folklorism on one hand, and to the culture industry on the other).

In the context of this narrative, calling the folklore boom a "heightening of awareness" became meaningful. The transformation of reality, industrial growth, and internal migration led to the coming together of the interior and Buenos Aires and to a comeback of music from the interior. It was therefore stated in the manifesto that "the boom of folk music is a sign of the maturity that Argentines have reached in knowing the country as it is today," and, metaphorically, that "the people of the interior have already founded Buenos Aires for the third time—this time from within."[18]

This new founding of Buenos Aires was not just cultural in nature, but was part of a political change of historic proportions as well. That is to say that besides adopting an aesthetic position, which was clear throughout the entire manifesto, there was also another stream of discourse in the manifesto that took a political and ideological stance. This type of discourse was evident in the various elements of the narrative I reconstruct here: in the people's fight with marketeers, the transformation of material conditions through human action, the heightening of awareness arising from these transformations, and popular art as being an expression of this heightened awareness. In other words, the members of the *nuevo cancionero* movement not only defined their identity in the collective as "popular artists" and inheritors of the "renovation" started by Luna and Yupanqui, but they also presented themselves as the recipients of a mission, a purpose that fit in perfectly with a global narrative: "May this heightening of awareness not be hidden from artists or the people."[19] *Nuevo cancionero* therefore outlined a genealogy by which it constructed a stylistic place, legitimated itself, defined who its enemies were, and sketched out a collective project in which the aesthetic and the political were intertwined.

## THE PROJECT

The construction of a genealogy was a central aspect of the position presented in the manifesto of the *nuevo cancionero* movement, but that was not all. There was also a plan presented that sketched out the aesthetic and ideological principles on which the identifying "we" was constructed. In order to explain and analyze these concepts more deeply, however, I do not base my comments exclusively on the manifesto; I also refer to the recordings produced at that time by some of the artists connected with the movement, songs found on these recordings, and specific paratext. In these works, the principles stated in the manifesto operated as discursive strategies but at the same time as a political platform, a means of self-legitimation, and a break with the classic paradigm. At the heart of these principles and strategies was the "tradition" versus "renovation" tension that appeared in the manifesto to define the *nuevo cancionero* movement.

Three principles were presented to help explain the mission of the *nuevo cancionero* movement. First of all, it had popular roots that were being reappraised because the identifying "we" was now constructed as part of a popular movement in which artists participated. Second, it was above all an artistic movement. Because of this, renovation, assimilation of "all modern forms of expression," and artistic freedom were insisted upon, as opposed to being subject to the traditional rules on which classic paradigm identity was based.[20] Third, the manifesto proposed an identity-building process anchored not in an idealized past but in both the country's present and the general populace instead. A number of strategies based on these three principles were evident in recordings. Without attempting to be exhaustive, I analyze some of these below.

A. In the classic paradigm, the representation of regional scenery and customs was tied to an idealized past that harbored key values. Song lyrics therefore mentioned traditions and constructed an identity. Amid this predominance of landscapes and customs, the *nuevo cancionero* movement reclaimed "man" and more specifically "modern man" as its central subject. Let us look at some examples.

In 1965, Oscar Matus independently published Mercedes Sosa's first recording. Called *Canciones con fundamento* (Principled songs), it both adopted a strong position and launched the career of an artist who would be central to the movement. On the back of the album jacket, text written by Armado Tejada Gómez introduced the singer as a member of the *nuevo cancionero* movement and stated the following: "This work is not just a recording: it is a *testimonial*." And later: "Her songs *document the interior of Argentina*. The land, but *with man being present there*. Man and his inner life. *Work, pain, persistent hope*, and the highly exuberant joy of being alive." In this text, it was also stated that the recording disdained "simple depiction of social customs and traditions and *folkloric picturesqueness* [of the type] found on postcards" (emphasis added).[21] How then, was the mission set forth in the manifesto put into practice? For one, the selection of songs on the entire album was in itself a strategy that helped to construct a speaker identified with the movement. Of the twelve songs on the recording, six belonged to the Matus–Tejada Gómez songwriting duo, three to Ramón Ayala, and only three to composers not part of the *nuevo cancionero* movement (Los Hermanos Núñez, Ariel Ramírez, and Aníbal Sampayo). Yet besides the choice of songwriters and composers, just looking at the names of the songs was enough to recognize the place given to "man" in them: "Zamba del riego" (Irrigation worker's zamba, by Matus and Tejada Gómez), "El cachapecero" (The ox cart driver, by Ramón Ayala),[22] "La de los humildes" (Poor people's zamba, by Matus and Tejada Gómez), "El cosechero" (The harvester, by Ramón Ayala), "Los inundados" (The people who have experienced a flood, by Ariel Ramírez and G. Aizemberg), and "La zafrera" (The female sugar cane harvester, by Matus and Tejada Gómez), and so on. Let us look at some song fragments.

| | |
|---|---|
| Se va tu caudal por el valle labrador | Your water flow passes through the hardworking/peasant valley |
| Y al amanecer sale a padecer | And at dawn comes out to endure |
| La pena del surco ajeno | The suffering of another's irrigation ditch |
| Verano y rigor, va de sol a sol | Summer and harshness, from morning until night lasts |
| La sombra del vendimiador. | The irrigation worker's shadow. |
| "Zamba del riego" | |
| Zambita para que canten | A little zamba so that |
| Los humildes de mi *pago* | The poor people of my *pago* can sing |
| Si hay que esperar la esperanza | If it is necessary to hope/wait for hope |
| Más vale esperar cantando. | It is best to wait for it by singing. |
| "La de los humildes" | |
| Rumbo a la cosecha cosechero yo seré | On the way to the harvest I will be a harvester |
| Y entre copos blancos mi esperanza cantaré | And among white puffs I will sing of my hope |
| Con manos curtidas dejaré en el algodón | With leatherlike hands I will leave in the cotton |
| Mi corazón. | My heart. |
| "El cosechero" | |

The idea, in other words, was to show the reality of the Argentine interior. Amid the landscape, however, working people and the man of the interior's duties appeared—a reality that corresponded not to an idealized past but to a real and troubled present instead.

Another interesting example is the second volume of *Folklore sin mirar atrás* (Folklore without looking back), by the Cuarteto Zupay (Zupay Quartet). This album was released under the Trova label in 1968. On the back cover, Miguel Smirnoff came up with a new category to describe this type of aesthetic concept:

"listening to the recordings made in the 1950s, and comparing them to recent ones by *avant-garde groups*, it is easy to see the difference produced by *evolution* that is as much internal as external" (emphasis added). The idea of an avant-garde music subject to transformative action was in itself a break with the classic paradigm. This transformative action amounted to a kind of "evolution" that recovered yet updated tradition in order to take modern man into account: "And if we sing songs about current reality, replacing the *rancho* [country home] and the *china* [wife] with a love song to our land, where does modern Argentine man come from? . . . That which is traditional does not suit a person who lives in Buenos Aires or Córdoba, has a car that theoretically speaking can go 240 kilometers per hour, . . . and who is up-to-date on books, theater, and films."[23] The choice of songs and songwriters was once again a key strategy in what was being asked in this question. This same approach to modern man was also reflected in the use of nontraditional genres like the ballad (e.g., "Balada para mi tierra" [Ballad for my land]), the addition of modern instruments, the [choice of] contemporary topics like the elderly being taken from their homes ("Por un viejo muerto" [For a dead old man]), and even in the title of the recording itself: *Folklore sin mirar atrás* (Folklore without looking back).

B. This was not just a matter of reflecting modern man and valuing the present. In the classic paradigm, social contradictions were erased so as to construct a national "we" anchored in a past considered to be a site filled with values. On the contrary, the *nuevo cancionero* movement wanted modern man to be shown in the context of exploitation, injustice, violence, and marginality. This view no longer involved an idealized image or the crystallization of certain canonic values (authenticity, generosity, loyalty, courage, love of country, etc.), but depicted man as suffering due to unjust social relations instead.

The connection of man to man, and of man to nature, changed radically in the *nuevo cancionero* movement. Although the landscape did not lose its magic, nature was now generally hostile, and man had to deal with it while he did difficult and dangerous jobs. Man now appeared in specific thematic roles connected to rural work and/or kinds of exploitation related to agricultural production. The *rancho* [family farm/home], the jungle, the rivers, and the deserts were no longer just part of the scenery; instead, they were now stages on which misery, marginality, and exploitation played out.

The idea, however, was not just to show the misery and exploitation of the man from the interior. Besides this, the goal was to express the awareness of being part of a popular movement that was linked to a destiny, which is why strong feelings connecting the work of the people with hope and struggle appeared in the songs.[24] No longer was there just a distancing from the past and a strong anchoring in the present, but there was also hope for a virtual narrative project involving the entire collective and projecting it into the future. Song went hand in hand with this hope and to some degree generated it. This concept was crucial for *nuevo cancionero* songwriters because the themes used in songs, the specific social spaces where songs were sung, and the profession of being a singer were all part of a strategy to construct a place for popular art in the collective mission:

| | |
|---|---|
| Como un canto de la tierra | Like a song from the land |
| Hay que cantar esta zamba | This zamba must be sung |
| Hermana de los humildes | Sister of the poor |
| Sembradora de esperanzas | Sower of hope |
| Alzada raíz de sangre | Root of blood raised up |
| Del fondo de la guitarra. | From the depths of my guitar. |

"La de los humildes"

This collective mission, this hopeful destiny that the manifesto talked about and that ran permanently through its songs, thus took the shape of rebel hope, or struggle. This facet of the fight against injustice was barely even suggested in the manifesto or in the first recordings made by *nuevo cancionero* artists, but it became more and more apparent as the 1960s went on. Popular struggles were depicted in songs along with a critical look at history, which led to—among other things—a rethinking of the role of the man from the interior (the gaucho, the rural worker) in the "popular" movement of which the *nuevo cancionero* was a part. In this context, the reframing of the Indian's role was especially interesting because it had been fairly ambiguous in the classic paradigm. Therefore, in "Zamba del riego," the lyrics were about a sleeping Huarpe [member of the indigenous group of the same name] waking up, in "Zamba del chaguanco" (Zamba of the Chaguanco Indian) about a Chaguanco Indian's misery, and in many other songs about his being a victim. Yet in "Canción para mi América" (Song for my America) by Daniel Viglietti, which was recorded by Mercedes Sosa on her album *Yo no canto por cantar* (I do not sing just for the sake of singing) in 1966, the Indian appeared in a new light because he was presented as a central figure in liberation battles.

Toward the end of the decade, this fight against injustice, including a call to action, became louder and louder in all of the artists connected with the *nuevo cancionero* movement. This was seen in album titles such as *Hasta la victoria* (Until victory, by Mercedes Sosa, 1972) and in songs recorded and sung as emblems of the movement: "Canción con todos" (Song with everyone, by César Isella), "Fuego de Animaná" (Animaná fire, by César Isella and Tejada Gómez), "Cuando tenga la tierra" (When I have the earth, by A. Petrocelli and D. Toro), "Plegaria de un labrador" (Prayer of a worker, by Víctor Jara), and so many others.[25]

C. The song titles just mentioned might make a person mistakenly think that the *nuevo cancionero* movement was concerned mainly with "mere content" or was perhaps of "low quality" rather than being focused on aesthetics or form. One of the movement's main principles, however, was to always be careful with the aesthetics and formal writing of its songs. Its political commitment and ideological position always went hand in hand with a demand for aesthetic rigor in which the artist's identity was at play in the context of its popular mission. For this reason, there was both a strong emphasis on formal writing and criticism of *facilismo* [that which can be done very easily with little effort].

From another perspective, in tandem with its defense of aesthetic rigor, the movement also distanced itself from the formal simplicity and repetition (both poetic and musical) characteristic of the classic paradigm, and importantly, from the repetition of successful models backed by the recording industry that tried to take the utmost advantage of the boom era. It was therefore stated in the manifesto that the *nuevo cancionero* movement "will discard, reject, and publically denounce, after doing case-by-case analysis, any coarse or inferior work that given its commercial purpose might insult the intelligence or morals of our people."[26]

Instead of *facilismo*, there was an intense search for musical and poetic quality in terms of seriousness, work, renovation, and experimentation. Not only the musicians' choice of songs but also their musical work consisted for the most part of making arrangements and using novel harmonic concepts other than parallel thirds, which were so common in folklore. This new type of singing, in which two voices sometimes had different melodic lines, often sung in falsetto, was an easily identifiable style; it required open-mindedness from the public, however, because it was far—and sometimes very far—away from the typical harmonizations of the classic paradigm.

A good example of this trend was the Cuarteto Zupay, which used ideas from classical choral music [art music] in its arrangements, such as harmonizations in fifths or sixths or basso continuo—clear references to the Baroque period. In addition, however, it added new sounds performed on modern instruments such as electric guitar or drums. In this fashion, rigor, experimentation, work, and seriousness were part of a discursive strategy of differentiation and rupture with the classic paradigm, but they also served to legitimate the movement's own artists who participated in its popular mission.

D. The "historical destiny" referred to in the manifesto of the *nuevo cancionero* movement regarding the popular movement that popular artists would be a part of was no longer presented as one taking place within the closed borders of the nation. As opposed to what was regional, yet always understood as being a particular expression of the nation, in the songs there was instead a thematic emphasis on recovering what was Latin American. This did not mean that there was ignorance about or rejection of regional elements. On the contrary, there was always importance given to expressing the whole country, with all its diverse genres and musical styles. The recovery of regional diversity as expressed in the manifesto, however, went hand in hand with the rejection of all closed-minded regionalism.[27] In this sense, Latin America appeared to be both a cultural and political frame of reference—a real contradiction with the ontologization of the national from a more or less conservative perspective.

This facet of the project was reflected in several aspects of the artistic output of the time. On one hand, there was a similar strategy used in paratext, in which there was a constant insistence on American roots; regarding song, these roots were often specifically indigenous. Another facet of the project was seen in the topics addressed in the songs. Some of the more important ones had a collective perspective that transcended any type of nationalism, such as "Canción del derrumbe indio" (Song of the Indian collapse) by Figueredo Armain, "Canción para mi América" by Viglietti, "América" by R. Herrera, and "Canción con todos" by Isella, and so on. But this Latin American perspective was also evident in the constant incorporation of songwriters and composers from other Latin American countries—like Víctor Jara, Daniel Viglietti, or Violeta Parra—as well as popular rhythms and genres from different regions of Latin America into the movement. This produced a tendency to collaborate that over time began to give the movement an ever wider and more extensive nature. As Mercedes Sosa put it, "our movement that was born here [in Mendoza] afterward really caught on in Latin America. With ease we talked about Joan Baez and Bob Dylan because they drew from the most refined elements of jazz to the profoundness of U.S. folklore [folk music]. We operated the same way here. Ten years after the emergence of the *nuevo cancionero*, I ended up singing with Joan Baez and being friends with her."[28]

E. All of these strategies made a contribution toward something that all of these works had in common: the construction of a speaker and listener connected to a new type of identity. There was no longer a "we" understood in terms of a "nation" expressed through different regional traditions, but more of a notion of both popular artists and the public as being critical, demanding, and subject to a heightening of awareness linked to a transcendent project instead. In other words, instead of the "we" having an ontological basis tied to an idealized past, the identity-shaping process had to do with an aesthetic and ideological goal understood in terms of freedom. As part of this goal, something that had not been relevant in folklore up until then became important according to the manifesto: the idea of youth having a generational identity, the insistence on the role of new generations, and the need to foster "formative dialogue with our youth."[29] At this stage, young people were portrayed as having some special characteristics. On one hand, just as occurred then with other fields of popular music production (e.g., Argentine rock), this music began to be recorded and heard at recitals more often. As a result, it became viewed more and more as pure entertainment unrelated to dance and as a vehicle for a message. On the other hand, youth was shown to have a major role as an agent of change, and especially of revolutionary change, even in music. Going a step further, drawing on Latin American topics and music from other countries was probably part of a strategy to connect Argentine youth to the political processes found on the rest of the continent. Lastly, new musical space was given to the new generations as a legitimizing strategy. In fact, what this music should appropriately be called within the realm of popular music began to be questioned; it was not called folklore very often. On the backs of album covers and in manifestos it was described as being the birth of something new, like post-folklore, that could be called Música Popular Argentina (Argentine Popular Music). This displacement could clearly be thought of in conjunction with other things found on quite a number of recordings made at the time: the addition of art music references, but also to what was modern; the abandonment of gaucho attire used by groups in the past and the use of urban, modern dress instead; the design of record jackets; and generally speaking, the process of identity construction that *nuevo cancionero* movement artists carried out.

## The Emergence of the *Nuevo Cancionero* Movement

The appearance of this movement, which had a new aesthetic and ideological plan for its works and doctrinal texts, produced great tension within the field of folklore: it unleashed a period of major discussion about what folklore was. The limits of folklore as defined in the classic paradigm were challenged, and controversy arose because the definition of what was and what was not folklore was at stake. I already briefly alluded to the social conditions that allowed this movement to appear in a field of production possessing such special traits. I now analyze in detail these social conditions.

According to the theoretical perspective I have adopted in this chapter, I must reiterate that I understand discursive production, in this case aesthetic, to be a social practice carried out by agents who are immersed in networks of specific relations. All discursive production can therefore be thought of as adopting a position, which is the end result of an agent's creation of options and strategies. These options and strategies can be explained and understood based on the agent's place (i.e., his or her competency) in these relational networks, which is determined by all of his or her abilities and trajectory.[30] Because of this, it was necessary for us to start by looking at the situation of artists who were part of this movement during the mid-1960s, as the field of folklore developed.

In order to be able to understand the circumstances that led to the appearance of the *nuevo cancionero* movement, however, it is necessary to have a wider perspective: it is important to analyze the field of folklore's place and its new aesthetic trends in the context of socio-global processes, and especially in the context of some discursive tendencies that were experienced in Argentine society during the 1960s.

## EXPANSION OF THE FIELD

The so-called folklore boom that began toward the end of the 1950s was a phenomenon that came about due to the establishment and expansion of the field of production. This establishment of the field was at the same time the result of stabilization in a market that had become attractive to recording companies, radio, and television. It did not involve, however, merely quantitative growth. Even when nobody was thinking about inventing strategies to openly break with the past, and long before the manifesto of the *nuevo cancionero* movement appeared, some artists—not just the pioneers recognized by the movement—had already developed innovative creative works that had obtained both recognition and legitimacy in the field. Because these works were accepted and canonized, they produced an opening effect that made it possible to consider using some of the musical, poetic, and even ideological concepts that the *nuevo cancionero* movement would eventually make explicit.

As for folk song's poetic elements, a kind of renewal had already been occurring in northern Argentina, especially in Salta, dating at least as far back as a group called La Carpa (The tent). According to Alicia Poderti, these young intellectuals, poets, narrators, and essay writers, who in 1944 banded together to publish a "bimonthly bulletin" (also called *La Carpa*), were unique because "they did not idealize the past and perceived the present as being full of conflicts, like a fragmented and chaotic reality."[31] With this renovating and demystifying attitude toward the past, they assumed a political position of struggle and rejected both folklorism and regionalism.[32] Poet Manuel J. Castilla, among others, followed these basic principles, which were similar to many of the important *nuevo cancionero* ones. Eventually, Castilla would play a major role in the renovation of folklore lyrics. Castilla's modernizing work and introduction to writing song lyrics for popular music was not just an isolated case. Other people, such as Jaime Dávalos and Hamlet Lima Quintana, would also make contributions toward creating a new poetic language in folklore, one far removed from purely decorative folkloric, gaucho, and regionalist elements. This innovation had to do with the fact that these artists were intellectuals: a good part of their innovations consisted of introducing discursive strategies associated with "cultured" poetry in song lyrics after avant-garde artists had appeared. From there they gradually positioned themselves in the field with a specific identity that made them stand out. They were "poets"—not collectors or performers, who would likely have had other views.

The important developments, however, were that this new language was accepted, that famous artists in the field (Los Chalchaleros, Los Fronterizos, etc.) recorded these new songs, and that these works existed alongside more traditional ones written in the classic paradigm vein. For these reasons, it can be said that a change began to occur in the expressive conditions within the field, and that new discursive strategies and forms of expression therefore became possible. Because the potential of these new possibilities was so great, when the *nuevo cancionero* movement's manifesto set forth its aesthetic and ideological principles, some of these artists joined the movement.

Musically speaking, something similar happened. Starting in the 1940s, musicians like Eduardo Falú and Ariel Ramírez had already been renovating musical composition, performance, and arrangements. This musical renovation was also connected to the academic training these musicians had obtained; although they did not use a decidedly avant-garde approach, they added stylistic elements taken from art music. What interests me here is that possessing this specific cultural capital allowed these musicians to add sounds, arrangements, genres, and instrumentation that expanded the limits of the field. This expansion, which took place around the time the *nuevo cancionero* movement appeared, produced some works that were accepted in the field and unanimously praised because they were considered to have reached maturity and the height of folklore. This is what happened with the album *Coronación del folklore* (Coronation of folklore, 1963), on which Ariel Ramírez's orchestra, Eduardo Falú, and Los Fronterizos performed together; *Romance por la muerte de Juan Lavalle* (Romance for the death of Juan Lavalle, 1965) by Falú and Ernesto Sábato; and above all, *La Misa Criolla* (The creole mass, 1964) by Ariel Ramírez. In all of these works, there was a dual purpose. The goal was to preserve folk roots and use folk music from the different regions of Argentina but at the same time to elevate and dignify that music by adding elements taken from art music, such as choral and orchestral arrangements.

At the time that the *nuevo cancionero* manifesto was launched, these musicians who had tried to elevate folk music had not only reached a privileged position in the field already, but they had also expanded its limits to the point of making audible many of the innovations that artists of the movement would eventually bring to this field of production.

## INTELLECTUALS AND POPULAR MUSIC: AN AVANT-GARDE FOLKLORE

According to Mercedes Sosa, she discovered a new world upon arriving in Mendoza in 1957 after having married Oscar Matus: "Soon I entered an unknown world: the world of writers, sculptors, painters, and intellectuals. I was dazzled by many of the creative, educated, and good people I met."[33] Antonio Di Benedetto, Carlos Alonso, Antonio Salonia, Chilean Iverna Codina, musician Tito Francia, editor Gildo D'Accursio, and many others were part of this group of intellectuals that was forming in Mendoza. A key organizer among them was Armando Tejada Gómez, a close friend of Oscar Matus. This nucleus of intellectuals would eventually be important regarding the emergence of the *nuevo cancionero* movement and would signal a new kind of connection with folklore.

Up to this point, the intellectuals who had helped to construct the field of folklore had come from nativist and traditionalist backgrounds associated with the many types of nationalism extant at the time—especially its conservative wing. As a consequence, the scientific study of folklore, a phenomenon that had appeared at the beginning of the century and had then evolved as a result of modernization, had found in these same intellectuals—many of whom were associated with the state—substantial support that had allowed for the collection and classification of folk materials.[34] During the 1930s and 1940s, this had led to the publication of numerous regional anthologies and songbooks as well as works written by key authors such as Carlos Vega, Félix Coluccio, and Augusto Raúl Cortazar.

During this same period and well into the 1950s, *Nativa* magazine became a place of refuge for people who since the 1920s had been fairly marginal in an intellectual field increasingly dominated by the various types of modernization and the avant-garde. According to this traditionalist view, protecting and developing native art forms was a patriotic act. Many intellectuals and ideas at the center of the classic paradigm then appeared in *Folklore* magazine from its 1961 creation and onward, thus showing that the intellectual continuity of nativism and folklore was now an established field of production.

The nucleus of intellectuals that formed in Mendoza in the years immediately preceding the appearance of the *nuevo cancionero* movement belonged to a completely different tradition called social literature, which was associated with leftist political culture. Having taken shape in Peronist times, this trend had been revitalized with the triumph of the Cuban Revolution. Some of these writers and intellectuals were later persecuted by the 1976–83 military regime, and the group of intellectuals who founded the *nuevo cancionero* was part of this tradition. In this intellectual world, the founding members of the movement discussed at length not only cultural and aesthetic problems of the time (the new novel, the new film, avant-garde aesthetics, the new place of song in the world, the opposition of elite versus popular art, etc.), but also political matters that would brand that entire generation: the fall of Peronism, Arturo Frondizi's rise to power, and the birth on the continent of a New Left influenced by the Cuban Revolution.

All of these people were part of a small group of intellectuals and artists, and it was in this world where their ideas began taking shape about the new aesthetic and political place that popular song should occupy. In addition, this was the network of specific relations in which their works in that realm began to be known. In this intellectual circle, circumstances were ripe for accepting the group's compositions performed by the voice of Mercedes Sosa. These same ideas and compositions were also accepted by other groups of intellectuals—such as ones in Montevideo, when Matus and Sosa set up household there in 1962. In Montevideo, they managed to gain radio exposure and the support of writers and artists like Carlos Núñez and Mario Benedetti. Matus and Sosa also got the backing of the Communist Party, which they joined shortly thereafter. By that time, Tejada Gómez and many other intellectuals had joined the Communist Party, as well.

The leftist culture of these intellectuals, especially their affiliation with the Communist Party, had great importance for the kind of connection with folklore that the *nuevo cancionero* movement proposed. In fact, as of 1946 folklore studies in the Soviet Union had taken a new path that could be summed up in the following two principles: (1) Folklore is an echo of the past but also expresses the present condition of the "popular" sectors. (2) Folklore has been and still is an arm of the proletariat in class struggles.[35] These concepts, which were associated with the basic ideas of the *nuevo cancionero* and clashed with the dominant "tradition" of the classic paradigm, were evident in all of the various offshoots of *nueva canción* [lit. new song, collective term for the folk-inspired protest music movements that emerged in multiple parts of Latin America] that appeared on the continent during those years and were supported by leftist intellectuals.

The acceptance of this aesthetic concept linked to popular song by circles of intellectuals explains why the *nuevo cancionero* movement was introduced by means of a manifesto. It also explains the avant-garde way used to present the movement's aesthetic and political principles. Considering how the people who would later found the movement started out, it is understandable why they decided to make a break with the classic paradigm: so as to eventually shed their marginal status in the field. They succeeded in introducing debate, pressuring artists into adopting a position, and, importantly, dividing the public along aesthetic and ideological criteria.

## THE POLITICIZATION OF DISCOURSE

What I have written up to this point is insufficient to explain how the movement developed, its progressive legitimization in the field of folklore, the coming-aboard of many artists, or, most importantly, their blockbuster success and international influence. In order to give a proper explanation, it is necessary to link this issue to some aspects of the social process that developed in Argentina after the fall of Peronism. Although an exhaustive analysis of the matter is beyond the scope of this chapter, I briefly outline its main features.

A. On one hand, from the time that President Juan Perón was overthrown [1955], the various governments that followed him until the mid-1960s suffered from a great crisis of legitimacy. The banning of Peronism resulted in a number of attempts to fill this void, all of which failed. This internal situation along with the Cuban Revolution's success and influence made possible the birth of a New Left that would have major importance all over the continent. Given these circumstances and the remaining Latin American dictatorships, some union and student groups became radicalized especially after 1966, and the critical, sometimes revolutionary, discourse of the Left kept expanding near the end of the decade.[36]

B. Moreover, in various parts of the world, including Latin America, popular song began to be revalued and conceived of as a vehicle for social change. A phenomenon called *Nueva Canción* then developed in Chile, Uruguay, Brazil, Cuba, France, and other European countries. An important occurrence related to this process was how Bob Dylan and Joan Baez had first changed rock music, followed by the Beatles. Using song as a vehicle of change became associated with the emerging youth phenomenon as a social identity and as a means of transformation; it was precisely in this period that the seeds of the Argentine rock movement were sown. The idea of youth being transformative, both aesthetically and politically speaking, ran through the entire *nueva canción* phenomenon and was a key aspect of the *nuevo cancionero* movement.

These briefly outlined traits of the Argentine social process between the middle and the end of the 1960s are key in helping us to understand the role that artists who followed *nuevo cancionero* principles played in symbolic struggles—battles that became more aggressive beginning in the early 1970s until 1976. Taking these characteristics into consideration, it is also understandable why this movement was broken up [desarticulado] during the 1976–83 military dictatorship by means of persecution and exile.

## Notes

1. Claudio Díaz, "Condiciones sociales y estrategias enunciativas en las canciones de Teresa Parodi," in *Lugares del decir: competencia social y estrategias discursivas*, ed. Danuta Teresa Mozejo and Ricardo Lionel (Rosario: Homo Sapiens, 2002), 211–39.

2. Editors' note: To develop his notion of paradigm, the author draws on the works of Tomas Kuhn, *La estructura de las revoluciones científicas* (Mexico City: Fondo de Cultura Económica, 1971), and Marc Angenot, *Interdiscursividades: de hegemonías y disidencias* (Córdoba: Editorial Universidad Nacional de Córdoba, 1998).

3. Liliana Clement, "Folklore: una disciplina científica. Algunos fundamentos epistemológicos," *Revista de investigaciones folklóricas* 17 (2002), 47–54.

4. Gabriel Ábalos, "Para una ontología simbólica de las tradiciones," paper presented at the Primer Congreso Universitario de Folklore (First University Conference on Folklore) (Córdoba, 2003).

5. Raymond Williams, *Marxismo y literatura* (Barcelona: Península, 1980; originally published in 1977, *Marxism and Literature*), 137.

6. Argentina's "centennial" took place in 1910, commemorating the founding of Argentina on May 25, 1810, during the May Revolution. At that time there was a lot of debate and reflection about the nation, and in that context the first texts having to do with "cultural nationalism" appeared, among them *El payador* (The gaucho minstrel) by Leopoldo Lugones; *La historia de la literatura argentina* (The history of Argentine literature) and *La restauración nacionalista* (The nationalist restoration) by Ricardo Rojas. These authors and books were influential in the formation of the classic paradigm of folklore.

7. Augusto Raúl Cortazar, who was a professor at the Universidad de Buenos Aires (University of Buenos Aires) and the Pontificia Universidad Católica Argentina (Pontifical Catholic University of Argentina), was one of the most important academic folklorists in Argentina. The Instituto Nacional de Musicología (National Musicology Institute) in Buenos Aires is named after Carlos Vega, one of the best-known and earliest ethnomusicologists in Argentina. Félix Coluccio was an Argentine researcher and prolific author of numerous books having to do with folklore. One of his best-known books was *Diccionario folklórico argentino* (1948, Dictionary of Argentine folklore).

8. The issue of "origin" is especially important in connection with "selective tradition." Michael Foucault, "Nietzsche, la genealogía, la historia," in *Microfísica del poder* (Madrid: Ediciones de La Piqueta, 1992 [1971]), drawing on Nietzsche's ideas, has shown the effects of power inherent in a proposed "origin." This is the total opposite of a theological view of history.

9. Claudio Monti and Adrián Weissberg, "Construcción de la imagen gauchesca: un enfoque cultural, escrito, filmado y encuestado," paper presented at the Primer Congreso Universitario de Folklore (Córdoba, 2003).

10. Translator's note: A *pago* is the place where a person is from, his or her home territory, and where he or she has (idealized) roots.

11. Although this is not the place to focus on it, the matter of indigenous roots in folklore is especially interesting since the greater part of the work of collectors and folklorists consisted of a policy of "rescuing" native culture. Not only that, this happened only twenty to thirty years after the nation had adopted a policy of exterminating indigenous peoples. For these reasons, the Indian's place in folklore has always been ambiguous. On one hand, there were a number of attempts to legitimate the Indian in the vein of Ricardo Rojas's *Eurindia* (1924). On the other hand, starting from the time that the gaucho was turned into a key symbol, the Indian continued to appear in many songs as an enemy or undervalued being. Generally speaking, the "rescuing" mentioned above was accompanied by idealization.

12. *Martín Fierro*, by Argentine author José Hernández, is an epic poem that Argentine national identity was based upon. The poem was originally published in two parts: *El gaucho Martín Fierro* (1872) and *La vuelta de Martín Fierro* (1879). In these two poems, Hernández sympathized with the plight of the gaucho, who was unjustly driven from his rural environment and forced to adapt to urban ways, which he did reluctantly. Hernández portrayed Martín Fierro as a *payador*: a gaucho musician who improvised and sang verses in song "duels" with other *payadores* accompanied by guitar.

13. Drafted by Armando Tejada Gómez, the manifesto (hereafter "Manifesto 1963") was published on February 11, 1963, in *Los Andes* [The Andes, a newspaper from Mendoza]. The head of Arts and Entertainment at *Los Andes* was Antonio Di Benedetto. On that same day, the movement was also presented at an artistic event at the Salón del Círculo de Periodistas (Meeting of the Journalists' Circle). Besides the artists who signed the manifesto at that time, Víctor Heredia, Marian Farías Gómez, Ramón Ayala, Los Trovadores, the Cuarteto Zupay, the Dúo Salteño, Horacio Guarany, Hamlet Lima Quintana, and others joined the movement later on.

14. Williams, *Marxismo y literatura.*

15. "Manifesto del nuevo cancionero," Página Oficial: Armando Tejada Gómez, www.tejadagomez.com.ar, accessed October 30, 2015.

16. Ibid.

17. This refers to the commodification and commercialization of tango.

18. "Manifesto 1963."

19. Ibid.

20. Ibid.

21. Armado Tejada Gómez, album text, *Mercedes Sosa: canciones con fundamento* (Buenos Aires: Producciones Matus, 1965).

22. In the jungle of Misiones Province, a *cachapecero* is a person who drives a *cachapé*, a cart pulled by oxen and used to drag trunks from sawmills and timberyards to the riverbank, where they are sent downstream on a raft—a practice still very common in the 1960s.

23. Miguel Smirnoff, album text, *Cuarteto Zupay: folklore sin mirar atrás*, vol. 2 (Buenos Aires: Trova, 1968).

24. "Manifesto 1963."

25. It is interesting to see that "Plegaria a un labrador" by Víctor Jara was part of the *Nuevo Cancionero* repertory. This particular song was an anthem of Chilean *nueva canción* [a similar folk music-inspired protest music movement that emerged in Chile in the 1960s]. Jara, a leader and singer of this movement, was assassinated right after the 1973 Chilean military coup.

26. "Manifesto 1963."

27. Ibid.

28. Quoted in Rodolfo Braceli, *Mercedes Sosa: La Negra* (Buenos Aires: Sudamericana, 2003), 96.

29. "Manifesto 1963."

30. For a more detailed analysis of the concept of "place," see the works of Ricardo Corta and Danuta Teresa Mozejko, "Producción discursiva: diversidad de sujetos," in *Lugares del decir: competencia social y estrategias discursivas*, ed. Danuta Teresa Mozejo and Ricardo Lionel (Rosario: Homo Sapiens, 2002), 9–42.

31. Alicia Poderti, *La narrativa del noroeste argentino* (Salta: Editorial Milor, 2000).

32. Ibid.

33. Mercedes Sosa quoted in Braceli, *Mercedes Sosa*, 93.

34. For a discussion regarding the development of the scientific study of folklore, see Ricardo Kaliman, "El 'provinciano cantor': definiciones del pueblo en las letras del folklore

argentino moderno," *Sociocriticism* 42, no. 1–2 (2002), 169–77; Carlos Vega, *La ciencia del folklore* (Buenos Aires: Editorial Nova, 1960).

35. Richard M. Dorson, "Teorías folklóricas acutales," in *Introducción al folklore*, ed. Robert Redfield, Guillermo E. Magrassi, and Manuel M. Rocca (Buenos Aires: Centro Editor de América Latina, 1991), 91–139.

36. María Matilde Ollier, *El fenómeno insurreccional y la cultura política, 1969–1973* (Buenos Aires: Centro Editor de América Latina, 1986).

# 11

# *Timba, Rumba*, and "Appropriation from the Inside"

IÑIGO SÁNCHEZ FUARROS

All of the sophisticated Blacks
Have gotten together
And we have decided
To not play any more rumba.
—Free Hole Negro, "Superfinos negros,"
from the album *Habana Blues B.S.O.*

The early 1990s were an especially precarious time for the Cuban people. Overnight, the country woke up to scarcity—empty shelves in stores and a population united by their confusion. It was the beginning of an uncertain epoch euphemistically christened the Special Period. The dissolution of the Soviet Union and the Council for Mutual Economic Assistance (Comecon)—the island's principal markets and providers—combined with Cuba's ineffective economic structure and the continuation of the U.S. embargo to create Cuba's greatest crisis of the twentieth century.

In terms of everyday life, the crisis involved a considerable reduction in the material prosperity and purchasing power of the Cuban people. In subjective terms, the repercussions were declared by a Cuban woman about the beginning of the Special Period: "There [was] nothing. Nothing. Do you understand?"[1] Power outages, drastic reductions in public transportation, food shortages, and runaway inflation pushed the public to its limits. Due to the gravity of the situation, the Cuban government was forced to undertake certain reforms in 1993. Generally

Originally published by Iñigo Sánchez Fuarros as "Timba, rumba y la 'apropiación desde dentro,'" *Revista Transcultural de Música / Transcultural Music Review* 9 (2005). Available at www.sibetrans.com/trans/publicacion/6/trans-9-2005. Translated by David Font-Navarrete with permission.

speaking, these economic and political reforms resulted in an opening of the Cuban regime.[2] While the reforms offered relief for some Cubans, uneven access to U.S. dollars (which became the "hard" currency) also provoked an increase in social inequality.[3] In this way, Cuban society entered a decade [the 1990s] of contradictions and uncertainty.

The soundtrack to this era followed the *clave* [rhythmic framework] of *timba* [Cuban music and dance genre]. This style of popular dance music emerged during the late 1980s and quickly became an important symbol for various sectors of the Cuban population. Thanks to influences from foreign musical styles, particular uses of traditional materials, the aggressiveness of arrangements, direct song lyrics, and provocative staging, *timba* connected with an audience eager for ways to express the reality of life in Cuba at the end of the twentieth century, as well as ways to articulate possible interventions. During these years, *timba* took shape as an alternative expressive space, distinct and contrary to official propaganda or particular positions forged in exile. In other words, *timba* developed with a purpose: to provide language for everyday life in which words are recovered again in order to describe reality.

This article does not analyze *timba*'s use for political, social, or cultural agendas, nor does it define it in musical terms.[4] Rather, I focus on a study of some of the processes by which *timba* is constructed and, more specifically, the process of appropriation. In this work, I approach *timba* as space of multiple appropriations, concentrating on the use of the socio-musical universe of *rumba* by *timba* musicians. This particular case does not nullify other forms of appropriation that might occur; in fact, they do occur at the nourishing breast of *timba*. Analyzing all of these forms of appropriations falls outside the scope of this article. In order to illustrate my exposition, I take advantage of some examples from the recordings by the most popular *timba* bands of the 1990s, especially NG La Banda, considered by many to be the movement's most seminal group.

## "Expropriation," Appropriation, and "Appropriation from the Inside"

The concept of appropriation acquires relevance in musicology through the debates surrounding "world music." In this scenario, the concept of appropriation is generally understood as an imperialist gesture; it is associated with notions of cultural power, control, and domination, often in the form of a Western [Euro-American] musician who appropriates "exotic" musics and transforms them into consumer objects subject to the commercial logic of capitalism.[5] The influence of postcolonial studies on this type of literature is obvious.[6]

Without needing to go further afield, the recent history of Cuban popular music offers a good example of this type of appropriation, which the Brazilian anthropologist José Jorge Carvalho has referred to as "expropriation":[7] the *Buena Vista Social Club* phenomenon. Produced by Ry Cooder, this album brought a team of elderly Cuban musicians to homes and stages throughout the United States, Canada, and Europe. Through [Cooder's] efforts, the project popularized a repertoire of old Cuban traditional music. In this way, an image was manufactured in which the island was reduced to an exotic paradise, polite and inoffensive, anchored in the flow of time, in accordance with the (Western) tastes to which the product was geared. Turned into a stunning phenomenon outside of the island, the project had important implications, not only for the subsequent development of Cuban popular music, but also for the whole of "world music" as a category.[8] The intense promotional campaign for the album culminated in the release of a film—also titled *Buena Vista Social Club*—by the renowned director Wim Wenders. This film captured moments during one of the international tours to promote the album, along with vignettes of life in Cuba, carefully edited in a narrative structure that is far from innocent, hiding a curious moral to the story, synthesized in the following quotation excerpted from Wim Wenders's official website: "The film [*Buena Vista Social Club*] helped immortalize both the music and its now-famous practitioners who had been living in near poverty, all but forgotten in their own country."[9]

Indeed, much of the success of *Buena Vista Social Club* was due precisely to the concocted history of the album's production, a skillfully manufactured fairy tale in which Ry Cooder presents himself first as a discoverer of talents forgotten in their own country, then as a charitable soul who rescues them from poverty and restores them to their rightful place: the theaters and auditoriums of the world. Meanwhile, the irony lies in the fact that *timba*—the island's truly popular music—remained silenced outside of Cuba due to the *Buena Vista Social Club* saga.

Returning to the topic at hand, some musicologists have nonetheless addressed the process of appropriation in more positive terms as an integral part of a local narrative that attempts to recover roots and preserve tradition. In a kind of polyphonic counterpoint, this "second voice" can be understood as a "melody of admiration, even homage and respect, a fundamental source of connectedness, creativity, and innovation."[10] This is precisely how Cuban musicologist Leonardo Acosta reads *timba*: "*Timba* is the heir to a long musical tradition of popular dance music, and we should approach it from that perspective."[11]

I believe that the thesis posited by Acosta is particularly pertinent to this discussion, although it also seems worthwhile to examine some of its assumptions. First, it assumes a relationship between *timba* and the tradition of Cuban popular musics as the result of a natural evolution. There is no doubt that *timba* must be understood in the global context of the development of Cuban popular music throughout the last century. However, tradition is not received passively; rather, it is inherited. It is thus necessary to account for the active complicity of those who receive tradition and eventually recognize and accept it. Second, this musicological approach assumes, implicitly or explicitly, the existence of fixed musical traditions with which actual musicians establish relationships of continuity or rejection. In light of recent musicological research, this approach is difficult to sustain. Therefore, I prefer to understand the relationship between *timba* and *rumba* as an *active* process of appropriation. As a parallel to the process of appropriation as "expropriation," I propose the use of a concept of "appropriation from the inside."

In this sense, an analysis that accounts for this dimension of "appropriation from the inside" necessarily emphasizes the active participation of individuals who present themselves as corollaries, culminations, or simply continuations of a previous tradition, in contrast to a musicological approach focused on tracking the survival or fidelity of that tradition. This change in focus enriches the concept of appropriation, allowing it to be read as an active process in two movements: selection and (in many cases) invention of a given tradition, and the subsequent utilization of that tradition. In my view of the relationship between *timba* and *rumba*, this process reveals a particular political position taken by *timba* musicians.

## En la calle

In 1989, the group NG La Banda (Nueva Generación La Banda, New Generation Band) burst onto the Cuban music scene with an unusual tour through the neighborhoods of the capital to introduce its second album, *En la calle* (In the street).[12] The album marks a turning point in the development of Cuban popular dance music, insofar as it contains the basis for a new style that would be consolidated during the 1990s and known by the generic term *timba*. Among the album's innovations that will become characteristic of *timba*, we can emphasize the prominence of *rumba* and other Afro-Cuban traditions, both on a musical level as well as in other aspects that are not strictly musical.[13] In this sense, the album cover of *En la calle* appears to illustrate this change rather well (fig. 11.1).[14]

The image is a snapshot in which the members of the band appear in a *solar* (tenement): the dirt floor, the buildings in the background, and the clotheslines framing the photograph all suggest an interior patio, characteristic of modest neighborhoods in Havana where residents would gather around drums and forge *rumba*. A Cuban musical genre with origins in the nineteenth century, *rumba* is

Fig. 11.1 CD cover of NG La Banda's *En la calle* (©1992 Qbadisc)

traditionally performed with percussion and voice. In that case, the percussion creates a repetitive base with a complex texture over which a solo percussionist and a solo (*guía* [guide]) singer improvise. Dancing—alone or in pairs, depending on the style of *rumba*—is an essential element of *rumba* performance, which reaches different levels of intensity depending on the degree of interaction between dancers, musicians, and audience.[15]

While it was a form of entertainment and distraction from daily chores, this spontaneous *rumba* also served—according to Leonardo Acosta—as a type of "chronicle of the home or *solar* in which everyday events are narrated, but which also covers aspects of social and political life."[16] However, let us return to the image. The musicians pose in impeccable suits; by contrast, the children in the image are half-dressed and appear somewhat puzzled by the camera. Sitting at the center of the image and painted a striking yellow, the *tumbadoras* (conga drums) are the axis around which the photograph's subjects are placed in a semicircle, "the space for rumba."[17] A unifying instrument, the *tumbadoras* here assume the metaphorical power of *rumba* as a vehicle for a certain sense of community that is ample and inclusive. The spontaneity—real or simulated—of the image is far from static and projects a dynamism that invites participation: the *tumbadoras* play in time with the *clave* [two wooden sticks] struck by one of the band members beside them while the rest of the musicians clap or simply laugh and smile.

In my view, this image synthesizes the complex symbiotic relationship maintained between the genres of *timba* and *rumba*.[18] Although it is ambiguous, the image perfectly captures the tension between tradition and modernity—that is, between movements of continuity and rupture. It also probes the borders between *rumba* and the more recent universe of *timba*. The following statement by Isaac Delgado, the lead singer of NG La Banda on the album, reinforces this idea and delves into the complex relationship between *timba* and *rumba*: "Today, people talk about *timba* as a new rhythm or trend in our contemporary popular music, but in reality *rumberos* [*rumba* experts] have been getting together since the old days to dance, tell it, and feel it. . . . Since then, the best at 'telling it and dancing it' are *timberos, the true timberos*" (emphasis added).[19]

What links exist between *timba* and *rumba*? What process of appropriation takes place between the two genres? I focus on three facets. First, there is an appropriation by *timba* and *rumba*'s physical and symbolic space—that is, the *solar*. Moreover, because *timba* recovers music's role as a tool for complaining and the musician's role as a chronicler of social life, as well as its emphasis on everyday life, *timba* also plays a role previously played by *rumba* in prerevolutionary Cuba. Finally, I discuss the way in which *timba* gathers some musical elements from *rumba* and incorporates them into its own compositional style.

## The Sound of the Neighborhood

If we return to the image discussed earlier, we can appreciate that the title is redundant and obvious: one does not need an especially keen eye to verify that the musicians were indeed photographed "in the street." Nonetheless, the title can be read less literally as a way to assume a position and give meaning in light of historical identification of *rumba* as "street" music—that is, subaltern and marginal, in contrast to other popular music that was interpreted in salons, dance halls, and ballrooms. The appropriation of *rumba* by the revolutionary government thus resulted in a reclamation of these spaces by *timba* during the 1990s.

However, NG La Banda's commitment to question this rigid distinction and occupy the space of the street did not end with a mere declaration of intentions. On the contrary, the group set out on a tour to bring its musical proposal—*timba*—to the neighborhoods and municipalities outside the usual circuits of dance music. This constituted an unprecedented event in the history of Cuban popular music.[20] Moreover, the subject matter of the neighborhoods was forcefully introduced into the band's songs. We need look no further than the song "La expresiva" (The expressive one) on the 1992 album, which offers a "tribute by NG La Banda to all the neighborhoods of Havana" through musical portraits, a series of choruses that appeal directly to the various neighborhoods. These continuous allusions to the neighborhoods of Havana by *timba* bands play into a certain rivalry between dancers from different areas of the city; at the same time, the allusions explicitly associate *timba*'s musical identity with Havana.

Originally, *rumba*'s space was restricted to the *solar*. Etymologically, the word "timba" sends us immediately to the interior patios where it was used as a synonym of *rumba*, a party, and where the exclamation "¡la timba está buena!" (the *timba* is good!) was used to celebrate good musicians, singers, and dancers, as well as the sweetness of a party. In this way, *timba* reclaimed the *solar* as its natural space, even if its real space is another. In this sense, I believe we can distinguish two overlapping dimensions. *Timba* is appropriated by the *solar*, albeit as an emotional space connecting to a given tradition through affective memories, fundamentally those of the city's Afro-Cuban population. Nonetheless, the real space of *timba*—the landscape of its songs and the audience they address—is the neighborhood. In this way, an interesting game of overlap and difference is created between these two urban genres, *rumba* and *timba*. *Timba* broadens the boundaries of the *solar* to the neighborhood, but it treats the neighborhood as if it were an old-fashioned *rumba solar*.

A good example of this overlap of spaces is found in another early work by NG La Banda, "Los Sitios entero" (All of Los Sitios) from the album *No se puede tapar el sol* (The sun can't be blocked). Los Sitios [lit. the places] is one of the neighborhoods in the municipality of Centro Habana. Essentially, the song is a sort of tribute to the neighborhood, which is populous, lower class, and well-known for its *rumberos*. Employing a technique known as *ataque por el estribillo* [lit. attack with the refrain],[21] the song begins directly with the chorus, whose refrain repeats throughout the composition:

| | |
|---|---|
| (Coro) Nací en La Habana. Soy habanero. | (Chorus) I was born in Havana. I'm a habanero. |
| Jesús María, Belén y Los Sitios enteros. | Jesús María, Belén, and all of Los Sitios. |

The lead singer develops the song over this refrain with a series of "guides" who sing the praises of the neighborhood and its idiosyncrasies. In the refrain of the chorus itself, the overlap of two spaces can be observed: as mentioned earlier, the neighborhood and the city are the real space of *timba*. In the middle of the composition, one of these "guides" sets up a change that leads to the main part of the song. A direct reference to *rumba*—the *rumbón* (a big *rumba* party)—anticipates what is coming:

| | |
|---|---|
| (Guía) Los Sitios me está esperando para tocar un *rumbón*, | (Lead) Los Sitios is waiting for me to play a *rumbón*, |
| y cuando suena la clave me palpita el corazón. | and when the clave plays my heart throbs. |
| Te digo, *rumbero*! | I'm telling you, *rumbero*! |

A long break by the drum set marks an entrance by the horn section. After a tutti passage and the sound of a single cowbell, the *rumba* "breaks out." The *solar* is embodied in the [musical] form of a *guaguancó* [a substyle of *rumba*], interpreted in a traditional way—with only percussion and vocals. From there, the lead singer offers his tribute to Los Sitios:

| | |
|---|---|
| (Guía) Pretendo con esta rumba homenajear a Los Sitios, que es un barrio . . . le-le-le-lele-lelelé, ¡güiro! bien bonito. | (Lead) With this rumba, I want to pay tribute to Los Sitios, a neighborhood that is . . . le-le-le-lele-lelelé, guiro! Very beautiful. |

In the context of the composition, *rumba* functions as a metonym for the *solar*: the *rumba* is a musical re-creation of the *solar*, which puts it in conversation with the neighborhood, and from there with the city, "all of Havana." We may ask whether the role played by the *solar* in *rumba*—not just a space for daily life, but an experiential space—is the same role played by the neighborhood in *timba*. Or, perhaps to the contrary, it is through *timba* that the neighborhood gets revenge on those who wanted to ignore it—hotels, media, and authorities—and thus conquers forbidden spaces such as nightclubs, radio, and export markets.

## "The Real Cuba"

The neighborhood's presence necessarily provokes the subject of *timba*, in the same way that the *solar* referenced the referential universe of *rumba* in its own historical moment. Unfortunately, there are few sonic or visual documents offering knowledge of how *rumba* sounded or was danced at the beginning of the twentieth century. For its part, a bibliography of secondary sources offers a portrait of *rumba* in which it functioned as "a public medium for expression for those who were not represented in the [mass] media."[22] These texts not only tell us about events inside the *solar*, but also discuss politics, including critiques of the oppression and mistreatment of Blacks in particular and Cubans in general at the hands of the United States or the Cuban government of the time, just as other Afro-Cuban artistic manifestations were repressed and condemned from within spheres of influence.[23]

Following the 1959 revolution, profound social transformations were enacted, aiming to eradicate neocolonial structures that still held sway in the heart of Cuban society. One of these transformations intended to elevate the status of folklore, recognizing it as an integral part of the national culture. As a result of this, according to the Cuban musicologist Argeliers León, *rumba* ceased to be "music of one sector, becoming a general expression of *Cubanness*" (emphasis added).[24] *Rumba* thus became a cultural symbol, acquiring the status of a national dance and becoming "folklorized" through the professionalization of its performers, the creation of dance companies and schools, and the proliferation of public spaces for its staging. *Rumba*'s inherent potential for social critique was thus defused, although *rumba* remains loaded with racial connotations—both positive and negative—in the collective memory, as Black music associated with values of marginality and protest.[25]

During the years of the Special Period, *timba* recovered some of *rumba*'s potential for criticism, taking up everyday life as a source of inspiration, leaving aside the sophisticated rhetorical artifice and rescuing the language of "the truth." This is demonstrated in some of NG La Banda's compositions, as well as other, younger groups such as Charanga Habanera or El Médico de la Salsa [the Doctor of Salsa, Manuel "Manolín" González Hernández].[26] Aside from these linguistic changes (stigmatized as vulgar, violent, chauvinist, and gaudy), *timba* puts uncomfortable subjects on the table that are (for various reasons) either hidden or prohibited by official censors. This is the case with Afro-Cuban religious cults, which occupy a prominent place in the thematic universe of some of *timba*'s most popular ensembles. Compositions such as "Santa palabra" (Holy word) deal openly with the predicaments surrounding these cults, whose practices were condemned or prohibited by official authorities during some historical moments.[27]

In other instances, musicians resort to allegory as a literary resource with which they can refer to the difficult sociopolitical situation of the moment, as in the case of the following chorus popularized at the beginning of the 1990s:

| | |
|---|---|
| (Coro) No se puede tapar | (Chorus) One can't block |
| el sol con un dedo, | the sun with a finger, |

| | |
|---|---|
| la verdad es la verdad, | the truth is the truth, |
| mala cara no quiero.[28] | [and] I don't want any frowning |

But occasionally, musicians are not so metaphorical. In the following chorus by singer Paulito FG, a critique of the state's constant demands for sacrifice is rather explicit:

| | |
|---|---|
| (Coro) San Dame y San Dame . . . | (Chorus) San Dame and San Dame [Saint Give Me]. . . |
| (Guía) Claro. | (Lead) Of course. |
| (Coro) y ¿San Toma dónde está? | (Chorus) And where is Saint Toma [Saint Take]? |
| (Guía) Si todo no es recibir, hay que dar a los demás . . . ¡también![29] | (Lead) If receiving isn't everything, then you need to give to others, too! |

Often, the music presents itself as a possible escape route or "antidote" to a lack of opportunity and an uncertain future. The following example from NG La Banda's first era of popularity should suffice [to demonstrate this]:

| | |
|---|---|
| (Guía) Si no bailan con NG La Banda seguro que el sol no les da. Así que . . . escucha como dice . . . | (Lead) If you don't dance with NG La Banda, it must be that the sun doesn't shine on you |
| (Coro) Ni el sol te da | (Chorus) The sun doesn't even shine on you |
| (Guía) Si tú no bailas conmigo . . .[30] | (Lead) If you don't dance with me . . . |

Along with the aforementioned topics, *timba* lyrics also discuss thorny issues that were inseparable from life during the Special Period: prostitution, new lifestyles, consumer culture, inequality, promiscuity, romantic deception, and so forth.[31] Moreover, this is done in a direct and explicit way, and it is not unusual for *timba*, as a whole, to be accused of poor taste and vulgarity. In fact, it is extremely significant that the same accusation of vulgarity leveled at *rumba* during the prerevolutionary era was used again during 1990s by Cuban musicology and other official sources in order to delegitimize *timba*, not only on the basis of its lyrics but also on the basis of its dance, which was perceived as shamelessly indecent and explicit.[32] In response to criticisms of his song lyrics, NG La Banda's leader and founder José Luis Cortés—also known as El Tosco [lit. the Coarse One]—defends himself by contending that elites ignore the tough reality of everyday life on the island: "We are Cubans, and we talk about the real Cuba in our songs."[33]

In this way, with an eye toward the neighborhood, *timba* recovers musicians' role as social chroniclers, as well as music's role as a tool of critique, taking the place that *rumba* had lost after being made an official cultural institution.

## "*Clave de rumba,* con guapería rumbera"

If *timba*'s will to appropriate space is clear and its lyrics intend to pick up the most critical functions of *rumba*, then *timba*'s appropriation of musical elements from *rumba* is just as evident. I briefly discuss three of these musical elements of interest.

First, *timba* adopts the *clave* [rhythmic framework] known as *clave de rumba*, in contrast to the tradition of Cuban popular dance music that is framed in the genre complex of [the Cuban] *son*. Significantly, Cuban music producer Ned Sublette has referred to *timba* as having "Rumba's clave with rumba's bravado" ("Clave de rumba, con guapería rumbera").[34] In terms of composition, this choice offers the rhythm sections of *timba* ensembles greater freedom to improvise and embellish, thereby bringing them closer to the spirit of *rumba*; this results in dense, complex arrangements and sounds with a strong emphasis on percussion. On the other hand, *rumba clave* (not coincidentally referred to as "Cuban clave") articulates a strong sense of Cubanness through its distinctive cadence, immediately conjuring an imaginary *rumba*, "the purest expression of Cuban identity."[35] Unlike *son* (the creolized relative of *timba*), the Cubanness to which *timba* clings is constructed on the basis of pride in Afro-Cuban heritage and its musical identification with musical genres like *rumba* that are associated with Blackness.

Second, the appropriation by *timba* of musical characteristics of *rumba* is even more evident in the importance both attribute to the chorus or refrain (*coro* or *estribillo*) in the structure of composition.[36] In the case of *rumba*, the call-and-response section is the decisive moment in a performance, a moment of great energy in which the *rumba* breaks open and initiates an intense dialogue among the lead singer, the chorus, and the *quinto* (lead conga drummer) with the participation of the dancers and the entire audience. For its part, *timba* treats the chorus as "the essence (*corpus esencial*) of the composition."[37] This view is corroborated by Juan Formell, one of the most prolific composers of Cuban popular dance music, for whom "the quality of the refrain is what decides the fate of a dance tune."[38] The specific weight of this section is important within the composition, to the point that songs often become a series of choruses. The *montuno* [final, repetitive, and semi-improvised section] of a song also tends to be the space reserved for improvisation; in live performance, this section allows songs to be extended ad infinitum according to the inspiration of the singer who improvises "leads" (*guías*) between one chorus and another, as well as the audience's response.

Third, the *montuno* is musically characterized by repetition of brief harmonic sequences and the reoccurrence of the piano *tumbao* [short, repeating accompaniment pattern], frequent changes in tempo, and a more prominent role played by percussion. All of this contributes to a progressive, segmented increase in musical intensity. This also leads also to a moment in which the dance reaches its maximum peak. The movements of dancers are made more extreme by the beat of the music, beginning what is known as the *despelote* [lit. chaos, frenzy, or mess]: a series of dizzying movements that are openly sexual and known by graphic and vivid names like "wobbly" [*el tembleque*, also a dessert] or "the blender" (*la batidora*). The musicians provoke the dancers with choruses whose language is simple, direct, colloquial, and habitually in the second-person singular form. In this way, the audience makes the chorus its own and the individual voice of the composer becomes a collective, community expression—a process that reaches its climax in the *despelote* section described above. The dancer thus becomes part of the sensual universe of the music; the *montuno* can thereby be considered the moment of true communion between the band and the audience.

In any case, the appropriation by *timba* of musical elements from *rumba* is expressed most clearly when *rumba* itself is incorporated into *timba* compositions. Sometimes it appears as an introduction, setting the atmosphere for the song ("El trágico," NG La Banda); in others, *rumba* acquires the status of an independent section within the composition, as in "Los Sitios enteros"; likewise, it is incorporated within *timba* arrangements and orchestration without ceasing to be perfectly recognizable ("De La Habana," Paulito FG). In this way, appropriation by *timba* during the Special Period is revealed to be about symbolic potential—critical, making identities cohesive, etc.—which was traditionally associated with *rumba* from the *solar* of prerevolutionary Cuba.

## Conclusion

I believe that understanding *timba* as a natural development in the tradition of Cuban dance music simplifies the cultural and social significance of the genre. In this sense, analyzing the relationships between *timba* and Cuban musical tradition, particularly *rumba*, through what I have called "appropriation from the inside," reveals a level of complexity overlooked by other types of analysis. Identifying themselves with *rumba*, *timba* groups return to the *solar* as a source of inspiration, recuperating musicians' role as social chroniclers and music's role as a tool of critique, thus reinstating the true values of *rumba* before it became incorporated into the official discourse and thereby cut off from its potential as an agent of social upheaval. *Timba* pays attention to tradition, chooses from the possibilities offered by it, appropriates the original sense of *rumba*, and thus offers an alternative space to think about Cuban reality, proposing new readings of the sense of community and "Cubanness."

## Notes

Acknowledgment: This article was written while I enjoyed a grant from the Formación del Profesorado Universitario, del Ministerio de Educación y Ciencia (AP2002-0142). A first version of it was presented at the VIII Congreso de la Sociedad Ibérica de Etnomusicología (SiBE), "¿A quien pertenece la música? La música como patrimonio y como cultura" (Zaragoza, March 25–28, 2004). I am grateful to Josep Martí for his valuable comments on the first version. Likewise, I thank Rubén López Cano for his suggestions and comments on this more recent version; there is no doubt they have greatly enriched the work. Gerardo de Cremona offered me hospitality and friendship, creating the conditions necessary to put this text together during a difficult time in my life, and I am grateful to him.

1. Isabel Holgado, *¡No es fácil! Mujeres cubanas y la crisis revolucionaria* (Barcelona: Icaria, 2000), 26.

2. Among various measures taken to alleviate the crisis, I highlight an opening of some economic sectors of the national economy to foreign investment, the expansion of the tourist industry, a timid legalization of self-employment, the free circulation of U.S. dollars, and the creation of agricultural markets. For a more detailed analysis of the economic, political, and social implications of the Special Period, see José A. Moreno, ed., *Cuba, Período Especial: perspectivas* (Havana: Editorial de Ciencias Sociales, 1998).

3. Archibald R. M. Ritter, "The Dual Currency: Bifurcation of Cuba's Economy in the 1990s," *CEPAL Review* 57 (1995), 113–31; "Entrepreneurship, Microenterprise and Public Policy in Cuba: Promotion, Containment or Asphyxiation," *Journal of Interamerican Studies and World Affairs* 40, no. 2 (1998), 63–94.

4. Other works that offer a general characterization of *timba* include the article by Cuban musicologists Neris González Bello and Liliana Casanella Cué, "La timba cubana: apuntes sobre un intergénero contemporáneo," *La Jiribilla* 76 (2002), www.lajiribilla.cu (accessed March 2004); the excellent monograph by Vicenzo Perna, *Timba: il suono della crisis* (Roma: Arcana, 2003), published in English translation as *Timba: The Sound of the Cuban Crisis* (Farnham, U.K.: Ashgate, 2005); and the concise introduction by Rubén López Cano, "El chico duro de La Habana: agresividad, desafío y cinismo en la timba cubana," *Latin American Music Review* 28, no. 1 (2007), 24–67. For a discussion of emic and etic definitions of *timba*, see Iñigo Sánchez Fuarros, "Timba y cubanidad: el aporte de la rumba en la música popular bailable cubana de los noventa" (PhD diss. in historical musicology, Royal Holloway, University of London, 2001).

5. See Asunción Barañano, Josep Martí, Gonzalo Abril, Francisco Cruces and José Jorge Carvalho, "World music, ¿el folklore de la globalización?" *TRANS—Revista Transcultural de Música* 7 (2003), www.sibetrans.com (accessed March 2004); Charles Keil and Steven Feld, *Music Grooves: Essays and Dialogues* (Chicago: University of Chicago Press, 1994).

6. See Georgina Born and David Hesmondhalgh, ed., *Western Music and Its Others: Difference, Representation and Appropriation in Music* (Berkeley: University of California Press, 2000).

7. José Jorge Carvalho, "La etnomusicología en tiempos de canibalismo musical: una reflexión a partir de las tradiciones musicales afro-americanas," *TRANS—Revista Transcultural de Música* 7 (2003), www.sibetrans.com/ (accessed March 2004).

8. Robert Neustadt, "Buena Vista Social Club versus La Charanga Habanera: The Politics of Cuban Rhythm," *Journal of Popular Music Studies* 14 (2002), 139–62.

9. See "Buena Vista Social Club," *Wim Wenders: The Official Site*, www.wim-wenders.com (accessed Sept. 2005).

10. Steven Feld, "Notes on World Beat," in *Music Grooves: Essays and Dialogues*, ed. Charles Keil and Steven Feld (Chicago: University of Chicago Press, 1994), 238–46, p. 238.

11. Leonardo Acosta, "La timba y sus antecedentes en la música popular cubana del siglo XX," *El Solar de la Timba* 3 (2003), www.solardelatimba.com (accessed March 2004).

12. José Luis Cortés, *En la calle* (CD Qbadisc Records 9002, 1992).

13. For an analysis of this album in terms of its implications regarding ethnicity, see Vicenzo Perna, "Dancing the Crisis, Singing the Past: Musical Dissonances in Cuba during the Periodo Especial," *Journal of Latin American Cultural Studies* 11, no. 2 (2002), 211–29.

14. The image discussed corresponds to the cover of the edition for *En la calle*, released on CD by the U.S.-based label Qbadisc in 1992. The CD compiled songs from the first two albums by NG La Banda (José Luis Cortés, *En la calle* [LP EGREM, 1989], and *No se puede tapar el sol* [LP EGREM, 1990]). The cover of the original 1989 LP edition of *En la calle* consists only of the group's name in large orange letters and the album title in black letters, a sober design consistent with the Cuban label's LPs from the era. In any case, the image on the cover of the Qbadisc edition is photographed professionally, staged perfectly, and featuring the musicians posed in specific ways. In my view, the existence of the various editions does not invalidate my argument. I am grateful to Kevin Moore, editor of the website *Timba: Home of Cuban Music on the Web!*, www.timba.com, for the information regarding the official cover of *En la calle* (1989).

15. The *rumba* complex consists of three styles, each of which has distinct characteristics. *Yambú* is a slow mode of *rumba* whose dance lacks the possessive pelvic movement known as *vacunao* [lit. the inoculation] and features movements imitating the labored movements of the elderly. *Guaguancó* is the best-known style; it is faster than *yambú* and danced by a couple that enact a game of attraction and rejection that culminates in the *vacunao*—that is, the symbolic possession of the woman by the man. Finally, *columbia* displays the most acrobatic choreography; danced only by men, its rhythm is fast and choppy.

16. Leonardo Acosta, "The Rumba, the Guaguancó and Tío Tom," in *Essays on Cuban Music: North American and Cuban Perspectives*, ed. Peter Manuel (New York: University Press of America, 1991), 51–73, p. 55.

17. Yvonne Daniel, *Rumba: Dance and Social Change in Contemporary Cuba* (Bloomington: Indiana University Press, 1995), 75.

18. Although this article is focused on the elements that *timba* borrows from *rumba*, another equally interesting view of the relationship would address the impact of *timba*'s eruption during the 1990s on *rumba*.

19. Isaac Delgado, "La rumba son ellos," *La Jiribilla* 26 (2001); www.lajiribilla.cu/ (accessed March 2004).

20. It is worth emphasizing the way this initiative soon crystallized in a stable circuit for popular dance music, providing younger orchestras access to audiences that would have otherwise been unavailable—in particular tourist venues. It is also interesting to note that *timba* groups were simultaneously taking the "neighborhood" and its predicaments to the heart of Havana's emerging musical scene, which was concentrated in exclusive hotels geared to international tourism, places to which the addressees of the songs had curiously restricted access (Perna, "Dancing the Crisis," 216).

21. López Cano, "El chico duro," 2.

22. Robin D. Moore, *Música y mestizaje: revolución artística y cambio social en La Habana, 1920–1940* (Madrid: Colibrí, 2002), 213.

23. The best-known *rumbero* of this era, Gonzalo Asensio (better known as Tío Tom), provided exemplary reflections of these events in the lyrics to his *rumbas*. One example is the following *guaguancó* denouncing an insult to a Cuban flag by U.S. Marines: "Listen Mister President / I want to know what you think / about the complaints / that Cubans have presented/ against those Americans / that have come from outside / to trample the flag/ of our Cuban land" (quoted in Acosta, "La timba y sus antecedentes").

24. Argeliers León, *Del canto y del tiempo* (Havana: Editorial Pueblo y Educación, 1981), 141.

25. On the subject of *rumba* and ethnicity, see Moore, *Música y mestizaje*.

26. Among innumerable examples, the discography of any of the aforementioned groups should suffice. Songs like "El trágico," "Crónica social," and "Picadillo de soya" by NG La Banda contain an excellent gallery of characters and situations during the Special Period; they are presented as being so starkly everyday that they become unrealistic.

27. "Santa palabra" is included in José Luis Cortés, *Cabaret Estelar* (MC Caribe Productions C-9463, 1995).

28. Cortés, *No se puede tapar el sol*.

29. Paulito Fernández Gallo, *Con la conciencia tranquila* (CD Nueva Fania NF108, 1997).

30. Cortés, *En la calle*.

31. See Neustadt, "Buena Vista Social Club"; Perna, *Timba*; López Cano, "El chico duro."

32. A good example of this accusatory discourse toward *timba* can be found in Liliana Casanellas Cué, "Textos para bailar: ¿una polémica actual?" *Salsa Cubana* 7–8 (1999), 12–15.

33. José Luis Cortés quoted in Judy Cantor, "Bring on the Cubans!," *Miami New Times*, June 19, 1997, www.miaminewtimes.com (accessed March 2004).

34. Ned Sublette, "Rumba 2001," *La Jiribilla* 26 (2001), www.lajiribilla.cu/ (accessed March 2004).

35. María Teresa Linares, "La más pura expresión de la cubanía," *La Jiribilla* 26 (2001), www.lajiribilla.cu (accessed March 2004).

36. This section is known as a *montuno*, which is how I refer to it henceforth.

37. Victoria Eli and María A. Alfonso, *La música entre Cuba y España: tradición e innovación* (Madrid: N.p., 1999).

38. Juan Formell quoted in Frank Padrón, "Sólo soy un Van Van," *Salsa Cubana* 7–8 (1998), 34.

# 12

# Gender and Brazilian Popular Music

## *A Study of Female Bands*

RODRIGO CANTOS SAVELLI GOMES
AND MARIA IGNÊZ CRUZ MELLO

This essay considers how gender, with its set-in structures of power, prestige, hierarchy, and discrimination, structures the discourse and the musical performances of the members of female bands in the area of Florianópolis, Santa Catarina [in southern Brazil].[1] Since music is one of the cultural manifestations closest to everyday life, this essay argues that music can be directly affected by the structures mentioned above, whether by reproducing, affirming, or challenging prevailing models and customs.[2] From an anthropological perspective—which features a methodology focused on the intense and frequent insertion of researchers in the field to observe various activities including music making, social interactions, culture, collectives, and individuals—this essay discusses the extent to which production by and musical discourses of female band members raise questions relating to the theme of gender. It analyzes how gender appears in social organization during musical performance, in lyrics, and narratives gleaned through personal interviews and testimonies, as well as through the musicians' compositional processes.

Despite great advances in the study of gender in various academic fields, some sectors of society have yet to explore all the varied aspects of gender relations; such is the case with female musical production. It is known that music has been for many centuries a field of male privilege. Recent studies have shown that, since

---

Originally published by Rodrigo Cantos Savelli Gomes and Maria Ignêz Cruz Mello as "Relações de gênero e a música popular brasileira: um estúdio sobre as bandas femininas," *Anais do XVII Congresso ANPPOM* (2007). Available at www.anppom.com.br. Translated by Kariann Goldschmitt with permission.

Plato's time, musical discourse has been grounded "in gendered metaphors, sexual difference, sexual attraction and repulsion" that privileged musical structures rooted in values predominantly reflecting the masculine point of view.[3] In the last few decades, studies in anthropology, musicology, history, psychology, and sociology have been exploring gender in various geographic, cultural, and socioeconomic contexts, which indicates new perspectives other than those of total masculine domination and thereby points to a system of "complementarity between genders,"[4] such as in the case of musicological studies of indigenous villages in Brazil.[5]

Nevertheless, studies of gender in the field of music remain recent and rare. In Brazil, the big themes that permeate discussions of gender—such as work, violence, and sexuality—have had little consequence in music scholarship.[6] In a preliminary survey, one can see that studies involving the question of gender in Brazilian music predominantly analyze a discourse embedded in lyrics, where they highlight female representations as well as stereotypes and images of women. The majority of these studies are guided by scholarly areas other than musicology, such as lyrics and literature,[7] social and political science,[8] and history and social history.[9] Another scholarly branch has been dedicated to locating women in music and identifying what functions they perform and their importance in the social context of their era. They also highlight biographical studies of women who had a significant impact on the music-making artistic environment of their time.[10]

Anthropology has given some prominence to the subject by looking at music and gender from other cultures, principally indigenous populations, as is the case of ethnomusicological studies carried out in indigenous villages in Brazil.[11] In the field of musicology, Joana Holanda presents an important discussion of gender in musical language in her dissertation on the works of two female composers; Helena Lopez da Silva makes useful reflections about the construction of gender identity in adolescence by studying the symbolic uses of music in schools.[12]

Thus, studies of gender in music are centered primarily on the following topics: studies of musical codes where representations of gender are analyzed as metaphors in traditional music theory and how women use this code to express their subjectivity; analyses and observations of musical performances, which seek to determine the greatest or smallest use of corporality, sensuality, and the differences and similarities of attitudes in musical performances between the sexes; reflections on discourse in lyrics (from operas to popular and folkloric song), which often mention affective, social, and moral relations between men and women; observations on the presence of women in musical environments, especially those exercising functions usually reserved for men, such as composers, bandleaders, drummers, bassists, and DJs.

In this way, the present article seeks to foment the debate about gender from an (ethno)musicological perspective. To do this, we conducted a regional and national survey with the goal of identifying the presence of women in Brazilian popular music groups, focusing especially on rock, samba, *pagode* [a variant or substyle of samba], and hip-hop. Our study initially consisted of a survey asking the following: which groups are all female; who are the band members and how many are there; where do they live; where do they perform; who is their public; and what are their instruments and musical styles?

Our methodology consisted of attending shows and rehearsals, unstructured observation, taking field notes, conducting semi-structured interviews, regularly distributing questionnaires, and consulting local magazines and newspapers. Another research tool we used was the internet, an important medium of communication that many popular music groups use to disseminate their work. Through blogs and sites like Orkut, Trama Virtual, MySpace, and YouTube, bands create their communities and social networks and host a variety of content—from musical recordings and music videos to touring schedule, photos, press releases, and forums—available to the general audience.

The use of these social networking tools greatly improved the status of several female groups in Brazil, providing their fans with preliminary contact through email and scraps,[13] and opening up the possibility to hear music, read reviews, and learn about the band's history and formation, therefore making it possible for fans to compare groups according to their ideologies, styles, musical genres, and subgenres.

In this discussion, we consider rock, hip-hop, *pagode*, samba, reggae, funk, and MPB [Música Popular Brasileira, urban popular music in Brazil] as genres, and use them as reference to distinguishing between the cited bands. Although bands, in forming their own style, identify with and have appropriated elements from various subgenres such as punk rock, pop, alternative, metal, stoner, rap, and hard-core, these are not considered in detail here.[14]

Some bands with feminist ideologies or attitudes have become prominent by using lyrics to express their desire for equality between the sexes and to challenge racial and sexual prejudice, or simply by declaring their feminist beliefs in interviews and testimonies. Curiously, all of the bands that we identified were from the rock genre, showing the women activists' preference for this genre. Among our investigated bands, the most notable were Bulimia [as in the eating disorder] (in Brasília), Close (in Olinda, Pernambuco), NoDolls (in Goiânia, Goiás), Cosmogonia (Cosmogony, in São Paulo), Dominatrix (in São Paulo), S.A.44 (in São Paulo), the Hats (in São Paulo), Female (in Belo Horizonte, Minas Gerais), Afasia (Aphasia, in Uberlândia, Minas Gerais), and Insana Z (Insane Z, in Ponta Grossa, Paraná).

Some distinguish themselves by exploring through their group name the novelty of their member makeup. For example, the rock-pop band Elas e Eu (They [feminine plural form] and I, in São Paulo) and the MPB group Ele por Elas (He for them [feminine plural form], in Rio de Janeiro) identify the gender of their members in their group name. Another group, the rock band Blush Azul (Blue blush, in Rio Branco, Acre), though it does not have a peculiar name like the others, subtitles itself "The band of the girls and the boy" ("a banda das garotas e do garoto"). In this manner, they also highlight the importance of declaring the gender of group members in the group's name.

Other bands made of women also pose the question of identifying that difference in their identity, presenting themselves as "strictly female band," or "band of just girls" as is the case with the rock groups Lazy Moon (in Cuiabá, Mato Grosso), Punk Rockake (in Curitiba, Paraná), RNA (in Serra, Espírito Santo), Ladies Die (in João Pessoa, Paraíba), Veno (in Rio de Janeiro), and the gospel band Jaspe (Jasper, in São Paulo).

In Florianópolis we found five musical groups formed of just women. Because of their geographic proximity, it was possible for us to carry out a more focused research project with these bands: we were able to attend their shows, take field notes, record audio, film, photograph, and conduct interviews and conversations with some of their band members.[15] For this reason, we focused on the following bands:

- Entre Elas (Between them [feminine plural form]): With eight musicians and a manager, this *pagode* group has been active for about a year; they do shows in bars and nightclubs, perform in the main events of the city and state, and occasionally participate in local radio and television programs.
- Declínio do Sistema (System decline): A hip-hop group consisting of three members, currently in the process of rebuilding the group (they are selecting new members) and, for that reason, have lately performed little. They work with their own music, exploring in their lyrics questions relating to women's themes and to sexual and racial prejudice.
- Dorotéia vai à Praia (Dorothy goes to the beach): With five members, this group has performed in many shows through the state of Santa Catarina in the last few years, thereby becoming one of the principle groups of rock 'n' roll in Florianópolis. However, they disbanded during this study due to the departure of some of their band members.
- Cabeça de Alface (Lettuce head): Founded in 2003 by three young musicians, two of whom are literature students at the Federal University of Santa Catarina. The group seeks to develop their own compositions in alternative rock style, with lyrics based in "nonsense" literature.[16] According to the band members, the themes center on the "aesthetics of nonsense and word play, taking language to its extremes." They are currently recording their first CD.
- Carpe Diem Septem: A rock group formed of five teenagers who from their inception sought to make a group of just women. Despite having little experience due to their youth, the group rehearsed regularly and has begun to perform their music in bars and at events in the city.

During this survey we noticed that the presence of women was more significant in rock than in other genres such as *pagode*, samba, reggae, and hip-hop: of the twenty-three bands with female members, nineteen were rock bands. The same finding was true in Florianópolis, where three of the five female bands were from rock 'n' roll.[17]

Women's preference for rock promoted the rise of a new category or subgenre known as "rock with female vocals."[18] It also prompted the organization of festivals that are specifically aimed at those groups. These include: Festival de Rock Feminino de Rio Claro (Female rock festival of Rio Claro, São Paulo); Festival Nacional de Punk Feminino (National festival of female punk rock, Goiânia); Festival de Música Mulheres no Volante de Juiz de Fora (Juiz de Fora women at the wheel music festival, Minas Gerais); the creation of [the station] Rádio Feminina (Women's radio, Goiânia), specializing in rock 'n' roll;[19] and finally, the creation of the radio program *Mundo Rock de Calcinha* (Panty rock world), affiliated with São Paulo's Mundo Rock (Rock world).[20]

Despite ample opportunities for women in this genre, rock is still understood to be a man's world, as many authors have confirmed.[21] Attributes like potency, strength, a "strong grip," physical endurance, and power are characteristics in rock that are more commonly linked to the [traditional] masculine ideal, while feminine characteristics of sensitivity, softness, and affectivity are not well assimilated in this genre. For this reason, rock fans did not always consider women's performances favorably because they considered that female presence an *impurity*, associating women with a more commercial style, subordinate to the taste of the major labels. To a certain extent, such judgment can be used to justify placing women's musical production in its own specific subgenre.[22]

On the other hand, many authors affirm that the presence of women is "more democratic among punk rock era musicians," represented in the United States by the Rock Against Sexism movement of the 1980s and Riot Grrrl of the 1990s that had as their objective "to promote more positive images of women in rock and to encourage women to form bands and play instruments, as well as to repudiate "the merely sexual treatment directed to women in music."[23] Nevertheless, all of these authors agree that, despite these movements, "rock continues to be a 'male-centered family.'"[24]

In this discussion we emphasize the statements of women interviewed through the course of our research. Although women still constitute the minority in the music business, being a woman no longer creates as much difficulty to establish oneself in this space, as expressed in the following statement by one interviewee:

> It used to be that women had to wear baggy pants, a ball cap, and had to dress sloppily to get into hip-hop. Women entering right now always wear heels and normal clothes as they always liked, with a short skirt.[25]

It is not just that prejudice is decreasing, but being a female band may also be an advantage when it comes to bar and nightclub hiring:

> The fact that we are all-women bands means that we are gaining entry to many parties due to people's curiosity.[26]

> In the beginning, a female band is always highly valued, because it isn't normal for you to see a band with women. It is always a novelty, something that always attracts the public, regardless of style or quality. So, it's necessary to take advantage of that to show one's potential. The problem shows itself when a band stands out and people start saying things like, "it's just because they are a band of only women."[27]

> Few women expose themselves to the rock scene. So of course, those who do, cause real surprise.[28]

> I think it is a differential; maybe it catches people's attention more.[29]

The justification for making a band of women appears, in some cases, to be motivated by the lack of availability of groups having those characteristics in the music market:

> There aren't groups of just women in Florianópolis.[30]

> The group began because they wanted a band of just women playing and, as there weren't any, they made their own. That was when the band began.[31]

In his research on rock in Florianópolis, Jacques reports men who say that things were perhaps "made easier" for women: "Because they are the minority, they are seen as a positive differential for bands, and to be part of them, they don't need to play as well as men, since they bring 'glamour.'"[32]

The fact that there exist few or no female groups is ultimately one of the main attractions for putting together a band of just women:

> We know that our differential is the fact that we are [a band] of just women, but we don't want that the issue to remain fixated on this; we want to be in places because of the quality of our sound . . . it's not enough just being women if we don't play well.[33]

Eccentricity is an important element, but it is surely not enough to keep one in the music business for long. Preoccupations with technical quality arose at many points in interviews:

> What matters is sound quality . . . improving equipment quality. . . . Since we are prioritizing that, it's going to be better if each of us takes classes on her instrument.[34]

Nevertheless, despite the gender differential being attractive, the exotic trait brings a certain embedded mistrust from prejudice, both from the public and from the players.

> In nightclubs it's like this—the guys want us to play, but they say "ah, I wanted to see you play earlier."[35]

> There is hesitation when the show's being arranged. There's a certain level of skepticism about a band made of women being able to do the trick.[36]

> It's necessary to prove that you are not at a festival, for example, just because you wear a skirt. You have to prove that you play like any another man. If you prove that, everything goes naturally.[37]

> Everyone stood still, waiting to see if you really know how to play.[38]

> [In] those days, a guy didn't want to close a deal with us to play at a party because we were five women, and he said to our face that we had to play poorly, so we never participated in the event.[39]

As for the dissimilarities between men and women in executing musical performances, Philip Brett and Elizabeth Wood raise the question of whether sexuality and gender are audible in the music itself. They discuss the controversy that arose from a *New York Times* article that, after analyzing recordings of lesbian composers, claims that "sexual preference, as well as sex, is inaudible" and emphasizes that it is an "inevitable conclusion." However, the authors argue that music "cannot be so easily separated from [its] context (of performance, venue, genre, and audience, as well as musical allusion): if stripped of all associations—which is impossible—[it] can yield no meaning."[40]

That is one of the questions that has puzzled and intrigued us in our investigation. To what extent can the factor of gender—and sexual orientation, as in the studies of Brett and Wood—be expressed in the musical production of men and women? The gender distinction becomes even greater when the theme is run through a compositional analysis (of scores), since the "musicological tradition was always much more invested in formal analyses than issues sensitive to the humanities," such as performance, shows, audiences, and sociocultural context, where no doubt the issue of gender emerges much more prominently.[41]

When asked whether or not there are differences between men and women in musical performance, female musicians pointed out that it is common for them to hear audience comparisons in this regard:

> If we make a mistake, it's because we are women. If we play well, they say that it's actually good considering we're women. If we play *really* well, they say that we simply did what we were supposed to.[42]

> We have already heard people say, "Well, they play well for being women."[43]

Although this might bring some discomfort—after all, it indirectly proposes a double standard—the question of differences and similarities between the sexes in musical performance, interpretation, and composition is a theme that remains underexplored in musicology.

> That issue of technique, that right there is where men and women can be equal . . . the only difference that you'll have is being able to tolerate playing for longer, more endurance, the strength of the beat, of being able to play the whole song with higher energy.[44]

Evidently, the "strength" they describe is more cultural than physical. Jacques observed that "many musicians, not just drummers, note that it is necessary to utilize the movement of body weight, not just so-called 'strength,' when playing an instrument."[45]

In hip-hop, technique doesn't present itself with the same degree of importance. As a result, the principal difference between men and women appears in the lyrics:

> We struggle on behalf of women, we show the reality of women . . . and that reality isn't shown by the guys. Our songs revolve around the women's cause, always the women's cause. We even have a CD that speaks of health, everything of the women's cause, of abortion, about the body, all of that.[46]

On the other hand, although the majority of reports attempt to minimize the differences between the sexes, a certain disqualification arose regarding female listeners:

> It's much easier to find men singing in bars and clubs who can tell what a good sound is than a woman. In *pagode* it's rare to see a woman playing, so it's rarer for them [women] to understand.[47]

> Women don't have much interest in music—there are still few of them. There are more men in the market because it interests them more.[48]

According to the testimonials, experience is an important factor and, since women are statistically less involved in music performance, consequently the number of women who are connoisseurs of good music is also lower.

Jacques also debates this issue, referring specifically to the world of rock, where he reveals that some authors tend to "relate to women more as fans," being that women's connection to music "is due more so to their interest in the idols than in the music."[49]

## Final Considerations

Through reports, observations, and research in various media, we sought to point out the various spaces that have been and are currently occupied by female groups in Brazilian popular music, the dialogues that are being established between those groups and feminist organizations, and the ways these musical groups have made possible a negation and transformation of existing gender roles.

Although rock is considered a male space, we observed that the participation of women and feminists in rock created an opening for the surge of a new category—rock with female vocals—as well as the promotion of musical events specifically for these women groups. These facts demonstrate that their participation through the years pegs women not merely as supporters, but also as conductors of significant transformations in this world of music.

In hip-hop—a musical genre that since its inception emerged as a "form of articulation by Afro-descendant youths against racism and prejudice"[50]—we noted that women, especially black women, are finding significant space to encourage discussions about women's causes, promoting women's awareness about issues such as abortion, health, and the use of contraception through their lyrics. This is also a locus for the dissemination of information about their civil rights, such as maternity leave, pensions for stay-at-home mothers and maids, and the denunciation of violence against women.

The growing participation of women in the music business—whether as producers or consumers—makes apparent the need for new research on this subject, which continues to be understudied despite the conquest of new spaces and growing visibility of female groups. However, new studies require a theoretical base and mastery of methodologies that can surpass the descriptive character and assist in the understanding of the specifics that gender has been building into the framework of artistic-musical expressions.

## Notes

Translator's note: "Gender" and "genre" come from the same Brazilian Portuguese word. The original title of this article, noted above, threw some ambiguity over which word was intended. The authors specify in a footnote in the original text that the phrase "relações de gênero" should be understood as "gender," whereas "gênero musical" means "genre." Thus, throughout this article, I opted for the streamlined translation of "gender" and "genre." Also, as noted by the authors, "Brazilian Popular Music" in the title and elsewhere in this article refers not to the genre MPB, but rather to popular music in Brazil more generally.

1. Following Christopher Small, *Música, sociedad, educación* (Madrid: Alianza, 1989; originally published in 1977 as *Music, Society, Education*) we do not refer to "performance" as linked to technical abilities and motor functions but rather as a social event where some individuals play and others listen. A performance is where the experience of doing and interaction among people is more relevant than the final product.

2. The article by Philip Brett and Elizabeth Wood, "Música lésbica e guei," *Revista Eletrônica de Musicologia (Curitiba)* 7, www.rem.ufpr.br, December 2002, translated and commented by Carlos Palombini, adjunct professor of musicology at the School of Music

at UFMG—reveals how and why discussions relating to sexual diversity (homosexuality, bisexuality, transsexuality, etc.), as well as the theme of gender, were kept at the margins of debates in *positivist* modern musicology. According to the authors, issues such as homosexuality and gender deflects the aspect of "music about itself"—a phenomenon of "absolute music"—representing a threat to the virile hegemony, to the status of science marked by the logic of rationality, the cult of the intellect, and the demonstration of force and seriousness, in an attempt to maintain itself as a force of truth and power. Thus, music moved away from the basic elements of ordinary, everyday life, focusing instead on mostly technical and rational aspects.

3. Maria Ignêz C. Mello, "Relações de gênero e musicologia: reflexões para uma análise do contexto brasileiro," in *Simpósio de Pesquisa em Música* (Annals), ed. Rogério Budasz, vol. 3 (Curitiba: Universidade Federal do Paraná, 2006), 69–74.

4. Maria Ignêz C. Mello, "Música, mito e ritual entre os Wauja do Alto Xingu" (PhD diss. in social anthropology, Universidade Federal de Santa Catarina, 2005), 287.

5. Acácio Tadeu de C. Piedade, "O canto do kawoká: música, cosmologia e filosofia entre os Wauja do Alto Xingu" (PhD diss. in social anthropology, Universidade Federal de Santa Catarina, 2004); Rafael de Menezes Bastos, "A musicológica kamayurá: para uma antropologia da comunicação no Alto Xingu" (Florianópolis: Universidade do Federal de Santa Catarina, 1999); Mello, "Música, mito e ritual."

6. Joana C. Holanda and Cristina Capparelli Gerling, "Estudos de gênero em música a partir da década de 90: escopo e abordagem," *Revista Associação Nacional de Música, Revista ANM–Rio de Janeiro* 15 (2005), and Mello, "Relações de gênero e musicologia," reveal that studies about music and gender have the largest coverage in countries like the United States and England and are thus considered to be forerunners in broaching the issue. According to the authors, the main vestiges began around the 1980s in the United States, with the first anthologies of scores by and biographies of women composers. In the 1990s, Susan McClary, *Feminine Endings: Music, Gender, and Sexuality* (Minneapolis: University of Minnesota Press, 1991), Lawrence Kramer, *Music as Cultural Practice, 1800–1900* (Berkeley: University of California Press, 1990), and Marcia J. Citron, *Gender and the Musical Canon* (Cambridge: Cambridge University Press, 1993), raised the first debates about gender metaphors in the musical code, showing how conventions and rhetorical constructions of musical theory and analysis can be replete with sexual metaphors constructed from sensations and impressions that reflect, for the most part, a masculine model. Still in the 1990s, other authors—such as Ellen Walterman, "Cassandra's Dream Song: A Literary Feminist Perspective," *Perspectives of New Music* 32, no. 2 (1994) 154–72; Suzanne G. Cusick, "Feminist Theory, Music Theory, and the Mind/Body Problem," *Perspectives of New Music* 32, no. 1 (1994), 8–27; Citron, *Gender and the Musical Canon*; and McClary, *Feminine Endings*—sought to perceive differential points in compositional structures and elaborations, arrangements and interpretations in feminine activities, to reveal how women find mechanisms to express their subjectivity in a musical system constructed in the patriarchal dominion.

7. Synval Beltrão, *A musa-mulher na canção brasileira* (São Paulo: Editora Liberdade, 1993); Maria Áurea Santa Cruz, *A musa sem máscara: a imagem da mulher na música popular brasileira* (Rio de Janeiro: Editora Rosa dos Tempos, 1992); Maria José S. Barbosa,

"A representação da mulher nas cantigas de capoeira," *Revue Internationale d'Études Lusophones* (Université de Nantes, France) 1 (2006), 137–52.

8. Neusa Meirelles Costa, "A mulher na música popular brasileira," www.samba-choro.com.br (accessed Oct. 2, 2006); Viviane Barbosa de Oliveira, "Quebrando o coco e fazendo a roça: gênero e identidade no cotidiano de quebradeiras de coco babaçu no Maranhão," in *Programa Mulher e Ciência, 1º Prêmio Construindo a Igualdade de Gênero—Redações e trabalhos científicos monográficos vencedores* (Brasília: Presidência da República, Secretaria Especial de Políticas para as Mulheres, 2006), 212–13.

9. Cleide Nogueira de Faria, "Puxando a sanfona e rasgando o nordeste: relações de gênero na música popular nordestina (1950–1990)," *Revista Eletrônica de Humanidades* 3, no. 5 (2002); Marina Haizenreder Ertzogue, "O canto das quebradeiras: cantigas de trabalho das mulheres extrativistas de Coco na Região Bico do Papagaio," *Revista Fragmento de Cultura* 12, no. 6 (2002), 1103–10; Ana Maria Veiga, "Mulheres em rádio e revista: imagens femininas na época de ouro da música (Rio de Janeiro 1930/1945)," in *Programa Mulher e Ciência, 1º Prêmio Construindo a Igualdade de Gênero—Redações e trabalhos científicos monográficos vencedores* (Brasília: Secretaria Especial de Políticas para as Mulheres, Presidência da República, 2006), 32–63; Maria Izilda S. de Matos, "Sensibilidades femininas: poética e música em Dolores Duran," *Labrys, Estudos Feministas* 5 (2004), www.tanianavarroswain.com.br/ (accessed Oct. 2, 2006).

10. Silvana Beeck Stival, "Chiquinha Gonzaga em Forrobodó" (master's thesis in literature, Universidade Federal de Santa Catarina, 2004); Nilcéia Cleide da Silva Baroncelli, *Mulheres compositoras: elenco e repertório* (São Paulo: Editora Roswitha Kempf, 1987); Adriana Chaves, "Mulheres no rock," www.mulheresnorock.pop.com.br/ (accessed Oct. 2, 2006); Rafael Sartori, "As mulheres e o rock 'n' roll," www.mulheresnorock.pop.com.br/ (accessed Oct. 2, 2006); Century Media, "O rock de saias, quem diria? Virou coisa de mulher!," www.mulheresnorock.pop.com.br/ (accessed Oct. 2, 2006); Alberto J. V. Pacheco and Adriana G. Kayama, "A cantora Lapinha e a presença musical feminina no Brasil colonial e imperial," in *Simpósio de Pesquisa em Música*, 7–12; Wivian Weller, "A presença feminina nas (sub)culturas juvenis: a arte de se tornar visível," *Revista Estudos Feministas, Florianópolis* 13, no. 1 (2005), 107–26; Edinha Diniz, *Chiquinha Gonzaga: Uma história de vida* (Rio de Janeiro: Editora Rosa dos Tempos, 1984); Carlos Kater, *Eunice Katunda: Musicista brasileira* (São Paulo: Annablume, 2001); Mariza Lira, *Chiquinha Gonzaga: grande compositora popular brasileira* (Rio de Janeiro: Funarte, 1978); Silvana Ruffier Scarinci, "Safo Novella: a voz da poeta grega reapropriada por Bárbara Strozzi (Veneza, 1619–1677)," in *Simpósio de Pesquisa em Música*, 13–20.

11. Mello, "Música, mito e ritual"; Piedade, "O canto do Kawoká"; Bastos, "A musicológica Kamayurá."

12. Joana C. Holanda, in her "Eunice Katunda (1915–1990) e Esther Scliar (1926–1978): Trajetórias individuais e análise de sonata para piano 'Sonata de Louvação' (1960) e 'Sonata para Piano' (1961)" (PhD diss., Universidade Federal do Rio Grande do Sul, 2006), investigated the music of Eunice Katunda and Esther Scliar, from their individual trajectories and an analysis of their respective musical works, *Worship Sonata* and *Sonata for Piano*. This research is an important reference for gender studies in music as it problematized

gender from the perspective of its sociocultural context; from the engagement of female composers in various movements such as "live music" groups, nationalism, the communist party (PCB, Partido Comunista Brasileiro); and also through their inalienable social identity as "women" subjects. Helena Lopes da Silva, "Música no espaço escolar e a construção da identidade de gênero: um estudo de caso" (master's thesis, Universidade Federal do Rio Grande do Sul, 2000).

13. Scraps are messages sent and received through Orkut and blogs. Their main characteristic is that they are public, allowing them to be read by any user. [Translator's note: At the height of Orkut's popularity, "scraps" also referred to comments on a blog.]

14. Following Tatyana de Alencar Jacques, "Comunidade rock e bandas independentes de Florianópolis: uma etnografia sobre socialidade e concepções musicais" (master's thesis, Universidade Federal de Santa Catarina, 2007), 10, with "appropriation," we refer to "the particular form with which musicians assimilate a determined musical characteristic, integrating it to their style."

15. With groups from other regions, we primarily made contact through the internet. With some of those, it was more effective to contact the bands and send them a questionnaire via email, as we did with S.A.44, RNA, Give Me A Break, Lazy Moon, Blush Azul, and the group Elas e Eu.

16. Lewis Carroll, Edward Lear, Samuel Beckett, and James Joyce are the main authors mentioned by the band members.

17. Although this article specifically studies women's groups, we also paid attention to mixed-gender groups in Florianópolis, primarily focusing on the presence of women in roles that are rarely attributed to them, such as drummers, bassists, composers, and producers. In spite of widening our focus, the evidence only changed slightly. Among the mixed-gender groups, we can cite Kratera (rock), Oh Sugar! (rock), Maltines (rock), Squadrão da Rima (Rhyme squad, hip-hop), Mary Black (hip-hop), Missiva (Missive, reggae), Black Diversity (funk) and Alessandra Sipriano and Band (pop/rock).

18. This category emerged at first from our interviews, but its common use was verified by other bands on websites.

19. Women's Radio (Rádio feminina) is an initiative of the Organização Punk Feminino (Feminine punk rock organization) that was born after the first Festival Nacional de Punk Feminino in 2006. Unlike the festival, which is restricted by genre and substyle of rock, the radio station is more inclusive, specializing in the broader rock 'n' roll genre, but still only playing bands featuring women singers. It can be heard on the internet at www.radiofeminina.cjb.net/.

20. *Mundo Rock de Calcinha* is a radio program that plays music by rock and metal bands made up of only females or with women on the vocals. It was founded in March 2007 by Gisele Santos, also founder of mundorock.net with more than seven years on the air. It can be heard at www.mundorockdecalcinha.com.

21. Jacques, "Comunidade rock e bandas"; Robert Walser, *Running with the Devil: Power, Gender, and Madness in Heavy Metal Music* (Middletown, Conn.: Wesleyan University Press, 1993); Chaves, "Mulheres no rock"; Media, "O rock de saias, quem diria?"; Sartori, "As mulheres e o rock 'n' roll."

22. Many authors use the idea of impurity through observations of discourses of various rock musicians that emphasize the "opposition between the purity of authenticity and the impurity of commercialized alienation" (Jacques, "Comunidade rock e bandas," 84).

23. Chaves, "Mulheres no rock"; Cohen quoted in Jacques, "Comunidade rock e bandas," 98; Media, "O rock de saias, quem diria?"

24. Jacques, "Comunidade rock e bandas," 98.

25. Jussara Pereira Lima, vocalist of the hip-hop group Declínio do Sistema, interview. She is also state coordinator of UNEGRO (União de Negros pela Igualdade), an organization of national scope, founded in Florianópolis in March 1994, with the goal of aiding in the eradication of racism and for better conditions for the exercise of citizens' rights.

26. Elisa Rebelo, manager of the *pagode* group Entre Elas, interview.

27. Giselle Xavier Lucena, bassist for the rock band Blush Azul, interview.

28. Fernanda dos Santos Martins, vocalist from the rock band S.A.44, interview.

29. Joana Feliciano, drummer from the band S.A.44, interview.

30. Pereira Lima interview.

31. Juliano Silveira, bassist from the rock band Oh, Sugar! from Florianópolis, interview. Today the band is no longer made of just women.

32. Jacques, "Comunidade rock e bandas," 99.

33. Rebelo interview.

34. Ibid.

35. Ibid.

36. Renata de Oliveira Figueiredo, drummer for the rock band RNA, interview.

37. Issaaf Santos Karhawi, bassist for the rock band Lazy Moon, interview.

38. Rebelo interview.

39. Paulete Costa dos Santos, bassist for the rock band RNA, interview.

40. Brett and Wood, "Música lésbica e guei."

41. Mello, "Relações de gênero e musicologia."

42. De Oliveira Figueiredo interview.

43. Rebelo interview.

44. Ibid.

45. Jacques, "Comunidade rock e bandas," 98.

46. Pereira Lima interview.

47. Rebelo interview.

48. Thanira Rates, vocalist, former member of the rock group Dorotéia va à Praia, interview.

49. Jacques, "Comunidade rock e bandas," 96.

50. Weller, "A presença feminina."

# PART THREE

# Alternate Genealogies, Marginal Ontologies, and Applied Ethnomusicology

Scholarly research about music and dance in Latin America and the Caribbean has historically been closely intertwined with ongoing concerns as to how to define the national character of each nation. The work of scholars during the first part of the twentieth century helped to identify and define the music and dance genres that would be deemed as coterminous with the official musical identity of a particular nation. In many cases, these scholars saw themselves as active contributors to larger nationalist projects (some of them even working under the direct or indirect auspices of the state), systematically identifying, documenting, and eventually inducting local forms of music and dance into emerging national canons. In Argentina, for example, the work of Carlos Vega and Isabel Aretz provided the foundation for what are still regarded as the central genres associated with Argentine folk music and dance.[1] This is not to say that these canons have not been redefined or updated over time, as is the case with Colombia and, to a lesser degree, Mexico, where new definitions of the nation during the last two decades of the twentieth century sought to incorporate a previously unacknowledged African cultural heritage, leading in turn to various attempts to expand the canon of officially recognized music and dance practices.[2] Yet, despite modifications and updates that have sought to be more inclusive, nationalist paradigms have remained an important, and not always directly recognized, influence on the epistemologies associated with Latin American music research, in terms of not only which musical practices are considered to form a part of the nation, but also which other practices remain at the margins.

While debates regarding the inclusion or exclusion of particular forms of music from different national canons can vary widely within the region, most iterations can be traced to the postcolonial struggle for national identity that took place in the region in the nineteenth century. Latin American elites considered a number of models through which to imagine and define their nations, models that in general exhibited two main concerns: an ethno-nationalist tendency that looked into the past as a means of linking nationhood to the idealized cultural legacy and grandeur of pre-Columbian societies (Aztecs, Incas, Mayas, Taínos, etc.), a way of undoing or sidestepping a colonial legacy deemed to have a detrimental effect on indigenous populations; and, a liberal humanist orientation that, at least in theory, regarded all (male) individuals, regardless of background, as potential citizens of the new nation, further suggesting that the national stock could be strengthened through the selective hybridization of Iberian, Amerindian, or African cultural heritages (although usually assuming that the latter two would play a subordinate role to the first).[3] Nationalist movements of the twentieth century drew on both of these strands, generating a series of models that responded to the specific social and historical circumstances of a particular locality, as well as to its particular history of race politics. These ranged from the neo-Aztec or Incan models associated with *indigenismo* (indigenism), to the cultural hybrid models associated with various flavors of *mestizaje* (term for the hybridization of European and indigenous traits) and *criollismo* (creolization), to the modernist appropriation of African or indigenous musical and cultural heritages that led to *afrocubanismo* (Afro-Cubanism) in Cuba and *antropofagia* (anthropophagy) in Brazil, to more universalist models, such as that of Mexican writer and philosopher José Vasconcelos, who posited that the cultural and racial mixing of European, indigenous, African, and Asian peoples in the Americas would produce a new *raza cósmica* (cosmic race) that would subsume all others.[4]

Yet, despite their apparent inclusiveness, these models tended to reproduce assumed inequalities regarding the musical and cultural heritages that they pointed to as sources of inspiration. One particularly persistent discrepancy was the tendency to regard indigenous people and their musical practices as belonging to a category ontologically distinct from that of other constituencies in the nation, a perspective linked to the belief that these communities occupied a primordial or premodern state. For some, this ontological difference was a way of claiming a specific type of national rootedness in the "original" populations of subsequently colonized territories. For others, it was a way of explaining what was perceived as the apparent lack of ability or interest on the part of indigenous populations to engage with nationalist projects promoted by the elite.

While from early in the twentieth century Latin American scholars had an interest in both indigenous and nonindigenous musical practices, the role that each of these musics had in those scholars' constructions of specific national imaginaries can be regarded as an example of how that type of ontological differentiation informed the various genealogies of Latin American music research. Research that was inspired by or intended to support particular nationalist projects emphasized or upheld mestizo or creolized musical practices as emblematic of the nation. Research on indigenous musics, on the other hand, generally took one of two paths. One focused on documenting so-called primitive forms of music making that were perceived as culturally separate from the modern nation. The other was invested in the analysis of indigenous musics inasmuch as they constituted vestigial or distorted manifestations of more sophisticated musical systems that flourished in the pre-Columbian era, rather than viable contemporary forms that could be inducted into the nationalist canon.

Carlos Vega's work is a good example of trends in other parts of Latin America. While early in his career he devoted some attention to indigenous musics and to the question of Inca music, his monumental anthologies of national dances omit mention of these practices, focusing instead on criollo music and dance. His systematic classification of Argentine musical instruments similarly maintains a distinction between criollo and "aboriginal" instruments.[5] The dichotomy between these two groups is elaborated in a number of publications, with Vega positing a tripartite set of musical domains: the first two, modern and folkloric, are constituted by contemporary and older musical forms that together belonged to the realm of history and literacy; the third, the primitive domain, refers to musics that continued to exist in a prehistoric and preliterate state.[6] Vega regarded the folkloric domain as being populated from above, as formerly new musical forms were displaced downward by emerging and more innovative ones. This dynamic environment continued to generate new compositions and dances, albeit following older modes of innovation, occasionally spilling back up into the modern domain as a source of inspiration, or strategically appropriating a few minor elements from the primitive domain (e.g., musical instruments, scales) for its own purposes. In contrast, he characterized the primitive realm as a living archaeological repository with little to no musical change or innovation.[7]

Vega's tripartite model echoed another common demarcation of musical phenomena by other scholars: that between musics of the pre-Columbian, colonial, and postcolonial eras. The overlap between the three parts of Vega's model and these three time periods was not coincidental. Vega's attempts to define the study of folklore in Argentina tended to reinforce prevailing attitudes regarding indigenous people held by many Latin American elite, despite his insistence that it was an ideologically neutral scientific enterprise. Vega's primitive category was not dissimilar from a pre-Columbian category that also ascribed the musics within it a particular kind of primordial timelessness or isolation. Colonial and postcolonial categories were deemed closer to one another, both because of the European cultural elements that were common to both and because of the generalized perception that the colonial period marked the start of the official written history of Latin America. Likewise, this ontological differentiation also influenced a type of academic division of labor among different scholars, with anthropologists, ethnologists, and linguists being the primary scholars interested in indigenous musical forms, and folklorists, historians, and musicologists being more interested in those other musical forms that could be more easily imagined as national. Vega himself tried to explain this apparent tendency, arguing that the disciplines of folklore and ethnography should be conceived as two complementary enterprises focused on the study of living cultures, with the former concerned with the expression of preliterate societies and the latter working firmly in the realm of oral and written history.

Although many of these paradigms and assumptions came to be questioned in the latter part of the twentieth century, their legacy is still felt in a number of ways in contemporary scholarship. Gonzalo Camacho Díaz's article (chapter 13) on the relationship between music, dance, and myth in the Huasteca region of Mexico offers a good example of how perceived ontological differences between indigenous and nonindigenous musics have led to different approaches and epistemological concerns. Whereas much research on Latin American folk and popular music has historically been concerned with issues of defining, documenting, and demarcating music and dance genres that are then used as a starting point from which to extrapolate to broader societal issues (see part 2), scholarship concerned with indigenous communities has provided alternative entry points for musical research. A particularly important line of inquiry has been the concern with understanding musical activity as circumscribed within larger indigenous worldviews, a research direction that has been greatly influenced by the growing anthropological interest in indigenous communities since the 1980s, particularly in Mexico, parts of Central America, and the Andean and Amazonian regions of South America. Camacho Díaz's work speaks well to this particular tradition, examining the various references to music and dance present within the myths associated with the deity Chicomexochitl. Beyond mapping out the relationship that Huastecan Nahua communities make between agriculture, civilization, and music making, the author also shows how Nahua cosmology strongly informs contemporary rituals, the roles of music and dance within them, and the aesthetic realization of these two forms of expressive culture.

Studies focused on the relevance and articulation of indigenous perspectives and categories through music and dance have provided a helpful counterpoint to the issue of ontological difference. They have helped to problematize and ultimately dismiss the characterization of indigenous communities as primitive, unchanging, and disengaged from the contemporary world, while at the same time providing alternate ways of acknowledging, accounting for, and more productively addressing important social, cultural, economic, and aesthetic differences that can exist between indigenous communities and other populations within a given country or region. Jorge Martínez Ulloa's work with urban Mapuche offers a particularly pertinent critique (chapter 14), arguing that the way in which Chilean scholars have constructed that population as Orientalized "others" denies the latter the possibility of being regarded as capable of effectively adapting to changing social realities like urbanization—this despite the fact that a growing majority of Mapuche in Chile live in urban areas.[8] Furthermore, he suggests that this romantic concern for the alleged purity and authenticity of Mapuche musical practices works against an understanding of the Mapuche as a subaltern group struggling for recognition and a degree of relative autonomy within a dominant nonindigenous (criollo) Chilean society. As a counter to this trend, Martínez Ulloa proposes a semiotic model as a means of understanding the transformation of Mapuche musical practices from rural to urban contexts. By focusing on the *palin*, a ritual game punctuated by music and dance, the author shows that its reinterpretation in urban settings exhibits a dual function, both as a ritual that strengthens the participants' connection to their Mapuche heritage, but also as a strategic spectacle aimed at the non-Mapuche spectators who have become an integral part of these events and designed to redefine outsiders' perceptions of what it means to be Mapuche.

Angela Lühning's reflection on the International Symposium of Ethnomusicology that took place in Brazil in 2000 (chapter 15) further explores the interactions between subaltern indigenous and hegemonic nonindigenous populations by shifting attention to the relationships that exist between musicians from the latter group and scholars from the former. While Brazilian nationalist models going back to the nineteenth century have acknowledged that both Amerindian and Afro-Brazilian cultural heritages have some role, indigenous communities have remained comparatively more geographically distant, less visible, and not as well integrated as their Afro-Brazilian and Luso-Brazilian counterparts. Recalling the various events that took place during the symposium, Lühning responds to many participants' apparent lack of familiarity with the musical practices of various indigenous and even some Afro-Brazilian communities. In particular, she was struck by how the presence and participation of members from these communities in the symposium contributed to a type of role reversal, which prompts her to ponder the development of a new type of ethnomusicology that is predicated on the equal partnership between scholars and culture bearers and the decentering of forms of knowledge associated with technology and the academy, which she sees as partly responsible for reinforcing the perceived ontological differentiation between both groups of participants. Lühning further posits that Brazil, like other Latin American countries, can be an interesting testing ground for this new mode of ethnomusicological scholarship, given that the prominent role that scholars have played at times within the elaboration of state cultural and educational policies can be instrumental in the development of more culturally sensitive approaches regarding the recognition of ethnic minorities as citizens of Brazil.

In some ways, Lühning's concerns are similar to those that arise in discussions on applied ethnomusicology in the United States. Yet, the absence of a single national cultural policy in the United States, the relative lack of involvement of U.S. scholars with state institutions, and the persistent tendency of ethnomusicologists to work with populations outside the United States have tended to stress aspects and issues associated with applied work. One particularly salient difference is the role that archives and research institutions with ties to the state can play in shaping the direction of music research, and how that direction can be informed by nationalist ideologies and priorities. Marina Alonso Bolaños's critique of the influence that institutions have had in shaping discourses and representations of music and indigeneity in Mexico (chapter 16) addresses this point directly, along the way also highlighting how different sociohistorical contexts have produced alternate ways of conceiving ethnomusicological and applied work. Charting the interrelationship between Mexican nationalism, state-sponsored research programs involving music, and ethnographic work on indigenous communities throughout the twentieth century, Alonso Bolaños shows how applied ethnomusicology in Mexico emerged during the second half of the twentieth century mainly as an institutional enterprise concerned with the production and dissemination of indigenous music in the form of various anthologies of field recordings. Some recording initiatives sponsored by these institutions created opportunities for recording and broadcasting projects led by indigenous people, which emphasized the role of different kinds of music in daily life. However, Alonso Bolaños argues that these projects came to be at odds with and were eventually overshadowed by other projects within those same institutions that continued to advocate for a more reified notion of indigenous music as primarily rooted in ritual performance and the use of pre-Columbian musical instruments.

While Afro-descendant populations in Latin America have also been marginalized by more socially, politically, and economically powerful groups, there has been less of a tendency to conceptualize these subaltern communities as ontologically distinct. A great deal of this discrepancy stems from the fact that Latin American elites have historically perceived Afro-descendant groups as having a position different from that of indigenous populations. Having been delivered to the Americas by European colonizers, in most cases unable to retain the languages spoken by their forebearers, and having also adopted and transformed a number of European or Amerindian cultural practices as their own, Afro-descendant populations have been perceived as lacking what anthropologist Shane Greene calls the "holy trinity" of ethno-cultural difference and recognition: territory, language, and culture.[9] There have been at least partial exceptions, particularly in countries where a comparative lack of an indigenous population or the existence of a large Afro-descendant population have led to the conceptualization of the latter as a mutually exclusive Other. Robin Moore's assessment of Fernando Ortiz's work, for example, shows that prior to and during the early days of *afrocubanismo* there was a tendency for the Cuban elite to envision Afro-Cuban populations in primitive and atavistic terms that legitimized their conceptualization as ontologically different.[10] In most cases, however, these characterizations did not endure into the latter part of the twentieth century, or the twenty-first, as has been the case for a number of indigenous groups.

Nonetheless, just as some scholars in Latin America have insisted that there is still a need to regard indigenous populations as culturally and qualitatively distinct (although not necessarily in ontological terms), others have come to argue that perhaps there is a similar need when it comes to some Afro-descendant populations. José Jorge de Carvalho's article regarding the relationships between some Afro-Brazilian forms of expressive culture, capitalism, and the state (chapter 17) makes such a case, at the same time also expanding the scope of issues associated with applied work and the role of academics in these dynamics that have been touched upon by some of the other authors in this section of the book. Echoing a point made by Lühning, he argues that more marginal populations in Brazil have a different relationship with their forms of expressive culture than the majority of other populations who find themselves more integrated into nationalist and capitalist processes that have been taking place in that country since the early part of the twentieth century. Carvalho articulates that difference by invoking the work of Walter Benjamin, positing that the induction of marginal Afro-Brazilian forms of music and dance into the cultural heritage and entertainment industries does not just recontextualize them by distancing them from ritual and communal contexts where these forms of expression perform necessary cultural work. It also undermines the agency and authority that local performers have over their expressive practices as they are introduced into new middle-class and largely non-Afro-Brazilian contexts, where the consumption of these forms is perceived as a celebration of Brazilian cultural diversity.

Carvalho's polemical account is notable for its focus on the often-unacknowledged role that scholars can have in this process. He argues that, throughout the twentieth century, the role of scholars in Brazil (and presumably in other parts of Latin America) has changed. Initially, scholars acted as official or unofficial agents of the state, individuals committed to the mapping of each country's musical diversity in the name of national integration. Later, as scholars became more aware of the disconnect between nationalist ideology, cultural policy, and the communities that the state was meant to serve, many tried to use their positions of influence in universities, state, and private institutions to speak on behalf of these communities. More recently, he suggests, the professionalization of the university system has required scholars to become producers of consumable knowledge (books, audio recordings, documentary films, music festivals, conferences, etc.). At the same time, a growing interest by the Brazilian middle class in the consumption of multiculturalism has prompted the culture and entertainment industries to seek more accessible and commodifiable forms of cultural difference, something that increasingly places scholars in the role of culture brokers whose own needs and priorities (as authors, performers, audio or video producers, concert promoters, faculty members seeking tenure, etc.) can come into conflict with the needs and priorities of those of whose expressive cultural practices these scholars are trying to research, support, and promote. Consequently, Carvalho advocates for scholars to examine their own research activities more critically and become more conscious of how their own actions can inadvertently reinforce myths about national integration and multicultural understanding that can act as masks for enduring social inequalities.

Javier F. León

## Notes

1. Carlos Vega, *La música popular argentina: canciones y danzas criollas* (Buenos Aires: Universidad de Buenos Aires, 1941); Isabel Aretz, *Música tradicional argentina: Tucumán, historia y folklore* (Tucumán: Universidad Nacional de Tucumán, 1946). For an in-depth discussion regarding the role that Vega, Aretz, and other scholars had in the shaping of Argentine folklore, see Oscar Chamosa, *The Argentine Folklore Movement: Sugar Elites, Criollo Workers, and the Politics of Cultural Nationalism, 1900–1955* (Tucson: University of Arizona Press, 2010).

2. For an analysis of the impact of this shift in nationalist ideology on Colombian music, see Peter Wade, *Music, Race and Nation: Música Tropical in Colombia* (Chicago:

University of Chicago Press, 2000). There has yet to be a similar music-centered study conducted in regards to Mexico's Third Root (Tercera Raíz) movement, which arguably has not been as strong an influence in the reshaping of Mexican nationalism. However, anthropologist Laura Lewis's work in the Costa Chica of Mexico provides an excellent overview of the relationships of emerging conceptions of Afro-Mexicanness, their relationship to older nationalist notions of indigeneity and *mestizaje*, and their impact on processes of identity formation at the local level; Laura A. Lewis, "Blacks, Black Indians, Afromexicans: The Dynamics of Race, Nation and Identity in a Moreno Mexican Community (Guerrero)," *American Ethnologist* 27, no. 4 (2000), 898–926. For examples of how these changing perspectives have informed the work of Latin American scholars, see Tomás Darío Gutiérrez Hinojosa, *Cultura vallenata: origen, teoría y pruebas* (Bogotá: Plaza & Janés Editores, 1992); Ronaldo Pérez Fernández, *La música afromestiza mexicana* (Xalapa: Universidad de Veracruz, 1990).

3. Mark Thurner, *From Two Republics to One Divided: Contradictions of Postcolonial Nationmaking in Andean Peru* (Durham, N.C.: Duke University Press, 1997), 3–12.

4. José Vasconcelos, *La raza cósmica, misión de la raza iberoamericana* (Madrid: Aguilar, 1966 [1925]).

5. Carlos Vega, *Los instrumentos musicales aborígenes y criollos de la Argentina* (Buenos Aires: Ediciones Centurión, 1946).

6. Carlos Vega, *Fraseología: proposición de un nueve método para la escritura y análisis de las ideas musicales y su aplicación al canto popular* (Buenos Aires: Universidad de Buenos Aires, 1941), 539–43; *La ciencia del folklore: con aportaciones a su definición y objeto y notas para su historia en la Argentina* (Buenos Aires: Editorial Nova, 1960), 13–51 and 87–141.

7. Vega's sense of the primitive category was clearly informed by European and Anglo-American scholarship of the late nineteenth and early twentieth centuries and was not dissimilar from how the term was used by comparative musicologists and other music scholars outside of Latin America at that time. A particularly pertinent example is Gilbert Chase's *Guide to the Music of Latin America* (Washington, D.C.: Library of Congress, 1945), which categorizes studies that today would be deemed ethnomusicological in scope under three musical categories: primitive, folk, and popular.

8. In his article, Martínez Ulloa cites statistics from the 1990s. Since then, the level of urbanization among the Mapuche has continued to increase. As of 2009, two-thirds of all Mapuche live in urban areas; see Jenniffer Thiers Quintana, "Santiago Mapuche: la dimensión indígena del espacio urbano en Chile," in *Actas del XIII Coloquio Internacional de Geocrítica: El control del espacio y los espacios de control*, ed. Quim Bonastra, Magno Vasconcelos Pereira Junior, and Maricarmen Tapia Gómez (Barcelona: Universitat Autònoma de Barcelona, 2014), 2.

9. Shane Greene, "Introduction: On Race, Roots/Routes, and Sovereignty in Latin America's Afro-Indigenous Multiculturalisms," *Journal of Latin American and Caribbean Anthropology* 12, no. 2 (2007), 345. Greene uses the term "holy trinity" in reference to contemporary Afro-Indigenous movements seeking recognition from the state as semi-sovereign communities akin, but not necessarily homologous, to indigenous groups that

have been afforded similar rights, a strategy that has been received with mixed results in the region. My invocation of his term points to the prior historical context that made such claims of recognition necessary: a time when Afro-descendant communities were generally not regarded as having the right to claim rootedness in Latin America due to their perceptions as outsiders or at least as partially acculturated into dominant colonial culture.

10. Robin Moore, "Representations of Afrocuban Expressive Culture in the Writings of Fernando Ortiz," *Latin American Music Review* 15, no. 1 (1994), 32–54.

# 13

# Myth, Music, and Dance

## *The Chicomexochitl*

GONZALO CAMACHO DÍAZ

Its exuberant vegetation is palpable proof that Mexico's Huasteca region is in the lap of fertility. Heading inland, one is delighted not only by the smell of oranges, coffee, tobacco, and banana but also by a musical and kinetic kaleidoscope for the eyes and ears. This is a place filled with history, stories, and myths, orally transmitted from generation to generation, where maize makes its presence felt and, in many cases, assumes the role of protagonist in the narratives. This article demonstrates that the myths and stories circulated in the Huasteca region are a vital source for music and dance knowledge in the region, especially when contrasted with corresponding cultural practices. To this end, it presents a brief analysis of a selection of Nahua myths and stories that refer to Chicomexochitl, the name given to maize in its anthropomorphized form and acting as the protagonist in these accounts.

As it is with many places in Mexico, maize is the basic food source of the Huastec people. Cultivated maize crops are part of the landscape that one sees along the extensive highways. Its presence in the fields, in the local markets, on open stoves in indigenous homes, in rituals, in offerings, and as objects used for divination reveals its importance as a fundamental subject matter, as much as in the culinary sense as in the Huasteca region's cultural expressions. In indigenous communities, maize is a dominant symbol that permits the articulation of other symbolic elements. Within this environment, a particular configuration of signs is established that gives an organic character to various cultural practices, filling

Originally published by Gonzalo Camacho Díaz as "Mito, música y danza: el Chicomexochitl," *Perspectiva Interdisciplinaria de Música* 2 (2008): 51–58. Translated by Randall Kohl with permission.

them with sense and coherence. Music and dance expressions are systematically embedded within this signifying field. For this reason, the study of such artistic forms of expression results in a new understanding of the culture of the peoples of this region.

The maize we know today is a product of the ancestral knowledge of the Mesoamerican people. Its domestication was achieved over centuries and involved a surprising transmutation from the small wild maize (*teocintle*) to its present-day variety. The process had an impact on the transformation of forms of production and on social and cultural structures of Mesoamerican communities. In a way, these changes were responsible for the emergence of myths as well as of music and dance practices that, symbolically, refer back to the origin and variety of the grain and to the ritual conduct associated with its production process.

Maize was an important symbol in Mesoamerican cultures and continues to occupy a privileged site in the imagination of contemporary indigenous communities. This would explain in part the presence of maize's numerous symbolic expressions projected onto the artistic practices within the Huastecan Nahua communities. Among the multiple myths and traditional tales of the Huasteca region, references to maize stand out that, as already mentioned, correspond to the mythical character Chicomexochitl, a Nahua name meaning "seven flower."[1] Chicomexochitl is a young incarnation of the grain represented in seed form; as such, he is thought of as a child version of maize. Its seedlike quality allows maize to be a symbol associated with germinating potential and with representations of the forces of creation and generation of life. It is not surprising then that, in this region, Chicomexochitl emerges as a civilizing hero, inventor of agricultural techniques, and creator of music and dance.

For the present analysis, through fieldwork and from bibliographic sources I collected several Nahua myths and stories that refer to Chicomexochitl. I reviewed the material to locate narrative tropes in which direct or indirect allusions to music and dance are made. Due to space limitations, I consider only passages essential to my argument. These passages are divided into two categories: the first group focuses on a particular characterization of Chicomexochitl that allows us to understand some general aspects of music and dance; the second group examines direct references between the Maize-Child and the music and dance expressions that are the subject of this article.

I begin by highlighting three aspects of the maize myth: the divine origin of Chicomexochitl; the agricultural cycle as a manifestation of the dispute between Chicomexochitl and his grandmother; and the sacrificial character of the mythic hero. These aspects are linked to the following characterizations of music and dance practices: they have a divine origin; they are, in large part, organized ac-

Fig. 13.1 A representation of Chicomexochitl made of cut paper found in the Xochicalli [lit. flower house, a type of altar] in the community of Acatepec, Hidalgo (Mexico), 2007 (Photograph by Lizette Alegre)

cording to the agricultural cycle; and they possess a sacrificial nature that musicians and dancers must observe.

Based on the myths reviewed, Chicomexochitl has both earthly as well as celestial origins. His mother is represented by a young virgin; the paternal figure is vague, at best associated with an archetypal class constituted mainly of birds. In many sources, the father is directly or indirectly represented by an ascending heavenly symbol, often a thrush. When the virgin is weaving or washing by the river, the thrush settles on a branch and drops a marble, stone, feather, or even a bit of excrement on the young woman's chest, abdomen, or mouth, resulting in her becoming pregnant.[2] Chicomexchitl is the product of this sacred conception, which shows the origin of the mythic hero by way of unifying the celestial and the earthly. The hero emerges from the fertile encounter of tectonic forces with astral seed. He is the firstborn fruit of a hierogamy [*hieros gamos*, lit. holy marriage] that gives men the basic sustenance for life.

The female figure is an important element within the development of the myth since she appears as the mother and grandmother. With the latter, Chicomexochitl begins a fight to the death, and from this battle the Maize-Child always emerges victorious. The aged woman embodies worn-out earth, representing the depletion of the fertilizing forces, while the young woman symbolizes the fertile land whose womb gives birth to the divine grain. In some versions of the myth, the Maize-Child kills the old woman by burning her, possibly an allusion to the agricultural system known as slash and burn. In this sense, the "burning" is the part that represents the whole. Its signifying force may derive from the empirical fact that ashes act as a natural fertilizer and from the observation of maize plants emerging from the ash-covered ground. Anuschka van 't Hooft and José Cerda Zepeda refer to this aspect as a central part of the myth: "The most common stories about the origin of maize deal with a prodigious child, whose evil grandmother puts him through several trials hoping for his death. The boy is able to defeat her, and from her body maize is born."[3]

The following passages validate this view. In the first, the grandmother's desire to kill the mythic hero is evident:

> When his grandmother arrived, [Chicomexochitl] became happy again: "Will we cut *ojites* again tomorrow?"[4] [She responds:] "So, you did not die? Now I will betray you to our ancestors who are on the other side of the sea, where they will surely kill you."[5]

The second refers to the birth of maize from the ashes of the old woman:

> The *Chikomexochitl* [seven flower] enclosed the little old woman and put her in the *temascal* [sweat lodge], afterward Chikomexochitl started to make a fire in the temascal and, later, the old woman finished burning up and she had become ashes; but Chikomexochitl took some of the ash and placed it in a *huaje* [seed pod of the lead tree], that was when Chikomexochitl was born, that was how Chikomexochitl made himself into maize.[6]

These passages suggest that the fight between Chicomexochitl and the grandmother is symbolic of the conflicting forces of the old, infertile earth and the grain that must germinate and emerge from the terrestrial core. In other words, it shows the antagonism between the destructive and regenerative forces of nature, whose struggle makes possible the periodic alternation of the unity of life—death gives way, in this case, to the agricultural cycle of maize. This cyclical character is expressed as much in the structure of music and dance genres associated with maize rituals, as in the moments of their performance.[7]

Indeed, a recurring character featured in the majority of Nahua music corresponds to a cyclical conception of time.[8] [This cyclicity] is linked to the construction of a particular perception of continuity in the unfolding of history, one that is socially interpreted as nonprogressive time, where chronological linearity is diluted. That is to say, it is a strategy to restore a sacred time and space in which gods and men establish a strong communicative connection.

The musical practices of the Nahua communities are also articulated within the annual cycle of patron saint celebrations, which tend to coincide with the agricultural cycle of maize. In this way, the diverse musical and dance expressions function as temporal and spatial markers of the various festive entities. Each celebration provides meaning to the distinct sound expressions that constitute it.

The sacrificial character of Chicomexochitl is observable in the mythic passages in which he gives his life for the humans: the mythic hero must die for the maize stalks to grow and become food for men. That is why in the Nahua communities of the Huasteca region we find expressions such as "the maize is our strength" and "the maize is our flesh" or "our blood."[9] In some versions of the myth, Chicomexochitl meets a deer and asks if it wants to be sacrificed for man, giving its flesh as food, which the animal refuses to do. Chicomexochitl then decides to sacrifice himself and prophesies to the deer that they will meet again at man's table:

> Afterward, he came across a deer next to a lake. The child asked it: "Do you want to take care of a family?" "I cannot take care of it. I don't want to," replied the deer. The child asked: "Who wants to suffer?" The deer said: "I do not want to suffer. I only want to suffer for myself." Then the boy replied: "I am going to suffer. I am going to feed the family."[10]

The sacrifice also appears in another version:

> And truly a bird did sing to the one they call *papán* [brown jay]. His father did not believe it and threw himself into the hills and became a deer. The child then said to his father: "We will meet again, and when we get home, the dogs and marksmen will chase you, and when we go to the altar of Our Mother, you will be the food and I will be the tortilla."[11]

Chicomexochitl's sacrificial character, revealed when he decided to die for men, has been interpreted by several [of my informants], including musicians and dancers, as the sacrifice taken up by Jesus Christ. For this reason, both divinities are conceived as one and the same: the Christ Child is an analogy for the Maize-Child. These beliefs are manifest in the *tlamanes* [giving thanks to the harvest] ceremony where a cross is constructed with three ears, called "elocruz" [*cruz de elote*], representing the image of the crucified Jesus Christ. Only boys are allowed to carry the ears that represent Chicomexochitl, pointing to the Maize-Child relationship.

Another example of this relationship can be observed during the Feast of Candlemas (Fiesta de la Candelaria) on February 2, which commemorates the child Jesus's presentation before the temple. On this date, the "blessing of the seeds" ceremony (*bendición de las sillas*) is performed in several communities of the Huasteca region. People carry ears of maize that represent the seed to the church to be blessed next to image of the Christ Child. Sometimes, an image is placed in a basket next to other seeds, [which] underscores the analogy between the Maize-Child and the Christ Child and the sacrificial character of Jesus Christ becoming a homology for that of Chicomexochitl.

Nahua believe that men should return the gifts given to them by a deity through sacrifices performed before and during corresponding rituals. Along with all-night music and dance performances, fasting prior to the celebration is thus among the sacrifices required to achieve ceremonial efficacy. Music and dance practices are conceived as sacrificial behavior and constitute the very expression of Nahua religiosity.

The above discussion makes clear that many of the musicians and dancers of the Nahua communities conceive of their activities as a sacrificial act and as a specific form of prayer. The sacrifice they make during the rituals bestows them with qualities that set them apart from the profane world and inscribe them within the universe of their divinities. Consequently, the community imparts onto them a sacred character, the same that is extended to the musical instruments and the dancers' costumes. Musicians and dancers acquire a symbolic power that is reflected as much in the ways they perceive the acquisition of music and dance knowledge as in their ability to cure certain diseases corresponding to native pathology.

## Chicomexochitl and His Links with Music and Dance

One aspect that should be underscored is Chicomexochitl's playful character. He appears as a mischievous and frolicsome boy with a conspicuously clever mind and as keeper of a special wisdom. On several occasions his tricks and games are associated with the act of playing a musical instrument or dancing. A dichotomy between work and play is apparent in the myths: while people work and toil in the fields, the boy spends his time playing music and dancing. However, when he chooses to perform his own chores in the field, he does these with great efficiency and speed, inventing new agricultural techniques or enlisting the help of a deity or wild animals. This provokes envy in the community's inhabitants, who are intent on destroying Chicomexochitl. However, each time that they claim to have killed him, he returns to life in the form of abundant ears of maize.

Music and dance appear in various myth versions directly linked to the Maize-Child. Such expressions are part of his activities and his character, as is shown here:

> Our young man continued his inclination toward music and dance. In short, the grandmother tried to trap him again. "Boy," Nanatzin said to him, "if you can't sit still, it's best that you do a job for me."[12]

It seems then that emphasis is placed not only on work but also on the importance of music and dance, sacralizing the playful character of the human being.

In the myths, Chicomexochitl is furthermore featured as the creator of musical instruments. Although reference is made to diverse musical artifacts used in the Huasteca region, the cane flute appears most often. Several musicians pointed out [to me] the similarity between the cane and the maize stalk, which apparently accounts for the presence of this aerophone in ceremonies pertaining to the first maize buds of the season. There also appear references to the sound characteristics of the flute, such as its piercing timbre, which provokes anger. Juan Hernández, from the community of Tepexititla, municipality of Huejutla Hidalgo, related the following: "When [Chicomexochitl] was a little older, he was always whistling; when he became a little older still he made a cane flute and he played all day long. Then a man said to the girl [Chicomexochitl's mother]: 'Why does your son cause a commotion? . . . We want to sleep and we can't sleep. Tell him to stop playing, to stop making a commotion.'"[13]

"Making a commotion" refers to a shrill and annoying sound—one of the reasons that the neighbors want to do away with Chicomexochitl. In the Huasteca region, some birds, among them the thrushes and the parrots, are considered "to make a commotion" or "to be labyrinthine," that is, "to have a shrill sound."[14] The similarity between the sounds produced on the flute and those made by the birds, in addition to the father-son parental relationship between the thrush and the Maize-Child, suggest that the shrill sound is part of the sonic characterization of the divine grain.

Chicomexochitl is also the inventor of music and this genesis connects him to the act of making musical instruments. Paulino Hernández Bautista and colleagues illustrate this thus: "Chicomexochitl was looking for a way to be able to play music and to dance: he finally found a cane and with it made a flute. He invented the flute and also music."[15]

Other musical instruments invented by the Maize-Child are the maracas and the tortoise shell, as illustrated in the following passages:

> "Well yes, grandmother, you sent me to see the *acamaya* [crawfish] and I went; I already met it, but I didn't let it eat me." Chicomexochitl made a fire and boiled the claw of the *acamaya* [freshwater crawfish]. Carefully, he pulled out the meat that was inside, ate it, and placed the animal's claw in the sun so it would dry. When the shell was dry, he placed little stones inside and used it as a shaker in order to continue his dances.[16]

> "With your adorned shell you are an attractive tortoise and should know that everyone will look at you and admire you; they will sing with you always; particularly when there are at celebrations, they will praise God with you singing and playing."

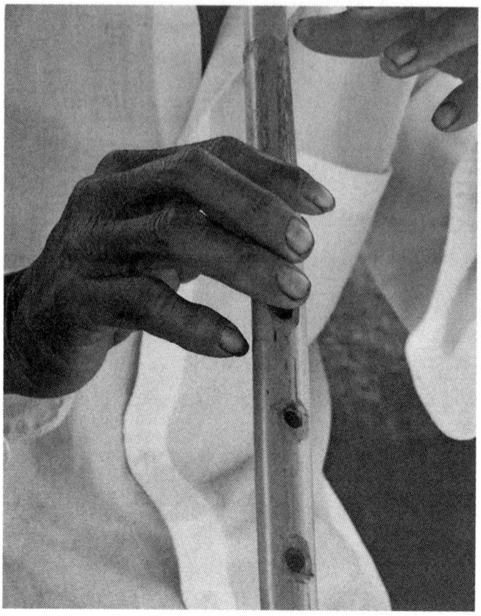

Fig. 13.2 Pedro Antonio Vargas holding a cane flute, Acatepec, Hidalgo (Mexico), 2007 (Photograph by Lizette Alegre)

> . . . For this reason, at the All Saints celebration they play, sing, and dance with the tortoise shell. So it was ordered by the boy Chicomexochitl.[17]

Another of Chicomexochitl's mythic deeds is that of being the creator of dance. As with music, this artistic expression is strongly connected to agricultural rituals. There are communities that refer to the "dance of the little maize," in which the dancing maize is represented by a boy and girl who execute corresponding steps and choreography to the beat of ritual music. Elsewhere, a "maize dance" performed in the fields is mentioned. In some Chicomexochitl ceremonies, all the participants dance in front of an altar.[18] Some inhabitants of the region consider the dancers' bodies to represent ears of maize.[19] Hernández Bautista and colleagues relate that "Our grandfathers say that the different dances were invented by that young man [Chicomexochitl]. He knew how to dance everything."[20]

The presence of music and dance in the Chicomexochitl myths speak of the ritual and symbolic importance of these artistic manifestations. For example, Enriqueta M. Olguín mentions that in a version [of a myth] compiled by Blas Castellón, "the father of the boy is a bird that talks and falls in love with the mother. He gets her pregnant by dancing."[21] This corresponds with what some of the Nahua communities' inhabitants observed about dancing being an important activity in the maize production process.

So, these eminently playful artistic expressions are transformed into inscribed and necessary activities within agricultural practice. That is to say, the music and

Fig. 13.3 Benito Martínez holding a tortoise shell, Tecacahuaco, Hidalgo (Mexico), 2007 (Photograph by Gonzalo Camacho Díaz)

dance practiced by the Maize-Child is linked to an emotional state characterized by "being happy" and "being content," as in this passage:

> It deals with getting into an oven in which firewood was placed beneath. The old woman made the boy get in. She covered any holes that there were, placed the firewood and lit it. After a long while, she deemed that Chicomexochitl was no longer alive and went to see but found him quite content; playing music and dancing to its rhythm.[22]

Some Huastecan musicians and shamans consider that the music and dance used in the agricultural ceremonies associated with maize are necessary so that the "little maize is happy." Also, they believe the objective of their practices is to produce happiness in the ritual participants, be they human or divine. The creation of a collective state of happiness can be interpreted as giving thanks to the Lords of the Earth for the food received. Felipe Hernández Chilocuil insists that the ritual maize songs, known as canaries (*canarios*), are festive and are played in order "to give happiness to the heart."

In the passages above we can observe that the origin of musical practices is directly associated with maize. Chicomexochitl offers this gift to men, who are expected to return it: "They will praise God by singing and playing music." In this sense, music and dance are part of the offerings made to the God of Maize, the Lord of the Hills, the Masters of the Earth. In some of the comments made by the Huastecan inhabitants, the adoration of maize is evident through the offerings, including the arts of sound and dance:

> In 1994, around the months of August and September, Chicomexochitl arrived. He was a few ears or grains of maize. He made himself present in different parts of our community. Everyone went to praise him wherever they came across him. They carried candles, *copalli* [incense resin], flowers, dance, and sometimes took a music band. . . . Some prayed, others sang. Different dances came and danced in front of Chicomexochitl. When they carried him to the designated place, they strewed flowers before him for the entire journey. Many people became emotional and cried.[23]

Collective memory also allows children to understand the relationship between maize and music and dance, as in the case of Magdalena Hernández Reyes from the community of Xocoyo Tuzantla in Tancahuitz de Santos, San Luis Potosí, who describes the following scene in a story she tells:

> Six years ago, a man was weeding his field around noon when he found a boy standing in the middle of it. The man spoke to him and said: "What are you doing there?" "Nothing," answered the boy, "I'm looking at the field that you have, it is very nice, there will be a good crop." The boy walked around without a shirt, his back freckled, and said to the man: "It would be good if you were to make a large meal, I will wait here, I want there to be some dancers that I know called 'the twigs,' two thousand of them. All the dancers that come to the party should bring guitars, violins, and *jaranas* [small guitar-like instruments]."[24]

As can be seen, this story is a retelling of the Chicomexochitl myth interwoven with the ritual life that Hernández Reyes surely has witnessed on many occasions. This narration demonstrates the self-replicating nature of myth and the effectiveness of cultural oral transmission.

## Conclusions

This article shows the relationships between mythology and music by demonstrating that through narrative forms we gain access to some aspects of musical knowledge. Myths are narrations consisting of a great deal of information distilled into symbols. They are communicative structures of a symbolic language used for cultural transmission, most notably in societies characterized by a considerable use of oral tradition. This text-code character allows for both a compression of knowledge and its organic articulation; set in a strong, emotional framework, it helps to capture the listeners' attention from the onset. In this way, webs of meaning (including affective meaning) are constructed between distinct cultural elements that mutually sustain each other, conforming to an efficient mnemonic system.

Conversely, music and dance practices help to demonstrate the content of the myths by reenacting parts of them within the rituals or, at least, by making reference to them by the very presence of these forms of artistic expressions. The instruments, the musical genres, the names of the songs, as well as the music and dance forms and structures, are vehicles for composite signifiers that, at the same time, reference the culture in question. By music and dance being present at any given event, and being part of a particular musical occasion with a specific intent, the two make an array of information available to the participants. Depending on cultural competence, particular strategies of reception, and new social contexts, the participants of the musical event will carry out a particular type of decoding which content will be integrated into other symbolic sets, which in turn will be interrelated to corresponding music and dance practices. This procedure makes it possible for such expressions to be part of a constant and unfinished process of articulation, interchange, and generation of signs.

Musical and dance activities are accompanied by a set of formulations that refer to these practices and that are placed in circulation as they become collectively accepted. Social censoring, through which these formulations must pass, turns into a procedure toward a determined consensus, constituting them finally into a public opinion regarding these same practices. In this way, "what is said" about music and dance becomes institutionalized, at the same time tracing certain vectors of meaning.

In the specific case presented here, we can conclude that "what is said" socially about music and dance, what is expressed about these forms in myths, like their tangible social practice in ritual events, are processes that authorize the construction of a narrative set, making possible a particular type of musical semiosis. This semiosis should be conceived as a dialectic between prior and new significations that allows for the remaking of earlier content and the shaping of new texts.

Finally, we can conclude that myth and other aspects of Nahua culture of the Huasteca region function as articulating agents of music and dance through the symbolic imagery of maize. Consequently, music and dance knowledge remains linked to other cultural aspects that, in turn, help to recall that knowledge. At the same time, the collective affect produced in large part by these artistic expressions redresses these other cultural aspects. The joining of music and dance practices with myth becomes a strategy of collective memory that courageously fights against forgetting.

## Notes

1. *Chicome* means "seven" and *xóchitl* "flower." It should be noted that seven is a mystical number closely connected to the Mesoamerican vision of the world. In fact, one of the ancient Mexican deities was Chicomecoatl (Seven Snakes), a representation of maize. In various contemporary Nahua communities belonging to the Huasteca region, seven corresponds to the four directions of the universe plus above, below, and center. This number also constitutes a semantic form, which refers to a sacred entity (Felipe Hernández Chilocuil, ethnographic interview, 1999).

2. Note the similarity of the Chicomexchitl creation myth to that of Huzilipochtli, who is also conceived as a result of a bough of feathers falling from the sky and impregnating the woman who will become his mother.

3. Anuschka van 't Hooft and José Cerda Zepeda, *Lo que relatan de antes: kuentos tének y nahuas de la Huasteca* (Pachuca, Hidalgo: Ediciones del Programa de Desarrollo Cultural de la Huasteca, 2003), 23.

4. An *ojite* is a tree used to make handles for tools, boxes, packing cases, and beehive frames. The seeds of the tree are high in protein, which is why the myth mentions looking for seeds in order to eat them.

5. Hilario Hernández, "Cuento de *Pilsintektsi*," in *Cuerpos de maíz: danzas agrícolas de la Huasteca*, ed. Amparo Sevilla (Mexico City: Consejo Nacional de Cultura y Arte, Ediciones del Programa de Desarrollo Cultural de la Huasteca, 2000), 182–89, p. 183.

6. Erasmo Montiel, "*Chikomexochitl*: siete flor, el maíz," in Sevilla, *Cuerpos de maíz*, 175–80, p. 176. The spelling here is as in the source.

7. See Alan R. Sandstrom, *Corn Is Our Blood: Culture and Ethnic Identity in a Contemporary Aztec Indian Village* (Norman: University of Oklahoma Press, 1991), 187.

8. For more information on this topic, see Gonzalo Camacho Díaz and Lizette Alegre González, "Corn Is Our Time" (paper presented at the 7th International Conference on Musical Signification, Imatra, Finland, 2001).

9. Among the Nahua of the Hausteca region, these phrases are frequently employed. Several authors have noted these notions. The anthropologist Alan Sandstrom (1991) used the phrase "corn is our blood" as the title of his book, which deals with this region's Nahua community.

10. Gonzalo Camacho Díaz and María Eugenia Jurado Barranco, "Xantolo: el retorno de los muertos" (thesis in ethnology, Escuela Nacional de Antropología e Historia, Mexico City, 1995), 268.

11. Hernández, "Cuento de *Pilsintektsi*," 186.

12. Paulino Hernández Bautista et al., "Chicomexochitl," in *Tradiciones, cuentos, ritos y creencias nahuas*, ed. José Barón Larios (Pachuca, Hidalgo: Gobierno del Estado de Hidalgo, Consejo Estatal para la Cultura y las Artes, 1994), 147–56, p. 153.

13. Juan Hernández quoted in Camacho Díaz and Jurado Barranco, "Xantolo," 267.

14. Editors' note: in the context of "hacer laberinto," *laberinto* (labyrinth) has multiple meanings. At one level it refers to what some would consider the incessant and annoying sound of birds (like the parrots mentioned in the text), but it is also a metaphor for creating chaos or confusion.

15. Hernández Bautista et al., "Chicomexochitl," 147.

16. Ibid., 151.

17. Ibid., 153.

18. Marco García Franco, "Fiesta del *Chikomexochitl*," in Sevilla, *Cuerpos de maíz*, 41–49, points out: "The shaman and his assistant take the maize while on the cob and place them in front of the altar until they make an enormous pile; then the women and the people who wish begin to dance around it" (47).

19. Sevilla, *Cuerpos de maíz*, includes several references to the dancers' bodies as ears of maize.

20. Hernández Bautista et al., "Chicomexochitl," 151.

21. Enriqueta M. Olguín, "Cómo nació Chicomexochitl," in *Huasteca II: prácticas agrícolas y medicina tradicional: arte y sociedad*, ed. Jesús Ruvalcaba and Graciela Alcalá (Mexico City: Centro de Investigaciones y Estudios Superiores en Antropología Social, Secretaria de Educación Pública, 1993), 115–39, p. 127.

22. Hernández Bautista et al., "Chicomexochitl," 155.

23. Agustín Martínez Medina, "Chicomexochitl," in Barón Larios, *Tradiciones, cuentos, ritos y creencias nahuas*, 157.

24. Hernández Chilocuil interview.

# 14

# Indigenous Music and Identity

## *Musical Spaces of Urban Mapuche Communities*

JORGE MARTÍNEZ ULLOA

> I do not know why *winkas* [non-Mapuche] insist on seeing us as we were 500 or 400 years ago: with spears and arrows, in shacks. . . . We do not see them with armor and horses and muskets.
>
> —Mapuche musician, Santiago de Chile

Indigenous music poses great theoretical problems. Is the concept of "music" used in Western and urban cultures similar or at least comparable to that used by preliterate ethnic groups? Does sound, the object of study of musicological inquiry, have the same conceptual and phenomenological characteristics in indigenous musicality? Given that perception is determined largely by one's own culture—through the descriptions of the "real"—can it be said that individuals from different cultures share the same environment, the same reality? Does indigenous music resonate with the outside observer as well? What do we perceive when we encounter a musicality that is "other"? Finally, what or who is indigenous?

From the very moment that humanity expressed itself, it established, willing or not, its inherent linguistic limitation: what is known is that which is named or can be named, and this determines [people's] precise relationship with reality. We come to know through descriptions, and it is language making that determines the nature of our relationship with reality and with each other.[1] However, the same language making entails, perhaps indirectly, the development of a certain sensibility that constantly destabilizes our own culture boundaries. Humans

---

Originally published by Jorge Martínez Ulloa, "La música indígena y la identidad: los espacios musicales de las comunidades de mapuche urbanos," *Revista Musical Chilena* 56, no. 198 (2002), 21–44. Available at www.revistamusicalchilena.uchile.cl. Translated by Emily Pinkerton and published with permission of *Revista Musical Chilena*.

know that they know, and this trait is possibly the foundation of their humanity; they relate to the world through descriptions, yet at the same time they are aware that these are descriptions, signs, or interpretations. With the manipulation of their language-making skills, of their knowledge, they are able to generate new descriptive spaces, new sensory realities, and ultimately innovate their cultural text in order to generate epitextual information to conjecture or glimpse new, yet unnamed, realities: the inaudible, the unforeseen.[2] Cultures, according to Jurij Lotman, possess a dual functionality: the creation of rules and a system for understanding and signifying (or naming) what is known as well as a system of probes to integrate new things.[3]

The possibility for translinguistic connections produces the dynamic quality of the signifying system. The analysis of epitextual data occurs within a communicative process[4] and permits the interaction between environment and the individual, the epigenesis of the cultural organism with his or her environment: what is Other can be something more than the negation of what is one's own.[5]

Another difficulty arises when the "otherness" of so-called "indigenous music" is only considered as a negation of one's self and one's cultural system. Doing so relegates that otherness to something that is deemed as the opposite of one's own musical nature, something that is exotic and strange.

A concern for the alleged purity of indigenous expressions leads criollo scholars to deny all value to expression they consider contaminated or compromised.[6] This view corresponds with an ideological value system that denies the Other the possibility of being something more than the mirror image of the scholars' own criollo culture; in short, it denies the possibility to be One [as opposed to Other] and therefore capable of change. This subaltern state of the Other also harkens back to ideological rigidity in which the Other's cultural and musical condition is considered static and self-referential.

Indigenous people and their music, obviously defined through this same ethnocentric lens, appear to the criollo as archaic sites of spiritual purity and simplicity,[7] related to magical and incomprehensible supernatural forces in a romantic naturalism that denies this Other music those qualities that the criollo find in their own music—that is, music's ability to be a part of and develop in response to current social and existential realities. In this regard, the epigraph of this essay is quite enlightening.

This article is based on several reflections about the current condition of Mapuche musicians in Santiago and the role of the concept of "Mapuche music" in the affirmation of their own identity and maintenance of their own culture—an affirmation that remains in tension and exchange with their own condition as economic and sociopolitical subalterns. For musicology, this borderline situation calls into question the type of hypothetical inquiries that have defined the discourse about music in Chilean criollo culture.

The place of Mapuche music, its transformations and epigenesis, its situation of alterity and subalternity in relation to criollo culture hegemony, and its communicative dynamism give reason for reflection on the roles of music in general as a space for social and cultural regeneration; much has been written on how culture and society shape the music that they produce, but less on how music reproduces the society that contains it.

The music of urban Mapuche, their ritual expressions, genres, and musical types offer an opportunity to reaffirm the permeability of all cultures, and the dynamic nature of musical-cultural production.

## The Mapuche: Migrants or Citizens?

Since the 1930s, a sustained and growing migratory flow has brought Mapuche from their communities of origin (in rural, southern Chile) to Santiago and other major urban centers. The General Population Census conducted in 1992 confirms that the majority of Chilean citizens who claim Mapuche ethnicity now live in urban conglomerations, especially the Santiago Metropolitan Region, the cities of Temuco (in the Ninth Region) and Valparaíso and Viña del Mar (in the Fifth Region).[8] This urbanization process has been accompanied by high levels of acculturation and loss of musical and cultural identity.[9]

Learning, using and maintaining language, customs, rituals, and traditional musical and cultural practices, as well as creating their own organizational structures, have characterized the Mapuche's struggle to maintain their cultural roots in large urban areas.[10] Evidently, this process of adaptation has prompted a reformulation of almost all of the aforementioned expressions. Language is learned not just as a first tongue and in the family setting, but rather in specialized schools or indigenous organizations or both. Similarly, traditional musical practices no longer adhere to the original communicative needs associated with rural areas. Organizational structures have acquired a territorial or neighborhood-based character that no longer exclusively relates to the organizational paradigms of *winka* [or *huinca*—i.e., criollo] culture—religious (Christian), political, or trade organizations—but rather Mapuche forms of organization like the *lofche*, clan-based expanded family councils.[11]

The situation for Mapuche culture in Chile has been very difficult. From the "Chilenization" to the military "pacification" campaigns,[12] the Chilean state has not recognized its multiethnic character, trying in various ways to negate and suppress Mapuche expressions. In the context of large urban centers, "the state of generalized prostration with which post-reservation Mapuche society struggles has brought as one of its principal consequences a supposed 'integration' into the Chilean state. This integration has taken place, however, in a context of inequality and latent unrest between both sectors."[13] Under such circumstances, some groups and individuals of Mapuche origin live a condition of identification by negation: contempt for their own origins and cultural heritage, which can lead to disintegration and acculturation, and, in extreme cases, to psychophysical disorders such as mental illnesses and alcoholism.[14] There are also tendencies toward social and cultural organizations that produce relatively exclusionary communities that invoke a static and reified notion of identity through the creation of [performing] groups devoted to "artistic promotion" [staged representations of traditional practices] where "Mapucheness" appears as a script to be enacted, as an evocation of a mythified rural existence and a negation of the possibility of living one's own culture in an urban setting.

The general frame of urban life places the Mapuche in a position of cultural subalternity, producing negative identifications and tendencies toward the creation of rigid, static cultural (folklorized) forms. Other urban Mapuche groups redefine their identity-defining cultural expressions, generating alternative semantic spaces within a criollo cultural context. This is the case with rogation ceremonies and ritual games such as the *nguillatun* or *palin*, which take place in the peripheral communities within cities, and have as their declared objective "to strengthen *newen*," that is, Mapuche power. In such spaces, criollo guests may redefine their own concepts of what they perceive as Mapuche, generating conditions for a more balanced relationship between both cultures. These transcultural spaces possess strong and distinctive musical and spiritual traits. Music as a vehicle for spirituality can foster positive identification in the Mapuche migrant, pride in his or her culture, and constitute a privileged space for the resolution of multiple social ills that marginality, negative identification, and subalternity have produced in urban Mapuche.

The main focus of this study is a redefinition of cultural and communicative forms within Mapuche musical spaces by means of a musicological model. This model addresses the motivating, signifying, and communicative aspects of urban Mapuche musicality, but it can also be applied to the musical life of any given culture.

From the moment that musical practices assume a role in the regeneration of culture, it becomes evident that there are strong tendencies toward particular configurations of what is defined as music. A study of the relationships between context (considered to be a signifying system, site of general competencies of music making) and text (considered to be the abstract model and nexus of these same competencies that is then realized in the communicative process) allows us to situate the role of innovation and tradition in music, individual creation and collective practice, continuity and change. Obviously, this study cannot disregard the motivations behind and social roles ascribed to the music-making act. Human groups create signifying systems, they generate communicative processes, in order to reproduce the conditions that make the existence of their own culture as such possible as well as the identification of individuals that recognize themselves within it. This space is defined as the pre-text: an understanding that motivations and social functions of musical activity predetermine the creation of musical texts, a group's own musical context. The dynamic relationship between pre-text, text, and context point to the role that the last plays as a frame for general competencies that shapes the social motivations behind music making: what is known determines in great measure what is considered necessary to do.

This theoretical framework lets us better understand the role of transformations and redefinitions within the musical expressions of urban Mapuche, as well as the roles of musical spaces in the maintenance of positive or negative identifying bonds. Until now, musicological studies—with the notable exception of writings in the anthropology of music[15]—considered linguistic elements separately from motivational aspects. This musicological practice has brought with it a certain isolation of the discipline within the social and human sciences because its consequence has been the undervaluing of music making as a space of cultural, and thus social, regeneration. Without falling into mechanical determinism or nonscientific universalism, one can assume that there are links between the needs of cultural regeneration and music making. These relationships, given the nonverbal characteristics of musical communication and the specific logics of music making, are not readily apparent or explicitly outlined. Nonetheless, no one can deny the central role of music in the self-identification of individuals and groups with their own culture. In order for a study of music to reveal such hidden relationships, it is necessary to move beyond the "fetish for notes," scores, or transcriptions as the only codes, and instead to think of musical text as an intersection of sonic and extra-sonic codes. If musical text is considered in this way, then context appears as the general framework of musical competencies, that is, as a historic or diachronic summation of texts, of intersections of codes. Context also presents itself as an intersection of non-situational, general codes. The relationship between context and text corresponds to the relationship between the signifying system and the communicative process of music making in each culture.

The texts of Mapuche musicality are not limited to sounds as variations of frequencies and tempos, but instead contain specific spatial and timbral dimensions as well as temporal contraction-dilation that make the transcription of such texts particularly complex. Proxemics, kinesics, and the type of anthropology conducted by Gregory Bateson are valid disciplinary instruments for understanding the polysemiotic nature of musical spaces.[16] Such spaces generate musical texts as multi-coded competencies, as intersections of multiple situational codes so that the musical context appears as the general framework for said intersections. Anthropology allows us to optimally grasp the musical pre-text; that is, the motivations and social functions behind the act of music making. The processes of identification, the modes of realizing musical expression, and semiotics allow us to approach the relationship between text and context as processes of signification and reproduction of competencies: as spaces of cultural regeneration.

Let me then introduce a tripartite semiotic model comprising of the three dimensions of pre-text, context, and text (respectively defined as the space spanned by the roles of and social motivations behind the act of music making, the signifying system of music making, and the communicative process itself). This model allows for the framing of collective and individual creation, of the role of tradition and innovation, of the presence of (paraconscious) social competencies for the decoding of music, and finally, of the role of identity and transcultural communication in a process of continuity and change.

Musicology's sonic fetishism has thus far impeded a constructive dialogue with other disciplines. As musicologists all know, it is difficult for academics from other disciplines to participate in musicology conferences; and when they do, their contributions are quickly called into question because of their supposed musical illiteracy. Conversely, the contributions of musicology are infrequently cited in the social sciences, to the point that it is commonly believed that musicians and musicologists do not possess discourses about society or culture. Following the proposed model, musicology can generate discourse about society and its cultural regeneration from the vantage point of music. If sound is a sign and as such the product of the same signifying systemic relationships that characterize entire cultural apparatuses, it is evident that an interdisciplinary space between musicology and other disciplines should be based on the notion of the nature of sound as sign.

## Pre-text, Text, and Context of the Musical Realm

The social existence of music is only guaranteed if, in the decodification of its message, one can verify the existence of a signifying system that encompasses both producers and receivers of the musical message. They must possess what Gino Stefani calls competencies, a series of capacities, aptitudes, and social forms of knowledge about making music.[17] These competencies, organized into a signifying system, are what we define here as context.

So then, of what context do we speak? Some argue that context is simply synonymous with that which is nonmusical or non-sonic. Musical context has been defined in numerous ways, from strictly musicological ones to ethnomusicological or anthropological ones. Among the former definitions, context appears only as a weak backdrop to the ineffable action of musicians and spectators.[18] In the latter, ever larger portions of context are incorporated until musical specifics are almost dissolved into the generality of cultural practices.[19] The first definition of context operates within a culture of written texts. On the other hand, the second way of considering context has been confined to preliterate areas or to oral traditions, where Western or criollo concepts of music may be called into question by culture bearers themselves.

Both definitions, however, are based on the idea of music making as embodied in sound but without specifying or delving deeply into the cultural dimensions of sound and lacking an awareness that what is defined as a sound is in reality a sign. A feature of the sign is its [ability] "to stand in place of something else." Therefore, a sign is a representation of reality (in this case acoustic) and not reality itself. In short, all signs—in order to have meaning—have a systemic relationship with the entire collection of signs of a culture, and culture reproduces itself precisely through this systemic relationship. By not defining music making as composed of signs, as possible representations of reality, one assumes that the very definition of sound seems "natural." If sound is equated with reality itself, one's understanding of context or text, however broad or narrow, is arbitrary: the definition of music making rests on the ideological position that there is only one possible concept of sound, because sound is supposedly a natural phenomenon.

Context, as it has been defined by musicology, does not have conceptual boundaries; it has neither a form nor a specific nature; and it is not clear whether it is applied to ideas or physical or systemic elements. All that musicologists seem to agree on is that context begins right where the "music itself" ends.[20]

Context is a general signifying system. It is made neither of things nor fixed environmental or physical data, but rather of signs and the relationships that they generate between one another. These signs can be musical semantics, musical grammars, theories, competencies, behaviors, aptitudes, perceptive strategies, and so on, that are the [musical] heritage of an entire community. That is, community in the sense of a group that communicates with itself.

The presence of this signifying system is realized within a communicative process. This process is also comprised of signs that belong to temporary and unique music-making occasions, and that do not constitute common heritage of an entire community.[21] The result of this communicative process is the musical event defined as a communicative space. In this space, text is defined as the aggregate of innovations made to the practices and building elements of the context.

If context is general, text is specific. Both operate as models that generate concrete occurrences: in the case of context, the concrete occurrence is the musical event as a social phenomenon; in the case of text, the musical event is the individual or unique occurrence.

Both text and context exist only to the extent that society finds strong motivation to reproduce itself through certain communicative processes. The regeneration of society is made through the reproduction of the culture that explains it, and the reproduction of culture through the generation of signs. Music exists beyond the capacity of the observer's ability to perceive music as a social occurrence. Thus, inasmuch as music is a space for the cultural reproduction of a society, it is a space for the reproduction of society itself. Music fulfills a series of motivations and roles in the reproduction of social mechanisms. In order to recognize this function of music, it is necessary to conceive of it as composed of signs, some of which will be acoustic in nature and others not. The combination of the social motivations and roles ascribed to music making is what this theoretical model defines as the pre-text.

Ultimately, pre-text determines the existence of context and text. The three poles of the model are related in dialectic fashion, since, although a general sense of pre-text exists a priori, it is the capacity of a culture to generate certain texts and contexts that condition the social motivations and roles of the pre-text: that which we can conceive informs what we desire.

Although the context generates the text as a negation of itself, the text—or the historical summation of texts—generates the context: the diachronic stabilization of a textual practice constitutes the raw material for context. The modalities of making music in any society inform the way in which music is reproduced and even the societal expectations regards to music. It is evident, nonetheless, that the principal and ultimately determining element will be given neither by improbable textual innovations nor by the contextual system (product of the former), but rather by the motivations and roles of cultural and social reproduction, that is, the pre-text.

By starting with the study of pre-text, musicology can generate an interdisciplinary space, a discourse about society from the specific point of view of music. If music making in a society is considered to be made up of signs, it will then be possible to determine, for example, how extramusical systems of signs are able to exert an influence on systems of signs that are strictly musical. This capacity of systems of signs in different signifying dimensions to act in analogous fashion is one of the ways through which new organizations of symbolic systems are created. This is the case with the compositional procedures of Western classical music. This analogous capacity of systems has been analyzed in the sphere of general semiotics by Charles Peirce.[22] What could be conceived as the invasion of the musical field by symbolic systems, procedures, outlines, and extramusical organizations explains how a society is generated—what forces act within society and are present in the musical event, conceived no longer as a series of organized sounds, but rather as a semiotic space that relates texts, contexts, and pre-texts associated with music making. It is, for example, no accident that the Cartesian precision of the Baroque corresponds to a tendency in music of that time to fix in very precise fashion what had so far been left to interpretive tradition: clarity and contours defined in philosophy as much as in music. The tyranny of numbers and mathematic rationality accompanied the European development of the banking system and of the simple mercantile economy and the rise of a particular good: money that served as a general signifier, so to speak, of the process of the exchange of goods. This environment informed the development of the figure of the composer as demiurge of musical meaning, separating him or her from having a specific instrumental role. Typically, the musical result of this process was the generation of macrostructures like those of a Bach or a Vivaldi, to give two examples.

Other cases of interconnections between generative sociocultural systems and music could be cited.[23] However, we should be wary of easy analogies. The processes are very intricate, and only through in-depth study of a concrete case study is it possible to unravel the complex signifying web of music making within a society. In order to illustrate the application of the semiotic model outlined here, I describe the reproduction of the rooting mechanisms of traditional music and the generation of a positive identity among Mapuche residing in urban areas, as well as the transcultural communicative spaces that these individuals generate by reproducing the conditions of their own identity consciousness within a *winka* (non-Mapuche) signifying system.

## The Musical Realm in Urban Mapuche Groups

The new reality lived by urban Mapuche obliges them to share a multicultural environment; more precisely, it situates them as a social group inscribed within a system of criollo (*winka*) cultural domination. In rural settings, although there are actually no communities so isolated as to be considered allegedly pure or completely isolated, Mapuche culture works preferentially as an overall social system: a subsistence economy based on agriculture and horticulture, a language (Mapudungun) learned within the family, and the endurance of beliefs, rites, and customs, forming a unified signifying system.[24] The production of texts follows innovation and variation within the norm. Since Mapuche sociocultural reproduction develops in a relatively homogeneous environment, the rural setting of Mapuche culture is characterized by a unified context and a text composed of variations within the norm, and the pre-text obeys social motivations and functions within a relatively slow process of change. These characteristics establish a homogeneous musical space with a strong presence of tradition: individual conflicts and specific social tensions are channeled and efficiently resolved through traditional mechanisms of belonging and identification. Correspondingly, there is a relatively stable linguistic and musical development; the level of different individual competencies is quite similar and only certain traditional figures with very defined roles stand out, such as the *longco*, *ngenpin* (owner of the word), and the *machi* (shaman).

Mapuche in urban settings are confronted with distinct pre-texts and contexts from which to forge their identity. Their communicative capacity depends on their subordinate position, caused by the negation that hegemonic cultural forms exercise [on Mapuche culture].[25]

In order for them to survive as Mapuche, the creation of an own constitutive space must pass through a process of acceptance by dominant institutions and of accommodation to criollo contextual norms. It must also go through a process of engaging with the temptation of redefining both Mapuche and hegemonic cultural forms, of generating new Mapuche musical-cultural texts that simultaneously feature a strong dose of innovation and a concern with tradition. This latter feature forms the basis for the definition of a symbolic and communicative Mapuche space inscribed within the criollo space.

Hence, the definition of a communicative Mapuche space within the criollo (*winka*) context is a requirement for the very survival of organized Mapuche groups. As specialized studies have rightly indicated, alcoholism and mental and somatic illnesses that affect a great portion of the (especially male) urban Mapuche population are the result of the negation that Mapuche inflict on themselves, on their culture, and on their identity.[26]

The members of the urban Mapuche community not only reinforce the role of the individual within the community, as in the case of ceremonies in rural areas, but also affirm their group identity as a unique and indivisible whole in opposition to the criollo environment surrounding them. The cultural homogeneity developed by ritual forms does not stem from internal dynamics within the community, as is the case in rural areas, but out of necessity to establish an identity through exclusivity and exclusion.[27]

We can then verify one of the first elements that characterize the urban Mapuche cultural pre-text: the overcoming of the idea of community—as the sum of the common elements between different individuals—in order to affirm the concept of identity, defined in this restricted sense as group of identical individuals in relation to nonidentical third parties, in this case, non-Mapuche. Identity, understood in this way, generates a closed and self-referential space in reference to the society within which it is contained. It is exclusionary, "what distinguishes us from . . ." This mode of identification seems to be the only possibility for subaltern cultural groups. In order to carve out a space for their own sociocultural articulation, it is necessary to delimit very precisely the elements of the signifying system (the context) that will be part of it as well as the individuals who will come together through this communicative action of the exchange of signs (the text) to reproduce their own culture.

Paradoxically, the reason for an identity affirmation based on exclusion is a concern with cultural dilution and the loss of identifying traits. This form of identification represents a new form of dependence in relation to the hegemonic culture; in defining themselves in exclusive terms, all individuals of the group are obliged to this one paradigm of what it means to be Mapuche. A sort of reified Mapuche, as it were, is produced, and the diversity necessary for the reproduction of culture is lost. Traditional culture is no longer lived, but rather is represented. Having lost the flexibility inherent to all communicative processes, the anchoring mechanisms of traditional identity formation become ossified.

Communication is the affirmation of variable identity: the sum of traits common to different individuals, the space spanned by the intersection of differences. It is the infinite process of exchange of difference. Culture, in general terms, can only be reproduced provided that it manifests itself through this communicative process. A culture that finds itself to be the heir of a closed, self-referential group due to the perpetuation of rigid paradigms in which communicative action is delimited loses its constitutive capacity. Instead of expression itself through cultural regeneration, it would do so through the act of cultural representation. This act of representation assumes the role of a monosemic sign of exclusivity, in this case a fixed notion of what it means to be Mapuche. This path generates new forms of dependence and cultural subordination, because it is a sign of the reification of a subaltern reality and, at the same time, of regenerative impotence.

Not all urban groups, however, define their identity in such a radically exclusive way. In some of them, the desire to engage with the *winka* surroundings is stronger. Based on this interest, they develop new, more open spaces of ritual and cultural reproduction, allowing non-Mapuche participants some participation by organizing new spaces for communicative exchange. Urban groups oscillate between these two strategies: (1) the embrace of a concept of identity as a form of exclusion within a rigid paradigm; and (2) the generation of redefined spaces based on the concept of communicative identity that allow for the participation and creation of specific roles for non-Mapuche. The first leads to new forms of dependence and cultural subordination; the second makes possible the reproduction of the traditional Mapuche culture, not in a static form but through the dialectic maintenance of its signifying anchors: not for the exhibition of particular signs of a reified Mapuche identity but as a mode of doing, speaking, and feeling Mapuche.

The first case is demonstrated through the creation of Mapuche folkloric groups. The folklorization or staging of Mapuche rituality adheres to gestures and signs rigorously fixed in conformity to a traditionality more stated than real. The second case is seen in the celebration of rites and ceremonies of traditional Mapuche culture in urban spaces—a practice that constitutes the first rupture in relation to the so-called canonical tradition—with the integral participation of non-Mapuche guests and with the creation of a space and communicative process that does not depend on a superficial sense of being Mapuche. In this dichotomy between the redefinition and adaptation of ritual forms and the staging of rites as forms of spectacle, the pre-text of Mapuche musicality in urban settings comes into play. This pre-text ultimately determines the context and the text of the Mapuche musical expressions in urban areas.

The context as a signifying system is composed of all those competencies, in this case musical, that allow a Mapuche to recognize a specific expression as such: a *choyke purrun* [rhea (ñandú) dance], a *trile purrun* [blackbird dance], and a *tayil* [sacred song] as varieties of the types *choyke purrun*, *trile purrun*, and *tayil*, respectively. It is evident that the specific *choyke purrun* the [Mapuche] observer witnesses is not the same as a general template of the dance: it possesses distinctive tangible traits specific to the occasion. Just as it is possible to speak of the *choyke purrun* as an ensemble of distinctive but generalizable traits, it is possible for the observer to put into play a whole series of strategies, theories, grammars, semantics, behaviors, and so on that recognize that specific *choyke purrun* as part of a type. To this end, and without the necessity to detail the linguistic and structural elements of the *choyke purrun* type,[28] Mapuche observers are fully conscious of their traditional culture and, hence, know when a *choyke purrun* is out of context, for example, or when this specific musical occurrence is incapable to conform to what traditionally would define a *choyke purrun*.

In a relatively isolated rural Mapuche community, [on the other hand,] contact with foreign people and cultures is quite sporadic. The capacity to signify as adequate a certain musical event is quite homogeneous and its dynamism is fundamentally endogenous. The variants of distinctive traits and, thus, of the competencies that facilitate their identification and decodification as cultural signs can be considered micro-variations. The context presents itself as a very homogeneous signifying system, of relatively slow development, with micro-variations present. For example, the acceptance of the accordion or the bugle in the *nguillatun* [rogation ceremony] has been a relatively slow process, with a limited geographic dispersion and over an extended time span. It is common to find in the same geographic area communities, even conservative ones, that make use of these innovations; the same thing occurs with the *trutruka* [long cane trumpet] made of plastic tubes or of copper pipes, coiled up instead of straight like the traditional instruments. The process of acquisition and establishment of innovations is quite slow and gradual, both in time and in space.

In urban groups, instances of contact with exogenous culture elements are numerous, enough so as to fear cultural dilution and loss of identity. As a result, imitation of the rural context, especially its more stable aspects, is common. The rural context is taken as a model of Mapuche identity, with distinctive traits of rural communities distant in time and space being deemed paradigmatic. The relative isolation of rural communities is taken as a legitimizing factor; from this isolation derives the perception—false and ideological—that the only way to preserve the characteristics of being Mapuche rests in preserving without variation the distinctive traits of the original musical events. This brings about a sort of immobility when it comes to the notion of variation.

To construct Mapuche musicality, urban groups maintain these traits as invariant, as a kind of script or libretto. This tendency to establish very precise traits generates a practice that is completely foreign to rural tradition, which relies on traditional mechanisms of cultural reproduction and stabilization and, thus, is fundamentally consensual and does not need legitimizing scripts. The practice of contextual rigidity in the urban area is symmetrical with a conception of one's own identity as exclusive; the boundaries of the Mapuche as a group are fixed from within, and the group is seen by its participants as a single individual rather than a group of individuals. Urban Mapuche are not aware that in rural contexts all micro-variation is structural variation. However, it is not the magnitude of the variation that defines its importance in the determination of context, but rather its function and its systematic importance.

The rigidity of context in these urban groups causes texts associated with innovation to be perceived as substantial threats to the identity and survival of the group. For this reason, the main tendency is to promote folkloric groups that establish their legitimacy through accurate or so-called authentic representations of traditional cultural elements. Paradoxically, this rigidity in the understanding of the differences between rural and urban context provokes the opposite effect: the *choyke purrun* as represented by the folkloric group on stage lacks its original [ritual] function; instead, it has become a dance spectacle. Reproducing the hermetic and unpremeditated nature of the rural setting in an urban environment ignores the true importance that the new context possesses. Treating the group as an individual, a closed and self-referential being instead of a whole of different individuals, leads to a new form of subordination. Indeed, Mapuche groups are rapidly consumed by urban audiovisual culture as a superficial expression of the exotic.

Some urban groups have come to understand that in an urban area contact cannot be avoided and that it is not a characteristic of Mapuche culture to be closed, hermetic, or self-referential. Rather, affirming Mapucheness consists in accepting a diversity of urban expressions in relation to the rural ones, and in considering the text of "the urban" as a variation of the norm. It is more important to maintain the functionality of these rites and ceremonies than their external and superficial aspects.

When the *palin* [ritual game] is played in Cerro Navia [urban area in the Santiago de Chile metropolitan region], various distinctive traits of this rite are altered. The declared motivation of the ritual continues to be substantially the same: to bestow strength on the male members of the group. The participation of non-Mapuche in the ritual is perceived as a subsequent reinforcement of its meaning; it is precisely these participants, in their traditional status as guests (*metrem*), who testify to the renewed power of the Mapuche. Beyond the use and presence of profoundly innovative distinctive traits, the contextual information is rightly reinforced through the affirmation of the traditional functionality of the ritual: the acquisition of blue force and its display.

In the *palin* instruments made of plastic and *kultrunes* [ceremonial drums] made of metal pots (washing pans) are used without causing the game to cease being a space for traditional cultural reproduction. Beyond the perpetuation of concrete elements, what remains important is the conservation of signs, of symbolic functionalities, because it is through these that culture is reproduced, and not through the maintenance of distinctive traits that have become decontextualized. If one is able to recognize that the pre-text of cultural reproduction is ensured by the form of speaking, doing, and feeling Mapuche, the new materials of these instruments is of little importance.

Yet, if the original traditional details are maintained in a context that is not original, the communicative process is falsified. Loyalty to distinctive (superficial and not essential) traits, the neglect of pre-textual function, becomes a negation of the Mapuche signifying context and places this representation within the frame of a *winka* spectacle and its signifying context. Culture is lived, not represented.

[For example,] José Ancán, who made videos with and about urban Mapuche youth, takes up in conscious and articulate fashion the oral quality of Mapuche cultural transmission.[29] The videos are organized as the means toward a new urban Mapuche orality. It is no coincidence that these videos, along with others created by participants in Mapuche student groups, are not articulated in the form of a documentary but rather are similar to the music video. The social value of *nutram*, of the tradition preserved orally by the elders, reemerges in a new form of urban orality with a power that does not possess corresponding criollo expressions. The videos [directed by Ancán] are more faithful to the Mapuche signifying context—to the doing, feeling, and speaking as a Mapuche—than any expression or representation that is evocative in nature.

Text, as an innovation of context, is not limited to linguistic information or sounds. Although the sounds of the folkloric group can be discerned as Mapuche, the absence of Mapuche functionality situates them as texts within a Western context: the representation of the exotic in the era of world music. A participant in a folkloric group that dresses as "Mapuche" for a stage performance fulfills a function of actor as defined within the context of Western culture. Conversely, when the same individual plays in a *palin* dressed in his everyday clothes, he is articulating a Mapuche text in a Mapuche signifying context. If the role of the observer is that which permits the distinction between ritual and spectacle, the actor in the Mapuche folkloric group represents Mapuche identity in accordance to Western blueprints; he knows he is being observed and he fulfills, consciously or not, the signifying formalities of the Western context, in a functionality that is theatrical in nature. In the *palin* of Cerro Navia, the non-Mapuche *metrem* are integrated into the Mapuche signifying context, for the reproduction of traditional culture takes place within the magical-ritual space of the *palin* and not on stage.

## Mapuche *Palin*

A *palin* consists of the confrontation of two groups of players, who—through the use of sticks with a curved end (*weñu*)—try to make a small leather ball (*pali*) pass across the end of the rival teams territory (*tripalwe*). The team that succeeds in doing so more than four times in a row is the winner. The *palin* is preceded by an invitation that the host team offers to the rival through a rogation ritual in which both teams participate. The rogations are made up of songs (*palin-ül*) performed in the moments prior to the game, during which the players greet each other by crossing their sticks above their heads (*afafan*). Following that, the players and musicians face off and the game itself begins. After the game, the *palin* continues with the ritual greeting that the host community offers to its guests (*metrem*) and with a final meal in which meat and drink are consumed.[30]

### THE CONTEXT OF THE URBAN *PALIN*

The context of the *palin* gives us, roughly speaking, the conditions in relation to which Mapuche will consider an event (or a series of events) to be a *palin*. A *palin* is composed of sounds and special actions that might be defined as music, present before and after what could be considered a game. [According to an outsider's description of the event,] "An entire tribe gathers in a large field; there they dance and make all their musical instruments sound: flutes, drums, *trutrukas*. Then, each picks his rival for the *palin*; the pairs make their bets and begin the fight right away."[31]

The first event that precedes the *palin* itself, and a common trait in these events, is the invitation. In the case of the urban *palin*, not only a single community, but also a number of people who are fairly representative of other groups and communities living in the metropolitan area are invited. A second element is the rogation, officiated by a *ngenpin* [lit. owner of the word, a male political and religious leader] or a *machi* [a shaman and religious leader, usually an older woman]. It consists of summoning spiritual energy or "blue force" represented by Kalfulikan [leader of the first Mapuche rebellion against Spain in 1553], who also represents the *kuyfi palife* [*palin* player of ancient times], bearer of the ancestors' force. Said force should move from the players of the host team (*palifes*) toward their invited adversaries, the *konas* [in this setting, non-Mapuche participants]. The formal structures of the songs, whether they take place in the rogations, or during the players' ceremonial greeting, are typical of all Mapuche music: repetition of a single musical phrase that is broken down into overlapping sections with a descending melodic contour eventually ending with an ending "tonic" pitch. The most frequently used intervals are those of a tritonic scale, with their origin in the natural harmonics produced by the *trutruka*. The rhythmic cells are superimpositions of binary meters on ternary [2:3], generating polyrhythm. The literary texts can be improvised, adding commentaries of reflections on a traditional theme. The use of space and of time is typical of other Mapuche contexts: East–West orientation and circular, counterclockwise motion. Specific spaces are designated for the game, for the libations with *mudai* [fermented grain beverage], for the rogation, and for the final meal. There are shelters located to one side of the field for the official guests (*metrem*). From a chronological perspective, the procedures also follow a sequence: formal invitation (according to lineage relationships), rogation, *afafan*, game, final greeting, collective meal, and dances.

### THE TEXT IN URBAN *PALIN*

This is a provisional articulation, which means that in addition to responding to the majority of the rules just described (contextual), every time a *palin* is held, new actions are established, some of which will endure. The establishment in time of certain specific customs will correspond to the pre-textual necessities, to the motivations of each community and group for having a *palin*. In the case of the urban *palin* in the communities of Santiago de Chile, the text is made up of linguistic elements—extracted from their context—and innovations. Among the latter, nontraditional invitations are common and extensive and may even include flyers; the daytime rogations (not at night as in the rural setting) are conducted by a self-appointed *machi*.[32] The teams are selected on-site, according to geographic criteria rather than lineage. The *afafan* is realized within each team and not between the two rival teams. The sonic element is constituted by two clearly defined moments: the songs and the game, with two groups of musicians performing and accompaniment uninterrupted by the events.

The text of the *palin*, in addition to being comprised of a group of topological and chronological signifying traits of syntactic Mapuche elements, is also composed of an uninterrupted and variable sonic flow in response to the variations of the game itself, whose organizing parameters seem to be related to changes in sonic and metric density. All of this concurs with what Carol Robertson has described as *chempralitun*, "the tone of growth or change," that is, a "tonic" pitch whose appearance is determined by the shift from one phase of the game to another, in analogy to the shift between temporal states present in the *tayil*.[33] The *chempralitun* in this case would be given by the fundamental of one of the *trutrukas* present.

### THE PRE-TEXT OF *PALIN*

If the pre-text is defined as the combination of the communicative motivations and functions that determine the very act of music making, of communicating by means of music, the pre-text of the *palin* will be constituted by the reasons that motivate the participants to hold a *palin*. The *palin* is organized as a magical setting in which a (culturally homogeneous) group summons mythic forces and characters in order to equip itself with the elements of those evoked forces. In the rogation that precedes the game, a *konkününguillatun* [religious ceremony] is conducted. In it, a blue stone [physical representation of the blue force being summoned] holds a central place and the evocation of the [blue] force of the *kuyfi palifes*. The *palin* is a place of magical sacrifice for obtaining power and good fortune. Historically, it is the gathering place for deciding and coordinating war plans or the fate of prisoners; important examples of this are cited by chroniclers and historians.[34] In the case of the urban *palin* of Santiago de Chile, the main goal is to give strength and self-assuredness to the men of the Mapuche Council of Cerro Navia.

When the players greet one another by striking their uplifted sticks, they are representing the aspect of the force as a product of the collective. This form is also seen in occasions of shamanic curing and is realized, in this case, by the assistants or guardian spirits of the *machi*.

Collective strength is the condition necessary to generate a sense of positive identity. It takes the entire community to assume the function of establishing cultural bonds between migrants and to generate a cultural-traditional practice of positive identification: pride in being Mapuche and the strength that comes from feeling that one is a brother (*peñi*). In reproducing the conditions of mythic and cultural-traditional identification of the group, the ritual symbolically establishes and reproduces the role of each individual in the community. *Palin* as a ritual represents the place of traditional power, of the blue force, of the power of the ancient players. It represents the identification of each participant with this power; it is the place of communal identification with the collective power, represented by the greeting. In the urban space, it also represents a way of making known to non-Mapuche the renewed power of the Mapuche; it is the occupation of a physical and symbolic space with the attributes of Mapuche culture, and it therefore constitutes a way of representing "the Mapuche" to *winkas*. In order to assume this role of representation, the traditional form of the ritual must be redefined so that the identifying behaviors constitute a process not merely of individual identification with the community, but rather of the entire community in relation to other groups that live in the city. It is of interest that those groups, and especially the criollos (*winka*), are able to recognize the power of the community, of "the Mapuche"; that they recognize and value each individual Mapuche as part of a complex cultural world; that they respect and fear their collective power. It is important moreover that the same identifying traits be included and recognized as traits of Mapucheness for non-Mapuche in all places where this ritual may occur. The urban *palin* operates as a ritual for those who take part (*el peñi*) and at the same time as a spectacle,[35] or better yet, as a demonstration for the criollos who attend as spectators and can confirm the existence of "the Mapuche." This semiotic duplicity of the urban *palin*, as ritual and as demonstration, represents the most characteristic trait of the pre-text.

To summarize, the pre-text of the *palin* consists of all those communicative functions that allow each urban Mapuche to speak, do, and feel as a Mapuche. The pre-text is speaking, doing, and feeling Mapuche power. This pre-text can be described via an outline of the implicit communicative functions. Inspired in the linguistic functions of Roman Jakobson,[36] the pre-text can be represented by the following model:

1) *Palin* as a "Mapuche way of speaking":
   - Informative function: The neighborhood is made acquainted with the existence of a strong Mapuche community because it is respectful of its tradition.
   - Identifying function: The Mapuche as individuals can enjoy traditional power—that is, a positive identity—as members of this community.
   - Discursive function: It is not enough to acknowledge that there is strength in the community. In order to be believable and authentic, it must be done so in "Mapuche style," that is, with the ritual of the blue force: the *palin*.
2) *Palin* as a "Mapuche way of doing":
   - Mediating function of actions: Music in *palin* underscores the roles of power and continuity: power like the warlike blowing of the *pifilka* [wooden flute]; continuity like the uninterrupted pulse of the *kultrun* and *wada* [shakers], idiophones that control the elemental forces.[37]
   - Conative function: This function produces results, orders, and commands. Evocation of the blue force in songs, the magic mediation of

the control of evoked forces, through the instruments, the demonstration of the existence of these forces in the game itself.

3) *Palin* as a "Mapuche way of feeling":
   - Communing function: In [Mapuche], the name for the "Mapuche Council of Cerro Navia in Santiago" translates to "united under a single thought" (*estar unidos por un solo pensamiento*). In the *palin* this mythical union is enacted and represented.
   - Regulating function of inner states: The Mapuche migrant feels Mapuche upon acting Mapuche, and upon taking on Mapuche expressivity in a precise signifying context.

## Conclusions

This article focuses on several reflections about the current condition of Mapuche musicians in Santiago de Chile and the role played by what they define as Mapuche music in the affirmation and reproduction of their own identity, in tension and in exchange with a situation of economic and sociopolitical subalternity. For any musicologist, this case puts to the test hypothetical inquiries that have defined discourses about music in Chilean criollo culture. In order to explore and to give an account of this transcultural space, it is necessary to generate a theoretical model that incorporates the epigenesis of the observer in relation to the observed: a feedback loop of signs that destabilizes one's own signifying system and allows one to incorporate epitextual data, that is, all the phenomena that in one's own culture are conceptualized as "noise."

The *palin* is a form of music making in Mapuche culture. As a communicative space it can by analyzed in a tripartite system that considers text, context, and pre-text. The text associated with that act of music making is presented as a combination of particular, distinctive, innovative traits in relation to contextual competencies. Context is a signifying system produced by the historical sum of texts of a given culture and as a marker that determines what can be considered pertinent text. And pre-text is the group of motivations and functions, the musical communicative space.

The pre-text of urban Mapuche *palin* consists of a combination of motivations that can be encompassed within the phrase "speaking, doing, and feeling Mapuche," in reproduction of identifying bonds with traditional Mapuche culture on the part of Mapuche migrants. This need is part of the general need of migrants to affirm a positive identity.

In fulfilling this communicative function, the urban *palin* is characterized as a ritual in that it represents the mythic site of Mapuche communal power, the blue force, the power of the ancestors, and the identification of the individual within the community culture. At the same time, it is organized as a demonstration-spectacle for the non-Mapuche, inasmuch as it should constitute a strong and positive expression of "Mapucheness."

The analysis of the *palin* in Cerro Navia in metropolitan Santiago allows us to provide an example of an "indigenous" musical expression, defined not only from the criollo perspective, but also through the perspective of its protagonists, where it is converted into a place for the formation of identity, for the cultural and social maintenance of a community. This expression, produced in a symbolic space of subalternity, succeeds in redefining traditional Mapuche context, generating a new, urban Mapuche signifying context and creating bases of identification for a cultural alternative to subalternity. It is no coincidence that this opportunity emerges when the majority of the people who identify as Mapuche live in urban areas and when conflict in rural communities is the product of the industrial impact of timber companies and consortia. It would be desirable for Chilean society and its institutions to come to an understanding of the multiethnic and multicultural character of the state and to create acceptable and respectful ways of coexistence for criollos and Mapuche: to overcome racism and protect and encourage cultural diversity, achieving dignified conditions of existence, typical of any modern nation.

## Notes

1. For Humberto Maturana, *El sentido de lo humano* (Santiago de Chile: Dolmen, 1994), 179, the term "relationship with reality" defines the "recurring distinctions within a co-ordinating domain of consensual behavioral coordinations."

2. They are defined as a combination of signs that, without being part of the signifying system, are nonetheless directly perceivable—information that even prior to any codification assumes mental reality, perhaps before possessing a specific form; see Jorge Martínez, "Hacia una musicología transcultural: el anclaje de la identidad musical tradicional en mapuche urbanos" (master's thesis in musicology, University of Chile, Santiago, 1996), 209–18.

3. Jurij Mihajlovič Lotman and Boris Andreevič Uspenskij, "Sul meccanismo semiotico della cultura," in *Tipologia della cultura*, transl. R. Faccani and M. Marzaduri, 2nd ed. (Milan: Bompiani, 1995), 62–64.

4. Umberto Eco, *Trattato di semiotica generale* (Milan: Bompiani, 1975), 19–20.

5. Maturana, *El sentido de lo humano*, 45, defines the epigenesis as the homeostatic mechanism that insures the functional stability of a complex organism in interaction with its environment, that is, the process that permits each individual to integrate the greatest possible number of interactions with the exterior and to do so in stable fashion. This process changes the individual and the environment.

6. Concepts such as Western and criollo are employed in their most typical sense. [Editors' note: Within the context of Chile's history of race politics, the term "criollo" denotes a

population and cultural formation that, while linking its origins to a European—especially Spanish—heritage, also claims a distinctive Chilean character, the result of the subordinate incorporation of indigenous, mestizo, or Afrodescendant cultural traits. As it pertains to this chapter, the term refers to what indigenous populations in Chile perceive as the dominant cultural, social, and economic hegemony from which they have been historically excluded. As such, the term can also be read as "nonindigenous" or even the local Chilean equivalent, "white," which the author sees as a related but distinct category from other (non-Chilean) Westerners].

7. Néstor García Canclini, "La puesta en escena de lo popular," in *Culturas híbridas: estrategias para salir de la modernidad* (Mexico City: Grijalbo, 1990), 195–96.

8. Instituto Nacional de Estadística, *Censo general de población 1992* (Santiago de Chile: Instituto Nacional de Estadística, 1993).

9. José Bengoa, *Historia del pueblo mapuche, siglos XIX y XX* (Santiago de Chile: Sur, 1985), 390.

10. Fernando Kilaleo, "Mapuche urbano," *Feley Kam Felelay*, no. 3 (1992), 7–12, p. 11.

11. José Ancán, "Rostros y voces tras las máscaras y los enmascaramientos: los mapuche urbanos," *Actas del Segundo Congreso Chileno de Antropología* (Santiago de Chile: Colegio de Antropólogos, 1997), 1:307–14; Jorge Martínez, "Mecanismos de anclaje de la identidad musical en mapuche urbanos," *Actas del Segundo Congreso Chileno de Antropología*, 1:325–37; Ramón Curivil, "Religión mapuche y cristianismo," in *¿Modernización o sabiduría en tierra mapuche?*, ed. Armando Marileo (Santiago de Chile: San Pablo, Centro de Estudios de la Realidad Contemporánea, 1995), 31–50; Cristián Parker Gumucio, "Modernización y cultura indígena mapuche," in *¿Modernización o sabiduría en tierra mapuche?*, 99–136.

12. Editors' note: The author is referring to the occupation and subsequent annexation of Mapuche territory (Araucanía) by the Chilean state during the latter part of the nineteenth century.

13. Ancán, "Rostros y voces," 308.

14. Claudia Briones de Lanata, "Resistencia y consentimiento en la identidad étnica de los mapuche araucanos," in *Sociedad y cultura mapuche: el cambio y la resistencia cultural* (Temuco: Sociedad Mapuche Lonko Kilapan, Centro Internacional de Investigación para el Desarrollo, 1992), 257–74; Nils Biedermann, "Enfermedad mental e identidad cultural en la etnia mapuche en Chile," in *Otras realidades, otras vías de acceso: psicología y psiquiatría transcultural en América Latina*, ed. Horacio Riquelme (Caracas: Nueva Sociedad, 1992), 101–12.

15. John Blacking, *How Musical Is Man?* (Seattle: University of Washington Press, 1973); María Ester Grebe, "Antropología de la música: nuevas orientaciones y aportes teóricos en la investigación musical," *Revista Musical Chilena* 35, no. 153 (1981), 52–74; María Ester Grebe, "Aportes y limitaciones del análisis musical en la investigación musicológica y etnomusicológica," *Revista Musical Chilena* 45, no. 175 (1991), 10–18.

16. Gregory Bateson, *Una unidad sagrada* (Barcelona: Editorial Gedisa, 1993; originally published in 1991 as *Sacred Unity*); Edward T. Hall, *La dimensione nascosta* (Milan: Bompiani, 1966; originally published in 1982 as *The Hidden Dimension*); Ray Birdwhistell, *Kinesics and Context* (Philadelphia: University of Pennsylvania Press, 1970).

17. Gino Stefani, *La competenza musicale* (Bologna: Cooperativa Libraria Universitaria Editrice Bologna, 1982).

18. In musicology, the interest in context has been limited to considering it as a portion of "extramusical" data that have no systemic relationship to the musical data, contained essentially in the score. Examples of this are the positions of Heinrich Schenker, Eduard Hanslick, Guido Adler, and Hugo Riemann. Currently, Carl Dalhaus has offered a more dynamic consideration of the social—contextual—in musicology.

19. Five different types of approaches to context in ethnomusicology can be cited: that of cultural anthropology, including authors like Alan Merriam and John Blacking, where cultural context practically engulfs musical data to the point of obscuring them; an anthropological-semiotic focus, represented for example by Steven Feld and Regula Burckhardt-Qureshi; one in a contrasting vein, represented by Simha Arom, where the objective is the study of music as an autonomous system, and larger or smaller portions of "extramusical" data—contextual—that are used to corroborate the musical-textual data; those that are in between, such as the approaches of Mantle Hood or Kwabena N'ketia, who speak about "musical cultures"; and the studies of Charles Seeger, for whom all musicology is ethnomusicology, and the latter is part of a vision of the world characterized by the music/word duality.

20. Ivo Supičić, "Subjects and Methods," in *Music and Society: A Guide for the Sociology of Music* (New York: Pendragon Press, 1987), 47–78.

21. This is perhaps the reason that it is possible to distinguish text as something unique, distinctive, new, as an unedited combination of social competencies that, therefore, becomes a new competency.

22. Charles S. Peirce, *Semiotica: i fondamenti della semiotica cognitiva*, ed. M. Bonfantini (Turin: Einaudi, 1980).

23. See the extensive writings of Theodor W. Adorno and János Maróthy, *Music and the Bourgeois: Music and the Proletarian* (Budapest: Académiai Kiadó, 1974), 131–47; Jacques Attali, *Noise: The Political Economy of Music* (Minneapolis: University of Minnesota Press, 1985); Konrad Boehmer, "Sociology of Music," *The New Grove Dictionary of Music and Musicians*, ed. Stanley Sadie (London: Macmillan, 1985), 17:432–39.

24. Bengoa, *Historia del pueblo mapuche*, 17.

25. Briones de Lanata, "Resistencia y consentimiento."

26. Biedermann, "Enfermedad mental," 105.

27. Horacio Riquelme, "Consumo de alcohol y cultura cotidiana en la población chilena," in *Otras realidades, otras vías de acceso: psicología y psiquiatría transcultural en América Latina* (Caracas: Nueva Sociedad, 1992), 18–20.

28. Martínez, "Hacia una musicología transcultural," 268–83.

29. Shown at the 2nd Chilean Congress of Anthropology, held in 1995 at the Austral University of Valdivia, Ancán's videos spurred an interesting debate about the video as an "oral" foundation of life stories.

30. There are a number of definitions of *palin*. Historically described by chroniclers like Sebastián de Covarrubias, Rodrigo Díaz de Caro, and Núñez de Pineda y Bascuñán, more recent writers like Father Alonso de Ovalle and Diego de Rosales referred to the game as *chueca*, the name for a variant of the game that developed during the colonial period

among mestizos and Spaniards (criollos). Mapuche chief Pascual Coña, in his memoirs transcribed by Wilhelm von Moesbach, offers an emic vision of what should be considered a *palin*. Finally, we find definitions of this game in Ernesto González, Ricardo Latcham, and Eugenio Pereira Salas. Records about the game of *chueca* can be found in the following works: Daniel Aeta, *Juegos y deportes* (Santiago de Chile: Nascimento, 1930), 140–44; Félix José Augusta, *Lecturas araucanas* (Temuco: Kushe, 1991 [1934]); Pascual Coña, *Testimonio de un cacique mapuche*, transcribed by Wilhelm von Moesbach (Santiago de Chile: Pehueno, 1984); Domingo Curaqueo, "El mapuche en la estructura social chilena," in *Las culturas de América en la época del descubrimiento* (Madrid: Comisión Nacional del V Centenario, 1985), 201–11; Ernesto González, *Kallfülikan, un canto mapuche*, pamphlet (Santiago de Chile: n.d.); Ricardo Latcham, "La organización social y las creencias de los antiguos araucanos," *Publicaciones del Museo de Etnología y Antropología de Chile* 3, no. 2–4 (1922); Rodolfo Lenz, "Chueca," in *Diccionario etimológico de las voces chilenas derivadas de lenguas indígenas americanas* (Santiago de Chile: Cervantes, 1904); Carlos Isamitt, "Cantos mágicos de los araucanos," *Revista de Arte* 1, no. 6 (1935), 8–13; Manuel Manquilef, *Comentarios del pueblo araucano II: la gimnasia nacional* (Santiago de Chile: Barcelona, 1914), 140–59; José Toribio Medina, *Cosas de la colonia, apuntes para la crónica del siglo XVIII* (Santiago de Chile: Ercilla, 1889); Víctor Nahuelpan, *Ulkantun, como motivación del quehacer cultural del pueblo mapuche* (Villarrica: Universidad Católica, 1982); Eugenio Pereira Salas, "Los juegos deportivos: la chueca," in *Juegos y alegrías coloniales en Chile* (Santiago de Chile: Zig-Zag, 1947), 125–37; Manuel Román, "Chueca," *Diccionario de chilenismos y otras voces y locuciones viciosas*, vol. 2 (Santiago de Chile: Imprenta de la Revista Católica, 1909).

31. Coña, *Testimonio de un cacique mapuche*, 28.

32. González, *Kallfülikan*, 245–63.

33. Carol E. Robertson, "Pulling the Ancestors: Performance Practice and Praxis in Mapuche Ordering," *Ethnomusicology* 23, no. 3 (1979), 411.

34. Augusta, *Lecturas araucanas*, 17–18; Pereira Salas, "Los juegos deportivos," 128.

35. It is important to point out that the sense of "spectacle" associated with the *palin* of Cerro Navia is something very different from the "shows" by Mapuche folkloric groups devoted to "artistic promotion." The latter represent—on a [professional] stage and with the use of theatrical techniques—gestures and traits associated with the rural *palin*, interpreting it as an evocation.

36. Roman Jakobson, "La lingüística y la poética," in *Estilo del lenguaje*, ed. Thomas A. Sebeok (Madrid: Ediciones Cátedra, 1974), 123–73.

37. It is known that the *kultrun*, commonly recognized as a membranophone instrument, has various hard objects inside it. In the ritual actions, the *machi* uses the *kultrun* as a membranophone and an idiophone; see María Ester Grebe, "El kultrún mapuche: un microcosmo simbólico," *Revista Musical Chilena* 27, no. 123 (1973), 3–42.

# 15

# Brazilian Ethnomusicology as Participatory Ethnomusicology

## *Anxieties Regarding Brazilian Musics*

ANGELA LÜHNING

During the "International Ethnomusicology Symposium: 500 Years of African and Indigenous Musics in Brazil" held at the School of Music at the Universidade Federal de Minas Gerais (UFMG, Federal University of Minas Gerais) in Belo Horizonte October 23–28, 2000, we attended and, without realizing it, we molded a meeting quite different from the conventional scientific symposium. It could be described as a participatory happening, going far beyond a symposium that might normally be classified as intellectual, academic, or scientific. But, in what way was it different or innovative? Aside from the customary roundtables with paper presentations and lectures, it offered film screenings and spontaneous musical presentations; practical workshops administered by representatives of diverse musical cultures, especially indigenous people of various Brazilian tribes; Afro-Brazilian *congado* practitioners; and musicians of the Bassari people of Senegal.[1] Over the course of the symposium, many questions and doubts emerged, and criticisms and misunderstandings arose, as did distress resulting from diametrically opposed expectations.[2]

People attended the International Ethnomusicology Symposium to hear and see, feel and learn, although with differing sets of prior knowledge, perspectives, and objectives. Access to new knowledge arrived through various routes: we

---

A longer version of this work was originally published by Angela Lühning as "Etnomusicologia brasileira como etnomusicologia participativa: inquietudes em relação às músicas brasileiras," in *Músicas africanas e indígenas no Brasil*, ed. Rosângela Pereira de Tugny and Ruben Caixeta de Queiroz (Belo Horizonte: Editora UFMG, 2006), 37–55. Translated by Holly Holmes and published with permission of Editora UFMG and with the consent of the author and the volume editors.

listened to many different types of music and sounds from live performances, recordings, films, and videos; we heard speeches and explanations about the previously heard material; and we enjoyed practical demonstrations, mixing individual interpretation, analysis, and practice. As a result, we learned from differing, yet complementary, formats. The most surprising result was the presence of the musically and culturally new (to avoid the antiquated term "exotic")—that is, new musical sonorities and realities within a space traditionally reserved for sounds resulting from Western musical conceptions. We even ended up discovering sounds from geographically nearby, as was the case with the indigenous Maxakalí people of Minas Gerais. The Maxakalí people and their musical culture, hitherto unknown [to us], became observable, audible, and visible—though not necessarily understood by the nonindigenous attendees.

We were and are, therefore, dealing with a translation problem in the literal sense. We found ourselves exposed not only to different languages but also to different expressive cultures that, according to the official discourse, should form part of a greater Brazilian national culture. We were confronted with the nagging question of whether it is possible to translate cultures and their meanings at all. Is that act of translation just an illusion? Each translation, after all, includes its intrinsic limitations and appears to carry a certain innate "untranslatability"—the expression of the absolutely unique, unmistakable, and incomparable that resides in each culture.

Social realities themselves seem to reinforce the impossibility rather than the possibility of a "translatability."[3] Does this finding mean that we should stop doing what we are doing and seeking what we are seeking? I don't believe so. Despite these limitations, we ought to seek more "translatability," more understanding between diverse worlds, in this particular case, between Brazil's many musical and social worlds. Finally, we ought to find other means of communication that can touch and reach everyone involved in those interactions we call "field" research—means of communication that do not lead to sterile academic texts that are unable to express the dense, complex, and contradictory nature of life. Often, we speak the languages of exclusion: intellectuals and academics at conferences speak by reading their written texts, intending to portray life, while those who are portrayed—the so-called informants, like the many protagonists present at the symposium in Belo Horizonte—speak with and through their bodies, which carry all of their experience and expertise, chanting, singing, playing and, sometimes, "speaking" just by playing a flute of deer bone, like Kanahma, an indigenous Waiwai [from the northern state of Pará].

One of the final moments of the International Ethnomusicology Symposium was extremely intense in emotion and meaning. It happened when all those present listened to melodies by the indigenous Waiwai flutist, who was re-creating and inventing in that moment something that had a sense of ritual, while, at the same time, having no pretension of it being a ritual. It was rather surprising to realize how far we are from being able to fully understand the sacred: in the School of Music auditorium, Kanahma played illuminated by just three candles—not because doing so made it a ritual, but simply to achieve a more appropriate ambience, imagining how he might normally play in a natural space, without electricity. However, the "paraphernalia" of the urban world was omnipresent during the creation and experience of this momentary and spontaneous quasi-ritual: camera flashes lit up, cell phones rang, little red lights on digital cameras blinked, and watches chirped, reminding us the entire time that it was only a re-creation. We were unable to leave the temporal reality of our digital world. We could not disconnect ourselves from it and therefore remained entirely in the temporal reality of that which is disposable, instantaneous, and extremely fleeting.

In fact, the issues of the presence and inclusion of technology and of representation were not discussed at the symposium. They should have and could have been, given that many of the participants recorded, filmed, and photographed everything, even before, during, and after a speech about copyright! We need to ask ourselves how we plan to use these innumerable documentations. Predictably, the voice of reason responds that they will be used only as a basis for study and to increase knowledge and delight as a source for future inspiration—certainly well-intentioned and reasonable uses. But this is also where doubts creep in: at the press of a button, a camera imperceptibly transforms into a powerful "weapon" in our hands. In our desperate search for the objective, measurable, and concretely palpable, we forget that the camera in and of itself has neither the sensitivity nor the ability to document the spiritual effort and mental preparation necessary to produce that so-called "final result," worthy of different or multiple recordings. The recording device is a child of the modern world, indivisible from its upbringing and generation: it wants the sound as soon as it is ready, uninterested in unutterable and invisible processes.

Strangely, many of us—colleagues by trade, the so-called ethnomusicologists and anthropologists with inclinations toward visual or audio documentation or both—feel troubled with this excess of exposure to technology. For ethical reasons, we suspect we may be going beyond what is permitted and acceptable. But who would have imagined that so many indigenous people, eager for equal access to worlds and modes of life different from their traditional systems, would feel highly appreciated by this process of documentation? Could it be that there is some kind of exaggerated paternalism that keeps us from seeing this issue in a more reasonable and unbiased way?

The witnessed moment, the moment that is "lived together,"[4] including the possibility of an understanding through the senses, transforms itself easily into the object of its own "research." In order to document that which is literally in the dark, nearly invisible but audible, that which we deem attainable by the power of modern technology, we forget how to experience that moment. This brief reflection on the issues of light and shadow brings other connotations, including questions about the construction of memory and its fixation through the sensory that, ultimately, is something bodily. Modern technology disables our ability to feel and to construct a sensory memory that would facilitate our future recollection of what had been "lived." Instead, we trust our future memory to the equipment that so ably records the moment in place of our personal memory. The question remains: is it possible to objectify the subjective, our subjective perception? Is it possible to linearly determine and express that which is extremely complex and multifaceted? Still, not even a purported simulacrum of reality, like film or video, succeeds in capturing everything. It will always be constrained by, and document the gaze of, those who operate the camera, sometimes sensitively and many times in a very limited way.

Yet, here comes the intervention of the rational stance: of course it is important to be able to show others—to students, to unconvinced and incredulous peers—our experience of the Waiwai performance, and all of the other filmed events. Would it not be a way to disseminate new knowledge about other realities, a contribution to a more multicultural perspective? Without a doubt, it is interesting, useful, and even necessary, but a potentially positive result depends entirely on what we will do with these sounds that belong to the world beyond the academy, these images of witnessed rituals, imprisoned in the "hearts" of electronic devices. And finally, at the heart of the matter comes the question concerning authorship: to whom do these repertories belong (in an ontological sense)?[5] That issue involves the necessity of definitions and discussions about ethical positions in relation to the possible implications that result from the actions of researchers, and not only in the area of music.

We also discussed the many faces of ritual and the sacred at the symposium. Obviously, all cultures have rituals. But it seems that the rituals of the Western world are more technical and bureaucratic than sacred; they are reflections of organization without an air of sacredness necessarily existing within them. We all enjoyed moments of the sacred in different forms of representation—the reflexive, meditative sacred and the happy, festive sacred—whether executed by the various participants of the symposium or shown in the form of film. Based on some reactions among the audience, it became apparent that we had forgotten that, contrary to Western notions, the sacred does not necessarily need to be "serious." It seems that we have lost familiarity with the sacred-ludic to the point of being overly cautious and concerned with its potentially misplaced presence, imagining that it must be something untouchable and nontransferable. Therefore, what people in Brazil customarily say, "the sacred is sacred," makes reflection impossible and for this reason impedes any action. (Perhaps the great respect we give to the sacred of the Other, treating it with such seriousness, hinders us from recognizing its possible function of transformation and adaptation through its joyful element, and in this way confounds even more our perception, which is directly linked to notions of scientific rigor.) On the other hand, we have seen cultures, such as that of the Bassari, where "music" exists only if it is connected to ritual. In other words, a perception of music for delight and entertainment does not exist.[6]

Other questions were raised (also in the subsequent journeys taken by some of the participants, like the Bassari, who later traveled to Salvador, the city with the largest concentration of Afro-Brazilians): what does the commonly used term to designate a player [of a musical instrument] or singer as a "musician" mean? From the Western point of view, an African person who plays an instrument well is by definition a "musician," since a piece of music presented with virtuosity fits the Western notion of music. Within this reasoning, what would be the music that one expects an "African musician" to play? A common answer, at least in Bahia, would be percussion-based music. But could it be thinkable that someone who plays well may not be considered a professional musician? On the other hand, is it imaginable that an African person sees himself or herself differently from what is projected onto them? And how might one understand this within a noncommodified and nonprofessional context? There exist so many different ways to make music or to be a musician. But what should we name this art form, one that forms a part of the context of a society, whether it assigns specific [performing] roles to people or not?

It may be easier to discuss these terminological questions in written form and without the protagonists who prompt these reflections present. However, the moment they are present, sharing the Western vision of the world and needing to be represented, then the dilemma becomes phenomenological in nature and nearly impossible for us to resolve. Instead of appreciating the competence and artful expression of the performers, we cloak ourselves in rigid and inflexible terminology, preventing us from understanding the complexity of performances that involve music making with all its communicative, ludic, social, religious, philosophical, and even professional and commodified aspects.

What do we then call people who are "simply" *people who make music,* who produce sounds and melodies, "musicians" without an accompanying adjective that augments, diminishes, details, or explains, like our approximate categories of "professional," "amateur," "dilettante," and "indigenous"? We are unfortunately too accustomed to employ the term "musician" in this way, which is obviously a result of the position that musicians have had and continue to have in Western culture, always thinking primarily about their professional status or position.

After these more general questions, I would like to touch on some of the specific questions that were raised during and after certain presentations or workshops. These questions point to the great gap between universal and local epistemologies in the very study of Brazilian musics. Just to give a few examples: it is commonly understood that traditionally only men [in Brazilian indigenous communities] play flutes, an understanding that is accompanied by a diverse set of mythological and practical explanations, despite some notable exceptions. For example, Dona Benvina, of the indigenous Pankararu group currently living in Minas Gerais, played her flute to conduct the *praiá* (the enchanted spirits of ancestors) who came with her to the symposium from Brejo dos Padres in the Pernambuco backlands.[7]

A similar question occurs regarding the drum ensembles within Afro-Brazilian religions, always played in groups of three, in which the largest or lowest pitched one is awarded the responsibility of guiding the presence of entities like *orixás*, *voduns*, *inquices*, and *caboclos*.[8] The drums are always played by men, while other instruments like the *xequerê* [beaded rattle made from a gourd] and *agogô* [single or multiple conical metal bells] can also be played by postmenopausal women. As explained by practitioners of these religions, after menopause women lose their reproductive function, which is fundamental to the [local] definition of gender and consequently to the division of labor and attributions between genders.[9]

Another issue, present in nearly all of the performances and in various musical styles, was that of repetition. Although the interpretations and explanations of the phenomenon were quite diverse, repetition is not a question of not knowing how to introduce difference or of not having inspiration; rather, it is part of complex creative processes associated with ritual preparations. As one of the Bassari performers observed, constant repetition leads people into a state of lightness and relaxed concentration and, at the same time, of emptiness that permits them to dance, sing, and play for many hours on end.

This same issue also raised questions about the notions of creation and composition, which until now have only been addressed in a very tentative way in ethnomusicology, questions that are situated at the point of convergence between the fields of ethnomusicology and composition. Indeed, one of the most interesting aspects is to look at these forms in contrast to Western musical procedures, since each creative form is responding to different ways of being, feeling, thinking, and engaging with [local] communities, on the one hand, and highlighting one's individuality, on the other. Certainly, the different [ideological] structures with which people view the matter of musical creation and innovation/repetition has to do with the very social organization and place within which the individual finds himself or herself, either as someone responsible for a collective or as an individual.[10]

Many of these matters remain open (they were not part of the symposium's official agenda), and many discussions at the symposium ended with contrary and contradictory expectations and proposals. Certainly, these multiple responses were the manifestation and result of the unusual and audacious circumstances: the opening of the doors of the academy to the sounds of so many Brazilian sonic worlds together with those who create and re-create those sounds. For many in attendance, this was the first direct contact with a variety of Brazilian sonorities: whether distant or geographically close, but long unnoticed, these sonorities are nevertheless a constitutive part of the whole, that is, of the world called Brazil. For many, it was also the first time they actually met the "faceless" [Other] that they had previously only encountered on CDs and in academic texts, a representation of identity and presence confined to paper.

Many also heard for the first time an indigenous language spoken, becoming aware that there are other languages [besides Portuguese] in Brazil. Indeed, the 180 extant indigenous languages and the remnants of various African languages remain confined to an existence at the level of exotic curiosity rather than being a part of present-day [official Brazilian] realities. But aside from the need to translate these languages into Brazilian Portuguese, it was necessary to translate the contents and meanings of markedly distinct cultures as well. This was accomplished by searching for new ways of building familiarity and, at the same time, recognizing existing limitations.

The greatest challenge of the International Ethnomusicology Symposium was to find a way to make possible an understanding between the ethnic groups present and the academic and nonacademic worlds, all with their diverse social and cultural experiences. Certainly, we are still far from having found the ideal way of communication. However, a path is taking shape, and the presence of the representatives of these most diverse cultures was crucial to learning the limits of academic discourse and legitimation. Who speaks about what or whom, for what reason, and in what way? Indeed, the roles between researchers and the researched were inverted at the symposium with the appearance of the first emic researchers, such as Ibã from the Kaxinawá indigenous group [from Acre state in northern Brazil], who presented a tape recording with songs by a village elder. The active voices of protagonists, often spiritual leaders and teachers of great life lessons, were new to the ears of the academy, and their discourses set a new tone. Why play recorded examples if there are people who can play live and even explain what they do? It is of course more expensive and challenging to organize live encounters, but these arguments should not have merit if we truly want to innovate and improve our musical understanding and hear the many existing sonorities in Brazil and around the world.

To bring these very musicians to a conference or symposium requires a great foundation of trust, something that exists—fortunately—in much of the research conducted in Brazil, though some is still lacking in this respect. We need to develop new ways of thinking, of building relationships and familiarity with different modes of life, of creation, performance, and reflection. This will enable us to accept and include [the Other] in official forums and in the so-called academic circles, keeping in check the postures of arrogant superiority (many times existing only in intellectual circles) and accepting attitudes of humility and of a willingness to learn about alternative types of knowledge.

Perplexity and the sensation of a complete reversal, pulling the supposedly safe ground out from under our feet, was certainly felt by many, and we surely had no answers in that very moment. But, paraphrasing [Bohemian-Austrian poet and novelist] Rainer Maria Rilke, we should love and live the questions that arise, so that later, when the right moment arrives, we can live the answers. Certainly, at the symposium we started to intuit, and may even have found, answers to our perplexity in facing this other way of joining modes of knowledge—practical, reflexive, and analytical. These concerns go beyond the search for an applied ethnomusicology, a widely acclaimed area of inquiry since its beginnings in the 1990s. These are reflections that in some way involve a reshaping of our own notion of science and of its social commitments outside of large centers of origin and domination, a procedure that requires the necessary reflection and scruples but that is extremely difficult to carry out. Not only ethnomusicology but many other disciplines in the humanities and beyond face similar questions.

To be sure, the symposium's attendees were enriched by new experiences. Some (e.g., students, professors, and other enthusiasts) were most interested in new knowledge. Others (indigenous people) came with expectations of belated and long-awaited recognition of their cultures by the rest of society, a society they are officially a part of, though only at its margins. Many have not understood that for this recognition to actually take place, each needs the other; to be able to recognize something, we need to be familiar with it first. In fact, recognition necessarily comes from knowledge. And this requires that we know, live, share, and even hear a recording or read about a subject as a form of *simulacrum*. We always end up knowing ourselves through the knowledge of others.

But, we have to acknowledge our own doubts and ask ourselves: What about the path of knowledge in general? What gives us the legitimacy to continue to document and try to understand the diversity of Brazil's musical worlds? We should enthusiastically embrace the presence of the protagonists of these various musical expressions, people who impart their real identity on that which they have done for so long, including all of the processes of transformation. At the same time, we should not forget that often those we see and hear are not the only people who express their local culture: these agents, who represent their peers, might in fact be better, or perhaps only less inhibited, freer from other obligations, or not encumbered by age or illness, in comparison with their peers. In fact, everyone is able to make cultural contact, for this is how they participate in the process of creative expression. However, I believe that what we least want is for these representatives to be seen as future individual artists who are to be integrated into a broad variety of commodified [music] markets, which is not necessarily in the best interest of those they represent. Thus, a general reflection about ethical procedures by those involved in the processes of exchange and mutual understanding becomes urgent. Also, there is a dire need for review and reflection on what limits should be set and not infringed upon in this search for a [new] model for the tenuous thread between necessity and expectation [desire] in [today's] consumerist and extremely commercial world.

But I also believe that one of the strongest cases that can be made for the importance of cultural visibility, exchange, knowledge, and recognition is the need to find new and alternative ways to deepen and expand how we envision the process of cultural education and socialization. We need to rethink ways, strategies, methods, and objectives on how to engage with cultural markets that operate on a foundation of mutual respect and sensible ethics.

Despite all of the aforementioned problems, and in light of the ongoing debates regarding the field of ethnomusicology, concerning its future as a scientific discipline and as a philosophical orientation, I believe that a more participatory and engaged ethnomusicology can develop possible answers to the many questions about the necessary integration and appreciation of all expressions of Brazilian culture. We need to rethink and accept in the most honest and open way the many different existing identities in this country.

To include the nature of Brazilian ethnomusicology in a more ample discussion is of fundamental importance to understanding ethnomusicology's viability as a path to be blazed. This issue is being raised at a moment when the continuation and the future of the sciences are being discussed, contributing to the consolidation of ethnomusicology as a discipline in Brazil. By finding its paths and its approaches, ethnomusicology enters the debate about multicultural education for different ethnic groups.

We need to ask in what way this new ethnomusicology should be different from other current ethnomusicological trends. Let us examine what kind of Brazilian ethnic music is included in CD collections produced outside of Brazil: in general there are few examples of Brazilian music, and these usually come from indigenous communities from the Xingu River or Amazon River or are related to Afro-Brazilian religious practices. Why? It seems that a desire to discover the different and the exotic still persists. Thus, musical styles that are deemed "less different" from European music or those produced by more ethnically mixed people have no place in these compilations. These few discs normally have no circulation in Brazil and usually lack liner notes in Portuguese. On the other hand, within Brazil's domestic production, there are few collections, or even other types of documentation, that include these ethnic traditions. These domestic collections are usually inclined to feature styles more in line with a vision of modern, urban, or national Brazilian musics, seeking styles that can be integrated into some "civilized" view of different musical styles. (Or, the collections take on a so-called folkloric classification, as much on the part of who releases the discs as on the part of who eventually consumes them.) Must these two approaches be mutually exclusive?

This small example shows that even today there is a great shortage of approaches and methods of documentation, and, therefore, a lack of comprehension of the diversity of Brazilian musics because they are simply unknown at the local, regional, national, or any other scope. If we look at which recordings circulate outside of Brazil (mostly "traditional" indigenous and Afro-descendant music) and what is produced for the Brazilian market, we notice a set of expectations and ascriptions that are incongruent and exclusionary. This is not the place to discuss this matter further, but whether intentional or accidental, it does not invalidate or undo the finding itself.[11]

What I propose for future symposia in the field of ethnomusicology is a discussion that stimulates a redefinition of certain concepts and behaviors, including an awareness of our obligations. This discussion should include all those involved in this fascinating, yet challenging, task of understanding the diverse musical cultures of Brazil—traditions that find themselves in constant processes of innovation and transformation, attesting to people's unbelievable strength of creativity.

Therefore, we ethnomusicologists should set as our goals the following.

1. Seek a greater understanding of the diverse Brazilian musical cultures as a key to the recognition of various cultural identities; this recognition is necessary for a respectful and dignified coexistence in a multicultural and multiethnic society.
2. Recognize that an understanding of Brazilian music is of fundamental importance for Brazil and, at the very least, it should have the same importance that it has in other countries.
3. Recognize that, after five hundred years of ignoring these diverse musical traditions for supposedly being inferior to and incompatible with Western art music, it is necessary to engage in an open and participatory

dialogue with the practitioners of these various traditions in order to elaborate a coherent way for recognizing these musical expressions.

4. Create a more participatory form of ethnomusicology. In Brazil, unlike in Europe, there exists a unique opportunity to bring together practitioners with scholars and educators interested in the greater visibility of these manifestations, thereby creating a practice of social commitment linked to the possible applications of ethnomusicological stances.[12]
5. Devise new modes of translation and interpretation of the various languages used in the performance, description, and analysis of the wide array of traditions and understand them in their own cultural context.
6. Address in a serious way matters of copyright, authorship, individual or collective participation, and professionalism, acknowledging that finding a consensus or general strategy of implementation may be a very complex matter. This will require basing operational definitions on a reexamination and revision of the very notions of artistic creation and conception, concepts that are currently based on Western notions that stem from and privilege the individual.
7. Create new participatory forms of discussion and approaches that no longer treat the protagonists of these musical styles as "objects" of research. This requires the inclusion of representatives and culture bearers of these diverse musical traditions, not only to illustrate or exemplify these traditions, but to assume the role of true and equal partners in public discussions of analyses and interpretations.
8. Find appropriate and unbiased ways of understanding processes of creation, abandoning approaches that understand these creative processes only by fixing them as written texts when they are expressed in so many other ways.
9. Consider in a serious, committed, and responsible way a new integration of all of the knowledge described above into processes of education, citizenship, and definition of local, regional, as well as personal cultural identities, making way for an open discussion and contributing to a creation of new models, focused on the matters of social responsibility and involvement.
10. "De-folklorize" the differentiated and multiple musical cultures in Brazil, understanding them instead as "serious" culture, deserving of focused and specific studies. To de-folklorize requires that those involved are sensitized and prepared to dialogue and search for a complex and detailed vision of Brazilian music and ethnomusicology. As an area of knowledge that studies Brazilian music as cultural expressions with diverse identities, ethnomusicology should propose providing visibility and should search

for multiple and reciprocal understandings through processes of continuous and constant approximation, exchange, and dialogue.

11. Synthesize the idea of ethnomusicology as an impetus to study and comprehend Brazil's rich and diverse cultures. Despite the academic need to know and discuss ethnomusicological texts written in other languages, and to translate them into Portuguese to offer a base of knowledge for interested people (especially when these studies pertain to Brazilian culture), publications in Portuguese about Brazilian culture need to be considered as equally important as those written in other languages. The time has come to recognize the necessity of carrying out projects, here and now, that are initiated, led, or accompanied by the protagonists [of the musical practices in question], resulting in a Brazilian ethnomusicology characterized by a distinctive and consistent participation of the social actors themselves.

This process will not be easy, because it involves deconstructing our own academic and scientific structures; a difficult task in a country where there has been a strong tendency to gauge its successes by the impact they have had abroad. This process necessarily relies on other presuppositions and points to other subsequent needs. However, it is an obligation for each one of us as sensitive human beings, observers, thinkers, and critics.

## Notes

1. Translator's note: I have understood *congueiros* to mean practitioners of *congado*, also referred to as *reinado* (see Glaura Lucas, "Diferentes perspectivas sobre o contexto e o significado do congado mineiro," in *Músicas africanas e indígenas no Brasil*, ed. Rosângela Pereira de Tugny and Ruben Caixeta de Queiroz [Belo Horizonte: Editora Universidade Federal de Minas Gerais, 2008], 75). Lucas defines *reinado* as "an afro-Brazilian religious manifestation, in its specificity in the state of Minas Gerais, fruit of the syncretism between European Catholicism and expressions of African religiousness, especially of Bantu origin."

2. While writing this paper, it became increasingly clearer that my own doubts as a participant of the symposium needed to be expressed through a more personal, sensitive, inquisitive discourse, since I was somewhat jolted by symposium events and their dynamics. I emphasize that, because of this, all of the statements are personal and subjective, although in various moments they were shared with colleagues who entered into heated discussions about what we experienced together.

3. See Peter Burke, *Kultureller Austausch* (Frankfurt am Main: Suhrkamp Verlag, 2000), for an analysis of the most varied phases and modalities of cultural contacts and exchanges, as well as conceptualizations in diverse areas of knowledge and during different times.

4. Translator's note: Here the author creates a play on words that interchanges "convivido" (meaning "coexisted, socialized with, or lived together") for the invented term

"comvivido": "com" (with) and "vivido," which can mean both "lived" and "experienced." I take the combination of these to mean "experienced and lived together."

5. After writing these reflections, I was reminded that questions of this type had been raised by Anthony Seeger in his excellent work, "Ethnomusicologists, Archives, Professional Organizations, and the Shifting Ethics of Intellectual Property," *Yearbook for Traditional Music* 28 (1996), 87–105; I recommended this article as a complementary reading.

6. Considering Huitzinger's concept of the *Homo ludens* [playing man], we may recognize that rituals do not necessarily need to be "serious." To the contrary, they can be ludic like *capoeira angola* or some types of indigenous *toré* [dance ceremony].

7. We can compare her playing with the flute tradition on the rereleased CD, *L. H. Corrêa de Azevedo: Music of Ceará and Minas Gerais* (Endangered Music Project) (1997, Rykodisc RCD 10404; also available as Smithsonian Folkways HRT 15019), recorded in the 1940s by Luis Heitor Corrêa de Azevedo in Pernambuco.

8. Translator's note: *Orixás*, *voduns*, *inquices*, and *caboclos* are terms used to indicate a pantheon of deities or spiritual beings in *candomblé* and refer to specific *nações*, or nations, based on linguistically descended groups of *yorubá*, *jêje*, and *bantu*, and various Amerindians, respectively.

9. I am thankful to Xavier Vatin for sharing his interesting observations regarding postmenopausal women who play the sacred drums in some *candomblé* houses in Salvador and the case of women who are conferred this activity when they assume masculine gender roles or a masculine stance.

10. See also chapter 2 of Peter Burke, *Popular Culture in Early Modern Europe*, 3rd rev. ed. (Farnham, U.K.: Ashgate, 2009, 1st ed. 1978), which raises interesting considerations about the questions of musical creation and transmission. [The author used a Portuguese translation of Burke's book, *Cultura popular na Idade Moderna* (São Paulo: Companhia das Letras, 1999).]

11. Within a world of creation and "production," in which, supposedly, only that which passes through some acceptance by a greater audience, by the media, or by critics is valuable. For many "musicians," their activity starts to have more importance at the moment in which someone registers or records it, permitting access to new knowledge that leads to recognition by others.

12. Various examples illustrate attempts to include Afro-Brazilian cultural elements in events organized by the cultural practitioners themselves. In the 1930s, there were two Afro-Brazilian conferences that attempted to integrate cultural manifestations in their programming. In 1934, representatives of Afro-religious cultures were brought to the stage of the Teatro Santa Isabel in Recife to present and contextualize their cultural universes. In Salvador in 1937, the reverse was attempted, when the participants of the conference were brought to various *casas de candomblé* [houses of *candomblé*, or sites of *candomblé* religious manifestation] to integrate themselves within a traditional space. *Candomblé* practitioners were among those who presented papers at the conference; see Lühning, "Acabe com este Santo, Pedrito vem aí . . . Mito e realidade da perseguição policial ao candomblé baiano entre 1920–42," *Revista USP* 28 (1996), 194–220.

Furthermore, various *casas de candomblé* in Salvador have attempted to reclaim their own histories and to unify—an unprecedented trend, since, despite having experienced similar challenges (persecution, prejudice), the various *casas* had never created a bond that went beyond spiritual kinship. Certainly, this is also due to the fact that each *casa* itself represents a closed world, without having a recognized central leadership. (Obviously, there were attempts at organization, like the Association of Afro-Brazilian Cults [Associação dos Cultos Afro-Brasileiros]; however, they were not able to achieve a real formal leadership.) Today, attempts at reimagining identities have been made through symposia, such as the "Alaindê Xirê" [held in a different venue each year, an annual festival of Afro-Brazilian religious manifestation with a particular emphasis on music], bringing together *alabés*, *xicarangomas*, and *runtós* [priest-musicians representing the Yoruba, Bantu, and Gbe linguistic groups, respectively] since 1998, as well as the Alabé Symposium at the Casa de Oxumaré [*casa de candomblé* in the Federação neighborhood of Salvador] a few years later. More recently, the Casa Branca [the first open *casa de candomblé*, named a National Historical Patrimony site in 1984 in Salvador] initiated a training project for young *alabé* apprentices. The First "As Folhas Sagradas" (The sacred leaves) Symposium, held in Salvador in 1993, had a profile that was at once more scientific and more informal, in which *candomblé* practitioners sought dialogue by making testimonies. However, until today, there has been no sign from academia that it is proposing to open its doors.

# 16

# Applied Ethnomusicology

## *A Critical History of Indigenous Music Studies in Mexico*

MARINA ALONSO BOLAÑOS

There has been a constant concern throughout the development of the so-called social and historical sciences: the search for a methodology that fits their specific nature.[1] Like other music scholars, I was convinced for many years that Mexican ethnomusicology continuously reflected on its own purpose, theories, and methods, what constituted a necessary phase in the development and consolidation of the discipline. We assumed that the mere task of historicizing ethnomusicology would result in defining its practice. Consequently, by locating the development of the discipline in a larger chronology, it seemed clear that the "precursors" of ethnomusicology had been studies with a folkloristic bent that gave way to a second stage, a discipline based on anthropology, and a final one that would be the intersection of several disciplinary fields.

Nevertheless, beyond this evolutionist framework, it is clear that Mexican ethnomusicologists did not systematically reflect on their role in the construction of knowledge. However, to understand the development of a discipline and the ways in which it has faced and attempted to explain, or has explained away, a changing reality, we need more than a review of the [music] scholarship; we need to correlate it to the intellectual orientations, traditions, and trends that constituted the discipline.

---

Originally published by Marina Alonso Bolaños as "La etnomusicología aplicada: una historia crítica de los estudios de la música indígena de México," in *Visiting Resource Professor Papers LLILAS* (Austin: University of Texas at Austin, 2008), http://lanic.utexas.edu/project/etext/llilas/vrp/mab.pdf. Translated by Andrés Amado with permission.

## The Construction of Mexican Identity

As Anne-Marie Thiesse notes, the processes of identity construction in Europe from the eighteenth to the twentieth centuries largely consisted in defining and promoting the heritage of each nation. A recovery and invention of a prestigious history, a series of heroes, a language, cultural monuments, folklore, local landscapes, particular mindsets, official emblems (anthem and flag), and picturesque depictions (dress, culinary specialties, or representative animals) created symbolic and material objects that nations used to represent themselves.[2]

Similarly, Latin American thinkers were invested in projects of identity construction in the early decades of the twentieth century.[3] Intellectuals in postrevolutionary Mexico were interested in establishing the origins of "Mexicanness." The so-called nationalist composers of the Generation of 1915, such as Manuel M. Ponce, Carlos Chávez, Candelario Huízar, and Silvestre Revueltas, aimed at participating in the construction of a cohesive image of "Mexicanness." They used motives from indigenous and popular music in their compositions, thus moving away from European composition models that had prevailed since the colonial period.

While Mexican composers of the nationalist period have been studied thoroughly, researchers who devoted their time to collecting and promoting Mexican vernacular musics have largely been forgotten, despite the fact that they too contributed to forging a national culture. Indeed, since the post-revolution years, public institutions have developed numerous projects for the study of indigenous music. Among the intellectuals involved in these projects were Rubén M. Campos, Gabriel Saldívar, Vicente T. Mendoza, Pablo Castellanos, Samuel Martí, E. Thomas Stanford, Henrietta Yurchenco, José Raúl Hellmer, Francisco Alvarado Pier, Irene Vázquez, Arturo Warman, Jas Reuter, Daniel Castañeda, Charles Boilès, Gertrude Kurath, and Francisco Domínguez. Their substantive body of work not only helped preserve and promote many forms of musical expression, it also laid the foundation for present-day research.

In the first decades of the twentieth century when the "great problems of the nation" were being discussed, Mexican anthropologists and archeologists endeavored to "rescue" indigenous contributions to the national culture. They sought and constructed an account of the past. In the context of searching for Mexico's prestigious past, the discipline of archeology gained great momentum. Music scholars turned to collecting songs and musical instruments as evidence of folkloric traits, and they described and classified Mexican music of Hispanic origin.[4]

During the first three decades of the twentieth century, the Department of Fine Arts of the Secretaría de Educación Pública (SEP, Ministry of Public Education) orchestrated so-called cultural missions with the goal of collecting data on regional music, its origins, and its instrumentation and contemporary use.[5] To this end, cultural missionaries had to follow a "schedule" for collecting dances, songs, and legends, and for transcribing theatrical plays.[6] In 1925 then-president [Plutarco Elías Calles] appointed Ignacio "Tata Nacho" Fernández Esperón as commissioner for the collection of vernacular music in the republic. The following year, Fernández Esperón reported on his travels throughout the country and shared his perception of the music of Michoacán, whose popular musical practices, he observed, were all imported from Guanajuato and Mexico City by itinerant singers. Similarly, he found that "the invasion of American 'jazz' music had already taken place, and local musical production no longer existed or, if it did, was difficult to hear." In his efforts to promote the music he collected, Fernández Esperón harmonized the pieces, "respecting the simplicity of the melodies and supplementing them with the most basic harmonic elements . . . so that when they are put to use, either by publishing them or performing them, . . . [they] maintain the naive spirit of their genesis."[7] Fernández Esperón's work influenced musical styles and genres throughout the country, especially in the west and south. His work was later used in Mexican cinema as the basis for representing popular music on sound tracks.

Moreover, the work of the SEP missionaries included "summoning local musicians and enthusiastic neighbors and organizing them so they may support community theater." These were important activities insofar as local musicians became actively engaged in the creative process [of local culture]. Yet, even though the SEP saw the benefit of expanding their ranks by including one music and choir teacher in 1926,[8] only in 1932 was a formal program established that would outline the work of music teachers in these missions. At that time, Genaro Vásquez [governor of Oaxaca 1925–28] gave a speech to prospective teachers involved in the "pedagogical dimension of folklore":

> Mexican folklore—namely our set of traditions, beliefs, and customs—no matter the perspective from which it is seen, responds to our psychology, it follows our ethnic instincts and your [Mexican] culture must serve the purpose of channeling and giving an artistic and beneficial form to whatever is innate in the [collective] soul of the people, but not to erase it or substitute it with exoticisms. . . .
>
> Use your enthusiasm to transform everything according to what progress requires; but preserving, as I said, whatever is essential to that [traditional] way of life.
>
> [Study] aboriginal dances and classify them as warrior dances, religious dances, or ironic dances; the outfits they wear. Describe the same; how are the dances learned so that they maintain a constant relationship with dancers from other parts of the country.[9]

The 1938–39 reports of the Department of Indigenous Affairs [founded by Vásquez] state that its educational programs provided some musical instruments, mostly wind and percussion, to support the creation of community bands. Interestingly, the areas where wind bands have a long tradition today often correspond to the places in which wind bands were promoted during the regime of Maximilian [Austrian Emperor of Mexico, 1864–67] and the presidency of Lázaro Cárdenas [1934–40]. This is the case, for example, for Oaxaca, Michoacán, and Guerrero.

Toward the 1960s, the emerging field of Mexican ethnomusicology adopted the name of the new discipline that had been launched in Bloomington, Indiana, but it did not embrace its conceptual and methodological models, so the use of the term "ethnomusicology" [in Mexico] seemed phony. Nevertheless, it seems that Mexican scholars did not dwell on the issue. In other words, the emerging Mexican ethnomusicology did not reject English-language [ethnomusicological] theories on the grounds that it critiqued evolutionist and functionalist postulates; scholars simply were not concerned with their relevance. Instead, Mexican ethnomusicologists were invested in preservation rather than descriptive or analytical projects. Another substantive distinction was that U.S. scholars studied *other cultures*, while Mexican scholars studied the music of their own country. These differences notwithstanding, from the late 1970s to the early 1990s the works of U.S.-based ethnomusicologists had greater circulation in Mexico and were often embraced without bias, as was the case with Alan Merriam's *The Anthropology of Music* (1964).

The earliest recordings were made by [Norwegian explorer and ethnographer] Karl Lumholtz, who recorded on wax cylinders some music of the indigenous peoples of Mexico's northeast. [U.S. anthropologist and ethnographer] Frances Densmore recorded [in the same area] in the 1920s. But it was not until much later in the twentieth century that researchers made in situ recordings that contributed to the creation of more accessible sound archives, in a similar vein to German musicologists who founded archives of world music at a moment of great interest in "rescuing" and promoting music through radio and sound recordings.[10] Between the 1940s and 1950s, the United Nations financed [U.S. ethnomusicologist, folklorist, and radio producer] Henrietta Yurchenco for the purpose of recording music of the Purépecha, the Yaqui, the Mayo, the Huichol, the Seri, the Rarámuri, and the Tzotzil.[11] From the late 1950s to the 1970s, Raúl Hellmer from the National Institute of Fine Arts, together with his student E. Thomas Stanford, launched a more systematic recording project. In the decades that followed, Stanford conducted various research projects, compiling recordings from more than four hundred indigenous and mestizo communities.[12]

In 1964 a group of anthropologists—including Guillermo Bonfil, Alonso Muñoz, Arturo Warman, and E. Thomas Stanford (students of Robert Weitlaner at Mexico's National School of Anthropology and History)—released an album containing field recordings. It attracted such attention that three years later the Instituto Nacional de Antropología e Historia (INAH, National Institute of Anthropology and History) proposed the publication of a series of recordings titled *Testimonio Musical de México* (Musical testament of Mexico) for the Museo Nacional de Antropología (National Museum of Anthropology).[13] The first albums in the series included field recordings compiled by this team of researchers while collecting items for the museum.

From then on, the production of recordings gained importance and various archives and sound libraries joined the project.[14] This is the moment when "applied ethnomusicology" was born. I use the term analogously to "applied anthropology," a branch of Mexican anthropology conceived by the *indigenismo* movement of the 1910s for the purpose of addressing indigenous issues.[15] Although connected to the academy, applied anthropology worked directly with the state to propose and implement public policy.

The pioneering recordings of the INAH series became a mandatory standard for Mexican music research. The series was used both for pedagogical purposes and radio broadcasts. Quite often, recorded pieces became part of the popular music repertoires of performers like Los Folkloristas, Amparo Ochoa, Oscar Chávez, and recently Lila Downs.

Before the heyday of the sound archives, researchers transcribed music in situ with the intention of divulging the roots of Mexican music or to compile songbooks. Transcribed music, particularly indigenous music, was often "arranged." Vicente T. Mendoza "corrected" pieces from the indigenous Otomí group as he transcribed them, because he believed that they were not structured correctly according to the canonical standards of Mexican music. Such transcriptions were a kind of "domestication of the savage sound."[16]

Some of the aforementioned scholars developed analytical models and modes of promoting indigenous music in the twentieth century. Although it was not their [intended] goal, they set precedents for important cultural policies to follow. These policies later influenced musicology in a dialogical way, emphasizing a scientific approach to the study of music. Based on those pioneering studies, broad areas of academic inquiry emerged in the 1980s and 1990s: the study of indigenous and mestizo musical genres; indigenous dance; organology, which included collection, construction, and classification of musical instruments; and popular music expressions of the oral tradition.

## Music and Ethnography

Until [the 1990s], traditional music was greatly neglected in Mexican ethnographies. Music was often considered as just an element within broader ceremonial contexts or as a form of recreation at community celebrations. This neglect was in part due to the methodological challenges of characterizing musical sound. On the one hand, it is an intangible phenomenon, and on the other, it is subject to a type of codification that is not universally understood, particularly its structure and notation.

I should also note that such lack of interest in musical subjects was also due to the inertia produced by the separation between the academy and institutional projects that occurred with the emergence of critical anthropology in 1968. It is worth remembering that, at that time, "the Magnificent Seven," a group of critical anthropologists, denounced the work of the Instituto Nacional Indigenista (INI, National Indigenist Institute) and other state projects of regional development for not addressing the needs of the indigenous populations, but instead seeking their acculturation and, thus, facilitating their ethnocide.[17]

That whole process had resulted in ethnographies that described music in a mechanical way, highlighting its alleged sacred character, one of the many stereotypes that led to music being divorced from its context. In fact, music was not even described or related to other aspects of the cultures that were being studied. Given that a number of scholars had helped to legitimize a single way of understanding indigenous music, whether for scientific or nationalist purposes, these attitudes informed state decisions on cultural policy.

In 1979, the INI created a network of radio broadcasters that aimed at reaching indigenous populations, promoting national culture through education, the valuing of local traditions, and encouraging the use of indigenous languages. Between 1994 and 1996, two *indigenista* projects on the research and promotion of intangible cultural heritage were launched: the recording project of radio broadcasters and that of the Department of Ethnomusicology. They were based on not only different but also contradictory premises.

The project of radio broadcasters involved the participation of indigenous peoples in the editing processes. As such, the musical selections did not adhere to the institutional canons of what was deemed "indigenous music"—a canon that considered "authentic" any music of a ritual nature that was performed with instruments considered to be pre-Hispanic in origin. In contrast, radio stations chose repertoires that better represented day-to-day lived realities in indigenous communities—for instance, songs that children learned in school or songs learned through public health promotional campaigns. Thus, not all pieces referenced nature or sacred subjects, but they did address more pragmatic aspects of daily life.

The recording project of the Department of Ethnomusicology subscribed to an *indigenista* philosophy that advocated the recognition of and respect toward indigenous cultures. Yet, the project leaders also determined which aspects of those indigenous cultures should be promoted: which ethnic groups were deemed worthy of consideration, which musical ensembles, and which repertoires. The liner notes accompanying these recordings foregrounded stereotypical representations of indigeneity. For example, the notes on indigenous recordings relating to the uprising of the Ejército Zapatista de Liberación Nacional (EZLN, Zapatista Army for National Liberation) state that indigenous societies are "an element of [our] cultural heritage" and that "they contribute to the history and cultural richness of the nation," as if indigenous societies were not subjects in themselves, but objects comparable to archaeological sites, architectural monuments, or the ecological environment. These notes imply a worldview in which history is not constructed but instead "imparted" through local traditions and practices.

Two years of political and social turmoil led the production of indigenous recordings to take different paths. The editing projects that radio broadcasters previously supported were transformed into independent projects. In Chiapas, indigenous groups began creating their own recordings, which they called independent recordings [*fonogramas independientes*].

In many instances, the independent publishing of recordings by local groups allowed both performers and listeners to "access modernity." In other words, new local interpretations of commercial music became a collective representation of modernity influenced by several factors, including the ways in which local and global media were accessed and an international presence that since the Zapatista uprising had prompted openness to more experimental forms of artistic expressions. On the other hand, the endurance of traditional music practices also meant that state and federal institutions, nongovernmental organizations, and so on continued to assert their interest in these musical practices, promoting them as static and romantic symbols of indigeneity. For instance, since the 1950s and 1960s, marimbas from Chiapas had been widely promoted [by these institutions and NGOs] as part of an "authentic" indigenous musical tradition, even though ten years earlier [the same institutions] had denounced the instrument as an intrusion and possible substitute for the traditional music of pipe and tabor ensembles.[18]

For their part, the above-mentioned INAH recording series *Testimonio Musical de México* also propelled the independent production of records, such as those by the Mixe band from Totontepec and the Santa María Band from Tlayacapan. The case of the Chimalapas Zoques [an ethnic group] of the isthmus of Oaxaca, on the other hand, illustrates the influence of institutional recordings on local music categories and their sense of ownership. The only song considered to belong to the Zoque regional *son* [tune] repertoire was "La migueleña" [The woman from San Miguel], which was written by Víctor Aquino, a Zapotec composer from the town of Juchitán [80 km to the west], and was later performed in Zoque language by various musicians from San Miguel Chimalapa. In the early 1970s, the renowned anthropologist Arturo Warman and his research team recorded and subsequently pressed this tune on an album. What is notable about this occasion is that the Zoque musicians promoted this recording among the people of San Miguel as evidence of the interest foreigners have in "Zoque music." Since then, "La migueleña" has been considered an example par excellence of [Zoque music]; Zapotecs do not dispute its authorship.

## Applied Ethnomusicology and Indigenous Music

The scholars mentioned above helped lay out the principles on which ensuing studies in applied ethnomusicology, the institutional incarnation of ethnomusicology, were based. Since the construction of knowledge regarding musical phenomena developed within institutions entrusted with preservation and promotion of cultural heritage, ethnomusicology was limited to a documentary practice whose primary aim became to preserve, not to explain. Consequently, music research had often been equated with the tasks of promoting and disseminating music.

Now, what does the concept of indigenous music entail for applied ethnomusicology? First, distinguishing indigenous music from other musics poses many problems because such distinction harks back to unresolved discussions regarding what constitutes indigeneity—especially when considering that the concept of indigenous music was created by the *indigenismo* movement of the [earlier] twentieth century. E. Thomas Stanford once asked the people of Los Altos de Chiapas what kind of music people played there. The locals replied that they played *sones* [tunes], not music; they thought that music was something that came through the radio.[19] This anecdote reminds us that the musical colonization of Mexico gave rise to a number of categories and hierarchies of music that we have yet to fully understand. This is why many of us still tend to mistakenly reduce indigenous musical practices to the performance of ritual music. That conflation speaks to one of the central concerns of applied ethnomusicology in Mexico: its preoccupation with finding the origins and purity of indigenous music, considered to be a link to nature and to the harmonious relationship among people of a given social group. For this reason, early projects [in applied ethnomusicology] forbade radio stations from broadcasting commercial music [in indigenous areas]: it was believed that these broadcasts would alter the musical taste of the listeners and would contribute to the demise or transformation of traditional music. Furthermore, they also insisted that indigenous music could only be that which exhibited pre-Hispanic traits and a ritualistic dimension.

Even though recordings would underscore the fact that indigenous music consists of a variety of musical styles, social functions, historical traditions, and syncretic notions of the fusion between pre-Hispanic and European elements, an emphasis on the sacred, the prioritizing of communal over the individual identity, and other markers of indigeneity remained as the primary devices framing each piece or track presented in an album.[20]

This view perpetuated romantic ideas about indigenous peoples that informed how [indigenous] radio broadcasters regarded both themselves and indigenous music. As a result, indigenous peoples have constantly been pressured to adapt their conceptualizations of self to the "logic of the Other," as demonstrated by notes written by indigenous researchers about forms of musical expression:[21] "Traditional dances and music as lived by the Teenek [Huasteco] people have great value, because they are used to honor and respect Mother Nature. We have conducted research by visiting several indigenous communities. They have had for many years, like many other peoples, their own special way of showing their feelings and communicating with supernatural beings. Thus, they make their offerings before god, but not an imposed god, but true gods, the very forces of nature, as our ancestors have taught us."[22]

The search for origins and rescuing of autochthonous and folk music remained—at least until the early 1990s—one of the fundamental concerns of institutional ethnomusicology. The unrestrained use of the notion of authenticity rendered that concept anachronistic and transformed applied ethnomusicology into an ahistorical discipline. A valorization of "true music," one with pre-Hispanic origins that exists only in the realm of discourse, or rather, is invented by institutions that promote cultural heritage, links these local vernacular forms of expression to a system of power that produces and maintains them in idealized forms—as evidenced by the slogans of the recording series of the INI and INAH: "To valorize anew and disseminate the authentic musical traditions of the country." According to [ethnomusicologist] Miguel Olmos, to speak of purity in the context of indigenous music is inadequate, given that, although music is a marker of identity that allows individuals to recognize each other through aesthetic stimuli, such stimuli change in response to cultural exchange, conquest, influence, contact, and so forth.[23]

It is worth remembering that Mexican anthropology originated from a romantic intellectual tradition, one that coexisted with Enlightenment notions of knowledge for knowledge's sake, and in which the search for a link between the pre-Hispanic past and the modern nation was a recurring leitmotif. This is well documented by Luis González, who observed that the Aztec fad during the war of independence and the early days of the nation equated indigeneity with Mexicanness, and that the trope of continuity was critical to sustaining that conflation.[24] Nevertheless, we know that today, as in the sixteenth to nineteenth centuries, "the preservation of ethnic identities is not incompatible with the adoption of new values and new cultural forms."[25]

The second concern of applied ethnomusicology (in its institutional incarnation) was the presumed opposition between tradition and modernity, and consequently, the relationship between music and its context. As stated in the liner notes from the recording of the Fourth Festival of Indigenous Music and Dance, organized by the INI in 1994, "Indigenous peoples are well-integrated societies, so it is difficult to speak specifically of music, dance, aesthetics, ethics, social norms, occupations, or community responsibilities as discrete areas of human activity or life itself. All are articulated, defined, and consolidated with one another. Many of the myths, customs, and rituals from which songs and dances, and much music, derive are based in essential cycles symbolically defined by the codes within each social unit, and thus are intimately related with activities, tasks, norms, and values that characterize each society."[26]

Undoubtedly, the goal of INI at that time was to highlight the importance of context in understanding indigenous music. However, by noting that musical phenomena are linked to society, this premise became an unexamined truism regarding indigenous music, one that assumes that legitimate forms of indigenous music are linked to a discretely bounded ritual worldview while dismissing what are perceived as "external" musical influences (e.g., regional popular music and commercial genres) without examining the type of social role and cultural work that these may have within those indigenous communities. In other words, it does not suffice to say that music is related to its context—one should point out how music and culture relate to each other.

This unfortunate misunderstanding regarding music and culture has resulted in another recurring problem: the classification of musical phenomena into either sacred or secular categories, into authentic traditional music and its re-creations, into traditional or commercial, indigenous or mestizo, indigenous rural or urban, and so on. These categories introduce a priori romanticized notions of indigeneity: Indians are good by nature, and therefore commercial music does nothing but pollute indigenous musical purity. Some maintain that indigenous music developed only in religious contexts; hence, it should not be considered "music" in the Western sense of the word, which includes notions of music as a form of entertainment. From this "purist" stance, an indigenous person taking payment for his or her work is seen as a capitalist intrusion; this may be true to some extent, but it should be studied further to elucidate why the indigenous person enters the marketplace in the first place.

## Final Remarks

Assessing the work of institutional indigenous music research projects in Mexico does not belie their contributions. In fact, the most notable works on Mexico's musical traditions that are considered classics today were produced within such institutional settings. My goal here is to highlight some of the more significant contradictions of such projects and the consequences that these contradictions have had in the construction of theoretical and methodological paradigms for the study of indigenous music today. I would like to add that ethnomusicology in Mexico has been largely excluded from debates within the anthropological sciences.

The notion of "indigenous music," which did not exist before the twentieth century, has been used in many generalizations and summations of information, even though there *cannot* be a single definition of "indigenous music" because it cannot be thought of as akin to a single musical genre. In other words, no definition of indigenous music can include all the diversity and contrasts that exist among indigenous communities. Guillermo Bonfil defined indigeneity as a meta-ethnic category that did not reference the cultural content of any specific group, but rather referred to the specific set of relationships between these groups and other entities within the social global system to which indigenous peoples belong.[27] If we are not aware of this, we run the risk of conflating an indigenous musical tradition with the music of poverty and marginalization. Consequently, it is better not to speak of indigenous music, but of Zoque music, Rarámuri music, or Yaqui music. Furthermore, we should differentiate between the musics of each group and within them, because different individuals use musical genres, style, lyrics, in different ways. Therefore, there is no single Zoque music but many Zoque musics that relate more to local identities than to the identity of the ethnic group per se.

This point is important because it draws our attention to local forms of musical expression, to observe the local dynamics of composition and performance. In other words, it forces us to engage with local realities rather than construct them from the outside. For instance, there are aesthetic concerns among local musicians regarding the transformation of their music that emerge at the moment of musical creation when musicians choose to emulate other musical forms and styles. They are aware of the fact that the repertoires performed by various groups have an important influence in the construction of local social identities. This is, for example, the case with the *onda grupera* [lit. the group wave—Mexican pop ballad and rock music], the *tambora sinaloense* [regional brass-based band], several genres of *música norteña* [lit. northern music—accordion-based regional music]—composed and performed by ensembles like Los Tigres del Norte, Los Tucanes [de Tijuana], and others—and the cumbias and the *rancheras anorteñadas* [rural-inspired popular music in *norteño* style]. All of these genres are to a great extent associated with migration[28] and other processes relating to recent social, political, and economic contexts of the indigenous regions of Mexico, processes that require further research.

## Notes

This article is part of a larger research project. Related findings that inspired this article are found in Marina Alonso Bolaños, *La invención de la música indígena de México: antropología e historia de las políticas culturales del siglo XX* (Buenos Aires: Editorial Sb, 2008).

1. Wilhelm Dilthey, *Introducción a las ciencias del espíritu: en la que se trata de fundamentar el estudio de la sociedad y la historia,* vol. 1 of *Obras de Wilhelm Dilthey*, ed. Eugenio Imaz (Mexico City: Fondo de Cultura Económica, 1978), 5.

2. Anne-Marie Thiesse, *La création des identités nationales: Europe XVIIIe–XXe siècle* (Paris: Seuil, 1999), 12–18.

3. Eduardo Devés Valdés, *Del Ariel de Rodó a la CEPAL (1900–1950)*, vol. 1 of *El pensamiento latinoamericano en el siglo XX: entre la modernización y la identidad* (Buenos Aires: Biblos, 2000), 25.

4. Arturo Chamorro, "La etnomusicología mexicana: un acercamiento a sus fuentes de estudio," in *Memoria del Primer Congreso de la Sociedad Mexicana de Musicología* (Tamaulipas: Dirección General de Asuntos Culturales, 1985), 80–95, p. 80.

5. Secretaría de Educación Pública, *Las Misiones Culturales en 1932–1933* (Mexico City: Secretaría de Educación Pública, 1933), 354.

6. Engracia Loyo, *Gobiernos revolucionarios y educación popular en México 1911–1928* (Mexico City: El Colegio de México, 1999), 310.

7. Secretaría de Educación Pública, *Boletín* 5, no. 2 (1926), 56–59.

8. Secretaría de Educación Pública, *Las Misiones Culturales en 1927* (Mexico City: Secretaría de Educación Pública, 1927), 4.

9. Ibid., 31.

10. Chamorro, "La etnomusicología mexicana," 88.

11. Gerard Béhague, "Latin America," in *Ethnomusicology: Historical and Regional Studies*, ed. Helen Myers (New York, London: The Norton/Grove Handbooks in Music), 472–94, p. 474.

12. These projects were financed by the Instituto Nacional de Antropología e Historia (INAH, National Institute of Anthropology and History), the Instituto Nacional Indigenista (INI, National Indigenist Institute), the Dirección General de Culturas Populares (General Office of Popular Cultures) of the Consejo Nacional para la Cultura y las Artes (CONACULTA, National Council for Culture and the Arts), and the Consejo Nacional de Ciencia y Tecnología (CONACYT, National Council for Science and Technology).

13. Marina Alonso Bolaños, "Fonoteca INAH, pionera en la difusión fonográfica de la música tradicional de México," in *No morirán mis cantos . . . : antología* (Mexico City: Fonograma del Consejo Nacional para la Culturas y las Artes, Instituto Nacional de Antropología e Historia, 1998), 1:4–7.

14. For example, the Department for the Study of Oral Music and Literature of the INAH, now the sound archive of the INAH; the National Fund for the Development of Mexican Popular Dance; the Ethnographic Audiovisual Archive of the INI; the Centro Nacional de Investigación, Documentación e Información Musical (CENIDIM, Carlos Chávez National Center for Musical Information and Documentation); the Archivo Regional de las Tradiciones Musicales, Colegio de Michoacán (College of Michoacán's

Regional Archive of Musical Traditions); and the General Office for Popular Cultures (Chamorro, "La etnomusicología mexicana," 89–91).

15. Translator's note: *Indigenismo* is an indigenist movement, a nationalist ideology emphasizing the value of Mexico's indigenous heritage.

16. To paraphrase Jack Goody, *La domesticación del pensamiento salvaje* (Madrid: Akal, 1985; originally *The Domestication of the Savage Mind*, 1977). Goody referred to changes in the processes of oral transmission stemming from the imposition of writing as the only legitimate way of preserving the memories of societies that received (but did not invent) alphabetic writing.

17. The researchers known as the Magnificent Seven were Guillermo Bonfil, Daniel Cazés, Margarita Nolasco, Mercedes Olivera, Ángel Palerm, Enrique Valencia, and Arturo Warman.

18. Henrietta Yurchenco, "La música indígena en Chiapas," in *América Indígena (Órgano Trimestral del Instituto Indigenista Interamericano)* 3, no. 4 (1943), 305–11.

19. E. Thomas Stanford, personal communication, 2005.

20. On markers of indigeneity, see Juan Pedro Viqueira, *Encrucijadas chiapanecas* (Mexico City: El Colegio de México and Editorial Tusquets, 2002).

21. On the "logic of the Other," see José Del Val, "Consideraciones generales en torno al Sistema Indigenista Interamericano" (Mexico City: Instituto Indigenista Interamericano, 1993), unpublished.

22. Benigno Robles, liner notes, *XEANT "La voz de las Huastecas,"* ed. Citlali Ruiz Ortiz and Leonardo Santiago (Mexico City: Comisión Nacional para el Desarrollo de los Pueblos Indígenas, 2006), 1.

23. Miguel Olmos, *El sabio de la fiesta: música y mitología en la región cahita-tarahumara* (Mexico City: Colección Biblioteca del Instituto Nacional de Antropología e Historia, 1998), 24.

24. Romantics believed that indigenous people were different from the rest of society by right, not only as a matter of fact; they believed that, therefore, the declaration of equality before the law would eventually solve the indigenous problem. Thus, Indians ceased to be Indians in 1821, when the Plan of Iguala was put forth; see Luis González y González, *El indio en la era liberal* (Mexico City: Clío, El Colegio Nacional, 1996), 157–58.

25. Federico Navarrete, *Las relaciones interétnicas en México* (Mexico City: México Nación Multicultural, Universidad Nacional Autónoma de México, 2004), 127.

26. José Antonio Ochoa et al., *Series Fonográficas Departamento de Etnomusicología*, ed. José Luis Sagredo (Mexico City: Instituto Nacional Indigenista, 1994).

27. Guillermo Bonfil, "Los pueblos indios, sus culturas y las políticas culturales," in *Obras escogidas de Guillermo Bonfil*, ed. Lina O. Güemes (Mexico City: Instituto Nacional Indigenista, Instituto Nacional de Antropología e Historia, Centro de Investigaciones y Estudios Superiores en Antropología Social, Dirección General de Cultural Populares, Secretaria de la Reforma Agraria, 1985), 2:352.

28. Marina Alonso Bolaños, "Canto rodado," in *Música sin fronteras: ensayos sobre migración, música e identidad*, ed. Fernando Híjar (Mexico City: Consejo Nacional para la Culturas y las Artes, Dirección General de Culturas Populares e Indígenas, 2006), 155–80.

# 17

# Metamorphosis of Afro-Brazilian Performance Traditions

## *From Cultural Heritage to the Entertainment Industry*

JOSÉ JORGE DE CARVALHO

This essay provides a set of reflections surrounding the intangible cultural heritage of Brazil, with emphasis on the performing arts (music, dance, theater, and storytelling) and related understandings and values of Afro-Brazilian communities. To accomplish this, it's necessary for me to articulate the following themes: (1) changes in the conception and objectives for documenting intangible cultural heritage; (2) changes in the role of researchers (ethnomusicologists, ethno-choreographers, anthropologists, sociologists, historians, specialists in oral literature, etc.) in the area of expressive culture; (3) important transformations in the structure of the Brazilian state that are taking place at this moment; (4) the serious problems of survival faced by the Afro-Brazilian communities holding these forms of performative knowledge; and (5) the hypertrophic role of entertainment in the contemporary era, as a consequence of the culture industry.

The issue of intangible cultural heritage requires a discussion about the performing arts that leads to an evaluation of the chronic inequality and discrimination affecting the culture bearers of these arts. At the same time, it requires a discussion of the positions adopted by researchers vis-à-vis the communities in which these popular and folk artists live. All of these factors are shaped today by the entertainment industry. I then discuss the spectacularization of the popular-

---

A longer version of this work was originally published by José Jorge de Carvalho as "Metamorfoses das tradições performáticas afro-brasileiras: de patrimônio cultural a indústria de entretenimento," *Série Antropologia* 354 (Brasília: Universidade de Brasília, 2004), 1–21. Translated by Peter Ermey with permission.

folk arts insofar as it is also the result of policies of the Brazilian state that actually support the culture industry and incentivize the commercial exploitation of these traditional artistic forms. I offer arguments that make it possible to articulate, albeit briefly, the historical specificities of each of these dimensions regarding the issue of traditional Afro-Brazilian cultural heritage today.

## Documentation and Diffusion of Intangible Heritage

The modern push for the documentation of the cultural heritage of humanity arose in the era of high imperialism, especially in the second half of the nineteenth century. At that time, the notion of heritage was global (or at least transnational). The large museums and archives of Berlin, Paris, and London were concerned about the so-called monuments of humanity, acquired by great scientific expeditions and then cataloged, archived, and preserved.

These archives privileged written works, with emphasis on the compilation of non-Western texts: Egyptian, Chinese, Arab, Persian, and Sumerian. Therefore, it was the large written archives of humanity that captured the interest of researchers—researchers who did not feel invested in the fate of the communities from which these documents originated. In principle, these researchers engaged with a past that they perceived as happening before "humanity," supposedly without a link to the groups of human beings that lived in the immediate vicinity of the archeological sites in which the researchers worked.

The invention of recording in the latter half of the nineteenth century changed the notion of archives, which accordingly began to document the music of living peoples—at least those seen as foreign to the Western world, and, in this sense, as bearers of radical cultural difference. The great phonographic archives of Berlin, London (the British Museum, and more recently, the British Institute of Recorded Sound), Paris, and Washington, D.C., were repositories for the recordings of Native North Americans, Africans, and Asians.

In all of these archives, the primary interest was comparative work, from which emerged the great hypotheses about the performing arts of humanity as a whole, especially in regard to music. As was the case with the creators of the written and archeological archives, researchers and theorists of the phonographic archives did not feel obligated to intervene politically on behalf of the communities that provided them with recorded material. From their perspective, such a distanced position was perfectly legitimate as long as they maintained the protected and self-justified role of the objective scientist. Furthermore, these researchers placed Western culture at the top of the human cultural hierarchy, failing to recognize that their comparative interest on decontextualized universals was ideologically defined.

The golden age of the great cultural archives in the last half of the nineteenth century in Europe gave way to the formation of national archives, which privileged traditional cultures considered representative of the people who constituted a given nation-state, a movement that started in Europe and soon moved to Latin America. The notion of heritage was expanded enormously to complement the materials already in the libraries, repositories of the treasured written record of the nation. Through audio and later film recordings, it was possible to put into the archives the materials associated with the oral traditions of peoples who brought diversity and uniqueness to the nation, as was the case with Mexico, Argentina, and Brazil during the first part of the twentieth century.

Let us now consider the relationship between the researcher and the folk and vernacular artist within the classic political-ideological framework of the nation-state.[1] Researchers (like Carlos Vega, Isabel Aretz, and Mário de Andrade) who would go into the field to record folk music imagined, despite significant differences in power, that the two parties involved in the process were united by a national bond, a type of mutual respect imagined by the researcher that helped to build the foundation of a new nation. Recordings of traditional music would be deposited in these national archives in the belief that the children of both the poor folk artist and the educated metropolitan could have future access to the memories and practices of earlier generations.

Despite the contact between these two actors, researchers continued their lives as members of the country's urban elite, while the keepers of folk and vernacular cultural heritage (farm workers, fishermen, cowhands, and artisans) continued with their rustic lives far from the metropolis.[2] The state discursively constructed a utopian sense of the nation, one that was defined by a minimally egalitarian imaginary, later disseminated by the educational system, which permitted researchers to maintain the belief that their projects were not opportunistic or predatory. They did not see themselves as appropriating the culture of folk and vernacular artists precisely because researchers saw their work as part of the effort to preserve the memory of the nation. Furthermore, their documentation was done without financial gain in mind.

In this period, researchers were constructed and valued as public servants who, as such, had an obligation to give their work back to society. Because of this, their identification with the object of study was high, and for some the collection of poetry and folk music becoming a lifetime passion. On the other hand, they did not get involved in the social, political, and economic dilemmas of the community, cultivating instead a different sense of politics.

An example of this model of research engagement, whose politics were rooted in culturalism, is that of Franz Boas, which developed when North American anthropology began to systematically study Native Americans as well as rural and African American communities. Boas defined the mission of the researcher (ethnographer, anthropologist, or cultural scientist) as defending and valuating the culture of those communities against the state, which had despised and mistreated them in the name of Eurocentrism.[3] Similarly, in ethnomusicology, Alan Lomax for a long time embodied the role of spokesperson on behalf of oppressed and marginalized musicians (such as blacks and poor workers), and his 1977 manifesto, "Appeal for Cultural Equality," remains relevant in this regard.[4]

## Researchers, the Nation-State, and the Entertainment Industry

The Boasian model (outlined above) was the first to establish an explicit political link between the researcher and the community, to speak truth to power. Within the context of that relationship, researchers aligned themselves with communities or ethnic groups and used the authority they derived from the state to defend the cultural dignity of those groups, demanding equal treatment and justice on their behalf in the eyes of that same state. By that act, researchers felt that they accomplished their mission. They sought to give back the aesthetic gifts they received from the community in which they conducted research by defending these practices within their specific academic fields and in the realm of ideas, distancing themselves from the field of politics in the strict sense of the term.

In the case of music practices, field recordings made by researchers in the 1950s did not hold any major commercial interest. At the most, researchers imagined that only other researchers would be interested in listening to what were deemed exotic musics from remote regions of the planet. Ethnomusicological recordings, therefore, had an objective much like that of the publication of a monograph or study: they were basically regarded as ethnographic documents.

For a long time, those ethnographic recordings did not necessarily have a potentially harmful effect on the communities from which they were collected because they circulated in a social environment outside of capitalist consumerism. In the 1970s, however, a dramatic change occurred: the production and publication of audiovisual materials began to be required as part of the professional development of innumerable ethnomusicologists. Many researchers then had to expand their work beyond what had been customary (teaching, writing academic textbooks, and giving lectures at conferences) in order to also dedicate efforts to the commercial publication of the music they had researched.

As culture industries interested in the exotic grew, the role of researchers as mediators of cultural consumption deepened. Researchers who had previously seen themselves in a category clearly separate from that occupied by the performing artists they researched now took on a secondary role that went beyond the dissemination of archival materials within strictly academic contexts. They became the producers of liner notes, photos, descriptions, and introductory materials for ethnographic recordings that were no longer published only by state institutions like the Berliner Phonogramm-Archiv, the Smithsonian, or the Musée de l'Homme [Museum of Man]. They also produced recordings for commercial labels in a recorded music industry that increasingly imposed on researchers the notion that their work needed to have market value. If researchers had previously contented themselves with the idea that their work contributed to intellectual pursuits, that the musical practices they researched helped to raise awareness about particular musical practices and folk and vernacular artists, now they were implicated as mediators of a complex capitalist structure linked to the industrial production of commercial recordings.

It is not pertinent here to analyze why the entertainment industry moved toward more exotic music. But it is important to note that there was a perverse synchronization between the commercialization of exotic musical performances and decolonization or cultural resistance. When researchers speak academically about a particular musical tradition, they indirectly mark it for potential use as a source of entertainment. Consequently, the record industry became interested in expanding its repertory of consumer products that featured these new exotic elements acquired by researchers.

The new message that the researcher promotes then, is no longer just one concerning politics, racism and ethnic discrimination, class inequalities, or cultural condescension, but also one concerning market relations. As such, researchers, operating in a paradoxical Samaritan logic of economic development, come to believe that, when they are able to achieve some economic benefit for a community, they can then be ethically justified in abandoning their role as objective scientist and public servant and in engaging with the culture industry.

This was a radical transformation of what the role of the researcher should be. The idea that an ethnomusicologist's field research, which aimed to collect and document traditions previously marginalized by the state, should be legitimized by financial gain, even for the financial gain of the musicians, would have been unthinkable under the logic of the researcher as public servant. Since the 1980s, however, researchers of folk and vernacular music, dance, and theater have increasingly become mediators of the commercialization of the people they research. We can cite a classic U.S. example that has held true since that time: researchers go to the field, return with their recordings, edit a compact disc, publish it commercially, later gather the musicians together to do shows and tours, become the group's spokespersons on those tours, give interviews to newspapers, and speak at universities and concert halls where the musicians perform. In sum, the researcher is transformed into a producer and presenter.

To summarize briefly, up to this point there have been three main changes in the relationship between ethnomusicologists and the musicians that they study. First, armchair researchers were completely removed from the dilemmas experienced by the communities whose music was stored in the archives in which they worked. Second, a generation later, the researcher was an intermediary, in line with an agenda of solidarity and decolonization; an example is Alan Lomax, who accepted the role of spokesperson on behalf of communities that faced problems dealing with more powerful institutions, while still maintaining his distance from these communities in terms of social class. Finally, as we discussed, researchers today act as mediators between the community and the cultural and entertainment industries for both contact and contract purposes.

In light of this last role, I propose elsewhere another transformation in the position of the researcher: ethnomusicologists who are no longer spokespersons, but listeners and activists that denounce the false contracts forged between the producers of entertainment and folk and vernacular musicians.[5]

## The Anthropophagic Attitude as Class and Race Ideologies

As I now turn to the main model of cultural ideology of the Brazilian nation-state, that famous modernist project, I critically analyze a classic phrase from the Anthropophagic Manifesto of Oswald de Andrade: "I'm only interested in what is not mine" (*Só me interessa o que não é meu*).[6] In reference to the relationship between elite metropolitan artists and Afro-Brazilian or indigenous communities, the author of the phrase does not question the privileges of class and race of the individual who can make this claim. For example, a choreographer from the Rio–São Paulo regions can "cannibalistically" appropriate from a particular performance style of a *tambor-de-crioula* [Afro-Brazilian dance associated with the religious celebrations for St. Benedict] from Maranhão [northeast Brazil]. However, not one artist from this *tambor-de-crioula* can exercise that same type of cultural cannibalism with the practices of a "highbrow" dance group that performs in the Municipal Theater of Rio de Janeiro, one that is supported, let's say, by a million-dollar subsidy from the Banco Itaú [a Brazilian bank] that allows that dance company to realize its goals of aesthetic anthropophagy.

The anthropophagic motto functions, in practice, as a kind of secret code of aesthetic impunity and privilege controlled by the dominant classes in Brazil. In that process of anthropophagy, which is obviously a one-way street, two interconnected groups celebrate their privilege over artists from indigenous and Afro-Brazilian communities, using symbols they claim to be national. These two groups are those that had no guilt or reservations about realizing this type of celebrated modernist cultural synthesis (cultural borrowings that over time turned into cultural theft), and those who grew out of this historical legacy and who today propose and manage intangible cultural heritage registries and inventories without politically problematizing the withdrawal of the state in favor of business marketing models with no long-term commitment to the very performance traditions that they celebrate.

I insist on questioning Oswald de Andrade's phrase, invoked so frequently (and which is emblematic of an attitude of arrogance), as well as the notion that it constitutes one of the few metaphors for the meeting between researchers and popular and folk artists in Brazil. Constantly referenced throughout the 1980s, the phrase legitimizes the continuous interventions of cultural appropriation and expropriation. "I'm only interested in what is not mine": I can take everything, not only because I like to do so, but because I have the power to do so. This attitude leads to the self-centered voracity of the [Brazilian] white cultural elite, requiring that all of the Afro-Brazilian and indigenous performance traditions, sacred or profane, be at their disposal, not only to satisfy their aesthetic appetite as consumers and performers, but also to try to resolve the ambivalence and political schizophrenia of its own Western identity and deep Eurocentrism.

## Sacred Performance or Entertainment

One of the questions intriguing many of us today is how to understand why, suddenly, a sector of the white middle class needs to re-create folk and vernacular traditions, going so far as sometimes directly invading the expressive space of popular and folk classes (above all of Afro-Brazilians). It is an attempt by the middle class to perform for itself this folk and vernacular culture as if it belonged to it, when historically it has been an emblem of resistance for Afro-Brazilian communities against the discrimination it still suffers at the hands of whites.

Before undertaking any specific discussion regarding ideology, I must say that what sustains that belief, that privileged game of knowing "the truth," is also the supposed right to be entertained in this era of the consumer-citizen. Therefore, I deem it necessary to theorize the concepts of spectacle and entertainment in reference to the notion of the culture industry, with its transnational tendencies, as a counterpoint to the analysis of the role of cultural policy in the current nation-state. This is helpful because entertainment is one of the two pillars of our urban capitalist way of life. To entertain means to stop time, to pause in order to dream how to be—or, rather, to dream to be that someone else (because we have access to them). It is to bracket a moment between labor activities that require focused attention and wear thin the utopian character of life. Although watching a show for two hours can create a pause, it returns us immediately thereafter to the same life as before.

It is this social and political filter of dense aesthetic-symbolic experience that is called entertainment. And only within the logic of entertainment is it possible to fantasize that folk and vernacular culture, the heritage and vital source of another community or ethnicity, class, or other racial group, can be captured and annexed as a cultural heritage available to our urban middle class.[7] That class able to pay for exotic entertainment is a middle class capable of accumulating disposable income. Nevertheless, to understand the phenomenon of the commodified staging of folk and vernacular culture in our era, we must also seek to understand, not only the motivations of those who consume the show or performance, but also the motivations of those who accept the transformation of their sacred rituals into shows transformed into commodities.

In the most common of cases, traditional rituals suffer a semiological and semantic reduction at the moment they are transformed into a commercial spectacle. A *cavalo marinho* [seahorse dance], for example, that lasts twelve hours in a neighborhood just outside Recife, is mutilated into a one-hour public show for the tourist circuit managed by the Office of Tourism.[8] It suffers a loss similar to that of literary works published in the *Reader's Digest*, which reduces the 1,800 pages of *War and Peace* into 200 pages of light reading. Furthermore, in some cases the mutilation can be counterproductive even to the logic of maximization of labor subscribed to by cultural producers of the entertainment industry.

In most cases, a group of performing artists is paid to present a show for the tourists in less time than the minimum necessary for those same artists to leave the performance feeling satisfied that they have achieved the expressive goals driving them internally. In other words, a group of performers receives a supposedly better value (better remuneration for less time spent working) that, however, operates under an inverse ideology of capitalist production motivated by the actions of the mediator and cultural brokers. In these instances, where the expressive language of a performance is sacrificed because audiences demand quick entertainment, cultural brokers buy the time that traditional artist groups seek to offer to their audiences, the gift of time expressed in the language of aesthetics, in order to kill it. In place of productivist logic in which more time equals more money, the artists receive extra money specifically so that they do not fully express themselves, so that they do not take more time than the time that consumers pay to be entertained—in the end, they are paid to be silent.

In such cases, performances are not just reduced or condensed, but they die, lacking the time they need to live. This is a time that is dense, open, and alive from the sacrifices made by those who have died. Yet, what consumers regard as traditional Afro-Brazilian song, dance, and poetry is, in fact, a stillborn simulacrum that haunts like a ghost from the machine-driven world of capitalist production. Paying for the show, which confirms the purchase and guarantees leisure time for the white consumer, also signifies the reduction of the time that folk and vernacular artists (almost always Afro-Brazilian) need in order to show their art in a humanizing context. This leads me to think that perhaps time itself should be regarded as one of the most important forms of intangible cultural heritage of indigenous and Afro-Brazilian communities. A type of heritage that is specifically threatened by the compression of time associated with the culture industries and contemporary capitalism.

My main interest here is in acknowledging the impact that leisure time has in the lives of folk and vernacular artists, a time that functions as a vehicle (in this case, objectified by the external demand of the cultural industry) for aesthetic relations. The impact on spectators who purchase that show is no less important, however. By agreeing to consume a condensed performance, spectators also buy, in a doubly schizophrenic maneuver, the absence of the time that is not available to them but which is necessary for a rich, complex, and long [non-commodified] performance. That temporal emptiness is not inert and only intensifies the effect of simulacrum (in the Baudrillardian sense of the diminution of contact with reality) that has already eroded spectators' lives, requiring them to buy leisure time to compensate for the absence of the time necessary to experience a complete and substantive (and, generally speaking, sacred) performance.

That same emptiness that audiences acquire (or absorb, or incorporate) is fed back mimetically to folk and vernacular artists, partially emptying them of the aura they seek to preserve when realizing a complete performance of their art. Spectators have little time at their disposal to be entertained and therefore pay for a simulacrum of a traditional performance. Conversely, artist groups have (too much?) time available to realize their art and, paradoxically, are paid not to enact the expressive mission of the rituals they seek to perpetuate. This is not a zero-sum game but a game that adds a corrosive influence to the social and historical experiences of artists as well as of spectators. In this way, a commodifying form levels and flattens out in a profound way the temporal poverty of a class that needs to be continually entertained with the temporal wealth of those in classes who are increasingly pressured to sell (partly in the form of silence) their ability to entertain.[9]

To understand the importance of the continuity of traditional performing arts is to appreciate the experience of a sense of time that cannot be encapsulated by the commodified performance paradigm. In the realm of the culture industry, semiological variety is synonymous with increased value. It is that consumer value (one that cannot stand the repetition of vocal, rhythmic, or instrumental signs) that insinuates itself dangerously into the promotion of archives of traditional oral heritage, particularly when the state reduces its involvement and begins to regard the traditions of Afro-Brazilian communities and indigenous nations (both lacking citizenship and access to resources and public services) as potential commodities to be freely exploited by the culture industry.[10]

## The Researcher's Responsibility

The advent of material culture registries tied to the growing spectacularization of the traditional performing arts [the staging of these practices as a form of commercial entertainment] involves a discussion of the transformations of the role of researchers vis-à-vis the performing arts culture-bearing communities as seen from the vantage point of the culture industries.

More than a moral dilemma, I believe that the discussion of positions currently occupied by researchers and their implications for communities being researched must be articulated within a framework of the notion of responsibility. Whether we as researchers are distant observers, spokespersons, shields, mediators, or converts who perform these musics, we must openly show to the institutions we belong to the ways in which we understand our responsibility toward the groups that we study and with which we interact. Responsibility implies a receptive attitude, providing answers and an interactive dialogue capable of establishing a bridge between the values and interests of our world and the values and interests of the world of folk and vernacular artists.

Due to a lack of clarity, or perhaps even conformity, we claim freedom of action and the right not to be questioned about research ethics when it comes to our interventions in the sacred performance practices of indigenous and Afro-Brazilian communities, something that is no more than outright impunity regarding the consequences of our actions.

A defensive stance very common among various researchers is to ascribe the power of resistance to local communities, to celebrate their ability to resignify foreign elements, and to favorably repurpose the capitalist relations of domination they have been subjected to by the various mediators of the culture industry (including many researchers). The curious thing about these cases is that, as members of the voracious-cannibalist class, researchers who seek to find communities and performative expressions that are not yet part of an established commercial entertainment circuit fail to acknowledge their role in the subsequent process of expropriation of these musical expressions, instead transferring that responsibility to folk and vernacular musicians themselves. These musicians then, are the ones who must be sufficiently powerful to absorb those external pressures and emerge victorious from the encounter. It is common, in fact, to hear a particularly perverse reiteration of the already-perverse anthropophagic precept, "I'm only interested in what is not mine." This is what indigenous and Afro-Brazilian groups are expected to say when they hybridize their cultural forms by incorporating new Western elements into their traditional forms. It is an excellent way to extricate ourselves from the problem we have caused: indigenous people and Afro-Brazilians, largely living on the edge between poverty and indigence, are charged with the responsibility of becoming powerful enough to manipulate in their favor the assault to which they are subjected by the culture industry. And, if they are incapable of manipulating the industry's agents, the failure will be that of indigenous peoples and Afro-Brazilians, not that of the culture industry!

This issue intersects with some theories regarding performance that have remained relevant for the last thirty years. One important strand to follow stems from Cuban theorist Inés Martiatu's critique of Eugenio Barba's theater anthropology.[11] Citing Barba's stay among the Yanomami indigenous group in Venezuela, and expanding on a reflexive self-critique initiated by Richard Schechner, Inés Martiatu stresses that the Yanomami never invited Bara and his theater company to visit them in the Amazonian rain-forest region where they live. As such, the fundamental responsibility for the consequences of that interaction for the Yanomami way of life must lie with Barba and his actors, not with an indigenous group that did not know they were creating something that was deemed [by Barba] a performance, a practice that is highly valued as an entertainment commodity among the more intellectual segments of Western societies.[12]

It is that notion of responsibility that I would like to incorporate into the current discussion regarding the relationship between researchers and folk and vernacular groups, whose horizon of artistic self-expression, in the majority of cases, is devoted to the performance of the sacred. The sacred, as I argue elsewhere, sets the limits of negotiation between culture-bearing communities and the agents of the culture industry, those who seek to turn traditional ritual art into a commodified performance.[13] Negotiation only makes sense when we consider that which is nonnegotiable (that line that cannot be crossed). Otherwise, it would not be a negotiation as much as a process of conquest, surrender, capitulation, complete submission, a loss of that which is sacred.

At the moment of negotiation, we must first focus on the mediators on behalf of the culture industry. We are the ones demanding that the *congado*, *jongo*, *maracatu*, and *tambor-de-crioula* [four Afro-Brazilian folk music and dance genres associated with religious rituals] engage with us. Popular and folk artists are not the "skilled negotiators." The skilled negotiators are the producers and entrepreneurs linked to the tourism and entertainment industries who help to weaken the state in order to assume a more irresponsible and autonomous position against it. They champion the notion of folk and vernacular performance as a form of value-added entertainment, leaving to the state the responsibility of inventorying and preserving it as intangible cultural heritage, as if [the state and the culture industry] were not part of the same social, economic, and racial networks. To a certain extent, we as researchers are also producing an ideological legitimation (under the guise of theory) by emphasizing in this process of unprecedented commodification the notions of negotiation, fusion, and hybridization of traditional cultures, without addressing the monumental economic inequalities regarding access to the spheres of power and decision making that are almost always unfavorable to indigenous and Afro-Brazilian communities.

Going deeper still, it is necessary to include an analysis of class in the discussion of intangible cultural heritage and its metamorphoses. Those who make cultural heritage policy belong to the same social networks as those who research folk and vernacular performances. Those researchers also act as mediators in the spectacularization of traditional performing arts, and now also borrow directly from said traditions, casting themselves in a role [as performers] previously exclusively occupied by folk and vernacular artists.

The crisis of the Brazilian state can also affect the researchers' perspective, generating new ambivalences about allegiance and even social and political identification. On one hand, the number of people who intermittently perform in popular and folk performances is growing. On the other hand, the notion of scientific neutrality continues to be invoked in regard to possible questions of authority and abuse of power and influence. From the perspective of citizenship, the question of responsibility can shift to the social mission of educational institutions (which are mostly public), for example graduate programs, the majority of which lack deep commitment to projects related to governance. Nonetheless, the most common attitude among these programs has been reactionary, accusing the state of unwarranted interference when it asks for some type of social commitment from those disciplines associated with the study of culture, as if it were an affront to academic freedom.

Who must assume more responsibility for the protection and promotion of intangible cultural heritage? The state, which demands a social commitment to local communities from research training programs devoted to the study of culture? Or educational institutions, which complain about the state, both for not providing them enough resources and for unjustifiably intervening with their scientific autonomy? Either way, until now there has been a tacit agreement between academia and the state to not assume their joint responsibility for the commercial exploitation of folk and vernacular performative knowledge and the lack of return benefits available to local communities as their performing traditions are made more accessible to broader audiences.

## From Mediation to Masquerade

We can summarize here questions to be discussed critically in some future forum about the policies governing research in the traditional performing arts in the era of the culture industry and the diminishing role of the state.

In many cases nowadays, researchers operate as brokers for the complex business interests associated with the culture industries. A conflict of the researchers' loyalties is at play here: who will their mediation serve better, the market or the community? To resolve this conflict, I think researchers must clearly inform the culture bearers and communities that they research of all of the agreements and consequences of their participation in the culture industries. Complementing the approach formulated by Franz Boas and Alan Lomax, it will be necessary for researchers to make an explicit commitment not only to become the groups' spokespersons or brokers within the entertainment marketplace, but also to become advocates for the group from the outside in, instructing the folk and vernacular artists about the rules and values of the capitalistic environment that desires and absorbs them. There is a still greater risk, in that our very work as mediators becomes ethically unsustainable. Instead of supporting a community in need in its fight for economic emancipation, this mediating role can actually contribute to a reproduction of our secular inequality, namely, the commodification of traditional performance practices of a historically marginal group as a new form of economic, racial, and class exploitation by a more economically and politically powerful group, this time with the endorsement of specialists from academia and from the state's cultural institutions.

In other cases, also frequent, researchers utilize their academic authority in the form of lectures and conference papers that combine modernist ideology with so-called postmodern theory to politically legitimize the cannibalization of traditional artistic forms by so-called highbrow or elite artists. The danger here is a new conflict of loyalties, equally unfavorable for the "native" or folk and vernacular artists. After all, these "highbrow" artists belong to the same social class as the researchers who talk about them and are interconnected by innumerable ties of interest and group reciprocity. These researchers' first instinct is to legitimize artistic cannibalism, "complicating it" theoretically by means of the notion of anthropophagic hybridity combined with the individualist ideology of artistic practice in modernity. In more extreme cases, researchers even take as their object of study the work of other research colleagues, placing them in the role of the "native" artist. In these cases, the conflict of interest is accentuated even more, leading not toward the critique, but toward a legitimation of the cannibalistic act.

Finally, there are cases in which researchers merge their roles as brokers and as anthropophagic artists, taking ownership of the performing art they are studying and placing themselves in the role of the "native" artist. There are various specific processes of appropriation at play. In some cases, researchers become just one more performer within a local folk and vernacular group. In other cases, researchers create a counterpart group that performs, for their own or others' entertainment, the same artistic forms they are studying. That situation, in which researchers assume the role of artists of the art they study and that is practiced by members of another social or racial group, creates a deep crisis of representation, an exhaustive analysis of which remains to be done.

Let us consider just a few of these points. In the first case, in which researchers present themselves as members of a traditional group, the crisis of representation could be resolved by claiming that their ability to represent an "other" artistic tradition through performance should be subjected to the aesthetic standards of the original group. However, the power difference between the two parties is so great that in many cases the group of folk and vernacular artists also depends on researchers for various types of support and must accept their participation without being able to express any possible disapproval or embarrassment generated by their presence of new (and usually sporadic) members in the group. The full acceptance, therefore, of researchers as occasional folk and vernacular artists is not entirely secured or guaranteed.

In the case of researchers who start their own counterpart "native" music and dance groups, the crisis of representation is even more pronounced, and the problems created by the large difference in power are even greater. On one hand, researchers will hone their ability to perform in their own social environment an art form from another social, ethnic, racial, and above all economic group. This is especially true because they are moving a performance tradition from its original marginal context to their own urban environment, which is generally middle class. This change in context also makes it immensely more difficult for the original communities to provide their own aesthetic assessment of researchers' ability to perform their artistic tradition, even if they are willing to do so.

Here the dangers are great. It can be that a poor or distorted rendition of the culture of the other begins to spread without that original community being able to voice its opinion. Changes for the sake of aesthetic or dramatic impact can take place, which can lead to serious losses at the symbolic level: acoustic musical instruments may be substituted with electronic instruments; there may be neglectful interventions transform the formal aspects of arrangement, melody, form, and order in which songs and dances are presented; vocal techniques may be altered or eliminated; rhythmic patterns may be simplified or have their character altered; performance attire may also change. If these things occur, who will make those responsible accountable? Will the original artists remain unprotected or even be excluded from the process of circulation of their own art? Who will guarantee that researcher or artists will return to the culture-bearing communities, opening themselves to critique and evaluation by the source artists?

An analysis of the social-, class-, and race-based motivations underlying the interest in appropriating an art form cultivated by those in another social and racial stratum still remains an open question. As an initial hypothesis, it is possible that this new form of cannibalism has emerged as a symptom of growing racial and class division in Brazil over the last decades, what has become almost an implicit form of structural segregation. It may be that the white middle class that demands and desires that researchers perform the musical and choreographed "native" traditions for them no longer tolerates the physical and symbolic proximity of actual "natives" in their spaces for living and socializing. On the other hand, probably due to Brazil's deep identity crisis—which is related to its alleged white, Western origins (an allegiance that endures and remains unresolved during the present historical moment when the country's dominant classes have come to generically celebrate subaltern identities as a means of defining themselves vis-à-vis the first world)—that middle class also feels compelled to establish symbolic bridges to the [formerly marginalized] African [and indigenous] legacies of the country. A solution some middle-class white Brazilians have found [to this identity crisis], apparently satisfying from a psychological perspective, is to experiment with the more explicit adoption of African cultural and aesthetic values, but without questioning their own role in the reproduction of the social and racial inequalities that those source communities continue to endure.[14]

## Race and Brazilian Performative Heritage

For the first time, probably, we [Brazilians] are recognizing as a legitimate subject for academic discussion that the notion of Brazilian intangible cultural heritage is not color-blind. It is racialized, as it is implicitly shown in the discourse of the academic elite, from Gilberto Freyre to today. The overwhelming majority of the performing arts that are being targeted for expropriation [as forms of commodified entertainment] are of African origin—as noted earlier, the *congado*, the *jongo*, the *maracatu*, the *tambor-de-crioula*—which, at the same time, continue to be performed by artists from Afro-Brazilian communities. Yet, the theorists and policy makers dealing with cultural heritage, as well as the researchers and mediators mentioned above, are overwhelmingly white. The use of these traditions as forms of entertainment, therefore, is a racializing operation; it is Afro-Brazilians from poor communities who put on their [musical] practices of African origin for the entertainment of a white middle class. So far, the discussion of cultural practices has not recognized the inextricable entanglement across the supposed cleavage between class and race. From now on, escaping to a vision of Brazilian society as *morena*, *mestiça*, or integrated is no longer tenable.[15] To show that a discussion about the racialization of the performing arts can no longer be postponed, it is enough to remember that, at this time, in the nation's various regional capitals we have white *maracatu*, white *capoeira* [a form of Afro-Brazilian martial art performed with musical accompaniment], white *tambor-de-crioula*, white *cacuriá* [dance performed during the Feast of the Holy Spirit in northeastern part of the country], white *jongo*, white *congado*, in addition to white samba schools, and white *pagode* [a substyle of samba], among other white versions of traditional

Afro-Brazilian performing arts. I offer two concrete examples regarding this new political-racial configuration of Afro-Brazilian culture. For the first, I visited a rehearsal of Maracatu Estrela Brilhante (Shining Star) in Recife in December 2002 in which twenty-seven of the thirty percussionists were from the white middle class. Second, in November 2003, I visited a presentation of the *berimbau* [a musical bow used to accompany capoeira performances] orchestra of the Grupo Nzinga de Capoeira Angola (Capoeira Angola Nzinga Ensemble) in Brasília at the headquarters of the Fundação Cultural Palmares (Cultural Foundation of Palmares), in which twenty-eight of the thirty *capoeira* players were white and middle class, and two were black.[16]

For more than half a century, [Brazilian] Freyrean ideologues from the social sciences promoted, both nationally and internationally, the notion that Afro-Brazilian culture did not suffer from segregation as did the African American culture in the United States, offering carnival and samba as the great examples of [racial] integration. Nothing was said, however, about the near-exclusive participation of Afro-Brazilians in the *congado mineiro* (from Minas Gerais), *afoxé baiano* ([music and dance genre associated with Carnaval] from Bahia), *ticumbi gaucho* ([music and dance genre associated with the Feast of Saint Benedict] from Rio Grande do Sul), *maracatu pernambucano* (from Pernambuco), *congada goiana* (from Goiás), *congo capixaba* (from Espírito Santo), *jongo fluminense* (from Rio de Janeiro), *congo paulista* (from São Paulo), and so on. There was a systematic erasure of the deep connection between poor Afro-Brazilian communities—*quilombos* [rural settlements, many originally founded by runaway slaves], rural districts, urban neighborhoods, and favelas—and these great traditions of African origin [carnival and samba] that have been identified as emblematic of [Brazil's] intangible cultural heritage. Samba was always mentioned [as an example] precisely because it was an expression of Afro-Brazilian culture that had been co-opted and expropriated by the white elite as a symbol of national integration.

Today, however, it is possible to perform *maracatu*, *capoeira*, or *congado* exclusively for the white middle class. The historic blackness associated with these traditions should come to the fore, inviting us to reconsider the false image of integration that up to now has sustained the theories about Brazilian intangible cultural heritage. In this new context, in which we encounter the appropriation of Afro-Brazilian traditions and performative knowledge by groups that are exclusively white, we cannot but underscore the fact that theorists about cultural heritage, "cannibalizing" artists, and researchers (with extremely few and rare exceptions) were always white.

I maintain that the requisite discussion here is not primarily accusatory, condemnatory, or inquisitorial, but specifically ethnographic. Given the existence of white *capoeira* and black *capoeira* groups, one must ask: why aren't there *capoeira* or *maracatu* groups with 50 percent white and 50 percent black participation? In this moment in our national history, then, we have Afro-Brazilian performance heritage being articulated by poor blacks and by rich whites. Obviously, class barriers are being imposed from above, accentuating even further the polarized chasm of race that is already so difficult to traverse (at least for now).

It is worth noting that not all appropriation or diffusion of performance traditions is necessarily negative or destructive. The June festivities [in honor of St. John the Baptist's birth], for example, have already completely spilled out of the rural context in which they were mostly found throughout the twentieth century. Nowadays, we have *arraiás* [huge tents with thatched roofs where the celebrations take place] for St. John that have thoroughly adapted to the lifestyles of all classes and social strata [in Brazil]. A *quadrilha* [square dance] performed by rich people at an *arraiá* in Lago Sul in Brasília, for example, is no less authentic than a *quadrilha* of field hands in a small village in Goiás. There has been, in fact, a free symbolic exchange without a type of class-based cooptation analogous to the race-based cooptation that characterized, for example, *samba carioca* [from Rio de Janeiro] during the Getúlio Vargas era [1930–45]. New meanings and values, added to the "original" performance of the *quadrilha*, cut across classes and social groups, making that tradition more polysemous and more deeply national, in the pluralistic sense of the term.

The story of this dance, which prompted the creation of the larger performative genre that we now know as *forró* [music and dance genre from the northeast, originally associated with patron saint celebrations], closely follows the steps outlined by the folklorist and cultural historian Carlos Vega in his theory of the cultural zigzag between the dominant and subaltern classes.[17] The *quadrilha* was brought to Brazil at the beginning of the nineteenth century by Princess Leopoldina, wife of Emperor Pedro I [r. 1824–34]. She came to Rio de Janeiro accompanied by a group of aristocrats from the Viennese court who happened to dance the quadrille, one of the typical dances of European nobility. It soon spread to the cabarets and bordellos of the city and was finally assimilated by the common people, not only in the capital but also in the interior of the country. The assimilation of the court quadrille by the folk and vernacular classes attenuated some signs associated with the aristocratic etiquette, making them untransferrable, while acquiring innumerable other diacritical signs associated with folk and vernacular culture: clothing, a "hick" style of speaking, facial expressions, body language, gender roles, as well as important changes in musical form and the use of musical instruments. Years later, that collection of signs was regarded by the upper classes as a model of a happy, contented, and relaxed life [associated with the countryside]. Later still, a new generation of the upper class began to reintroduce the dance into their midst, no longer the "original" quadrille (the one that traveled from Vienna to Rio de Janeiro), but the folk and vernacular *quadrilha* danced in fields, markets, and public spaces of the villages in the interior of the country.

In this sense, then, the "label of origin" is always a convention, a decision by the cultural unconscious in relation to a historical narrative that defines the copy as an object of desire and emulation. A symbol of a different way of life that possesses some type of positive expressivity that a group feels it lacks, something that allows the group to change its outlook by expressing new things using a new language, or reinforce a preexisting perspective, only with a new language appropriated from another racial, class, or ethnic group. Origin, following here the line of thought outlined by Walter Benjamin, does not refer to genesis, to a type of ground zero before which nothing existed (a type of argument that was practically demolished by Derrida's theory of signs). Rather, it refers to the pre-emergence of the symbol (*Ursprung*), from the past to the present. Simply and prosaically, it refers to the historical emergence of a previously existing cultural matrix. As such, it deserves to be respected, because we receive, inherit, or extract from those who transmit it (in a peaceful or violent way) the ever-fragmentary symbolic legacy that we call intangible cultural heritage.[18]

This caveat must be stated in order to not let ourselves fall into a purist, static, or reifying view regarding expressive culture traditions. We are dealing with a phenomenon of expropriation and aesthetic, symbolic, and economic cannibalization with very specific characteristics.[19] For example, there are already cases of groups and cultural associations made up of members of the white middle class that perform sacred rituals, like the Dance of St. Gonzalo, transforming them into copies or barely simulations, inasmuch as they do not exhibit any [religious] devotion to the saint. The issue pertains not only to the resignification and reterritorialization of traditional symbols in urban and metropolitan contexts, a theme already amply discussed in the anthropological, sociological, and historical literature. What worries many scholars at this time is the expropriation of those traditions as forms of commodified entertainment or as an unprecedented exercise of power. In the first instance, mediation by researchers might not be favorable for the community. In the second case, the authorship of folk and vernacular artists and the zeal that communities have for their sacred traditions can be trampled by a social and racial group with more opportunities for social mobility, a group that decides to perform those "other" traditions, disconnecting them in the process from a local sense of identity and belonging, historical religious consciousness, aesthetic creation, originality, a source for self-esteem, and political resistance.

Given that Afro-Brazilian performance traditions are now also performed by middle-class whites for a public that is equally white and middle class, I propose that we now consider updating how we deal with this type of expressive and political structure. Rather than conceptualizing it as commonsense genre differentiation, it should be regarded as a strategic displacement of expressive signs that function, by way of a staging performances removed from daily life contexts, as a new mode of seduction within the same group that cannibalized them from a source community. Simplifying the argument, this masquerade inverts the process most commonly discussed by postcolonial theory regarding the lucid and critical mimesis of dominant forms by subaltern subjects, using an oblique or ironic style.

This subaltern mode of critical resistance oscillates between two models. On the one side, there is irony or burlesque dramatization of the supposed seriousness of the customs and etiquette of dominant groups, as exemplified by the seminal documentary by Jean Rouch, *Les Maîtres Fous*, and the essays about mimesis and alterity by Michael Taussig.[20] On the other side, there is the generation of a threat to the authority of the dominant group by means of a symbolic terror, one that also makes use of a mask of resistance that is effective, not because it resorts to an objectifying form of subaltern power, but because of its control of rhetorical communication; in other words, by the convincing character of a threatening staging. Examples of analyses of this type, again, can be found in the ethnography of Colombian shamanism by Michael Taussig and in essays by Homi Bhabha.[21]

In counterpoint to what Frederic Jameson calls the "antagonistic dialogue of class voices," in the case analyzed here it is the seemingly more privileged subject (the white middle class as opposed to poor black communities) that must perform a masquerade of subaltern culture to entertain itself and communicate between its peers.[22] The symbolic relations of power and domination in this case are considerably complex, and I cannot do more than summarize the idea of the masquerade as an alternative theoretical scheme to interpret this difficult-to-define phenomenon of cultural appropriation.

What I call a masquerade basically refers to a staging, done by white middle-class artists (many of whom are researchers of folk and vernacular culture) for an audience that is also white and middle class, utilizing a semiotic cloak that renews itself by means of a triple displacement: a performance tradition of African origin, preserved and practiced by lower-class blacks, and historically created to strengthen a form of alterity previously undermined (although at the same time constructed) by the violence of slavery, later becoming a vehicle for communication for a white upper class that primarily identifies with Western culture.

In Brazil we had a previous and similar iteration of this form of staging: when the *lundu* [a nineteenth-century dance] went from the slave living quarters to the parlors of slave owners' houses. At that time, white maidens wearing Luso-

Brazilian clothes staged the dance for young white men; this dance was previously performed, in the barnyard, by black female slaves for young black male slaves.

That type of masquerade, already well studied in the Brazilian case, was very common in slave societies of the New World in the nineteenth century. Its most immediate equivalents are the *danzón* [Afro-Cuban music and dance genre from the turn of the twentieth century] and other Afro-Cuban dances, studied by Alejo Carpentier, that made their way to the salons of the white Cuban elite. There was also the *bomba*, a musical form of the slaves of Puerto Rico and studied by Ángel Quintero Rivera, that like *lundu* "ascended" socially through a process of mimesis. Another notable example to contrast with these three Latin American cases are the minstrels of the United States in the nineteenth century: whites, the dominant ethnicity, painted their faces black and played the musical repertoire of U.S. blacks.[23] These four examples address a type of racial and class division (and conflict) typical of the formation of the slave nations in the Americas.

The point I want to highlight here is that this racial masquerade returned precisely at a time of general decolonization and the struggle against racism in the New World, particularly in Brazil. Different from the decolonizing mimesis of the subaltern mentioned above—which we can call progressive in that it permits a new field of expression and consequently brings to light the specific contradictions of colonial societies—that resurgence of the masquerade of the white elite risks having a regressive and destructive impact on both groups involved. It can be regressive for the educated white middle class to the extent that it reinforces a Freyrean nostalgia for a naive and innocent appropriation of Afro-Brazilian culture, forgetting that the severe social and racial antagonism of contemporary Brazil requires a different attitude of whites (above all those at universities or with a college education) supposedly committed to the universalization of citizenship. The masquerade would therefore function as the opposite of the fight for affirmative action: instead of helping to make way for black artists, some white youths are practically barring them from the urban musical scene and occupying their places, even if temporarily—which is doubly problematic because, beyond its staging, it calls attention to the attitude that Afro-Brazilian performance traditions are disposable, as disposable and temporary as all objects of consumption.

The masquerade can also be highly destructive to black performing artists, to the extent that they begin to see themselves reflected in a new mirror that can dictate and impose new iterations of subalternity. That mirror is connected to the racist aesthetic values conditioned by the media and the culture industry, whose mechanisms of diffusion cannot be controlled. Furthermore, this unwanted negative perspective emerges exactly at a time when these artists are gaining prominence as a result of the work of civil and other organizations and new pressures for the state to address their demands by rising above older iterations of subalternity associated with the marginalization and invisibility associated with the chronic post-slavery neglect.

In this sense, by questioning the historicized opposition between the oral and written traditions, Derridean deconstruction forces us to recognize all natives as authors, each one emerging in an unstable and singular point from incessant dissemination.[24] The question regarding the ownership of Afro-Brazilian cultural practices, therefore, becomes an extension of the notion of copyright as applied to Afro-Brazilian performing artists in the face of interventions, mimesis, reproductions, and offshoots carried out by artists and researchers from the white middle class. The recognition of this copyright (more than anything else) constitutes full acceptance of the alterity of Afro-Brazilian cultural heritage and the explicit commitment to the defense of its dignity.

## Basic Policy Principles

Finally, I suggest some basic guiding principles for how researchers, as participants committed to national integration, should relate to culture bearers of intangible cultural heritage-bearing communities, principally those of indigenous and Afro-Brazilian descent.

1. Recognize performative knowledge as a form of ownership. This should be the starting point for determining the researcher's position in relation to local communities, regardless of current legal debates [in Brazil] about the legitimacy of communal rights and calls for the reduction of time that these performative practices are protected by copyright law.
2. Be critical of the growing popularity of the notion of collective ownership of music, dances, and dramatic forms, as well as the notion of the "public domain," both of which simultaneously are false and conveniently reinforce the notion of cultural cannibalism.
3. Commit to returning to culture-bearing communities the materials, publications, and public performances that researchers produce in their capacity as specialists in the traditions that they preserve. Commit to social inclusion and attempt to contribute to the formulation of public policies, preferably in the form of affirmative action, that allows for a reduction of the racial and ethnic inequality that maintains the keepers of valued traditions and practices of African and indigenous origin in Brazil in the worst socioeconomic conditions. Through their inclusion in socially and politically privileged spaces, folk and vernacular artists will be better equipped to communicate their performative forms of knowledge in the way that they deem most appropriate.

I maintain, once again, on the exploratory and still unfinished nature of these reflections, set out with the sole objective of opening a frank and open discussion.

## Notes

Special thanks to Letícia Vianna for encouraging me to publish these ideas, which are still under development; and to Rosângela Tugny, who also urged me to share these reflections at a conference at the Universidade Federal de Minas Gerais (UFMG, Federal University of Minas Gerais) School of Music. I discussed these topics along with various students from the departments of Traditional Brazilian Cultures and the Anthropology of Art at Universidade de Brasília (UnB, University of Brasília) and with various other students and colleagues, including Carlos Henrique Siqueira, Daniel Menezes, Ernesto de Carvalho, Inés María Martiatu, Maria Inês de Almeida, Luís Ferreira, and Paula Vilas.

1. Editors' note: Like most Portuguese and Spanish-speaking scholars, the author uses the term "popular" to denote folk and vernacular musical and cultural practices, rather than commodified and mass-mediated musical and cultural forms as the term tends to imply in English, although there can be some overlap between the two usages. For the purposes of this chapter, the term "popular" is translated as "folk and vernacular" to avoid confusion with the English usage.

2. Emblematic of this structure was the relationship, close in some ways and distant in others, between Mário de Andrade and the *coco* player Chico Antônio from Rio Grande do Norte, for three decades: Mário de Andrade had his intellectual dilemmas and his links to the dominant class, and Chico Antônio would live his own dilemmas of an illiterate of the poor class. I theorize about this relationship between Chico Antônio and Mário de Andrade in José Jorge de Carvalho, *A sensibilidade modernista face às tradições populares* (Brasília: Universidade de Brasília, 2000).

3. For an analysis of the Boasian vocation of anthropology and its current crisis, see Paul Rabinow, "Humanism as Nihilism: The Bracketing of Truth and Seriousness in American Cultural Anthropology," in *Social Science as Moral Inquiry*, ed. Norma Haan et al. (New York: Columbia University Press, 1983), 52–75.

4. See Alan Lomax, "Appeal for Cultural Equity," *Journal of Communication* 27 (1977), 125–38.

5. See José Jorge de Carvalho, *La etnomusicología en tiempos de canibalismo musical: una reflexión a partir de las tradiciones musicales afroamericanas* (Brasília: Universidade de Brasília, 2003).

6. Editors' note: In the late 1920s and early 1930s, Andrade's notion of cannibalism (*antropofagia*) became an important part of Brazilian national imaginary. Andrade argued that one of Brazil's greatest national traits was its ability to consume other cultures (European, indigenous, African) for its own ends.

7. I suggest here in a line of argument separate from this theory of entertainment that it is possible for the formulation of another radical critique of the famous Anthropophagic Manifesto: "only what isn't mine can entertain me."

8. Editors' note: The seahorse dance (*cavalo marinho*) is a dance-drama associated with the Feast of the Epiphany (January 6).

9. For more on the transformations of time in Western art, see João Adolfo Hansen, "A temporalidade na cultura contemporânea," in *Conversas no ateliê: palestras sobre artes e humanidades*, ed. Vera Pallamin and Joaci Pereira Furtado (São Paulo: Faculdade de Arquitetura e Urbanismo, Universidade de São Paulo, 2002), 11–26.

10. That position is explicitly defended, and without any critique to the possible destructive consequences that the capitalist consumption of exotic cultural traditions can have for the communities that perform them, by Joaquim Falcão, "Patrimônio imaterial: um sistema sustentável de proteção," *Tempo Brasileiro* 147 (2001), 163–80.

11. Editors' note: A noted Italian experimental theater director based in Denmark, Eugenio Barba is best known for the development of what he terms "theater anthropology," the cross-cultural study of performative techniques that he believes are used by performers of different cultures to achieve a heightened or "extra-quotidian" form of autonomy. Barba's theories are well-known in Latin America, where the director has given numerous lectures and workshops going back to the late 1970s. Most relevant to this article, Barba is also known for organizing performance "barters" with local populations that he deems as not having had prior experience with Western theater (e.g., members of the Amazonian Yanomami community in Venezuela). For a more detailed discussion about Barba's ideas and their influence on Latin American theater, see Javier F. León, "The 'Danza de las Cañas': Music, Theatre and Afroperuvian Modernity," *Ethnomusicology Forum* 16, no. 1 (2007), 127–55, pp. 140–42. See also Ian Watson, *Negotiating Cultures: Eugenio Barba and the Intercultural Debate* (New York: Palgrave, 2002).

12. See Inés María Martiatu, *El rito como representación* (Havana: Ediciones Unión, 2000), and Richard Schechner, "Del ritual al teatro y de vuelta: la trenza de la eficacia y el entretenimiento," in *Performance: teoría and practica interculturales* (Buenos Aires: Universidad de Buenos Aires, 2000).

13. See Carvalho, *La etnomusicología en tiempos de canibalismo musical.*

14. I refer here to the arguments about the crisis of institutions and white Brazilian identity that I developed in an essay written in the centennial year of abolition in Brazil; José Jorge de Carvalho, "Mestiçagem e segregação," *Humanidades* 19 (1988), 35–39.

15. Translator's note: Lit. dark or brown, "morena" is an ambiguous term that can be used to refer to people with dark hair and features, a "Moorish" phenotype, but also as a euphemism for people of African descent; "mestiça" refers to people of mixed African, European, and Native American heritages.

16. For a discussion of the Grupo Nzinga-DF, see Telma Litwinczik, *A valorização da capoeira angola por brancos universitários: estudo de caso no grupo Nzinga-DF* (Brasília: Departamento de Antropologia, Universidade de Brasília, 2003).

Editors' note: Palmares was Brazil's largest and most famous *quilombo*, a settlement where escaped slaves lived away from the control of Brazilian slave owners. Such settlements existed also in the Caribbean region, where they were called *palenques* (in Spanish).

17. See Carlos Vega, *La ciencia del folklore* (Buenos Aires: Editorial Nova, 1960).

18. Walter Benjamin, *Origem do drama barroco alemão* (São Paulo: Brasiliense, 1984), 67–68, "The original is never found in the world of raw facts and manifestos, and its rhythm only reveals itself as a double vision that recognizes it, on one hand, as restoration and reproduction, and on the other hand, because of this, as incomplete and unfinished."

19. For a conceptual frame regarding the phenomena of cannibalism and spectacularization of folk and vernacular cultures, see José Jorge de Carvalho, "'Espectacularização' e 'canibalização' das culturas populares na América Latina," *Revista Anthropológicas* 21, no. 1 (2010), 39–76.

20. For a detailed analysis of *Les Maîtres Fous*, see Paul Stoller, *The Cinematic Griot: The Ethnography of Jean Rouch* (Chicago: University of Chicago Press, 1992); about grotesque mimesis of the North Americans by the Kuna of Panama, see Michael Taussig, *Mimesis and Alterity: A Particular History of the Senses* (New York: Routledge, 1992).

21. See Michael Taussig, *Xamanismo, colonialismo e o homem selvagem* (São Paulo: Paz e Terra, 1993), and Homi Bhabha, *O local da cultura* (Belo Horizonte: Editora da Universidade Federal de Minas Gerais, 1998).

22. See Fredric Jameson, *O inconsciente político* (São Paulo: Editora Ática, 1992), 77.

23. See Alejo Carpentier, *La música en Cuba* (Mexico City: Fondo de Cultura Económica, 1946); Ángel Quintero Rivera, *Salsa, sabor y control* (Mexico City: Siglo Veintiuno Editores, 1998); and Eric Lott, *Love and Theft: Blackface Minstrelsy and the American Working Class* (Oxford: Oxford University Press, 1995).

24. See, for example, Jacques Derrida, "A diferença," in *Margens da filosofia* (Campinas: Papirus, 1991).

# Contributors

## Editors

JAVIER F. LEÓN received his PhD in ethnomusicology at the University of Texas at Austin. He is currently the Director of the Latin American Music Center of the Indiana University Jacobs School of Music. Previously, he has been Assistant Professor in the Department of Folklore and Ethnomusicology at Indiana University and in the Newcomb Department of Music and the Roger Thayer Stone for Latin American Studies at Tulane University. His work has been published in multiple journals, including *Latin American Music Review*, *Black Music Research Journal*, *Ethnomusicology Forum*, and the volumes *Music and Cultural Rights* (2009), *A tres bandas: mestizaje, sincretismo e hibridación en el espacio sonoro iberoamericano* (2011), and *Música popular y sociedad en el Perú contemporáneo* (2015). He is also the editor of the special Music and Neoliberalism issue in the journal *Culture, Theory and Critique* (2014). His current research deals with music, cultural policy, heritage safeguarding, and the neoliberalization of the culture industries in Latin America.

HELENA SIMONETT received her PhD in ethnomusicology from the University of California, Los Angeles. She is currently Assistant Professor of Latin American Studies and the Blair School of Music at Vanderbilt University and serves as Associate Director of the Center for Latin American Studies. She conducted extensive research on Mexican popular music and its transnational diffusion and currently explores the role of indigenous music and dance in northwestern Mexico. Her publications include *Banda: Mexican Musical Life across Borders* (2001) and *En Sinaloa nací: historia de la música de banda* (2004). She is guest editor of "Music for Being," *The World of Music* 51, no. 2 (2009); guest editor (with Julio Mendívil) of the 2016 issue of *TRANS-Revista Transcultural de Música (TRANS-Transcultural Music Review)* on indigenous music in Latin America; and the editor of *The Accordion in the Americas: Klezmer, Polka, Tango, Zydeco, and More!* (2012). With Bernardo Esquer López, she produced the children's book *Ca'anáriam—Hombre que no hizo fuego* (2012) in Yoreme and Spanish language (with English translation).

## Authors

MARINA ALONSO BOLAÑOS is an Associate Researcher at the Sound Archive of the Instituto Nacional de Antropología e Historia (National Institute of Anthropology and History), Mexico. She received degrees in ethnology from the Escuela Nacional de Antropología e Historia (National School of Anthropology and History), anthropology from the Universidad Nacional Autónoma de México (National Autonomous University of Mexico) and a doctoral degree in history from the Colegio de México (College of Mexico). She specializes in space, normative systems, worldviews, and musical practices in the Chiapas region, in particular the Zoque. Her publications include *La invención de la música indígena de México: antropología e historia de las políticas culturales del siglo XX* (2008; The invention of indigenous music in Mexico), *Los pueblos indígenas de Chiapas: atlas etnográfico* (with Margarita Nolasco, 2008; The indigenous peoples of Chiapas), *Los zoques de Oaxaca: un viaje por los Chimalapas* (with Leopoldo Trejo, 2009; The Zoque of Oaxaca), and *Creando mundos, entrelazando realidades: cosmovisiones y mitologías en el México indígena* (with Catharine Good Eshelman, 2015; Indigenous world views and mythologies of Mexico).

GONZALO CAMACHO DÍAZ is a surgeon and also holds a PhD in social anthropology from the Escuela Nacional de Antropología e Historia (National School of Anthropology and History), Mexico City. He is currently a tenured professor in the Department of Music at the Universidad Nacional Autónoma de México (UNAM, National Autonomous University of Mexico). He has produced several CDs, and his publications include "El vuelo de la golondrina: música, y migración en la Huasteca" (in *Música sin fronteras*, 2006; The swallow's flight) and "La cumbia de los ancestros: música ritual y mass media en la Huasteca" (in *Equilibrio, intercambio y reciprocidad*, 2007; Cumbia of the ancestors). He is also coeditor of *Reflexiones sobre semiología musical* (with Susana González Aktories, 2011; Reflections about musical semiology).

JOSÉ JORGE DE CARVALHO holds a PhD in social anthropology (ethnomusicology) from Queen's University in Belfast. He is Professor of Anthropology at the Universidade de Brasília (University of Brasília) and Director of the Instituto de Inclusão no Ensino Superior e na Pesquisa (Institute for Inclusion in Advanced Education and Research). He is an advocate of affirmative action policies at the university and the creator of Knowledge Encounters, a project for the inclusion of indigenous, Afro-Brazilian, and vernacular elders as university faculty. His books include *Cantos sagrados do Xangô do Recife* (1993; Sacred songs of Xangô and Recife), *O Quilombo do Rio das Rãs* (1996; The Quilombo of Rio das Rãs), *Las culturas afroamericanas en Iberoamérica* (2005; Afro-American cultures in Latin America), and *Inclusão étnica e racial no Brasil* (2005; Ethnic and racial inclusion in Brazil).

CLAUDIO F. DÍAZ holds a master's degree in social semiotics and a PhD in literature from the Universidad Nacional de Córdoba (National University of Córdoba), Argentina, where he is a tenured Professor in the Sociología del Discurso (Sociology of Discourse) program and Director of the Escuela de Letras (Department of Letters) at the Facultad de Filosofía y Humanidades (School of Philosphy and the Humanities). He leads a research team that focuses on socio-discursive approaches to the study of popular music. His publications include *Libro de viajes y extravíos: un recorrido por el rock argentino (1965–1985)* (2005; Book of travels and digressions), *Variaciones sobre el "ser nacional": una aproximación sociodiscursiva al folklore argentino* (2010; Variations on "being national"), *Bailar en San Antonio: testimonios y reflexiones sobre el Encuentro Nacional Cultural de San Antonio de Arredondo* (with Florencia Páez and Natalia Díaz, 2013; To dance in San Antonio), and editor of *Fisuras en el sentido: músicas populares y luchas simbólicas* (2015; Fissures of meaning).

RODRIGO CANTOS SAVELLI GOMES was a recipient of the Scientific Initiative Scholarship Program at the Universidade do Estado de Santa Catarina (Santa Catarina State University), Brazil. He received his bachelor's degree in music at this institution under the mentorship of Maria Ignêz Cruz Mello.

JUAN PABLO GONZÁLEZ is Director of the Instituto de Música (Music Institute) of the Universidad Alberto Hurtado (Alberto Hurtado University), Santiago de Chile, and Professor at the Instituto de Historia (History Institute) of the Pontificia Universidad Católica de Chile (Pontifical Catholic University of Chile). He obtained his PhD in musicology at the University of California, Los Angeles. His main focus of interest is the social history of Chilean and Latin American popular music during the twentieth century. His latest books are an expanded second edition of *En busca de la música chilena: crónica y antología de una historia sonora* (with the late José Miguel Varas, 2013; In search of Chile's music) and *Pensar la música desde América Latina: problemas e interrogantes* (2013; Thinking music from Latin America).

RUBÉN LÓPEZ-CANO has a PhD in musicology and is Professor at the Escola Superior de Música de Catalunya (Catalonia College of Music), Spain. His research deals with musical rhetoric and semiotics, musical cognition, urban popular music, sampling and digital music culture, diaspora, the body and subjectivity in music, artistic research, and music research epistemologies. He is the author of *Música plurifocal* (1997; Plurifocal music), *Música y retórica en el barroco* (2012; Music and rhetoric in the Baroque), and *Investigación artística en música: problemas, métodos, paradigmas, experiencias y modelos* (with Úrsula San Cristóbal, 2014; Artistic research in music).

ANGELA E. LÜHNING received her PhD in ethnomusicology from the Freie Universität Berlin (Free University of Berlin), Germany, and is Professor in the School of Music at the Universidade Federal da Bahia (Federal University of Bahia), Brazil. She has published multiple books, articles, and children's literature in a variety of topics, including indigenous and Afro-Brazilian music, memory and transmission processes, music in historical contexts and historical recordings, music in *candomblé*, ethnomusicology and participatory processes, community cultures and social education, and on Pierre Fatumbi Verger and his oeuvre. She is also Director of the Pierre Verger Foundation, where she coordinates research and organizes projects with underprivileged youths.

JORGE MARTÍNEZ ULLOA is a composer and musicologist. He studied composition, electronic music, and informatics at Conservatorio di Musica Luigi Cherubini (Luigi Cherubini Music Conservatory) in Florence, Italy, later receiving a master's degree in musicology from the Universidad de Chile (University of Chile). He is Professor of Music at the Pontificia Universidad Católica de Valparaiso (Pontifical Catholic University of Valparaíso) and the Universidad de Chile. He has published a number of articles dealing with musical semiotics, analysis of contemporary art music, music informatics, and ethnomusicology. He also maintains a catalog of over 150 compositions that have been premiered in venues in Europe and the Americas.

MARIA IGNÊZ CRUZ MELLO received her PhD in social anthropology from the Universidade Federal de Santa Catarina (Federal University of Santa Catarina), Brazil. The late Dr. Cruz was Professor of Ethnomusicology at the Department of Music of the Universidade do Estado de Santa Catarina (Santa Catarina State University) and Director of the Music, Culture, and Society Research Group. Her research interests included music from the Amazonian region, popular music, music cognition, and music and gender. Her publications included multiple articles in conference and symposia proceedings, as well as the essay "Músicas de homens, músicas de mulheres: interconexões musicais e assimetrias de gênero entre os índios Wauja" (in *Gênero, Cultura e Poder*, 2004; Men's music, women's music).

JULIO MENDÍVIL is a Peruvian musician, ethnomusicologist (PhD, Universität zu Köln [University of Cologne]), and Professor at the Johann Wolfgang Goethe-Universität Frankfurt am Main (Goethe University Frankfurt). His publications include *Todas las voces: artículos sobre música popular* (2001; All the voices: essays on popular music), *Ein musikalisches Stück Heimat: ethnographische Beobachtungen zum deutschen Schlager* (2008; A musical piece of home) and *Del juju al uauco: un estudio arqueomusicológico de las flautas globulares cerradas de cráneo de cérvido en la región Chinchaysuyu del Imperio de los Incas* (2009; From the Juju to the Uauco: an archaeomusicological study of globular deer flutes in the Chinchaysuyu Region of the Inca Empire). He has also been Associate Researcher at the Hochschule für Musik, Theater und Medien Hannover (University of Music, Drama, and Media in Hannover) and Director of the Center for World Music at the Universität Hildesheim (University of Hildesheim), Germany. He currently serves as Chair of the executive board for the Latin American branch of the Society for the Study of Popular Music.

CARLOS MIÑANA BLASCO received his PhD in anthropology from the Universitat de Barcelona (University of Barcelona), Spain. He is currently Associate Professor of Anthropology and Professor of the Master's Program in Musicology at the Universidad Nacional de Colombia (National University of Colombia), Bogotá. His field research has been mainly focused in the Southwestern Andean region of Colombia and embraces the areas of anthropology, ethnomusicology, and education. He has developed collaborative research projects with the Nasa and Yanacona indigenous communities. His publications include *Kuvi: música de flautas entre los paeces* (1994; Kuvi: flute music among the Páez), *De fastos a fiestas: navidad y chirimías en Popayán* (1997; From pomp to fiesta: Christmas and the Chirimía in Popayán), and contributions to multiple journals and edited volumes.

RAÚL R. ROMERO holds a PhD in ethnomusicology at Harvard University. He is Professor of Music in the Faculty of Performing Arts at the Pontificia Universidad Católica del Perú (Pontifical Catholic University of Perú), Lima, where he is also the founding Director of the Instituto de Etnomusicología (Institute of Ethnomusicology). He is the author of several books and articles, including *Debating the Past: Music, Memory and Identity in the Andes* (2001) and *Andinos y tropicales: la cumbia peruana en la ciudad global* (2007; Andeans and tropicals: Peruvian *cumbia* in the global city). He is currently writing about nationalism in twentieth-century Peruvian art music.

IÑIGO SÁNCHEZ FUARROS is a Postdoctoral Research Fellow at the Instituto de Etnomusicologia–Centro de Estudos em Música é Dança (INET-MD, Institute of Ethnomusicology and the Center for the Study of Music and Dance) at the

Universidade Nova de Lisboa (New University of Lisbon). He holds a PhD in anthropology from the Universitat de Barcelona (University of Barcelona), Spain. His publications include the monograph *"Cubaneando" en Barcelona: música, migración y experiencia urbana* (2012; "Cubaneando" in Barcelona: music, migration and the urban experience), and contributions to multiple journals and edited volumes, including the volumes *Musical Performance and the Changing City* (2013) and *Toward an Anthropology of Ambient Sound* (forthcoming). His current work focuses on the role and significance of music in processes of urban change. He is the editor of *TRANS-Revista Transcultural de Música* (*TRANS-Transcultural Music Review*).

CARLOS SANDRONI received his PhD in musicology from the Université François-Rabelais de Tours (University of Tours), France. He is Adjunct Professor in the Music Department at the Universidade Federal de Pernambuco (Federal University of Pernambuco), Brazil. His publications include *Mário contra Macunaíma: política e cultura em Mário de Andrade* (1988; Mário against Macunaíma), *Samba de roda no Recôncavo baiano* (with Márcia Sant'Anna, 2007; Samba de roda in Bahian Recôncavo Region), *Feitiço decente: transformações do samba no Rio de Janeiro, 1917–1933* (2012 [2001]; Casting a proper spell), and *Patrimônio cultural em discussão: novas perspectivas teórico-metodológicas* (with Sandro Guimarães de Salles, 2014; Debating cultural heritage). His main research interests are ethnomusicology, popular music history, and intangible cultural heritage studies.

CAROLINA SANTAMARÍA-DELGADO received her PhD in ethnomusicology from the University of Pittsburgh under the auspices of the Fulbright Program. She directed the Master of Music at the Pontificia Universidad Javeriana (Pontifical Xavierian University) in Bogotá and is currently Professor of Music at the Universidad de Antioquia (University of Antioquía) in Medellín. Her research focuses on Latin American popular music and has been published in a number of journals. She has also served as editor for the *Cuadernos de Música, Artes Visuales y Artes Escénicas* (Journal of Music, Visual, and Performing Arts). Her most recent book is *Vitrolas, rocolas y radioteatros: hábitos de escucha de la música popular en Medellín, 1930–1950* (2014; Victrolas, jukeboxes, and radio theater).

RODRIGO TORRES ALVARADO studied music in Chile, Spain, and France, completing his Diploma of Advanced Studies at the Université Paris 8 (Paris 8 University). He is Associate Professor in the Department of Arts at the Universidad de Chile (University of Chile), where he runs the Archivo de Música Tradicional (Traditional Music Archives) and the Centro de Documentación e Investigación Musical (CEDIM, Musical Documentation Center). He also supervises the Master in Musicology Program. He has published articles, books, CDs, and documentary films on Chilean popular and traditional music.

ALEJANDRO VERA is Associate Professor at the Institute of Music of the Pontificia Universidad Católica de Chile (Pontifical Catholic University of Chile). He holds a PhD in musicology from the Universidad Autónoma de Madrid (Autonomous University of Madrid). His research focuses mainly on seventeenth- and eighteenth-century Spanish and Latin American music. His publications include articles in *Acta Musicologica*, *Early Music*, and *Latin American Music Review*, and the books *Música vocal profana en el Madrid de Felipe IV* (2002; Secular vocal music in Felipe IV's Madrid) and *Santiago de Murcia: cifras selectas de guitarra* (2011). He is the 2002 recipient of the Emilio Pujol Music Research Award (Spain) and the 2008 Otto Mayer-Serra International Music Research Award (Mexico).

## Translators

JUAN CAMILO AGUDELO is a PhD student in ethnomusicology at the University of Texas at Austin. He holds a bachelor's degree in the history of science from Harvard University and a master of music in ethnomusicology from the University of Texas at Austin. His thesis research focused on *gaita* musicians from Colombia's Caribbean coast and their multiple discourses of tradition as *gaita* music expanded beyond the region. His current research investigates how cosmopolitan DJs are using Colombian *cumbia* to represent Latino identity.

ANDRÉS AMADO holds a PhD in ethnomusicology from the University of Texas at Austin and is currently Assistant Professor of Ethnomusicology and Musicology at the University of Texas Rio Grande Valley. His research interests focus on issues of race, ethnicity, cosmopolitanism, and musical nationalism in Latin America, particularly Guatemala. He is also interested in historical research in ethnomusicology. He has worked as Assistant Editor of the *Latin American Music Review*.

MONA-LYNN COURTEAU is a Freelance Editor specializing in academic works in ethnomusicology, music, cultural and social anthropology, and Latin American studies. She coedited *Genres: Caribbean and Latin America*, volume 9 of the *Bloomsbury Encyclopedia of Popular Music of the World* (2014). She holds a master of arts in ethnomusicology and is based in Auckland, New Zealand.

PETER ERMEY has a Bachelor of Arts in Biology from Brown University and a Master of Arts in Folklore and Ethnomusicology from Indiana University. He produced and directed an ethnographic film, *Um Dom de Deus*, about the folia do Divino celebrations in the Central West region of Brazil that premiered in Pirenópolis, Goiás, in 2007. He currently teaches at Indiana University and American Military University. His research interests include Brazilian folk music, technology, and public policy.

JANE L. FLORINE earned her PhD in ethnomusicology from the Florida State University and is currently Professor of Music (Ethnomusicology and Musicology) at Chicago State University. Among her publications are the monographs *Cuarteto Music and Dancing from Argentina: In Search of the Tunga-Tunga in Córdoba* (2001) and *Cosquín, una cosecha de coplas: música y significado cultural en el Festival Nacional de Folklore argentino* (forthcoming; Cosquín, a Harvest of Song). Her main research area is popular music from Argentina (especially folklore), and her work has been supported with Fulbright, Fulbright-Hays, and National Endowment for the Humanities Fellowships.

DAVID FONT-NAVARRETE is an artist, musician, and ethnomusicologist. He earned a bachelor's degree from Antioch College; a master's from the University of Maryland, College Park; and a PhD from York University. Currently a Lecturing Fellow in Duke University's Thompson Writing Program, his publications include a forthcoming monograph on Afro-Cuban Lucumí music (cowritten with Kenneth Schweitzer), and articles on Ayan/Aña (cowritten with Akinsola Akiwowo), Congotronics, Sublime Frequencies, Miami and Global Bass, and Bugarabu. His current research project—*At the Edge of Tradition*—explores the confluence of cultural traditions, avant-garde art, and anthropology.

KARIANN GOLDSCHMITT received her PhD in musicology from the University of California, Los Angeles, and is Assistant Professor of Ethnomusicology at Wellesley College. She has previously held teaching posts at University of Cambridge, New College of Florida, and Colby College. She studies popular music's relationship to the global media industries since World War II with a focus on Brazilian music and national branding. Her research has appeared in *Luso-Brazilian Review*, *Popular Music and Society*, and *The Oxford Handbook of Mobile Music Studies* (2014).

HOLLY HOLMES is a Freelance Portuguese-English Translator and Copywriter in Tucson, Arizona. She is a candidate for the PhD in ethnomusicology at the University of Illinois at Urbana-Champaign, and in 2015 she was certified as a translator by the Chartered Institute of Linguists in the United Kingdom. Her doctoral dissertation focuses on regionalism and politics in the music of composer Milton Nascimento during the Brazilian military dictatorship (1964–85). She is a contributor to *Researching Music Censorship*, edited by Annemette Kirkegaard, Jan Sverre Knudsen, Jonas Otterbeck, and Helmi Järviluoma-Mäkelä (forthcoming 2016).

SYDNEY HUTCHINSON holds a PhD in ethnomusicology from New York University and is currently Assistant Professor of ethnomusicology at Syracuse University. She is the editor of *Salsa World: A Global Dance in Local Contexts* (2013) and author of *From Quebradita to Duranguense: Dance in Mexican American Youth Culture* (2007) as well as numerous articles on Caribbean music, dance, gender, and place. Hutchinson is currently completing a book on the performance of gender in Dominican music with support from an American Association of University Women fellowship.

MICHAEL IYANAGA has a PhD in ethnomusicology from the University of California, Los Angeles. He is currently a Mellon Faculty Fellow in Latin American Studies at the College of William and Mary. He has taught at the Universidade Federal da Paraíba (Federal University of Paraíba) and the Universidade Federal de Pernambuco, as well as at UCLA and the College of William and Mary. His publications appear in *Ethnomusicology*, *Música e Cultura*, and *Latin American Music Review*, as well as a number of other journals. His research interests include music and religion in the African Diaspora.

RANDALL C. KOHL holds a master's degree in ethnomusicology from the University of Hawai'i and a doctorate in history and regional studies from the Universidad Veracruzana (University of Veracruz). His research interests include guitar-based traditions such as Hawaiian slack key and the Veracruz *son jarocho*, as well as the general areas of historical ethnomusicology and the sociology of music. He is currently a tenured professor on the music faculty of the Universidad Veracruzana and a member of Mexico's National System of Researchers. His published works include *Ecos de "La bamba": una historia etnomusicológica sobre el son jarocho de Veracruz, 1946–1959* (2007; Echoes of La Bamba), *Escritos de un náufrago habitual: ensayos sobre el son jarocho y otros temas etnomusicológicos* (2011; Writings of a habitual castaway), and *Declaraciones del son* (2013; Declarations of the *son*).

MICHAEL S. O'BRIEN is Assistant Professor at the College of Charleston. He earned a PhD in ethnomusicology from the University of Texas at Austin. His research focuses on popular music in Argentina, particularly tango and *murga*, and their relation to populism, cultural politics, and public space.

EMILY PINKERTON researches traditional music in Chile, focusing on folk revivals, organology, and the performance of gender. She holds a PhD in ethnomusicology from the University of Texas at Austin, and her investigation of *canto a lo poeta* and the twenty-five-string Chilean *guitarrón* was supported by the Fulbright Commission and the Organization of American States. She is Instructor of Latin American music at the University of Pittsburgh as well as a touring artist who blends North American and South American traditions in her compositions.

MARYSOL QUEVEDO is a PhD candidate in the musicology program at Indiana University. She has served as Editor and Researcher at Indiana University's Latin

American Music Center. She is currently completing a dissertation on art music in Cuba after the 1959 revolution, examining the relationship between music composition, national identity, and the Cuban socialist regime. Her research interests include Spanish Baroque stage and theater music, twentieth- and twenty-first-century Latin American art and popular music, as well as performance of gender and ethnicity in contemporary music.

JONATHAN RITTER holds a PhD in ethnomusicology from the University of California, Los Angeles, where he studied under Anthony Seeger. He is currently Associate Professor of Music and Chair of the Latin American Studies Program at the University of California, Riverside. A specialist in the musics of the Andean region, he is coeditor of *Music in the Post-9/11 World* (2007) and author of *We Bear Witness with Our Song: The Politics of Music and Violence in the Peruvian Andes* (forthcoming).

GREGORY J. ROBINSON is Associate Professor of Music at George Mason University. He earned his PhD in anthropology of music at the University of Pennsylvania. His research has been published in *Ethnomusicology*, and his forthcoming book centers on traditional music for accordion and guitar in Chilean Patagonia. It traces the ways in which local, national, and transnational affinities and identifications interact with various forms of conviviality, informing definitions of tradition that accrue to this repertoire. Other research areas include rurally oriented music in Argentina and contemporary media representations of classic rock.

JUAN EDUARDO WOLF holds a PhD in folklore and ethnomusicology from Indiana University and is currently Assistant Professor of ethnomusicology at the University of Oregon. His current book project deals with expressions of Blackness in music-dance along Chile's northern border, particularly in relation to the movement to have Afro-descendants legally recognized by the Chilean state. He has also written on *lakita* panpipe practice in that region and coauthored an instructional text on the Inga variety of Quechua spoken in Colombia's Putumayo Valley.

# Index

The University of Illinois Press
is a founding member of the
Association of American University Presses.

Composed in 10.5/13 Adobe Minion Pro
at the University of Illinois Press
Manufactured by Sheridan Books, Inc.

University of Illinois Press
1325 South Oak Street
Champaign, IL 61820-6903
www.press.uillinois.edu